North Carolina
JOURNEYS

A Journey Through
Africa, Asia
and the Pacific Realm

TEACHER'S EDITION
VOLUME 1

Gibbs Smith, Publisher
Salt Lake City

NC STATE UNIVERSITY

*This series is dedicated to Burt and Pauline Beers
for their dedication to history and social studies education,
but most importantly for their dedication to North Carolina's students.*

Published by
Gibbs Smith, Publisher
P.O. Box 667
Layton, UT 84041
800-748-5439
www.NCJourneys.com

Cover Design: Jeremy C. Munns

Printed and bound in China
ISBN 978-1-4236-0237-8

13 12 11 10 09 08 07   10 9 8 7 6 5 4 3 2 1

*Gibbs Smith, Publisher wishes to thank all the contributors
to the second and third editions of this series.*

Gibbs Smith, Publisher

Julie Dumont Rabinowitz
Managing Editor

Christopher Harlos, Ph.D.
Editor

Susan A. Myers, Aimee Stoddard
Copy Editors

Jeremy C. Munns
Lead Designer

**Michelle Brown, Alan Connell,
Robert Jones, John Vehar**
Designers

Janis J. Hansen
Photo Editor

Lynn P. Roundtree, Wendy Knight
Photo Researchers

Content Specialists

Writers

Linda Scher
Raleigh, North Carolina

Elisabeth Gaynor Ellis
New York, New York

Area Specialists

Joel Cline
Meteorology, National Weather Service
Raleigh, North Carolina

David P. Gilmartin, Ph.D.
South Asia
North Carolina State University

Akram F. Khater, Ph.D.
Islam
North Carolina State University

Tom Parker
Terrorism Consultant
Bard College

Tony K. Stewart, Ph.D.
South Asia
North Carolina State University

Kenneth P. Vickery, Ph.D.
Africa
North Carolina State University

Douglas C. Wilms, Ph.D.
Geography
East Carolina University

Curriculum Specialists

Mary Vann Eslinger
Social Studies Consultant
Morehead City, North Carolina

Jacqueline Boykin
Social Studies Consultant
Williamston, North Carolina

Candy Beal, Ph.D.
Middle Grades Social Studies Education
North Carolina State University

Consulting Teachers

Susan O. Collatz
Mooresville, North Carolina

Rose H. Cooper
Carthage, North Carolina

Karen Fichter
Zebulon GT Magnet Middle School
Cary, North Carolina

Greg Giles
Raleigh, North Carolina

Ann Hamzé
C. M. Eppes Middle School
Greenville, North Carolina

Leah Harkness
Apex, North Carolina

Amy L. Hayden
Apex, North Carolina

Kevin C. Martin
Teacher Consultant
Raleigh, North Carolina

Barbara B. Massey
Thomas Jefferson Middle School
Winston-Salem, North Carolina

Margaret Parrish
Raleigh, North Carolina

William E. Pitts
Educational Consultant
Wake Forest, North Carolina

Arvil R. Sale
Boone, North Carolina

Stacey Anne Samuel
Wilmington, North Carolina

Judy Simpson
Mt. Airy, North Carolina

Rebecca Stevens
Greensboro, North Carolina

Sue Trent
Charlotte, North Carolina

Laurie Walsh
Teacher Consultant
Bend, Oregon

Karen Watts
Wilkesboro, North Carolina

NC State University

Humanities Extension/Publications

James W. Clark, Ph.D.
Director & Professor of English

Burton F. Beers, Ph.D.
Editor Emeritus
Humanities Publications &
Professor of History

Regina Higgins, Ph.D.
Editor
Humanities Publications

James Alchediak
Chief Videographer & Lecturer
in Communications

Pamela H. Ellis
Administrative Assistant

Lisa Morgan
Bookkeeper

Zachary H. Jackson
Editorial Assistant
Humanities Publications

Pallavi Talwar
Editorial Assistant
Humanities Publications

Frances Higgins
Editorial Assistant
Humanities Publications

Editorial Support

Bryan Smithoy
Copy Editor
Warrenton, North Carolina

Contents

Introduction — T4

CONNECT with *North Carolina Journeys* T4

The Contributions of North Carolina
Teachers to the Making of These Books T5

NCJourneys.com — T6

Student Edition Features — T8

Teacher's Edition Features — T12

Teacher's Resource Guide Features — T16

Teaching Methods — T18

Teaching Social Studies
Using North Carolina Journeys T18

Skill Lessons T22

Diversity in *North Carolina Journeys* T24

Character and Values Education
in *North Carolina Journeys* T25

Teaching Social Studies
to the English Language Learner T26

Maps and the Five Themes of Geography T27

Seminars and Debates T28

Teacher Resources — T30

North Carolina Grade 7
Social Studies Standard Course of Study T30

National Geography Standards T32

Pacing Guide and Teaching Strategy Activities T33

Calendar of Important Cultural
and Historical Events T34

Information on Cultural, Historical, and
Natural Resources in North Carolina T35

Volume 1

CHAPTER 1
A Journey on the Internet 2

UNIT 1
Africa Foundations 14

CHAPTER 2
A Diversity of People and Lands 16

CHAPTER 3
Historical Foundations of Africa 38

CHAPTER 4
Enduring Traditions 60

CHAPTER 5
Africa and the World 80

UNIT 2
Africa Today: Regions 102

CHAPTER 6
North Africa 104

CHAPTER 7
West Africa 126

CHAPTER 8
Central Africa 146

CHAPTER 9
East Africa 164

CHAPTER 10
Southern Africa 184

UNIT 3
Southwest Asia 202

CHAPTER 11
Lands and People of Southwest Asia .. 204

CHAPTER 12
**Southwest Asia's
Enduring Traditions** 226

CHAPTER 13
Economy and Government 246

CHAPTER 14
Society and Culture 270

Volume 2

UNIT 4

South Asia 290

CHAPTER 15
The Lands of South Asia 292

CHAPTER 16
South Asia's Enduring Traditions 312

CHAPTER 17
Modern India 332

CHAPTER 18
Other Nations of South Asia 352

UNIT 5

East Asia and Southeast Asia 372

CHAPTER 19
Lands and People of East Asia and Southeast Asia 374

CHAPTER 20
China's Enduring Traditions 394

CHAPTER 21
China Today 414

CHAPTER 22
Korea 434

CHAPTER 23
Japan's Enduring Traditions 454

CHAPTER 24
Modern Japan 476

CHAPTER 25
Southeast Asia 496

UNIT 6

The Pacific Realm 520

CHAPTER 26
Australia and New Zealand 522

CHAPTER 27
Oceania 546

Appendix 566

Contents

Greetings from Gibbs Smith, Publisher

It is with great joy that we bring you *North Carolina Journeys*. We believe in the power of a book, and we feel each of these textbooks is a special gathering place for ideas, compelling images, great stories, and thought-provoking questions and activities. In the pages of these books, there is energy to launch you and your students into riveting discussions.

One reason why we choose to publish only social studies textbooks is that we believe in the importance of social studies education. It is a unifying subject—one that supports all kinds of connections. To be honest, that word "connect" is central to this entire program. As an educator, you know the power of making connections. You see this every day. Here are some connections you will find in *North Carolina Journeys*.

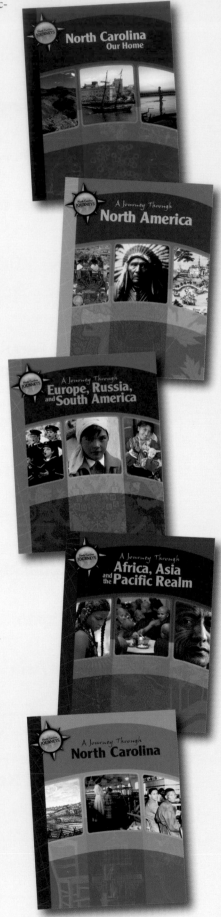

COURSE OF STUDY

The North Carolina Social Studies Standard Course of Study is the true foundation and framework for each book in the series. Because of that, these books give you everything you need to successfully teach the curriculum without a lot of extra stuff that does not pertain to what you need to teach.

NORTH CAROLINA CREATED

Educators and scholars from the Tar Heel state were instrumental in creating these materials. North Carolina scholars and writers crafted the content of each book. North Carolina educators who well know the challenges and joys of teaching social studies in today's classrooms wrote all of the activities in the Teacher's Editions.

INTEGRATION

You'll find activities that integrate Math, Science, Reading/Language Arts, Technology, Fine Arts, and Character Education objectives from North Carolina's Standard Course of Study. "Integration is the way," as Cathy Wilson from Wilmington puts it. This program supports that approach and provides tools for you to connect your social studies instruction with other curriculum areas.

INVITING

You'll find your students will connect with the content of these books because they will be engaged. For a change, these textbooks will be something your students will enjoy reading. The narrative shares the stories of real people and the images are meaningful and poignant.

END-OF-GRADE TESTS AND ELL SUPPORT

This program helps students prepare for important End-of-Grade Tests, especially those in reading and writing. All of the chapter assessments are written in the style of the North Carolina Reading Comprehension End-of-Grade Test. North Carolina educators also designed meaningful ELL teaching tips as well as novice and intermediate ELL extensions for many activities. They also wrote Modified Lesson Plans for English Language Learners.

CORRELATED ACTIVITIES

Paideia seminars, Socratic seminars, research activities, Skill Lessons, projects for multiple intelligences, problem based learning activities, Go to the Source activities, and more all bring a wealth of ideas to your classroom. *North Carolina Journeys* are true "best practices" guides to teaching social studies in North Carolina.

USEFUL TECHNOLOGY

Technology makes all the materials of *North Carolina Journeys* accessible in many media. At **NCJourneys.com** you and your students will find a wealth of tools, including online books, worksheets, digital storytelling activities, interactive atlases, and more. **NCJourneys.com** also provides customizable tests through the *ExamView® Assessment Suite*.

These are just some examples of the connections you can find in *North Carolina Journeys*. We hope you enjoy exploring these books and learning new things about the world and your state each time you and your students dip into these pages. The possibilities are truly endless.

Enjoy!

Carrie Gibson
Textbook Director
Gibbs Smith, Publisher

The Contributions of North Carolina Teachers to the Making of These Books

In shaping the books in *North Carolina Journeys*, the editors and Gibbs Smith, Publisher have drawn together the talents of university scholars and more than 50 outstanding North Carolina fourth, fifth, sixth, seventh, and eighth grade teachers. Each individual in this remarkable group has been selected with care. Their special knowledge and skills has led to a unique collaboration—one that gives our state's teachers and students materials that support teaching and learning in North Carolina's unique social studies curriculum.

Students in fourth grade begin their journeys through the world in North Carolina and then move on in successive grades for an introduction to North America, then to South America and Europe before completing these journeys with Africa, Asia, Australia, and the Pacific Realm. Eighth grade then returns students to their home state for studies in North Carolina history. This is a curriculum that requires editors to rely upon the expertise of scholars in the world's geography, religions, languages, economics, governments, cultures, and history. North Carolina is blessed with outstanding scholars in all of these fields, and their expertise has made these books richer, more accurate, and in tune with current scholarship.

Experts in social studies education were called upon to draft the Go to the Source primary resource activities and Skills Lessons. They developed projects and assignments for evaluating student progress and created modified sheltered instruction lesson plans for English Language Learner students. The assessments in the series reflect their knowledge of the field and also of North Carolina's testing environment.

You can see by looking at the list of contributors that *North Carolina Journeys* has drawn consulting Social Studies teachers from virtually every corner of North Carolina. Collectively their experience embraces a broad range of classroom environments. All came to the project with recommendations indicating that, irrespective of environment, each had enjoyed remarkable success.

Consulting teachers were organized into groups reflecting the grade that they taught. Their work with the editors and with one another commenced as the manuscripts for each text began to take shape. As a group these teachers met with the editors in Raleigh but they also consulted with one another and with the editors via the Internet. It was work that consumed summers, school vacations, and weekends. The teachers undertook a number of vital tasks: linking daily lessons with the state's curriculum objectives; suggesting teaching strategies, pacing, and classroom activities; and identifying resources to augment almost every subject.

Textbooks for Every Classroom

The mix of scholarship and service in this edition of *North Carolina Journeys*, we trust, has produced books with features that facilitate a variety of teaching styles. At each grade level, teachers using the Student and Teacher's Editions, the Teacher's Resource Guide, and the companion Web site, **NCJourneys.com**, will find that they have in hand all necessary resources to meet curriculum guidelines as well as integrate other curricula into the social studies.

Other teachers should find it easy to incorporate the books into their individual styles, leading students in discussions, assigning independent projects, augmenting—or even making substitutes for—textbook content. The driving force behind the publication of this series has been the determination to write books that each teacher will claim as an effective teaching tool and that students will enjoy on their social studies journeys.

Burton F. Beers, Ph.D.
Emeritus Editor and Professor of History
North Carolina State University

About NCJourneys.com

NCJourneys.com is where you will find electronic resources specifically designed for *A Journey Through Africa, Asia, and the Pacifc Realm.* The following are some of features of **NCJourneys.com.** This site supports the textbook, enchances learning, and provides user-friendly ways to incorporate technology in your social studies instruction.

Online Book

At **NCJourneys.com,** you and your students can access the entire content of *A Journey Through Africa, Asia, and the Pacific Realm.* The content is searchable, and your students will be able to click on all vocabulary terms to read their definition. In addition, all of the maps in the book and several of the images are tied into the online text where they appear in the book.

Audio Book

At **NCJourneys.com,** you will find the entire audio recording of *A Journey Through Africa, Asia, and the Pacific Realm.* This is the same recording provided on the Audio Book CD.

Interactive Games and Digital Storytelling

NCJourneys.com includes learning games developed by the award-wining instructional designers at LetterPress Software, Inc. The following programs are just an example of the types of programs you will find at **NCJourneys.com:**

World Geography and History Programs

These interactive programs present an exciting approach for learning about world geography and history topics. The following programs are an example of what you will find at **NCJourneys.com:**

Conquerors of the World
Cross the plains of Europe and Asia with Hannibal, Charlemagne, and Suleiman the Magnificent.

Ships of History
This program presents the major ships of history: from the simple outrigger canoe used by the Polynesians to the luxurious ocean liners enjoyed today.

Interactive Atlas

The *Interactive Atlas Collection* is designed to help students learn and identify the locations, capitals, and other facts about North Carolina and the countries of the world. Separated into continents and regions, each lesson provides students with an opportunity to explore maps of the state or countries. This exploration section is supported by games and extension activities. The extension activities will help students learn new facts about each location. The following programs are included in the *Interactive Atlas Collection*:

North Carolina	Europe Geography
Africa Geography	North America Geography
America's States and Capitals	South America Geography
East Asia Geography	West Asia Geography

Exam View Assessment Suite

ExamView Assessment Suite is an industry standard assessment program available at **NCJourneys.com**. It is a user-friendly assessment program that helps you create custom assessments. The program comes loaded with questions from all of *A Journey Through Africa, Asia, and the Pacific Realm's* chapter assessments. All questions are written in the style of the North Carolina Reading Comprehension End-of-Grade Test. *ExamView Assessment Suite* provides you the opportunity to create multiple versions of the same test with corresponding answer keys. *ExamView Assessment Suite* also allows you to track student progress in an accessible way.

Image Banks

Several images from *A Journey Through Africa, Asia, and the Pacific Realm* are organized in chapter image banks. You or your students can use these images in PowerPoint presentations or a variety of other ways.

Digital Transparencies of Maps and Graphic Organizers

At **NCJourneys.com** you and your students have access to digital files of all of the maps in the book. You can also download all the graphic organizers and blank maps of the Teacher's Resource Guide. Use these to files for digital projectors or create your own hardcopy transparencies for the images you will use most.

Digital Students Worksheets

You will never have to worry about losing a worksheet from the Teacher's Resource Guide, because all of the student worksheets are available at **NCJourneys.com.**

Web site Links

You and your students will find links to the web sites mentioned in the Teacher's Edition activities and the Chapter Resources sections.

Facilitating Exchange

This space will provide a special community for North Carolina teachers to share ideas about social studies instruction. You are bound to find creative lesson plans and materials to give a boost to your teaching.

Unit

Units present information on the geography or history of an entire region within Africa, Asia, and the Pacific Realm. Generally, they are comprised of three to five chapters. Units are arranged so that subject matter is relevant and can be taught as a whole.

Unit Opener Text

This opener uses a dramatic or unique written item to catch the interest of the reader about the unit to come.

Chapter

Each chapter is a unified presentation of an important aspect of the region covered in that unit. Each chapter usually contains three lessons.

Chapter Opener Text

Chapter openers contain some written item of interest drawn from the text or from some aspect of the text to catch the interest of the reader.

Unit Opener Illustration

A large photo or painting connects to the text in a way that is striking in terms of aesthetics and in meaning to the unit.

Locator Map

A map of the world highlights the region that is being studied in the unit.

Unit Preview

Provides the student with information about each chapter in one-sentence descriptions.

Chapter Opener Map

A half- or full-page map shows the region to be studied.

Eyewitness to History

Eyewitness to History is a two-page spread found in each chapter. This feature presents a person, place, or artifact that has changed over time. It expands on the idea of the geographical theme of place by showing historical changes to that place over time. Most *Eyewitness* features contain a map that illustrates the location of the topic. The emphasis of this feature is geographical, yet it teaches important historical data.

Chapter Preview

Provides short descriptions of each lesson.

Chapter Opener Illustrations

Works of arts or photographs connect to the Chapter Opener text and chapter topic.

Lesson

Each lesson begins with a preview of key ideas and key terms.

Lesson Review

"Fact Follow-Up" and "Talk About It" questions that test students' knowlege of the lesson.

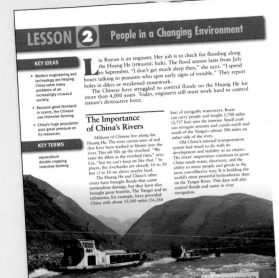

Photographs

Captions have a question related to the content.

Key Terms

Important terms are boldfaced, highlighted, and defined in context.

Skill Lesson

Skills from the North Carolina Social Studies Curriculum are presented in conjunction with the text as a one or two-page spread, just before the Chapter Review.

Go to the Source

Allows students to analyze a primary source that relates to the content of the chapter. The questions and activities familiarize students with different types of primary sources and also build content-reading skills.

Chapter Review

The Chapter Review contains four elements and is found at the end of each chapter.

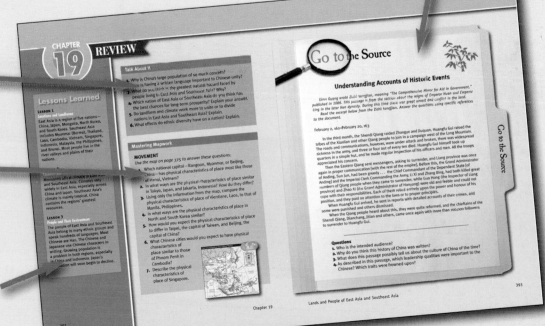

Talk About It

Critical thinking questions about the chapter

Mastering Mapwork

A review of the map skills based upon the Five Themes of Geography

Lessons Learned

Summary review of the chapter lessons.

Special Features

These features are designed to capture student interest and to offer further avenues for research and learning. Special features also offer students who are visual learners additional opportunities for better understanding.

A Journey to...

This feature highlights a specific part of life in the region being studied. It focuses on a particular place to tell a story or describe what daily life is like in that place. This feature expands on the geographical themes of human-environmental interaction and place.

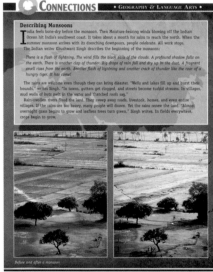

Word Origins

This feature explains how certain words came into use and gives the definition of the word from its original source. This feature helps students remember important place names or terms.

Geography Connections

Geography Connections takes up one aspect of the arts, language arts, math, or science to explore the themes of geography. This feature is ideal for integrating geography with other subjects. It expands on the themes of geography and shows how another subject can be connected to the geographic theme.

What Would You Do?

This feature focuses on a conflict within a region and asks the students to think of possible solutions. These are critical thinking questions that are excellent writing prompts. Students are encouraged to consider questions from the point-of-view of people living in the region.

Customs

Customs highlights a custom from the countries or regions studied in the chapter. The purpose of this feature is to broaden the student's knowledge of how people live in their world. This feature could serve as a starting place for class discussion.

Maps

Maps are invaluable tools in teaching social studies. They are especially vital in a curriculum that focuses upon cultural geography, as does the North Carolina Standard Course of Study for grades 4–7. A professional map publisher, Mapping Specialists of Madison, Wisconsin, drew maps for each grade level according to specifications from *North Carolina Journeys* editors and designers. Dr. Douglas Wilms, Professor Emeritus of Geography at East Carolina University, served as the series' geographical consultant. The maps in the series meet the highest standards of production, design, accuracy, and up-to-date geographical and historical scholarship.

Maps introduce every chapter. Maps within lessons extend the information provided in written form to a visual form that meets the needs of all learning levels. Map activities end every chapter. Within the appendix is an atlas full of maps.

Title

The map title gives students and teachers a short description of the map's purpose. The map title begins with the region covered (such as North Carolina, the United States, Western Europe, or Africa). The title concludes with a short description of the type of map shown (physical, political, political/physical, climate, vegetation, population, resources and economic activities, distribution, largest cities, and so on).

Locator Map

On the top right of the map is a small locator map of the world. The location covered by the chapter opener map is highlighted so that students and teachers can locate the region within the world.

Scale

Every map includes a scale bar reflecting miles and kilometers.

Key

Every map includes this vital tool to show the meaning of the symbols or colors used on the maps.

Map Body

The map itself includes colors that indicate proper elevations on physical maps, distinguish nations on political maps, show population distribution on population maps, show varieties of vegetation on vegetation maps, show climate distribution on climate maps, and show ownership of territories through time on historical maps. Text references to places in the region under discussion are labeled on the map. Longitude lines, latitude lines, the Equator, Tropic of Cancer, Tropic of Capricorn, International Date Line, and the prime meridian are present and labeled. The map projections vary by map, depending on what is depicted. Mapping Specialists used projections that show the least amount of distortion.

Caption

The map captions used on all lesson maps begin with a word that shows the theme (or themes) of geography that the map displays. After the theme is a short description of the map. Finally, there is a question that relates the map back to the lesson. Often these are higher order thinking questions. Answers are contained in this Teacher Edition.

Unit Opener Pages

Each unit opens with four pages of suggestions and activities for teaching that unit in the Teacher's Edition, and two wrap-around margin pages with map activities and a career feature, *Social Studies at Work*.

Unit Opening Statement

This describes the image used in the Student Edition unit opener and the content of the unit.

Unit Planner

The Unit Planner helps you prepare to teach the unit. Preparing the Unit offers suggestions about integrations and reminders about where to find ancillary material. Unit Teaching Strategies suggest concepts to emphasize and alternate ways to approach the material in the textbook.

Unit Lesson Plan

This organizer lays out the unit. It provides a summary of each lesson, an Essential Question to organize instruction of each lesson, and a Suggested Time in which to teach the lesson to allow you to pace yourself. See page T33 in the Teacher's Edition for alternative pacing guides, including suggestions for block schedules.

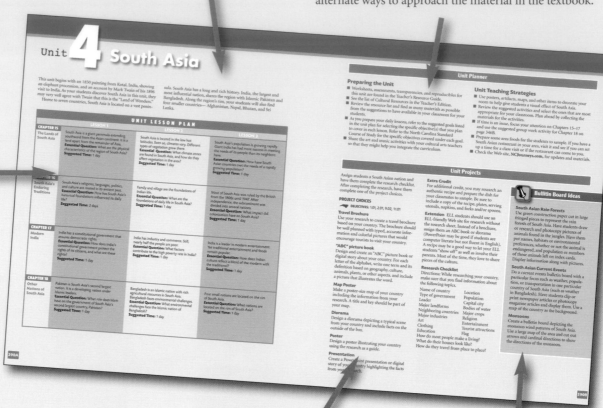

Unit Activities

Every activity in the textbook is labeled with the North Carolina social studies curriculum objectives—marked with this symbol. Each unit begins with a Unit Introductory Activity and Unit Culminating Activity. The Introductory Activity is designed to introduce students to the region or topics to be studied in the unit. The Culminating Activity of each unit encourages students to create a product at the conclusion of their unit study that builds upon their work in the previous unit. Unit Technology, Science, and Math Activities are designed to offer you opportunities to integrate the other curriculums into social studies using concepts from the unit.

Unit Projects

The Unit Projects offer a choice of five student projects for each unit, reflecting different aspects of the multiple intelligences. Students may work on these as they study the unit or after they complete their study of the unit.

Bulletin Board Ideas

The bulletin board ideas were created by North Carolina teachers. Adjust and expand them according to your needs. With some changes, ideas can be taken from one region and used in another.

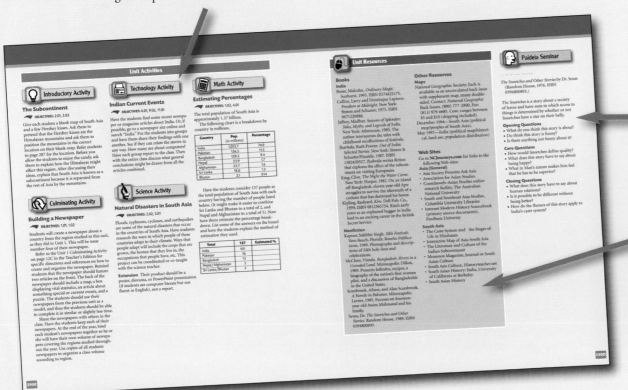

Paideia Seminar

Each unit offers a Paideia Seminar addressing themes from the unit.

Unit Resources

Unit Resources suggests "teacher-tested" resources for the unit, including books, videos, online material, and maps.

Social Studies at Work

This feature discusses a North Carolina person with a job requiring social studies skills and/or knowledge. These features are designed to be read aloud to the class or photocopied and distributed for students to read themselves. Each feature provides an activity for the class to do and suggestions about where to find out more information about the person or their job.

Unit Opener Map Activity

The Unit Opener Map Activity orients the student to the area of the world to be studied in the unit. Each map activity in the series is identified with a special graphic and labeled with the matching National Geography Standards (see page T32 in the Teacher's Edition) and the related geographic themes.

Unit and Chapter Teaching Strategies

In each unit and chapter, there are suggested teaching strategies for you to consider when planning your lessons. Due to the magnitude of information and activities in this book, the suggested strategies will help you organize your lessons, pace yourself through your year, and make the best use of your allotted time to teach social studies. These strategies were developed by experienced teachers in each grade level and will offer solutions and ideas to help you plan.

Prior to starting the year or semester, read over the suggested teaching strategies for each unit and chapter in order to prioritize the concepts that you will teach throughout the year. You will also find that there are numerous ideas and strategies for integrating social studies with other disciplines and suggestions for working with different populations of students. By planning ahead, you can pace yourself through the curriculum, meet the demands of the North Carolina Standard Course of Study and pique the interest of the students with all of the exciting and challenging ideas that the book has to offer.

Rose Cooper
Moore County Public Schools

Paideia

Paideia (pronounced pa•DAY•uh) is the Greek word for the education of the whole child. The Paideia Program was first articulated in a book entitled *The Paideia Proposal* (1982) by philosopher Mortimer Adler. The program is dedicated to the idea that American classrooms can be made simultaneously more rigorous and more inclusive.

The application of the Paideia Program in the classroom is based on what Adler termed the three "columns" of teaching and learning: didactic instruction of information, coaching of intellectual skills, and seminar discussion of ideas and values. Together, these three types of instruction enhance the literacy, problem solving, and thinking skills of students. Teachers integrate these three types of instruction in units of study called Paideia Coached Projects, so named because the focus of each unit is a performance or production of value to an audience outside the classroom. Examples of Coached Projects include historical reenactments and interpretations, documentary research and publication, and activist social service projects.

In taking the study of history and society beyond the walls of the classroom, Paideia Coached Projects often involve the integration of traditional "social studies" with other subject areas.

At the heart of each successful Coached Project is the Paideia Seminar, an intellectual dialogue about ideas and values facilitated by open-ended questions about a text. In a Paideia Seminar, students explore and personalize the concepts inherent to a body of information and set of skills. Imagine for a moment elementary students engaged in an intellectual discussion about the value of a flag as a symbol, middle school students comparing the concepts of freedom and responsibility as represented in political speeches from two historical periods, or high school students engaged in analyzing a series of maps that offer a variety of data about a geographical region. In each instance, students are learning to think and speak for themselves about the curriculum.

See page T28 in the Teacher's Edition for guidelines on conducting a Paideia Seminar.

Chapter Opening Pages

Each chapter opens with two pages of suggestions and activities for teaching the chapter in the Teacher's Edition, and two wrap-around margin pages with activities and resources.

Social Studies Strands

The North Carolina Standard Course of Study Social Studies Strands are listed along with major concepts of the chapter.

North Carolina Standard Course of Study

The main North Carolina Standard Course of Study for the Social Studies Competency Goals addressed in the chapter are listed here.

Activities and Integrations Organizer

This organizer lists all the activities found in the chapter. The activities are grouped according to their curriculum integration. If an activity has more than one integration, for example, a writing prompt that addresses language arts and character education, it is listed under each heading. The objectives/traits are listed to the right of each activity title.

Assessments

The assessments written for each chapter can be used as a complete set or be broken into components. The assessments were designed to complement the North Carolina End of Grade Testing Program.

Analogies

Each chapter provides an analogies activity that can be used as an instructional strategy to help students better understand new material. Analogies are useful to help students make associations with prior knowledge.

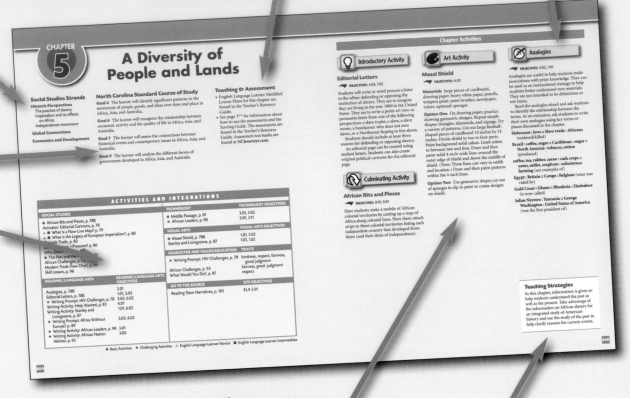

Activator

The Activator provides a suggestion to quickly introduce students to the theme of the chapter.

Writing Prompt

The Writing Prompt is a chapter-specific prompt to assist you in integrating the language arts curriculum with your social studies instruction. These are aligned with the state writing assessments.

Chapter Activities

Each chapter begins with a Chapter Introductory Activity, designed to introduce students to the region or topics to be studied in the chapter. The Culminating Activity is designed to reinforce the concepts studied in the chapter and conclude the chapter. The art activity may be done in class or in conjunction with the art specialist.

Teaching Strategies

Teaching Strategies suggest concepts to emphasize and alternate ways to approach the material in the textbook.

Map Activity

The Map Activity reinforces concepts illustrated in the chapter opening map. Each map activity is identified with a special graphic and labeled with the matching National Geography Standards (see page T37 in the Teacher's Edition) and the related geographic themes.

Chapter Resources

Chapter Resources suggest "teacher-tested" resources for the chapter, including books, audiovisuals, maps, and online material.

Additional Features

Lesson Opener

Each lesson begins with the main North Carolina Standard Course of Study for the Social Studies objectives covered in the lesson, noted by this symbol ➤.

Caption Answers

Caption Answers are given where appropriate.

Discussion Questions

These suggested questions are designed to help your class discuss important concepts and make connections between new material and prior knowledge. Often, students are asked to relate what they are studying to North Carolina or their community.

Activities

Several different types of activities can be found in each chapter.

Teacher Notes

Teacher Notes provide background information, teaching suggestions, or clarifications.

Background Information

Provides additional information related to a topic covered in the lesson.

Lesson Review

Lesson Review answers are found at the end of each lesson.

Name Origin

Name Origin details the origins of place names.

ELL Teaching Tips

ELL Teaching Tips offer suggestions for addressing the special needs of English Language Learner (ELL) students (also described as English as a Second Language [ESL] students).

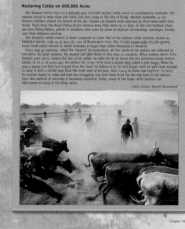

It's a Fact

It's a Fact lists facts about each nation in the region or about the topic covered in the chapter.

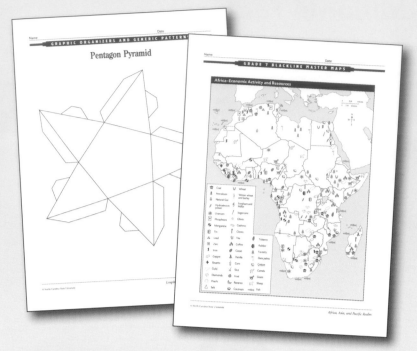

The teacher materials for *North Carolina Journeys* include a grade-level Teacher's Resource Guide. This binder contains all of the ancillary materials to supplement the Teacher's Edition. The Teacher's Resource Guide includes Worksheets, Assessments, English Language Learner (ELL) Worksheets, Modified Lesson Plans for ELL learners, Blackline Master Maps, Graphic Organizers, and Generic Patterns. All of the material in the Teacher's Resource Guide is available at **NCJourneys.com.**

Worksheets

Each chapter contains worksheets for that chapter to be used in conjunction with specific lessons. Each chapter in the series has a Key Terms Vocabulary Review worksheet, which reviews the Key Terms from the chapter.

Every lesson in the series has a Reading Guide worksheet to help reinforce important facts from the lesson. These should be used in conjunction with—but not in place of—the Lesson Review found in the Student Edition. Chapter Review worksheets in the Teacher's Resource Guide assess content recall.

Other worksheets vary by chapter and by lesson. All of the worksheets in the Worksheet section of the Teacher's Resource Guide are listed on the Table of Contents found in the front of the Teacher's Resource Guide.

Assessments

North Carolina Journeys presents numerous opportunities for assessing students' work and understanding. Some assessments are formal; others are informal. Both formal and informal assessments seek to measure students' understanding of important content information and social studies terms and methodologies. Formal assessments include Lesson Reviews, Chapter Reviews, and three-part student assessments following each chapter. Teachers may informally assess students' work on unit and chapter activities suggested in the Teacher's Edition of the textbook. Many of these activities give suggestions for informal assessments. Skill Lessons for each chapter of the textbook are accompanied by teaching suggestions that include informal assessments.

Formal Assessments

Lesson Reviews follow each lesson in the textbook. The Fact Follow-Up features assess content recall; the Think About It features encourage students to synthesize information, to take and support positions, and/or to explain phenomena or events. As students respond to items in the Lesson Reviews, they build skills in reading, analyzing, and interpreting social studies materials as well as in applying decision-making and problem-solving techniques.

Chapter Reviews include Talk About It, Mastering Mapwork, Becoming Better Readers, and Go to the Source.

All formal chapter assessments are derived from the Lesson Reviews and Chapter Reviews. The formal assessment for each chapter contains three elements:

■ Items designed to check students' recall and understanding of content information. For grades 6 and 7, there are 15 items. Every item in this section is taken from either Lesson Review or Chapter

Review items.

■ Map questions that assess students' abilities to read and interpret information from maps and/or charts. The five map questions for each chapter are designed for students to use a textbook map to respond to questions that will assess map reading skills, synthesizing skills, and their abilities to use the Five Themes of Geography.

■ Reading Response items engage students in reading a passage and responding to questions about the passage. There are five reading assessment items following each paragraph which use the same format as the End-of-Grade assessment.

■ Essay questions designed to measure students' capacities to synthesize information and express their opinions or points-of-view in well-constructed short responses or essays.

Recall and understanding items, reading assessment items, and map assessments all follow a multiple choice format and are congruent with the testing conventions used by the North Carolina State Board of Education in its assessment programs. There is a general scoring guide for all essay questions that approximates the analytic scoring model used in the North Carolina Writing Assessment for grades 4, 7, and 10. No attempt is made to replicate the analytic scoring model exactly since the essay questions deal with content materials in the social studies; additionally, the analytic scoring model used by the state of North Carolina is lengthier and more cumbersome than would be appropriate for use by teachers on a weekly basis.

Blackline Master Maps

The set of Blackline Master maps complements the maps in the Student Edition, including many of the maps found in the atlas of the textbook. This set includes a blackline map of North Carolina and the United States at all grade levels.

Graphic Organizers and Generic Patterns

Included with the Teacher's Resource Guide is a set of graphic organizers and patterns. All of the organizers and patterns are listed on the Table of Contents found in the front of the guide.

Graphic Organizers

The set of graphic organizers is based upon recommendations from the North Carolina Department of Public Instruction. These can be used with any grade level in a multitude of ways. References to specific graphic organizers are made throughout the Teacher's Edition.

Generic Patterns

This is a set of patterns helpful to social studies teachers. The patterns include cubes, pyramids, fact or country wheels, question catchers, and a myriad of other shapes. References to specific patterns are made throughout the Teacher's Edition.

English Language Learner Support

Worksheets

In addition to the suggested activity adaptations for ELL students in the Teacher's Edition, a set of worksheets for ELL students is included in the Teacher's Resource Guide. All of the worksheets referenced in the activity adaptations as well as stand-alone worksheets can be found by chapter in the Teacher's Resource Guide.

Modified Lesson Plans

The Teacher's Resource Guide includes a set of Modified Lesson Plans to help ELL students learn the rigorous content of the Social Studies Standard Course of Study without knowing a lot of English. Suggested modifications and alternative lesson plans adapt the content of each chapter for ELLs.

As a general practice, ELLs tend to spend their first couple of years learning English vocabulary. In the past, this has meant predominantly "survival skills" like body parts, colors, and general greetings. Since the No Child Left Behind legislation, however, this is not nearly enough for them to prepare for the rigorous End of Grade testing at the end of each school year. ELLs now are expected to be exposed to the Standard Course of Study in each content area. While they may not learn every objective in the same way as other students, they should be able to access much of the material and make sense of it as they learn the academic English needed to succeed in school. The lesson plans and modifications provide a non-verbal or alternative method of assessing student learning and will help your ELLs become a more productive part of your classroom.

Writing Assignment and Essay Question Scoring Guide

The individual features of the essay for the purposes of this scoring guide are Main Idea, Support and Elaboration, Organization, Conventions, and Synthesis.

1 Responds to the prompt by giving the topic or main idea of the essay. No supporting detail or elaboration. Lacks logical organization. Lacks control of grammatical conventions appropriate to the writing task. Little or no use of appropriate social studies vocabulary. Response is fragmentary with no synthesis of individual features of the essay form.

2 Responds to the prompt by stating the topic or main idea of the essay. Minimal supporting detail. Some attempt at logical organization. Exhibits minimal control of grammatical conventions appropriate to the writing task. Minimal or flawed use of appropriate social studies vocabulary. Response is more extended, but there is no clear synthesis of the individual features of the essay form.

3 Responds to the prompt by clearly stating the topic or main idea of the essay. Supporting detail is evident, though there may be errors of fact. Organization is logical. Grammar and language usage shows few flaws. Attempt is made to use appropriate social studies vocabulary. Response is extended but lacks synthesis.

4 Responds to the prompt by clearly stating the topic of main idea of the essay. Sufficient supporting detail with no errors of fact. Logical organization. Exhibits reasonable control of grammatical conventions appropriate to the writing task. Uses simple and compound sentences. Pertinent social studies vocabulary is used. Response is extended, but the organization and language usage of the essay do not achieve a synthesis of the individual features of the essay form.

5 Response to the prompt is clear. Supporting detail is present, has no errors of fact, and is appropriately elaborated or explained. Organization is logical. Exhibits reasonable control of grammatical conventions appropriate to the writing task. Simple, compound, and complex sentences are used. Social studies vocabulary is appropriately used. The extended response shows clear organization with a synthesis of the individual features of the essay form.

Teaching Social Studies Using *North Carolina Journeys*

Integration is the Way!

Teaching across the curriculum is a successful teaching strategy used in elementary and middle schools everywhere. Educators have created successful interdisciplinary units by integrating subject areas. Students have enjoyed product-based lessons that mix core subjects with specialty areas. But one dilemma usually arises for teachers: From which subject area should a teaching team base the unit? Social studies is the one subject that can creatively integrate the curriculum.

Social studies is a bottomless well of subject potential that can be successfully tapped to incorporate all areas. The *North Carolina Journeys* Teacher Edition and Teacher Resource Guide are valuable tools for planning across the curriculum. Social studies incorporates the teaching of math, reading and language arts, science, character education, physical education, and all the creative arts and technologies. Integrating all subjects through social studies opens tremendous opportunities for all students. Here are some examples:

During the study of Europe, for instance, a language arts teacher can incorporate countless related grade-level novels and test them through such programs as Reading Renaissance and Accelerated Reader. Comprehension skills can be polished through text, chapter, and review questions in each book of the series. Many meaningful social studies writing prompts are provided for practicing personal narratives and argumentative writing. Reading strategies and English Language Learner lessons round out the wide variety of language arts integrations to hone student skills through *North Carolina Journeys*.

Math teachers can integrate challenging *North Carolina Journeys* math lessons. Various math curriculum lessons are written into each grade level. Many opportunities to teach math through graphing, ratios, and word problems open up when students use maps and charts in geography lessons. From the history of algebra to the use of math facts, *North Carolina Journeys* offers countless numerical challenges for every available grade level, written to match the state curriculum.

Social studies naturally blends much of history and science—from discussions about improvements in transportation methods to the development of information technology. Students can study inventions, the scientific method, astronomy, and medical breakthroughs from all cultures. From the Chinese invention of gunpowder and the Arab's development of the Astrolabe to Copernicus, Galileo, Sir Isaac Newton, Leeuwenhoek's microscope, and the Curies' discovery of radium, science lessons are prevalent in *North Carolina Journeys*.

Opportunities to incorporate technology education with social studies are abundant in *North Carolina Journeys*. The Teacher Edition is filled with activities and suggestions incorporating Internet use, challenging database and spreadsheet activities, and multimedia technology projects. These provide all educators with the inspiration to soundly integrate social studies with computer skills. Students will have loads of fun in the process.

Social studies can be the launching pad for the character education, creative arts, and physical education, too. Cultures from five continents provide diverse musical, artistic, architectural, and athletic studies to be tapped for awesome instruction across the curriculum. Students are faced with thought-provoking questions about other cultures and our own culture from which to draw moral lessons.

North Carolina's demands on teachers are increasing. Only creative, curriculum-based activities can stir student excitement. Integrating technology, Gardner's Intelligences, and differentiated learning comes naturally in *North Carolina Journeys*. Seemlessly integrated units await you—use them!

Eric Flore
New Hanover County Public Schools

Geography and Language Arts

The ability to communicate with others is essential in a world that is growing smaller each day. Our very existence depends on it. Improving students' written and oral communication skills is easily accomplished through integrating North Carolina's social studies curriculum with other academic subjects and the arts.

North Carolina Journeys includes segments called *Connections*. These short features expand upon geographical concepts while creating a bridge to other academic and enrichment subjects. Just as "no man is an island…" (John Donne), social studies should not be taught in isolation. *Connections* creates the opportunity for students to see the interdisciplinary aspects of social studies as more than just dates, names, or places on a map.

Tapping on prior knowledge or experience with literature, *Connections: Geography and Language Arts* helps students better relate to a region's environment or history. Brief glimpses of a region's poetry, proverbs, and summaries of films, folktales, novels, and plays allow students a miniature and more intimate close-up of life that reflects on similarities of values among the world's cultures rather than differences. Middle school students can more readily identify with, and respond to, a historical event from the point of view of a well-defined fictional character. A poet's carefully chosen words paint environmental landscapes that can capture students' imaginations.

Integrating Language Arts

Through mini-integrated units, language arts and social studies teachers share unique teaching moments emphasizing writing skills that branch across curriculum barriers. A delicate web is woven between the two subjects. Like a spider's web it appears gossamer fragile, but in reality the bonds being developed are as strong as fine-milled wire. The textbook and its features, such as Connections, provide an amazing number of spin-offs that impact the North Carolina Writing Test. My students have analyzed poems and phrases from novelists, short story authors, and dramatists, identifying literary techniques, elaboration, and vocabulary that appeals to the senses. Since imitation is the highest form of flattery, students enjoy trying to emulate the works they have read in *Connections*.

Connections also help us as we prepare our students for North Carolina's End of Grade Test in reading. Several different forms of reading are included in end of grade testing, such as folktales, poems, or essays based on summaries of films, novels, or plays. The features and suggested activities allow students to practice their skills in reading and analyzing different genres.

Each new example serves as a springboard for class discussions, writing prompts, and possibilities for new mini-integrated units. Middle school students enjoy the active, meaningful involvement of cross-curriculum reading and writing. They also exhibit better retention when concepts are covered in both social studies and language arts rather than when they are taught in the isolation of just one subject.

The opportunities available help create, in both the students and teacher, an appreciation and respect for cultural diversity. By fostering exploration into each region's literature, teachers have the unique opportunity to encourage students to make their own "connections" and become life-long learners.

Susan Collatz
Iredell-Statesville School System

Social Studies and Math

Social studies provides many opportunities for teachers to integrate other curriculum areas into the study of people and cultures. By integrating language arts, science, math, music, visual arts, and technology into social studies, students can gain a richer understanding of the state and world in which they live. Integrating subjects can also provide students with the chances to make real-world connections with the various disciplines.

Whether students are studying France, Russia, Kenya, or China, social studies and math connections are frequently encountered. Throughout this text series there are numerous opportunities for middle school teachers to integrate geography and math. One example is through the *Connections: Geography and Math* features. In these sections, students will use math concepts coupled with a geography or social studies concept. Estimating, measuring, and graphing are only a few of the many math competencies addressed throughout this text. Teachers will also find that every unit and every chapter includes options for math integrations. These unit and chapter activities are closely aligned with the math skills students are required to master at each grade level.

By using the various opportunities presented in this text to integrate math into social studies, or by developing your own math integrations, you can provide new avenues for students to master both social studies and math goals and objectives.

Eric Eaton
Polk County Public Schools

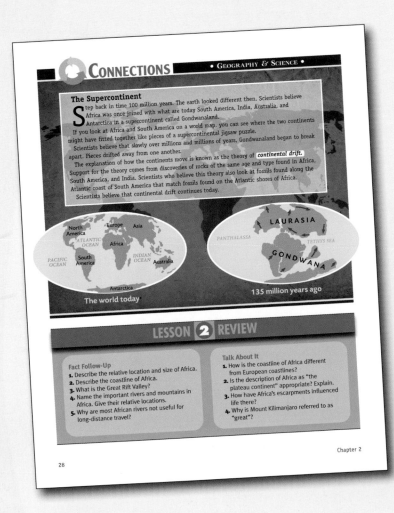

Social Studies and Science

Because middle school students learn best in an atmosphere of integrated curricula, the developers of this textbook series have made a concerted effort to incorporate all disciplines, including science, throughout the books. In the sixth and seventh grade Teacher's Editions, each unit, as well as most chapters, includes a specific science activity. The goals and objectives for each of these activities are labeled according to the North Carolina Standard Course of Study.

As a result of this science integration, middle school students will develop an understanding of inquiry through the use of research materials and technology. After identifying problems, students will acquire information; present their findings in such various formats as spreadsheets, databases, and posters; and then be able to interpret the data. Using the principles of scientific inquiry, students will focus on such issues as human impact on the environment, especially the negative effects of land and air pollution and resulting diseases. Students will use their scientific skills by developing hypotheses for the causes of these problems and possible solutions for them.

Through the integration of science in this textbook, students will combine a deeper appreciation of the scientific process in the context of civic responsibility. Through the implementation of an integrated curriculum for middle school students, we prepare the next generation so that they will have a greater insight into the problems facing our global community while providing them with the skills necessary to discover and implement solutions.

Karen Watts
Wilkes County Public Schools

Social Studies and Technology

Technology is easily integrated into the social studies curriculum. It provides the teacher with a teaching tool that is current and updated often. The North Carolina Standard Course of Study has a very strong computer strand for each grade. The emphasis of this strand culminates with a test in the eighth grade. This makes the use of technology in the social studies classroom a must.

Word processing and desktop publishing can engage students in a multitude of projects. Students can create theirs own newsletters, newspapers, and mini-books using these technologies. This allows for authentic research and delivery of a quality product. The technology itself can be a motivator to students who often have a hard time putting their thoughts on paper because the mechanics of handwriting are so difficult and the editing is so tedious.

Databases offer a way of looking at regions. Students can create the databases and use the data that they have gleaned from current sources to compare economies, population, and incomes so that they can make generalizations about these regions.

Spreadsheets offer a way for students to model outcomes in an experimental way. What will the population be for a country if the rate of growth continues in a constant manner? What happens to the population density if migration continues for 20 years? Student can make predictions and test their validity.

Writing scripts and creating plays and video tapes to share with classmates makes events come alive to the students. PowerPoint and other multimedia tools allow students to be creative and use their writing skills.

Technology offers a new frontier for teachers and students to use in learning about the regions of the world. Integrate, motivate, and watch the excitement of your students as they take possession of their learning.

Arvil R. Sale
Watauga County Public Schools

Skill Lessons

Using the Skill Lessons

Skill Lessons, suggested unit and chapter activities, and the assessments in *North Carolina Journeys* teach, practice, and assess the skills in the North Carolina Social Studies Curriculum: (1) reading social studies materials and increasing social studies vocabulary; (2) accessing a variety of sources; gathering, synthesizing, and reporting information; (3) analyzing, interpreting, creating, and using resources and materials; (4) applying decision-making and problem-solving techniques to world issues; and (5) incorporating computer technology effectively in the learning process. These skills are consistent with and parallel to the skills identified in voluntary national standards for social studies and geography.

Why Teach Social Studies Skills

Some Skill Lessons deal with one or two aspects of these skills; others, with the skills in their entirety. Though aspects of skills may be introduced in isolation, skills are not taught in isolation. Lessons are based on the content information in each chapter and students learn or practice skills as they broaden content understandings. Thus students simultaneously become more knowledgeable and more skillful. The skills process becomes the means through which the content is learned.

Like values and attitudes, skills may be "taught or caught." However, social studies skills that are not taught are only rarely caught. To make the social studies skills their own, some students need to have skills modeled by the teacher. Then they must practice the skills with guidance. Skill Lessons in the text provide opportunities for students to practice these skills with increasingly complex information. In Skill Lessons that ask them to compare their own work with that of other classmates, students monitor and evaluate their own work as well as learn from the work of others.

Reading in Social Studies

North Carolina Journeys contains explicit strategies to enhance students' skill in reading social studies materials, in increasing social studies vocabulary, and analyzing, interpreting, creating, and using resources and materials (Skill Competency Goals 1 and 3). Strategies are located in the suggested activities for each unit and chapter found in the Teacher's Edition. Skill Lessons for each chapter use reading strategies, involving students in reading for meaning, drawing inferences, detecting cause and effect, recognizing bias, and recognizing and using social studies terms. There are numerous opportunities for students to use such reading materials as maps, charts, graphs, photographs, and artifacts. The reading and map items for each chapter assessment underscore the importance of gaining skill in reading social studies materials. These items also serve as opportunities for teachers to assess student understanding and, if need be, to reteach basic skills of reading in the content area of social studies.

As students progress through *North Carolina Journeys*, they encounter increasingly challenging opportunities to practice using a variety of information sources and research skills (Skill Competency Goal 2). Skill Lessons and suggested activities in the Teacher's Edition use maps, charts, globes, atlases, and other reference works.

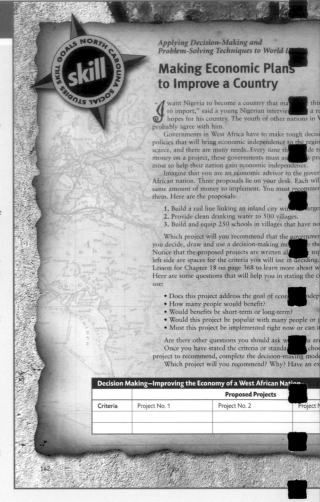

Students transfer information from one medium to another as they create presentations in newspapers, books, computer-generated displays, and so forth.

Decision Making and Problem Solving

Skills in applying decision-making and problem-solving strategies (Skill Competency Goal 4) lie at the very heart of social studies. These skills are embedded in numerous suggested activities and Skill Lessons. Students create graphic organizers and other note-making devices that help them examine conflicting viewpoints, develop hypotheses, predict outcomes, offer solutions, and draw conclusions. In chapter assessments, essay questions give students additional opportunities to practice making decisions and to support them with reasoned arguments. In civic life, group as well as individual decision-making and problem-solving skills are basic competencies. Both Skill Lessons and suggested classroom activities provide many small group activities involving decision making and problem solving.

A young student in Burkina Faso

Chapter 7   West Africa   143

Skill Lesson Review

1. Which project did you recommend? Why?
   Answers will vary. Ask students to share their ideas.
2. What criteria did you establish to help you make
   your decision? Did the criteria help you? Which
   criterion was most important to you? *Answers
   will vary. The balance between health concerns and
   trade expansion is the issue here.*
3. Did you consider recommending parts of
   proposed projects — providing clean drinking

   water to 250 villages and building 125 schools,
   for example? *Answers will vary. The class could
   discuss this possibility and create a combination of
   its own.*
4. What other projects could you suggest to help
   West African nations become economically
   independent? *Answers will vary. Loans to small
   businesses and farms would help, and so would
   building a communications system.*

143

Throughout *North Carolina Journeys* there are suggested activities for incorporating computer technology in the learning process (Skill Competency Goal 5). In every unit of every grade level, the Teacher's Edition suggests individual, small group, and whole class activities that make use of computer technology. Skill Lessons in the series encourage such activities as well. In particular, it is suggested that students engage in online searches for information as a part of special projects and ongoing classroom activities. From time to time, there are suggestions for using computer technology to create finished products. Scattered throughout the series are suggestions for using various Web sites and conducting searches.

Two skill areas that are addressed in the curriculum's social studies strands are embedded in *North Carolina Journeys*. Civic participation skills ranging from contacting public officials to engaging in hypothetical situations as advisors to government decision-makers are explicitly included in the curriculum, and are addressed in the Government and Active Citizenship Strand. Skills in understanding viewpoints other than one's

own are important tools for citizenship in an increasingly diverse and complex nation and world, and are addressed by the Individual Identity and Development Strand. Direct teaching of these strands and skills is a part of *North Carolina Journeys*.

Because geography is basic to learning about world regions, these Skill Lessons emphasize acquiring and using geographic information of increasing complexity. The Five Themes of Geography identified by the National Geographic Society and the National Council for Geographic Education are taught early in the year's work as tools for analyzing world areas.

Students who learn and practice social studies skills over the course of the school year will have learned about world areas important to their own future. They also will have grown more skillful in finding and using information, in making decisions and solving problems, in solving problems, and in dealing with unfamiliar people, places, and ideas as they become responsible citizens.

Diversity in *North Carolina Journeys*

What a wonderful gift we teachers have in our diverse students! Diversity has always presented us with a challenge. We have become masters of meeting the needs of those who differ from the "norm," whether those differences are due to abilities, learning needs, languages, or emotional needs. We must take all our students, love them, and teach them to the best of our abilities.

When many of us began our teaching careers, our classrooms were full of children who were mostly Caucasian or African American. Students and teachers were trying to become accustomed to integration. This often meant moving into a new community and attending school with students and teachers who were different from us. We met the challenge and succeeded.

As the years went by, we would occasionally encounter a student from another country. Although there were not many of these students, their presence enriched our classrooms.

But, my, how the world has shrunk! Now we have students from all parts of the world—Latin America, Europe, Africa, and Asia. They have moved here for the very same reason our ancestors came to the United States—to accept the promise of a better life from the greatest nation in the world. With them come new challenges of understanding cultures and languages. We can make this job a joy by accepting the differences of our students and learning from them. They can introduce their classmates to places they may never have had the opportunity to visit.

It has been said that no one learns more than when they teach. Whether you are an experienced teacher or one who is just starting in your teaching adventure, social studies is the subject that offers more learning opportunities than any other. Its subject is people. Through social studies we can teach understanding and compassion not only about the differences that separate us but also about the sameness that unites us. By studying the cultures, both past and present, of North Carolina, the United States, our hemisphere and our world, we can teach our students to find out the unusual and different, and not to be judgmental about these. We can teach them that it is the big things that unite us: the love of children and family, a religion that is meaningful, compassion for others, respect for nature, and the value of hard work.

Pat Brooks Ellington
New Hanover County Schools

Over the last several decades, the North Carolina classroom has gained diversity through the rediscovery of our long-established cultural groups and through the naturalization of new citizens. In the same manner that our students' cultural heritages differ, the countries that we teach about are also diverse within their borders. As social studies teachers we bear the responsibility of recognizing cultural diversity, providing students with opportunities to continue learning about countries and cultures, and most importantly, equipping students with the means to continue learning about the world beyond the borders of the United States.

No two students are identical. Through social studies we learn that no two peoples of the world are identical. We discover that there are differences between regions of a country as well as regions of the world. Through our studies we also recognize the temporal aspects of change in cultures. Certainly the nations of Africa in the twenty-first century are immeasurably different from the colonies of the 1950s.

Along with the recognition of spatial and temporal diversity within the world's regions and nations, it is critical to realize we can neither learn all there is to know about a country, nor can all we know be conveyed. However, just as an architect first draws the exterior of a house before adding interior rooms, so we must present generalities before accentuating the details. If details become the focus of classroom lessons, then we risk promoting a few ingrained stereotypes instead of addressing the multiplicity of cultures and values within a region.

As role models, we must recognize diversity. Our challenge is to appreciate and teach diversity more effectively. Students or members of the community who have lived in other countries are primary resources. Let them share what is often a source of intense pride for them. Furthermore, keep abreast of current events. Look beyond the headlines into other events: holiday celebrations, political campaigns, drama, art, and major sports events. Not only will this highlight the diverse ways of celebrating life throughout the world, it will also remind us of our similarities.

Still, how do we convey diversity to students who are more concerned with "fitting in" than they are with breaking stereotypes? First, show your enthusiasm; then share the experiences you have had with other cultures. Next, have your students reverse roles and imagine how an outsider might view the United States. *North Carolina Journeys* offers opportunities for this type of study. Critical self-evaluation is the first step in appreciating diversity in others.

Ann Hamzé
Pitt County Public Schools

Character and Values Education in *North Carolina Journeys*

Character Education is an important part of educating students today. Addressing the needs of the student through character education allows the teacher the opportunity to model and simulate the positive outcomes of good character choices. The issues and decisions simulated in the classroom that address character education may affect positive choices on behalf of the student later in life.

In order to have an effective character education program the school must have an effective moral community. This environment will provide students the opportunity for appropriate moral action. In this character education environment, various character education activities will provide intentional, proactive, and comprehensive approaches to the core values identified in the school's curriculum. Character education promotes the identified core ethical values as the basis of good character.

The idea of "character" must be comprehensively defined to include thinking, feeling, and behaving. This understanding will help students make moral decisions and provide a process for students to develop their own intrinsic motivation to have moral character.

Character education activities will help the classroom become an active, engaging environment where the teacher can guide and direct students to making good moral choices. This process will help the students consider the appropriate moral options when faced with future real-life situations.

Michele L. Woodson
Alamance County Public Schools

Since 1996, North Carolina's educational agencies have joined 28 other states integrating character and values education into its curriculums. *North Carolina Journeys* continues to offer activities, strategies, and a special margin feature on the ten targeted character traits (eight are named in N.C. Senate Bill 1139; six are identified in the U.S. Office of Education grant funding a partnership in character education—there is some overlap in the lists). These traits are

Respect

Responsibility

Kindness

Integrity

Fairness (Justice)

Good Citizenship

Courage

Perseverance

Self-discipline

Good Judgment

Many goals and objectives in the North Carolina Standard Course of Study for the Social Studies have topics and applications of these character and value traits.

What Would You Do? is one margin feature that focuses on a regional conflict and challenges the students to think of possible solutions. These are critical thinking questions using one or more of the character traits encouraging students to defend a point of view. Every chapter in every unit has one of the special character-based margin features.

Many of the writing prompts and Paideia seminars as well as some projects and activities emphasize these character and value traits. All are itemized in the Activities and Integrations Organizer found with every chapter.

One useful Web site to gain additional insight into the North Carolina Character Education Partnership is **http://www.ncpublicschools.org/nccep**. An annotated bibliography, model units, and model lesson plans are just some of the links and features found through this site.

Margaret Parrish
Wake County Public Schools
Department of Public Instruction

Teaching Social Studies to the English Language Learner

As at no other time in the public schools of the United States, and certainly in the state of North Carolina, children for whom English is not the language of the home are filling the classrooms. Although our English Language Learners (ELL) may come from any corner of the world, their plight is underscored by the relatively recent influx of children from Mexico to our state. Brought by parents who have made their way here seeking employment, these children add another instructional challenge for the classroom teacher.

ELLs come to our classrooms with numerous needs and bring various gifts. As individuals, they are as different from one another as are you and I. But as a group they do have an essential commonality—their temporary limitation in English precludes their immediate access and understanding of the Standard Course of Study. And as educators we have both a legal and ethical obligation to teach children, regardless of their home language.

Suggestions are made in this series of books for gaining participation of ELLs and providing access to the curriculum. These suggestions and activities are designed not only to help ELL students gain academic content but also to assist them in developing cognitive academic language proficiency.

How fortunate we are to have these young ambassadors from all around the world in our classrooms. The insights and knowledge they bring to us are waiting to be shared. Including new English learners in classroom activities has two potential benefits. First, it will increase their understanding of content and English language. And secondly, it emphasizes for English-speaking American students that other perspectives and patterns of living are a large part of today's world.

Tim Hart
Senior Administrator, ELL
Wake County Public Schools

Addressing the Needs of the English Language Learner

We have chosen ELL (English Language Learner) to refer to students whose English language proficiency is limited. Other terms in current use are ESL (English as a Second Language), LEP (Limited English Proficiency), ESOL (English to Speakers of Other Languages), and EFL (English as a Foreign Language). These terms are often used interchangeably.

ELL adapted activities are noted on the Activities and Integrations chart on each Chapter Opener A page. ELL worksheets are included in the Teacher's Resource Guide.

Cultural Considerations

- Some ELLs may use inappropriate language, not realizing that some English words they have learned are not to be used in the classroom.
- Many ELLs will want to do homework and tests together. While American teachers may regard this as cheating, the students may not consider this to be a rule infraction unless specifically instructed not to work together.
- Competition is a new concept for many ELLs. They may be afraid or unwilling to participate in games or activities involving individual competition. Generally, group competition is more familiar to them.
- Many ELLs will be afraid to "lose face" in front of their peers. They may simply say "I don't know" rather than take the risk to answer a question.
- When introducing a new activity, allowing ELLs to observe first will help them to be more comfortable when asked to participate.
- Some ELLs may be reluctant to try new foods. Be aware of religious dietary restrictions.
- Some ELLs are comfortable with physical touch; they may be more openly affectionate than their American counterparts. Others are the opposite, and may avoid even a casual hug.
- In some cultures, it is downgrading for a teacher to pat a student on the head.

Reminder Tips

- Some ELLs may have adequate social language, yet their understanding of academic terms may be limited. A student who converses well with his classmates may experience difficulty when asked a review question in class.
- Many ELLs have not learned cursive writing. Please type or print!
- Map activities are great for ELLs!
- ELLs may be given a word bank to help them correctly complete crossword puzzles.
- Provide ELLs photocopies of student notes (or an outline) during or after lectures or videos.
- Spanish-speaking ELLs may use a Spanish glossary to help them comprehend new vocabulary.
- Provide additional terms from each chapter for ELLs to define (in English or in their native language).
- Encourage ELLs to use their native language dictionaries to look up unfamiliar words.
- For some assignments, some ELLs may need the number of questions reduced.
- ELLs benefit from seeing other students' projects. Provide the ELLs an extra day to turn theirs in.
- Do not expect ELLs to compare and contrast another unfamiliar culture with American life.
- Some ELLs may experience a "silent period" of six to twelve months. While not yet talking, they are still learning English!
- When a new ELL enters mid-year, ask another student to work through "getting acquainted with the textbook" with the new ELL.
- With some written exercises, ELLs may not understand the directions. Help them get started by working the first few questions together.
- Activators that provide visual clues for the material to be introduced are great activities for ELLs.
- Analogies and true/false items are extremely difficult for ELLs to correctly answer.

- Help ELLs find needed information by highlighting key words in worksheet questions.
- For multiple-choice items, cross out one or two incorrect answers to help ELLs choose the correct answer from fewer options.
- Mneumonic memory devices are not generally helpful to ELLs.

- New Word List—Have ELLs preview the chapter, observe the illustrations, and identify 10 to 20 unfamiliar English words and look them up in their native language dictionaries.

ELL Resources

For links to ELL resource Web sites, please visit
NCJourneys.com

Maps and the Five Themes of Geography

This text, in its effort to promote the understanding of major world regions, includes many maps. Maps are models of the real world, and as reference tools are integral parts of the text. Each map should be studied thoroughly, as important information may be gleaned from each of them, whether they depict cities, countries, population information, economic activities, or such natural features as deserts, islands, water resources, climatic types, and elevation.

Allow your students the time to think about and discuss what appears on each map, making sure they understand the map's title, legend, and scale. Be prepared to help them with directions and latitude and longitude. Allow them to review all data presented on the map and draw some conclusions about the area under study. These activities, sometimes called the "map habit," will enhance the student's understanding of the Five Themes of Geography.

The Five Themes of Geography provide us with a framework for looking at the earth. The understanding of each theme is readily enhanced with consistent map activities.

Location

Every place on earth has a "global address," a location, and we use latitude and longitude to determine absolute location—the first of two types of location. The second type, relative location, is simply the location of one place relative to another. North Carolina, for example, is located in the southeastern part of North America but is also located in the northeastern part of the South.

Place: Physical and Human Characteristics

Every place has a personality that is determined by the interaction of both its physical (landforms, climate) and human (population, settlement patterns) characteristics. Think of your home town: What are its special physical and human characteristics?

Human-Environmental Interaction

This theme explores the interaction between people and their environment. People can modify their environment by cutting trees and draining swamps, and by polluting the air and rivers. Sometimes the environment can adversely effect people, such as happened in 1999 when Hurricane Floyd hit North Carolina, in 2004 when the Tsunami devastated the Asian coastline, or in 2005 when Hurricane Katrina hit New Orleans and the Gulf Coast.

Movement

People are scattered across the earth and continue to move from one place to another. World trade involves the shipment of all sorts of commodities across the globe. And ideas move also as more and more people access television, telephones, and the Internet.

Regions

Because the earth is so large and so complex, geographers have organized it into regions—broad geographical areas distinguished by similar features. Regions can be physical (such as North Carolina's Piedmont) or cultural (such as a language or religious concentration). When we talk about visiting New England or the Midwest or the Southwest we are regionalizing parts of the United States.

Geography is a way of thinking, observing, and appreciating the earth. A good way to promote geographic learning is by promoting the "map habit." In addition to the maps throughout the text, note also all of the Atlas maps at the back of the text. These will allow students to compare one major world region with another.

Dr. Douglas C. Wilms
Professor Emeritus, Geography
East Carolina University

Seminars and Debates

Paideia Seminar Guidelines

A Paideia Seminar is a collaborative, intellectual dialogue about a text, facilitated with open-ended questions. The two developmental learning goals of a Paideia Seminar are to help students develop both social and intellectual skills. Specific objectives for a Paideia Seminar center around increased understanding of the curricular ideas and values.

A Paideia Seminar evolves as three steps; (1a) *pre-seminar content* preparation for analysis of ideas and values in the text (usually through reading), and (1b) *pre-seminar process* to prepare for the whole group dialogue; (2) *Seminar* to discuss the ideas and values of the text; (3a) *post-seminar process* to assess both individual and group participation in the communicative event, and
(3b) *post-seminar content* for student application of the ideas and values (usually through writing).

Following a brief introduction, or "pre-seminar," where the teacher provides the class with necessary background information, the discussion questions (divided into three categories) lead the students through a critical examination of the text and their reaction to it.

Opening questions are intended to quickly put the possibilities of the text into play and should thus be quite general and "open ended." Ideally, opening questions should elicit the greatest variety of responses and work best with maximum participation. Some good opening questions:

> What might be another good title for this text?
> What do you think is the main idea?
> What do you notice first about this text?

Core questions will require critical interpretation on the part of the student, and thus responses will likely vary. Because core questions are intended to foster a close reading of the text, however, it is important for students to understand that any interpretation needs to be supported by evidence within the text itself. Some other core questions:

> How does the beginning of this text relate to the end?
> What tensions do you notice in the text?
> What is the difference between _____ and _____?
> How does the image of the _____ contribute to your reading of the poem?

Closing questions are intended to help students examine the rhetorical import of the text within the larger frameworks of local and global experience.

> How can the message of the text be applied to your/ our current situation?
> What action, if any, does the text request of the reader?
> What would happen if readers complied with that request?

Ask follow-up questions at any point in the discussion to help students elaborate upon and refine their thoughts on the text.

For example, teachers can simply rephrase the comment, "so you're saying ..." Or, they can ask probing questions about previous comments such as:

> What do you mean when you say _____?
> What would lead you to that conclusion?
> How does that relate with what you said about _____?

Save a few minutes at the end of the allotted time for a few post-seminar questions such as:

> What did you like about our discussion?
> Did the discussion change your views about the text in any way?
> Did the discussion change your view about _____ in any way?

Socratic Seminar Guidelines

A Socratic Seminar is a guided group discussion exploring issues. The seminar encourages students toward more rigorous thinking and to explore multiple meanings. Students share, analyze, evaluate, and synthesize their work.

The teacher and the students sit in a circle. The teacher starts off the discussion by asking a question based on the text. The leader listens to student responses and guides the conversation. The teacher uses clarification questions, probing assumption questions, probing reasons and evidence questions, questions about viewpoints and perspectives, questions that probe implications and consequences, and questions about the initial question. Students speak one at a time, respectful of one another's opinions. This technique enables students to think for themselves and to formulate opinions. At the end of the seminar, students can write about what they learned.

Possible Socratic Seminar Topics
- Think These Through prompts in the Lesson Reviews
- Picture captions
- What Would You Do? features

Guide to Student Debates

A debate is a formal public argument for or against a proposal. The affirmative side supports the idea. The negative side opposes it. Both sides take part. The proposal must be stated in a positive way. It should be something that is debatable, is of interest to the audience, states only one problem, has clear wording, and suits the age of the debaters. Below are suggested guidelines for a formal student debate.

The affirmative speakers support and try to prove these issues:
■ The present situation needs to be changed.
■ The ideas proposed are practical ways to change.
■ Change would make the situation better.

The negative speakers are against the proposal, and only need to prove one of the following in order to win the debate:
■ There is no need to change the present situation.
■ The situation does not require a big change.
■ Change will make things worse.

The debate judges (other students in the class) then vote on "which side did the better debating?" Criteria:

1. better organized
2. better evidence
3. courteous and effective speakers

The debate is made up of two parts:

1. First, the affirmative and the negative sides present their arguments.
2. Next, the two sides answer each other's arguments.

Gathering Evidence

The students must do research on a debate topic so that they will have evidence to support the speeches. The audience is made up of the teacher and the other students in the class.

Outline

Debate Information
A. Proposition_____
B. Affirmative Side
1. Supporting arguments and evidence
2.
3.
4.
5.

Affirmative Plan (to implement the proposal and demonstrate the benefits of the proposal)

C. Negative Side
1. Arguments against the affirmative's position or plan
2.
3.
4.
5.

Negative Plan (countering the affirmative plan, demonstrating the disadvantages of the affirmative, or aadvocating to sty with the Status quo.)

Each side should be made up of three or four people who need to search for evidence in a variety of sources. Printed materials, online information, surveys, questionnaires, photos, signs, and drawings may be used. Remind students that expert advice and research carries more wcight with the judges than students' personal opinions.

North Carolina Grade 7 Social Studies Standard Course of Study

The focus for seventh grade is on the continued development of knowledge and skills acquired in the fourth, fifth, and sixth grade studies of North Carolina, the United States, and Europe and South America by considering, comparing, and connecting those studies to the study of Africa, Asia, and Australia. As students examine social, economic, and political institutions they analyze similarities and differences among societies. While concepts are drawn from history and the social sciences, the primary discipline is geography, especially cultural geography. This focus provides students with a framework for studying local, regional, national, and global issues that concern them, for understanding the interdependence of the world in which they live, and for making informed judgments as active citizens.

Strands: Geographic Relationships, Historic Perspectives, Economics and Development, Government and Active Citizenship, Global Connections, Technological Influences and Society, Individual Identity and Development, Cultures and Diversity

Competency Goal 1 The learner will use the five themes of geography and geographic tools to answer geographic questions and analyze geographic concepts.

OBJECTIVES

1.01 Create maps, charts, graphs, databases, and models as tools to illustrate information about different people, places and regions in Africa, Asia, and Australia.

1.02 Generate, interpret, and manipulate information from tools such as maps, globes, charts, graphs, databases, and models to pose and answer questions about space and place, environment and society, and spatial dynamics and connections.

1.03 Use tools such as maps, globes, graphs, charts, databases, models, and artifacts to compare data on different countries of Africa, Asia, and Australia and to identify patterns as well as similarities and differences.

Competency Goal 2 The learner will assess the relationship between physical environment and cultural characteristics of selected societies and regions of Africa, Asia, and Australia.

OBJECTIVES

2.01 Identify key physical characteristics such as landforms, water forms, and climate and evaluate their influence on the development of cultures in selected African, Asian and Australian regions.

2.02 Describe factors that influence changes in distribution patterns of population, resources, and climate in selected regions of Africa, Asia, and Australia and evaluate their impact on the environment.

2.03 Examine factors such as climate change, location of resources, and environmental challenges that influence human migration and assess their significance in the development of selected cultures in Africa, Asia, and Australia.

Competency Goal 3 The learner will analyze the impact of interactions between humans and their physical environments in Africa, Asia, and Australia.

OBJECTIVES

3.01 Identify ways in which people of selected areas in Africa, Asia, and Australia have used, altered, and adapted to their environments in order to meet their needs and evaluate the impact of their actions on the development of cultures and regions.

3.02 Describe the environmental impact of regional activities such as deforestation, urbanization, and industrialization and evaluate their significance to the global community.

3.03 Examine the development and use of tools and technologies and assess their influence on the human ability to use, modify, or adapt to their environment.

3.04 Describe how physical processes such as erosion, earthquakes, and volcanoes have resulted in physical patterns on the earth's surface and analyze the effects on human activities.

Competency Goal 4 The learner will identify significant patterns in the movement of people, goods, and ideas over time and place in Africa, Asia, and Australia.

OBJECTIVES

4.01 Describe the patterns of and motives for migrations of people, and evaluate the impact on the political, economic, and social development of selected societies and regions.

4.02 Identify the main commodities of trade over time in selected areas of Africa, Asia, and Australia and evaluate their significance for the economic, political, and social development of cultures and regions.

4.03 Examine key ethical ideas and values deriving from religious, artistic, political, economic, and educational traditions, as well as their diffusion over time, and assess their influence on the development of selected societies and regions in Africa, Asia, and Australia.

Competency Goal 5 The learner will evaluate the varied ways people of Africa, Asia, and Australia make decisions about the allocation and use of economic resources.

OBJECTIVES

5.01 Describe the relationship between the location of natural resources, and economic development, and analyze the impact on selected cultures, countries, and regions in Africa, Asia, and Australia.

5.02 Examine the different economic systems, (traditional, command, and market), developed in selected societies in Africa, Asia, and Australia, and assess their effectiveness in meeting basic needs.

5.03 Explain how the allocation of scarce resources requires economic systems to make basic decisions regarding the production and distribution of goods and services, and evaluate the impact on the standard of living in selected societies and regions of Africa, Asia, and Australia.

5.04 Describe the relationship between specialization and interdependence, and analyze its influence on the development of regional and global trade patterns.

Competency Goal 6 The learner will recognize the relationship between economic activity and the quality of life in Africa, Asia, and Australia.

OBJECTIVES

6.01 Describe different levels of economic development and assess their connections to standard of living indicators such as purchasing power, literacy rate, and life expectancy.

6.02 Examine the influence of education and technology on productivity and economic development in selected nations and regions of Africa, Asia, and Australia.

6.03 Describe the effects of over-specialization and evaluate their impact on the standard of living.

| Competency Goal **7** | The learner will assess the connections between historical events and contemporary issues in Africa, Asia, and Australia. |

OBJECTIVES

7.01 Identify historical events such as invasions, conquests, and migrations and evaluate their relationship to current issues.

7.02 Examine the causes of key historical events in selected areas of Africa, Asia, and Australia and analyze the short- and long-range effects on political, economic, and social institutions.

| Competency Goal **8** | The learner will assess the influence and contributions of individuals and cultural groups in Africa, Asia, and Australia. |

OBJECTIVES

8.01 Describe the role of key historical figures and evaluate their impact on past and present societies in Africa, Asia, and Australia.

8.02 Describe the role of key groups such as Mongols, Arabs, and Bantu and evaluate their impact on historical and contemporary societies of Africa, Asia, and Australia.

8.03 Identify major discoveries, innovations, and inventions and assess their influence on societies past and present.

| Competency Goal **9** | The learner will analyze the different forms of government developed in Africa, Asia, and Australia. |

OBJECTIVES

9.01 Trace the historical development of governments, including traditional, colonial, and national in selected societies, and assess their effects on the respective contemporary political systems.

9.02 Describe how different types of governments such as democracies, dictatorships, monarchies, and oligarchies in Africa, Asia, and Australia carry out legislative, executive, and judicial functions and evaluate the effectiveness of each.

9.03 Identify the ways in which governments in selected areas of Africa, Asia, and Australia deal with issues of justice and injustice, and assess the influence of cultural values on their practices and expectations.

9.04 Describe how different governments in Africa, Asia, and Australia select leaders and establish laws in comparison to the United States and analyze the strengths and weaknesses of each.

| Competency Goal **10** | The learner will compare the rights and civic responsibilities of individuals in political structures in Africa, Asia, and Australia. |

OBJECTIVES

10.01 Trace the development of relationships between individuals and their governments in selected cultures of Africa, Asia, and Australia, and evaluate the changes that have evolved over time.

10.02 Identify various sources of citizens' rights and responsibilities, such as constitutions, traditions, and religious law, and analyze how they are incorporated into different government structures.

10.03 Describe rights and responsibilities of citizens in selected contemporary societies in Africa, Asia, and Australia, comparing them to each other and to the United States.

10.04 Examine the rights, roles, and status of individuals in selected cultures of Africa, Asia, and Australia, and assess their importance in relation to the general welfare.

| Competency Goal **11** | The learner will recognize the common characteristics of different cultures in Africa, Asia, and Australia. |

OBJECTIVES

11.01 Identify the concepts associated with culture such as language, religion, family, and ethnic identity, and analyze how they can link and separate societies.

11.02 Examine the basic needs and wants of all human beings and assess the influence of factors such as environment, values, and beliefs in creating different cultural responses.

11.03 Compare characteristics of political, economic, religious, and social institutions of selected cultures and evaluate their similarities and differences.

11.04 Identify examples of economic, political, and social changes, such as agrarian to industrial economies, monarchical to democratic governments, and the roles of women and minorities, and analyze their impact on culture.

| Competency Goal **12** | The learner will assess the influence of major religions, ethical beliefs, and values on cultures in Africa, Asia, and Australia. |

OBJECTIVES

12.01 Examine the major belief systems in selected regions of Africa, Asia, and Australia, and analyze their impact on cultural values, practices, and institutions.

12.02 Describe the relationship between and cultural values of selected societies of Africa, Asia, and Australia and their art, architecture, music, and literature, and assess their significance in contemporary culture.

12.03 Identify examples of cultural borrowing, such as language, traditions, and technology, and evaluate their importance in the development of selected societies in Africa, Asia, and Australia.

| Competency Goal **13** | The learner will describe the historic, economic, and cultural connections among North Carolina, the United States, Africa, Asia, and Australia. |

OBJECTIVES

13.01 Identify historical movements such as colonization, revolution, emerging democracies, migration, and immigration that link North Carolina and the United States to selected societies of Africa, Asia, and Australia, and evaluate their influence on local, state, regional, national, and international communities.

13.02 Describe the diverse cultural connections that have influenced the development of language, art, music, and belief systems in North Carolina and the United States and analyze their role in creating a changing cultural mosaic.

13.03 Examine the role and importance of foreign-owned businesses and trade between North Carolina and the nations of Africa, Asia, and Australia, and assess the effects on local, state, regional, and national economies and cultures.

National Geography Standards

These standards are developed and published by the National Geographic Society, **www.nationalgeographic.org**.

Description	Standard	Element
How to Use Maps and Other Geographic Representations, Tools, and Technologies to Acquire, Process, and Report Information from a Spatial Perspective	1	1: The World in Spatial Terms
How to Use Mental Maps to Organize Information About People, Places, and Environments in a Spatial Context	2	1: The World in Spatial Terms
How to Analyze the Spatial Organization of People, Places, and Environments on Earth's Surface	3	1: The World in Spatial Terms
The Physical and Human Characteristics of Places	4	2: Places and Regions
That People Create Regions to Interpret Earth's Complexity	5	2: Places and Regions
How Culture and Experience Influence People's Perceptions of Places and Regions	6	2: Places and Regions
The Physical Processes that Shape the Patterns of Earth's Surface	7	3: Physical Systems
The Characteristics and Spatial Distribution of Ecosystems on Earth's Surface	8	3: Physical Systems
The Characteristics, Distribution, and Migration of Human Population on Earth's Surface	9	4: Human Systems
The Characteristics, Distribution, and Complexity of Earth's Cultural Mosaics	10	4: Human Systems
The Patterns and Networks of Economic Interdependence on Earth's Surface	11	4: Human Systems
The Processes, Patterns, and Functions of Human Settlement	12	4: Human Systems
How the Forces of Cooperation and Conflict Among People Influence the Division and Control of Earth's Surface	13	4: Human Systems
How Human Actions Modify the Physical Environment	14	5: Environment and Society
How Physical Systems Affect Human Systems	15	5: Environment and Society
The Changes that Occur in the Meaning, Use, Distribution, and Importance of Resources	16	5: Environment and Society
How to Apply Geography to Interpret the Past	17	6: The Uses of Geography
How to Apply Geography to Interpret the Present and Plan for the Future	18	6: The Uses of Geography

Pacing Guide and Teaching Strategy Activities

This textbook is intended to be used as a resource for teachers. Teachers cannot expect to use all of the materials included in the Teacher's Edition or the Teacher's Resource Guide. Here are several suggestions to help you organize your presentation of the material throughout the school year in order to cover the goals and objectives of the North Carolina Standard Course of Study.

Notes on Block Scheduling

During a 90-minute block, it will be extremely difficult for students to stay in their seats the entire time. An important strategy for teachers is to plan a variety of activities that will enable students to move around from time to time.

It will be necessary to focus on concepts rather than strict content in order to meet the goals for the Standard Course of Study. Prioritize according to the needs and ability levels of your students.

Alternate Pacing Guide

Traditional Schedule

4 weeks Review of Geography, Chapter 1
4 weeks Australia/New Zealand/Oceania (begin with mainly "Western" cultures familiar to students)
9 weeks Southwest Asia and South Asia
9 weeks Africa
9 weeks Asia

Block Scheduling

Semester

1 week   Introduction, Review of Five Themes, basic landforms and bodies of water
1 weeks Australia, New Zealand, Oceania
4 weeks Southwest Asia and South Asia
5 weeks Africa
5 weeks Asia

The Pacific Realm can be moved to the end of the semester.

Four-Week Block

4 weeks Geography, Australia, New Zealand, Oceania
4 weeks Southwest Asia (could include North Africa) and South Asia
4 weeks Africa
4 weeks Asia

Units must be developed to last four weeks. Do not carry units over from one block of time to another.

Alternate Teaching Strategy—Introduction to Geography and Cultures Through Religion

Begin with Southwest Asia, Unit 3, focusing on the religions. They are a major focal point throughout the book. After Southwest Asia, move to Africa, moving from north to south. From Africa, cover the remainder of the countries as they are presented in the book. This can be used in both a traditional or block schedule by rearranging the units/blocks.

Social Studies Student Notebook

In order to help students improve their organizational skills, require them to keep a social studies notebook with the following elements:

Vocabulary Section: Students should keep their daily vocabulary words in one section of their notebook so that they are compiling a glossary.

Note Section: In this section, students keep their notes, reading guides, and graphic organizers; good to review for tests.

Homework/classwork/handouts: In this section, students keep their independent work.

Extra Credit Section: In this section, students can earn extra credit by collecting current events. They should include the article and write a summary or main idea underneath it.

Calendar of Important Cultural and Historical Events

This list reflects important dates of holidays, festivals, and commemorations, and celebrations that relate to the study of social studies in seventh grade. Some holidays are listed with the actual date of the holiday instead of the observed date, which may differ from year to year.

JANUARY
National Book Month

3rd Monday—Martin Luther King, Jr. Day (United States)
 1 Independence Day (Cameroon);
   Independence Day (Western Samoa);
   New Year's Day (all)
 6 Epiphany (Orthodox Christianity)
 8 Adults' Day (Japan)
 15 Arbor Day (Jordan)
 24 Chinese New Year
 26 Australia Day

FEBRUARY
Black History Month

Lent begins 40 days of sacrifice leading up to Easter.
3rd Monday—Presidents' Day (United States)
 4 Independence Day (Sri Lanka)
 6 Waitangi Day (New Zealand)
 14 Literacy Day (Liberia)
 22 Mother's Day (India)
 28 Peace Memorial Day (Taiwan)

MARCH
Women's History Month

Purim, also known as Feast of Lots (Judaism);
Holi, a Hindu holiday (India, Malaysia, Surinam)
 1 Women of Color Day (all)
 2 Independence Day (Morocco)
 3 Throne Day (Morocco)
 13 Decoration Day (Liberia)
 14 David Livingston arrives in Cape Town (1841)
 17 St. Patrick's Day (Ireland, United States)
 21 No Ruz [New Year's Day] (Iran)
 22 Arab League Day (Egypt, Iraq, Lebanon, Saudi Arabia, Syria, and Yemen)

APRIL

Easter usually falls in early April or at the end of March.
 1 April Fools' Day (United States)
   Planting Day (China)
 4 Independence Day (Senegal)
 16 Family Day (South Africa)
 17 Independence Day (Cambodia)
 22 Earth Day (United States)
 25 Anzac Day (Australia, New Zealand)
 26 National Independence Day (Israel)
 27 Nelson Mandela elected president in South Africa's first election open to all races (1994); Freedom Day (South Africa)
 30 Buddha's Birthday (Hong Kong, Korea)

MAY
Asian Pacific Heritage Month

Last Monday—Memorial Day (United States)
 1 Labor Day (Aruba, Belize, Belgium, Brazil, Chile, France, Germany, Hong Kong, Italy, Malaysia, Mexico, Singapore, Switzerland, Venezuela)
 3 Constitution Memorial Day (Japan)
 5 Children's Day (Japan, Korea)
 7 Wesak Day (Singapore)
 8 Teacher's Day (United States)
 20 Day of Hatred (Cambodia)
 25 Africa Day; Independence Day (Jordan)

JUNE
 1 International Children's Day
 6 Memorial Day (Korea)
 19 Independence Day (Kuwait)
 25 Dragon Boat Festival (China)

JULY
 1 Independence Day (Rwanda)
 4 Independence Day (United States)
 5 Peace and Unity Day (Rwanda)
 7 Independence Day (Solomon Islands)
 14 African Community Day (Senegal)
 20 Neil Armstrong becomes first person to set foot on the moon (1969); Ocean Day (Japan); Peace and Freedom Day (Cyprus)

AUGUST

Onam falls on Shravan Day in August or September (India).
 3 Independence Day (Niger)
 9 National Women's Day (South Africa)
 15 Independence Day (India)
 17 Independence Day (Indonesia)
 24 Flag Day (Liberia)

SEPTEMBER
National Hispanic Heritage Month

Rosh Hashanah is a Jewish holiday to atone for wrong over ten days that cannot begin on a Sunday, Wednesday, or Friday, leading to Yom Kippur, which may not fall on a Friday or a Sunday. These days are determined by the Hebrew calendar, not the Gregorian calendar.
1st Monday—Labor Day (United States)
Full moon—Mooncake Festival (Singapore)
 1 Teacher's Day (China—not established)
 2 Japan signs treaty to end World War II; Father's Day (Australia, New Zealand)
 3 Independence Day (Qatar)
 15 Respect for the Aged Day (Japan)
 16 Independence Day (Singapore)
 22 Feast of the Ancestors (Cambodia)
 24 Heritage Day (South Africa)
 28 Confucius' Birthday (Taiwan)

OCTOBER

2nd Sunday—White Sunday (Western Samoa)
2nd Monday—Columbus Day (United States)
 1 Labor Day (Australia); National Day (Hong Kong)
 2 Mid-Autumn Festival (Hong Kong)
 10 National Day (Taiwan)
 16 World Food Day (all)
 17 Mother's Day (Malawi)
 20 Kenyatta Day (Kenya)
 22 Labor Day (New Zealand)
 31 Halloween (United States)

NOVEMBER
American Indian Heritage Month

2nd week—Geography Awareness Week
4th Thursday—Thanksgiving Day (United States)
1st Tuesday—Election Day (United States)
 1 Recreation Day (Tasmania)
 3 Culture Day (Japan)
 11 Veterans Day (United States)
 14 Children's Day (India)
 15 Shichi-Go-Sen "Five-Seven-Three" (Japan)
 23 Labor Thanksgiving Day (Japan)

DECEMBER

The Muslim holiday of Ramadan is a month-long period based on a lunar calendar, though it generally falls in the month of December. Hanukkah falls in the month of December and is the Jewish eight-day festival of lights.
 12 Independence Day (Kenya)
 25 Christmas Day (most Protestants and Catholics)
 26 Family Day (Namibia)

Information on Cultural, Historical, and Natural Resources in North Carolina

These resources are listed by North Carolina region. Addresses, phone numbers, and Web sites were accurate at the time of publication but may have since changed. Please call ahead before visiting with your class to make arrangements.

Links to these sites are also available at **NCJourneys.com**

Mountain Region

HISTORIC SITES

Cradle of Forestry in America National Historic Site
1001 Pisgah Highway
Brevard, NC 28712
(800) 660-0671
www.cradleofforestry.com

Carl Sandburg Home National Historic Site
928 Little River Road
Flat Rock, NC 28731
(828) 693-4178
www.nps.gov/carl

Zebulon B. Vance Birthplace
State Historic Site
911 Reems Creek Road
Weaverville, NC 28787
(828) 645-6706
www.ah.dcr.state.nc.us/sections/hs/vance/vance.htm

Thomas Wolfe Memorial
State Historic Site
52 Market Street
Asheville, NC 28801
(828) 253-8304
www.ah.dcr.state.nc.us/sections/hs/wolfe/wolfe.htm

MUSEUMS, AQUARIUMS, PLANE-TARIUMS, ART CENTERS, AND HISTORIC HOMES

Appalachian Cultural Museum
University Hall Drive
Boone, NC 28607
(828) 262-3117
www.museum.appstate.edu

Appalachian Heritage Museum
129 Mystery Hill Lane
Blowing Rock, NC 28605
(800) 438-7500, (828) 264-2792
www.mysteryhill-nc.com/heritage.html

Asheville Art Museum
2 South Pack Square
Asheville, NC 28801
(800) 935-0204
www.ashevilleart.org

Biltmore Estate
1 North Pack Square
Asheville, NC 28801
(800) 624-1575
www.biltmore.com

John C. Campbell Folk School
Route 1 off U.S. Highway 64 East
Brasstown, NC 28902
(800) FOLK SCH
www.folkschool.com

Cherokee Historical Museum
87 Peachtree Street
Murphy, NC 28906
(828) 837-6792
http://www.tib.com/cchm/

Cherokee Indian Reservation Visitor Center
Main Street
Cherokee, NC 28719
(800) 438-1601
www.cherokee-nc.com

Colburn Gem & Mineral Museum
2 South Pack Square
Asheville, NC 28801
(828) 254-7162
http://main.nc.us/colburn

Folk Art Center & Southern Highland Craft Guild
Milepost 382, Blue Ridge Parkway
Asheville, NC 28805
(828) 298-7928
www.southernhighlandguild.org

Grandfather Mountain Nature Museum
U.S. Highway 221 North/
Blue Ridge Parkway
Linville, NC 28646
(800) 468-7325
www.grandfather.com/museum/natmuseum/natmus.htm

Hiddenite Center
Church Street
Hiddenite, NC 28636
(828) 632-6966
www.hiddenite.appstate.edu

Hickory Ridge Homestead Living History Museum
P.O. Box 295
Boone, NC 28607
(828) 264-2120
www.boonenc.org/saha/hrh/

Mountain Farm Museum
150 Highway 441 North
Cherokee, NC 28719
(828) 497-1900
www.westernncattractions.com/mountain.htm

Mountain Gateway Museum
Water Street at Catawba Street
Old Fort, NC 28762
(828) 668-9259
www.faahomepage.org/town/enter.html

Mountain Heritage Center
Robins Administration Building
Western Carolina University Campus
Cullowhee, NC 28723
(828) 227-7129
www.wcu.edu/mhc

Museum of North Carolina Handi-crafts
307 Shelton Street
Waynesville, NC 28786
(828) 452-1551
www.geocities.com/Heartland/Valley/6225/page19.html

Museum of North Carolina Minerals
Blue Ridge Parkway
at Highway 226
Spruce Pine, NC 28777
(540) 587 0966
www.blueridgeparkway.info/museum_nc_minerals.htm

North Carolina Homespun Museum
111 Grovewood Road
Asheville, NC 28804
(828) 253-7651
www.grovewood.com/nchomespun.htm

Oconaluftee Indian Village
U.S. Highway 441/Drama Road
Cherokee, NC 28719
(704) 497-2315
www.westernncattractions.com/village.htm

Penland School of Crafts
Conley Ridge Road
Penland, NC 28765
(828) 765-2359
www.penland.org

Smith-McDowell House Museum
283 Victoria Road
Asheville, NC 28801
(828) 253-9231
www.wnchistory.org/smhmwebpage.htm

Waldensian Museum
109 E. Main Street
Valdese, NC 28690
(828) 874-2531
www.valdese.com/museum.htm

Western North Carolina Air Museum
1340 Gilbert Street
Hendersonville, NC 28792
(800) 828-4244
www.wncairmuseum.com

Western North Carolina Nature Center
75 Gashes Creek Road
Asheville, NC 28805
(828) 298-5600
http://wildwnc.org

PARKS, NATIONAL FORESTS, ZOOS, NATURE CENTERS, AND BOTANICAL GARDENS

Appalachian National Scenic Trail
Pisgah National Forest & Great Smoky Mountains National Park
(304) 535-6331
www.nps.gov/appa

Asheville Botanical Gardens
151 W.T. Weaver Boulevard
Asheville, NC 28804
(828) 252-5190
www.ashevillebotanicalgardens.org

Crowders Mountain State Park
S.R. 1125/522 Park Office Lane
Kings Mountain, NC 28086
(704) 853-5375
www.ils.unc.edu/parkproject/visit/crmo/home.html

Fontana Dam
Highway 28
Fontana Dam, NC 28733
(800) 467-1388
www.main.nc.us/graham/fontanad.html

Great Smoky Mountains National Park
107 Park Headquarters Road
Gatlinburg, TN 37738
(888) 355-1849
www.nps.gov/grsm

Lake James State Park
Lake James Road, Highway 126
Marion, NC 28752
(828) 652-5047
www.ils.unc.edu/parkproject/visit/laja/home.html

Joyce Kilmer Memorial Forest
Route 1, Box 247 (Mailing Address)
Highlands, NC 28741
(828) 479-6431
www.main.nc.us/graham/hiking/joycekil.html

Mount Jefferson State Park
U.S. Highway 221
Jefferson, NC 28640
(336) 246-9653
www.ils.unc.edu/parkproject/visit/moje/home.html

Mount Mitchell State Park
Highway 128 off the
Blue Ridge Parkway
Burnsville, NC 28714
(828) 675-4611
www.ils.unc.edu/parkproject/visit/momi/home.html

Nantahala National Forest
Route 1, Box 247
Highlands, NC 28741
(828) 257-4200
www.cs.unca.edu/nfsnc

New River State Park
N.C. Highway 88 at S. R. 1588
Jefferson, NC 28640
(336) 982-2587
www.ils.unc.edu/parkproject/visit/neri/home.html

Pisgah National Forest
Pisgah Forest, NC 28768
(828) 257-4200
www.cs.unca.edu/nfsnc

South Mountains State Park
3001 South Mountains State Park Avenue
Morganton, NC 28655
(828) 433-4772

Stone Mountain State Park
S.R. 1002 at U.S. Highway 21
Roaring Gap, NC 28668
(336) 957-8185
www.ils.unc.edu/parkproject/visit/stmo/home.html

Piedmont Region

HISTORIC SITES

Alamance Battleground
State Historic Site
5803 South N.C. Highway 62
Burlington, NC 27215
(336) 227-4785
www.ah.dcr.state.nc.us/sections/hs/alamance/alamanc.htm

Bennett Place State Historic Site
4409 Bennett Memorial Road
Durham, NC 27705
(919) 383-4345
www.ah.dcr.state.nc.us/sections/hs/bennett/benett.htm

Charlotte Hawkins Brown Memorial
State Historic Site
6136 Burlington Road
Sedalia, NC 27342
(336) 449-4846
www.ah.dcr.state.nc.us/sections/hs/chb/chb.htm

Burwell School State Historic Site
319 North Churton Street
Hillsborough, NC 27278
(919) 733-4276
www.presnc.org/guide/piedmont.html#orange

Duke Homestead
State Historic Site
2828 Duke Homestead Road
Durham, NC 27705
(919) 477-5498
www.ah.dcr.state.nc.us/sections/hs/duke/duke.htm

Fort Dobbs State Historic Site
438 Fort Dobbs Road
Statesville, NC 28677
(704) 873-5866
www.ah.dcr.state.nc.us/sections/hs/dobbs/dobbs.htm

Horne Creek Living Historical Farm State Historic Site
320 Hauser Road
Pinnacle, NC 27043
(336) 325-2298
www.ah.dcr.state.nc.us/sections/hs/horne/horne.htm

House in the Horseshoe
State Historic Site
324 Alston House Road
Sanford, NC 27330
(910) 947-2051
www.ah.dcr.state.nc.us/sections/hs/horsesho/horsesho.htm

North Carolina State Capitol
State Historic Site
1 East Edenton Street
Raleigh, NC 27601
(919) 733-3456
www.ah.dcr.state.nc.us/sections/capitol/default.htm

James K. Polk Memorial
State Historic Site
Highway 521
Pineville, NC 28134
(704) 889-7145
www.ah.dcr.state.nc.us/sections/hs/polk/polk.htm

Reed Gold Mine State Historic Site
9621 Reed Mine Road
Stanfield, NC 28163
(704) 721-4653
www.ah.dcr.state.nc.us/sections/hs/reed/reed.htm

Historic Stagville
5825 Old Oxford Highway
Durham, NC 27722-1217
(919) 620-0120
www.ah.dcr.state.nc.us/sections/do/stagvill/default.htm

Town Creek Indian Mound State Historic Site
S.R. 1160
Mount Gilead, NC 27306
(910) 439-6802
www.ah.dcr.state.nc.us/sections/hs/town/town.htm

MUSEUMS, AQUARIUMS, PLANETARIUMS, ARTS CENTERS, AND HISTORIC HOMES

Ackland Art Museum
Franklin Street at
South Columbia Street
UNC-CH Campus
Chapel Hill, NC 27599-3400
(919) 966-5736
www.unc.edu/depts/ackland

American Classic Motorcycle Museum
1170 U.S. Highway 64 West
Asheboro, NC 27203
(910) 629-9564

The ArtsCenter
300 East Main Street
Carrboro, NC 27510
(919) 929-2787
www.carrboro.com/artscenter.html

Artspace, Inc.
201 East Davie Street
Raleigh, NC 27601
(919) 821-2787
http://artspace.citysearch.com/3.html

Ayr Mount Historic Home
376 St. Mary's Road
Hillsborough, NC 27278
(919) 732-6886
www.co.orange.nc.us/ercd/commissions/hpc.htm

Blandwood Mansion
447 West Washington Street
Greensboro, NC 27401
(336) 272-5003
www.blandwood.org

Catawba Science Center
243 Third Avenue Northeast
Hickory, NC 28601
(828) 322-8169
www.catawbascience.org

Charlotte Museum of History
3500 Shamrock Drive
Charlotte, NC 28215
(704) 568-1774
www.charlottemuseum.org

Chinqua-Penn Plantation
2138 Wentworth Street
Reidsville, NC 27320
(336) 349-4576
www.chinquapenn.com

Cleveland County Historical Museum
Courtsquare
Shelby, NC 28150
(704) 482-8186

Alexander Dickson House
150 East King Street
Hillsborough, NC 27278
(919) 732-7741
www.historichillsborough.org/alliance5.html

Discovery Place
301 North Tryon Street
Charlotte, NC 28202
(704) 372-6261
www.discoveryplace.org

Duke University Museum of Art
Campus Drive
Duke East Campus
Durham, NC 27706
(919) 684-5135
www.duke.edu/web/duma

Executive Mansion
200 North Blount Street
Raleigh, NC 27601
(919) 733-3456
www.ah.dcr.state.nc.us/sections/capitol/default.htm

Exploris
201 East Hargett Street
Raleigh, NC 27603
(919) 834-4040
www.exploris.org/visit

Furniture Discovery Center
101 West Green Drive
High Point, NC 27260
(336) 887-3876
www.furniturediscovery.org

Gaston County Museum of Art and History
131 West Main Street
Dallas, NC 28034
(704) 866-3437
www.upress.virginia.edu/epub/pyatt/dall01.html

Granville County Museum
110 Court Street
Oxford, NC 27565
(919) 693-9706
www.oxfordnc.org/museum.html

Green Hill Center for North Carolina Art
200 North Davie Street
Greensboro, NC 27401
(336) 333-7460
www.greenhillcenter.org

Greensboro Historical Museum
130 Summit Avenue
Greensboro, NC 27401
(336) 373-2204
www.greensborohistory.org

Greensboro Natural Science Center
4301 Lawndale Drive
Greensboro, NC 27455
(336) 288-3769
www.greensboro.com/sciencecenter

Hayti Heritage Center
804 Old Fayetteville Street
Durham, NC 27701
(919) 683-1709
www.durham-nc.com/group/features/hayti_heritage.html

Hickory Museum of Art
243 Third Avenue Northeast
Hickory, NC 28601
(327) 327-8576
www.hickorymuseumofart.org/hma_frames.html

High Point Museum
1859 Lexington Avenue
High Point, NC 27262
(336) 885-1859
www.high-point.net/dept/museum

Historic Bethabara Park
2147 Bethabara Road
Winston-Salem, NC 27106
(336) 924-8191
www.bethabarapark.org/legend.htm

Horizons Unlimited Educational Center
1636 Parkview Circle
Salisbury, NC 28144
(704) 639-3004
www.ee.enr.state.nc.us/eec Horizons.htm

Joel Lane House
St. Mary's Street at West Hargett Street
Raleigh, NC 27601
(919) 833-3431
www.geocities.com/joellane_raleigh

Historic Latta Plantation
5225 Sample Road
Huntersville, NC 28078
(704) 875-2312
www.lattaplantation.org

International Civil Rights Center and Museum
132 South Elm Street
Greensboro, NC 27401
(910) 373-2043
www.unitedwaygso.org/intouch/3u0wyz8w.htm

Mendenhall Plantation
603 West Main Street
Jamestown, NC 27282
(910) 454-3810
www.high-point.net/dept/museum/images/historical_buildings.htm

Mint Museum of Art
2730 Randolph Road
Charlotte, NC 28207
(704) 337-2000
www.mintmuseum.org

Mordecai Historic Park
1 Mimosa Street
Raleigh, NC 27604
(919) 833-6404
http://capitalareapreservation.org/park.html

Morehead Planetarium
East Franklin Street
UNC-CH Campus
Chapel Hill, NC 27599-3480
(919) 962-1236
www.morehead.unc.edu

Museum of Early Southern Decorative Arts
924 South Main Street
Winston-Salem, NC 27101
(888) 653-7253
www.oldsalem.org/mesda.html

Museum of the New South
324 North College Street
Charlotte, NC 28202
(704) 333-1887
www.museumofthenewsouth.org

North Carolina Auto Racing Hall of Fame and Museum
119 Knob Hill
Mooresville, NC 28115
(704) 663-5331
www.ncarhof.com

North Carolina Central University Art Museum
433 Murray Avenue
Durham, NC 27704
(919) 560-6211
www.nccu.edu/artmuseum

North Carolina Collection Gallery
Wilson Library
UNC-CH Campus
Chapel Hill, NC 27599-3930
(919) 962-1172
www.presnc.org/guide/piedmont.html#orange

North Carolina Mapscape
Piedmont Environmental Center
1220 Penny Road
High Point, NC 27265
(336) 883-8531
www.piedmontenvironmental.com/mapscape.html

North Carolina Museum of Art
2110 Blue Ridge Road
Raleigh, NC 27607
(919) 839-6262
http://ncartmuseum.org

North Carolina Museum of History
5 East Edenton Street
Raleigh, NC 27601
(919) 715-0200
http://ncmuseumofhistory.org/

North Carolina Museum of Life and Science
433 Murray Avenue
Durham, NC 27704
(919) 220-5429
www.ncmls.org

North Carolina State Museum of Natural Sciences
102 North Salisbury Street
Raleigh, NC 27603
1-877-4NATSCI
www.naturalsciences.org

North Carolina Transportation Museum
411 South Salisbury Avenue
Spencer, NC 28159
(704) 636-2889
www.ci.salisbury.nc.us/nctrans/

Old Salem
600 South Main Street
Winston-Salem, NC 27101
(888) 653-7253
www.oldsalem.org

Orange County Historical Museum
201 North Churton Street
Hillsborough, NC 27278
(919) 732-2201
www.chapelhillpreservation.com/local.htm

Angela Peterson Doll and Miniature Museum
101 West Green Drive
High Point, NC 27260
(336) 885-DOLL

Mattye Reed African Heritage Center
1601 East Market Street
Greensboro, NC 27401
(336) 334-7108
www.ncculturetour.org/MRAHC.htm

Reynolda House Museum of American Art
2250 Reynolda Road
Winston-Salem, NC 27106
(336) 725-5325
www.reynoldahouse.org

SciWorks
400 West Hanes Mill Road
Winston-Salem, NC 27105
(336) 767-6730
www.sciworks.org

Schiele Museum of Natural History and Planetarium
1500 East Garrison Boulevard
Gastonia, NC 28054
(704) 866-6900
www.schielemuseum.org

Seagrove-Jugtown Pottery Museum
Post Office Box 531
Seagrove, NC 27341
(336) 873-8040
www.ncpotterycenter.com

Southeastern Center for Contemporary Art
750 Marguerite Drive
Winston-Salem, NC 27106
(336) 725-1904
www.secca.org/home1.html

**Spirit Square Center
for Arts and Education**
345 North College Street
Charlotte, NC 28202
(704) 372-9664
www.performingartsctr.org/

Wake Forest University Museum of Anthropology
Wake Forest Drive
Winston-Salem, NC 27109-7267
(336) 758-5282
www.wfu.edu/MOA

**Weatherspoon Art Gallery
(UNC-Greensboro)**
Spring Garden Street at Tate Street
Greensboro, NC 27403
(336) 334-5770
www.uncg.edu/wag

PARKS, NATIONAL FORESTS, ZOOS, NATURE CENTERS, AND BOTANICAL GARDENS

Boone's Cave State Park
S.R. 150
Lexington, NC 27292
(704) 982-4402

Concord Zoo
1643 Simplicity Road
Concord, NC 28025
(704) 782-3149

Sarah P. Duke Memorial Gardens
Anderson Street
Duke University West Campus
Durham, NC 27706
(919) 668-5100
www.hr.duke.edu/dukegardens/dukegardens.html

Lake Norman State Park
159 Inland Sea Lane
Troutman, NC 28166
(704) 528-6350
www.ils.unc.edu/parkproject/visit/lano/home.html

Duke University Primate Center
3705 Erwin Road
Durham, NC 27705
(919) 489-3364
www.duke.edu/web/primate

Eno River State Park
6101 Cole Mill Road
Durham, NC 27705
(919) 383-1686
www.ils.unc.edu/parkproject/visit/enri.home.html

Falls Lake State Recreation Area
13304 Creedmoor Road
Wake Forest, NC 27587
(919) 676-1027
www.ils.unc.edu/parkproject/visit/fala/home.html

**Guilford Courthouse
National Military Park**
2332 New Garden Road
Greensboro, NC 27410
(910) 288-1776
www.nps.gov/guco

Hanging Rock State Park
S.R. 1101
Danbury, NC 27016
(336) 593-8480
www.ils.unc.edu/parkproject/visit/haro/home.html

Jordan Lake State Park
280 State Park Road
Apex, NC 27502
(919) 362-0586
www.ils.unc.edu/parkproject/visit/jord/home.html

Kerr Lake State Park
Recreation Area
269 Glasshouse Road
Henderson, NC 27536
(252) 438-7791
www.ils.unc.edu/parkproject/visit/kela/home.html

Medoc Mountain State Park
S.R. 1002
Hollister, NC 27844
(252) 586-6588
www.ils.unc.edu/parkproject/visit/memo/home.html

Morrow Mountain State Park
49104 Morrow Mountain Road
Albemarle, NC 28001
(704) 982-4402
www.ils.unc.edu/parkproject/visit/momo/home.html

North Carolina Botanical Garden
Old Mason Farm Road at U.S.
Highway 15-501 Bypass
Chapel Hill, NC 27599-3375
(919) 962-0522
www.unc.edu/depts/ncbg

North Carolina Zoological Park
4401 Zoo Parkway
Asheboro, NC 27203
(800) 488-0444
www.nczoo.org

Pee Dee National Wildlife Refuge
U.S. Highway 52
Wadesboro, NC 28170
(704) 694-4424
http://meckbirds.org/PeeDee/

Pilot Mountain State Park
U.S. Highway 52
Pinnacle, NC 27043
(336) 325-2355
www.ils.unc.edu/parkproject/visit/pimo/home.html

Raven Rock State Park
S.R. 1314/Raven Rock Road
Lillington, NC 27546
(910) 893-4888
www.ils.unc.edu/parkproject/visit/raro/home.html

William B. Umstead State Park
U.S. Highway 70
Raleigh, NC 27612
(919) 571-4170
www.ils.unc.edu/parkproject/visit/wium/history.html

Uwharrie National Forest
N.C. Highway 27
Troy, NC 27371
(910) 576-6391
www.cs.unca.edu/nfsnc/recreation/uwharrie/index.htm

Coastal Plain Region

HISTORIC SITES

Charles B. Aycock Birthplace
State Historic Site
264 Governor Aycock Road
Fremont, NC 27830
(919) 242-5581
www.ah.dcr.state.nc.us/sections/hs/aycock/aycock.htm

Bath State Historic Site
207 Carteret Street
Bath, NC 27808
(252) 923-3971
www.ah.dcr.state.nc.us/sections/hs/bath/bath.htm

Battleship North Carolina
Battleship Drive
Eagle Island
Wilmington, NC 28401
(910) 251-5797
www.battleshipnc.com

Beaufort State Historic Site
100 Block of Turner Street
Beaufort, NC 28516
(919) 728-5225
www.beaufort-nc.com/bythesea

Bentonville Battleground
State Historic Site
5466 Harper House Road
Four Oaks, NC 27524
(910) 594-0789
www.ah.dcr.state.nc.us/sections/hs/bentonvi/bentonvi.htm

**Brunswick Town
State Historic Site**
8884 St. Phillips Road
Winnabow, NC 28479
(910) 371-6613
www.arch.dcr.state.nc.us/amonth/brunstwn.htm

Cape Hatteras Lighthouse
N.C. Highway 12
Buxton, NC 27920
(252) 995-4474
www.nps.gov/caha

**CSS Neuse State Historic Site
& Governor Richard
Caswell Memorial**
2612 West Vernon Avenue
Kinston, NC 28501
(252) 522-2091
www.ah.dcr.state.nc.us/sections/hs/neuse/neuse.htm

Elizabeth II State Historic Site
Manteo Waterfront
Manteo, NC 27954
(252) 473-1144
www.outerbanks.com/elizabeth2/

Fort Branch State Historic Site
S.R. 1416/Fort Branch Road
Hamilton, NC 27840
1-800-776-8566
www.fortbranchcivilwarsite.com

**Fort Raleigh National
Historic Site**
U.S. Highway 64
Manteo, NC 27954
(252) 473-5772
www.nps.gov/fora

Historic Edenton
108 North Broad Street
Edenton, NC 27932
(252) 482-2637
www.ah.dcr.state.nc.us/sections/hs/iredell/iredell.htm

**Historic Halifax State
Historic Site**
Dobbs Street at St. David Street
Halifax, NC 27839
(252) 583-7191
www.ah.dcr.state.nc.us/sections/hs/halifax/halifax.htm

James Iredell House
State Historic Site
105 East Church Street
Edenton, NC 27932
(252) 482-2637
www.ah.dcr.state.nc.us/sections/hs/iredell/iredell.htm

Moores Creek National Battlefield
200 Moores Creek Road
Currie, NC 28435
(910) 283-5591
www.nps.gov/mocr

Somerset Place State Historic Site
2572 Lake Shore Road
Creswell, NC 27928
(252) 797-4650
www.ah.dcr.state.nc.us/sections/hs/somerset/somerset.htm

**Tryon Palace Historic Sites
and Gardens**
610 Pollock Street
New Bern, NC 28562
1-800-767-1560
www.tryonpalace.org

Wright Brothers National Memorial
U.S. Highway 158
Kill Devil Hills, NC 27948
(252) 441-7430
www.nps.gov/wrbr

MUSEUMS, AQUARIUMS, PLANETARIUMS, ARTS CENTERS, AND HISTORIC HOMES

Attmore-Oliver House Museum
510 Pollock Street
New Bern, NC 28562
(252) 638-8558
www.pamlico-nc.com/historicnewbern/index.htm#Attmore-Oliver House Museum

Bellamy Mansion
503 Market Street
Wilmington, NC 28401
(910) 251-3700
www.bellamymansionmuseum.org

Blount-Bridgers House
130 Bridgers Street
Tarboro, NC 27886
(919) 823-4159
www.artcom.com/museums/vs/af/27886.htm

Cape Fear Museum
814 Market Street
Wilmington, NC 28401
(910) 341-4350
www.co.new-hanover.nc.us/cfm/CFMmain.htm

Country Doctor Museum
6642 Peele Road
Bailey, NC 27807
(252) 235-4165
www.ncmsalliance.org/doctormuseum.htm

**82nd Airborne Division War
Memorial Museum**
Ardennes Street at Gela Street
Fort Bragg, NC 28307-0119
(910) 432-5307
www.fayetteville.net/museum/82ndAirborne/

Fayetteville Museum of Art
839 Stamper Road
Fayetteville, NC 28303
(910) 485-5121
www.fmoa.org

**Graveyard of the
Atlantic Museum**
N.C. Highway 12
Hatteras Village, NC 27943
(252) 986-2995
www.hatteras-nc.com/
atlanticgraveyard

Greenville Museum of Art
802 South Evans Street
Greenville, NC 27834
(864) 271-7570
www.greenvillemuseum.org

Hope Plantation
132 Hope House Road
Windsor, NC 27983
(252) 794-3140
www.albemarle-nc.com/hope

Imagination Station
224 East Nash Street
Wilson, NC 27893
(252) 291-5113
www.imaginescience.org

**Indian Museum of
the Carolinas**
607 Turnpike Road
Laurinburg, NC 28352
(910) 276-5880

**John F. Kennedy Special
Warfare Museum**
Ardennes Street
Fort Bragg, NC 28307
(910) 432-1533
www.bragg.army.mil/answers/
museums.htm

Museum of the Albemarle
1116 U.S. Highway 17 South
Elizabeth City, NC 28337
(252) 335-1453
www.albemarle-nc.com/MOA

Museum of the Cape Fear
801 Arsenal Avenue
Fayetteville, NC 28305
(910) 486-1330
www.ncmuseumofhistory.org/
reg_msms.htm

**Museum of the Native American Resource
Center**
Old Main Building
UNC-Pembroke
Pembroke, NC 28372
(910) 521-6282
www.uncp.edu/nativemuseum

**National Railroad Museum
and Hall of Fame**
2 Main Street
Hamlet, NC 28345
(910) 582-3317
www.micropublishing.com/
railroad

Newbold-White House
Harvey Point Road
Hertford, NC 27944
(252) 426-7567
www.albemarle-nc.com/
newbold-white

North Carolina Aquarium
2201 Fort Fisher Boulevard South
Kure Beach, NC 28449
(910) 458-8257
www.aquariums.state.nc.us/
ff/index.htm

North Carolina Aquarium
Airport Road
Manteo, NC 27954
(252) 473-3493
www.aquariums.state.nc.us/
ri/index.htm

North Carolina Aquarium
1 Roosevelt Drive
Pine Knoll Shores, NC 28512
(252) 247-4003
www.aquariums.state.nc.us/
pks/index.htm

North Carolina Maritime Museum
315 Front Street
Beaufort, NC 28516
(252) 728-7317
www.ah.dcr.state.nc.us/sections/
maritime/default.htm

Orton Plantation Gardens
9149 Orton Road Southeast
Wilmington, NC 28405
(910) 371-6851
www.seewilmington.com/orton.
htm

Poplar Grove Plantation
10200 U.S. Highway 17 North
Wilmington, NC 28405
(910) 686-9518
www.poplargrove.com

**Robeson Planetarium—
Science & Technology Center**
S.R. 72-711
Lumberton, NC 28358
(910) 671-6015
www.robesonsky.com

Rocky Mount Arts Center
1173 Nashville Road
Rocky Mount, NC 27803
(252) 972-1164
www.ci.rocky-mount.nc.us/
artscenter

**Rocky Mount Children's
Museum**
1610 Gay Street
Rocky Mount, NC 27801
(252) 972-1167
www.ci.rocky-mount.nc.us/
museum

St. John's Museum of Art
114 Orange Street
Wilmington, NC 28401
(910) 763-0281
www.stjohnsmuseum.com

Tobacco Farm Life Museum
709 Church Street
Kenly, NC 27542
(919) 284-3431
www.tobmuseum.bbnp.com

Wayne County Museum
116 North William Street
Goldsboro, NC 27530
(765) 962-5756

Weymouth Center
555 East Connecticut Avenue
Southern Pines, NC 28387
(910) 692-6261
www.weymouthcenter.org

PARKS, NATIONAL FORESTS, ZOOS, NATURE CENTERS, AND BOTANICAL GARDENS

**Alligator River National
Wildlife Refuge**
Manteo, NC 27954 (Mailing Address)
(252) 473-1131
www.outer-banks.com/
alligator-river

Bodie Island Lighthouse
South Nags Head, NC 27959
(252) 473-2111
www.outerbanks.com/bodielight

Cape Fear Botanical Garden
536 North Eastern Boulevard
Fayetteville, NC 28301
(910) 486-0221
www.capefearbg.org

Cape Hatteras National Seashore
Route 1, Box 675
Manteo, NC 27954
(252) 473-2111
www.nps.gov/caha

Cape Lookout National Seashore
131 Charles Street
Harkers Island, NC 28531
(252) 728-2250
www.nps.gov/calo

Carolina Beach State Park
S.R. 1573 & S.R. 1534
Carolina Beach, NC 28428
(910) 458-8206
www.ils.unc.edu/parkproject/
visit/cabe/home.html

Cliffs of the Neuse State Park
345-A Park Entrance Road
Seven Springs, NC 28578
(919) 778-6234
www.ils.unc.edu/parkproject/
visit/clne/home.html

Croatan National Forest
141 East Fisher Avenue
New Bern, NC 28560
(252) 638-5628
www.cs.unca.edu/nfsnc

Currituck Lighthouse
Corolla, NC 27927
(252) 453-8152
www.currituckbeachlight.com

**Dismal Swamp Canal National Wildlife
Refuge**
2356 Highway 17 North
South Mills, NC 27976
(757) 986-3705
www.albemarle-nc.com/gates/gdsnwr

**Fort Fisher State
Recreational Area**
1610 Fort Fisher Boulevard
Kure Beach, NC 28449
(910) 458-5798
www.ils.unc.edu/parkproject/
visit/fofi/home.html

Fort Macon State Park
East Fort Macon Road
Atlantic Beach, NC 28512
(252) 726-3775
www.ils.unc.edu/parkproject/
visit/foma/home.html

Goose Creek State Park
2190 Camp Leach Road
Washington, NC 27889
(252) 923-2191
www.ils.unc.edu/parkproject/
visit/gocr/home.html

Hammocks Beach State Park
1572 Hammocks Beach Road
Swansboro, NC 28584
(910) 326-4881
www.ils.unc.edu/parkproject/
visit/habe/home.html

Jockey's Ridge State Park
West Carolista Drive
Nags Head, NC 27959
(252) 441-7132
www.jockeysridgestatepark.com

Jones Lake State Park
113 Jones Lake Drive
Elizabethtown, NC 28337
(910) 588-4550
www.ils.unc.edu/parkproject/
visit/jone/home.html

Lake Waccamaw State Park
1866 State Park Road
Lake Waccamaw, NC 28450
(910) 646-4748
www.ils.unc.edu/parkproject/
visit/lawa/home.html

Lumber River State Park
S.R. 2246
Orrum, NC 28369
(910) 628-9844
www.ils.unc.edu/parkproject/
visit/luri/home.html

**Mattamuskeet National
Wildlife Refuge**
Highway 94
Swan Quarter, NC 27885
(252) 926-4021
www.albemarle-nc.com/
mattamuskeet/refugee

Merchants Millpond State Park
S.R. 1403
Gatesville, NC 27938
(252) 357-1191
www.ils.unc.edu/parkproject/
visit/memi/home.html

Ocracoke Lighthouse
Ocracoke, NC 27960
(252) 928-4531
www.ocracoke-nc.com/light

**Pea Island National
Wildlife Refuge**
N.C. Highway 12
Rodanthe, NC 27968
(252) 987-2394
www.hatteras-nc.com/peaisland

Pettigrew State Park
2252 Lake Shore Road
Creswell, NC 27928
(252) 797-4475
www.ils.unc.edu/parkproject/
visit/pett/home.html

Teddy Roosevelt
State Natural Area 82
P.O. Box 127
Atlantic Beach, NC 28512-0127
(919) 726-3775

Sandhills Horticultural Gardens
2200 Airport Road
Pinehurst, NC 28374
(910) 695-3882
www.sandhills.cc.nc.us/lsg/
hort.html

Singletary Lake State Park
6707 N.C. Highway 53
Kelly, NC 28448
(910) 669-2928
www.ils.unc.edu/parkproject/
visit/sila/home.html

Waynesborough State Park
801 U.S. Highway 117 South
Goldsboro, NC 27530
(919) 778-6234
www.ils.unc.edu/parkproject/
visit/wayn/home.html

Weymouth Woods State Park
1024 Fort Bragg Road
Southern Pines, NC 28387
(910) 692-2167
www.ils.unc.edu/parkproject/
visit/wewo/home.html

STATE AND FEDERAL AGENCIES AND NON-PROFIT GROUPS

Blue Ridge Parkway Superintendent
400 BB&T Building
One Pack Square
Asheville, NC 28801
(800) PARKWATCH
www.blueridgeparkway.org

Capital Area Visitor Center
301 North Blount Street
Raleigh, NC 27601
(919) 733-3456
www.ah.dcr.state.nc.us/sections/
capitol/vc/vc.htm

National Forests in North Carolina
P.O. Box 2750
Asheville, NC 28802
(828) 257-4200
www.cs.unca.edu/nfsnc

Nature Conservancy of North Carolina
101 Conner Drive
Chapel Hill, NC 27514
(919) 403-8558
http://nature.org/wherewework/
northamerica/states/north
carolina/home.htm

North Carolina Aquariums
417 North Blount Street
Raleigh, NC 27601
(919) 733-2290
www.aquariums.state.nc.us

North Carolina Arts Council
221 East Lane Street
Raleigh, NC 27601
(919) 733-2111
www.ncarts.org

North Carolina Collection
Louis Round Wilson Library
University of North Carolina
Chapel Hill, NC 27599-3930
(919) 962-1172
www.lib.unc.edu/ncc

North Carolina Department of Agriculture
Public Affairs Office
116 West Jones Street
Raleigh, NC 27603
(919) 733-7125
www.ncagr.com

North Carolina Department of Archaeology & Historic Preservation
507 North Blount Street
Raleigh, NC 27604
(919) 733-7342
www.arch.dcr.state.nc.us

North Carolina Department of Environment, Health, & Natural Resources
Environmental Education Office
512 North Salisbury Street
Raleigh, NC 27604
(919) 715-5381
www.cehn.org/cehn/
resourceguide/ncdehnr.html

North Carolina Division of Archives & History
109 East Jones Street
Raleigh, NC 27601
(919) 733-7305
www.ah.dcr.state.nc.us/
default.htm

North Carolina Division of Coastal Management
P.O. Box 27687
Raleigh, NC 27611
(919) 733-2293
http://dcm2.enr.state.nc.us

North Carolina Division of Forest Resources
512 North Salisbury Street
Raleigh, NC 27604-1189
(919) 733-2162
www.dfr.state.nc.us

North Carolina Division of Parks & Recreation
P.O. Box 27687
Raleigh, NC 27611-7687
(919) 733-4181
www.ils.unc.edu/parkproject/
ncparks.html

North Carolina Division of Travel and Tourism
301 North Wilmington Street
Raleigh, NC 27601-2825
1-800-VISIT-NC
www.visitnc.com

North Carolina Folklife Office
407 North Person Street
Raleigh, NC 27601
(919) 733-7897
www.ncarts.org

North Carolina General Assembly
Legislative Building
16 West Jones Street
Raleigh, NC 27603
(919) 733-4111
www.itpi.dpi.state.nc.us/
caroclips/raleigh/legbuilding.html

North Carolina Historic Sites
109 East Jones Street
Raleigh, NC 27601
(919) 733-7862
www.ah.dcr.state.nc.us/
sections/hs/default.htm

North Carolina Secretary of State's Office
Publisher, North Carolina Manual
300 North Salisbury Street
Raleigh, NC 27603
(919) 807-2155
www.secstate.state.nc.us

North Carolina Symphony
2 East South Street
Raleigh, NC 27601
(919) 733-2750
www.ncsymphony.org

North Carolina Wildlife Resources Commission
512 North Salisbury Street
Raleigh, NC 27604-1188
(919) 733-7123
http://216.27.49.98

Preservation North Carolina
101 St. Mary's Street
Raleigh, NC 27605
(919) 832-3652
www.presnc.org

State Library of North Carolina
109 East Jones Street
Raleigh, NC 27601-2807
(919) 733-3683
http://statelibrary.dcr.state.nc.us/NC
SLHOME.htm

UNC Center for Public Television
Public Affairs
10 T.W. Alexander Drive
Research Triangle Park, NC 27709
1-888-292-7070
www.unctv.org

University of North Carolina General Administration
Communications Office
910 Raleigh Road
Chapel Hill, NC 27599-9000
(919) 962-1000
www.northcarolina.edu

General Resources

El Pueblo, Inc.
4 N. Blount Street, Suite 200.
Raleigh, NC 27601
Phone 919-835-1525
Fax 919-835-1526
www.elpueblo.org/english/
index.html

National Humanities Center
7 Alexander Drive, P.O. Box 12256
Research Triangle Park, North
Carolina 27709-2256
Phone: (919) 549-0661
Fax: (919) 990-8535
www.nhc.rtp.nc.us/index.htm

World View
University of North Carolina at
Chapel Hill
CB #8011
UNC-Chapel Hill
Chapel Hill, NC 27599-8011
tel: (919)962-9264
fax: (919)962-6794
worldview@unc.edu
www.unc.edu/world/staff.shtml

North Carolina Geographic Alliance
www.ngsednet.org/community/in
dex.cfm?community_id=180

North Carolina Council for the Social Studies
www.ncsocialstudies.com

National Council for the Social Studies
8555 Sixteenth Street
Suite 500
Silver Spring, Maryland 20910
Telephone: 301 588-1800
Fax: 301 588-2049
Publications Orders: 1 800 683-0812
www.ncss.org

Contents

CHAPTER 1 A Journey on the Internet — 2

Unit 1 — Africa's Foundations — 14

CHAPTER 2 A Diversity of People and Lands — 16
- Lesson 1 Africa's Diverse Population 18
- Lesson 2 Location and Landforms 23
- Lesson 3 Climate and Vegetation 29
- Chapter Review 36

CHAPTER 3 Historical Foundations of Africa — 38
- Lesson 1 Early Civilizations 40
- Lesson 2 West African Kingdoms 48
- Lesson 3 East African City-States and Zimbabwe .. 53
- Chapter Review 58

CHAPTER 4 Enduring Traditions — 60
- Lesson 1 Families and Villages 62
- Lesson 2 Traditional Ways of Life 68
- Lesson 3 Religious Foundations 72
- Chapter Review 78

CHAPTER 5 Africa and the World — 80
- Lesson 1 Africa and the Slave Trade 82
- Lesson 2 European Imperialism in Africa 86
- Lesson 3 Independence and After 92
- Chapter Review 100

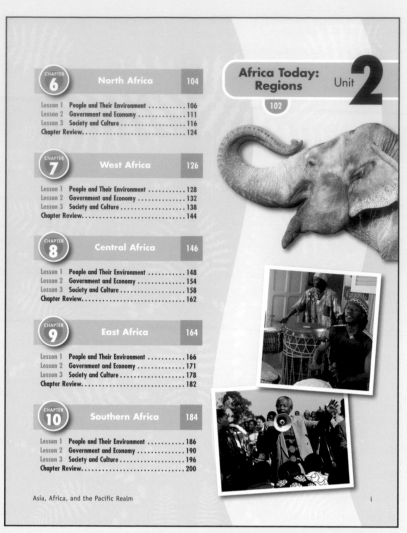

CHAPTER 6 North Africa — 104
- Lesson 1 People and Their Environment 106
- Lesson 2 Government and Economy 111
- Lesson 3 Society and Culture 116
- Chapter Review 124

CHAPTER 7 West Africa — 126
- Lesson 1 People and Their Environment 128
- Lesson 2 Government and Economy 132
- Lesson 3 Society and Culture 138
- Chapter Review 144

CHAPTER 8 Central Africa — 146
- Lesson 1 People and Their Environment 148
- Lesson 2 Government and Economy 154
- Lesson 3 Society and Culture 158
- Chapter Review 162

CHAPTER 9 East Africa — 164
- Lesson 1 People and Their Environment 166
- Lesson 2 Government and Economy 171
- Lesson 3 Society and Culture 178
- Chapter Review 182

CHAPTER 10 Southern Africa — 184
- Lesson 1 People and Their Environment 186
- Lesson 2 Government and Economy 190
- Lesson 3 Society and Culture 196
- Chapter Review 200

Africa Today: Regions — Unit 2 — 102

Unit 3 — Southwest Asia — 202

CHAPTER 11 Lands and People of Southwest Asia — 204
- Lesson 1 Location and Landforms 206
- Lesson 2 Climates and Resources 211
- Lesson 3 People and Their Environment 218
- Chapter Review 224

CHAPTER 12 Southwest Asia's Enduring Traditions — 226
- Lesson 1 Roots and Southwest Asian Societies 228
- Lesson 2 Three World Religions 233
- Lesson 3 Shaping Modern Southwest Asia 237
- Chapter Review 244

CHAPTER 13 Economy and Government — 246
- Lesson 1 Economy 248
- Lesson 2 Governments of the Middle East 254
- Lesson 3 Other Governments of the Regions 261
- Chapter Review 268

CHAPTER 14 Society and Culture — 270
- Lesson 1 Many Different Cultures 272
- Lesson 2 Islamic Societies and Cultures 277
- Lesson 3 Israeli Society and Culture 281
- Chapter Review 288

CHAPTER 15 The Lands of South Asia — 292
- Lesson 1 Location, Landforms, and Regions 294
- Lesson 2 Climates and the Land 299
- Lesson 3 People and Their Environment 304
- Chapter Review 310

CHAPTER 16 South Asia's Enduring Traditions — 312
- Lesson 1 History's Impact on South Asia 314
- Lesson 2 Family and Village Life 320
- Lesson 3 South Asia Divided 323
- Chapter Review 330

CHAPTER 17 Modern India — 332
- Lesson 1 Government and Politics 334
- Lesson 2 Economic Development 337
- Lesson 3 Climate and Vegetation 344
- Chapter Review 350

CHAPTER 18 Other Nations of South Asia — 352
- Lesson 1 Pakistan 354
- Lesson 2 Bangladesh 359
- Lesson 3 Island and Mountain Nations of South Asia .. 362
- Chapter Review 370

South Asia — Unit 4 — 290

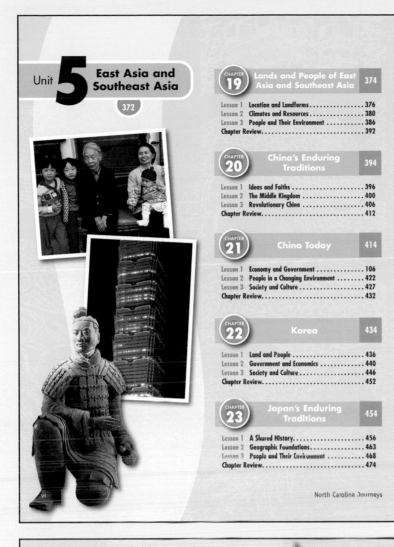

Unit 5 — East Asia and Southeast Asia
372

CHAPTER 19 — Lands and People of East Asia and Southeast Asia ... 374
Lesson 1 Location and Landforms 376
Lesson 2 Climates and Resources 380
Lesson 3 People and Their Environment 386
Chapter Review 392

CHAPTER 20 — China's Enduring Traditions ... 394
Lesson 1 Ideas and Faiths 396
Lesson 2 The Middle Kingdom 400
Lesson 3 Revolutionary China 406
Chapter Review 412

CHAPTER 21 — China Today ... 414
Lesson 1 Economy and Government 106
Lesson 2 People in a Changing Environment 422
Lesson 3 Society and Culture 427
Chapter Review 432

CHAPTER 22 — Korea ... 434
Lesson 1 Land and People 436
Lesson 2 Government and Economics 440
Lesson 3 Society and Culture 446
Chapter Review 452

CHAPTER 23 — Japan's Enduring Traditions ... 454
Lesson 1 A Shared History 456
Lesson 2 Geographic Foundations 463
Lesson 3 People and Their Environment 468
Chapter Review 474

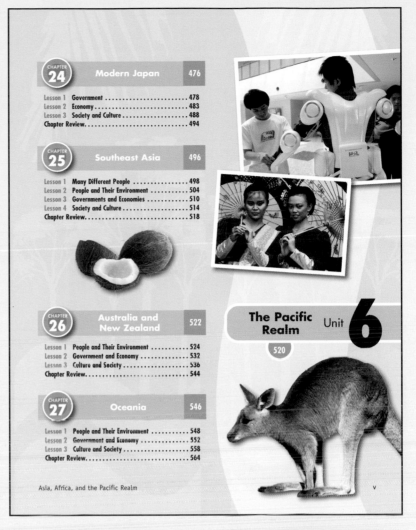

CHAPTER 24 — Modern Japan ... 476
Lesson 1 Government 478
Lesson 2 Economy 483
Lesson 3 Society and Culture 488
Chapter Review 494

CHAPTER 25 — Southeast Asia ... 496
Lesson 1 Many Different People 498
Lesson 2 People and Their Environment 504
Lesson 3 Governments and Economies 510
Lesson 4 Society and Culture 514
Chapter Review 518

The Pacific Realm — Unit 6
520

CHAPTER 26 — Australia and New Zealand ... 522
Lesson 1 People and Their Environment 524
Lesson 2 Government and Economy 532
Lesson 3 Culture and Society 536
Chapter Review 544

CHAPTER 27 — Oceania ... 546
Lesson 1 People and Their Environment 548
Lesson 2 Government and Economy 552
Lesson 3 Culture and Society 558
Chapter Review 564

Appendix
Atlas 567
Geography Review 588
Governments 592
Dictionary of Geographic Terms 594
Gazetteer 596
Glossary 604
Index 615
Credits 630

Eyewitness to History
Kilimanjaro—Mountain of Greatness 26
Sailing the Nile Through Time 44
Village Markets 64
Stanley and Livingstone 88
The Suez Canal 118
The Ivory Trade 134
Rivers Through Time 150
Madagascar 174
The Struggle Against Apartheid 192
Sources of Water Through History 214
City Life in Southwest Asia 250
Jerusalem: The City of the Faithful 283
India's Holiest City 296
Gandhi's Salt March 326
India's Railways 340
Growing Tea in Sri Lanka 364
Singapore: Tiger of Asia 388
Early Chinese Achievements 402
Hong Kong 418
The Korean War 442
Dropping the Bomb 460
Becoming Emperor 480
The Vietnam War 500
Australia's Gold Rush 528
Wayfinding Through the Ocean 560

Skill Lessons
Using Geography's Five Themes 12
Using Geography's Themes: Location 34
Using Geography's Themes:
  Human-Environmental Interaction 56
Using Geography's Themes:
  Characteristics of Place 76
Using Geography's Themes: Movement 98
Using Geography's Themes: Region 122
Making Economic Plans
  to Improve a Country 142
Obstacles to Development 161
Preserving Wildlife 181
Defeating Apartheid 199
Using Maps to Understand
  Southwest Asia 222
Organizing Information
  Using a Time Line 242
Dealing with Change
  in Southwest Asia 267
Diversity in the Middle East 286
Comparing Landform
  Subregions in South Asia 309
Change Through
  Nonviolent Resistance 329
Planning Improvements in India 349
Comparing Nations in South Asia 368
Locating a Factory in Asia 391
Obstacles to Development 411
Achieving Democracy in China 431
Perspectives on Living
  in a Divided Nation 451
Planning with Population Profiles 473
Cooperation with Outsiders 492
World Influences Shaping
  Southeast Asia 517
Diversity in Australia 542
The Changing Pacific Islands 563

A Journey to...
Mali: Timbuktu—
  Meeting of Camel and Canoe 51
West Africa: Slavery—The Experience of
  Millions of Africans 84
Burkina Faso:
  The Panafrican Film Festival 141
Addis Ababa: Linking Village to City 180
Lebanon: Land of Contrasts 210
Cyprus: A Divided Island 266
Modern India: India's Information
  Technology Industry 346
Karachi: Life Amid
  the Hustle and Bustle 358
South China: Life Aboard a Junk 409
Cheju Do: Women of the Sea 449
Tokyo: Crowds,
  Cherry Blossoms, and Crows 485
The Outback: Mustering Cattle
  on 600,000 Acres 538

Connections
• **GEOGRAPHY & THE ARTS** •
Central African Art 180
Visions of Beauty 278
The Taj Mahal 315
Oceanic Art 555

• **GEOGRAPHY & LANGUAGE ARTS** •
Stories and Poetry About the Land 70
South Africa Protest Theater 197
Describing Monsoons 301
The Thousand Cranes 469

• **GEOGRAPHY & MATH** •
Ancient Mathematicians 240

• **GEOGRAPHY & SCIENCE** •
The Supercontinent 28
Desert Wildlife 108
Silk 384
The Three Gorges Dam 424
Ring of Fire 506

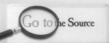

Go to the Source

Comparing Poetry and Maps 37
Reading Ancient Writings 59
Understanding Myths 79
Reading Slave Narratives 101
Understanding Government Documents . . 125
Using Letters as Primary Sources 145
Analyzing Historic Speeches 163
Analyzing Speeches
    as Primary Sources 183
Analyzing National Symbols 201
Using Evidence to Make Predictions 225
Comparing Documents and Statistics 245
Analyzing a Political Cartoon 269

Identifying Causes & Predicting Effects . . . 289
Analyzing Historic Documents 311
Understanding Protest Movements 331
Identifying Point-of-View 351
Understanding Press Conferences 371
Understanding Accounts
    of Historic Events 393
Interpreting Sayings 413
Comparing National Symbols 434
Understanding Context 453
Understanding Culture
    through Ceremonies 475
Analyzing Art as an Artifact 495
Analyzing Public
    Awareness Campaigns 519
Analyzing Historic Documents 545
Interpreting Statistics 565

Maps

Africa—Physical 17
Africa—Population 20
Africa—Climate 35
Africa—Natural Vegetation 35
Africa—Early Civilizations 39
Africa—Economic Activity
    and Resources 61
Africa—Religions 75
Slave Trade, 1701–1810 81
European Possessions
    in Africa, 1880–1914 90
European Possessions in Africa, 1850 90
North Africa—Political 105
West Africa—Political 127
Central Africa—Political 147
East Africa—Political 165
Southern Africa—Political 185
Southwest Asia—Political/Physical 205
Southwest Asia—Vegetation 212
Southwest Asia—Economic Activity
    and Resources 213
Southwest Asia—Population Density 219
Southwest Asia—Early Civilizations 227
Southwest Asia—Major Religions 233
Major Areas of Islamic Expansion 238
The Middle East Nations 247
The Northern Tier 263
The Arabian Peninsula 271
South Asia–Political/Physical 293
Monsoon Winds 300
South Asia—Natural Vegetation 303
South Asia—Population Density 305

South Asia—Major Languages 313
South Asia—Buddhism and
    Hinduism to A.D. 500 317
South Asia—British Rule to 1900 325
Republic of Modern India 333
South Asia—Economic Activity
    and Resources 338
Other Nations of South Asia—
    Political/Physical 353
East Asia and Southeast Asia—
    Political/Physical 375
East Asia and Southeast Asia—
    Population Density 381
Contemporary China—Political 395
Birthplace of Ancient China 401
China's Size 404
Spheres of Influence in China, 1914 408
China—Economic Activity
    and Resources 415
North and South Korea—
    Political/Physical 435
North and South Korea—Economic
    Activity and Resources 435
Japan—Political/Physical 455
Japan's Empire, 1895–1946 462
Japan's Size 467
Japan—Economic Activity
    and Resources 477
Southeast Asia—Poltical/Physical 497
Southeast Asia—Economic Activity
    and Resources 497
Australia/New Zealand—
    Political/Physical 523
Australia/New Zealand—Economic
    Activity and Resources 523
Australia/New Zealand—
    Population Density 531
Oceania—Political/Physical 547

CHAPTER 1

A Journey on the Internet

Social Studies Strands

Geographic Relationships

Technological Influences and Society
Communication

Cultures and Diversity
Family life
Celebrations

North Carolina Standard Course of Study

Goal 2 The learner will assess the relationship between physical environment and cultural characteristics of selected societies and regions of Africa, Asia, and Australia.

Goal 3 The learner will analyze the impact of interactions between humans and their physical environments in Africa, Asia, and Australia.

Goal 11 The learner will recognize the common characteristics of different cultures in Africa, Asia, and Australia.

Goal 12 The learner will assess the influence of major religions, ethical beliefs, and values on cultures in Africa, Asia, and Australia.

Introduction

This chapter introduces the students to Africa, Asia, and the Pacific Realm (Australia, New Zealand, and Oceania) through the Internet. A seventh grader e-mails other seventh graders asking for information about their daily lives or important celebrations that happen in their countries. Students respond to her requests from Morocco, Egypt, Lebanon, Australia, China, Japan, the Cook Islands, and other nations. Cultural events such as parades, holidays, and religious celebrations offer students an interesting introduction to the countries they will be studying. These countries are so far away from the United States that many students often have a difficult time relating to them. With the use of the Internet and information about cultural activities, you should be able to make these countries more immediate for your students.

Visit **NCJourneys.com** for more resources on Africa, Asia, and the Pacific Realm.

Teaching & Assessment

• English Language Learner Modified Lesson Plans for this chapter are found in the Teacher Resource Guide.

• *ExamView® Assessment Suite* is provided at **NCJourneys.com.** It includes customizable assessments for all chapters. Paper tests are also available in the Teacher Resource Guide. See pages T16–T17 for information about how to use the assessments and the Scoring Guide.

Worksheets

Worksheets and answer keys are found both in the Teacher Resource Guide and at **NCJourneys.com**, including Reading Guides, Reading Strategies, Chapter Reviews, English Language Learner and others.

ACTIVITIES AND INTEGRATIONS

SOCIAL STUDIES

- ● Five Themes of Geography Project, p. 2B
- ■ Around a Part of the World, p. 3
- Guest Speaker, p. 6
- Global Slant, p. 9
- ★ Governments Around the World, p. 10
- Skill Lesson: Using Geography's Five Themes, p. 13

READING/LANGUAGE ARTS	READING/LANGUAGE ARTS OBJECTIVES
Analogies, p. 2B	2.01, 5.01
Activator, p. 2	1.01, 2.01
Writing Prompt: Trip to Africa, p. 2	3.02, 6.01, 6.02
Writing Back, p. 4	4.03, 11.3
▲ ■ Seeing the Internet as a Great Circle Route, p. 6	1.03, 1.04, 2.01
Hometown and the Five Themes, p. 9	5.01, 5.02
★ Embassy Contact, p. 9	2.01
Where Would I Like to Visit?, p. 11	1.01, 6.01, 6.02
● Five Themes of Geography Poem, p. 13	5.01, 5.02

MATHEMATICS	MATHEMATICS OBJECTIVES
▲ ■ How Long Does It Take?, p. 2B	1.02
▲ Stripped Gore Map/Globe, p. 5	3.01

TECHNOLOGY	TECHNOLOGY OBJECTIVES
▲ ■ Seeing the Internet as a Great Circle Route, p. 6	1.02
■ Mapping the Internet, p. 7	1.02
Population Pyramid, p. 10	3.05, 3.06

VISUAL ARTS	VISUAL ARTS OBJECTIVES
▲ Passport, p. 2B	4.01
Create-a-Continent, p. 8	1.01, 6.01
● Five Themes of Geography Poem, p. 13	5.01, 5.02

CHARACTER AND VALUES EDUCATION	TRAITS
● Writing Prompt: Trip to Africa, p. 2	integrity, responsibility

● Basic Activities ★ Challenging Activities ▲ English Language Learner Novice ■ English Language Learner Intermediate

Introductory Activity

How Long Does It Take?

 OBJECTIVES: 1.02

Have students calculate the number of hours of travel time required to get from Raleigh to the cities listed below at different rates of speed:

Airplane	450 miles per hour
Automobile	60 miles per hour
Bicycle	15 miles per hour
Walking	3 miles per hour

Raleigh, North Carolina, to:

Tangier, Morocco (3,979 miles): Airplane, 8.8 hours; Automobile, 66.8 hours; Bicycle, 265.3 hours; Walking 1,326 hours

Khartoum, Sudan (6,729 miles): Airplane, 15 hours; Automobile, 112.2 hours; Bicycle, 448 hours; Walking, 2,243 hours

Johannesburg, South Africa (8,132 miles): Airplane, 18.7 hours; Automobile, 135 hours; Bicycle, 542.1 hours; Walking, 271 hours

 **Culminating Activity**

Five Themes of Geography Project

 OBJECTIVES: 1.01

Students may work alone or in pairs. The skill lesson on pages 12–13 reviews the Five Themes of Geography.

Objective To display Geography's Five Themes in pictures and writing.

Review Geography's Five Themes:
1. Location: Absolute and Relative
2. Place: Physical and Cultural
3. Human-Environmental Interaction: Dependence, Adaptation, and Modification
4. Movement: People, Goods, and Ideas
5. Region: Common Characteristics

Materials several *National Geographic* magazines or travel-related magazines, ledger paper, scissors, glue, pencil, and writing pen (dark blue or black)

Procedure Hand out magazines, scissors, ledger paper, and glue.

Have students find an article in their magazine about a country or region discussed in this chapter. Students should look through the article for pictures that reflect the Five Themes of Geography. In most cases, students should try to find more than one picture per theme (some themes can be subdivided into two or more categories).

Have students cut out the pictures and place them into these categories: location, place, human-environmental interaction, movement, and region.

Pictures should be trimmed so they will all fit on only one side of the ledger paper. Students must leave space for the collage's title, themes, subthemes and captions. This will involve some trial and error. It is recommended that students lightly outline the areas where the pictures will be located. They should then write the title, themes, subthemes, and captions before gluing the pictures to the paper. The title of the collage will be "The Five Themes of _____." Beneath each picture students should write the name of the theme, subtheme (such as Location, Absolute), and a brief caption explaining how the picture represents the theme. Students should be able to explain how the pictures represent each of the themes of geography.

Extension Have ELL students define the Five Themes using a native-language dictionary or translator. All ELL students should be able to do this activity if caption writing is reduced.

 Art Activity

Passport

 OBJECTIVES: 4.01

At the beginning of the year, students will create a passport to present to the teacher as they travel through the various countries in the seventh grade curriculum. As a means of passing through customs, teachers can stamp the passport with the date they begin the study. Students will create a stamp representing the country at the end of the unit as a means of exiting. Students can use a school picture from the previous year to include in their passport.

Obtain a copy of the application for a passport at a U.S. Post Office or online so students can see what is involved in getting one (visit **NCJourneys.com**). If possible, show an actual passport to students.

Extension ELL students could bring in a real passport (if they have one) to show their classmates what one would look like.

 Analogies

 OBJECTIVES: 1.02

Analogies are useful to help students make associations with prior knowledge. They can be used as an instructional strategy to help students better understand new materials. They are not intended to be definitions or test items.

Read the analogies aloud and ask students to identify the relationship between the terms. As an extension, ask students to write their own analogies using places discussed in the chapter.

Extension For intermediate ELL students, model and provide additional explanations.

country : region :: county : state
   (is a unit of)

email : computer :: letter : stationary
   (is a form of communication)

research : information :: question : answer
   (is an action that leads to)

point-of-view : culture :: favorite sports team : where you live (is influenced by)

Teaching Strategies

- This chapter is a good opportunity to discuss student's misconceptions about the regions they will study in seventh grade.
- Review with students the basics elements of geography, landforms, location, and climate using the Geography Review and the Dictionary of Geographic Terms in the Appendix.
- Review with students the different systems of government found in the world using the Types of Governments feature in the Appendix.
- Use the Getting to Know Your Textbook Worksheets in the Teacher's Resource Guide to familiarize students with the resources in this book.

Activator

 OBJECTIVES: 2.02

Activators are great tools to use in order to "hook" the attention of the students. Reading picture books or stories is an excellent way to build interest in the subject and integrate language arts into the social studies curriculum.

On the Same Day in March by Marilyn Singer (HarperCollins, 2000. ISBN 0060281871.)

Writing Prompt

 OBJECTIVES: 1.02

Evaluative

Imagine that your parents are planning a trip to Africa, Asia, and the Pacific Realm. The trip will last six weeks and visit several places in each of these world regions. Would you like to go with your parents or would you rather stay at home? Write or word process a letter to your parents to persuade them to either let you go with them or stay at home with a friend or relative while they are gone.

As you write your letter, remember to
- state your preference clearly.
- give at least three reasons and explain them fully.
- write in well-organized paragraphs and complete sentences.
- use good grammar, spelling, punctuation, and capitalization.
- include an introduction and conclusion and that the parts fit together.

CHAPTER 1

A Journey on the Internet

Rabat, Morocco

Abidjan, Ivory Coast (Côte d'Ivoire)

0 — 500 mi
0 — 500 km

Kendra, a North Carolina seventh grader, used the Internet to contact young people from the nations of Africa, Asia, and the Pacific Realm. She discovered a path into a growing network where geographic and cultural information can be shared among people throughout the world. Join Kendra and other young people to learn about the culture, the land, and the lives of people in Africa, Asia, and the Pacific Realm.

From: Kendra in North Carolina, United States
Subject: Ways of Life in Africa, Asia, and the Pacific Realm
....
My social studies teacher said we could use the Internet to post notes on bulletin boards of nations in Africa, Asia, and the Pacific Realm. Please send photos and information about culture—holidays and festivals, clothing, language, religions—almost anything that shows how you live in those regions. I will share what you send with my seventh grade class.

From: Sibille in Abidjan (ab·ih·JAHN), Ivory Coast
Subject: Aboure-Ashanti (ah·BOO·rih ah·SHANT·ih) Age Class Ceremony
....
Bonjour, Kendra. My family traveled from our big city to my father's village, Yaou, to see my cousins. In that West African village, boys and girls stay in groups that share the same age. They learn and do village chores together. My cousins graduated to the next age class. The girls wore traditional dresses of brilliant colors. They painted their faces white, and they waved white cloth as they paraded through the village. The ceremony ended with the girls dancing together.

Chapter 1

2

Chapter Resources

Print Resources
Nonfiction

Arnold, Caroline. *The Geography Book: Activities for Exploring, Mapping, and Enjoying Your World.* Wiley, John & Sons, 2001. ISBN 0471412368.

Bell, Neill. *The Book of Where.* Scholastic, 1982.

Benscoter, Dee and Geri Harris. *Social Studies Activities Kids Can't Resist: 40 Sensational Activities for the Topics You Teach.* Teaching Resources, 2002. ISBN 100439297036.

Davis, Kenneth C. *Don't Know Much About Geography.* Morrow, William & Co., 1993. ISBN 0380713799.

Exploring Your World. National Geographic Society, 1995.

Julio, Susan. *Great Map Games (Grades 3-6).* Scholastic, 2000. ISBN 100439077532.

Kapi Wynn. *Geography Coloring Book.* Prentice Hall, 2002. ISBN 10013101472.

Knowlton, Jack. *Geography from A to Z: A Picture Glossary* (picture book), HarperTrophy, 1997. ISBN 100064460991.

Kretzer, Marilyn, Marlene Slobin, and

Madella Williams. *Making Social Studies Come Alive (Grades 4-8)* Scholastic, 1999. ISBN 100590963813.

Literature Based Map Skills. Sniffen Court Books, 1994.

Menzel, Peter Material, Charles C. Mann, Paul Kennedy. *World: A Global Family Portrait.* Sierra Club Books, 1995 ISBN 10087156430.

Menzel, Peter and Faith D'Aluisio, *Hungry Planet: What the World Eats.* Publisher: Ten Speed Press, 2005. ISBN 101580086810.

Nickelsen, Leann. *Comprehension Activities*

From: Ahmed in Rabat (ra·BAHT), Morocco
Subject: Feast of the Throne Celebration
....

My uncle danced at the Feast of the Throne ceremony when King Hassan II became king of Morocco in 1961. He talks about it still. He and his friends wore their finest robes and turbans. The headgear and the loose-fitting robes protect our people from the hot desert sun.

From: Maureen in Nairobi, Kenya
Subject: Kenya Schools
National Drama Festival
....

My school's drama club is competing in the Kenya Schools National Drama Festival. It's the most important drama event in Kenya—involving 3,000 students from schools and colleges. There will be more than 150 performances, and awards will be given for best performances, actors, producers, and choreographers. Many plays and dances deal with issues important to Kenyans.

From: Edward in Mokhotlong (mahk·haht·long), Lesotho (leh·so·toe)
Subject: Grandfather's hat
....

My grandfather and his friends wear hats that remind them of their childhoods in the stormy Drakensburg Mountains. He told me that to protect themselves from bolts of lightning, they wear the cone-shaped hats. Those hats are filled with charms to ward off lightning strikes.

Journey on the Internet

3

Map Activity

Around a Part of the World

NATIONAL GEOGRAPHY STANDARDS: 1, 3, 4, 5, 6
GEOGRAPHIC THEMES: Region, Place
OBJECTIVES: 1.02

Have students look at a world map or globe. Cover all parts of the world except the area to be studied. Ask students why they think these countries are studied together. Have students search Chapter 1 for similarities. As a class, have them list what they believe are similarities.

Follow-up question: Any new ideas about these countries after the discussion? Are these countries more or less alike than the students thought?

For Reading In Social Studies And Science. Teaching Resources, 2003. ISBN 100439098386.

Silver, James F. *Geography Curriculum Activities: Ready-To-Use Lessons and Skillsheets for Grades 5-12.* Prentice Hall, 2001. ISBN 100130425915.

---. *Ready-To-Use World Geography Activities for Grades 5-12.* Center for Applied Research in Education, 1992. ISBN 100876289456.

Singleton, Laurel. *G is for Geography.*

Boulder: Social Science Consortium, 1993. ISBN 0899943705.

Smith, David. *Mapping the World by Heart Lite.* Tom Snyder Productions, 2003. ISBN 10159009383.

VanCleave, Janice. *Geography for Every Kid.* John Wiley & Sons, 1993. ISBN 0471598429.

Van Tine, Elizabeth, Shirley Lee, Camille Cooper, and Barbara White. *Super Social Studies! (Grades 4-8).* Scholastic, 1999. ISBN 100439050081.

Maps
Millennium Map Series (double-sided, laminated, write-on/wipe-off surfaces). National Geographic Society catalog, (800) 368-2728. Cost is $23.95 per map. These can also be ordered as back issues.

- February 1999—Biodiversity
- August 1999—Cultures
- February 1998—Exploration
- May 1998—Physical earth
- October 1998—Population

continued next page...

Writing Activity

Writing Back

OBJECTIVES: 4.03, 11.01

Assign students to cooperative groups. Each group is to reply to one of the responses sent to Kendra in Chapter 1. What would be their next question? Why? Ask students to compose a letter giving more information about their school and culture. Post their letters on a bulletin board.

Using the Internet, your class can start a cultural exchange with students in Africa, Asia, or the Pacific Realm.

Teacher Notes

The Southern Ocean

The ocean current that flows from west to east around Antarctica plays a crucial role in global ocean circulation. The region where the cold waters of this current meet and mingle with the warmer waters of the other oceans forms the Antarctic Convergence. Scientists have determined this is a separate body of water and a unique ecologic region. In 2000, the International Hydrographic Organization formally recognized this as the fifth world ocean—the Southern Ocean—by combining the southern portions of the Atlantic Ocean, Indian Ocean, and Pacific Ocean. The Southern Ocean extends from the coast of Antarctica north to 60°S. The size rank of the world's five oceans (largest to smallest) is: Pacific, Atlantic, Indian, Southern, and Arctic.

From: Kendra in North Carolina, United States
Subject: Religions in Asia

I want to find out about other kinds of cultural events. I found homepages on Southwest Asia, the birthplace of three major religions—Judaism, Christianity, and Islam. How are cultural events centered around religions there and elsewhere?

From: Leila in Jerusalem, Israel
Subject: Easter

Hello, Kendra. You probably know that Jerusalem is a Holy City for Jews, Muslims, and Christians. My family looks forward to spending Easter—the holiest day of Christianity—in Jerusalem. My father, sister, and I always go to sunrise services on the Mount of Olives. That's where people will find the site of Gethsemane, where Jesus prayed before he was arrested and crucified.

From: Benjamin in Jerusalem
Subject: Bar Mitzvah

I am thirteen and I am studying the Torah—the Jewish Law. I studied it before my bar mitzvah. At this special service, I became a "son of the Law," an adult responsible for my own faith. My bar mitzvah was at the Western Wall, the site of the Jewish Temple built by King Solomon. The rabbi (teacher), my father, and brother stand behind me. I am holding the scrolls of the Torah.

4

Chapter Resources (continued)

Web Sites

Links to the following Web sites are found at **NCJourneys.com**.

Multinational Partnerships/ Agreements

- European Union (**EU**)
- Free Trade Agreement of the Americas (FTAA)
- International Monetary Fund (IMF)
- Kyoto Protocol

- North American Free Trade Agreement (NAFTA)
- North Atlantic Treaty Organization (NATO)
- Organization of American States (OAS)
- United Nations
- United Nations Member States
- United Nations (electronic field trip)
- What is the Group of Eight? (G-8)
- The World Bank
- World Health Organization (WHO)

- World Trade Organization (WTO)

International Information

- CIA World Factbook
- Country Profiles
- E-Conflict World Encyclopedia
- Embassies
- Global Statistics
- Flags of all Countries
- Flags of the World
- License Plates of the World
- News Resource

From: Hussein in Tehran, Iran
Subject: Nowruz

Here in Iran we celebrate Nowruz, our new year's festival, on the spring equinox every year. We wear new clothes and exchange gifts. We eat sweets to sweeten our lives for the rest of the year. It is a time to visit family and friends.

0   250 mi   500 mi
0   250 km 500 km

From: Mahmut in Istanbul, Turkey, Southwest Asia
Subject: Dashing through the snow

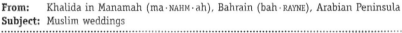

Kendra: Culture can be seen in other ways besides religions and festivals. The environment affects how people live, so it affects culture. Here's a picture you can download from my father's village. An open sleigh is the taxi. Eastern Turkey's cold, cold winter and lack of technology mean our cousins' lives are much different from the way we live in Istanbul. We have a car and my father has this computer :-)

From: Khalida in Manamah (ma·NAHM·ah), Bahrain (bah·RAYNE), Arabian Peninsula
Subject: Muslim weddings

I went with my parents to my Aunt Fatima's wedding last month. On the eve of her wedding, my mother and I went to the "lailat al henna," a females-only celebration to honor Fatima. My mother and Fatima's mother dressed Fatima's hands in jewels and drew beautiful patterns on her hands with henna dye. On the wedding day, after the blessings of the imam (our prayer leader), she and her husband sat apart on one side of a huge room. Aunt Fatima followed the custom of remaining silent during the reception. My sister and her friends danced without partners because it would be unseemly for men and women to dance together in public.

A Journey on the Internet

5

Map Activity

Stripped/Gore Map—Globe

NATIONAL GEOGRAPHY STANDARDS: 1
GEOGRAPHIC THEMES: Location
OBJECTIVES: 1.02

Students can make a small, personal globe using a stripped/gore map projection to better locate regions (Africa, Asia, and Pacific Realm) or locations from this chapter and to study map distortion.

Review with students that flat maps, even stripped/gore projections, are too distorted to make perfect globes; a globe is the only true model of earth. Other map projections (including the equal-area projection on page 17 used frequently throughout this book) cannot be formed into earth's sphere shape. To recreate a sphere, eight- or twelve-gore/stripped projections make the best "globes."

Distribute the stripped/gore projection handout found in the Teacher's Resource Guide. Have students locate and label the five oceans and color them blue. Students are to locate and label seven continents and color each continent a different color (not the same blue as oceans). Only after completing the labeling and coloring do students cut out this projection along lines. Students may choose to put a wad of crumpled paper inside his or her globe. Each point of a strip/gore is lightly glued together at points A and B. Polar circle can have a piece of string attached (before North Polar circle is glued) to create a hanging fixture.

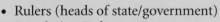

- Rulers (heads of state/government)
- Population Reference Bureau
- Tourism Offices Worldwide Directory
- Then and Now (nation name changes)
- Country Background Notes, U.S. Department of State
- Country Background Notes, U.S. Department of State
- Countires and Regions, U.S. Department of State
- Student Resources, U.S. Department of State

- Virtual World Tours
- World Communities
- World Currency
- World Flag Database
- World Photo Gallery
- Worldskip (news, information, products, and services from 220 countries)

Translators
- Google Language Tools
- Language Translator
- Worldlingo

Current Events
- The New York Times Learning Network (Pointers to over 400 international newspapers, categorized by country.)

Geography and Maps
- Atlas Query, NOAA
- Earth Observing Center
- Geographic Encyclopedia
- Geography Songlist
- Graphic Maps and World Atlas

continued next page...

Activity

Seeing the Internet as a Great Circle Route

OBJECTIVES: 1.02, 3.03

Assign students (as many as 27) to represent Kendra, Sibille, Ahmed. . . Glennis. Each is to identify "who they are" and where they live as they read aloud "their" e-mail.

Reading aloud should be done while standing in circle or on areas of classroom floor representing 27 locations in the Internet journey (or playground map). As each student completes reading, s/he tosses yarn ball representing fiber optic connections between himself/herself and Kendra. Kendra should start the yarn-ball toss holding onto one end of yarn and continuing to catch the yarn ball each time Sibille, Ahmed . . . Glennis tosses it to her. Each student representing Sibille, Ahmed. . . Glennis also must hold onto their portion of yarn before tossing the ball back to Kendra.

After Glennis has tossed yarn ball to Kendra from the final reading, all students are to carefully lay overlapping yarn design onto floor. This overlapping image is the great circle route established by the Internet illustrating the geographic theme of movement. Discuss with students the speed at which this Internet communication can occur, how interconnected these 27 students are though scattered over four world regions, and how and why technology links our world with yarn ball representing fiber optic networks. Discuss great-circle-route theory as used by airlines and Internet providers.

Students can also place pushpins or sticky notes on large wall or screen map of the world to locate each nation in Africa, Asia, and Pacific as well as North Carolina or identify each nation on laminated desk map or blackline master world map.

Extension Assign ELL students to work with partners.

From: Sharda in Davangere (da·VAHN·gih·ray), India
Subject: Folk Dancing

My little sister, Lalinni, was chosen to dance at a school festival. Dancing is a common way to worship among Hindus. The Hindu God Shiva is often shown as the god of the dance. When my sister was chosen, my mother spent many hours making her costume. I helped her practice her dance. Before dawn, we woke up to help Lalinni dress and put on the proper makeup and jewelry.

From: Agasanur in Kerala (KER·ah·lah), India
Subject: Onamisa Harvest Festival

Our biggest festival lasts ten days during autumn. My friends and I dance around a colorful display of flowers and food. My father and brothers row boats to the rhythm of drums and cymbals, and my mother makes flower carpets. Flowers grow well in our tropical climate. We have this festival to celebrate a good harvest and to honor an ancient king.

From: Mohan in Kerala (KER·ah·lah), India
Subject: Kathakali (kah·thah·KAHL·ee)

I have been waiting forever, or so it seems, to be old enough to perform Kathakali-dance-drama. I have been practicing for years, but it will be many more years before I can perform all of the steps my father knows. On the evening of the dance, my father painted my face green, to signify my role as a hero. At midnight we met the drummers on the street. We danced to their drumbeats while acting out ancient Hindu stories.

6

Chapter 1

Activity

Guest Speaker

OBJECTIVES: 12.02

Have an ELL parent or adult friend who speaks English come to class to teach a folk dance from India.

Students could research folk dances from India on the Internet and make a poster or digital storybook to demonstrate what they learned.

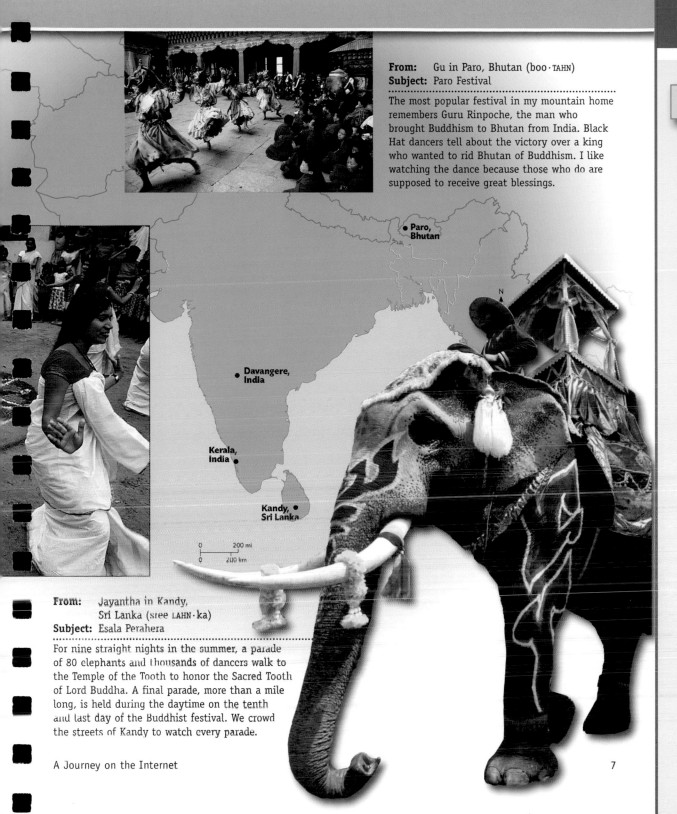

From: Gu in Paro, Bhutan (boo·TAHN)
Subject: Paro Festival
....
The most popular festival in my mountain home remembers Guru Rinpoche, the man who brought Buddhism to Bhutan from India. Black Hat dancers tell about the victory over a king who wanted to rid Bhutan of Buddhism. I like watching the dance because those who do are supposed to receive great blessings.

● Paro, Bhutan

● Davangere, India

Kerala, India ●

Kandy, ● Sri Lanka

0   200 mi
0   200 km

From: Jayantha in Kandy,
            Sri Lanka (sree LAHN·ka)
Subject: Esala Perahera
....
For nine straight nights in the summer, a parade of 80 elephants and thousands of dancers walk to the Temple of the Tooth to honor the Sacred Tooth of Lord Buddha. A final parade, more than a mile long, is held during the daytime on the tenth and last day of the Buddhist festival. We crowd the streets of Kandy to watch every parade.

A Journey on the Internet   7

Activity

Mapping the Internet

OBJECTIVES: 3.03

Divide the class into groups of six. Provide each group with the list of words (below) and ask them to use the words on a poster illustrating the structure of a computer network. Note: Students may disagree about some of the terms, so encourage them to look up and modify definitions, or, with the introduction of new technology, add new words to the illustration. Once completed, display the posters in the classroom. Without making specific reference to a particular poster, briefly discuss with the class the elements of "cyberspace geography." Have each group explain the process by which they designed the poster.

Router: the "traffic cop" that puts the data on the best route.
Web server: holds the files for individual Web sites.
DNS server: translates the URL (the ".com") to an IP address.
E-mail server: place where a person's e-mail is stored.
Dial-up modem: the most common telephone connection to the Internet Service Provider.
DSL modem: also a telephone connection, DSL is faster and allows voice and digital data to travel over the line at the same time.
Cable modem: links the home to the network through the TV cable.

Chapter Resources (continued)

Geography and Maps (continued)
- Google Earth
- Latitude/Longitude Distance Calculator
- Library of Congress Map Collections
- National Geographic
- National Geographic Map Machine
- National Geographic Education
- Osher Map Collection
- Perry-Castaneda Library, Map Collection

Geology, Climate and Weather
- Earthquakes
- Hurricane Hunters

- National Climatic Data Center, Asheville, North Carolina
- National Hurricane Center (with links to international agencies)
- National Invasive Species Information Center, USDA
- National Weather Service
- National Geodetic Survey (GPS data)
- Natural Hazards Gateway, USGS (international information on earthquakes, etc.)
- State Climate Office of North Carolina
- The Tornado Project
- The Weather Channel

Economics
- Currency Converter
- EduStock (Contains tutorials on the stock market, picking a stock, and a stock market simulation.)

Documentaries and Teacher Resources
- British Broadcasting Corporation (BBC) Schools—Teachers
- History Channel Classroom
- Public Broadcasting Service (PBS) Programming

Activity

Create-a-Continent

OBJECTIVES: 2.01

Have students review the Dictionary of Geographic terms in the appendix. Students will learn landforms and water bodies that will be discussed throughout the year. Divide the class into pairs. They are to imagine they are explorers and have just discovered a new continent. Using a list of specific landforms and water bodies, students will design their continent on paper and then will build it out of clay on cardboard (such as drink flats). Give students a day to sketch their continents and to decide on the colors of clay needed. Have them prepare the clay at home and bring it in on a specified day. After students create their clay continents, they must present it to the teacher and identify land and water bodies as requested by the teacher.

Clay recipe
1 cup water
2 teaspoons cream of tartar
1 cup flour
1 tablespoon cooking oil
½ cup salt
food coloring

Tell students to use liquid cooking oil and they must use cream of tartar. Clay should not be sticky—too much water. DO NOT USE SUGAR!

Combine dry ingredients in a saucepan and combine liquid ingredients in a cup. Stir the liquids into the dry ingredients. Cook over medium heat for approximately 3 minutes, stirring. When the mixture has the texture of play dough or cookie dough, remove from the heat. Knead until smooth (not long), and store in airtight container.

Terms to be Included

hill	river source	lake
mountain	river mouth	strait
plateau	bay or gulf	river
plain	sea or ocean	atoll
peninsula	archipelago	delta
lagoon	isthmus	

From: Chou in Beijing (bay·JIN), China
Subject: Lunar New Year Festival

Our New Year Festival is supposed to last three days, but most people celebrate for more than a week. They have spent a month cleaning house, buying new clothes, and cooking meals, so they want to have fun as long as possible. We visit relatives and friends, pay respects to ancestors, and attend parades. The color red is everywhere because it represents good fortune. My parents give me hung-pao, little red packets of money. By tradition, everyone becomes one day older on the New Year. Happy Birthday, everyone!

From: Losang in Lhasa (LAHS·ah), Tibet (Xizang [SHE·dzang], China)
Subject: Tibetan New Year

Boy monks dance and hold sticks to drive away evil during our five-day Tibetan New Year. In the "ceremony of the dying year," older monks like myself wear demons' masks to scare off evil spirits. The day before, we made an offering of food and drink to the Buddha. On the last day, we throw wheat flour on each other as a symbol of gathering luck for the new year.

Lhasa, Tibet
(Xizang, China)

From: Liu in Shanghai (shang·HIGH), China
Subject: Dragon Dance

Ribbons of color swirl over and among dragon dancers. We celebrate Chinese New Year in Shanghai by dancing, wearing red, and exploding firecrackers.

As a follow-up activity, have students create a word search. Instead of giving a word bank, they are to write the definitions and leave blanks. The person solving the word search must fill in the blanks and then look for those words in the puzzle.

Writing Extension Students are to imagine they are the explorers who discovered their continents. They should keep a diary of their adventure and describe what they see (this will help students with elaboration).

Extension Assign ELL students this activity without the follow-up activities.

From: Toyotaro in Kyoto (key·OH·toe), Japan
Subject: Gion Festival

We have a festival that celebrates our city, Kyoto. In 869, the city was saved from an epidemic. The head priest of the Gion Shrine led a procession to thank the gods. Now men and boys ride a huge ancient cart through Kyoto to the Gion Shrine. We play flutes and drums and throw straw good-luck favors. Two priests from the shrine lead each float. Floats are almost 35 feet tall and decorated with paintings and tapestries.

From: Hiko in Nikko (NIK·oh), Japan
Subject: Toshogu Shrine Festival

My father helps my brother, Takakazu, adjust his helmet on Toshogu Shrine Festival Day. Hundreds of men and boys dress in authentic samurai costumes. We walk to the burial site of Ieyasu, the leader who united Japan and enforced law through the great warriors called samurai.

From: Ki Woo in Seoul (sole), South Korea
Subject: Autumn Harvest Festival

Last September my family joined millions of people on the trains and highways for Ch'usok, the autumn harvest festival. Koreans travel to the villages of their ancestors. We returned to Kochang. There we visited the graves of our ancestors and prayed to them for a good harvest for the country. Later my brothers and I danced to celebrate the end of the hot summer

A Journey on the Internet

9

Activity

Global Slant

OBJECTIVES: 1.02

Have students review the information about location and climate in the appendix. Have each student label the parts of a globe (Equator, Tropics, meridians, parallels, and so forth). Discuss the tilt of the earth on its axis, and discuss the differences between revolution and rotation.

Have students write or word process an expository paper on the reasons the seasons change.

Extension Students may integrate ten science curriculum by extending their study of climate to include an understanding of the atmosphere and how changes to the atmosphere, such as greenhouse gases, combine to affect climate, vegetation, and weather system.

Writing Activity

Hometown and the Five Themes

OBJECTIVES: 1.02

Here are three ways to practice using the Five Themes of Geography in writing exercises:
- Have students create a Five Themes graphic organizer of their hometown.
- Using the Five Themes, students will write a poem about their hometown.
- Have students write a persuasive letter to a business. Using elements from the Five Themes, convince the business to settle in their hometown.

Extension Have ELL students create a digital story, PowerPoint Presentation, Web page, collage, or poster to demonstrate The Five Themes in their own hometown.

Research Activity

Embassy Contact

OBJECTIVES: 1.03

Using Web site addresses in the *World Almanac* (or visit **NCJourneys.com**), have students write the embassies of countries that will be studied during the course of the year. Assign each student a different country. Write a letter to that country requesting information. Do this at the beginning of the year since it often takes a long time for materials to come. Include student's name and school address so the student will receive the mail. Watch the excitement grow as students begin receiving their own mail. This teaches letter writing and technology skills.

Activity

Governments Around the World

OBJECTIVES: 9.01, 9.02

Have students review the information about the types of constitutional and nonconstitutional governments in the Appendix. Using this information, have students choose one country from each region they will study this year. Using a graphic organizer or a spreadsheet, have the students classify the governments of those countries based on the criteria described in the Appendix. Discourage students from choosing countries used as examples in the Appendix.

 Activity

Population Pyramid

OBJECTIVES: 1.02

A population pyramid is a graph of the population of an area, such as a country or town, using age and sex groupings. The pyramid is arranged with the youngest age group at the bottom and the eldest at the top, at intervals of five to ten years. The pyramid is split down the middle with one side showing male groups and the other side female. Population pyramids are a useful way of summarizing the demographic characteristics of an area. Their shape reflects changes in birth rate and death rate.

1. List all population data for a nation in a spreadsheet such as Microsoft Excel. It should be changed to a percentage so that it can be compared. List the data for males and females by age or age spans. An example of the breakdown may be 0–4, 5–9, 10–14, 15–19, 20–24, 25–29, 30–34, 35–39, 40–44, 45–49, 50–54, 55–59, 60–64, 65–69, 70–74, 75–79, 80+.
2. After listing as negative numbers those data pertaining to males—Excel requires these negative numbers to graph the data appropriately—select the data for both males and females, as well as age category labels. Under Insert, select Chart. From the chart type, select the bar chart Cluster Bar from the chart

wizard and follow the prompts for steps 2–4.
3. Click on the Vertical Axis and select Format. From Options tab, set the overlap to 100 and the gap width to 0.
4. Click on either data series from the chart and select Format. From Options tab, set the overlap to 100 and the gap width to 0.
5. Click on the Horizontal Axis and select Format. From the Numbers tab, select the Custom Number format and enter in the following: 0;0. Doing this will eliminate the negative signs.
6. Complete the chart by adding the appropriate

labels to designate males and females, and by designating that the age and sex distribution is a percent, if appropriate. Apply any other formatting, such as altering the colors of the bars in the pyramid and removing the gridlines.

Visit **NCJourneys.com** for links to the following data sources:

- **U.S. Census Bureau**
- **United Nations Population Information Network**

From: Kendra in North Carolina, United States
Subject: The Pacific Realm

It seems to me that many of the celebrations that I have read about are tied to religious ideas. Some are for good fortune and most of them are fun. Who can send me information about celebrations in the Pacific Realm—Australia, New Zealand, and the islands of the South Pacific?

From: Nitya in Bang Pa In, Thailand
Subject: Loi Krathong Lotus Festival

My friends and I are surrounded by lotus blossoms during Loi Krathong, the floating lotus festival. After sunset, everyone heads for a river to launch lotus-shaped paper boats filled with lighted candles. The river is so pretty with sparkling lanterns reflected in the water. They symbolize the flowering of the human spirit. The night ends with fireworks.

From: Arifin in Sumba, Indonesia
Subject: Pasola Festival

Horsemen from my village gallop to meet other horsemen in a day-long mock battle during the Pasola Festival. The thin spears they carry are blunted, but they can still injure. Pasola lasts for eight days. We believe it helps our harvests be fruitful and makes sure that the newborn babies are healthy.

10

From: Ton in Tay Ninh, Vietnam
Subject: Cao Dai Noon meditation

In my Cao Dai faith, we sit and pray during noon meditation in the Great Temple. The orange building has a red roof, blue shutters and balcony, golden thrones, and silver stars and clouds on the ceiling. Dragons are painted brightly on the pillars. My religion blends Buddhist, Daoist, and Confucian beliefs to respect life, avoid meat, and live simply.

From: Fobora in Menyamya (men·YAHM·yah), Papua New Guinea
Subject: Waratambar

Hello Kendra. We celebrate Waratambar. It is a harvest feast of thanks like your Thanksgiving in the United States. Our festival blends ancient customs with our Christian beliefs. My father and his friends paint their faces yellow and wear headdresses of moss, collars of flowers, and waist coverings of ferns. They sing songs about God's gifts of creation. They act out ancient wars in their dances.

Cook Islands

From: Miria in Cook Islands
Subject: Constitution Day

Hi, Kendra! I love to dance any time, but dancing during Constitution Day celebrations is special. We celebrate independence from New Zealand by competing for the national dance championships. Our schools send teams from all over the Cook Islands to compete. We dress in white hats and grass skirts and swing baskets as we dance to drumming. Finally, the judges choose one team as the winner. Maybe next year :-) We had fun anyway.

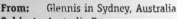

From: Glennis in Sydney, Australia
Subject: Australia Day

G'day, Kendra. My friends and I won the honor of carrying a banner in this year's Australia Day parade. The celebration is the anniversary of the first British settlement in Australia, way back in 1788. Captain Arthur Phillip and a boatload of convicts settled at the site of my hometown, Sydney. They built a colony for prisoners from Great Britain. A strange way for a nation to begin, right mate? But I'm glad they did. Our banner also symbolizes the importance of the Aborigines in our country's history.

A Journey on the Internet

11

Writing Activity

Where Would I Like to Visit?

OBJECTIVES: 2.06

Have students choose one nation that they will study this year. It should be a nation that interests them and that they would like to visit. Students will write or word process an essay describing why that country interests them, why they would like to visit it, and what they would like to know more about the country—food, culture, religious practices, government, and so on.

Have students research on the Internet or in magazines images of the country that they find intriguing. Students should include in their essay an explanation of why that image of the country fascinates them.

Extension ELL students can make a collage to "explain" why a country interests them. They should research using ELL-friendly Web sites.

Teaching This Skill Lesson

Materials Needed texts, maps, atlases, Internet, encyclopedias, pencils, paper

Classroom Organization Subdivide the class into five groups of approximately equal size. Each group will review *one* of the key ideas or one of the Five Themes of Geography.

Beginning the Lesson List each of the Five Themes on chalkboard or overhead. Review the themes with students and assess for understanding. Make sure students can explain each theme in their own words. Tell them each group will be using the information in Chapter 1 and other resources to practice using the Five Themes.

Lesson Development Make sure each group understands its assignment and that every student is working. It may be advisable to assign individual roles. Suggestion: one reader for each piece of material (such as map, Internet, atlas, encyclopedia), one or two fact checkers (to check that all the information readers are finding is consistent, to question inconsistencies), one or two writer/recorder/reporters.

Conclusion Each group is to report its findings. Other class members may ask questions about reports. In discussion, ask which themes were easier, more difficult to use. Why are there five themes? Are all needed?

Extension Using a large wall map of the world or a projection of a digital atlas, help students pinpoint places Kendra "visited" on the Internet. For each place, review the Five Themes information with students, asking questions from all five groups as each site is pinpointed.

To ensure students' understanding of the Five Themes, post them in the classroom and refer to them in future lessons.

Accessing a Variety of Sources; Gathering, Synthesizing, and Reporting Information

Using Geography's Five Themes

Suppose Kendra is your classmate and she is telling your class about what she has learned on the Internet. The first questions everyone asks are about the people, places, and events she discovered.

Kendra uses one of the school's maps to show the nations where she has communicated with other students. She talks about the e-mails she has received, and shows the photographs she has downloaded. Everyone listens because they will have an assignment based on Kendra's experiences.

Getting Organized

You will serve on one of five teams. Each team will collect data for oral reports on "The Land and People of Africa, Asia, and the Pacific Realm." You may use some reference books, but Kendra's pictures and e-mail will provide the main source of material.

The Five Themes and Key Questions

You probably have studied the Five Themes of Geography before. Geographers use the themes to ask key questions that help them understand places. These questions help them gather facts and organize those facts into ideas.

To understand how these key questions and themes may be used, the Five Themes of Geography are reviewed below. Do not be too concerned if you cannot answer everything. You will be studying geography's themes through the weeks to come. Here are the assignments:

Team No. 1
Theme: Location

Your assignment—apply the geographers' first key question, "Where is this place?" to Kendra's "trip." Use a classroom map or atlas to describe the locations of Africa, Asia, and the Pacific Realm. Use the same resources to describe the locations of the places described in Kendra's e-mail. Recall that geographers describe location in two ways.

1. Absolute location is given with latitude and longitude.
2. Relative location can be described by telling where a place is found in relation to other places. For example, how can you use Europe to describe Africa's location?

Team No. 2
Theme: Place

Your assignment—use the geographers' two ways of answering a second question, "What is this place like?"

1. Physical characteristics. Geographers use natural landforms, climate, and plants and animals to describe a place.
2. Human characteristics. Geographers use cities, roads, farms, dams, and other things made by people to describe a place. They also include the people of a place, including their language, religion, food, sports, economy, and government.

Find enough information from Kendra's e-mails to describe how each place she visited by computer might be similar to or different from other places based upon their physical characteristics.

The photographs show many festivals and religious observances—key signs of culture. How do the photographs reveal information about these cultural (human) characteristics?

Team No. 3
Theme: Human-Environmental Interaction

Geographers usually ask a series of questions when they use this theme. In what ways have people living in a place adapted—or adjusted—their ways of life so they can live in cold, hot, dry, or other types of environments? How have people tried to change their environment? What have been the consequences of these efforts?

Your assignment—find out how the people who wrote to Kendra adapted to and changed their environments. Kendra was online during autumn. Did that make a difference in the regions where she sent e-mail? What evidence in the photos or e-mail shows how people adapt to climate? Did she receive any evidence of people changing their environments? Did these efforts seem to improve people's lives? Did they see changes that made life worse?

Team No. 4
Theme: Movement

When geographers think about this theme, they most often have in mind the movement of people, goods, and ideas. Geographers, for example, want to learn how a place may be affected by the movement of Western ideas to East Asia. Spectators at the Oi River Boat Festival (right) are dressed in Western-style clothing. Participants are dressed in traditional Japanese costumes.

Your assignment—look closely at Kendra's e-mails and photographs for similar evidence of movement. Does there seem to be more exchange of people, goods, and ideas in some places than in others? How are people's lives affected? How do festivals and the practices of religion show the theme of movement?

Oi River Boat Festival, Japan

Team No. 5
Theme: Region

Geographers define a region as a group of places bound together by one or more characteristics. For example, places that are located in mountains and have much the same climate and vegetation would be part of a mountain region. Do Kendra's e-mails show places that have characteristics in common? Places that are quite different?

What evidence is there that shows common characteristics within Africa? within Asia? How do regions within those continents differ?

Although Kendra does not speak of regions as geographers might, her e-mails and pictures indicate that she may have been communicating at times within one region, and at other times from one region to another. Your assignment is to determine which she does more often.

Writing Activity

Five Themes of Geography Poem

OBJECTIVES: 1.01

Have students select a country they will study this year and write a poem about it.

Line one: Location—Name of country of area

Line Two: Place—two or three words to describe setting

Line Three: Human-Environment Interaction—three words that tell what people do in this area

Line Four: Movement—short phrase that describes movement of people, goods or ideas

Line Five: Region—two or three words to describe the religion, a holiday or special event in this area

Line Six: A short phrase to describe why you like this place so much

Final copy of the poem should be printed on the center of a map of the place. Physically or digitally paste small pictures matching the poem around the border.

Skill Lesson Review

Note: Use in discussions with students after completing the skill lesson.

1. Which resources were easiest and most difficult to use? *Important points: Encourage students to discuss their difficulties, coaching them if advisable in the use of these materials that they will be using from time to time throughout the year. Note that students may well find maps most difficult and that it may be necessary to review elementary map reading skills.*

2. Which of the Five Themes of Geography was easiest to use in this activity? Which was most difficult? Explain why. *Important points: Encourage student discussion, using any opportunity that presents itself to reteach the Five Themes of Geography. It is likely that students' understanding of the Five Themes may be minimal at this point; encourage them by telling them that they will be using the Five Themes in the first skill lessons of the year.*

Africa Foundations

...e of the Sphinx and one of the Great Pyramids of Egypt. The text suggests that the buses visiting these sites are like time machines, taking their passengers back in history. This unit will serve the same purpose for your students, taking them back in time to understand the foundations and important early civilizations of Africa.

Because of Africa's geography, its growing population is unevenly distributed across the continent. The past also has influenced Africa, where some of the world's most important civilizations have flourished. In the more recent past, Africa has suffered under the transatlantic slave trade and a century of European colonial rule. Most countries did not become independent until after World War II. Today, traditions continue to influence the people of Africa.

UNIT LESSON PLAN

	LESSON 1	LESSON 2	LESSON 3
CHAPTER 2 **A Diversity of People and Lands**	Africa's population is unevenly distributed, rapidly growing, and spread among thousands of ethnic groups. **Essential Question:** Who are the diverse groups of people in Africa, and where do they live? **Suggested Time:** 1 day	Africa is a large continent mainly covered by a plateau. Other important features are its smooth coastline, the Great Rift Valley, mountains, and rivers. **Essential Question:** What major landforms and physical features are found in Africa? **Suggested Time:** 1 day	Climates in Africa are mainly influenced by distance from the Equator. These climates determine the major zones of vegetation. **Essential Question:** How do Africa's different climate zones affect its vegetation? **Suggested Time:** 1 day
CHAPTER 3 **Historical Foundations of Africa**	Egypt, Kush, and Axum were early African civilizations that developed along the Nile River and Red Sea. **Essential Question:** What forces contributed to the rise of African kingdoms along the Nile River and the Red Sea? **Suggested Time:** 1 day	Ghana, Mali, and Songhai were West African kingdoms that controlled the gold and salt trade. **Essential Question:** What impact did the early West African kingdoms have on the gold and salt trade? **Suggested Time:** 1 day	Mombasa, Sofala, and Kilwa developed as trading centers on the Indian Ocean. Zimbabwe grew as an inland trade site. **Essential Question :** How did the East African kingdoms develop as trading centers? **Suggested Time:** 1 day
CHAPTER 4 **Enduring Traditions**	Africans have roles as members of their families and their villages. **Essential Question:** How do Africans interact with one another within their families and communities? **Suggested Time:** 1 day	Most Africans either farmed or herded. Those ways of life are still important. **Essential Question:** What is the traditional way of life for many Africans? **Suggested Time:** 1 day	Traditional African religions include belief in a Supreme Being and respect for ancestors. Those traditions often mix today with Christianity and Islam. **Essential Question:** What are the beliefs of traditional African religions, and how have these beliefs been influenced by Christianity and Islam? **Suggested Time:** 1 day
CHAPTER 5 **Africa and the World**	Slavery was an ancient practice. The Atlantic slave trade, which began after the European conquest of the Americas, cost millions of Africans their lives or freedom. **Essential Question:** What impact did the Atlantic slave trade have on Africa? **Suggested Time:** 1 day	European imperialism brought almost all of Africa under European rule in the late 1800s. **Essential Question:** How did European imperialism affect Africa? **Suggested Time:** 1 day	African countries won independence after World War II. They are still struggling with the effects of imperialism. **Essential Question:** What forces brought about the collapse of European imperialism in the post–World War II world, and what are the lingering effects of European imperialism on Africa? **Suggested Time:** 1 day

Preparing the Unit

- Worksheets, assessments, and reproducibles for this unit are found in the Teacher's Resource Guide.
- See the list of Cultural Resources in the Teacher's Edition.
- After previewing the suggested resources and activities, share them with your art teacher, music teacher, language arts teacher, and others, so that they may be integrated with your curriculum. Integrating the curriculum and ideas will also help you in pacing.

Unit Teaching Strategies

- Before you begin your study of Africa, decorate your room with pictures and posters from Africa. If possible, find African objects such as statues, masks, or other artifacts from Africa to give the room an African feel. See the bulletin board ideas for additional help.

- Use the Unit 1 Introductory Activity to begin your study of Afri...
- You can also give students a visual aid by viewing a video on Africa such as *African Journey*, or North Carolina State University Humanities Extension/Publications videos.
- As you begin the unit, assign projects and due dates to students so that they can begin working on them as they learn about Africa. Projects may be completed independently, in pairs, or in cooperative groups. In order to maximize your time, give students a list of choices and ask them to choose one of the projects to complete. Provide a rubric and clear expectations for the project. Set a due date near the end of your study of Unit 1.
- To cover the material on Africa, study Unit 1 as a class. This will provide the background needed for the teaching strategies in Unit 2.
- Check **NCJourneys.com** for updates and materials.

Unit Projects

Students will have seven days to complete their project. They have the option of choosing one of five different projects. Suggested report format: two pages in length, word processed, and double spaced. This format is for all projects below except for the Country Poster/Digital Slide Show.

PROJECT CHOICES

OBJECTIVES: 1.01, 4.01, 7.02

Slave Trade Project/Movie Review

Students will research on the West African Slave trade. They should also rent and view the movie *Amistad*. (This movie is rated R, so a parent will need to rent it and view it with, or before, their child. Students not allowed to rent the movie may read the book.) They will write a film review following the outline provided in the Teacher's Resource Guide.

Biography of a Famous African

Students will investigate the life and achievements of a famous African from ancient or modern history. The biography must include a brief history of the person; his or her country of origin and its capital city; the reason(s) why this person is famous; the time periods he or she lived in; a map of his or her country; a picture or drawing of the person; his or her educational background; his or her job; his or her biggest achievement; and the student's opinion of the person's overall role in African history.

Country Poster/Digital Slide Show

Students will choose an African country and create a poster or digital slide show. The display must depict the following items: the capital city; the country's current population; a brief history of the nation; a map of the country; its flag; its natural resources; animals living in that country; a place the student would like to visit; and the economy of the country or ways people make a living. The poster or digital slide show should be colorful and evocative of Africa.

Report on Imperialism in Africa

Students will research imperialism in Africa. The report must include the reasons why European countries wanted colonies, what they did in Africa with their colonies, and the ways in which African colonies gained their independence from Europeans. The report should include a bibliography citing at least three resources in addition to the textbook.

Ancient Civilizations

Students must choose an ancient African civilization and either write a report, create a poster, or create a digital story about it. The project must include the following information: the history of the civilization including when it was formed, how it rose to power, and how and when it declined; the factors leading to its collapse; a description of its most famous ruler, a description of the ways of life followed by its people; the religion(s) of the civilization; a map of the civilization; and a picture or drawing of a significant feature of the civilization.

Bulletin Board Ideas

Current Events

Have students clip items from newspapers and magazines that relate to the countries in the region they are studying. Have them do this for two or three weeks prior to the unit study. At the time you begin the unit, let students choose the most interesting or relevant articles. Provide a large map of the region. Let students star those places the articles refer to; then use the map as a backdrop for the articles.

African Place Names

Place a large map of Africa on the bulletin board. Cover the names of the larger cities or of the countries. Cover names of rivers and mountain ranges. Have clues posted nearby. Allow room for students to post answers. When a correct guess is made, remove its cover.

Slave Trade Routes

Create a slave trade map between Africa and the Americas. Show routes of traders from the interior to the coast. Show areas where people were kept until they had to sail. Show areas where they were sent in North, Middle, and South America.

Who Knows What About Africa?

OBJECTIVES: 1.01

Give each student a copy of the worksheet in the Teacher's Resource Guide and allow them 10 to 15 minutes to find people who know the answers. Encourage students to move around the classroom and try to get the name of a different student for each statement. Explain to students before they get started that there may be some blank statements at the end of the allotted time because there may not be anyone in the class who knows the answer. Once students have completed the task, have a discussion about each statement pointing out places on a map to give students a visual. The discussion will allow you to determine the misconceptions students may have and give a fuller introduction about Africa.

Culminating Activity

Building a Newspaper

OBJECTIVES: 1.01, 2.02

Assign each student a country from the region studied in this unit. Students will create a newspaper about their assigned country. They will be limited to only the front and back of one sheet of paper. Each side must have two columns. They must include the following information:

A banner headline (16-point font) identifying their country. Be creative with the name, perhaps using alliteration or words that would be meaningful to the country. Make certain this is centered. The remainder of the newspaper should be 12-point font.

The paper should feature two articles on the front. One should be a short article that would attract a visitor, or students may write a letter to someone about a visit to one major place in the country.

The second article should be a feature approximately one to one and one half columns in length.

The back of the newspaper should include either a physical, political, or thematic map of the country and a box displaying vital information of the country.

Include population, religion, per capita GNP, and other information. A good source for this information is the CIA World Factbook online or an almanac (visit NCJourneys.com for links). Additionally, students should graph information about the country (for example, economic activity or a climograph). The graph may come from another activity that the class has done while studying the region. Doing this in Microsoft Works will help prepare students for the computer test.

Lastly, the back should have an article about something special from the country or important current events and a puzzle. A wordsearch, jumble, or crossword puzzles about the country created by the student are possible ideas.

Students should list themselves on the bottom of the back page as the editor in chief. They should also include in small type at the bottom of the back page a bibliography of the sources from which they found their information in MLA format.

Keep each of the newspapers. At the end of the year, bind each student's newspapers together so the student will have a book of newspapers covering the regions studied throughout the year. You could give students copies of other students' papers and organize the booklet according to region.

An alternative to a newpaper could be a class Web site.

Science Activity

African Air Pollution

OBJECTIVES: 2.02

African cities face significant challenges from air pollution. Students will evaluate how humans impact air quality in African cities, including the potential point and non-point sources of air pollution as well as the financial and economic trade-offs of economic development.

Students should, using either a graphic organizer or spreadsheet, choose three cities in Africa and identify at least three significant types of pollution and possible effects, using the Clean Air Initiative in Sub-Sarahan Africa's Web site (link found at **NCJourneys.com**) and others. Then students should consider and identify the relationship of each type of pollution to the

economy of that country. What are the economic trade-offs involved in reducing or eliminating the source of pollution? What effect could these trade-offs possibly have on the economic development of the region?

Finally, students should use the information to write or word process a letter to the leader of that nation suggesting ways to decrease pollution with the least economic impact.

Technology Activity

Current Events

OBJECTIVES: 1.02

Have students use Internet sources to find current events about Africa. In class, group the stories by the section categories used in United States newspapers (politics, sports, business, living). Display on a bulletin board. If students discover an imbalance in news coverage, discuss the possible reasons why. Finally, students should analyze the points-of-view of African newspapers on world issues and issues relating to the United States.

Math Activity

Population Percentages

OBJECTIVES: 1.02

Africa has approximately 900 million people, which is roughly 15 percent of the world's population. What is the population of the world? Find this number by using the percent formula.

Hint Use the percent ratio Rate (R) = Percentage (P part) and 100 = Whole (W)

Example
20% of whole equals percentage
20% of whole equals 20
$\frac{20}{100} = \frac{20}{W}$
cross multiply 20 x W = 20 x 100
20W = 2000
divide $\frac{20W}{20} = \frac{2000}{20}$
W = 100

Answer The world's population is approximately 6 billion.

Extension Assist ELL students by setting up the problem for them

Unit Resources

Fiction

Greaves, Nick. *When Hippo Was Hairy: And Other Tales from Africa.* New York: Barron's Educational Series, 1988. ISBN 0812045483. Thirty-six folk tales about animals from Zulu, East African, and Ndebele traditions.

Language Arts Writing Connections

Story Starters on Ancient Africa. Story Starters on Ancient Egypt. Heinrich Enterprises. This series takes a time period and helps the students develop a story using extensive vocabulary to help create characters, setting, and plot.

Nonfiction

Appiah, Kwame Anthony, and Henry Louis, Jr. Gates (Ed.). *Africana: The Encyclopedia of the African and African American Experience.* Basic Civitas Books, 1999. ISBN 100195223284.

Ayo, Yvonne. *Eyewitness Africa.* Dorling Kindersley, 2000. ISBN 0789460300.

Fossey, Dian. *Gorillas in the Mist.* Phoenix Press, 2001. ISBN 100753811413.

Hart, George. *Eyewitness Ancient Egypt.* 2000. ISBN 0789457849.

Reader. John, *Africa: A Biography of the Continent.* Vintage Books, 1999. ISBN 10067973869X.

Audiovisual

Africa. National Geographic Society and Nature Co-production (8-part series). 1-800-336-1917, AFRICA, PO Box 2284, South Burlington, VT 05407

Art in Africa. North Carolina State University Humanities Extension/Publications, 2001.

Living in Africa: Africa, South of the Sahara. North Carolina State University Humanities Extension/Publications, 1998.

Living in Africa: Meet Zimbabwe's Young Scholars. North Carolina State University Humanities Extension/Publications, 1998.

Wonders of the African World with Henry Louis Gates Jr. PBSVideo. 1999.

Maps

National Geographic Society
Each is available as an uncirculated back issue with supplement map, many double-sided.

Contact: *National Geographic* Back Issues
(800) 777-2800, Fax: (813)979-6685
Cost: ranges between $5 and $10 (shipping included)

February 1997—Dawn of Humans
December 1971—includes a physical map and a cultural map of Africa
December 1990—includes a political map and a map of Africa threatened
January 1995—Egypt's Nile Valley
April 2001—recreated drawing of Thebes, time line/Egypt's Nile Valley, dynasties

Web Sites

Go to **NCJourneys.com** for links to the following Web sites:

- Africa: A Continent Revealed Map Exhibit
- Africa for Kids, PBS Kids
- Africa Resource Center
- *Africa* Series Companion Web Site
- Africam (live Web cam of African game parks)
- African Voices Exhibit at the Smithsonian Institution
- All Africa (news service for Africa)
- American Museum of Natural History African Artifacts
- *Hopes on the Horizon* PBS Companion Web Site
- National Museum of African Art, Smithsonian Museum
- National Geographic: Africa
- The Story of Africa, BBC
- *Wonders of the African World* Companion Web Site

Paideia Seminar

"Ozymandias"

OBJECTIVES: 11.02

A Paideia seminar is a formal discussion based on a text. The teacher asks only open-ended questions. Students must read and study the text, listen to other students' comments, think critically, and respond with their thoughts and with responses to the thoughts of others. Higher order thinking is evident because students are required to summarize, analyze, synthesize, compare and contrast, and use logic to defend and challenge ideas.

Have the class read "Ozymandias" by Percy Shelley (1818). Visit **NCJourneys.com** for a link to the poem.

A possible theme for the seminar discussion is immortality.

Opening Questions

- What scene does this poem describe?
- What is its central theme?

Core Questions

- What are the different voices in this poem?
- What does the description suggest about the speaker's attitude toward the scene?
- How do you react to Ozymandias' self-description as "king of kings"?
- How does the idea of "decay" work in this poem?

Closing Questions

- What does this poem suggest to you about the place of art in nature?
- What does it suggest about human vanity?

Sphinx and pyramids at Giza

The locator map is a Robinson projection with approximately a 12 percent distortion of the earth. Brainstorm and discuss why Africa is often depicted in the center of this equal-area type of projection. Discuss that Africa is the only world region (with Gulf of Guinea) intersected by both the Equator and prime meridian. Have students fold a sheet of 8½-inch by 11-inch paper into fourths. Using horizontal fold as the Equator and vertical fold as the prime meridian, assign students to use mental mapping skills to sketch Africa's outline shape on this folded sheet of paper. File the mental maps in a portfolio to revisit at end of "Unit 1" study to redo and compare with map sketched at beginning of unit's study.

Extension For ELL students, model and provide additional explanation.

Egypt's buses are like time machines. Climb aboard one in Cairo for a ride to Giza. The trip is short, but when the bus stops near the Great Sphinx or a nearby pyramid, you have traveled back almost 5,000 years. At that time, workers cut, moved, and placed gigantic stones to form pyramids more than 400 feet (120 meters) high.

Africa's great ancient traditions are not just tourist attractions. Africans today are inspired by past achievements to build modern societies.

14   Unit 1

Social Studies at Work

Social Studies at Work: Public Service Official

A public service official is someone who is elected or appointed to serve in a government office.

Meet Senator Elizabeth Hanford Dole
One of North Carolina's Most Famous Citizens

Elizabeth Hanford Dole, a native North Carolinian, is known throughout the world. Her lifetime of success began as a student in Salisbury where, by the time she was in second grade, her teacher noted on Dole's report card that "she tries so hard to do everything exactly right—and she succeeds."

This pursuit of academic excellence led Dole to attend Duke University. She then studied at the University of Oxford in England and earned a master's degree in education and a law degree from Harvard University.

After graduating, Dole went to work in the White House as executive director of President Lyndon Johnson's Committee on Consumer Interests. President Richard Nixon appointed Dole to the Federal Trade Commission.

Dole is only one of a handful of women to hold a prestigious post in the Cabinet. She is the only women to have been appointed to lead two different departments under two different presidents. President Ronald Reagan chose Dole to lead the

14

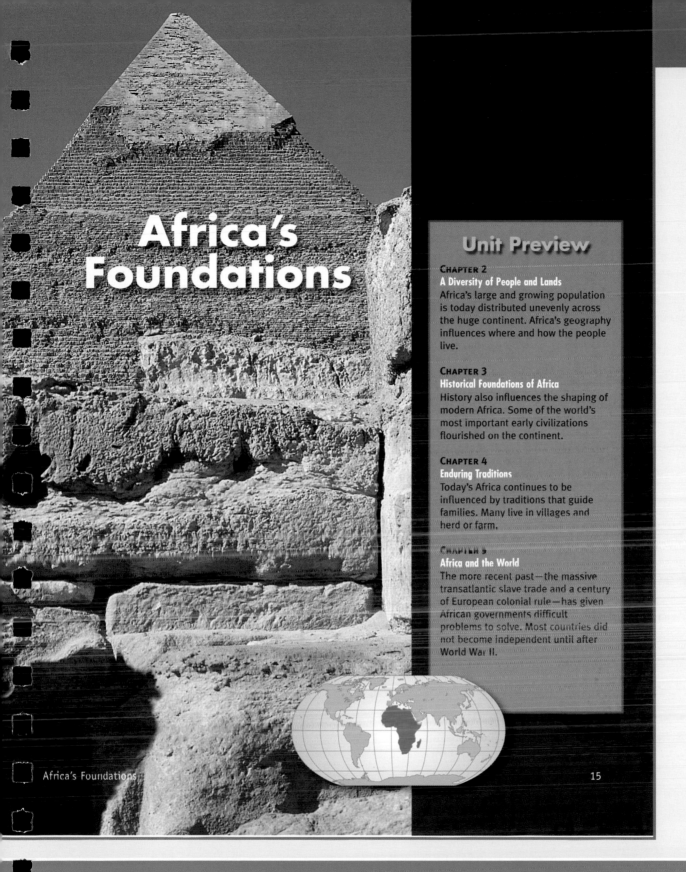

Africa's Foundations

Unit Preview

CHAPTER 2
A Diversity of People and Lands
Africa's large and growing population is today distributed unevenly across the huge continent. Africa's geography influences where and how the people live.

CHAPTER 3
Historical Foundations of Africa
History also influences the shaping of modern Africa. Some of the world's most important early civilizations flourished on the continent.

CHAPTER 4
Enduring Traditions
Today's Africa continues to be influenced by traditions that guide families. Many live in villages and herd or farm.

CHAPTER 5
Africa and the World
The more recent past—the massive transatlantic slave trade and a century of European colonial rule—has given African governments difficult problems to solve. Most countries did not become independent until after World War II.

Africa's Foundations   15

Transportation Department and President George H. W. Bush named her Secretary of the Department of Labor.

All these important jobs were just the beginning for Dole. She spent several years as director of the American Red Cross. She led nearly 30,000 staff members and more than a million volunteers. The Red Cross comes to the rescue when disaster strikes—whether it's a hurricane in North Carolina or a famine in Somalia.

Dole is probably most famous for her role in politics. First as the wife of Senator and presidential candidate Bob Dole. Second, as a presidential candidate herself. In 2002, she was elected senator from North Carolina.

Public Servant for a Day
Imagine that you have been appointed the director of a local disaster relief agency. Think about the kinds of natural disasters (that means weather- or nature-related) your town is likely to face someday. a hurricane? a tornado? a snowstorm? What does your agency need to do to get prepared to help when a crisis hits? Make a list of all the supplies and volunteer assistance you think you'll need.

Find Out More
Visit **NCJourneys.com** for a link to the American Red Cross Web site to find out more about its important work both locally and abroad. On the Red Cross page, click on international`services for a look at current relief efforts throughout the world.

CHAPTER 2

A Diversity of People and Lands

Social Studies Strands

Geographic Relationships
Physical features
Absolute and relative location
Climate and vegetation

Cultures and Diversity

Worksheets

Worksheets and answer keys are found both in the Teacher Resource Guide and at **NCJourneys.com**, including Reading Guides, Reading Strategies, Chapter Reviews, English Language Learner and others.

North Carolina Standard Course of Study

Goal 2 The learner will assess the relationship between physical environment and cultural characteristics of selected societies and regions of Africa, Asia, and Australia.

Goal 3 The learner will analyze the impact of interactions between humans and their physical environments in Africa, Asia, and Australia.

Goal 4 The learner will identify significant patterns in the movement of people, goods, and ideas over time and place in Africa, Asia, and Australia.

Goal 5 The learner will evaluate the varied ways of people of Africa, Asia, and Australia make decisions about the allocation and use of economic resources.

Teaching & Assessment

- English Language Learner Modified Lesson Plans for this chapter are found in the Teacher Resource Guide.

- *ExamView® Assessment Suite* is provided at **NCJourneys.com**. It includes customizable assessments for all chapters. Paper tests are also available in the Teacher Resource Guide. See pages T16–T17 for information about how to use the assessments and the Scoring Guide.

ACTIVITIES AND INTEGRATIONS

SOCIAL STUDIES	
Vegetation Rubbings of Africa, p. 16b	
★ ■ Population Exploration, p. 16b	
▲ Activator: *Ashanti to Zulu,* p. 16	
▲ Categorize Africa's Physical Characteristics, p. 17	
● ▲ No-Bake Edible Map, p. 18	
▲ Just How Large is Africa, p. 23	
Mount Kilimanjaro, p. 27	
Continental Drift Theory, p. 28	
The Baobab Tree, p. 29	
Africa—Climate, p. 34	
Skill Lesson: Using Geography's Themes: Location, p. 35	

READING/LANGUAGE ARTS	READING/LANGUAGE ARTS OBJECTIVES
Analogies, p. 16b	2.01
Writing Prompt: Africa's Development, p. 16	1.01, 3.01, 3.03
A Poem of an African Country, p. 19	1.01, 1.02, 2.01, 2.02, 6.01
★ Creative Writing, p. 24	1.01, 1.03, 6.01, 6.02
Creation Stories, p. 25	1.02, 1.03, 6.01, 6.02
■ Kilimanjaro: Mountain of Greatness, p. 26	1.01, 2.01
Go to the Source: Comparing Poetry and Maps, p. 37	2.01, 3.01, 4.01, 5.01, 5.02

SCIENCE	SCIENCE OBJECTIVES
Africa and the Atlantic, p. 32	3.05

MATHEMATICS	MATHEMATICS OBJECTIVES
▲ Where Have All the People Gone? p. 20	4.01
● ▲ Swahili Math, p. 20	1.02
★ ■ Illustration of Population Growth, p. 21	1.01, 1.02, 1.03
■ Rain Forest Word Problem, p. 31	1.02
★ ▲ African Dodecahedron, p. 33	3.01

TECHNOLOGY	TECHNOLOGY OBJECTIVES
★ ■ Illustration of Population Growth, p. 21	1.09, 1.10, 1.11, 3.05
How to Make a Climograph in Microsoft Excel, p. 30	1.09, 1.10, 1.11, 3.05

VISUAL ARTS	VISUAL ARTS OBJECTIVES
● ▲ Mask Making, p. 16b	1.02, 5.01
★ ▲ African Dodecahedron, p. 33	4.01

CHARACTER AND VALUES EDUCATION	TRAITS
Writing Prompt: Africa's Development, p. 16	good citizenship
What Would You Do?, p. 31	respect

● Basic Activities ★ Challenging Activities ▲ English Language Learner Novice ■ English Language Learner Intermediate

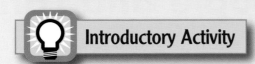 **Introductory Activity**

Vegetation Rubbings of Africa

 **OBJECTIVES:** 1.01, 1.02

Trace the Africa—Natural Vegetation map (page 35) onto large paper using a projector. Have students re-create the map by texturing different colored crayon or pastel rubbings of the varying types of vegetation. Place the items to be rubbed under the paper, then rub the side of a crayon or pastel across the top. The texture will come through. An arrangement of tropical plant or houseplant leaves may be rubbed over the area for tropical rain forest. Have students be creative about what to use for the other areas, such as sand rubbings for the desert or grass for the grasslands. Discuss the role that vegetation plays in Africa.

 **Culminating Activity**

Population Exploration

 **OBJECTIVES:** 2.02

Review with students the population distribution map for Africa found on page 20, and note areas of dense and sparse population. Divide them into cooperative groups, each group having one kind of map (resource, land use, rainfall, physical features, climate, disease, distribution, for example). Have each group determine reasons for population clusters (and scattering) based on their map information.

Regroup students (jigsaw pattern) into groups with each different map represented and have these groups come up with a list of reasons why "Africa's population is unevenly distributed."

For this "Thinking and Writing as a Geographer" activity, have students in a group create a graphic organizer for an essay on the topic "Reasons for Africa's Population Distribution."

From the graphic organizer and group discussion, have students write or word process their essays and then bring them back to the group for editing and proofing. Students will hand in their final essays.

Extension For intermediate ELL students, model and provide additional explanations. ELL's may participate in the group but not write essays.

 **Art Activity**

Mask Making

 **OBJECTIVES:** 12.03

For Africans, masks have been important in many different ceremonies, festivals, and rites. Research and view in books or on the Internet examples of different styles of masks: realistic, animalistic, abstract, and expressionistic. Students should design a mask on paper first and then construct it. Sturdy plastic/paper plates may be used as bases. Students may glue or tape on extra shapes and then use papier-mâché. Finish masks by painting and gluing on decorations. Ask students to explain the symbolism of their masks.

Extension For novice ELL students, model and provide additional explanations.

 **Analogies**

 **OBJECTIVES:** 1.02

Analogies are useful to help students make associations with prior knowledge. They can be used as an instructional strategy to help students better understand new materials. They are not intended to be definitions or test items.

Read the analogies aloud and ask students to identify the relationship between the terms. As an extension, ask students to write their own analogies using key terms or places discussed in the chapter.

Extension For intermediate ELL students, model and provide additional explanations.

large : small :: urban : rural
(is the opposite of)

dirty : unclean :: diversity : variety
(is the same as)

hill : mountain :: mesa : plateau
(is smaller than)

Loire Valley : France :: Great Rift Valley : East Africa (is located in)

temperate climates : middle latitudes :: tropical climates : low latitudes
(are found in)

wet : dry :: drought : flood
(is the opposite of)

Teaching Strategies

- Use the pictures throughout the chapter to illustrate the diversity of land and people in Africa.

Activator

OBJECTIVES: 12.01, 13.02

Activators are great tools to use in order to "hook" the attention of the students. Reading picture books or stories is an excellent way to build interest in the subject and is also a great way to integrate language arts into the social studies curriculum.

Ashanti to Zulu: African Traditions by Margaret W. Musgrove. (Puffin Books, 1980. ISBN 0140546049.)

OR

Find a variety of pictures or postcards depicting the different regions, village and suburban life, and wildlife. Divide the class into small groups. Explain that when we study foreign countries, we often focus on differences when in fact we have much in common. Give each group a picture. Ask them to brainstorm the ways in which the United States is like the picture. After five minutes of brainstorming, have each group share their best answer and the picture with the class.

Extension Have ELL intermediate students compare picture to their native country when brainstorming.

Writing Prompt

OBJECTIVES: 2.03

Evaluative

The African continent has a rich variety of land features, climates, and vegetation zones. Do you think that Africa's physical geography has hurt its development more than it has helped? Explain your opinion in an essay.

As you write or word process your essay, remember to

- state your opinion clearly.
- give at least three reasons and explain them fully.
- use examples to support your reasons.
- write in complete sentences and paragraph form.
- organize your ideas and include an introduction and a conclusion.
- use good grammar, spelling, punctuation, and capitalization.

CHAPTER 2

A Diversity of People and Lands

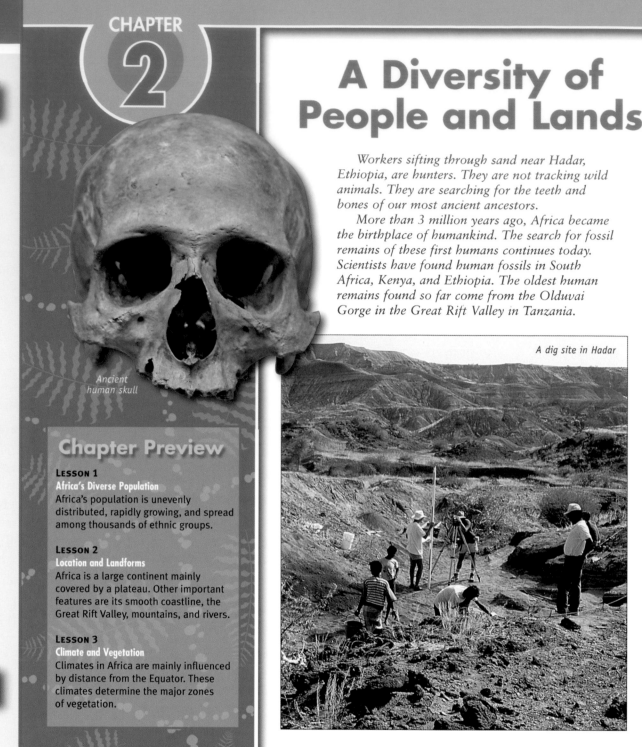

Workers sifting through sand near Hadar, Ethiopia, are hunters. They are not tracking wild animals. They are searching for the teeth and bones of our most ancient ancestors.

More than 3 million years ago, Africa became the birthplace of humankind. The search for fossil remains of these first humans continues today. Scientists have found human fossils in South Africa, Kenya, and Ethiopia. The oldest human remains found so far come from the Olduvai Gorge in the Great Rift Valley in Tanzania.

Ancient human skull

A dig site in Hadar

Chapter Preview

LESSON 1
Africa's Diverse Population
Africa's population is unevenly distributed, rapidly growing, and spread among thousands of ethnic groups.

LESSON 2
Location and Landforms
Africa is a large continent mainly covered by a plateau. Other important features are its smooth coastline, the Great Rift Valley, mountains, and rivers.

LESSON 3
Climate and Vegetation
Climates in Africa are mainly influenced by distance from the Equator. These climates determine the major zones of vegetation.

16

Chapter 2

Chapter Resources

Print Resources

Africa in Transition. Southern Center for International Studies, 2000. ISBN 0935082247. Resource of background essays, maps, charts, and lesson plans.

Chambers, Catherine. *Drought* (Disaster in Nature series). Heinemann Library, 2001. ISBN 157572426X. Examines drought disasters, discussing what causes them, how they affect people, and how we can compensate for them. Includes a section on the drought in the Sahel region of Africa.

Hull, Robert. *Stories from West Africa.* Raintree Steck-Vaughn, 2000. ISBN 0739813331.

Iliffe, John. *The African AIDS Epidemic: A History,* James Currey, 2006. ISBN 0852558902.

Musgrove, Margaret W. *Ashanti to Zulu: African Traditions.* Puffin Books, 1980. ISBN 0140546049.

Africa–Physical

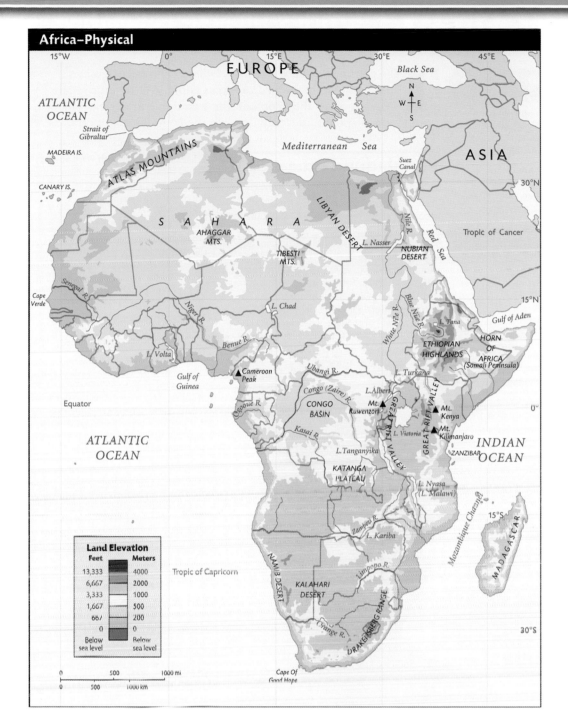

Map Activity

Categorize Africa's Physical Characteristics Map Activity

NATIONAL GEOGRAPHY STANDARDS: 1, 4

GEOGRAPHIC THEMES: Place

OBJECTIVES: 1.02, 1.03, 2.01

Using the "Africa-Physical" map transparency from the Teacher's Resource Guide and the map on this page, have students itemize on chart paper/board the physical place characteristics found on this African continental map and bodies of water adjacent to Africa. Divide the class into small groups to categorize physical features as to deserts, mountains, other landforms, rivers, lakes, other water bodies. As an oral review of categories is conducted, note with students how much of Africa is 3,333 feet (1,000 m) or less in elevation on the earth's second-largest continent.

Audiovisual

Africa in Transition. Southern Center for International Studies, 2000. Eight-part video.

The Elephants of Africa. Nature. WNET Video Distribution, P.O. Box 2284, South Burlington, VT 05407.

Web Sites

Links to the following Web sites are found at **NCJourneys.com.**

• Climate Prediction Center Africa Desk, NOAA

• Florida's National Geographic Alliance; Lesson plans of six activities developed on geography and African rivers.

• Mt. Kilimanjaro Geology News, The Geology Society

• Nature: The Elephants of Africa Companion Web Site

• U.S. Geological Survey; *The Dynamic Earth: The Story of Plate Tectonics* online version

• World Wise School site (Peace Corps); *Water in West Africa* (Photos, stories, and lesson plans for 25 African nations.

OBJECTIVES: 2.02, 3.02, 4.01

Discussion Questions

1 Why would people settle near bodies of water? What would enable them to move away from these areas?

 Caption Answer

Nigeria, the Nile River valley, Ethiopia, Malawi, the southeast coast of Africa, the areas around Lake Victoria, and the coastal areas of Morocco, Algeria, and Tunisia.

Activity

The No-Bake Edible Map

OBJECTIVES: 2.01

The objective of this activity is to locate the physical features of Africa. Caution: before constructing this map, ask if any student is allergic to peanuts. This recipe contains peanut butter.

Divide the class into pairs. Give each pair a piece of wax paper and a ball of dough (recipe follows). Place the following supplies in small containers on a central table:
- graham cracker crumbs
- green sprinkles
- blue icing
- mini chocolate chips
- red candy strips
- brown sugar
- rubber gloves (optional)

Students should pat out the dough into the shape of the African continent. Using the directions below, students should locate the physical features of Africa. Before eating the maps, students must show the map to the teacher, or the students should evaluate the maps of the other classmates.

Dough Recipe
2 cups smooth peanut butter
2½ cups powdered milk
2½ cups powdered sugar
2 cups white corn syrup

Mix all ingredients together and form small balls. This makes about 25 small balls of dough.

LESSON 1 Africa's Diverse Population

KEY IDEAS

- Africa's population is unevenly distributed, mainly rural, and growing rapidly.
- Africa's population is diverse, made up of more than 2,000 ethnic groups.

KEY TERMS

diversity
epidemic
ethnic group
Swahili

The continent where scientists believe humans originated is now the home of about 813 million people. A little more than 13 percent of all the people in the world live in Africa. This population is spread unevenly through the continent.

Population Patterns

Most Africans live in places where trade, industry, climate, soil, or natural resources allow large numbers of people to support their families. As the map on page 20 shows, areas of heaviest settlement in North Africa are in the fertile farmlands along the Nile River in Egypt and in the cities of Algeria, Tunisia, and Morocco.

Other heavily settled areas are southern Nigeria and nearby parts of West Africa, lands near Lake Victoria, and the highlands of East Africa. Rich volcanic soil and ample rainfall have made those places well suited to farming.

A Samburu girl of Gambia balances a bowl on her head. The Samburu, like most people in Africa, live where resources support them. **What areas in Africa are heavily populated?**

Johannesburg, South Africa, and nearby cities are centers of mining and industry. This area first attracted large numbers of European settlers and African migrant workers because of the gold found in nearby mines.

The bar graph on page 20 shows how these population patterns affect the populations of African countries. Nigeria contains by far the largest population with 131.5 million people. Ethiopia at 77.4 million and Egypt at 74 million are the next most populous countries. Each has slightly more than half as many people as Nigeria. The Democratic Republic of the Congo has 50 million people.

Vast areas of Africa—such as the deserts, semi-arid areas like the Sahel (seh·HAYL) and tropical rain forests—are less populated. These areas lack the rich soil, the rainfall, or the mineral resources to support large populations. Relatively few people have settled in areas that are breeding grounds for the tsetse (TEET·see) fly and other insects that spread deadly diseases.

Rapid Population Growth

Another key feature of Africa's population is rapid growth. Africa is the fastest growing region in the world. By 2025, the United Nations projects that Africa's population will grow to 1.454 billion people.

Worldwide, but especially in Sub-Saharan Africa, HIV/AIDS (Human Immunodeficiency Virus/Acquired Immunodeficiency Syndrome) continues to be a challenge to development. The growing *epidemic* reverses economic and social gains. It robs millions of people of

18   Chapter 2

Make the dough the night before and bring it in, or have students mix the dough during class and then form their maps.

brown graham cracker crumbs: Sahara Desert, Namib Desert, Kalahari Desert

green sprinkles: rain forest

brown sugar: Mediterranean vegetation zone along the northwest, southeast vegetation zone

blue icing: Nile River, Zambezi River, Orange River, Lake Tanganyika, Limpopo River, Lake Victoria, Senegal River, Lake Nyasa, Congo (Zaire) River, Lake Chad

mini chocolate chips: Mount Kenya, Mount Kilimanjaro, Ethiopian Highlands, Atlas Mountains, Drakensberg Range

red candy strips: prime meridian, Tropic of Cancer, Equator, Tropic of Capricorn

Extension For novice ELL students, model and provide additional explanations.

their health and lives. It also widens the gap between rich and poor and leaves millions of children orphaned each year.

Although HIV/AIDS has caused a slow-down in the population growth rate, Africa's population is still growing. Sub-Saharan Africa is both the world's poorest and fastest-growing region.

Rapid population growth makes progress difficult. Many African nations cannot meet the needs of their people for medical care, safe drinking water, and good housing.

Population experts give several reasons for Africa's rapid population growth. Due to vaccination programs, improvements in health care, and better housing, people are living longer. The infant mortality rate in many African countries is still high, but children who survive their early years are living longer.

Furthermore, in rural areas, most Africans are farmers. They need many children to help with the farm work and then to care for aging parents. In Eritrea, the nation with the most rapid population growth rate in Africa—4.26 percent, the average woman has five children.

Rural families are not likely to give up having many children anytime soon.

Parents see children as a blessing. Many African proverbs stress the importance of each child. The Ibo (EE·boh) people of Nigeria ask, "Gini ka nnwa"—"What counts for more than a child?" A West African proverb comments on how children contribute to family life as workers: "Each extra mouth comes attached to two extra hands."

A woman prepares a meal in her village near Lake Volta in Ghana. **Why do many Africans have large families?**

Cape Town, the largest city in South Africa, has a population of more than 3.5 million. **Why is Africa growing rapidly in both rural and urban areas?**

A Diversity of People and Lands

19

Discussion Questions

1 Why does Africa have one of the fastest-growing populations in the world?

2 What regions in North Carolina are growing this rapidly?

3 Compare a rural area in North Carolina to a rural area in West Africa.

4 What are some vaccinations that are available in the United States? If these vaccines were available in Africa, what effect might they have? (Students use the Internet to find out more.)

 Caption Answer

People have had large families because the infant mortality rate in Africa has been high. Improvements to health care are helping people live longer. Farming families often have many children to help on the farm.

 Caption Answer

Health care has improved. People are living longer. Children are seen as a blessing.

 Writing Activity

A Poem of an African Country

 OBJECTIVES: 1.01, 2.01

Choose a country in Africa. Research the following: neighboring countries, important bodies of water, physical features, and climate and vegetation. Have students create their own graphic organizer and fill in their information.

Using this information, students are to write a poem describing the physical characteristics of the country studied. They must have at least one example from each of the categories above. The poem does not have to rhyme or have a meter. Have students write their poems on an outline map of Africa.

Extension ELL students can use ELL-friendly Web sites to do research on the country. Intermediate students' poems should have only one or two words per line if needed. Novice students should stop at the graphic organizer.

 Background Information

HIV/AIDS Crisis

For much of Africa, the HIV/AIDS epidemic has devastated the society and infrastructure.. Almost two-thirds of all people living with HIV in the world live in sub-Saharan Africa—an estimated 24.7 million in 2006.

By early 2005, more than 20 million Africans had died of AIDS. An estimated 12 million children under 17 in sub-Saharan Africa have lost one or both parents to AIDS. African families often consist of 10 or more dependents, so the loss of a breadwinner can be devastating.

With the exception of such countries as South Africa, nations in sub-Saharan Africa lack welfare systems. Eastern and Southern Africa have suffered greatly.

Kenya, Zimbabwe, and urban areas of Burkina Faso have begun to see a leveling or a decline from the peak rates of infection. But this success is limited. By 2006, Botswana's national HIV infection rate was 24.1 percent, Namibia's was 19.6 percent, and Swaziland's was 33.4 percent. Experts fear that HIV infection combined with new drug-resistent tuberculosis may trigger a spike in deaths in the near future.

Caption Answer

Areas near the ocean, lakes, and rivers as well as grasslands have high densities of population. Desert, rain forest, and mountainous regions have low densitites of population.

 Map Activity

Where Have All the People Gone?

NATIONAL GEOGRAPHY STANDARDS: 1, 4, 9, 12

GEOGRAPHIC THEMES: Location, Place

OBJECTIVES: 2.02, 2.03

In a discussion with the class, classify all nations with population density less than five people per square mile (less than two people per square kilometer) and all nations with population density more than 250 people per square mile (more than 100 people per square kilometer). Using data from a current almanac or the Internet and a spreadsheet, have small groups of students design horizontal bar graphs (in both ascending and descending order of population density) for the ten nations not represented in the Africa—Population graph on page 20.

Option Five small groups can each be assigned one African region: North, West, Central, East, or Southern Africa, to design a population bar graph. Have each student analyze the graphs and then write a clarification paper on: Some African nations have a higher or lower population density than other nations. Give three reasons explaining why this might be so.

Extension Do not assign the writing portion for ELL students.

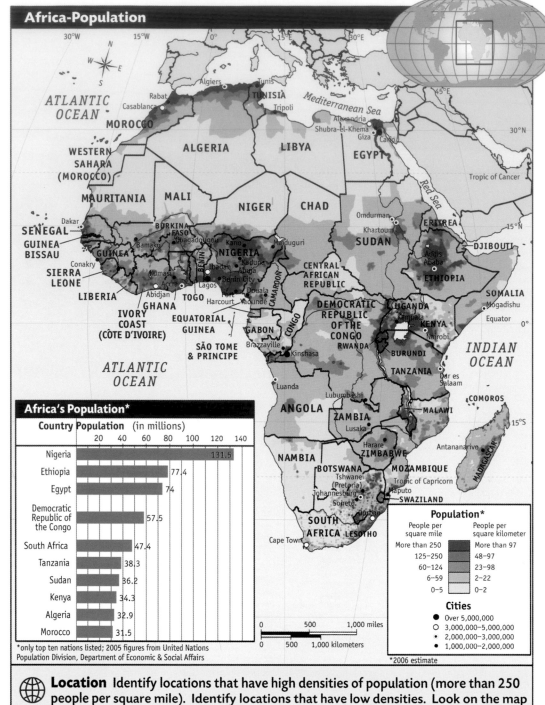

Africa-Population

Africa's Population*

Country — Population (in millions)

Country	Population
Nigeria	131.5
Ethiopia	77.4
Egypt	74
Democratic Republic of the Congo	57.5
South Africa	47.4
Tanzania	38.3
Sudan	36.2
Kenya	34.3
Algeria	32.9
Morocco	31.5

*only top ten nations listed; 2005 figures from United Nations Population Division, Department of Economic & Social Affairs

Population*

People per square mile	People per square kilometer
More than 250	More than 97
125–250	48–97
60–124	23–98
6–59	2–22
0–5	0–2

Cities
- ● Over 5,000,000
- ○ 3,000,000–5,000,000
- · 2,000,000–3,000,000
- · 1,000,000–2,000,000

*2006 estimate

Location Identify locations that have high densities of population (more than 250 people per square mile). Identify locations that have low densities. Look on the map on page 17. *What landforms create conditions for high densities of population? for low densities?*

Chapter 2

 Math Activity

Swahili Math

OBJECTIVES: 4.07

Have students use the Swahili numbers below to answer these math problems in Swahili.

moja = one
mbili = two
tatu = three
nne = four
taro = five

sita = six
saba = seven
nave = eight
tisa = nine
kumi = ten

1. moja + taro =
2. saba + mbili =
3. tatu + nne =
4. kumi – saba =
5. saba – sita =
6. tatu – moja =
7. saba – tatu =
8. kumi – moja =
9. kumi – saba =
10. tisa – naye =

11. tatu x mbili =
12. taro x mbili =
13. tisa / tatu =
14. nave / mbili =
15. kumi / mbili =
16. nave / nne =
17. moja / moja =
18. tatu / tatu =
19. kumi / moja =
20. kumi / taro =

Rural and Urban

Africa's population is largely rural. Two thirds of Africa's people live in villages in the countryside. In the East African country of Burundi (buh·RUN·dih), nine out of ten people live in rural areas. East Africa has the highest percentage of rural dwellers. Only in South Africa and such North African countries as Libya, Algeria, and Tunisia do more than half of the people live in cities.

Throughout Africa, urban areas are growing rapidly. In 2006, more than 9 million people lived in Lagos (LAH·gos), Nigeria. By 2010, it is predicted to be one of the world's five largest cities.

Since 1970, the city of Kinshasha (kin·SHAH·sa), Democratic Republic of Congo, has increased its population from 500,000 people to about 8.1 million. The population of Nouakchott (nuh·AHK·shat), Mauritania (mawr·uh·TAY·nee·ah), is more than six times what it was in 1977.

Farmers are moving to the cities because they hope for greater economic opportunities. Younger people move to find jobs. Cities grow as people seeking better lives arrive. Urban growth is increasing. By 2025, it is likely that less than half of Africa's people will live in villages.

Customs

African families give their children names that have special meanings. Young people might have regular names used at school, but then have special names used only at home. One child's name at home, Neng'otonye, means "one who is loved most by her parents." Houda means "guidance." Aseye means "rejoice." Does your family give similar nicknames?

A farm in northern Rwanda shows the rural quality of most African nations. **How and why is that changing?**

A Diversity of People and Lands

21

Discussion Questions

1 What is meant by rural?

2 What factors contribute to the dramatic population growth in such places as Lagos, Kinshasa, and Nouakchott?

3 How are the customs of these places changing as a result of the population growth?

4 In the United States, approximately 75 percent of the population lives in urban areas. How would life be different in the United States if more people lived in rural areas?

5 What regions in North Carolina have the highest percentage of new populations?

6 Do we have people moving to our community or leaving our community? Why do you think this movement is occurring?

Caption Answer

More people, especially young people, want a different type of life in urban areas.

Activity

Illustration of Population Growth

OBJECTIVES: 2.01

To illustrate population growth, have students imagine that they are negotiating a new allowance with their parents. Propose a base allowance of $1/week (or $10/week). Ask them to calculate how long it will take to double their weekly allowance based on a weekly growth rate of 4.2 percent. Encourage the use of the calculator or spreadsheet.

WEEK 1	$1.00	WEEK 1	$10.00
2	1.04	2	10.42
3	1.09	3	10.86
4	1.13	4	11.32
5	1.18	5	11.80
6	1.23	6	12.30
7	1.28	7	12.82
8	1.34	8	13.36
9	1.39	9	13.92
10	1.42	10	14.50
11	1.50	11	15.11
12	1.57	12	15.74
13	1.64	13	16.40
14	1.70	14	17.09
15	1.78	15	17.81
16	1.86	16	18.56
17	1.93	17	19.34
18	2.01	18	20.15

Next, assign each student a country in Africa. Have them look up the rate of natural increase in an almanac or on the United Nations' Cyber Schoolbus Web site (link found at **NCJourneys.com**). Using the country's current population as the base, have them use a computer spreadsheet program to determine how many years it would take for the population to double.

Extension Assign a peer tutor to help ELL students complete the spreadsheet.

Discussion Questions

1 What challenges face a nation where several languages are spoken?

2 Why is knowing multiple languages beneficial?

3 How has diversity in our community helped enrich our culture?

Caption Answer

The many languages reflect the many different ethnic groups within Africa.

Caption Answer

An ethnic group is a large group of people with the same cultural background, who are united by language, religion, ancestry, or ancestors' place of origin.

This court building in South Africa illustrates the many languages spoken on the continent. **How is language a sign of diversity in Africa?**

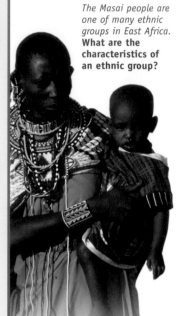

The Masai people are one of many ethnic groups in East Africa. **What are the characteristics of an ethnic group?**

Diversity of People

What do the phrases *bonjour, soh-bay-doh,* and *mou-doh-boh-no* all have in common? Each is a way of saying "good morning" in three of the many different languages spoken in the West African country of Togo.

Tiny Togo contains only 4.5 million people. Yet its people belong to 40 different ethnic groups. An ***ethnic group*** is a large collection of people with the same cultural background, united by language, religion, ancestry, or ancestors' place of origin.

Togo's ethnic and language diversity is not unusual. *Diversity* means differing from one another. Africa is a place of diversity because many different ethnic groups live there. Nigeria has 250 ethnic groups who speak 100 different languages. Africans belong to more than 2,000 ethnic groups and speak more than 1,000 languages.

Some languages are spoken by more than one ethnic group. North of the Sahara Desert, in countries such as Algeria, Libya, Tunisia, and Egypt, people speak languages that are mainly dialects, or variations, of Arabic or Berber languages.

The greatest diversity in languages occurs south of the Sahara. Thousands of people throughout West Africa speak Hausa (HOW·sah), a language used for trade. *Swahili* (swa·HEE·lee), an African, mostly Bantu, language with many words borrowed from Arabic, is spoken throughout parts of East Africa. In Nairobi, Kenya's capital, many Kenyans speak three languages—English, Swahili, and the language of their own ethnic group.

English and French are also common throughout the continent, especially in countries where no one African language is spoken by large numbers of people. English and French took root in parts of Africa because the United Kingdom and France ruled colonies there.

Africa's many languages are a basis of its cultural heritage. Its cultures reflect landforms and climates that separated some ethnic groups and drew others together on the continent.

WORD ORIGINS

Swahili comes from the place where language first was spoken. Arabic and African people met on the coast of East Africa, where they joined their cultures and created a new language. Swahili comes from the Arabic word sahil, which means "coast." Swahili means "people of the coast."

LESSON 1 REVIEW

Fact Follow-Up
1. Where in Africa do most people live?
2. What are some reasons why Africa's population is growing rapidly?
3. Why is population in Africa moving from rural to urban areas?
4. Which area has the most language diversity?

Talk About It
1. Explain how Africa's population patterns are affected by the continent's landforms.
2. What are some positive and negative results of Africa's rapid population growth?
3. How do Africa's languages reflect its landforms?

LESSON 1 REVIEW

Fact Follow-Up Answers
1. Population is distributed unevenly throughout the continent, with most people living where climate, soil fertility, or other natural resources can support large populations. Areas of densest settlement in the north include the Nile River valley and the cities of Algeria, Tunisia, and Morocco. Southern Nigeria, parts of West Africa, and the highlands of East Africa are densely populated. In Southern Africa, Johannesburg and nearby cities support large populations.
2. Vaccination programs have lowered the death rate. Though infant mortality is still high, children who survive the early years live longer. In rural areas, most people are farmers who need many children to help with farm work and then care for aged parents.
3. Though Africa is largely rural, urban population is growing as people move to cities for greater economic opportunities and a search for better ways of life.

4. The greatest language diversity occurs south of the Sahara.

Talk About It Answers
1. The deserts, semiarid areas like the Sahel, and tropical rain forests are sparsely populated, lacking rainfall, rich soil, or mineral resources to support large populations. Most people live in areas that have climate, soil, and/or natural resources to support large populations.
2. Positive results include the fact that improved health care and vaccination programs are working. Negative results include the fact that rapid population growth makes economic progress difficult.
3. Africa's people, dispersed because of landforms such as deserts, mountain ranges, and rain forests, developed great language diversity, with more than 1,000 languages being spoken on the continent.

OBJECTIVES: 2.01, 3.01, 5.01

Africa is the second-largest continent on earth. Only Asia is larger. Three countries the size of the contiguous United States could fit inside this continent with room to spare. The continent is almost as wide as it is long, stretching almost 5,000 miles (8,050 kilometers) from east to west and more than 6,000 miles (9,660 km) from north to south.

Location

Africa's closest neighbors to the north are Europe and Asia. It is bordered on the west by the Atlantic Ocean and on the east by the Indian Ocean. The Mediterranean Sea separates Africa from Europe to the north. The Red Sea separates it from Asia to the northeast.

The continent is divided into 54 countries. Some nations are quite large. Sudan, Africa's largest nation in area, is one third the size of the contiguous United States. Others are much smaller. Djibouti (je·BOUT·ih) is less than one fifth the size of North Carolina.

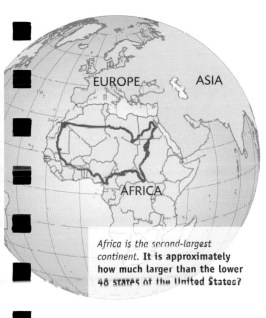

EUROPE   ASIA

AFRICA

Africa is the second-largest continent. **It is approximately how much larger than the lower 48 states of the United States?**

Features of the Land

One geographer has called Africa "the plateau continent." The name fits. Most of Africa is *plateau,* high flat or gently rolling land. Its edges drop abruptly to the sea, forming steep cliffs called *escarpments.* Some of these cliffs rise from 2,000 feet (600 m) to more than 4,000 feet (1,200 m) over the coastal lowlands, especially in southern Africa.

Because so much of Africa is plateau, the continent has a narrow coastal plain. One striking feature of Africa's coast is its evenness. Compare Africa with other continents on a world map or globe. Africa lacks peninsulas such as Asia has in India and Malaysia. No seas stretch into the interior as the Mediterranean and Black Seas do in Europe. Seaways do not open up the continent as the St. Lawrence River does in North America.

The even coastline contains few inlets or bays to form good harbors. Also, waterfalls and rapids near the mouths of Africa's rivers cause an abrupt drop from the plateau to the coastal plains. Boats cannot easily move upstream and downstream.

Above these barriers, Africans have traveled by land and water throughout the interior of the continent. Few early city-states sprang up along the coast; most early African kingdoms and empires developed in the interior. Rapids limited explorations into the interior by Europeans. In modern times, rapids made it difficult to establish transportation links between the coast and the interior.

KEY IDEAS

- Africa is east of the Atlantic Ocean, west of the Indian Ocean, and south of the Mediterranean Sea.

- Africa's chief land features are a plateau, the Great Rift Valley, the Eastern Highlands, the Atlas Mountains, and the Drakensberg Mountains.

- Africa's coastal plain is even and narrow.

- Africa's long rivers are interrupted by numerous waterfalls.

KEY TERMS

cataracts
continental drift
escarpments
plateau

Discussion Questions

1 How do you think the geography of Africa affected its history and exploration?

2 How is the geography of Africa both similar to and different from that of the three regions of North Carolina?

3 Which region in North Carolina best resembles the landforms found in Africa? How?

 **Caption Answer**

About three times larger

 Map Activity

Just How Large Is Africa?

NATIONAL GEOGRAPHY STANDARDS: 3
GEOGRAPHIC THEMES: Location
OBJECTIVES: 1.03

Locate maps of Africa and the contiguous United States drawn to the same scale (enlarge the map on page 28) and give students the outlines if you cannot locate

maps drawn to scale). Using clear transparency film or white tissue paper, have several students trace the boundary outline of the African continent. Have the rest of the class trace the boundary outline of the contiguous 48 United States using color transparency film or tissue paper. Have students with African outlines tape those outlines onto darker sheets of construction paper. Instruct students with United States outlines to superimpose three (almost four) onto each African outline, positioning the United States so that it remains mostly within Africa's boundary.

Identify with the class the students who choose to rotate, flip, or overlap the United States outlines to accomplish the task.

To gain some perspective on just how large Africa is, discuss with students the concept of traveling on Interstate Highway 40 from Wilmington, North Carolina, to Barstow, California, three times consecutively.

Discussion Questions

1 What are the geographic features of the Great Rift Valley?

2 Based on the information about the Great Rift Valley, do you know of any similar geographical features in the United States?

Steep cliffs that drop into the sea from the plateau

Narrow coastal plains and western highlands and mountains

Eastern highlands with Mount Kilimanjaro, the Atlas Mountains in the Northwest, and the Drakensberg Mountains in the Southeast

Creative Writing

OBJECTIVES: 2.01

After reading the legend on page 26 and listening to additional African legends such as *A Story, A Story* by Gail E. Hailey (Atheneum, 1988. ISBN 0689712014.), *African Folk Tales* by Hugh Vernon-Jackson (Dover, 1999. ISBN 0486405532.), or *The Fire on the Mountain and Other Stories from Ethiopia and Eritrea* by Harold Courlander (1995. ISBN 0805036520.), ask students to identify a landform in Africa and make up a legend that might explain its origin.

The plateau of Africa forms an escarpment as shown here in Cape Town, South Africa. **What is an escarpment?**

The Great Rift Valley cuts deeply into the plateau in Kenya and throughout eastern Africa. **What are Africa's other major landforms?**

Morocco's Atlas Mountains tower over the Rdat Valley in North Africa. **What are Africa's other major mountain ranges? Where are they located?**

24

Great Rift Valley

The Great Rift Valley in eastern Africa offers one of the most striking features of the African landscape. The Great Rift is best seen from the air. It is a giant trench gouged out of the plateau. It is so long and wide that it can be seen from space.

Stretching more than 6,000 miles (9,660 km) from the Red Sea south into southern Africa, the Great Rift is more than a mile deep in places. This huge ditch is the result of shifting movements of the earth's crusts that began between 25 and 35 million years ago. This movement caused faults, huge cracks, to appear in the earth's surface. In some places the earth's crust sank. In others it was pushed up. The movement created high parallel cliffs between 20 and 60 miles (32 and 97 km) apart. Over time, large lakes were created.

The forces that created the Great Rift Valley are still at work. Deep below the surface, the earth's crust is shifting slowly. Scientists predict that in a few more million years water will fill the valley, making this part of East Africa a huge island.

Mountains and Highlands

In Tanzania (tan·za h·NEE·AH), in East Africa, a legend describes the origins of the mountains there:

Long, long ago the earth was smooth and flat and even all over. But one day, [the earth] arose and wanted to talk to the sky. When the two of them finished talking, the earth took leave of the sky and started to return. But she did not reach home everywhere. Some parts of her became tired on the way and had to stop where they were....These are the hills and mountains.

 It's a Fact

Africa

■ Scientists believe that Africa's regular coastline and escarpments are a result of continental drift. Africa was the central portion of Gondwana (see Connections, page 28). When other portions broke off, they drifted away while Africa remained stationary. With no tectonic plates bumping into it, Africa did not develop high mountain ranges.

■ Unemployment rates for many African nations run between 20 percent and 35 percent. Due to the political turmoil there, Zimbabwe's unemployment rate in 2005 was estimated to be 80 percent.

■ Many Africans are underemployed, working only part-time without benefits.

■ In 2005, about 60 percent of Africans were within reach of a cell phone signal, the lowest level of coverage in the world. However, one in 11 Africans have a cell phone. In contrast, there is only one landline phone for every 33 people in Africa.

It is easy to link this legend to the mountains and Ethiopian Highlands that make up the eastern highlands. Some mountain peaks in East Africa seem to touch the sky. Mount Kilimanjaro (kil·ih·man·JAR·oh), Africa's highest peak, towers 19,340 feet (5,802 m) above surrounding flat grasslands.

Other major mountain ranges in Africa include the Atlas Mountains in the northwest and the Drakensberg (DRAHK·enz·burg) Mountains in the southeast.

Lakes and Rivers

Africa has few lakes. Yet the continent's three largest are among the largest in the world. Lakes Victoria, Tanganyika (tan·gan·YEE·ka), and Nyasa (nigh·AS·ah) are located in the Eastern Highlands at elevations above 1,500 feet (450 m). All are population centers. People use their lifegiving waters for drinking, irrigation, and transportation.

Compared to other continents, Africa has few rivers. Those few are well known for their size and length. The Nile, for example, is the world's longest river at 4,145 miles (6,673 km). Its source flows from near the center of the continent northward into the Mediterranean Sea.

The source of the Nile was a mystery

and a challenge to European explorers for years. The dangerous search for where the Nile begins captured the imaginations of several European explorers in the 1800s.

The Congo River, another major river, crosses the Equator twice as it winds through Central Africa. The Niger (NIGH·jer) flows through West Africa. Other important rivers are the Zambezi and Limpopo (lim·PO·po) Rivers in East Africa, and the Orange River in South Africa.

Although many of Africa's rivers are long, their usefulness for transportation is limited. Waterfalls and shallow rapids cascade over escarpments from the plateau to the coastal plains near the ocean. In many places at the mouths of rivers, water levels can be low. Rivers also become too shallow for navigation during the dry season.

The falls and rapids that limit travel also have some benefits. Water power harnessed by dams creates electricity. The Congo River drops nearly 900 feet (270 m) as it pours over *cataracts*—large waterfalls and rapids—on its course to the Atlantic Ocean. Along the way, the Congo River powers dams that generate electricity for Kinshasa, the capital of the Democratic Republic of the Congo.

The Falls of the Blue Nile in Ethiopia are one of many cataracts on African rivers. **How do falls affect movement of people and goods?**

A Diversity of People and Lands   25

Discussion Questions

1 Name four regions in Africa.

2 What regions in Africa have mountain ranges?

3 Name the important rivers in Africa. Explain why Africa's lakes are described as life-giving waters.

4 What advantages has the Nile River given Africans over the past 200 years?

5 How do we use rivers and lakes? How would our lives be different if these waters became polluted or dried up?

 Caption Answer

Falls slow movement because they make it difficult to travel the full length of the river in either direction.

 **Writing Activity**

Creation Stories

OBJECTIVES: 12.01, 12.02, 12.03

After students have read the creation legend found in Tanzania, have them compare it to creation stories with which they are familiar, such as one from Native American, Greek, or Norse mythology. Students can use graphic organizers for the comparisons. As a follow-up, have students write their own creation story as to how something in nature came about.

Extension ELL students can draw an explanation instead of writing one.

 Teacher Notes

Mount Kilimanjaro

GPS measurements in the last decade have indicated that the height of Mount Kilimanjaro is 5,892 meters above sea level. That is three meters shorter than the height recorded on maps prior to the GPS measurement. This explains discrepancies between the measurement given in the text here and older resources.

Background Information

Rivers Wet and Dry

Africa contains five of the world's largest drainage basins. The Congo (Zaire), Niger, Nile, Orange, and Zambezi Rivers all flow into the sea. However, only the largest rivers in each of these drainage basins can count on heavy flow year-round. Smaller rivers and streams dry up during the year. In most regions of Africa, yearly runoff is low. Only the Niger River in West Africa and the Congo River in Central Africa have high runoff year-round. This is in part because of the high evaporation rates all over Africa. Although snow falls on the Atlas Mountains and East Africa's highest peaks have glaciers, nowhere in Africa is melted snow an important water source.

Map Activity

Kilimanjaro: Mountain of Greatness

NATIONAL GEOGRAPHY STANDARDS: 4, 7, 17
GEOGRAPHIC THEMES: Location, Place
OBJECTIVES: 3.04

Using the background map in the feature, have students identify the two East African nations impacted by the location of Mount Kilimanjaro. Have students speculate which country lays claim to this great peak being within its territory and why it does so. Have students explain why Kilimanjaro is nicknamed the "mountain of great-ness" and "mountain of caravans." Discuss the significance of the follow-ing to the mountain and surrounding area: its visibility 100 miles away; its location 200 miles from the Equator; and its proximity to the Great Rift Valley and Olduvai Gorge. Have each student create his/her own nickname for Mount Kilimanjaro, Kibo, and/or Arrow Glacier and explain its signifi-cance.

Extension ELLs may make their own physical geography map.

ELL Teaching Tips

Learning Styles

Most new ELL students learn best kines-thetically. Don't expect them to sit and listen to lectures. Use lots of gestures, drawings, or other visual aids. Give students hands-on activities to complete.

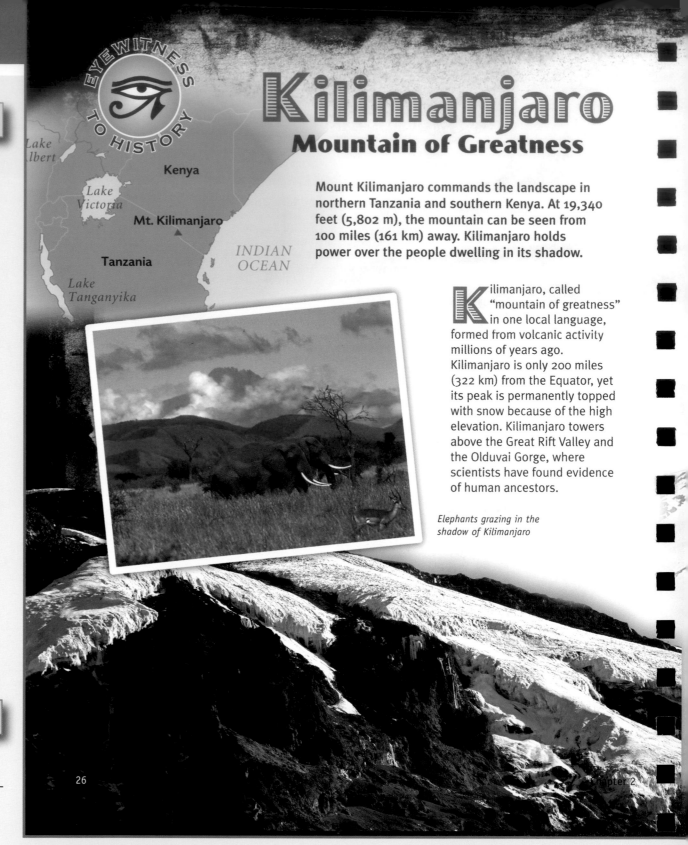

EYEWITNESS TO HISTORY

Kilimanjaro
Mountain of Greatness

Lake Albert

Kenya

Lake Victoria

Mt. Kilimanjaro

Tanzania

INDIAN OCEAN

Lake Tanganyika

Mount Kilimanjaro commands the landscape in northern Tanzania and southern Kenya. At 19,340 feet (5,802 m), the mountain can be seen from 100 miles (161 km) away. Kilimanjaro holds power over the people dwelling in its shadow.

Kilimanjaro, called "mountain of greatness" in one local language, formed from volcanic activity millions of years ago. Kilimanjaro is only 200 miles (322 km) from the Equator, yet its peak is permanently topped with snow because of the high elevation. Kilimanjaro towers above the Great Rift Valley and the Olduvai Gorge, where scientists have found evidence of human ancestors.

Elephants grazing in the shadow of Kilimanjaro

26

Chapter 2

Teacher Notes

Global Warming

Global warming is also affecting the famous "snows" (actually the glaciers) of the mountain. Researchers have documented from mapping and aerial observation that about 82 percent of the ice fields were lost between the time they were first mapped in 1912 and 2000.

The first written reference to Mount Kilimanjaro was by the ancient Greek astronomer Ptolemy. Arabians and Persians sailed across the Arabian Sea and Indian Ocean to trade with merchants in East African market towns. They saw and reported the icy heights of the mountain. They may have used it as a landmark, just as African traders did who called Kilimanjaro "mountain of caravans." Africa's highest mountain and the highest freestanding mountain in the world remained relatively unknown to modern Europeans until 1848. The local Chagga people called it "Kilema Kyaro," meaning "that which cannot be conquered" or "that which makes a journey impossible."

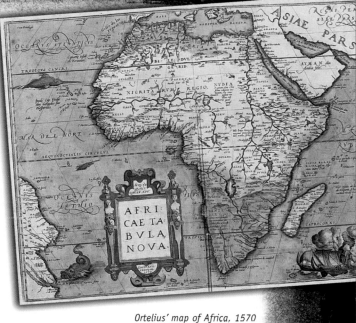

Ortelius' map of Africa, 1570

Today, Kilimanjaro attracts tourists who want to climb to the crater's edge (left). Climbers can stand at the edge of the ice field and see the volcanic center of the main peak called Kibo. Most tourists trek up the eastern slopes. Native climbers often ascend Arrow Glacier by a rocky wall. This approach is not recommended for tourists.

Carabiners used by mountain climbers

A Diversity of People and Lands 27

Discussion Questions

1 From reading this legend, how important do you think nature and land are to the people who wrote it? How does this view compare to the Native Americans' view of the land?

 Eyewitness Activity

Mount Kilimanjaro

OBJECTIVES: 2.01, 13.03

• Have students create an acrostic that emphasizes facts about Mount Kilimanjaro. Students will write a sentence for each letter in the word Kilimanjaro using the first letter as the starter for the sentence.

• Based on the information in the feature, have students create a Web site, digital story, PowerPoint Presentation, or brochure illustrating facts about Mount Kilimanjaro.

• Have students plan an itinerary for a trip to Mount Kilimanjaro. For this activity, additional research from the Internet or travel agencies will be needed. To plan an effective itinerary for the trip, students should include what they will need, where they will go, when and for how long they will go, and the cost.

Extension Assign novice ELL students to do the acrostic on a poster with illustrations. Intermediate ELL students should do the acrostic and brochure only. Use an ELL-friendly Web site for research.

Activity

Continental Drift Theory

OBJECTIVES: 3.04

Have students research the continental drift theory. Make sure students understand they will need information about plate tectonics, Pangaea, Laurasia, Gondwanaland, and Dr. Alfred Wegener.

Have students write or word-process a letter to Dr. Wegener discussing his scientific theory of continental drift. Their letter should show agreement or disagreement with his ideas. Clearly, students should make a decisive statement and elaborate on it. Elements of the letter should include an introduction of the topic, support for the agreement or disagreement, and the subjects of plate tectonics, Pangaea, Laurasia, and Gondwanaland.

As a differentiation, students may write a persuasive letter trying to convince Dr. Wegener of a different theory.

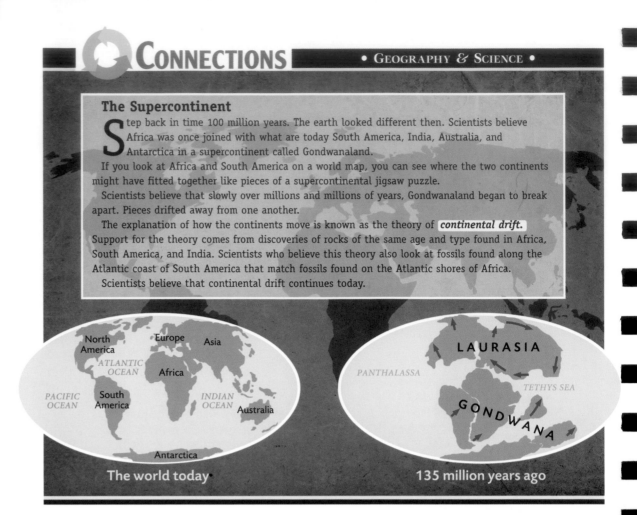

CONNECTIONS • GEOGRAPHY & SCIENCE •

The Supercontinent

Step back in time 100 million years. The earth looked different then. Scientists believe Africa was once joined with what are today South America, India, Australia, and Antarctica in a supercontinent called Gondwanaland.

If you look at Africa and South America on a world map, you can see where the two continents might have fitted together like pieces of a supercontinental jigsaw puzzle.

Scientists believe that slowly over millions and millions of years, Gondwanaland began to break apart. Pieces drifted away from one another.

The explanation of how the continents move is known as the theory of *continental drift.* Support for the theory comes from discoveries of rocks of the same age and type found in Africa, South America, and India. Scientists who believe this theory also look at fossils found along the Atlantic coast of South America that match fossils found on the Atlantic shores of Africa.

Scientists believe that continental drift continues today.

The world today • 135 million years ago

LESSON 2 REVIEW

Fact Follow-Up
1. Describe the relative location and size of Africa.
2. Describe the coastline of Africa.
3. What is the Great Rift Valley?
4. Name the important rivers and mountains in Africa. Give their relative locations.
5. Why are most African rivers not useful for long-distance travel?

Talk About It
1. How is the coastline of Africa different from European coastlines?
2. Is the description of Africa as "the plateau continent" appropriate? Explain.
3. How have Africa's escarpments influenced life there?
4. Why is Mount Kilimanjaro referred to as "great"?

LESSON 2 REVIEW

Fact Follow-Up Answers
1. Africa is bordered by the Atlantic Ocean to the west, the Indian Ocean to the east, the Mediterranean Sea to the north, and the Red Sea to the northeast. It is the second largest continent in the world.
2. The coastline has a narrow coastal plain falling from escarpments. The coastline is even, with no seas or peninsulas and there are few inlets or bays to form good harbors.
3. The Great Rift Valley in eastern Africa stretches more than 6,000 miles from the Red Sea in the north into southern Africa and is more than a mile deep in places. It is such a prominent earth feature that it can be seen from space.
4. The Nile River flows from near the center of the continent north-ward into the Mediterranean Sea. The Congo winds through Central Africa, crossing the Equator twice, emptying into the Atlantic Ocean. The Zambezi and Limpopo Rivers in East Africa and the Orange River in South Africa are other major rivers. In East Africa there are mountains including Mount Kilimanjaro, the continent's tallest peak, and the eastern highlands. Other major ranges include the Atlas Mountains in the Northwest and the Drakensberg Mountains in the Southeast.
5. Waterfalls and rapids cascading over escarpments from the coastal plains as well as rivers becoming too shallow for navigation during the dry season make most African rivers unsuitable for long-distance travel.

LESSON ③ Climate and Vegetation

Many people think of deserts or jungles when they imagine Africa. Much of Africa is neither. Vast grasslands and savanna cover much of the continent. Africa has a rich variety of climates that allows many types of vegetation to grow.

African Climates and Location

The Equator divides the continent almost in half (see map, page 35). The sun's rays hit the Equator most directly, giving places there the highest temperatures. Away from the Equator, going north or south, temperatures generally decrease.

Find the latitude lines on the map labeled "Tropic of Cancer" and "Tropic of Capricorn." Within these two lines equally distant from the Equator lies the climate zone known as the *Tropics*. Areas within the Tropics are generally hot year-round. Only the southern tip of Africa and the northern area near the Mediterranean Sea are outside the Tropics.

Tropical climates are dry and hot or wet and hot, except where the elevations of mountains or highlands affect climate.

Africa's tropical climates range from extremely wet to extremely dry. In wet rain forest areas close to the Equator, heavy rains fall every day. In savanna climates north and south of the rain forests, rain is seasonal. A wet season of rainfall follows a dry season. Scarcely any rain falls in arid areas such as the Sahara Desert.

The climate is mildest in the areas farthest from the Equator. That is why the northern and southern ends of the continent have a Mediterranean, or a Marine West Coast climate. Although summers can be quite dry, winters often have much more rainfall than drier African climate zones.

KEY IDEAS

- Africa's climates are influenced by nearness to the Equator and by elevation.
- Africa's climates affect vegetation.
- Africa's vegetation zones are rain forest, savanna, desert, and grasslands.
- Uncertain rainfall creates harsh conditions in many parts of Africa.

KEY TERMS

drought
leaching
Sahel
savannas
Tropics

Kenya has a hot and dry climate, except during the rainy season. **In what overall climate zone is Kenya and most of Africa?**

A Diversity of People and Lands

29

OBJECTIVES: 2.02, 3.02, 5.03

Discussion Questions

1 What kind of clothes would you need in the Tropics in the winter? in the summer?

2 How would you compare our climate to that of Africa?

3 Where is North Carolina relative to the Equator? How does this affect our climate? What other factors affect the climate in our community?

4 How does the geography in the picture differ from the region where we live?

 **Caption Answer**

In the climate zone known as the Tropics

Activity

The Baobab Tree

OBJECTIVES: 3.01

The baobab tree is a succulent plant with spiny limbs that stores water. Water-storing plants are important to Africa. Because of the lack of moisture and poor soil, vegetation is sparse. The baobab tree is shaped like a bottle. The trunk is filled with moist pulp and can be as big as 30 feet in diameter. There are no leaves on the baobab trees during dry season. It has large flowers, pollinated by bats, and oblong-shaped fruit. The fruit, bark, and leaves can be eaten.

Design a garden for inside the classroom or somewhere on the campus (plant one if possible). Include beans, carrots, corn, pumpkins, sunflowers, tomatoes, or other vegetables appropriate to our climate. Have students sketch their ideas for the garden. Research plants found in continental America that require very little rainfall for survival. Compare their physical form to those that need more rainfall to grow. List results; have groups discuss findings. Students may keep garden journals about plant growth, failure, and harvest.

Design an African garden or landscape. Students should research the types of plants that could be grown in it and detail the type of environment that would support it.

Extension ELL students should use an ELL-friendly Web site for research and make a collage or poster to show their findings.

Talk About It Answers

1. Africa's coastline is very even with few inlets or bays to allow for good harbors. No seas like the Mediterranean and Black Seas in Europe stretch into the interior of the continent.

2. Important points: Students should take a position and support it with reasons. Note: Most of the continent is plateau, dropping abruptly to the sea over escarpments.

3. Escarpments have prevented or hindered river trade, making transportation inland from the oceans difficult. They have also served to discourage invaders.

4. It is great because of its height, because it is a snowcapped mountain located only 200 miles from the Equator, because it has been used as a landmark since ancient times, and because of the legends that surround it.

Caption Answer

Grass with few trees and bushes

Activity

How to Make a Climograph in Microsoft Excel

 OBJECTIVES: 2.02

Climographs are used to compare the temperature and precipitation of a nation or area over time.

Open Excel and make a new spreadsheet. Highlight cells B1 to M1 and move your cursor to Format. Pull down to Column and over to Width. Change the width to 6 in order to be able to see all the columns at once.

Click in cell B1 and type "Jan." Move your cursor to the edge of the cell and drag it to cell M1. The months of the year will fill themselves in. Click on cell A2 and type the word "precipitation," then click on cell A3 and type the word "temperature." Using your source, fill in the precipitation and temperature for each month of the year.

Highlight cells A1 through M3. Click on the chart icon on the ruler bar. In the Chart Type dialogue box, choose Custom Chart. Pull down to Line/Column on 2 Axis. Click on Next but do not press finish. In the Chart Source Data dialogue box, make sure Rows is chosen to create this type of graph. Click on Next. In the Chart Options dialog box, fill in the title.

The title should be "Climograph for ____." For the category X axis type "Months of the Year." For the Y axis type "Precipitation in Inches." Skip the second category X. Type "Temperature in Fahrenheit" in the secondary value Y axis. Note: The sample chart changes as you type so you can check to see if you are making a mistake.

Click on the Gridlines section and choose to show the major gridlines for the Y axis. Click on the Legends section and decide where you want the legend to appear on your chart. If you want the actual numbers to appear on your climograph, click on the Data Labels (this may make your chart look messy). Click on the Data Tables if you want your data to appear on the same page. After making these decisions, click on Next.

Climates and Elevation

Elevation affects climate, especially in eastern and southern Africa. There the plateau tilts upward. As elevation increases, temperature decreases (see maps, pages 17 and 35).

Close to the Equator in East Africa, visitors see snowcapped mountain peaks. Snow never melts on those peaks, whose temperatures remain low year-round. Areas with high elevation in parts of southern Africa have a mild climate, even when their location is close to the Equator.

Vegetation

Climate has a direct impact on African vegetation. Both temperature and rainfall affect vegetation (see map, page 35).

Rain Forests

Along the Equator, both heat and rainfall are plentiful. Thick, lush tropical rain forests thrive here.

The rain forest is one of the most complex natural habitats in the world. A single tree can have as many as 50 kinds of plants growing on it. Ferns, vines, orchids, creepers, and air plants attached to a tree take nourishment from air, rain, and the tree.

High temperatures and constant rainfall create this rich variety of vegetation. The Equator's hot and wet climate is ideal for plant and animal life to thrive.

It might seem that rain forest soils would be fertile. Normally, decaying plants help renew the soil, making it more fertile. Yet constant and heavy rains in the rain forest cause the nutrients in the soil to dissolve and wash away. This process, called *leaching,* quickly wears out the soil.

At one time, tropical rain forests covered the wide band of land along the Equator. Today, such forests are being harvested across much of West Africa. Rain forests remain thick near the coast (see map, page 35).

Central Africa along the Equator still has large areas of rain forest. Farming, logging, mining, and road building might one day be threats to these areas as well. Rain forests are seen as places where farms may be located, especially where food is scarce and the population is growing. Timber from the rain forest brings high prices on the world market.

The Mount Kenya rain forest is lush in contrast to a savanna. **What grows on the savanna?**

30

Chapter 2

In the Chart Location dialogue box decide if you would like to have your chart appear on a new page or on top of your spreadsheet. Click on Finish and look at your chart.

On the menu bar under View, pull down to Tool Bars. Click beside Chart. This toolbar will appear on the screen. Choose Value Axis on the chart toolbar. Click next to the words, choosing the icon that looks like a hand pointing to a chart. In the Format Axis dialog box, choose the Scale box. For maximum type "12" and for major unit type "2". For minor unit type "1". Press Okay. Choose Secondary Value Axis on the chart toolbar. Click on the icon again. In the Format Axis dialog box, choose the Scale Box. For minimum, type "-30" and for maximum type "90"—for major unit type "10" and for minor unit type "5"—then press Okay.

If you hold the chooser down for a moment the name of the area will appear. Go to the chart toolbar to change something about that area. For example, click on the background of your chart and hold for a moment. The words Plot Area will appear. Choose Plot Area from the chart toolbar and click on the hand icon. In the Format Plot Area dialogue box, choose Custom Color and pick a color for your background. Use this method to change other aspects of your chart.

Savanna

Away from the Equator, the rain becomes less constant. *Savannas,* large open areas of grass with few trees and bushes, appear. Savanna, or grasslands, make up the largest vegetation zone south of the Sahara. Rain falls only in summer in the savanna.

Although the savanna contains few trees, they are dramatic sights. Tall baobab trees stretch to the sky with their spindly branches. They can be seen from a distance because they are the only trees growing on the savanna.

Desert

Beyond the savanna to the north or south of the Equator, little rain falls. The trees start to disappear and grasses become shorter until, finally, they blend into the desert.

North of the Equator, the desert is huge. The Sahara is the world's largest desert, a bone-dry expanse of rock, gravel, and sand. Average rainfall of 8 inches (20 centimeters) a year can be less or none at all. The Sahara stretches more than 3,100 miles (4,991 km) across the continent from the Atlantic Ocean to the Red Sea. Its elevation ranges from 100 feet (30 m) below sea level to more than 11,000 feet (3,300 m) above. It occupies an area equal in size to the continental United States, and covers one quarter of the continent.

Two deserts lie south of the Equator. The Namib (nahm·ib) and Kalahari (kal·ah·HAR·ih) are smaller than the Sahara. Both are just as hot and dry.

African deserts are not all flat or colorless. Rugged mountain ranges rise above rocky wastes, or shifting dunes are spotted with tough shrubs. Sometimes the desert can be a surprising rainbow of orange, yellow, and pink dunes.

Dry Grasslands

South of the Sahara is semi-arid land of dry grasslands called the *Sahel.* A band 200 to 700 miles (322 to 1,127 km) wide, the Sahel stretches across the continent between the desert and the savanna (see map, pages 127). With more rainfall than

the desert, the Sahel still receives only 4 to 24 inches (10 to 61 cm) a year. In some years it may not rain at all. The Sahel's high temperatures mean that even when it does rain, up to 90 percent of the moisture quickly evaporates.

The savanna in Tanzania is mostly grassland, except where tall baobab or other trees grow. **What effect do rainfall amounts have on vegetation?**

Temperate Grasslands

On the northern and southern coasts, small areas have adequate rainfall and temperatures that encourage farming. These areas produce crops that cannot grow anywhere else on the continent.

Farmers in Algeria, Morocco, and Tunisia harvest crops of citrus fruit, grapes, and olives. In southern Africa, farmers are able to raise wheat, barley, and other grains.

What would YOU do?

In some parts of Africa, water is scarce. Hosts greet guests in their homes with an offering of water to drink. This welcome often poses a difficult problem for visitors. Hosts may be offended if the water is refused. But the water may not have been purified or treated. It could be unsafe to drink. How would you respond politely to the offer of water?

A Diversity of People and Lands

31

Discussion Questions

1 How does elevation affect climate?

2 Contrast the rain forests, savannas, and deserts.

3 How important do you think the tropical rain forests are? What can be done to protect them?

4 Is harvesting a threat to the vegetation found in Africa? How?

5 Compare our vegetation to the vegetation found in the rain forests of Africa.

6 How does what is happening in the rain forests compare to what is happening to the forests in North Carolina? What are the reasons for cutting the timber? How would North Carolina be affected if the production of logging and mining industries were limited?

7 Which of the regions mentioned do you think has the highest population density? Why?

 Caption Answer

Large amounts of rainfall mean more vegetation.

 Math Activity

Rain Forest Word Problem

OBJECTIVES: 5.02, 5.03, 6.01

The rain forest is a source of many rare trees. The trees provide lumber that is an important source of income for the local tribesman. If a tree containing 37½ board feet of lumber is sold for $2.50 per board foot, how much would the tribesman receive?

Answer $93.75

Extension Assist ELL students by setting up the problem for them.

 Background Information

Sunshine and Stormy Weather

Rainfall is a key factor in Africa's climate. In much of Africa rain comes in intense but short bursts during the wet seasons. Often it beats down as thunderstorms. Such storms occur an average of 242 days a year in Kampala, Uganda. Some areas are exceptions to this rainfall pattern. In south central Africa, summer rain usually comes in bursts that last several days with inter-vening clear spells. Occasionally tropical cyclones bring intense rainfall to southeast Africa, but in general Africa has relatively few rain days each year. Because of the high incidence of thunderstorms over much of the continent, British Geographer Ieuan Griffiths has labeled Africa the "continent of sunshine and storm."

31

Discussion Questions

1 What kinds of adaptations would people have to make living in areas of uncertain rainfall?

2 What crops are grown in our area? How would this change if we had a change in climate?

3 How do you think Cairo has managed to survive if it only receives one inch of rain per year?

4 How do our lives change when there is a drought?

Caption Answer

It evaporates in the hot temperatures. The heat causes this to happen.

Research Activity

Africa and the Atlantic

OBJECTIVES: 2.02, 2.03

Have students explore the ways in which the climate of Africa contributes to world weather systems, specifically the formation of hurricanes in the Atlantic Ocean. Students should examine evidence that atmospheric properties can be studied to predict weather hazards. Students should use the Internet for research and identify the key terms to use to search for appropriate data. What is the relationship between rain in the Sahel and storm systems in the Atlantic?

The dry grasslands of Niger are part of the Sahel, which receives less rain than the savanna but more than the desert. **What happens to the small amount of rain that does fall? Why?**

Uncertain Rainfall

Botswana (baht·SWAN·ah) in southern Africa is a country partially covered by the Kalahari Desert. Water's importance is reflected in the Botswanians' language. In Botswana, people greet each other with a single word: pula. Botswana's money and its national motto are also pula, the word for rain. This word's use shows how important water becomes in dry lands.

Taken as a whole, the African continent receives generous rain. However, this rain is unevenly distributed. Many large areas have too little precipitation. On average, about 1 inch (2.5 cm) of rain falls a year in Cairo, Egypt, a city built in the desert. Nairobi (nigh·ROH·bih), Kenya, in the eastern highlands, averages almost 38 inches (97 cm) of rain a year.

Some land in Africa receives less than 20 inches (51 cm) of rain a year. Irrigation

LESSON **3** REVIEW

Fact Follow-Up Answers

1. Only the southern tip of the continent and the northern area near the Mediterranean Sea lie outside the Tropics. In Africa, there are wet, savanna, and desert tropical climates. North Africa and Southern Africa have Mediterranean or Marine West Coast climates.

2. High temperatures and constant rainfall create a rich variety of vegetation. A single tree can have as many as 50 kinds of plants growing on it, including ferns, vines, orchids, creepers, and air plants.

3. A savanna is a large, open area of grassland with few trees such as the baobab and low bushes. In

Africa, savannas are located south of the Sahel in a broad band that crosses the continent.

4. The giant Sahara is located north of the Equator. The Namib lies south of the Equator along the Atlantic coastline, and the Kalahari is inland in Southern Africa.

5. The Sahel stretches between the Sahara Desert to the north and the savanna to the south. It is a semiarid area of dry grasslands with more rainfall than the desert and less than the savanna. The high temperatures of the Sahel dry up about 90 percent of the moisture from rainfall almost immediately.

is necessary to raise crops because the limited rainfall does not wet the soil enough for seeds to grow to maturity. The soil has no extra moisture to support the young plants. Plants quickly wilt and die without this base of water.

Drought, a period of time when there is very little rain or no rain at all, is a constant threat in many countries. Periods of little rainfall can last for years, sometimes spanning a decade. Even where rainfall is high enough to support farm crops, farmers face uncertainty. This

uncertainty is the most distinctive feature of the rainfall pattern in most African nations. Farmers cannot always be sure when the rains will come or if they will last. Only tropical rain forest areas can count on constant rainfall.

Even when rain does come as expected, it can hurt as well as help the farmer. Rain often falls in short, hard-hitting bursts or thunderstorms. These downpours can do great damage. They flatten crops, cause the soil to erode, and flood roads.

Very little rain falls in the Egyptian desert, so crops cannot grow there without irrigation. **What effect does uneven distribution of rain have on Africa?**

LESSON 3 REVIEW

Fact Follow-Up
1. What climate zones are found in Africa?
2. Describe the vegetation in a rain forest.
3. What is a savanna? Where in Africa are savannas located?
4. What deserts are located in Africa?
5. What is the Sahel? Describe its climate.

Talk About It
1. How does elevation affect climate in Africa?
2. How is rainfall both a benefit and a burden to Africa?
3. Why is water Africa's most precious resource?
4. Would you prefer to visit an African rain forest or a desert? Explain your choice.

A Diversity of People and Lands

33

Talk About It Answers
1. As altitude or elevation increases, temperature decreases. Mountain peaks such as Mount Kilimanjaro near the Equator have snowcapped peaks all year. Areas with high elevation in Southern Africa have a mild climate, despite their location close to the Equator.
2. Africa, as a continent, receives adequate rainfall. However, rain falls unevenly, providing a contrast between the almost-constant rainfall of the tropical rain forest and the bone-dry deserts. Areas of Africa experience long

droughts, and when rain does fall in these areas floods and soil erosion result.
3. Rainfall in Africa is uncertain, except in the rain forests, so water for drinking and irrigation is precious. All life on earth depends on water. Since much of Africa has too little of it, water is the essential and most precious resource.
4. Important points: Students should choose one and support that choice with accurate details.

Caption Answer

Africa's uneven settlement and uneven production of food comes from uneven distribution of rain.

Activity

African Dodecahedron

 OBJECTIVES: 1.01, 1.03, 2.01

Materials strips of paper with all African countries' names—one on each strip; container (bag) for drawing countries' names; 12 handout dodecahedron patterns per student; colored pencils, markers, and crayons; scissors, glue/glue sticks, and rulers; textbook and other research materials; and optional string

Preparation Assign each student a different African nation. Copy the dodecahedron pattern reducing as desired (pattern makes a shape about the size of a soccer ball).

Students will illustrate in words, drawings, and graphs 12 aspects of their African country on the faces of the dodecahedron (inside the dashed lines). One face must contain the country's name. Aspects to consider: outline map of the country, flag, population, ethnic groups, major land and water features, important statistics (Human Development Index, GDP per capita, literacy rates, life expectancies, infant mortality, age distribution, urban population, or arable land), major languages, chief religions, capital/major cities, government characteristics, imports/exports, main crops, livestock, or industries, mineral resources, monetary unit, trading partners, health characteristics, important landmarks, famous people, membership in international organizations, and country's Web site.

Form dodecahedron by gluing five outer edges to other faces' edge—(edges can be glued outward or inward depending on student's preference). String can be attached inside one edge for hanging. Students will present final products as an introduction to their study of Africa.

Extension ELL students may need to work with partner to complete. Do not assign the presentation.

Map Activity

Africa—Climate

NATIONAL GEOGRAPHY STANDARDS: 1, 3, 4, 8
GEOGRAPHIC THEMES: Location, Place, Region
OBJECTIVES: 2.02

Before this map is used, an introduction/review of how world climates correlate with latitude should be offered to the students (use the Geography Review in the Appendix). Using the world climate map in the atlas, give four major climates with ten specific climate types and each season's yearly precipitation. From this chapter's reading it is necessary to note which African climates fit within the world climate type-seasons:

Africa	World
Tropical Rain Forest	Tropical Wet
Tropical Savanna	Tropical Wet and Dry
Mediterranean	Mediterranean
Humid Subtropical	Humid Subtropical
Marine West Coast	Marine West Coast
Steppe	Semiarid
Desert	Arid
Undifferentiated Highlands	Highland

Discuss with students that climatologists and cartographers often use various terms for climates that are synonymous.

Have students answer the following questions:

1. Which is the largest of the eight climates found in Africa? *Desert*
2. From the reading on the next page, what is the unique name given to the steppe climate located north of the Equator in Africa? *Sahel*
3. Africa's rain forests are located in which hemispheres? *Northern and Southern, Western and Eastern*
4. What can be misunderstood about the location of Africa's Mediterranean climate areas? *Not all are literally located along the Mediterranean Sea; one area is in the southern region around the Cape of Good Hope and Cape Town.*
5. Which hemisphere(s) contains Africa's humid subtropical climate? *Southern and Eastern*
6. Tropical climates usually extend from 0° to 23.5° north and south of the Equator. Is this accurate for Africa's savanna climate? *no*
7. In which hemisphere(s) are Africa's highlands located? *Northern, Southern, Eastern*
8. What climate(s) is found on the island of Madagascar? *Tropical Rain Forest, Tropical Savanna, Steppe*
9. Define undifferentiated. *Things that cannot be distinguished as being dissimilar or distinct.* Why are Africa's highland climates described this way? *Elevation (or altitude above sea level) and temperature determine the highland climate's characteristics more than latitude and precipitation.*

Extension Intermediate ELL students can answer questions.

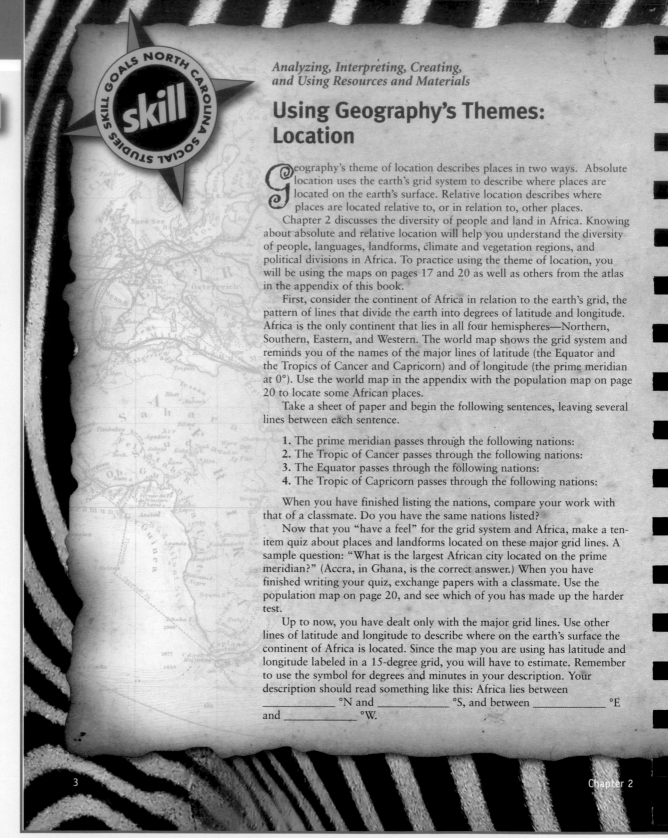

GOALS NORTH CAROLINA SOCIAL STUDIES SKILL

skill

Analyzing, Interpreting, Creating, and Using Resources and Materials

Using Geography's Themes: Location

Geography's theme of location describes places in two ways. Absolute location uses the earth's grid system to describe where places are located on the earth's surface. Relative location describes where places are located relative to, or in relation to, other places.

Chapter 2 discusses the diversity of people and land in Africa. Knowing about absolute and relative location will help you understand the diversity of people, languages, landforms, climate and vegetation regions, and political divisions in Africa. To practice using the theme of location, you will be using the maps on pages 17 and 20 as well as others from the atlas in the appendix of this book.

First, consider the continent of Africa in relation to the earth's grid, the pattern of lines that divide the earth into degrees of latitude and longitude. Africa is the only continent that lies in all four hemispheres—Northern, Southern, Eastern, and Western. The world map shows the grid system and reminds you of the names of the major lines of latitude (the Equator and the Tropics of Cancer and Capricorn) and of longitude (the prime meridian at 0°). Use the world map in the appendix with the population map on page 20 to locate some African places.

Take a sheet of paper and begin the following sentences, leaving several lines between each sentence.

1. The prime meridian passes through the following nations:
2. The Tropic of Cancer passes through the following nations:
3. The Equator passes through the following nations:
4. The Tropic of Capricorn passes through the following nations:

When you have finished listing the nations, compare your work with that of a classmate. Do you have the same nations listed?

Now that you "have a feel" for the grid system and Africa, make a ten-item quiz about places and landforms located on these major grid lines. A sample question: "What is the largest African city located on the prime meridian?" (Accra, in Ghana, is the correct answer.) When you have finished writing your quiz, exchange papers with a classmate. Use the population map on page 20, and see which of you has made up the harder test.

Up to now, you have dealt only with the major grid lines. Use other lines of latitude and longitude to describe where on the earth's surface the continent of Africa is located. Since the map you are using has latitude and longitude labeled in a 15-degree grid, you will have to estimate. Remember to use the symbol for degrees and minutes in your description. Your description should read something like this: Africa lies between _____°N and _____°S, and between _____°E and _____°W.

3

Chapter 2

Do you now feel comfortable using the grid system to describe the absolute location of places in Africa? Now, you will use a part of the population map found on page 20—the grid system and some political markings such as city names and national boundaries.

When you described Africa as lying between _____ °N and _____ °S, you were describing Africa's absolute location. A description of the continent's absolute and relative location might be written something like this: "Africa is surrounded by major bodies of water—the Mediterranean Sea on its northern edge; the Atlantic Ocean on the west and Indian Ocean on the east." Or you might write, "The Sahel stretches across Africa from the Atlantic Ocean to the Red Sea in a band that forms the southern border of the Sahara Desert." Generally, relative location describes where a place is in relation to other places. Words like "lies between," "north of," and "along the Congo River," are words that describe relative location.

Look now at the physical map on page 17. Find the Equator where it crosses Lake Victoria. What other landforms of Africa are crossed by the Equator? What landforms are crossed by the Tropic of Cancer? the Tropic of Capricorn? The answers to these questions describe the relative location of those landforms.

The lake's location may be described in other ways. Are there mountains or rivers near Lake Victoria? In what general area of Africa does it lie? Use the map to describe the relative location of Lake Victoria in as many ways as you can. Compare your list with a classmate's.

Use the natural vegetation map, left, with the other maps in the chapter to describe the landforms and vegetation of nations in Africa. Make another short quiz. Try to stump a partner with such questions as "What are the major landforms and vegetation of the Democratic Republic of the Congo? of Libya? of Madagascar?"

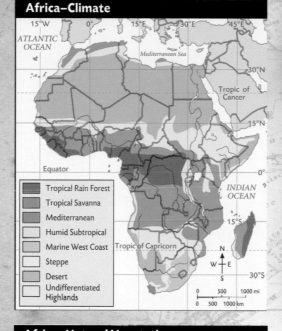

Africa–Climate

- Tropical Rain Forest
- Tropical Savanna
- Mediterranean
- Humid Subtropical
- Marine West Coast
- Steppe
- Desert
- Undifferentiated Highlands

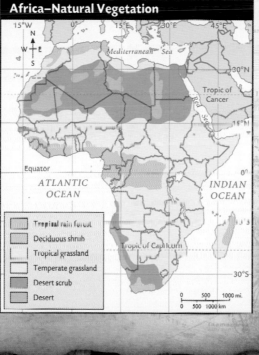

Africa–Natural Vegetation

- Tropical rain forest
- Deciduous shrub
- Tropical grassland
- Temperate grassland
- Desert scrub
- Desert

Teaching This Skill Lesson

Materials Needed textbooks, a variety of maps of Africa (from atlases, encyclopedias, or other resources), paper, pencils

Classroom Organization Students may work individually and/or in pairs.

Beginning the Lesson Review the theme of location, making certain students understand the difference between relative and absolute. Tell students they will be using their textbook maps of Africa and other maps to practice using the theme of location.

Lesson Development Monitor students as they construct ten-item quizzes on absolute location. If students are working individually and having problems, pairing students may be a solution. Allow students to exchange papers and complete quizzes made by other students. Next, have students construct quizzes on relative location. Remind students they will be using different kinds of maps: population density, physical, and so forth. Tell them that absolute location can be determined only with maps that use the grid system but that a variety of maps can be used to work with relative location.

Conclusion Ask students which location—relative or absolute—was easier, more difficult to use. Why is it important to be able to use both absolute and relative location?

Extension For intermediate ELL students, model and provide additional explanations.

Skill Lesson Review

1. How many African nations are located on coastlines? *Thirty. Three others are islands.*
2. How many capital cities are located on coastlines? *Twenty-two. Ten more are on lakes or rivers.*
3. What are the relative and absolute locations of the following places?
   a. Addis Ababa, Ethiopia–*south of Eritrea, west of Somalia, east of Sudan, and north of Kenya; 9°N, 38°E.*
   b. Kalahari Desert–*south Africa; between 22° and 25°S latitude, between 15° and 25°E.*
   c. Nile River–*northeast Africa.; between 32°N and the Equator, between 30° and 32°E.*
   d. Luanda, Angola–*southwest Africa, on the Atlantic coast; 8°S, 12°E.*
   e. Bamako, Mali–*on the Niger River, northeast of Guinea, south of Mauritania, west of Burkina Faso; 13°N, 8°W.*
4. Which of the places above was easiest to describe relatively? absolutely? *The Nile is easiest to describe relatively. The easiest to describe absolutely were the cities.*
5. When do you think it is more useful to use absolute location? relative location? Why? *Absolute location is useful in identifying a city or other precise location. Relative location works better for large, sprawling landforms.*

35

Talk About It

1. Important points: Students should make a choice and support that choice with facts. Note: There are more than 1,000 spoken languages in Africa. The landforms include plateaus, escarpments, highlands and mountains, plains, an even coastline, and the Great Rift Valley.

2. Important points: Students should take a position and support it with reasons. Note: Rapid population growth makes economic progress difficult, but families, especially rural families, believe that having many children is important.

3. River transportation from interior of the continent to its coastlines has been affected by cataracts and by the steep escarpment that drops from the plateau to the narrow coastal plain. Ocean transportation has been affected by the even coastline with its lack of bays and good harbors. Settlement patterns have been less affected by the landform than by the availability of arable land, water, and other resources.

4. With abundant water, population would probably be more widely dispersed. A predictable water supply would enable farmers to produce larger crop yields, ensuring an agricultural surplus that could be sold. It is possible that increased industrialization and a more diversified economy would result.

5. Important points: Students should choose one vegetation zone and explain the choice. Note: Vegetation zones are rain forest, savanna, desert, dry grasslands, and temperate grasslands.

6. Important points: Students should choose and explain logical differences including the following: ease of transportation between coastlines and interior areas; improved movement of people and goods; possibly more navigable rivers would have encouraged earlier European exploration and imperialism.

CHAPTER 2 REVIEW

Lessons Learned

LESSON 1
Africa's Diverse Population

Africa's population is growing rapidly. It is unevenly distributed, creating high densities in southern Nigeria, the cities of North Africa, and the fertile lands of East Africa. Most people live in rural areas, but cities are gaining population quickly. Africa is a place of diversity. Its people belong to more than 2,000 ethnic groups and speak more than 1,000 languages.

LESSON 2
Location and Landforms

Africa is dominated by a large plateau. A narrow coastal plain, uninterrupted by bays or gulfs, does not provide any natural harbors. The Great Rift Valley, the Eastern Highlands, and two mountain ranges are other major landforms. Rapids and waterfalls make travel difficult on such major rivers as the Nile, Zaire, Niger, and Zambezi.

LESSON 3
Climate and Vegetation

Climates in Africa are mainly determined by nearness to the Equator. Places closest to the Equator have tropical climates. The northern and southern ends of Africa experience Mediterranean climates. Desert climates cover parts of Africa. Climate creates different zones of vegetation: rain forests, savanna, dry grasslands (the Sahel), desert, and bands of temperate grasslands. Rain is not spread evenly across the continent.

36

Talk About It

1. Which is more diverse—Africa's landforms or its languages? Explain your answer.
2. Should African governments try to control population growth? Explain your answer.
3. How has Africa's being a "plateau continent" affected transportation and settlement patterns?
4. If there were abundant water in Africa, how would life there change? Explain.
5. If you were able to visit one of Africa's vegetation zones, which would you choose to visit? Explain why.
6. How would life in Africa be different if the continent had more navigable rivers? Explain.

Mastering Mapwork

Use the map on page 17 to answer these questions.
1. Locate 30°E longitude. What major rivers are crossed by this line of longitude?
2. Describe the absolute and relative locations of the Atlas Mountains.
3. What desert is located nearest the southwest coast of the African continent? Describe its absolute location.
4. What lake is located nearest to 15°N latitude and 15°E longitude? What is the relative location of this lake?
5. Locate the Sahara Desert.

Chapter 2

Mastering Mapwork

1. Ubangi, Zambezi, Limpopo, and Orange
2. The mountains lie between 15°W and 15°E latitude and just north of 30°N longitude. The Atlas lie in extreme northwestern Africa and are bounded by the Sahara Desert to the south, the Atlantic Ocean to the west and northwest, and the Mediterranean Sea to the north.

3. The Namib Desert lies between latitudes 15°S and 30°S and along 15°E longitude.
4. Lake Chad is located where the national boundaries of Nigeria, Niger, Chad, and Cameroon converge.
5. The Sahara stretches from the Atlantic Ocean to the Red Sea across the entire African continent. It is located roughly between 15°N and 30°N.

Go to the Source

Comparing Poetry and Maps

Jonathan Swift poked fun at maps of Africa in his poem, below. The map below, "A new and exact Map of Africa and the Islands thereunto belonging" by W. Hollar (1666), is an example of the type of map Swift found to be sub-standard.

Read the poem and study the map. Answer the questions using specific references to the documents.

> *So Geographers, in Afric-maps*
> *With Savage-Pictures fill their Gaps;*
> *And o'er unhabitable Downs,*
> *Place Elephants for want of Towns.*

> *—Jonathan Swift, from* Poetry, a Rhapsody, *1733*

Questions

1. What does "with savage pictures fill their gaps" mean? What evidence of this do you see on the map?
2. In the eighteenth century, what might have been the impact or effect on European opinion of Africa after looking at the map (below) or the map described in the 1733 poem?

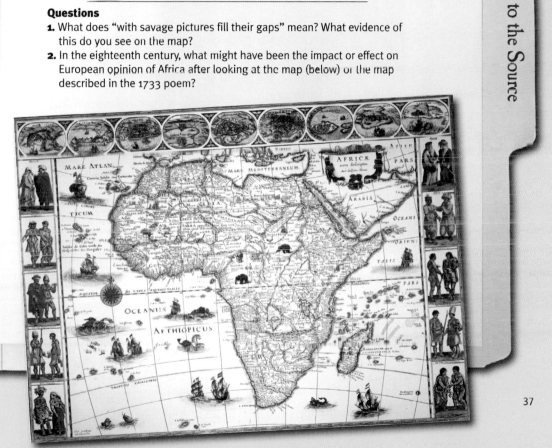

37

How to Use the Chapter Review

There are three sections in the Chapter Review: Talk About It, Mastering Mapwork, and Go to the Source. Use the Vocabulary Worksheets and the Chapter Review Worksheet in the Teacher's Resource Guide for additional reinforcement and preparation for the Chapter Assessments. The chapter and lesson reviews and the Chapter Review Worksheets are the basis of the assessment for each chapter.

Talk About It questions encourage students to speculate about the content of the chapter and are suitable for class or small-group discussion. They are not intended to be assigned for homework.

Mastering Mapwork has students apply one or more of the Five Themes of Geography to maps within the chapter.

Go to the Source activities allow students to analyze a primary source that relates to the content of the chapter. The questions and activities familiarize students with different types of primary sources and also build content-reading skills.

Go to the Source

OBJECTIVES: 7.01; Skills 3.05, 4.03

Plutarch wrote in *Life of Theseus*, "As geographers, Sosius, crowd into the edges of their maps parts of the world which they do not know about, adding notes in the margin to the effect that beyond this lies nothing but sandy deserts full of wild beasts, and unapproachable bogs." Swift echoes this sentiment about the ignorance of geographers in his poem. Swift plays up the ironic theme that the geographers of the sixteenth and early seventeenth centuries, in seeking to clarify a region through the creation of a map, end up making the place they are mapping more obscure and clouded through fanciful illustrations.

Vocabulary help: "for want of" means "the lack of;" "Downs" are rolling, treeless highlands with little soil.

Discuss with students the role of geographers and cartogrpahers today. What are our expectations of the maps and information we use? How do we know information, whether a map or even a textbook, is accurate? For more information on this topic, see "Creating Africa. A Brief Tour of European Cartography of Africa," by Jonathan T. Reynolds, Northern Kentucky University (visit **NCJourneys.com** for a link).

ANSWERS

1. They filled the places that were unknown or "empty" on their maps with pictures of wild animals or monsters. There are sea monsters, elephants, lions, and other animals drawn randomly on this map.

2. Important points: The reader should infer from the poem that geographers knew little of the actual human and physical geography of Africa. Therefore Europeans may have concluded that Africa was full of savage people and wild animals. This may have contributed to the European idea of Africa as a "dark" and unknown continent and later to European exploitation of Africa resources.

CHAPTER 3

Historical Foundations of Africa

Social Studies Strands

Historic Perspectives
Ancient kingdoms
Development
Forms of government
Economy
Contributions to society

North Carolina Standard Course of Study

Goal 4 The learner will identify significant patterns in the movement of people, goods, and ideas over time and place in Africa, Asia, and Australia.

Goal 8 The learner will assess the influence and contribution of individuals and cultural groups in Africa, Asia, and Australia.

Goal 11 The learner will recognize the common characteristics of different cultures in Africa, Asia, and Australia.

Goal 12 The learner will assess the influence of major religions, ethical beliefs, and values on cultures in Africa, Asia, and Australia.

Teaching & Assessment

• English Language Learner Modified Lesson Plans for this chapter are found in the Teacher Resource Guide.

• *ExamView® Assessment Suite* is provided at **NCJourneys.com**. It includes customizable assessments for all chapters. Paper tests are also available in the Teacher Resource Guide. See pages T16–T17 for information about how to use the assessments and the Scoring Guide.

Worksheets

Worksheets and answer keys are found both in the Teacher Resource Guide and at **NCJourneys.com**, including Reading Guides, Reading Strategies, Chapter Reviews, English Language Learner and others.

ACTIVITIES AND INTEGRATIONS

SOCIAL STUDIES

African Kingdom Class Presentations, p. 38B
Activator: *The Winged Cat,* p. 38
● African Culture Hearths, p. 39
Sailing the Nile, p. 44
Sailing The Nile Through Time, p. 45
★ Islamic Expansion, p. 51
★ Visit This City-State, p. 53
Skill Lesson: Using Geography's Themes: Human-Environmental Interaction, p. 56

READING/LANGUAGE ARTS	READING/LANGUAGE ARTS OBJECTIVES
▲ ■ Into the Afterlife, p. 38B	3.01, 3.03
Analogies, p. 38B	2.01
Writing Prompt: Great Personal Contribution, p. 38	1.01, 3.01, 3.03
■ Writing Activity: The Nile, p. 40	3.01
● Research Activity: Salt, p. 48	2.02
Go to the Source: Reading Ancient Writings, p. 59	2.01, 4.01, 4.02

MATHEMATICS	MATHEMATICS OBJECTIVES
● Obelisk, p. 38B	3.01
● Equilateral Triangle Math Word Problem, p. 42	2.01

TECHNOLOGY	TECHNOLOGY OBJECTIVES
■ Find Out About It, p. 43	1.20, 3.10, 3.11
★ Axum Trade Chart, p. 47	3.10, 3.11

VISUAL ARTS	VISUAL ARTS OBJECTIVES
● Obelisk, p. 38B	5.01, 5.02
■ Find Out About It, p. 43	1.01, 1.02, 1.05
★ Illustrated Map, p. 51	4.03, 5.01, 7.01

CHARACTER AND VALUES EDUCATION	TRAITS
What Would You Do?, p. 43	respect, good judgment
▲ ■ Leaving Home, p. 54	good citizenship, respect, perseverence

● Basic Activities ★ Challenging Activities ▲ English Language Learner Novice ■ English Language Learner Intermediate

 **Introductory Activity**

Into the Afterlife

OBJECTIVES: 12.01, 12.02

The pharaohs and members of the royal families were buried in pyramids and tombs filled with not only gold and precious jewels but also furniture, jars of wine, oil, and grain. Occasionally, a pet or servant would join the deceased to serve them in the afterlife.

What five items would students want to take into the afterlife and why? Remind them that they will have only a standard coffin, not a pyramid. After students have come up with their individual lists, create a class list and graph the top ten items.

Extension Novice ELL students may need to draw pictures of items instead of writing a list.

 **Culminating Activity**

African Kingdom Class Presentations

OBJECTIVES: 4.01, 7.01

Break the class into five groups. Assign to each one of the kingdoms of Kush, Axum, Mali, Ghana, and Songhai. Each group is to prepare a 15 minute presentation about the contributions of its kingdom. Groups should include visual aides in their presentation.

 Art Activity

Obelisk

OBJECTIVES: 12.1

The obelisk is a tapered monolithic pillar originating in ancient Egypt, and usually made of Aswan red granite. The Assyrians had a black obelisk designed with cuneiform on its sides. The four sides are often called faces (north face, south face, and so on). An obelisk has a wider square/rectangular base and a pyramidal top. Typically, the entrance of ancient Egyptian temples would be marked by a pair of obelisks. "Cleopatra's Needles" are two especially famous obelisks because they were presented as gifts in the nineteenth century to Britain (placed on the Thames in London) and the United States (in New York City's Central Park). Many Americans are also familiar with two other important obelisks—the Washington Monument and one commemorating the Battle of Bunker Hill. Students will design an obelisk with their name or life story told in hieroglyphics or cuneiform.

Materials obelisk pattern—copied and/or with tracing paper (see the Teacher's Resource Guide for pattern); paper, card stock, or sandpaper; scissors, colored pencils, paint, markers, and/or crayons; and glue stick

Duplicate obelisk pattern using copy machine or tracing paper. Using card stock is helpful but sandpaper adds an even better texture. Using colored pencils, paint, markers, or crayons, decorate the outside using hieroglyphics and/or cartouches that tell events in each student's life. Cut out the obelisk (including the dot where small arrows are shown). Turn obelisk over and fold along the score lines, beginning with the long lines. Turn the obelisk over to the front and spread glue over the long tab on the side of the obelisk. Turn the obelisk over again and fold the sides around to form the main body. Press the glued tab on the inside of the sides being joined together. Fold the top section of the obelisk, and place glue along the top's tabs. Glue these top tabs to the inside of the obelisk's top. Fold down and glue the tab at the base of the obelisk. Glue the base tab to the inside to form the bottom of the obelisk.

 **Analogies**

OBJECTIVES: 8.01, 4.02

Analogies are useful to help students make associations with prior knowledge. They can be used as an instructional strategy to help students better understand new materials. They are not intended to be definitions or test items.

Read the analogies aloud and ask students to identify the relationship between the terms. As an extension, ask students to write their own analogies using key terms or places discussed in the chapter.

Emperor : Rome :: Pharaoh : Egypt (ruled)

Pittsburgh : Ohio River :: Khartoum : Nile River (is at the confluence of)

Mansa Musa : Mali :: Sunni Ali : Songhai (ruled)

gold : West Africa :: salt : Sahara Desert (is found in)

sailboats : East African city-states :: camels : West African Kingdoms (were used to transport goods in)

Teaching Strategies

Pace yourself through Chapter 3 and be selective in your activities with ancient Egypt. Because of the fascination with Egypt there is a tendency to dwell on this subject, which sometimes causes other important concepts to be skimmed lightly.

If there is a high level of interest, assign some independent projects to students so that they may work on them as you complete your study of historical foundations. Use an activator or introductory activity to introduce the chapter to the students.

Activator

OBJECTIVES: 12.01, 12.02

"Hook" the attention of the students by reading a picture book or story.

The Winged Cat: A Tale of Ancient Egypt by Deborah Lattimore. Harper-Collins, 1992. ISBN 0060236353.

Summary This story helps students understand the ancient beliefs of the Egyptians. It also gives details that describe the Egyptian belief in the after-world.

OR

Instruct the students to read the chapter opener. Explain that we know a lot about the ancient Egyptian civilization because of the treasures found in the pyramids. Divide the class into teams or groups of three to four and have them brainstorm a list of items that they would put in a tomb to depict life in the twenty-first century. Compare their lists and compare their items with some of the items found in the pyramids.

Extension ELL students could do this with a group as directed.

Writing Prompt

OBJECTIVES: 8.01

Evaluative

Throughout history, there have been many outstanding people who are famous for their achievements. Which person do you think made the greatest contribution to the world? Select one and tell why you believe they are the most outstanding.

As you write your paper, remember to :

• name the person you believe was most outstanding.

• state at least three reasons and explain fully why you thing they made the greatest contributions.

• give examples to support your reasons and explain them fully.

• write in complete sentences and paragraph form.

• organize your ideas and include an introduction and a conclusion.

• use good grammar, spelling, punctuation, and capitalization.

38

CHAPTER 3

Historical Foundations of Africa

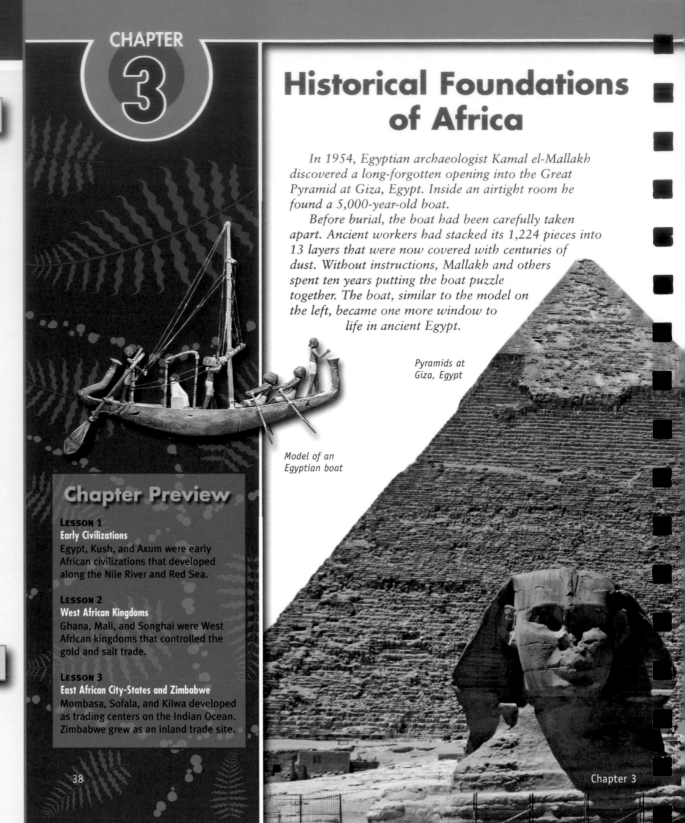

In 1954, Egyptian archaeologist Kamal el-Mallakh discovered a long-forgotten opening into the Great Pyramid at Giza, Egypt. Inside an airtight room he found a 5,000-year-old boat.

Before burial, the boat had been carefully taken apart. Ancient workers had stacked its 1,224 pieces into 13 layers that were now covered with centuries of dust. Without instructions, Mallakh and others spent ten years putting the boat puzzle together. The boat, similar to the model on the left, became one more window to life in ancient Egypt.

Pyramids at Giza, Egypt

Model of an Egyptian boat

Chapter Preview

LESSON 1
Early Civilizations
Egypt, Kush, and Axum were early African civilizations that developed along the Nile River and Red Sea.

LESSON 2
West African Kingdoms
Ghana, Mali, and Songhai were West African kingdoms that controlled the gold and salt trade.

LESSON 3
East African City-States and Zimbabwe
Mombasa, Sofala, and Kilwa developed as trading centers on the Indian Ocean. Zimbabwe grew as an inland trade site.

38

Chapter 3

Chapter Resources

Audiovisual
Pyramids, PBS Video, (800) 344-3337

Print Resources
African Civilization series; Franklin Watts, 1998:
• Bessire, Mark. *Great Zimbabwe*. ISBN 0531202852.
• Conrad, David. *The Songhay Empire*. ISBN 0531202844.
• Green, Rebecca. *The Empire of Ghana*. ISBN 0531202763.

• Haynes, Joyce. *Egyptian Dynasties*. ISBN 0531202801.
• Russmann, Edna. *Nubian Kingdoms*. ISBN 0531202836.
• Thompson, Carol. *The Empire of Mali*. ISBN 0531202771.
• Wilson, Thomas. *City States of the Swahili Coast*. ISBN 053120281X.
Benanav, Michael. *Men of Salt: Crossing the Sahara on the Caravan of White Gold*. Lyons Press, 2006. ISBN 101592287727.
Der Manuelian, Peter. *Hieroglyphs from A to*

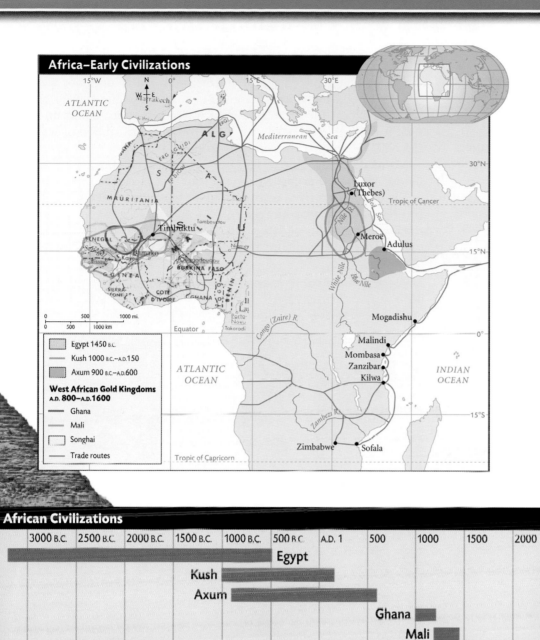

Africa–Early Civilizations

Egypt 1450 B.C.
Kush 1000 B.C.–A.D.150
Axum 900 B.C.–A.D.600

West African Gold Kingdoms
A.D. 800–A.D.1600
Ghana
Mali
Songhai
Trade routes

Map Activity

African Culture Hearths

NATIONAL GEOGRAPHY STANDARDS: 6, 10
GEOGRAPHIC THEMES: Place, Movement
OBJECTIVES: 4.01, 5.01

Define culture hearth (a specific place where a distinctive culture originated). Ask students why they think the word "hearth" is used in this term. Using the Africa—Early Civilizations map on page 39 and the African Civilizations time line, assign students to explain why Egypt is a major hearth in Africa, why Axum and Songhai are secondary hearths in Africa, and how ideas and materials flowed between these civilizations.

African Civilizations

	3000 B.C.	2500 B.C.	2000 B.C.	1500 B.C.	1000 B.C.	500 B.C.	A.D. 1	500	1000	1500	2000
Egypt											
Kush											
Axum											
Ghana											
Mali											
Songhai											
East African city-states											
Zimbabwe											

Historical Foundations of Africa

39

Z. Scholastic, 1996. ISBN 0590400088. McKissack, Patricia and Fredrick McKissack. *The Royal Kingdoms of Ghana, Mali and Songhay: Life in Medieval Africa.* Henry Holt, 1995. ISBN 0805042598.

Magazine Back issues

Cobblestone Publishing Company:
- *Alexandria Under the Ptolemies.* (*Calliope* magazine 2001–02).
- *Ancient Nubia.* ISBN 038240792X.

- *Egypt: Old and New.* ISBN 0382405560.
- *Egyptian Tomb Builders.* ISBN 0382445767.
- *Mansa Musa, King of Mali.* ISBN 0382444809.
- *Pharaohs of Egypt.* ISBN 0382406036.
- *Queens of Egypt.* ISBN 0382405897.
- *Science & Medicine in Ancient Egypt.* ISBN 032408934.
- *Tombs and Pyramids at Giza.* (*Calliope* magazine 2001–02).

Web Sites

Links to these at **NCJourneys.com.**
- The British Museum Student tours (inlcude treasures and mummies from ancient Sudan and Egypt)
- Egyptian Collection, Metropolitan Museum of Art
- Egyptian and Nubian Collections, Museum of Fine Arts
- Timbucktoo, Mali; History Channel Classroom
- Tutankhamun and the Golden Age of the Pharaohs Traveling Exhibit

OBJECTIVES: 2.02, 3.02, 4.01

Discussion Questions

1 Art is one way of recording everyday life. What was life like in ancient Egypt based upon this picture?

2 Do we have any rivers in either the United States or North Carolina that are as important to us as the Nile is to Egypt? Why or why not?

3 Name the regions in North Carolina that are fertile because of rivers.

Caption Answer

The Nile River deposited fertile silt along its banks.

Writing Activity

The Nile

 OBJECTIVES: 3.01

Give students the following writing prompts:

Clarification Explain what Herodotus meant when he said "Egypt is the gift of the Nile."

Prediction How would the history of Egypt have been different had the Nile *not* flowed through Egypt?

LESSON 1 Early Civilizations

KEY IDEAS

- Annual flooding of the Nile provided fertile soil to ancient Egyptians, who grew surplus food grains.

- Successful farming supported the ancient Egyptian civilization, which was led by pharaohs and priests.

- The Kingdom of Kush near the Red Sea developed as a part of Egypt, then as an independent kingdom.

- Axum, nearer the Red Sea than Kush, grew in importance as its city of Adulus controlled trade with the Mediterranean.

KEY TERMS

delta
pharaohs
pyramids

At first glance, Egypt in northeastern Africa does not seem a promising place for a great civilization of the ancient world. Except for a thin ribbon of water with green banks on either side, it is all desert. Luckily for the Egyptians, this ribbon of water is the Nile, the longest river in the world.

At its delta, the Nile widens into a broad area of many streams before emptying into the Mediterranean Sea. A *delta* is an area of land at the mouth of a river, often triangular in shape, made by the deposits of silt and sand carried by the river.

The green banks on either side of the river make up the Nile River valley. This valley contains some of the richest farmland in the world.

This wall painting of an Egyptian couple sowing and tilling their field was found in the man's tomb in the Valley of the Nobles of Thebes. **How did parts of Egypt become so fertile?**

Chapter 3

Egypt— The Gift of the Nile

Then and now, the Nile River is Egypt's lifeline. Greek historian Herodotus visited Egypt 2,500 years ago. "Egypt is the gift of the Nile," he said.

Herodotus knew that the Nile floods its banks every year. It spreads the fertile silt it has carried more than 4,000 miles (6,440 km). The Nile flows from the mountains and lakes of East Africa.

The soil spread by the yearly floods was so rich that ancient Egyptian farmers could easily grow more than enough food for themselves and their families. Farmers grew about three times as much grain as they needed. The farmers fed others with this surplus food. Those who did not have to farm for a living became craftspeople or traders. Some became leaders of communities that grew along the Nile.

Pharaohs and Farmers

By 3500 B.C., two kingdoms had developed in Egypt along the Nile. The union of the kingdoms in 3100 B.C. marks the beginning of Egyptian civilization. Rulers called *pharaohs* (FAY R·ohs) led Egypt. The civilization produced works of art and architecture that still amaze us.

Egyptian society depended on Nile River Valley farmers. Every harvest, farmers turned over their surplus grain to the pharaoh's tax collectors. This system allowed the pharaoh, his family, and court to live a life of luxury. The taxes paid the government officials and priests. They could purchase such luxuries as ebony, ivory, and ostrich feathers from regions south of the Sahara. Egyptian rulers

bought wood, spices, incense, and precious stones from Asia.

When farmers were not working their land, they were likely to be busy draining marshes and digging channels to bring water into their fields. Government officials organized these irrigation plans. They also directed the building of huge stone statues, temples, and royal tombs. These construction projects were closely linked to the religious beliefs of the ancient Egyptians. Many of these structures still stand today as monuments to this civilization.

The gold funeral mask of King Tutankhamen illustrates the wealth of Egyptian pharaohs. **How did they acquire their wealth?**

The Nile is the world's longest river. **Why was Egypt called "The gift of the Nile?"**

Discussion Questions

1 Herodotus said "Egypt is the gift of the Nile." What is the evidence to support this statement?

2 Consider the gold funeral mask of King Tutankhamen. What level of sophistication had the Egyptian culture reached?

3 Some historians say the development of agriculture was the most important factor in the beginnings of civilization. Would you agree with this?

4 How would the history of Egypt be different if the Nile River did not exist?

5 How would a "Nile River" in a developing country change the lives of its people?

6 What are some of the architectural designs we use today that were given to us by the Egyptians?

7 What are other gifts given to our civilization by the Egyptians?

8 How do dams cause problems for people living downstream when there is an abundance of rainfall?

 Caption Answer

Farmers turned their surplus harvests over to the pharaoh's tax collectors.

 Caption Answer

The Nile's silt created rich soil. This allowed farmers to grow enough food to support communities.

 ELL Teaching Tips

Welcoming Newcomers

If possible, have more advanced ELL students who speak the newcomers' languages take your new students on a tour of the important places in your school, such as the bathroom, office, or cafeteria. Make sure they also explain to the students what the expectations are for the classroom.

41

Discussion Questions

1 Why do you think so many ancient civilizations have their gods and goddesses represent aspects of nature?

2 What similarities are there between the religions of the Egyptians and the ancient Greeks?

3 Why do you think the Egyptians built such elaborate structures as the pyramids?

4 Why were rulers buried with so many of their personal possessions?

5 How would you compare monuments and statues of presidents and/or war heroes to the great pyramids?

6 Pyramids were elaborate "houses" for the dead. What are some funeral customs or practices we have? Why are these rituals so important for the living?

7 Is the practice of burying symbols of wealth the same in the United States as it is in Africa? If yes, how and in what way?

Caption Answer

Egyptians believed that people needed things from their earthly life in the afterlife, so people were buried with tools and treasures.

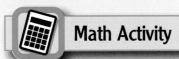

Math Activity

Equilateral Triangle Math Word Problem

 OBJECTIVES: 3.03

The felucca is a traditional sailing vessel on the Nile. This sailboat has a sail that is a right triangle. If one leg is 12 feet and the other leg is 20 feet, what is the hypotenuse?

Answer 23.3 feet

Extension Assist ELL students by setting up the problem for them.

Egyptian Religion

Egyptians believed in many gods. They worshiped a sun god and a wind god. They believed in such animal gods as the jackal, snake, and crocodile. The Nile River itself held a special place among Egypt's gods.

Ramses' tomb at Thebes, Egypt (above), was surrounded by images of the pharaoh as a god. The pyramids at Giza (below) still tower over the landscape today. **How do Egyptian burial practices illustrate the beliefs of the ancient civilization?**

Egypt's pharaohs claimed that they were the children of the gods worshiped by the Egyptians. The pharaohs held great power because the Egyptians thought the pharaohs were godlike.

The pharaohs used their power to build a strong government. Priests and government officials carried out their orders, enforced laws, and made sure society ran smoothly. Pharaohs led Egypt for more than 3,000 years.

The Egyptians believed that after a person died, his or her life continued. In the afterlife, the dead would need many of the tools and treasures of their earthly existence.

The pharaohs ordered huge stone tombs known as *pyramids* built for themselves. When they died, the symbols of their wealth and power—precious stones, gold jewelry, and incense—were buried with them.

Construction of the pyramids was an enormous, backbreaking, and sometimes bone-crushing task. It required the work of thousands of workers. The workers were sometimes slaves. The largest and most famous pyramid was the Great Pyramid (see photo on page 38). This tomb of the pharaoh, known as Khufu, (KUH·foo) was built in 2600 B.C. The Great Pyramid covers 13 acres (5.2 square hectometers) at its base, about seven city blocks. It is as tall as a 40-story building.

42

Chapter 3

It's a Fact

Ancient Egypt

We owe many things to the ancient Egyptian civilization: toothbrushes (chew sticks) and toothpaste (made from powdered pumice mixed with wine vinegar), cosmetics for both men and women (eyeliner, eye shadow, lipstick, hair dye, rouge, perfume, and skin cream—many of which were found in King Tut's tomb), bronze razors, and early shampoo—Egyptians mixed citrus juice with water to help remove excess oil from hair.

What would YOU do?

International agreements restrict who can take artifacts from the nation where they were originally found. The government must give permission if someone wants to take an object considered to be a national treasure. Otherwise, the object may be considered stolen. In 1912, the bust of Nefertiti was taken to Germany without Egypt's permission. Later, in the 1930s, Egypt asked for it back, but Hitler refused to give it up. He said that it was his beloved possession and that it would remain in Germany forever.

Egypt is now taking legal action to take back five different artifacts it believes are "national icons" from museums in the United States, the United Kingdom, Germany, and France. Yet these objects have been owned by these museums for decades. They allow many visitors to see the wonders of Ancient Egypt without having to travel far. Should these items be given back to Egypt?

Decline of Ancient Egypt

Egypt had no foreign invaders for more than 1,500 years. Its desert landforms offered some protection. Deserts surrounded the Nile to the east and west.

Foreign forces began to attack Egypt beginning around 1100 B.C. Assaults by the Assyrians and Persians weakened Egypt. Finally in 332 B.C., Alexander the Great of Greece conquered the kingdom and ended the power of the pharaohs. After Alexander's death, one of his generals, Ptolemy, took control of Egypt.

Kush and Egypt

Kush (kush) was Egypt's neighbor and trading partner on the Nile long before Egypt became a great kingdom. While Egypt's pharaohs built a civilization in the northern Nile Valley, Kush developed to the south.

Both Egypt and Kush were on the Nile. Their locations encouraged contacts between them. Yet travel on the Nile was not as easy as the map on page 39 may suggest. South of ancient Egypt, the Nile's waters tumble over a series of six cataracts. The first of these waterfalls stood between the Egyptians and Kush. This made the movement of people and freight slow and dangerous.

Egypt was a desert country with few natural resources. It looked to Kush and other places for raw materials, such as stone and timber, and for the fine goods favored by royalty. Egyptian traders traveled south (up the Nile) in search of these goods.

Egypt took direct control of Kush around 1500 B.C. The Egyptians built forts along the Nile to make sure that trade was not disrupted. Towns and temples grew along this part of the Nile.

Egypt ruled Kush for the next 500 years. The Kushites adopted parts of Egyptian culture, especially Egyptian religious beliefs and its spoken and written language.

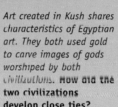

Art created in Kush shares characteristics of Egyptian art. They both used gold to carve images of gods worshiped by both civilizations. **How did the two civilizations develop close ties?**

Historical Foundations of Africa

43

Discussion Questions

1 Egypt took control of Kush to protect its own interests. Is there ever a time when it is justified for a country to take over another for its own interests?

2 Why do you think the Assyrians and Persians were able to weaken and conquer Egypt?

3 Egypt and Kush had difficulty communicating with each other. What enabled them to build a strong relationship?

Caption Answer

They were trading partners.

Activity

Find Out About It

OBJECTIVES: 8.03

Have students research the following areas of the ancient Egyptian civilizations: mathematics, science, writing, medicine, agriculture, and government. Students should display the results of their research in one of two ways. First, on poster board, cut out the large shape of a pyramid and have the students write and illustrate their facts in the pyramid. Display in the classroom.

Second, Expand the activity and have students illustrate individual pyramids to form a larger pyramid. Distribute pre-cut triangles copied on legal-size paper. Have students lay triangles on the floor to form a pyramid. Number each triangle, beginning at the apex. Have each student illustrate a triangle with information researched. Completed triangles are assembled to form a larger pyramid. Display in the classroom or in a prominent location in the school.

Extension ELL students should use an ELL-friendly Web site for research. An alternate activity is to have students build a pyramid out of croutons, stuffing mix cubes, or marshmallows to display in the classroom.

Map Activity

Sailing the Nile

NATIONAL GEOGRAPHY STANDARDS: 1, 4, 7, 14

GEOGRAPHIC THEMES: Location, Place, Movement, Human-Environmental Interaction

OBJECTIVES: 2.01, 2.02, 2.03

Using the background map, have students identify: the sources of the Nile *(Ethiopian Highlands and Lake Victoria)*, the tributaries of the Nile *(Blue Nile and White Nile)*, the countries crossed by the flow of the Nile *(Ethiopia, Uganda, Sudan, and Egypt)*, and the lakes impacted/created by the Nile *(Victoria and Nasser—also Kyoga and Albert)*.

Discuss with students that rivers can flow in any direction (north, west, etc.), but they usually flow from a source to a large body of water. Carefully research and examine with students the directions that different rivers flow. Note that the Nile is not the only river on earth that flows north. Have students speculate on the significance of the size, impact, and location of the delta at the mouth of the Nile. Guide students into understanding that the Nile is an exotic river crossing deserts, with cataracts along its channel and man-made reservoirs.

Extension For novice ELL students, model and provide additional explanations. Assign students to work with a partner.

EYEWITNESS TO HISTORY

Sailing the Nile Through Time

The longest river in Africa and the world, the Nile was worshiped as one of the gods of Egyptian civilization. Today, Africans still depend upon its waters for food, energy, and transportation.

Two rivers flow north out of East Africa to form the Nile. The Blue Nile tumbles out of the Ethiopian Highlands, carrying topsoil torn from the earth by tropical rains. The White Nile begins in Lake Victoria and grows in the swamp region of southern Sudan. There it nourishes the papyrus (left), a reed used by the ancient Egyptians to make paper. Khartoum is located at the confluence of the two rivers. The united Nile runs through the desert, over a series of cataracts, then along the fertile strips created by its own flood waters in the valley of Egypt. The Nile drains into the Mediterranean Sea.

Ancient Greek poets wrote about the Nile. In *The Odysssey*, Homer calls the Nile Aigyptos. The Greeks built a great city, Alexandria, where the Nile flows into the Mediterranean.

Homer

Fifteen species of poisonous snakes, crocodiles (right), and hippopotamuses (left) still challenge those who live along the Nile.

Map labels: Mediterranean Sea, Cairo, EGYPT, Nile River, Aswan, L. Nasser, Red Sea, SUDAN, Khartoum, ERITREA, Blue Nile, L. Tana, SOMALIA, ETHIOPIA, Cataracts, DEMOCRATIC REPUBLIC OF CONGO, White Nile, L. Albert, UGANDA, L. Turkana, KENYA, L. Victoria, RWANDA, TANZANIA

44

Chapter 3

Out of the fertile soil carried by the Nile grew the ancient Egyptian culture. On the banks of the Nile rose the pyramids outside Cairo at Giza (below). Great pharaohs were buried with boats, such as those that sailed on the Nile.

In modern times, the Nile filled Lake Nasser, after the Aswan High Dam (right) was built for irrigation and to control flooding. Because of the dam, the Nile makes greater amounts of land arable. Controlled in some measure, the Nile flows on through human history waiting for the next chapter to be written.

Boats sailing the Nile

Historical Foundations of Africa

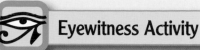 **Eyewitness Activity**

Sailing the Nile Through Time

OBJECTIVES: 1.01, 1.02, 1.03

Use one or more of the following activities to reinforce the significance of the Nile River to world civilization.

• After reading the information about the Nile, have students construct a graphic organizer emphasizing information from the text. Selects an appropriate graphic organizer form the templates in the Teacher's Resource Guide.

• Ask students to write or word process a paper explaining how the Nile River has affected Egypt.

• Read the story *Croco'nile* by Roy Gerrard to the class (Sunburst, 2001. ISBN 0374416117). After listening to the story, students can draw a picture illustrating a scene from the Nile River.

Extension ELL students can draw a picture of the scene.

Discussion Questions

1 How did Kush become free of Egyptian rule?

2 How did the transition from the Bronze Age to the Iron Age affect early civilizations in Egypt?

3 What is a crossroads? What benefits would come from living in an area considered a crossroads?

4 How did the relative location of Kush make it a crossroads?

5 How important is trade for a country to become wealthy?

6 Why was it safer to transport goods by water rather than by land?

7 Many people say that competition in business is healthy. How is this true?

8 What do you think would happen to the powers of the Middle East if we were no longer dependent on its oil?

Caption Answer

The decline of the Roman Empire and the resulting loss of trade

Caption Answer

Egypt became weak from fighting within the country. Kush used that time to break away from Egypt and eventually conquer it. After Assyria conquered Egypt, Kush developed a civilization of its own.

The flat-topped pyramids at Meroë are artifacts of the Kush civilization.
What led to the decline of Kush?

This granite monument carved in a Meroë temple honors a king of Kush.
How did Kush become free of Egyptian influence?

The Kingdom of Kush

Fighting within the kingdom and foreign invasions weakened Egypt by about 1000 B.C. Kush broke away and became an independent kingdom. Kush's rulers steadily gained in wealth and power.

The army of Kush conquered Egypt around 730 B.C. The victorious king had an account of his conquest of the Egyptian city of Memphis carved on a granite monument.

The kings of Kush ruled Egypt for about 70 years. They adopted more Egyptian beliefs and customs, such as praying to Egyptian gods and having their names carved on Egyptian temples.

Kushite control of Egypt ended with the invasion of Assyrians from the East. Armed with iron weapons, the Assyrians easily conquered Egypt. Egyptian soldiers fought with weapons of copper and bronze, no match for iron weapons.

The rulers of Kush continued to govern their kingdom, although they were pushed out of Egypt. They moved the center of government south. Their new capital, Meroë (MEHR·eh·WEE), grew on the banks of the Nile near the sixth cataract.

Here Kush became wealthy and influential. Kush's location near the Red Sea made it the crossroads for trade between Asia and the Mediterranean world. Meroë's merchants shipped ivory, leopard skins, ostrich feathers, ebony, and gold to Egypt and beyond to Greece and Rome.

Kush developed a civilization of its own as its power grew. Kushites used their own written and spoken language. Eventually, they stopped following Egyptian gods. The Kushites continued to bury their rulers in royal pyramid tombs similar to the tombs of the pharaohs, but they created their own style of pyramids. Kushite pyramids had steeper sides and flat tops instead of pointed ones.

Kush remained a powerful empire in Africa for around 450 years. Egypt and the Roman Empire bought trade goods from Kush between 250 B.C. and A.D. 200. As the Roman Empire declined, fewer buyers wanted the luxury goods from Kush. Kush's foreign trade decreased because of competition from Axum (ACK·sum), another kingdom on the Red Sea. By A.D. 300, the people of Kush had abandoned Meroë and the kingdom was collapsing.

46

Background Information

Christianity in Egypt and Ethiopia

The Ethiopian Orthodox Church is one of the oldest Christian sects in the world. Today the people of Ethiopia continue the commitment to the Christian faith that began with Axum's King Ezana. In the fifth century a theological dispute led the Church in Egypt and Ethiopia to separate from Rome and Constantinople. Today about 37 percent of Ethiopians are Christians, and another 47 percent are Muslims. About 12 percent follow animist religions. In largely Muslim Egypt, Coptic Christians are a small minority, about 10 percent. Coptic Christian churches in Egypt hold church services in Arabic, but clergy read portions of the liturgy in the ancient Coptic language, basically the Egyptian language written with Greek letters.

The Kingdom of Axum

Axum opened directly onto the Red Sea. It replaced Meroë, and Kush, as a center of African trade with the cities of the Mediterranean, India, and the Arabian Peninsula. From Meroë, traders had to haul their goods overland to the Red Sea. Such travel by land was difficult and dangerous.

Axum's Red Sea port city of Adulus (AH·duhl·us) (see map, page 39) gave Axum an advantage in taking control of the trade. At Adulus, merchants came to buy ivory, gold, and perfumes from the African interior. Traders carried their goods north to Egypt and across the Mediterranean to Rome and Byzantium. Other merchants traveled east to Arabia and across the Indian Ocean to India.

By the A.D. 200s, Axum had become the most impressive kingdom in Africa or Southwest Asia. It controlled smaller kingdoms across the Red Sea in Arabia. On the African continent, it ruled much of the most fertile areas of the upper Nile.

Axum minted its own coins of gold, silver, and copper. Its farmers raised large herds of cattle and produced a variety of crops. Architects and engineers of Axum built 100-foot (30-m) towers to honor their leaders.

King Ezana, Axum's most powerful ruler, led his soldiers in destroying Meroë. In A.D. 324, King Ezana converted to Christianity. After his conversion, the people of Axum also accepted Christianity.

In the 600s, Muslim armies took control of Egypt and North Africa, spreading Islam and cutting Axum off from other Christian countries. With the support of the Christian Church, Axum withstood the spread of Islam. It became "a Christian island in a Muslim sea," according to one historian. By then, Axum's position as a trading power had been lost to Arab traders.

Much of Axum's wealth disappeared when it lost its foreign trade. In the early 800s, Axum's rulers led their people south into the highlands of what is today Ethiopia. Over time, the kingdom of Ethiopia replaced what had been Axum. A lasting legacy of Axum is the Christian faith of the Ethiopian people.

North African Christians of the sixth and seventh century A.D. painted religious images on wood, such as this one of Christ and a local religious leader. **How did Axum become a center of Christianity in Africa?**

Discussion Questions

1 What characteristics make a great civilization?

2 What qualities and characteristics enabled Axum to grow powerful and impressive?

3 What legacy do you want our country to leave?

4 What do you want your legacy to be?

Caption Answer

King Ezana converted to Christianity in A.D. 324.

Research Activity

Axum Trade Chart

OBJECTIVES: 4.02

Have students research the goods traded at Axum and create a web or flow chart illustrating what goods were traded, where they came from, where they were traded to, and the type of transportation that brought the goods into and out of Axum.

LESSON 1 REVIEW

Fact Follow-Up
1. How does the Nile River enrich Egypt?
2. Describe the economy of ancient Egypt.
3. How did the pharaohs prepare for the afterlife?
4. Describe the relative locations of Egypt, Kush, and Axium.
5. How was Kush able to conquer Egypt?
6. Contrast the economies of Kush and Axium.

Talk About It
1. Could Egypt have developed its civilization without the Nile River? Explain your answer.
2. Which was the "greatest" civilization—Egypt, Axum, or Kush?
3. How did the relative locations of Egypt and Kush influence their civilizations? Which civilization was easiest to invade? Why?

LESSON 1 REVIEW

Fact Follow-Up Answers
1. The flooding of the Nile brings silt down the river, enriching the soil so that productive agriculture is possible.
2. Egypt's rich soil along the Nile produced an agricultural surplus to support artisans, merchants, and the government.
3. The pharaohs ordered huge stone tombs known as pyramids built for themselves. In the pyramid, the pharaohs were buried with the symbols of their wealth and power that they would need in the afterlife.
4. Egypt was located in northeastern Africa along the Nile River; Kush was located south of Egypt, also along the Nile. Axum was located southeast of Kush and Egypt on the Red Sea.
5. Egypt was weakened by fighting within the country and by foreign invasions. Kush took the opportunity to break away and then to conquer Egypt.
6. Kush, located on the Nile River, was able to trade stone, timber, and other goods from farther south. Kush traded with Egypt, southern Africa, Rome, and Greece. Axum, located on the Red Sea, traded with the interior of Africa, Egypt, Rome, Byzantium, and India. Axum also grew wealthy from its cattle farming and rich agriculture.

Talk About It Answers
1. Important points: Students should support their position. The predictable annual flooding of the Nile was important.
2. Important points: Students should choose one civilization and support that choice with facts. Note that Egypt is best remembered because of the monuments that remain.
3. Both were ports; both were located on the Nile River. Wealth and ideas from other parts of the world were accessible to them by water. Both could be invaded by water: Egypt from the Mediterranean Sea and the Nile River, Kush from other Nile River civilizations. The Nile was a benefit and a hazard to both.

OBJECTIVES: 4.02, 5.01, 8.01

Discussion Questions

1 What elements are most important to building a civilization— having natural resources, building capabilities, a location on trade routes, or other elements? Why?

2 What role would a well-trained army play in keeping a country powerful? Is the army the most important characteristic?

3 How did Ghana become rich by trading products it did not produce?

4 How did building a strong army and an efficient government help Ghana evolve as a powerful kingdom?

5 What was the importance of gold to Ghana between A.D. 300 and 1600?

6 What has made the United States such a powerful country? How has location contributed to its power?

Arab traders

Salt

 OBJECTIVES: 4.02

Using the Internet, have students research the salt trade in Africa. Where was the salt mined? How was it mined? What kingdoms traded the salt? Why was salt an important commodity in Africa? Have students create and illustrate a map showing the routes of the salt trade.

LESSON **2** West African Kingdoms

- West African kingdoms developed by controlling the trade of salt from the Sahara and gold from along the Senegal and Niger Rivers.

- Ghana, then Mali and Songhai, grew by collecting taxes on salt and gold traded through the kingdoms.

- Islamic leaders of Mali and Songhai made Timbuktu into a center of Islamic culture and learning.

KEY TERMS

mansa

Camels cross the desert. **Who used camels to carry goods to trade in Ghana?**

Common salt that we pour on French fries and shake over popcorn plays an important part in the story of ancient Ghana (GAHN·ah), Mali (MAH·lee), and Songhai (song·HIGH). These West African kingdoms grew out of the trade in salt and gold between 300 and 1600.

In the Sahara Desert oasis city of Taghaza (tahg·HAZ·ah), salt was so common that people made their houses from slabs of it. They could easily dig it out of the ground. In the Sahara, salt was not a precious mineral but rather an ordinary building brick.

In tropical climates, salt is vital to health. Large amounts of salt are lost as people sweat. Without enough salt, the human body goes into convulsions, then paralysis, and finally death occurs. This means that in places where salt was scarce, it was worth its weight in gold. Merchants did indeed trade it for gold. The kingdoms of West Africa controlled this trade.

Golden Ghana

The people of Ghana produced neither gold nor salt. Yet they became rich by trading both. Ghana's location helped it become the first of the trading empires in West Africa. Ghana sat on the trade route between the Sahara, the main source of salt, and the gold fields of the Senegal (sen·ih·GAWL) River to the south. Its location enabled Ghana's rulers to profit from the salt and gold exchange.

Arab traders from the cities of North Africa and desert nomads skilled at traveling long distances by camel led the trade. Arab traders carried salt south on a caravan route that went through the market towns of Ghana. Traders from the West African savanna carried gold north to Ghana. There traders bargained salt for gold.

Ghana's rulers made money because merchants exchanged salt and gold in towns under their control. Goods passing through the kingdom were taxed. The kingdom also was enriched by taxes on lands and crops.

Ghana built a well-trained army and an efficient government with the taxes it collected. By the 900s, Ghana ruled an area larger than any European government of that time. A Spanish visitor marveled at the size and wealth of Ghana's towns. He had seen nothing like them at home.

In 1076, Ghana came under attack from North African desert peoples. Ghana's soldiers eventually drove off these invaders, but the fighting interfered with trading. Ghana lost its hold on the gold-salt trade and the kingdom broke into smaller parts.

Chapter 3

Discussion Questions

1 How did the discovery of gold fields along the Niger River lead to the expansion and development of Mali?

2 Who were the Malinke, and where did they originate?

3 What do you think life would have been like if you had been a camel caravan guide during the period of the gold-salt trade?

4 What role has gold played in the history of the United States? Is there anything, such as gold, that you would be willing to face great dangers to obtain?

Mali Takes Over the Gold Trade

As older gold mines near the Atlantic coast ran out of the precious metal, new ones opened to the east. Miners uncovered gold fields along the upper Niger River in the eleventh and twelfth centuries. To reach the mines, traders tracked new routes across the Sahara and the savanna.

In the 1200s, the Malinke (mah·LING·kee) people took control of the gold-salt trade from Ghana. The Malinke army claimed most of the land that had belonged to Ghana.

Malinke rulers greatly expanded this empire known as Mali (MAH·lee). At its peak in the 1300s, Mali stretched from the Atlantic coast to a bend in the Niger River. There, new trade routes through the Sahara came to an end. Upriver, Mali built the great city Timbuktu (tim·buck·TOO), in the Niger River valley.

The leader of the Mali people was called the *mansa*, or chief. The wealth of the mansa of Mali came from taxes they charged on goods passing through the kingdom. Another source of wealth was the tributes, or gifts, paid to Mali's rulers by chiefs of surrounding lands. The chiefs usually gave farm crops to the Mali leaders.

Mali was located on more fertile lands than Ghana. So most people in the kingdom of Mali farmed. Rice, millet, yams, and beans provided an abundant food supply. Farmers gave some of their harvest to the government as tribute—a form of taxation.

Rulers strengthened their hold on power with taxes and tribute. They bought horses and weapons for their armies. With more equipment they expanded their area of control even farther. At the kingdom's peak, two thirds of the gold in use in Europe and North Africa came from trade controlled by Mali.

Islam in Mali

Mali's rulers were the religious as well as the political leaders of their people. Most followed the Muslim faith. In 1325, Mansa Musa, Mali's most famous ruler, made a pilgrimage to Mecca, the holiest city in the Muslim world.

Camel caravan guides controlled the West African gold-salt trade. **How did Ghana's and Mali's locations help them become trade centers?**

 **Caption Answer**

Ghana sat on the trade route between the Sahara and the gold fields of the Senegal River to the south. Mali included land from the Atlantic to a bend in the Niger River where trade routes ended.

Historical Foundations of Africa

Discussion Questions

1 How did Timbuktu become the center of Muslim learning in Africa?

2 What were the contributions of Timbuktu? Why were they important?

3 What role did religion have in the history of Timbuktu?

Caption Answer

Mansa Musa made a pilgrimage to Mecca, and then Muslim scholars returned with Mansa Musa to Timbuktu.

Customs

In the seventh century, Muslims conquered North Africa, bringing their religion, Islam, to the continent. Islam came with camel caravans to West Africa. Arab merchants in East Africa introduced the faith there.

In West Africa the mud walls and towers of large mosques became a dramatic addition to the region's architecture.

This mosque in Timbuktu reflects the importance of Islam to the Mali culture. **How did Timbuktu become a center of Muslim learning in Africa?**

50

Chapter 3

Background Information

Mansa Musa's Golden Touch

Mansa Musa's stopover in Egypt on the way to Mecca made Mali and its sovereign famous far and wide. At the beginning of his pilgrimage in 1324, Mansa Musa stopped at the royal court in Cairo. According to contemporary accounts, he came on horseback with hundreds of slaves and soldiers, freely distributing magnificent gifts along the way. Mali's ruler gave away so much gold in Cairo that the price of this precious metal tumbled in Egypt and remained low for more than a decade. Despite his wealth and generosity to the Egyptians, Mali's ruler gets low marks in Malinke oral traditions. He is scolded for squandering the kingdom's gold and weakening the empire.

Muslim scholars from Mecca went back to Mali with Mansa Musa. They made Timbuktu a center of Muslim learning. The people of Mali described their city's role as the heart of Islam in Africa: "Salt comes from the north, gold from the south, but the word of God and the treasures of wisdom are only to be found in Timbuktu." This saying meant that Timbuktu's leadership in gold and salt trade was not as important as the city's leadership in Muslim teaching.

After Mansa Musa died, the members of the royal family competed with one another for power. This fighting weakened Mali. A leader of the Songhai people challenged the weaker Mali for control of the gold trade.

On an early map of West Africa, Mansa Musa of Mali (bottom right corner) holds a gold nugget. **Who was Mansa Musa?**

A Journey to MALI

Timbuktu—
Meeting of Camel and Canoe

If you lived in the Middle Ages, you might have heard of a place called Timbuktu. It was such a place of mystery and distance that when people wanted to refer to something from far away they used Timbuktu as their symbol for remoteness.

Timbuktu sits on the edge of the Sahara Desert, north of the Niger River. Camel caravans arrived in Timbuktu with salt from the Sahara. Canoes filled with gold floated down from the upper Niger River. So many traders came that Timbuktu became known as "the meeting place of the camel and the canoe."

Blacksmiths traded their metalwork for carved ivory and hammered gold. Only prayers and meals interrupted the brisk trade of the day.

Timbuktu was the trading hub of the Mali and Songhai kingdoms in West Africa for almost 300 years, beginning soon after its founding in 1100. After Mali leader Mansa Musa's pilgrimage to Mecca, the city became an Islamic cultural center.

Islamic scholars established schools and built mosques. African traveler Leo Africanus wrote in the sixteenth century of the "great stores of doctors, judges, priests, and other learned men" in Timbuktu.

Caravan approaching Timbuktu

Discussion Questions

1 In many civilizations adversaries had to fight for control of the government after the death of a leader. Can you name any examples of this from history or around the world?

2 What factors contributed to the development of Timbuktu as a major trading center?

3 Why do you think the United States has such peaceful transfers of power?

Caption Answer

Mansa Musa was Mali's most famous ruler.

Activity

Islamic Expansion

OBJECTIVES: 4.03, 8.02, 11.03

After reading the *A Journey to* feature on Mali, break the class into cooperative groups. Using historical atlases, encyclopedias, or the Internet, have the groups research the role of Arab traders in the expansion of Islam into Africa and other parts of the world. What institutions were brought with Islamic scholars or Arab traders? How did the ideas of Islam and these institutions change African societies?

Have students record their information using graphic organizers.

Have the groups share their findings with the class. Discuss as a class the role of Islam in Africa before European Imperialism.

Map Activity

Illustrated Map

OBJECTIVES: 1.01, 4.02

Discuss the photograph of the map of Africa on this page with the class. What do the illustrations show readers about what was considered important in Africa at the time the map was drawn? Have students illustrate a map of North Carolina or their county demonstrating what they consider to be important today.

Discussion Questions

1 What enabled Sunni Ali to take control of Mali?

2 Compare the contributions made by Mansa Musa to those made by Askia Muhammad.

3 How was Sunni Ali important to the gold trade?

4 Overall, how important has Islam been in the history of West African kingdoms? Why?

5 Who are some of the great leaders we have had in the United States? What characteristics do you think a great leader must have? Must a great leader be ruthless to maintain control?

6 For the United States to remain strong, do you think it is crucial for the government to keep creating new weapons and technology? When do you think "enough is enough"?

7 Would you prefer to be remembered for power, wealth, or intellectual accomplishments? Why?

 **Caption Answer**

Horses were used in both trade and the army.

Songhai

Songhai's founder, Sunni Ali, captured the city of Timbuktu from Mali in 1464. He later added Ghana and other lands nearby to his kingdom.

Among the Songhai people, Sunni Ali is remembered as a skilled and sometimes ruthless fighter. The Songhai thought of Sunni Ali as a great hero and honored him for his conquests. The Arab writer Mahmud el Kati described him as "always conqueror, never conquered."

After Sunni Ali, Songhai's most important leader was Askia Muhammad. Like Mansa Musa, Askia Muhammad was a follower of Islam who made a pilgrimage to Mecca. On his return, he added to Timbuktu's fame as a center of learning by attracting Islamic teachers and poets to its schools. By the 1500s, Timbuktu had three universities and a population of more than 50,000.

As in Mali, the ruler's wealth came from taxes on trade and tribute of crops from the farmers of the Songhai empire. The Songhai empire lasted 125 years—a shorter time than the empires of Ghana or Mali. Songhai fell in 1591 to invaders from Morocco. The invading army fought with guns and cannons, the latest weapons of the time.

Songhai forces could not defend the empire against such weapons. The Moroccan conquest ended 600 years of West African empires. Trade continued, but the golden age of empire was over. West African empires are still remembered for their power, wealth, and intellectual accomplishments.

This terracotta equestrian figure was made in ancient Mali sometime between the thirteenth and fifteenth centuries. **Why were horses important in the kingdom of Mali?**

LESSON 2 REVIEW

Fact Follow-Up
1. How did gold and salt enrich ancient Ghana?
2. How did relative location help Ghana become a powerful kingdom?
3. Who were Mansa Musa and Sunni Ali? What did they accomplish?
4. Describe the relative locations of Ghana, Mali, and Songhai.
5. With what other places did these three civilizations trade?

Talk About It
1. Which of these three civilizations was the "greatest"? Explain your answer.
2. Could Ghana have developed a great civilization without trading? Explain.
3. In what ways were the civilizations of Ghana and Mali alike? How were they different?
4. Why do you think these three areas in West Africa developed great civilizations while others did not? Explain.

LESSON 2 REVIEW

Fact Follow-Up Answers
1. Ghana produced neither salt nor gold but was enriched by taxing the trade in these commodities as caravans bearing these products passed through their towns.
2. Ghana was located on the trading routes between the Sahara Desert, where salt was produced, and Senegal, where gold was mined.
3. Mansa Musa was Mali's most famous ruler. He made a pilgrimage to Mecca and established contacts with Islamic scholars resulting in the creation of Timbuktu as a center of Muslim learning in Africa. Sunni Ali was ruler of Songhai and a great and feared warrior. He captured Timbuktu in 1464.
4. All are located in the bulge of western Africa. Ghana, located in central western Africa, was conquered by Mali, whose borders extended far beyond what Ghana's had been, reaching west to the Atlantic Ocean and east to the center of Africa. Songhai stretched as far east and west as Mali, passing through the other two kingdoms.
5. All three traded with Europe, North Africa, and the Arabian Peninsula.

LESSON 3 — East African City-States and Zimbabwe

From 500 to 1500, wealthy city-states grew up along the eastern coast of Africa. A *city-state* is an independent city that has its own government and controls the lands surrounding it. The wealth of these city-states came mainly from trade, similar to the West African kingdoms of Ghana, Mali, and Songhai. Yet the East African trade grew eastward over the Indian Ocean, not across the Sahara Desert.

Trade Along the Indian Ocean

Most of the trade goods in East Africa went by boat across the Indian Ocean. Traders exchanged gold, ivory, slaves, and animal skins for tea, silk, and porcelain. Precious goods from China, India, and other parts of Asia were exchanged in busy marketplaces of Indian Ocean ports.

Climate and geography made the East African coast ideal for traders sailing back and forth across the Indian Ocean. Strong winter winds blew steadily toward Africa,

filling the sails of ships from India and the Arabian Peninsula. In summer, the wind patterns reversed, blowing away from Africa and toward Asia. Travel was easy across the Indian Ocean. Regular trade routes developed across this ocean much sooner than on Africa's Atlantic coast.

Some 40 city-states existed along the coast of East Africa from Mogadishu (mah·gah·DISH·oo) (in present-day Somalia) to Sofala (so·FAH·lah) (in present-day Mozambique). Muslims from Arabia and Persia traded in these ports for goods brought from inland areas of Africa.

KEY IDEAS

- East African city-states grew as centers of trade with India, Arabia, and Persia.

- Arabic and African people mixed in the eastern trading cities, creating a new language and bringing Islam to that part of Africa.

- Zimbabwe developed as a trading center between inland gold fields and eastern cities.

KEY TERMS

city-state

Modern-day dhows sail from Tanzania on the Indian Ocean. These boats are similar to those that sailed from East African city-states. **With whom did the city-states trade?**

Historical Foundations of Africa 53

OBJECTIVES: 3.01, 4.02, 11.01

Discussion Questions

1 Why were there so many independent city-states along the eastern coast of Africa?

2 How would life in North Carolina be different if each city were its own city-state? Do you think the rights of the individual could be better protected in a city-state?

3 Compare and contrast the city-states to your local government.

Caption Answer

East African city-states traded with China, India, and other parts of Asia.

Activity

Visit This City-State

OBJECTIVES: 4.02, 4.03

Using an outline map of Africa (found in the Teacher's Resource Guide), have students locate the East African city-states of Sofala, Mogadishu, Kilwa, Mombasa, Zanzibar, and Zimbabwe. Have students research one of those city-states and prepare a flyer, digital story, or PowerPoint presentation promoting it. They might tell traders why they should come to trade in their city-state. Students must give the location, climate, goods available, and any interesting facts about the culture.

Extension ELL students should use an ELL-friendly Web site for research. Novice students should create a collage instead of a flyer or computer product.

Talk About It Answers

1. Important points: Students should choose one of the three and support that choice with reasons. Note: Mali produced Timbuktu, the center of Islamic learning.

2. Important points: Students should take a position and support it with reasons. Note: Ghana had no greater natural resources than the areas surrounding it; it was the management of the gold and salt trade that enriched Ghana.

3. Both were located in West Africa, both were on trading routes between North Africa and areas to the south, and both were active traders. In Mali, which was larger than Ghana, the political leadership was also the religious leadership. Mali, because of Islam, cultivated ties with Southwest Asia and developed Timbuktu as a center of Islamic learning.

4. Important points: Students should respond to the question and support their explanation with facts. Note: What distinguished these three kingdoms from other areas was their control of the trade in gold and salt.

Discussion Questions

1 Why was it important for languages such as Swahili to develop?

2 Why did new cultures develop along the coast of Africa?

3 How did the trade winds affect Africa's economy?

4 What are some examples of the ways cultures have blended in your community? How do you think this has helped strengthen your community?

5 Which city in North Carolina do you think is the richest and most important? What has made that city so important? If you were going to create the ideal city, what characteristics would it have?

Caption Answer

It influenced the architecture, a new language developed, and Islam spread.

Activity

Leaving Home

OBJECTIVES: 3.02, 4.01, 5.03

Around 1450, the people of Zimbabwe left their walled city, possibly because of soil exhaustion caused by the demand for food. This is an example of human-environmental interaction. Discuss as a class problems facing the world today due to demands of people, such as the depletion of rain forests. Have students pair up and decide on an issue to research. Students should define the problem, identify the causes or demands creating the problem, and point out the short- and long-term effects. Have students create a poster, ad, or rap/song that will draw attention to the issue.

As an expansion the class can prepare a proposal for their community leaders on how to solve the problem.

Extension ELL students should use an ELL-friendly Web site for research and draw a poster.

Cultures Come Together

Many of these traders tired of the six-month journey across the sea. They married African women and settled along the coast. City-states, such as Malindi (ma·LIN·dih) and Mombasa (mahm·BAHS·ah) (in present-day Kenya), Kilwa (KIL·wah) (in present-day Tanzania), the island of Zanzibar (ZAN·zih·bar), and Sofala became their homes.

Cultures mixed in the coastal trading towns. A new language called Swahili developed. This language combined Arabic words and the language of Bantu-speaking African peoples. Arab traders spread their religion. Mosques, the houses of worship for Muslims, became a common sight in the coastal towns.

Many port cities were small. They consisted of a few stone houses and a mosque. Kilwa and Mombasa, and other cities spread along the coast, looked rich as successful Arab and Swahili traders built homes made entirely of coral stone.

By 1200, Kilwa was the richest East African city-state. Gold brought from inland areas of southern Africa was the greatest export. Inland peoples also traded ivory and slaves for spices and incense as well as Arab traders' cloth, beads, and imported pottery.

Portuguese explorer Nuña da Cunha visited Mombasa in 1528. He observed how "the men and women go very bravely [dressed] with many fine [clothes] of silk and gold in abundance. This is a place of great traffic and has a good harbor in which are [anchored boats] of many kinds." In the early 1500s, the Portuguese attacked and took control of many of the East African city-states. The northern ports resisted the Portuguese longer than the southern ones, but by the end of the century the entire coast was controlled by Portugal.

This door carved in Zanzibar (right) and today's Mombasa (below) show the meeting of Arabic and African cultures in East Africa. **How did that encounter affect East Africa?**

54

Background Information

Great Zimbabwe

The word *Zimbabwe* means "houses of stone" and comes from the Shona language. Among the treasures excavated at Great Zimbabwe were glass beads, Chinese ceramics from the Ming dynasty and glazed Persia earthenware. These artifacts link Great Zimbabwe to the trading centers at Sofala and Kilwa on the east African coast where Arab traders lived. In 1891, when Europeans first began excavating these ruins, many mistakenly believed these extraordinary pillars and carvings had been built by the ancient Phoenicians. This explanation of Zimbabwe's origins fit with the colonial myth that Africa had no history of its own. Archaeological expeditions in 1905 and 1929 unlocked the mystery of Zimbabwe's origins and confirmed its construction by local Shona people.

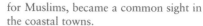

Great Zimbabwe

The kingdom of Great Zimbabwe (zim·BOB·way) grew in southern Africa between the Zambezi and Limpopo Rivers. It existed as a trading kingdom from the early eleventh to the mid-fifteenth century.

The people of Zimbabwe grew wealthy from trade with the East African city-states. As city-states like Kilwa grew rich, so did Zimbabwe. From artifacts found at Zimbabwe, archaeologists know that its rulers used dinnerware from Persia and China.

Zimbabwe's location contributed to its prosperity. With gold fields to its west and coastal trading cities to its east, Zimbabwe's rulers found ways to control and tax the trade. Zimbabwe's people also were successful farmers and cattle herders. In about 1450, the people of Zimbabwe left their walled kingdom. Is it possible that farming or grazing cattle had worn out the soil around Zimbabwe. With less food available, the people had to move.

The walls of Zimbabwe still stand more than 500 years after the kingdom's palace was completed.
How did this location contribute to the kingdom's success?

Word Origins

Modern-day Zimbabwe is named for the capital of the kingdom that dominated trade for 400 years between East Africa and South Africa. **Zimbabwe** means "great stone house." High stone walls surrounded the royal center. Parts of this wall are more than 30 feet (9 m) tall and 15 feet (4.5 m) thick. Some of the wall still stands.

Discussion Questions

1 Why did the Portuguese want control of Mombasa?

2 How did the location of Zimbabwe contribute to its prosperity?

3 Agree or disagree: Location is the most important of the Five Themes of Geography in determining the success of a country.

Caption Answer

Zimbabwe's rulers found ways to tax the and control the trade of gold from the west and goods from the coastal trading cities to its east.

LESSON 3 REVIEW

Fact Follow-Up
1. Compare East African city-states with the kingdoms in West Africa.
2. With what world areas did the East African city-states trade?
3. How did the Swahili language develop?
4. Name the important city-states in ancient East Africa. Give reasons for their importance.
5. Describe the remains of Great Zimbabwe.

Talk About It
1. Why was Zimbabwe described as "Great"?
2. Could the city-states of East Africa have prospered without trade? Explain your answer.
3. How did the relative location of Kilwa, Mombasa, and Zanzibar benefit those city-states of East Africa?

LESSON 3 REVIEW

Fact Follow-Up Answers
1. Both lay on trade routes, but the kingdoms of West Africa were larger than the city-states of East Africa. West African kingdoms stretched from the interior of the continent to the Atlantic coastline, whereas the city-states of East Africa were located along the coastlines of the Indian Ocean. The kingdoms concentrated on overland trade; the city-states had both inland and oceangoing trade.
2. They traded with China, India, other parts of Asia, and with the interior of Africa.
3. It developed out of a need for African and Arabic traders to communicate in coastal trading towns. It resulted from Arabic words for products being introduced into the Bantu language.
4. Kilwa, the richest, was an exchange point for gold, ivory, spices, incense, and slaves traded for cloth, beads, and pottery. Mombasa developed because of its excellent harbor. Zimbabwe was a kingdom as well as a city-state that traded gold for goods from as far away as China.
5. Parts of the stone walls of the kingdom remain. Certain sections are more than 30 feet high and 15 feet thick. Artifacts of the kingdom include dinnerware from Persia and China.

Talk About It Answers
1. The kingdom had large herds and fertile farmland, but its great wealth came from its location between the gold fields and the East African city-states. Zimbabwe's rulers controlled and taxed the trade in gold.
2. Important points: Students should take a position and explain it. Note: With the exception of Zimbabwe's fertile soil, the city-states lacked abundant valuable natural resources.
3. Their location on or near the coast of East Africa lay between the gold-rich inland areas and the Asian merchant trade on the coast. The business of trading was carried on in these city-states.

Teaching This Skill Lesson

Materials Needed textbooks, other maps of Africa, paper, pencils

Classroom Organization Students may work individually, in pairs, or in *small* groups.

Beginning the Lesson Review human-environmental interaction by asking a question such as "How have *you* changed the environment today?" or "Think back over your day. How many ways have you seen that people living right here have changed the environment?" And review inferencing with a question such as this: "Yesterday I went into a store and saw _____ on sale. Why would that be on sale?" or "When I went to the video store recently, there were many copies of the movie that was all rented out just three weeks ago. Why?" Lead students to understand that they can see something or know a fact about something and make an educated guess about it—an inference. Tell them they will be making inferences about human-environmental interaction. Sketch the graphic organizer described in the text on page 56 on the chalkboard to illustrate to students how their paper should be marked for note-making.

Lesson Development Monitor students as they make notes of their observations and inferences from the observations, checking to see that they are making extended notes about the three photographs on page 57. If their notes are too sketchy, ask such questions as "What more can you observe?" If their inferences are limited, ask such questions as "What else do you think this might mean?"

Conclusion Ask students to share some of the inferences they made. Record these on the chalkboard. Allow students to challenge inferences, then see if they can support these challenges with information from the text. Question to ensure that students have a working understanding of both human-environmental interaction and inferencing.

Analyzing, Interpreting, Creating, and Using Resources and Materials

Using Geography's Themes: Human-Environmental Interaction

All these headlines appeared in newspapers and magazines within a few weeks. Each headline refers to situations in Africa. What do they have in common? If you answered "the environment," you are very good at synthesizing (analyzing, then bringing together) your thoughts. If you happened to mention people and how people affect and are affected by the environment, you are an excellent synthesizer.

Another of geography's themes, human-environmental interaction, examines how the natural environment affects people, how they live, and how people, in turn, affect the environment. Think about how you are influenced by the physical environment: in the foods you eat, the clothing you wear, the kind of home you live in, your leisure activities.

How do you influence the physical environment? By using water and mineral resources? by consuming natural products? by leaving litter?

All of us together interact with the physical environment as we build houses, cut down trees, change the earth's surface by farming or building roads, pollute rivers and oceans, even tunnel through mountains or divert rivers.

The African continent displays varied examples of human-environmental interaction. The top photograph on page 57 was taken in the vast wastes of the Sahara Desert. It shows an area of little human impact on the environment. How have humans today interacted with this area? How might this pattern of interaction change in the future? For example, what would a photograph of the same place look like if oil were discovered under the sand?

Now examine the middle photograph of a traditional village in West Africa. What conclusions can you draw about ways that the environment has affected people's lives. How have the villagers changed the environment?

Take a sheet of paper, divide it in half lengthwise, and label the halves "Humans Affect the Environment" and "The Environment Affects Humans." Next, "read" the photograph of the traditional village. Make notes (or record examples, as the geographers would say) of humans affecting the environment and of the environment affecting humans.

First, note what you actually can see in the photograph. Then draw a line across the page. Beneath the line, make notes of what you cannot actually see but can infer. (An inference is an "educated guess." If, for example, you see deep snow or outdoor ice skating, you would not infer that the photograph was made near the Equator.)

Pay special attention to vegetation, clothing, and housing as you make your inferences. Look for signs that show the effects on types of transportation.

1,000-Day Drought Devastates Crops

Activists Gear Up for Earth Day

Tornado Leaves Hundreds Homeless

A Delicate Balance

When you have finished, compare notes with a classmate. Be sure to question inferences that you do not believe are accurate. What can you learn from each other?

Use the same process with the bottom photograph of urban Cape Town, South Africa. How do your notes and those of your classmate about the photograph differ? How can you account for the differences? Discuss these questions with a classmate.

You are now ready to tackle an analysis of human-environmental interaction in ancient Egypt and the Valley of the Nile. You will be re-reading Lesson 1 in this chapter and making notes.

Before you begin, examine the map of the area on page 39 or on page 44. You might want to draw a free-hand map of the course of the Nile for your note making, using the river as the divider between "Humans Affect the Environment" on the west bank of the river and "The Environment Affects Humans" on the east bank of the river. If not, simply divide a sheet of paper lengthwise and label each half.

Remember to note first what you actually read or see in photographs from Lesson 1. Then note your inferences. When you have finished, discuss your work with a classmate. Again ask why you might have different notes.

To extend your understanding of human-environmental interaction in the Nile River valley, skim Chapter 6 on contemporary North Africa. How have the patterns of human-environmental interaction changed over time? Why do you think they have changed in these ways?

Sahara Desert

Ivory Coast village

Cape Town, South Africa

Historical Foundations of Africa

57

Discussion Questions

1 Apply this process of analyzing human-environmental interaction to Native Americans in North Carolina before the arrival of the Europeans.

2 Reexamine the photographs in the skill lesson. What evidence do you find that the advance of science and technology helps humans change their environment? Explain.

 Skill Lesson Review

1. In ancient Egypt, which had more impact: humans on the environment or the environment on humans? *Important points: Students should take a position and support the position with reasons. The desert environment encouraged people to settle along the banks of the Nile; flooding of the Nile enabled Egyptians to grow surplus food. People, however, changed the environment with their farms, cities, and monuments.*

2. What does the phrase "living in harmony with the environment" mean to you? Where in Africa do you think there is most harmony with the environment? Explain. *Important points: Disturbing the environment as little as possible, taking from the environment only what is needed for life. Students should choose one place (area) in Africa and explain the choice.*

3. "A Delicate Balance" was one of the newspaper headlines used in this lesson. What does it mean? *Balancing the needs of people with the needs of the environment.*

4. Which skill is easier for you to use: inference or synthesis? Why do you think this is so? *Important points: Students should state a preference and explain why they prefer either inference or synthesis.*

5. Where in the world would you expect to find the most and the least evidence of human-environmental interaction? Why? *Important points: Students should choose two places or world areas and explain the choice. Note that the most evidence would likely be found in highly industrialized nations; the least evidence in harsh climates with sparse population.*

6. Apply this process of analyzing human-environmental interaction to one of the following ancient civilizations: a. Ghana b. Kush c. Zimbabwe. *Important points: Students should choose one of the three civilizations and analyze human-environmental interaction in that civilization, using detailed explanations. Note the importance of landforms, resources, and relative location.*

Talk About It

1. The yearly flooding of the Nile brought silt to produce rich soil. This helped Egyptian farmers grow more than enough for themselves and others.

2. The pharaohs ordered that pyramids be constructed for them when they died. Many items were buried with the pharaohs. The pyramids remain, and some of the symbols of power buried with the pharaohs also were preserved. The dry climate and the shifting desert sands that covered many of these monuments may have helped preserve them. The wetter climates of East and West Africa would likely have rotted any artifacts not made of stones or other hard substances.

3. Important points: Students should choose a civilization and give reasons for the choice. Note: We know about religion in Egypt because artifacts were preserved. Mali was a center of Islam.

4. Important points: Students should choose a position and support it with reasons. Note: The wealth of Ghana, Mali, and Songhai came from trade. Egypt depended on both its own agriculture and trade.

5. Important points: Students should support any explanation with reasons. Note: Trade routes changed; invaders took over; the readily available supply of gold dwindled.

6. Important points: Students should mention resources, government, religion, and economic activities. Great kingdoms can be built on agriculture or on trade. But for kingdoms to last, resources must last.

CHAPTER 3 REVIEW

Lessons Learned

LESSON 1
Early Civilizations
Egyptian civilization grew along the Nile. Surplus food raised on the fertile banks of the river allowed the Egyptian civilization to grow. Pharaohs were government and religious leaders of Egypt. The Kingdom of Kush was first dominated by Egypt, then developed as a trading center based in Meroë. The Kingdom of Axum succeeded Kush as a center of African trade with the Mediterranean. It became the heart of early Christianity in Africa.

LESSON 2
West African Kingdoms
West African kingdoms followed each other as the center for trade. First Ghana, then Mali, then Songhai developed as trading posts for the salt-gold trade. Mali and Songhai were important early centers of Islam. Both kingdoms encouraged the development of Timbuktu as a Muslim city.

LESSON 3
East African City-States and Zimbabwe
Winds blowing toward and away from the East African coast helped settlements along the Indian Ocean become market cities for trade with India, Arabia, and Persia. Mombasa, Sofala, and Kilwa grew as city-states that controlled trade from Africa. Great Zimbabwe grew as a trading center between inland gold mines of southern Africa and the coastal ports controlled by East African city-states.

58

Talk About It

1. How was Egypt "the gift of the Nile"?
2. Why did the Egyptian civilization leave more remains or artifacts than those of West Africa or East Africa? Explain.
3. In which ancient civilization do you think religion was most important? Explain.
4. Was trade more important for West African civilizations than for Egypt? Explain.
5. Why do you think these ancient African civilizations rose and then fell? Give as many reasons as you can.
6. What might later civilizations have learned from Egypt? from Great Zimbabwe?

Mastering Mapwork

HUMAN-ENVIRONMENTAL INTERACTION

Use the map on page 39 to answer these questions:
1. On this map of early civilizations, what features indicate human-environmental interaction?
2. Which area depicted on this map shows the least evidence of human-environmental interaction?
3. Using only the information on this map, which of these—the Nile River or the area around Timbuktu—would indicate more evidence of human-environmental interaction? Explain your answer.
4. What evidences of human-environmental interaction would you expect to observe along the trade routes depicted on this map?
5. How might evidence of human-environmental interaction differ in Timbuktu and Zanzibar?

Mastering Mapwork

1. Trade routes, cities, the boundaries of kingdoms and city-states.

2. The area of Central Africa lying north of the Congo (Zaire) River and south of 15°N latitude.

3. Important points: Students should choose one area and support the choice with evidence taken from the map. Note the number of trade routes and the areas they cover.

4. In general, one would expect to observe tracks left by humans and animals; perhaps one would observe camping spots from overnight stops by traders or even villages that had grown up to serve the needs of traders passing by. One would also be likely to observe deforestation, as trees would have been cut for firewood.

5. Timbuktu is located in a fairly arid region of West Africa; Zanzibar is located in East Africa on the Indian Ocean. Evidences of human-environmental interaction would differ because of Timbuktu's location on overland trade routes and available vegetation and building materials, and because of Zanzibar's location on oceangoing trade routes. In Zanzibar one would expect to observe warehouses and docks to accommodate oceangoing trade.

  **Go to the Source**

Reading Ancient Writings

Ancient Egyptians wrote many things, from religious texts to love poems, using hieroglyphics. These writings give historians information about everyday life in ancient Egypt.

Read this excerpt from the Autobiography of Bekenkhonsu. Answer the questions using specific references to the document.

Hereditary prince, count, High Priest of Amon, Beknekhonsu, triumphant; he says:

I was a truthful witness, profitable to his lord, extolling the instructions of the god, . . . performing the excellent ceremonies in the midst of his temple. I was chief overseer of works in the house of Amon, satisfying the excellent heart of his lord. O all ye people, take account in your hearts; ye who are on earth, who shall come after me, in millions of millions of years . . . I will inform you of my character while I was upon earth, in every office which I administered, since my birth.

I passed four years in extreme childhood.

I passed twelve years as a youth, while I was chief of the training stable of King Menmare.

I acted as priest of Amon, during four years.

I acted as divine father of Amon, during twelve years.

I acted as third prophet of Amon, during fifteen years.

I acted as second prophet of Amon, during twelve years.

He favoured me, he distinguished me, because of my rare merit. He appointed me to be High Priest of Amon during twenty-seven years.

I was a good father to my serf-laborers, training their classes, giving my hand [to] him who was in trouble, preserving alive him who was in misfortune, performing the excellent duties in his temple. I was chief overseer of works before Thebes for his son, who came forth from his limbs, King Ramses II, given life, maker of monuments for his father, Amon, who place him on his throne.

. . . I performed the excellent duties in the house of Amon, being chief overseer of works of my lord. I made for him a temple (called) Ramses-Meriamon-Hearer-of-Petitions, at the upper portal of the house of Amon. I erected obelisks therein, of granite, whose beauty approached heaven. . . .

_____

Questions

1. Why would Beknekhonsu have wanted these details of his life written on his tomb?
2. Today we learn the details of a person who has recently died in an obituary. What parts of Beknekhonsu's life were omitted?
3. What does this reveal about life as a priest in ancient Egypt?

Go to the Source (side tab)

Historical Foundations of Africa

59

 **Go to the Source**

OBJECTIVES: 3.03; Skills 3.05, 4.06

The entire inscription of the "The Autobiography of Bekenkhonsu" is available online (link found at **NCJourneys.com**).

After the age of four, Bekenkhonsu was educated as a noble for 12 years. During the last years of the reign of Seti I Menmare, Bekenkhonsu became a priest. He served Amen for 43 years, and then was appointed First Prophet by Ramses II. This was one of the most powerful positions in the country. He died at the age of eighty-six, which was unusual.

ANSWERS

1. Important points: Students should give reasons why a person in Beknekhonsu's position in society would want to list his accomplishments. Because the ancient Egyptians believed in an afterlife, the priest might be listing his accomplishments in order to have more status in his afterlife. Perhaps the more one did in the name of Amon, the better one's afterlife.

2. He reveals that he lived a long life (86 years) and that he served as a priest and an architect or builder. Lacking are personal details such as marriage and children. This might mean that priests did not marry or that marriage and family were not important enough to mention.

3. Important points: Answers should reflect one or more of the aspects or roles of authority, responsibility, self-discipline, or spirituality. Answers may also describe how ancient Egyptian priests differ from religious leaders today.

 How to Use the Chapter Review

There are three sections in the Chapter Review: Talk About It, Mastering Mapwork, and Go to the Source. Use the Vocabulary Worksheets and the Chapter Review Worksheet in the Teacher's Resource Guide for additional reinforcement and preparation for the Chapter Assessments. The chapter and lesson reviews and the Chapter Review Worksheets are the basis of the assessment for each chapter.

Talk About It questions encourage students to speculate about the content of the chapter and are suitable for class or small-group discussion. They are not intended to be assigned for homework.

Mastering Mapwork has students apply one or more of the Five Themes of Geography to maps within the chapter.

Go to the Source activities allow students to analyze a primary source that relates to the content of the chapter. The questions and activities familiarize students with different types of primary sources and also build content-reading skills.

A Diversity of People and Lands

Social Studies Strands

Cultures and Diversity
Families
Traditions
Ways of living
Religions

Individual Developmental Identity

North Carolina Standard Course of Study

Goal 3 The learner will analyze the impact of interactions between humans and their physical environments in Africa, Asia, and Australia.

Goal 10 The learner will compare the rights and civic responsibilities of individuals in political structures in Africa, Asia, and Australia.

Goal 11 The learner will recognize the common characteristics of different cultures in Africa, Asia, and Australia.

Goal 12 The learner will assess the influence of major religions, ethical beliefs, and values on cultures in Africa, Asia, and Australia.

Teaching & Assessment

- English Language Learner Modified Lesson Plans for this chapter are found in the Teacher Resource Guide.

- *ExamView® Assessment Suite* is provided at **NCJourneys.com.** It includes customizable assessments for all chapters. Paper tests are also available in the Teacher Resource Guide. See pages T16–T17 for information about how to use the assessments and the Scoring Guide.

Worksheets

Worksheets and answer keys are found both in the Teacher Resource Guide and at **NCJourneys.com**, including Reading Guides, Reading Strategies, Chapter Reviews, English Language Learner and others.

ACTIVITIES AND INTEGRATIONS

SOCIAL STUDIES

Linear Descent Chart, p. 60b
▲ ■ Differing Values, p. 60b
Activator: *The Village of Round and Square Houses,* p. 60
● Is this Economy Primary, Secondary, or Tertiary, p. 61
★ ■ Family Activities, p. 63
● Village Markets, p. 64
Symbols with New Meanings, p. 72
★ Distinguishing African Beliefs, p. 75
Skill Lesson: Using Geography's Themes: Place, p. 76

READING/LANGUAGE ARTS	READING/LANGUAGE ARTS OBJECTIVES
Analogies, p. 60b	2.01
Writing Prompt: Family Jobs, p. 60	3.03
★ Ashanti to Zulu Jigsaw, p. 62	1.01
■ Family Responsibilities Cinquain Poem, p. 63	5.02
▲ Talk to an Ancestor, p. 72	1.02
Creative Writing, p. 68	5.01, 6.01
Go to the Source: Understanding Myths, p. 79	2.01, 4.01, 5.01, 5.02

MATHEMATICS	MATHEMATICS OBJECTIVES
Grain Farmer Math Problem, p. 71	1.02, 2.02

TECHNOLOGY	TECHNOLOGY OBJECTIVES
★ ■ Family Activities, p. 63	2.05, 3.01
● Oral Traditions and Folktales, p. 73	2.05
★ Distinguishing African Beliefs, p. 75	1.16, 2.05

VISUAL ARTS	VISUAL ARTS OBJECTIVES
● Yoruba Headress, p. 60b	1.01, 5.01
Dahomey Wall Hangings, p. 65	4.01, 5.01
Symbols with New Meanings, p. 72	1.01, 2.03
African Traditions Booklet, p. 74	4.01, 4.02

CHARACTER AND VALUES EDUCATION	TRAITS
Writing Prompt: Family Jobs, p. 60	responsibility, respect, good judgment, self discipline
What Would You Do?, p. 63	respect

● Basic Activities ★ Challenging Activities ▲ English Language Learner Novice ■ English Language Learner Intermediate

Introductory Activity

Linear Descent Chart

OBJECTIVES: 9.01, 11.04, 12.01

Patrilineal and matrilineal descents are ways of defining families and sometimes leaders in African countries. Explain to students that the Ashanti group is one that traditionally uses a matrilineal descent. As a result, when the king dies, his son does not become king. It is the sister's son who becomes king. Have students complete a chart for their families. Use patrilineal and matrilineal lines. Have students show through these lines of descent who would be "king."

Extension Assign ELL students to define matrilineal, patrilineal, and descendant in their native language first using a native language dictionary. Use good modeling strategies to ensure that ELL students understand directions.

 Culminating Activity

Differing Values

OBJECTIVES: 4.01, 4.03, 8.02

Chapter 4 explores African values. As a class, complete the following questionnaire as it relates to Africa. To help compare African and American values, have students answer the questions about the United States with a parent or guardian for homework.

1. Why do people get married?
2. How do people decide on marriage partners?
3. When couples get married, with whom do they live?
4. Who usually pays for the wedding?
5. List possible family members (or those in your home). Beside each name write the responsibilities of each in the home.
6. How are the elderly treated?
7. What activities are provided for family members who live away from each other to get together?
8. Who usually makes the major decisions concerning money, discipline, and conflicts?
9. If there is a disagreement between two family members, how would it be solved?
10. Describe one family member's job.

Extension This is a good opportunity for ELL students to share some of their culture. Use the **WorldLingo** Web site (link found at NCJourneys.com) to translate the questionnaire. ELL students should answer it with their parents about their culture. Novices may draw a picture to share with the class for one answer on the questionnaire. Intermediates may read a few answers to the class.

 Art Activity

Yoruba Headdress

OBJECTIVES: 12.02

Materials construction paper or heavier card stock 24 inches by 14 inches, tempera paint, sponges, clear tape or glue, paintbrushes, pencils, rulers, scissors, practice paper, big flat trays for paint, newspapers

To make the design, cut sponges into nonrepresentational shapes: triangles, diamonds, rectangles, and so on. On practice sheet of paper create designs by repeating sponge prints. Create at least four designs for finished headdress. One dip in the paint will make multiple prints. Repeat best designs horizontally on a 14-inch by 24-inch sheet of colored construction paper. Create new designs/patterns with alternating colors and/or by combining shapes. Let it dry.

To make the headdress, fold the 24-inch side around student's head to fit. Mark where it needs to be taped or glued. If glue is applied, then hold for about 35 to 40 seconds before moving on. Cut five 2-inch slits at the top of the headdress. When gluing or taping, roll the paper into a slight conical shape. Tape or glue at the bottom. Round the cut pieces at the top so that they are meeting in the middle. Glue or use clear tape.

 Analogies

OBJECTIVES: 12.01

Analogies are useful to help students make associations with prior knowledge. They can be used as an instructional strategy to help students better understand new materials. They are not intended to be definitions or test items.

Read the analogies aloud and ask students to identify the relationship between the terms. As an extension, ask students to write their own analogies using key terms or places discussed in the chapter.

atom : compound :: nuclear family : extended family (is smaller than)

father : mother :: patrilineal : matrilineal (is opposite of)

chief and elders : village council :: mayor and council members : city council (serve in)

camels : desert :: cattle : East Africa (are raised in)

Islam : North Africa :: Christianity : South Africa (is found in/is the major religion of)

Teaching Strategies

Use an activator or introductory activity to introduce the chapter to the students. Emphasize the importance of tradition in African society. Tradition will be a recurring theme throughout the course.

Discussion Questions

1 What are some examples of special ways of rearing children and celebrating births and marriages in North Carolina?

Activator

OBJECTIVES: 11.01

Activators are great tools to use in order to "hook" the attention of the students. Reading stories builds interest in the subject.

The Village of Round and Square Houses by Ann Grifalconi. (Little, Brown, 1986. ISBN 0316328626.)

Summary The storyteller explains why the women live in round houses and the men live in square houses.

OR

Ask the students to brainstorm some traditions that their families practice, such as holidays, birthdays, or religious observances. Ask students to participate in a pair/share with a partner about their family traditions and then ask for volunteers to share some that are interesting. To give them a jump start, share one of your favorite traditions with the class.

Extension ELL students may draw pictures in place of the interview.

Writing Prompt

OBJECTIVES: 11.01, 11.02

Evaluative

Every person in a family has certain jobs and responsibilities. In your opinion, who in your family has the most important job? Explain your answer.

As you write or word process your paper, remember to

- name the person you believe has the most important job.
- give at least three reasons and explain them fully.
- give examples to support your reasons.
- write in complete sentences and paragraph form.
- organize your ideas and include an introduction and a conclusion.
- use good grammar, spelling, punctuation, and capitalization.

CHAPTER 4

Yoruba helmet mask

Chapter Preview

LESSON 1
Families and Villages
Africans have roles as members of their families and their villages.

LESSON 2
Traditional Ways of Life
Most Africans either farmed or herded. Those ways of life are still important.

LESSON 3
Religious Foundations
Traditional African religions include belief in a Supreme Being and respect for ancestors. Those traditions often mix today with Christianity and Islam.

Enduring Traditions

Wambui Njama, the bride, and Jomo Kimathi, the groom, are to be married in their Kenyan village. On the wedding day, Jomo's sisters, aunts, and female cousins will come to Wambui's home to take her to the ceremony (below). First they will fight a mock battle with Wambui's female relatives. Wambui and Jomo's Kikuyu (kih·KOO·yoo) people practice this tradition.

Each of Africa's thousands of ethnic groups has its own art (left), and special ways of rearing children, celebrating births and marriages, and sharing the sorrows of death. With such a wide variety of ethnic groups, patterns of living in Africa differ greatly.

Masai Wedding, Kenya

Chapter 4

Chapter Resources

Print Resources

Bedford-Pierce, Sophia. *African Proverbs.* Peter Pauper Press, 1962. ISBN 0880880252.

Courlander, Harold. *A Treasury of African Folklore: The Oral Literature, Traditions, Myths, Legends, Epics, Tales, Recollections, Wisdom, Sayings, and Humor of Africa.* Marlowe, 1996. ISBN 1569248168.

Golding, Vivien. *Traditions from Africa.*

Raintree Steck-Vaughn, 1999. ISBN 0817253823. Describes a variety of African traditions, including food, festivals, music, and toys.

Web Sites

Links to the following Web sites are found at **NCJourneys.com.**

- African Lives (Series of occasional articles from the *Washington Post* chronicles the joys and struggles in the everyday lives of

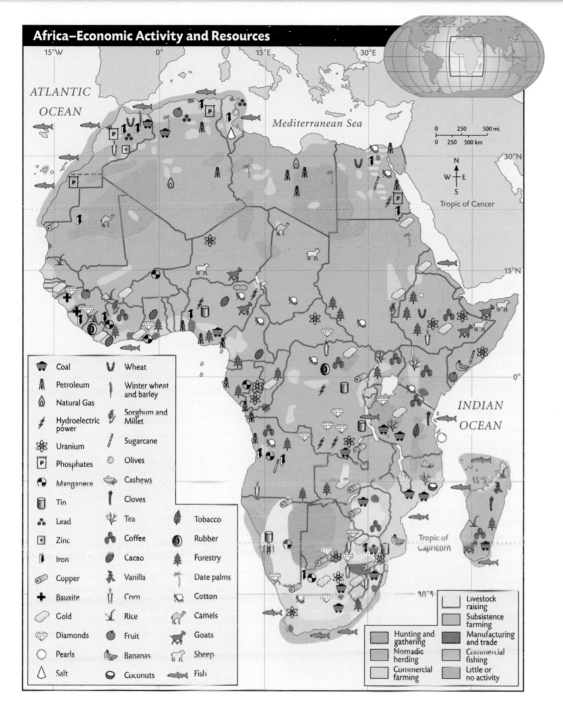

Africa–Economic Activity and Resources

15°W 0° 15°E 30°E

ATLANTIC OCEAN

Mediterranean Sea

0   250   500 mi.
0 250 500 km

Tropic of Cancer

30°N

15°N

0°

INDIAN OCEAN

15°S

Tropic of Capricorn

30°S

Legend:

Coal	Wheat
Petroleum	Winter wheat and barley
Natural Gas	Sorghum and Millet
Hydroelectric power	Sugarcane
Uranium	Olives
Phosphates	Cashews
Manganese	Cloves
Tin	Tea
Lead	Coffee
Zinc	Cacao
Iron	Vanilla
Copper	Corn
Bauxite	Rice
Gold	Fruit
Diamonds	Bananas
Pearls	Coconuts
Salt	

Tobacco	
Rubber	
Forestry	
Date palms	
Cotton	
Camels	
Goats	
Sheep	
Fish	

Livestock raising
Subsistence farming
Hunting and gathering
Nomadic herding
Commercial farming
Manufacturing and trade
Commercial fishing
Little or no activity

Enduring Traditions   61

Is This Economy Primary, Secondary, Tertiary, or Quaternary?

NATIONAL GEOGRAPHY STANDARDS: 1, 16

GEOGRAPHIC THEMES: Location, Place, Human-Environmental Interaction, Movement, Region

OBJECTIVES: 1.02, 5.01

Display the map transparency while students examine and speculate why some areas have "little or no activity" (desert, game reserves). Discuss that nomadic herding, hunting and gathering, livestock raising, commercial farming, subsistence farming, and commercial fishing are traditional economic activities that have existed in Africa since humans established cultures and exploration/colonization impacted these cultures.

Introduce students to primary economic activities (agriculture, mining). Examine and discuss why manufacturing and trade areas are so limited in Africa (developing economies are more primary than secondary). Introduce **primary activities**: those in which workers and the environment come into direct, active contact, that is, farming, fishing, mining; **secondary activities**: those in which workers take raw materials and produce something as a finished product, for example, manufacturing; **tertiary activities**: jobs promoting, distributing, selling, or using what is made from raw materials, for example, education, finance, office work, retailing; and **quaternary activities**: those responsible for collecting, processing, and manipulating information, that is, business management, or data processing.

Using map transparency, trace map onto shower liner or large sheet of paper. Collect symbols for each resource to tape (with double-sided tape) onto map, for example, a lump of coal, a stoppered vial of petroleum/gasoline/kerosene, a piece of copper wiring, a small plastic animal for cattle, or grapes from a craft store. Any resource that cannot be found should be illustrated with the chemical element symbol or drawn illustration. As resources are placed onto the map have students explain each symbol and whether activity or resource is primary, secondary, tertiary, or quaternary.

African peoples. Caution: Some details in articles may be unsuitable.)
- African Mythology, Encyclopedia Mythica (Includes short description of more than 100 names related to African mythology.)
- African Art and Rituals of Divination, Metropolitan Museum of Art
- Afropop Worldwide
- The Baobab Project, Harvard University
- The British Museum Africa Collection
- CK Ladzekpo - African Music and Dance

(Pictures, short descriptions, and music of West Africa—particularly drumming.)
- Dance Drummer (includes video clips of West African drums)
- Mint Museum, African Art Collection
- Museum of African Art
- National Museum of African Art
- North Carolina Museum of Art, African Art Collection
- Radio Africa

OBJECTIVES: 10.03, 11.01, 11.04

Discussion Questions

1 Give examples of ways in which different ethnic groups work together to create strong communities?

2 What are some of the advantages/disadvantages of arranged marriages?

3 Would arranged marriages be successful in our society today?

4 What are some traditional values that people in the United States share?

5 Do you think that the family is the cornerstone of American society?

6 Situation: You are the child of an immigrant family with a traditional background who has been raised in the United States. Your parents announce they have arranged a marriage for you. Describe your feelings.

 Caption Answer

It shows the groom is serious about marriage and can support a wife.

 Activity

Ashanti to Zulu Jigsaw

OBJECTIVES: 11.02

After reading *Ashanti to Zulu* by Margaret Musgrove (Penguin Putnam, 1980. ISBN 0140546049.), go through each page and ask the students to identify the elements highlighted in each illustration. The elements are usually a man, woman, child, their living quarters, an artifact, and an animal. Explain to the class that they will be given a tribe or region of Africa and will be required to find each of the six elements.

Divide the class into groups of four or five and assign a region or tribe for their research. Pass out a graphic organizer with one of the six elements listed in each grid (six squares). Instruct the students that they will be doing group work in the "jigsaw" manner, meaning each student will go and research, trying to find information on each of the six elements, and then the group will come back together

KEY IDEAS

- Marriage builds ties between families. Extended families of married children and grandchildren are important in African societies.

- African families trace their ancestry through either the father or the mother.

- All age groups play important roles in traditional village life. Elders govern those villages.

KEY TERMS

age grade
arranged marriage
bridewealth
elders
extended family
lineage
matrilineal
patrilineal

In many parts of Africa, especially south of the Sahara, a single country may be home to many different ethnic groups. As you have read, Nigeria's 131.5 million people belong to more than 250 different groups. Even small countries contain many groups. Togo has more than 40 ethnic groups. The people of Sierra Leone in West Africa are members of more than 18 ethnic groups.

With so many ethnic groups, customs differ. Yet like people everywhere, traditional values have helped Africans build strong communities, share joys, and withstand hardships.

Marriage and Family

The family is the cornerstone of traditional African society. Marriage is much more than a union between two people. It builds and strengthens ties between families.

The visiting and celebrating during Wambui and Jomo's wedding will continue for eight days. On the eighth day, Wambui officially becomes a member of her husband's family. Jomo's family celebrates the addition of Wambui to their family group and the linking of the two families.

In fewer and fewer African societies a marriage like the one between Wambui and Jomo would be an **arranged marriage.** In this type of marriage, parents decide whom their children will marry. Even in places where most marriages are arranged, some people will make their own choice of marriage partners.

In traditional African societies, marriages may include the giving of money, goods, cattle, or services by the husband to his new wife's family. This gift, called **bridewealth,** is usually given before the marriage to show that the groom is serious about marrying the bride and that he has the resources to support her. The payment also acknowledges that the bride's family is losing a valuable worker that the husband's family is gaining.

Extended Families

Traditional African families have several generations of relatives living together. Called an **extended family,** the group may include a husband and wife, their unmarried children, and some of their married children with their families.

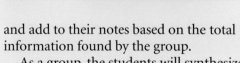

Cattle often are included in the gifts given by a new husband to his wife's family. **What is the purpose of this gift, called bridewealth?**

62

Chapter 4

and add to their notes based on the total information found by the group.

As a group, the students will synthesize the information and write six different paragraphs, one for each element, that will later be shared with the entire class. Before the presentations, make another graphic organizer with the six elements across the top of the page and each of the tribes or regions down the left-hand side of the page. Then, as each group gives its presentations, individuals at their desks can jot down highlights of each element.

To check for understanding, the students can be split into teams and given clues regarding a particular tribe or region. The points the team receives will be based on how many clues are given. For example, guessing the region/tribe after one clue will earn the team five points. However, if it takes the team four clues, then the team will earn one point.

Extension ELL students should use an ELL-friendly Web site for research. Peer tutors may assist the student in finding and completing the information.

Among Muslims, a man may have several wives. That custom is more common in West Africa than in East Africa.

Within the village, several generations may share a single house with many rooms. Others have smaller houses grouped in a common living area. Such living arrangements bring family members together every day.

Many Africans are moving into cities. As they move, members of their extended families remain behind. The crowded living conditions in cities do not make it easy for extended families to stay together. Africa remains a place where most people live in villages and traditions are strong.

Tracing Family Lineage

In African societies, every person belongs not only to a family but also to a much larger lineage group. **Lineage** is the term for tracing descent from a single ancestor.

In Africa, some ethnic groups trace a person's descent either through the mother's female lineage or the father's male lineage. A group that traces its descent through the father's family belongs to a *patrilineal* descent group. In a patrilineal descent group, sons and their wives and children remain a part of the father's extended family after marriage. When a daughter of the family marries, she joins the household of her husband.

Many West and Central African peoples, such as the Ashanti of Ghana, trace relationships through the female line. Tracing descent through the female line is called *matrilineal* descent. If you belonged to such a group, your family would include all your mother's children, your mother's sisters and their children, and your mother's brothers. Brothers are expected to play an important part in the upbringing of their sister's children.

Understanding who belongs to a family is important because of the tradition of putting the needs of the family

An extended family in Morocco includes grandparents, parents, unmarried aunts and uncles, and grandchildren. **How are extended families affected by more people moving to cities?**

before those of the individual. Individuals depend on their relatives for help. As long as a family member has food, shelter, or anything else to share, he or she is expected to share it with other family members.

Each family member has a duty to look after one another. Every member has responsibilities. A young child of age four or five is expected to look after younger sisters and brothers. Children of farmers will help with planting, harvesting, or caring for livestock. As adults, young people are expected to take care of their parents when they become old or sick. When parents die, their children give them a proper funeral and burial.

What would YOU do?

Because there are so many ethnic groups in Africa, thousands of languages are spoken. People resort to a single language at times for commerce, but there is no one single language in Africa. Do you think Africa needs one single language for communication? What would you recommend? Why?

 Research Activity

Family Activities

OBJECTIVES: 11.01

Have students research and prepare their own family trees. A good Web site to start with is Rootsweb (visit **NCJourneys.com** for a link) (Note that this activity may be problematic for adopted children. Have them research their adoptive parent's family trees.)

Have students interview an older family member about his or her life and the role he or she played in the family. They should write a paragraph describing what they learned in the interview.

Have students choose a role within their own family and write a poem explaining the importance of that role.

Extension Have ELL students use the **WorldLingo** Web site to translate the Web site for this activity. Novice students may draw a picture defining their role in their family and complete their interview in their native language. Intermediate students should write a simple paragraph in English about the interview.

Discussion Questions

1 In our culture, what might be used as bridewealth?

2 What are some advantages/disadvantages to living in an extended family?

3 In extended families, who is more important—the individual or the group? Why are the needs of the family put before the needs of the individual?

4 In the United States, why is there so much emphasis placed on the individual?

5 What are some responsibilities attached to being a family member? What responsibilities do you have as a member of your family?

6 In your community, what individuals other than your family play a part in your life? What are their roles?

 Caption Answer

Migration to the cities means the extended families are weakened. They often cannot stay together.

Writing Activity

Family Responsibilities Cinquain Poem

OBJECTIVES: 11.01

In African society, each family member has responsibilities and a duty to look after one another. Children help with younger siblings or help with farms or herds of animals. Children are also expected to care for their parents as they age. Have students think about the role they have in their family, as well as their responsibilities. They should write a cinquain poem explaining their role.

Cinquain: 5 lines:
2 syllables
4 syllables
6 syllables
8 syllables
2 syllables

Extension Assign novice ELL students to write five words to describe their role in their family. Intermediate ELL students should write a five-line poem. Give credit for incorrect attempts at matching syllables to pattern.

Eyewitness Activity

Village Markets

OBJECTIVES: 5.02

Help students achieve a better understanding of markets with one or more of the following activities:

- Create a village market in your classroom. Divide the students into small groups of two to four students. Assign each group a product to make for the market, such as jewelry, food, paper design (see Dahomey Wall Hangings activity, page 65), or other goods. Once the products are completed, invite another class or parents and administrators to visit your market and purchase the products. Students can also participate in the art of bargaining, and an economics lesson can easily be incorporated into the study of the village market.
- Have students complete a graphic organizer comparing the village market with a downtown shopping district, a "big box" store such as Wal-Mart, or a shopping mall.
- To give students a more personal view of the village market, read to your class *My Rows and Piles of Coins* by Tololwa M. Mollel (Clarion, 1999. ISBN 0395751861).
- After reading the Eyewitness account and hearing the story, ask students to write about something that they really want and to explain how they will earn money to buy it. For a class project, plan a field trip and have students brainstorm ways the class can earn money to pay for the trip. To make the project more meaningful, you should actually carry out the plans for raising the money and go on the trip.

Extension ELL students should be able to do all but the writing portion of this activity.

EYEWITNESS TO HISTORY

Village Markets

Bright-eyed women guard their wares at the market. Young children run yelling and playing. Older youth call out the rates of the day's prices all over town. In ancient times and today, the open-air market has been a center of African village life.

Camel market, Cairo

In North Africa, indigo blue cloth caught the attention of European explorers. Moroccan leather and Berber carpets found their way to Mediterranean marketplaces.

Goods were sold in great marketplaces in Timbuktu, Zimbabwe, Sofala, Mombasa, and Mogadishu. Smaller local markets kept villages alive. Women sold crops from their gardens or cloth from their looms. Herders sold hunks of cheese or baby goats. Camel merchants met at distant oases.

Brass ankle ornament

As trade developed between regions, the smaller markets sold more kinds of jewelry, tools, livestock, and crops. Not only were woven cotton cloth and colorful cotton threads sold, but also dyed wool. Gleaming jewelry of brass, gold, silver, and copper appeared from locked boxes.

Chapter 4

Market in Banjul, Gambia

An ancient traveler might still recognize today's marketplaces. The noise, lively confusion, and smells are not too far removed from the past. Many of the food, crafts, and art look the same. Today, fresh vegetables bring an earthy smell to the air of Zinder, Niger. Camel merchants still meet at oases. Merchants wait for buyers to purchase colorful food containers made from calabashes (gourds) and copper.

Kente cloth

Vendors also sell blue jeans, sneakers, and T-shirts alongside traditional kente cloth, a fabric of original African design.

Market in Kano, Nigeria

Enduring Traditions

65

Art Activity

Dahomey Wall Hangings

OBJECTIVES: 12.02

In the West African country of Benin, talented craftsmen design and make Dahomey wall hangings, once a royal art form, to sell to tourists. Students may experience this art form by making their own Dahomey wall hangings out of paper. For samples of this art form, visit the online gallery of Ralph Proctor Gallery (link found at **NCJourneys.com**).

Materials black construction paper, colorful construction paper, glue, scissors, thin black markers

Design and cut out traditional African shapes and symbols from the colored construction paper. Arrange the shapes on the black construction paper and glue them in place. Use the markers to add detail. You can also add marks around each symbol to represent stitches. Once they are complete, hang them around the classroom to use as decorations.

Extension Ask African ELL students if anyone can bring in a real one to share with the class.

It's a Fact

African Society

■ Many African societies transmit their early histories orally. In West Africa the oral historians are called griots. Training to become a griot begins early, around the age of five. It is not uncommon for a griot to be able to recite a village's history going back 300 to 400 years, reciting villagers' names and family occurrences.

■ In many parts of Africa, family members will intervene in the domestic affairs of married couples to resolve conflict. In some cases, marriages will be dissolved if no children are involved.

65

Discussion Questions

1 Does the well-known African proverb that says "it takes a village to raise a child" have any consequences in today's society?

2 Do you think we put too much or not enough responsibility on young people today? Why?

3 What rites of passage do we celebrate as children grow into adulthood?

4 What are some responsibilities young people in your age grade should accept?

5 What organizations/institutions in our society help build strong bonds of loyalty and support?

 **Caption Answer**

Young people keep traditions, share ceremonies of celebration within their group, and work together.

Building Community in the Village

A well-known African proverb says "It takes a village to raise a child." This saying suggests the shared responsibility that villagers feel for one another. Villagers play an important part in each other's daily lives.

In some African societies, the process that trains young people to become leaders in their villages begins with the **age grade** system. In this system, young people are divided into groupings of boys and girls of about the same age.

Every age grade has responsibilities. When an age grade is young, the children might be responsible for keeping village paths cleared and cleaning the markets for market day. As the children grow older, they might take on a larger project, such as building a school or library.

Aboure-Ashanti girls walk to a dance festival in the Ivory Coast. **How do you think the age grade system helps keep such traditions alive?**

Those of the same age grade also share ceremonies marking the move from one age grade to another. These shared experiences build strong bonds of loyalty and support that last a lifetime.

Among the Ibo of Nigeria, men in the thirties and forties age grade serve as an informal police force. They enforce rules laid down by the **elders,** respected older leaders who make laws for the village. When they are in their fifties, they become the elders. Those men in an age grade sixty and over serve as judges. They settle conflicts and punish lawbreakers.

During their years together, Ibo age-mates build strong ties. When a member of their age grade dies, the others often aid in the support or schooling of his children. Ibo women also belong to age grades. Women take part in community-service projects, and they sometimes assume political roles in the community.

Chapter 4

 Background Information

Working Together

Among some African peoples, polygamy, having more than one wife, is an accepted practice. The wives develop close relationships and support one another in daily duties. A new wife is welcomed as an extra helper. Among the Masai in Kenya, each wife lives with her children in her own house and the husband divides his time equally among wives. The duties of the wives include child care, cooking and feeding the family, and milking the herds. Among the Ewe in Ghana and Togo, the husband as well as each wife has a separate house. For the Hausa of Nigeria polygamy is an accepted Muslim practice and a symbol of prestige. Having more than one family is seen as a sign of wealth.

Governing the Village

Rule by elders is a common system of governing in rural Africa. Respect for age, a central value of many African societies, is reflected in this Masai (ma·SIGH) saying: "In the beginning we are foolish, but with experience we become wise." Elders pass on the beliefs and customs of their culture. The high value put on their teaching is expressed in the Yoruba (YOR·uh·bah) saying: "The young cannot teach tradition to the old."

Village councils led by chiefs and elders encourage villagers to solve problems cooperatively. Leaders try to persuade others to see their points of view. Villagers often talk through a problem until everyone sitting in on the discussion agrees to a solution.

Village councils and other local forms of government were successful for centuries. They allowed many African villagers to live orderly and peaceful lives. Such ethnic groups as the Ibo and Yoruba consisted of many thousands of people who lived in loosely connected villages. Local village leaders maintained the safety and stability of these communities even

A Toposa village elder in Sudan addresses other villagers who have awaited his decisions and guidance. **What other roles do elders have in villages?**

when part of a larger governmental structure.

European colonists challenged the authority of village leaders. Modern African nations have claimed control over the villages, yet villagers still look to village elders for leadership.

Discussion Questions

1 Respect for elders is a central value of many African societies. What are some other important values in African society? What are some central values we have? Do you think any of these are changing?

2 What lessons, if any, can the young teach the elderly? What lessons, if any, can the elderly teach the young?

3 What is the purpose of government? What is its primary responsibility?

4 Problems and issues in some African villages are handled through persuasion. Why do national issues need to be handled differently?

5 Why do many villagers still have allegiance to the village rather than to the national government?

6 Why do you think many in African society hold such a high respect for age?

7 Does our society hold the same high regard for elders? Explain.

 **Caption Answer**

They settle arguments, make laws, and judge wrongdoing. They listen to the problems of the village.

LESSON **1** REVIEW

Fact Follow-Up

1. What is an arranged marriage? Who arranges it?
2. Describe an extended family.
3. What are patrilineal and matrilineal descents?
4. What is the purpose of the age grade system?
5. How have traditional villages been governed? How has village authority been challenged?

Talk About It

1. What are some advantages and disadvantages of arranged marriages?
2. Are families more important in traditional African society than they are in our society? Explain.
3. How do age grade groups contribute to strengthening family and community ties?
4. What rituals or rites of passage in the United States are similar to age-grade ceremonies?

LESSON **1** REVIEW

Fact Follow-Up Answers

1. In an arranged marriage, parents decide whom the children will marry.
2. An extended family includes several generations of relatives (perhaps including uncles, aunts, and cousins) living together. Such a family might include a husband and wife, their unmarried children, and some of their married children with their families.
3. In patrilineal descent, a group traces its descent through the males in the father's family. In matrilineal descent, a group traces its descent through the females in the mother's family.
4. The age grade system is a process that trains young people to become leaders in their villages. It keeps villagers learning together as they take on more responsibilities in their villages.
5. Traditional villages have been governed by elders. Village councils led by chiefs and elders encourage villagers to solve problems cooperatively. European colonists challenged the authority of village leaders. Recently, African nations have claimed control over the villages.

Talk About It Answers

1. Among the advantages are guarantees of family support for the young couple, a predictable future, and carrying on important family traditions. However, under the system of arranged marriages, young people do not choose their own mates, and marriages might not be based on love.
2. Important points: Students should take a position and support it with reasons. Note: African families provide financial as well as emotional support; responsibilities are owed by families to newlyweds as well as by the newlyweds to families; freedom of individuals may be more valued in the West.
3. The shared responsibility and ceremonies encourage trust and closeness, encourage young people to develop leadership, and teach them to share responsibilities and learn important traditions.
4. Important points: Students should give examples and support their choices. Note: Religious, sports, school, scouting, family or other traditions are possible examples.

 **OBJECTIVES:** 2.03, 3.01, 5.01

Discussion Questions

1 Can you think of a relationship for us that would be comparable to that of the Hausa and Fulani?

2 How do the Hausa and Fulani work together?

3 Why do farmers in Africa have several fields where no crops grow?

4 How important is agriculture in African society?

5 How have current farming practices in Africa hurt the environment? What are practices we use that help protect the environment?

6 What climate conditions in North Carolina are the same and/or different to those in Nigeria for farming? Are the roles of men and women in farming the same in Africa as they are in North Carolina?

 Caption Answer

Subsistence farmers are small farmers who produce enough for their own needs. Many farmers practice shifting agriculture, which means that they clear and burn brush, and use the ashes to fertilize the soil. When the soil is depleted, they move on to new land.

LESSON **2** Traditional Ways of Life

KEY IDEAS

- Many Africans still survive through small farming.
- The types of crops grown by African farmers depend on the climate.
- Herding is another traditional way of life in Africa.

KEY TERMS

shifting agriculture
subsistence farmers

The Hausa and Fulani peoples of West Africa have a long history of working closely in ways that help both groups. During the wet season, Hausa farmers grow such crops as sorghum and millet. During the dry season after the grain harvest, herds of cattle belonging to Fulani herders pass through the farmland.

Hausa farmers let the Fulani herders stay for days or weeks with their cattle grazing on the vegetation left in the fields after the harvest. The cattle dung fertilizes the fields. The soil becomes enriched and ready for planting. When the rains return, the Hausa replant. The Fulani return to pastures along the Niger River.

Agriculture

In Africa today, as in the past, farming is the main way for many people to make a living. Soil, climate, and water resources have always influenced the ways Africans farm.

Subsistence Farming

Where there has been enough rainfall, people have lived in villages, raising crops on the fields surrounding their homes. Most are small farmers, sometimes called *subsistence farmers,* who produce enough food for their own needs. They may have a small field with corn or wheat and a garden with vegetables. They may also own chickens, cows, or goats. Farmers sell any excess produce in the local market or trade it for other goods.

African farmers often practice *shifting agriculture.* They clear and then burn trees and brush from fields near their village. The ashes fertilize the soil. Three or four years later the soil loses its fertility and the land is abandoned. Farmers shift

A farmer in Angola works the fields. **What does it mean to be a subsistence farmer? How do farmers deal with poor soil?**

68

Chapter 4

 Writing Activity

Creative Writing

 **OBJECTIVES:** 2.01

After reading the legend on page 26 and listening to additional African legends such as *A Story, A Story* by Gail E. Hailey (Atheneum, 1988. ISBN 0689712014.),

African Folk Tales by Hugh Vernon-Jackson (Dover, 1999. ISBN 0486405532.), or *The Fire on the Mountain and Other Stories from Ethiopia and Eritrea* by Harold Courlander (1995. ISBN 0805036520.), ask students to identify a landform in Africa and make up a legend that might explain its origin.

their crops to new fields created in the same manner. If the old fields regain their fertility, they will be farmed again. Population growth is making it harder to practice shifting agriculture because less and less land is available for farmers. The quality of the land is very poor.

The work roles of African farmers vary by ethnic group and time of year. Muslim customs prevent some women from working outside. Yet sub-Saharan women do much of the farming. They grow nearly three quarters of the food. They plant, weed, and harvest crops. They prepare and cook food. They often sell their raw or cooked foods in the marketplace.

Types of Crops

Farmers in different parts of Africa grow crops suited to their environment (see map, page 61). Crops vary by climate and vegetation zones. In the mild climates of northwestern and southwestern Africa, farmers raise grapes, olives, and figs along with winter wheat and barley.

Yams, corn, millet, and sorghum are major food crops in the grasslands of the drier savanna. In Nigeria in West Africa, yams are the basic food of the Ibo. Traditionally, the Ibo grew yams and other root crops in gardens surrounding their homes. They planted oil palms and other trees near the gardens.

Some farming takes place in the oases of the Sahara. Farmers are limited in their choice of crops because their land receives such little rainfall in a year. They must irrigate their crops. Oasis dwellers of the Algerian Sahara grow date palm trees. Deep roots allow these trees to obtain water and survive high temperatures.

Oasis farmers nourish the palm trees with well water. They use a method hundreds of years old. A donkey or camel is harnessed to the balancing arms of a rope-and-pulley arrangement, called a shaduf, which is attached to a well. The

animal methodically goes around and around in a circle, moving the pulley ropes to raise buckets of water from deep in the ground. The squeaking of the shaduf's balancing arms echoes through the oasis all day long.

Farmers plow terraced fields in the mild climate of Madagascar (mad·ah·GAS·car). Zebu cows graze on land where rice and wheat have been harvested. **How does climate affect farming in other places in Africa?**

WORD ORIGINS

The **yam**, a starchy tuber similar to a sweet potato, is one of the most common vegetables grown and eaten in Africa. Many West Africans eat yams at nearly every meal. The word probably comes from the Fulani (FU·lah·nee) word nyami, which means "eat."

Discussion Questions

1 What part do women play in farming?

2 According to the text, how are Africans able to farm even in areas such as the Sahara?

3 By using the information in the photograph, what evidence is there to support the idea that this is a traditional society?

4 How has climate affected the lifestyles of people in Africa?

5 How does climate affect the agricultural products we have in the various regions of North Carolina?

6 How could farming in Africa change with the use of technology that we have in the United States?

Caption Answer

Crops vary by climate and vegetation zones. Much depends on available rainfall. Farmers in drier or desert climates may use other means to water plants. Northeastern and southeastern African farmers grow grapes, olives, and figs; farmers in the grasslands grow yams, corn, and millet; oasis dwellers of the Algerian Sahara grow date palm trees.

Discussion Questions

1 How would your life be different if you had to migrate according to the seasons? What possessions would you value?

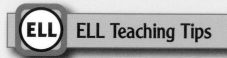

ELL Teaching Tips

Use the Cultures in Your Classroom

Tie the cultures of your ELLs to your lesson. These children with diverse backgrounds have stories and experiences that are unique. Teachers should build on the background knowledge and cultures their students bring from their home countries.

Herders

Herding—raising animals and protecting them while they graze—has been an important way of life in Africa. Wherever rainfall has been too little or too uncertain or the soil has been too poor for farming, the people have herded livestock. In areas with more rainfall, herders often raise cattle. In drier regions, they are more likely to keep sheep, goats, or camels.

In North Africa, the Tuareg in southern Algeria raise camels, sheep, and goats. They are often nomadic, moving from their homes to fresh grazing land. In ancient times, the Tuaregs also made their living by trading. They benefited from the trans-Saharan trade in gold and salt.

South of the Sahara in the Sahel and savanna, land is used by cattle herders. In the savanna, many herders do not continually move from place to place. Instead, they migrate once from their dry season grazing grounds along a swamp to their wet season ones on higher ground. Some might settle in one spot, such as a place near a river. Sometimes groups divide so that their animals may more easily find grass.

CONNECTIONS · GEOGRAPHY & LANGUAGE ARTS ·

Stories and Poetry About the Land

Stories and poems tell us about a people and their land. In the poem *In the Field*, A. R. H. Attah of Ghana paints a picture of a woman farming:

You are always in the field
Carrying
Loads on the head
A baby asleep on the back
Pounding
Clearing
Tilling
My mother, you are always working
So much that I can't even tell the
Difference
Between You and the fields
What a strange beauty.

The narrator knows the importance of land and farming and how hard his mother works in the fields.

In Africa, the oral tradition, or telling of poetry and narrative, has a long history. For a people on the move, such as a nomadic group following a herd, oral storytelling was a way to keep alive the stories and the situations that created them.

An Ethiopian proverb states that "When the heart overflows, it comes out through the mouth."

Maybe folktales remain popular in Africa because they give expression to strong emotions.

Folktales were often told around the fires and on journeys. One story of the Ashanti tells about a farmer who leaves his field because his yam speaks to him. He meets a weaver who scoffs and then joins the farmer in running away. Why? His bundle of cloth speaks. The two men talk to a fisherman who laughs at them until his fishtrap says that hearing a yam speak is amazing.

The story ends with the men being told by their king to stop the foolishness and to go back to their work. The last words of the story are spoken by the king's footstool. We understand through this funny story that work rules, even during extraordinary happenings.

African folktales and poetry bring enjoyment to the people. Poems and stories reveal the daily life of the people to readers and listeners outside of that culture.

A woman pounding rice, Ivory Coast

Background Information

The Deadly Tsetse Fly

The tiny tsetse fly has had a tremendous impact on land use in parts of East, Central, and West Africa. In areas where the tsetse fly is prevalent, the land is uninhabitable for humans, horses, or cattle.

The insect carries a parasite that causes a deadly disease called nagana in cattle and horses and causes sleeping sickness in humans. The flies breed along lakeshores and riversides and in areas of moderate rainfall. Efforts to control it have included massive insecticide sprayings, radiation to sterilize male flies, the clearing of large land areas around villages, and the removal of villages to disease-free areas. Political instability has hurt control efforts.

A young Masai herder tends cattle in Kenya.
How does Masai culture reflect the importance of cattle to the people?

The Samburu and Masai of Kenya and Tanzania, and the Tutsi of Rwanda and Burundi raise cattle (see map, page 61). A milder climate makes this possible.

In some societies, livestock form a key part of social life. For example, among the Masai, cattle represent wealth and status. The more cattle a Masai owns, the greater his standing in the community. When a Masai child is five months old, he or she is taken to the cattle pen for a special name-giving ceremony. To the Masai, the cattle pen is a place of honor.

The Dinka herders of Ethiopia and Sudan do not eat the meat of their cattle. Milk and cheese are key parts of the Dinka diet. A nutritious drink is made from a mixture of blood drawn from the neck of a living cow and milk.

The cow provides the Dinka with other basic needs. Dung is used as fertilizer and dried as fuel for cooking fires. Sleeping mats, rain covers, and sandals come from hides and skins. The horns serve as scoops and containers.

LESSON 2 REVIEW

Fact Follow-Up
1. How do the Fulani and Hausa people work together?
2. What is subsistence farming?
3. Describe the role of women in traditional agriculture.
4. What crops are grown on traditional farms?
5. What animals are raised in herding areas?

Talk About It
1. Describe the relative location of subsistence farming and herding economies.
2. How does subsistence farming illustrate human-environmental interaction?
3. Which traditional economic activity contributes most to building strong community and family ties? Why?

Enduring Traditions

71

Discussion Questions

1 How does the use of cattle by the Dinka compare to the use of the buffalo by the Native Americans?

2 What impact would a drought have on a cattle-based society such as the Masai's?

3 What part does livestock play in the lives of many East Africans?

4 What crops in North Carolina require migratory workers?

 **Caption Answer**

Children are named at five months in a special ceremony that takes place in a cattle pen, a place of honor to the Masai.

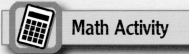 **Math Activity**

Grain Farmer Math Problem

OBJECTIVES: 3.01

A farmer is buying grain. He brings his own sacks to take the grain home. He brings a sack that is 2 feet tall, 6 inches wide, and 18 inches long. How many cubic feet of grain would this sack hold?

His other sack is larger. It is 3 feet tall, 1 foot wide, and 2 feet long. How much grain will it hold? Compare the volume of these sacks. What is the ratio?

Answer
1. 216 cubic feet
2. 864 cubic feet
3. 1/4

Extension Assist ELL students by setting up the problem for them.

LESSON 2 REVIEW

Fact Follow-Up Answers
1. Fulani herders pass through the Hausa farmland during the dry season. The Hausa let the Fulani stay because cattle that graze on the vegetation remaining from the harvest leave dung that fertilizes the farmland for planting.
2. Subsistence farming is small farming that produces enough food to meet the farmer's own needs. Sometimes there is a little left over to share, trade, or sell.
3. African women do much of the farming. They grow nearly three quarters of the food in Africa south of the Sahara. Women plant, weed, and harvest crops. They prepare and cook food, and sell raw or cooked food in the marketplace.
4. Traditionally, the crops grown—yams, corn, millet, and sorghum grown in grasslands areas—are those that feed families. Grapes, olives, and figs are grown in the northwestern and southeastern areas of the continent.

5. In North Africa, herders raise camels, sheep, and goats. South of the Sahara and in East Africa, herders raise cattle in areas free from tsetse flies.

Talk About It Answers
1. Farming areas are located in northwestern, western, and southeastern Africa. Herding areas are located in North Africa, in the Sahel and savanna areas south of the Sahara Desert, and in areas of West and East Africa where the tsetse fly is not a threat.
2. The farmers use the land in areas where rainfall is sufficient to raise crops to feed themselves. Subsistence farming generally takes animals out of the soil without replacing them.
3. Important points: Students should take a position and explain it. Note: Farmers usually stay in one place and so form ties with neighbors. Herders move constantly but have strong ties among themselves.

OBJECTIVES: 11.01, 11.03, 12.01

Discussion Questions

1 Why does Africa have so many different religious beliefs?

2 Although there are hundreds of religious beliefs, what are some common beliefs shared by most Africans?

3 How do traditional religions in Africa vary?

4 Do you think it is a strength or a weakness that Africa does not have a common religion? Why?

5 Why do the traditional (indigenous) religions put emphasis on nature?

6 Compare the traditional concept of the African belief in the Supreme Being to God in a monotheistic religion.

Caption Answer

The belief in a Supreme Being, in lesser gods and spirits, and in nature spirits.

Activity

Talk to an Ancestor

OBJECTIVES: 4.01, 8.01

Note Be aware that there may be students who have suffered recent deaths in their families.

The Swazi of South Africa have unique relationships with their ancestors; they speak of them and to them as if they were alive. Have students first talk with parents and/or grandparents, then choose a not-too-recent ancestor to "talk to." (Note: If students have difficulty identifying an ancestor, have them create a "fictional" ancestor to "talk to.")

In a paragraph, students should write about the deeds or actions of a chosen ancestor. On what occasion would this occur? In a second paragraph, students will include three questions for the ancestor to answer. Remind students that they will someday be someone's ancestor. Have them write in a paragraph what deeds or actions they hope their descendants will say about them.

Extension Assign novice ELL students to draw themselves talking to an ancestor. Intermediate ELL students should illustrate their deeds or actions.

LESSON ③ Religious Foundations

- Traditional African religions hold beliefs in a Supreme Being and lesser gods who are related to specific activities.

- Respect for ancestors is an important part of traditional African religions.

- Christianity and Islam are widely practiced in Africa and are influenced by traditional African religions.

KEY TERMS

ancestors

Africans developed rich religious traditions long before the coming of Islam and Christianity. African Christians and Muslims often kept many of those traditions, even as they practiced their new faiths.

A young Christian couple travels from the city where they live to their home village whenever they are ill. A traditional healer there calls upon the spirit world to cure sickness. A Muslim fisherman who prays to Allah five times each day also sacrifices a chicken to the spirit of the river to guarantee a good catch.

Traditional African Religions

Africa has never had a single religion. Because of the continent's many ethnic groups and great size, there are hundreds of different religious beliefs (see map, page 75).

Traditional African religions do share some beliefs. Most believe in a Supreme Being who created all the world. This Supreme Being does not actively direct what happens in the world. Other lesser spirits listen to and pass on the concerns of humans to the Supreme Being.

From one ethnic group to another, the lesser gods and spirits that surround the Supreme Being vary in number and in their roles. Nature spirits such as trees, rivers, and wind can bring good luck or bad. Illness or other troubles may be because someone has behaved badly, making one of the spirits angry.

The Yoruba name for the Supreme Being is Olorun. The Yoruba believe in more than 400 other spirits, including gods of

African art, such as this Yoruba headdress from Nigeria, is used in traditional religious rites. **What belief do most traditional religions hold in common?**

72

rain, forest, and sea. The Yoruba call these lesser spirits *orishas* (oh·rish·ahz). The Yoruba believe the orishas assist Olorun. Orishas have names and special roles among humans. Oya is the goddess of the Niger River.

Certain spirits are associated with particular occupations or needs. Before going out to fish, fishermen will ask the sea god to keep them safe and ensure a good catch. Although the Yoruba do not worship Olorun directly, they often end their prayer to the lesser gods with the words "May Olorun accept it."

Among the Kikuyu of East Africa, Mount Kenya is a sacred mountain. Early European explorers who observed Kikuyu men and women facing the mountain thought the Kikuyu were praying to the mountain. In fact, the Kikuyu were praying to the spirits of their ancestors, not the mountain.

Ancestors are both family members who have recently died and those who died in the distant past. Ancestors hold a special place in African religions. Ancestors are recalled in stories and songs that explain how people are related to one another through the generations.

Followers of African religions believe that when a person dies, he or she becomes a spirit with powers greater than the living. When a relative dies, his or her spirit continues to be involved in the life of the community. Ancestors connect the Supreme Being with relatives still alive.

Chapter 4

Art Activity

Symbols with New Meanings

OBJECTIVES: 4.03, 12.02

Materials potatoes or synthetic sponges, black tempera paint or acrylic paint, and T-shirts

Students should design symbols related to religious cultures and beliefs studied in Chapter 4. Use the new symbols to create new descriptions of traditional African beliefs. A discussion prompt: How helpful are symbols?

Extension Students can make stamps of their symbols. Stamps can be made with various materials. The easiest but least permanent are potato stamps, which can be painted with black tempera paint or textile dyes and printed on paper or cloth. Flat sheets of synthetic sponge can be cut into symbols and pasted onto wood blocks. Linoleum blocks can be carved by more advanced students. For a permanent design, use acrylic paint or oil-based painting ink. See your art teacher for assistance.

Groups of Ashanti attend a healing ceremony in a Ghana village. **How do healers help followers of traditional African religions?**

Ancestors understand the problems humans face and can protect their descendants or warn them when they are doing wrong or making a mistake.

In the religious life of the Swazi of South Africa, each family has special observances that remember the ancestors. Many of these take place at births, marriages, and deaths or during an important life change, such as moving into a new house. The Swazi do not worship their ancestors. The Swazi speak of them and to them as if they were alive. Their tone is not always respectful. They sometimes scold the spirits or question their actions.

In rural villages, when family members cannot understand why a loved one is stricken with illness, they might turn to a healer for help. Healers try to find the causes of problems through prayers, contact with the spirits, and herbal medicines.

Many members of the Zulu ethnic group in South Africa have converted to Christianity. Yet many continue to turn to healers to find the causes of misfortunes, such as a poor harvest or a serious illness. Typically, Zulu healers also use prayers and herbal medicines to solve these problems.

Christianity

Two major religions— Christianity and Islam—have many followers in Africa. About 85 percent of Africans belong to one of these two faiths. There are about the same numbers of Christians and Muslims.

Christianity first came to Africa through Egypt. Alexandria became a center of Christianity in the ancient world. Coptic Christians, an important denomination in Africa, descend from that early center of Christianity.

Throughout the rest of Africa, the earliest efforts to spread Christianity began when European missionaries followed European explorers into the interior of Africa. The missionaries translated the Bible into African languages. This contributed to the spread of the religion.

Since then, Christianity has found many converts among Africans. African Christians have created church services that reflect traditional African culture, including drumming and dancing. Africans have found creative ways to blend traditional religious practices with Christianity.

John Paul II visited Africa 14 times during his more than 26 years as pope of the Roman Catholic Church. **When and how did Christianity spread through Africa?**

Enduring Traditions

73

Discussion Questions

1 How do attitudes toward death in Africa differ from those in the United States?

2 Although ancestors in the United States are not as central to day-to-day life as they are in Africa, what evidence is there that they are still important here?

3 Compare/contrast the importance of ancestors in the African religion with those of the religions practiced in the United States.

4 Do we have healers in our society? Do they hold the same role as the healers of African religions?

5 Describe how Christianity spread through Africa.

6 In what ways have Americans included beliefs and customs from other cultures into their own?

 **Caption Answer**

Healers help people try to find the causes of problems through prayers, contact with the spirits, and herbal medicines.

Caption Answer

Christianity came to Africa through Egypt in ancient times.

 Research Activity

Oral Traditions and Folktales

OBJECTIVES: 4.03

Divide students into cooperative groups of two or three. Have them research African folktales and bring in the lists of ones they find. Then have each group read a different story. They must explain the meaning in a short paper. As an extension of this activity have students reenact their story or create a puppet show for the class. If you have an opportunity, videotape the stories and show them to younger classes. In addition to the Internet, anthologies of folktales from around the world are useful. Check your local library or a local college library for these anthologies.

Background Information

Religion in Africa

While noting that there are many exceptions, African scholar Jocelyn Murray has called Christianity and Islam religions of the cities. Traditional religions are usually closely tied to a specific area, a local or household shrine where reverence for a clan ancestor is shown, and a specific community of people. In urban areas people from many parts of the country mix. One of the strengths of both Islam and Christianity has been the ability of these world religions to bring together people from many different cultural and ethnic backgrounds.

Caption Answer

Islam came to Africa through North Africa over 1,000 years ago.

Activity

African Traditions Booklet

 OBJECTIVES: 1.01, 4.03, 11.01, 12.02

Materials four 8½ inch by 11-inch sheets of unlined paper; scissors; stapler/staples; colored pencils, markers, and crayons; rulers

Students will design a fold over or flap booklet including African traditions on family, villages, marriage, lineage, farming, herding, and religions.

The top fold must include the student's name with the title. With provided paper, students are to stack the three sheets so that the top edges are 1½ inches apart. Instruct students to fold up each bottom edge to create another 1½-inch-wide section. Finally have them staple twice along the bottom fold, and then turn the book so that the staples are at the top. Top title fold must be stapled to remaining pages so that page numbers show with each page's topic across the bottom of its page.

Have students use the textbook and other resources to illustrate one topic per page of their book. They should illustrate each topic. The booklets can be used for review and/or displayed.

Extension For ELL students, keep writing to a minimum; use peer tutors to help assemble the booklet as needed.

A mosque in Cairo is a sign of the presence of Islam in Africa. **When and where did Islam first come to Africa?**

Islam in Africa

Islam was founded in the seventh century in Arabia by the prophet Muhammad. This new faith spread quickly into North Africa. Within four centuries, most Egyptians had converted to Islam. Egyptian Christians had become a minority.

Islam spread from North Africa to other parts of Africa. South of the Sahara, Islam spread slowly. Muslim traders introduced Islam to West Africa, as they traveled south along the desert gold-salt trade routes. As you have read in Chapter 3, the rulers of Mali and Songhai accepted Islam and transformed Timbuktu into a center of Islamic culture. Arab traders settling in the East African coastal cities brought Islam to that part of Africa.

Islam did not require Africans to reject all traditional religious practices. Many African converts accepted such key practices of Islam as praying five times a day, fasting during the month of Ramadan, and making a pilgrimage to Mecca. They often ignored practices that did not fit local custom, such as the veiling of women.

Customs

Many Africans worship as Christians or Muslims. Those who do often include practices from local traditions. The owner of a new car may go to the elders of his village to ask for guidance from his ancestors. He may also ask for prayers to the god of iron. Finally, he may take his car to his church for the minister's blessing.

74

Chapter 4

Map Activity

Distinguishing African Beliefs

NATIONAL GEOGRAPHY STANDARDS: 3, 6, 10
GEOGRAPHIC THEMES: Location, Place, Movement, Region
 OBJECTIVES: 1.01, 11.03

In small groups, assign students to research and identify the major beliefs and characteristics of Christian denominations (Roman Catholic, Protestant, Eastern

Orthodox), Islamic sects (Sunni, Shiite), and traditional beliefs (shamanist, animism) found throughout Africa. Assign one group to research why Judaism is found in three main parts of Africa. Have students create a graphic organizer listing the major features they are to research. Have each group present its findings using visual aids (graphic organizers, multimedia presentation). Discuss as a large group why some areas of Africa would have "undetermined" religions.

Extension Intermediate ELL students should work in groups while novice students observe.

LESSON ③ REVIEW

Fact Follow-Up Answers

1. Most traditional African religions believe in a Supreme Being who created the world and in lesser spirits who listen to and pass on the concerns of humans to the Supreme Being.
2. Nature spirits such as trees, rivers, and wind can bring good luck or bad luck. Illness or other troubles may be the result of someone behaving badly and making one of the spirits angry.
3. Ancestors hold a special place in African religions. They are recalled in stories and songs that explain how people are related to one another through the generations. Ancestors are not gods but are believed to connect the Supreme Being with living relatives.

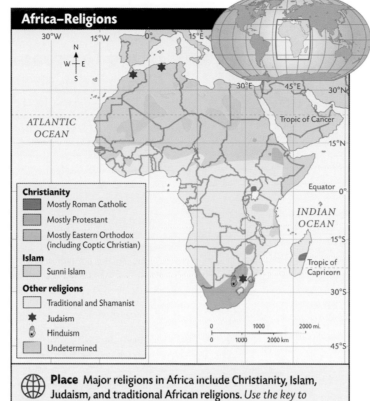

Africa–Religions

Christianity
- Mostly Roman Catholic
- Mostly Protestant
- Mostly Eastern Orthodox (including Coptic Christian)

Islam
- Sunni Islam

Other religions
- Traditional and Shamanist
- ★ Judaism
- Hinduism
- Undetermined

Place Major religions in Africa include Christianity, Islam, Judaism, and traditional African religions. *Use the key to locate the religions found in Africa.*

LESSON 3 REVIEW

Fact Follow-Up

1. Describe similarities in traditional African religions.
2. Describe the role of nature in traditional religions.
3. What place do ancestors hold in traditional religions?
4. How did Christianity spread to Africa?
5. How did Islam spread in Africa?

Talk About It

1. Why do forces of nature hold great religious importance in traditional African societies?
2. Why have Christianity and Islam gained followers in Africa?
3. How have African believers changed Christianity and Islam? Why did this happen?

Discussion Questions

1 How did Islam spread in Africa?

2 How have African believers changed Christianity and Islam?

3 Why are traditional religious practices incorporated into a new religion?

4 Why has Islam been accepted so readily in Africa?

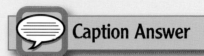 **Caption Answer**

Mostly Protestant: South Africa, Swaziland, southwestern Namibia, and northeastern Zimbabwe. Ethiopian Orthodox: Ethiopia

Mostly Roman Catholic: Madagascar

Mostly Sunni Muslim: all of North Africa; East Africa—northern Sudan, Somalia, north and eastern Ethiopia, central and eastern Tanzania; West Africa—Mauritania, Gambia, Mali, Niger, parts of Ivory Coast, Guinea, Guinea-Bissau, and Senegal; South Africa—northeastern Mozambique

Traditional and Shamanist: Southern Africa—South Africa, Botswana, Namibia, Angola, Zambia, Zimbabwe, Mozambique, Lesotho, Malawi, Swaziland; West Africa—Nigeria, Benin, Togo, Ghana, Ivory Coast, Liberia, Sierra Leone, Burkina Faso, and southern Mali; Central Africa—southwest Chad, Central African Republic, Zaire, Congo, Gabon, Equatorial Guinea, Cameroon; East Africa—southern Sudan, southwestern Ethiopia, Uganda, Rwanda, Burundi, Kenya, and Madagascar

Judaism: the cities of Algiers and Rabat in North Africa and Pretoria in South Africa

---

4. Christianity first came to Africa through Egypt. Alexandria was a center of Christianity in the ancient world. King Ezana brought Christianity to Axum, which later became Ethiopia. Later, European missionaries in the nineteenth century spread Christianity throughout the rest of Africa.
5. Islam first came to Africa through North Africa. Muslim traders introduced Islam to West Africa. Muslim traders settling in East African coastal cities brought Islam to that part of Africa.

Talk About It Answers

1. According to traditional religion, the forces of nature are spirits that assist the Supreme Being. Traditional farmers and herders depend on the bounties of nature and respect the nature spirits that can bring them luck or misfortune.
2. Both religions found ways to adapt to traditional African culture. Christians translated the Bible into African languages, for instance.
3. African Christians have created services with drumming and dancing, and blended traditional practices with the Christian religion. Many African Muslims accept the key practices of Islam but do not require women to be veiled. Converts to both religions wanted to keep their own cultures as well as the practices of the two religions.

Teaching This Skill Lesson

Materials Needed textbooks, maps, atlases, reference books, paper, pencils

Classroom Organization preferably pairs or small groups

Beginning the Lesson Review geographic themes of location and human-environmental interaction. Ask students to think about a favorite place, picture it in their minds, and jot down words to describe that place. Ask for a volunteer to describe a favorite place and make notes on the chalkboard. Then ask a question such as "Which of these was made by people and which was natural or made by nature?" Have students categorize the notes using natural and people-made as categories. Tell students that all places have both physical (natural) and cultural (made by people), or human, characteristics and that the physical and cultural characteristics are another of geography's themes.

Developing the Lesson Monitor as students complete a sketch of the chart on page 77, making sure they can distinguish between the physical and human characteristics of places. Help students choose three cities in different parts of Africa, referring them to cities named in Chapters 6 through 10. (Each student may choose different cities, though duplications are fine.) In class or for homework, have each student describe one of the cities in a web chart or data retrieval chart like the one on page 77. Monitor as students complete this task. Students may complete the assignment on the other two cities as an extended homework assignment.

Conclusion Have students write a short paper comparing location, human-environmental interaction, and physical and cultural (human) characteristics of place of the cities they have chosen. Students should use the standard format for writing descriptive and comparative paragraphs.

Extension As you introduce each of Chapters 6 through 10, ask students what they already know about these regions based on cities they have analyzed.

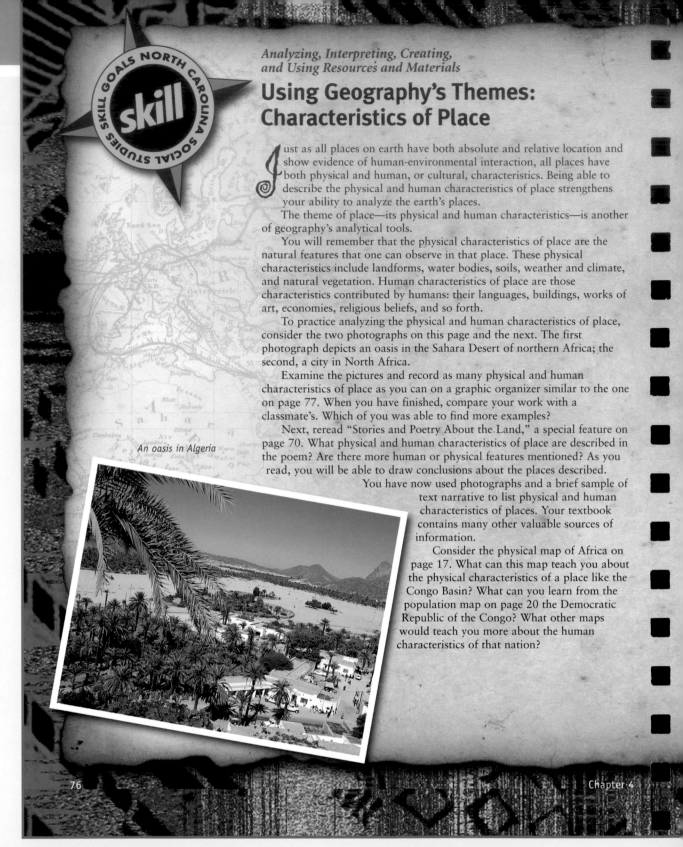

SKILL GOALS NORTH CAROLINA SOCIAL STUDIES

Analyzing, Interpreting, Creating, and Using Resources and Materials

Using Geography's Themes: Characteristics of Place

Just as all places on earth have both absolute and relative location and show evidence of human-environmental interaction, all places have both physical and human, or cultural, characteristics. Being able to describe the physical and human characteristics of place strengthens your ability to analyze the earth's places.

The theme of place—its physical and human characteristics—is another of geography's analytical tools.

You will remember that the physical characteristics of place are the natural features that one can observe in that place. These physical characteristics include landforms, water bodies, soils, weather and climate, and natural vegetation. Human characteristics of place are those characteristics contributed by humans: their languages, buildings, works of art, economies, religious beliefs, and so forth.

To practice analyzing the physical and human characteristics of place, consider the two photographs on this page and the next. The first photograph depicts an oasis in the Sahara Desert of northern Africa; the second, a city in North Africa.

Examine the pictures and record as many physical and human characteristics of place as you can on a graphic organizer similar to the one on page 77. When you have finished, compare your work with a classmate's. Which of you was able to find more examples?

Next, reread "Stories and Poetry About the Land," a special feature on page 70. What physical and human characteristics of place are described in the poem? Are there more human or physical features mentioned? As you read, you will be able to draw conclusions about the places described.

You have now used photographs and a brief sample of text narrative to list physical and human characteristics of places. Your textbook contains many other valuable sources of information.

Consider the physical map of Africa on page 17. What can this map teach you about the physical characteristics of a place like the Congo Basin? What can you learn from the population map on page 20 the Democratic Republic of the Congo? What other maps would teach you more about the human characteristics of that nation?

An oasis in Algeria

76

Chapter 4

Extension ELL students should draw a picture of their favorite place and label the physical and cultural characteristics after defining these terms in native language using a native language dictionary.

Finally, skim the appendix at the end of this book. What features in the appendix are good sources of information about the physical and/or human characteristics of place?

You will find that classroom resources and the media center can help you as well. For example, how can an encyclopedia be used to learn about place? What about an atlas or a resource like the World Almanac?

You have now used three of geography's five themes to analyze, organize, and describe places in Africa: location, human-environmental interaction, and place.

You may now understand enough of geography's tools to use them yourself. Choose three cities in different parts of Africa. Using the text, classroom resources, and materials in the media center, pull together data about location and place. Organize the data so it may be presented on a web chart, a data retrieval chart, or in an essay. The form in which you present your data is less important than demonstrating how well you can use geography's themes to do the following:

1. Find the places easily.
2. Compare human-environmental interaction in the three places.
3. Describe those three places.

Imagine that you are preparing this material for the members of your class. Here are some questions to help you begin collecting data for each theme.

Locating Africa How will you help your audience find the continent's relative location? absolute location?

Locating Three African Cities Which map will you ask your audience to use? Do you think that you should first give your audience the relative or absolute locations of the three cities?

Human-Environmental Interaction What two or three things best describe for each place (1) the environment's impact on the people and (2) the people's impact on the environment?

Place Again, what two or three things best describe for each city (1) its physical characteristics and (2) its human characteristics?

Mountain village in Morocco

Describing Two Places

	Physical Characteristics	Human Characteristics
Desert Oasis	1.	1.
	2.	2.
	3.	3.
North African City	1.	1.
	2.	2.
	3.	3.

Skill Lesson Review

1. How do physical and human characteristics of places change from place to place along the Equator? What are the most important causes of variety in physical characteristics? in human characteristics? *Elevation affects climate and temperature, even along the Equator. Population, and therefore human characteristics, is affected by climate and vegetation as well as by ethnicity and traditions.*

2. Which is of more use in explaining life in a traditional village: the physical or human characteristics of place? Why? *Important points: Students should choose explanation and explain it. Villages grow where climate and vegetation can support them, but traditional village life is shaped by human characteristics.*

3. How do the physical characteristics of a place influence its human characteristics? Explain with as many examples as possible. *Explanations*

should include the influence of physical characteristics on economic activity, on food production, on the ease of moving from one pace to another.

4. Which is easier for you to analyze: the physical or the human characteristics of a place? Why do you think this is true? *Important points: Students should state which is easier for them and explain why. Most physical characteristics can be read on a map. Human characteristics require more research.*

5. How does knowing about the physical and human characteristics of a place help you understand that area? *Descriptions of the physical and human characteristics of place give information on the environment within which people live and how they have altered it. Thus, these descriptions are useful in understanding the area.*

Talk About It

1. They began as economic arrangements and continue because they honor the tradition of the family as the most important social unit in African society.

2. The tradition of women working the land associates women with the territory and the village in some cultures. A connection with a certain area would thus be through women more than men. This might account for the development of matrilineal descent patterns.

3. Important points: Students should choose a position and explain that choice. Note: Africans blended some cultural traditions with Christianity.

4. Answers should emphasize the differences between working one area of land and roaming over a large territory with herds.

5. Finding city housing large enough for an entire extended family would be difficult. When extended families are living both in villages and cities, the ties between them tend to weaken.

6. Important points: Students should take a position and support it with reasons. Note: economic importance of children in traditional societies, importance of children as caregivers for the elderly.

7. Important points: Students should choose one idea and explain how that idea could help American society. Note: possible imports include village life, village councils, rule by elders, age grade system, family responsibility system.

8. In patrilineal societies, descent would be through sons, and the social, economic, and political positions of males might be higher. In matrilineal societies, descent would be through daughters, and the social, economic, and political positions of females might be higher.

9. Important points: Encourage students to suggest such examples as church youth groups, peer groups, and class and club organizations in schools. Organizations such as Boys and Girls Clubs, 4-H, and scouting might be mentioned. Lead students to state similarities and differences between these examples and the age grade system.

CHAPTER 4 REVIEW

Lessons Learned

LESSON 1
Families and Villages
In traditional African societies, marriages strengthen the ties between families. Every family member has a role to play in the family, which includes aunts, uncles, and grandparents. Village life is governed by elders who direct the activities of different age groups.

LESSON 2
Traditional Ways of Life
Many farmers in Africa are small farmers who often practice shifting agriculture. Crops differ according to the climate and landscape. Herding of cattle is another traditional activity. Some ethnic groups combine farming and herding.

LESSON 3
Religious Foundations
Religions in Africa include traditional practices of belief in a Supreme Being, lesser spirits connected to the natural world, and respect for ancestors. Christianity came to Africa through Egypt and was later spread by European missionaries. Islam came to Africa through North Africa and was spread through Muslim traders. The practice of both religions today includes a mix of traditional practices and the beliefs of those faiths. These faiths shape everyday life.

78

Talk About It

1. How have practices like bridewealth been important in traditional societies?
2. Is there any connection between the importance of women in agriculture and the development of matrilineal descent patterns? Explain your answer.
3. Is African Christianity more Christian or more African? Explain your answer.
4. Apply the geographic theme of human-environment interaction to traditional agricultural and herding economies.
5. Why would the movement of people into cities break down the extended family?
6. Is rearing children more important in traditional African societies than in our own? Explain your answer.
7. If you could import one African idea from this chapter to help American society, what would it be? Explain why.
8. How might patrilineal and matrilineal societies differ?
9. Is there any practice in American society that is similar to the age grade system in traditional African societies?

Mastering Mapwork

PHYSICAL AND HUMAN CHARACTERISTICS OF PLACE

Use the map on page 61 to answer these questions:

1. Using the information from the map and what you have learned from this chapter, describe the physical characteristics of places lying along the Tropic of Capricorn.
2. Locate the intersection of 15°N latitude and 30°E longitude on the map. Using the information from the map and what you have learned from this chapter, what human characteristics of place would you expect to observe?
3. Locate the intersection of 25°S latitude and 30°E longitude. What human characteristics of place would you expect to observe in this area?

Mastering Mapwork

1. Most areas lie either in desert or semiarid grassland areas.

2. This is an area of nomadic herding and small or subsistence farming. Yams can be grown in this area. Small farmers tend to live in villages with their croplands located outside the villages.

3. In this general area, there is mining of phosphates, copper, uranium, iron, and diamonds. It is an area of commercial farming and livestock raising.

Go to the Source

Understanding Myths

Tales such as this have passed from generation to generation through storytelling. Historians learn about a culture's values and ways of life from its stories.

Read this folktale, "Waxes and Wanes," from southern Nigeria. Answer the questions using specific references from the document.

There was once an old woman who was very poor, and lived in a small mud hut thatched with mats made from the leaves of the tombo palm in the bush. She was often very hungry, as there was no one to look after her.

In the olden days the moon used often to come down to the earth, although she lived most of the time in the sky. The moon was a fat woman with a skin of hide, and she was full of fat meat. She was quite round, and in the night used to give plenty of light. The moon was sorry for the poor starving old woman, so she came to her and said, "You may cut some of my meat away for your food." This the old woman did every evening, and the moon got smaller and smaller until you could scarcely see her at all. Of course this made her give very little light, and all the people began to grumble in consequence, and to ask why it was that the moon was getting so thin.

At last the people went to the old woman's house where there happened to be a little girl sleeping. She had been there for some little time, and had seen the moon come down every evening, and the old woman go out with her knife and carve her daily supply of meat out of the moon. As she was very frightened, she told the people all about it, so they determined to set a watch on the movements of the old woman.

That very night the moon came down as usual, and the old woman went out with her knife and basket to get her food; but before she could carve any meat all the people rushed out shouting, and the moon was so frightened that she went back again into the sky, and never came down again to the earth. The old woman was left to starve in the bush.

Ever since that time the moon has hidden herself most of the day, as she was so frightened, and she still gets very thin once a month, but later on she gets fat again, and when she is quite fat she gives plenty of light all the night; but this does not last very long, and she begins to get thinner and thinner, in the same way as she did when the old woman was carving her meat from her.

Questions

1. Explain why people might create such a story. How might the old woman's behavior be contrary to values in an African village?
2. What role do these stories have in today's society?

Go to the Source

Go to the Source

OBJECTIVES: 1.03, 12.02; Skills 3.05

Myths have long been used by many cultures to explain natural phenomena as well as provide moral or religious instruction. Discuss with students how historians and anthropologists can use details from the myths to understand more about the culture and its values at a given period in time.

Other African myths can be found at the Sacred Texts Web site (Visit **NCJourneys.com** for a link).

ANSWERS

1. Folk stories are part of the oral history of Africa. In many cultures creation myths explained natural phenomena. Africans used the story of the old woman to explain why the moon grew smaller.

   This chapter speaks of a shared responsibility villagers have to one another. The old woman's actions were selfish and the rest of the village women reacted by isolating her.

2. Important points: Students should choose a myth and compare it—it can be from any area that they have studied in the past, including Norse, Greek, or Roman mythology, Egyptian myths, or Native American folktales. Note: Creation myths explain why people are on earth or how certain things came to be.

How to Use the Chapter Review

There are three sections in the Chapter Review: Talk About It, Mastering Mapwork, and Go to the Source. Use the Vocabulary Worksheets and the Chapter Review Worksheet in the Teacher's Resource Guide for additional reinforcement and preparation for the Chapter Assessments. The chapter and lesson reviews and the Chapter Review Worksheets are the basis of the assessment for each chapter.

Talk About It questions encourage students to speculate about the content of the chapter and are suitable for class or small-group discussion. They are not intended to be assigned for homework.

Mastering Mapwork has students apply one or more of the Five Themes of Geography to maps within the chapter.

Go to the Source activities allow students to analyze a primary source that relates to the content of the chapter. The questions and activities familiarize students with different types of primary sources and also build content-reading skills.

CHAPTER 5

A Diversity of People and Lands

Social Studies Strands

Historic Perspectives
The practice of slavery
Imperialism and its effects
on Africa
Independence movement

Global Connections

Economics and Development

North Carolina Standard Course of Study

Goal 4 The learner will identify significant patterns in the movement of people, goods, and ideas over time and place in Africa, Asia, and Australia.

Goal 6 The learner will recognize the relationship between economic activity and the quality of life in Africa, Asia, and Australia.

Goal 7 The learner will assess the connections between historical events and contemporary issues in Africa, Asia, and Australia.

Goal 9 The learner will analyze the different forms of government developed in Africa, Asia, and Australia.

Teaching & Assessment

• English Language Learner Modified Lesson Plans for this chapter are found in the Teacher Resource Guide.

• *ExamView® Assessment Suite* is provided at **NCJourneys.com.** It includes customizable assessments for all chapters. Paper tests are also available in the Teacher Resource Guide. See pages T16–T17 for information about how to use the assessments and the Scoring Guide.

Worksheets

Worksheets and answer keys are found both in the Teacher Resource Guide and at **NCJourneys.com**, including Reading Guides, Reading Strategies, Chapter Reviews, English Language Learner and others.

ACTIVITIES AND INTEGRATIONS

SOCIAL STUDIES

● African Bits and Pieces, p. 80B
Activator: Editorial Cartoons, p. 80
▲ ■ What is a Flow-Line Map? p. 81
▲ ■ What is the Legacy of European Imperialism?, p. 82
 Triangle Trade, p. 84
Dr. Livingstone, I Presume? p. 88
Who Owns What? p. 90
● The Past and the Present p. 93
African Challenges, p. 95
Modern Trade Flow Chart, p. 96
Skill Lesson: Using Geography's Themes: Movement, p. 98

READING/LANGUAGE ARTS	READING/LANGUAGE ARTS OBJECTIVES
Editorial Letters, p. 80B	1.01, 3.03
Analogies, p. 80B	2.01
★ Writing Prompt: HIV Challenges, p. 80	3.03, 6.02
Help Wanted, p. 87	4.01
Stanley and Livingstone, p. 89	1.01, 6.02
★ Africa Without Europe? p. 91	3.03, 6.02
★ African Leaders, p. 92	3.01
Go to the Source: Reading Slave Narratives, p. 101	2.01, 4.01, 4.02

TECHNOLOGY	TECHNOLOGY OBJECTIVES
● Middle Passage, p. 83	3.01, 3.02
★ African Leaders, p. 92	3.01, 3.11

VISUAL ARTS	VISUAL ARTS OBJECTIVES
● Masai Shield, p. 80B	1.01, 5.02
Stanley and Livingstone, p. 89	1.01, 1.02

CHARACTER AND VALUES EDUCATION	TRAITS
★ Writing Prompt: HIV Challenges, p. 80	kindness, respect, fairness, good judgment
What Would You Do?, p. 87	respect
African Challenges, p. 95	fairness, good judgment

● Basic Activities   ★ Challenging Activities   ▲ English Language Learner Novice   ■ English Language Learner Intermediate

Introductory Activity

Editorial Letters

🔶 **OBJECTIVES:** 4.03, 7.02

Students will write or word process a letter to the editor defending or opposing the institution of slavery. They are to imagine they are living in the year 1800 in the United States. They are to write a point-of-view or persuasive letter from one of the following perspectives: a slave trader, a slave, a slave owner, a Southerner who does not own slaves, or a Northerner hoping to free slaves.

Students should include at least three reasons for defending or opposing slavery.

An editorial page can be created using student letters. Students can also create original political cartoons for the editorial page.

 **Culminating Activity**

African Bits and Pieces

🔶 **OBJECTIVES:** 8.01, 9.01

Have students make a mobile of African colonial territories by cutting up a map of Africa along colonial lines. Have them attach strips to these colonial territories listing each independent country that developed from them (and their dates of independence).

 Art Activity

Masai Shield

🔶 **OBJECTIVES:** 4.03

Materials large pieces of cardboard, drawing paper, heavy white paper, pencils, tempera paint, paint brushes, newspaper, rulers; optional: sponges

Option One On drawing paper, practice drawing geometric designs. Repeat simple shapes: triangles, diamonds, and zigzags. Try a variety of patterns. Cut out large football-shaped pieces of cardboard 18 inches by 24 inches. Divide shield in two to four parts. Paint background solid colors. Limit colors to between two and four. Draw and then paint solid 4-inch-wide lines around the outer edge of shield and down the middle of shield. (Note: These lines can vary in width and location.) Draw and then paint patterns within the 4-inch lines.

Option Two Use geometric shapes cut out of sponges to dip in paint to create designs on shield.

 Analogies

🔶 **OBJECTIVES:** 4.02, 7.01

Analogies are useful to help students make associations with prior knowledge. They can be used as an instructional strategy to help students better understand new materials. They are not intended to be definitions or test items.

Read the analogies aloud and ask students to identify the relationship between the terms. As an extension, ask students to write their own analogies using key terms or places discussed in the chapter.

Holocaust : Jews :: Slave trade : Africans (enslaved/killed)

Brazil : coffee, sugar :: Caribbean : sugar :: North America : tobacco, cotton (produced)

coffee, tea, rubber, cacao : cash crops :: yams, millet, sorghum : subsistence farming (are examples of)

Egypt : Britain :: Congo : Belgium (once was ruled by)

Gold Coast : Ghana :: Rhodesia : Zimbabwe (is now called)

Julius Nyerere : Tanzania :: George Washington : United States of America (was the first president of)

Teaching Strategies

In this chapter, information is given to help students understand the past as well as the present. Take advantage of the information on African slavery for an integrated study of American history and use the study of the past to help clarify reasons for current events.

Activator

OBJECTIVES: 4.03, 10.04

Have your students bring in examples of editorial cartoons. After everyone has had a chance to look at them and understand what is being said, have students be editorial cartoonists at the abolitionist newspaper *The Liberator*. Have students draw a political cartoon that denounces slavery.

Extension Assign intermediate ELL students to work with a peer tutor.

Writing Prompt

OBJECTIVES: 10.04

Problem-Solution

Sub-Saharan Africa remains the center of the world AIDS crisis, with two-thirds of all people living with HIV. The rates of HIV infection in some African countries range from 13 to 36 percent among the adult population. Although Nigeria's current rate of infection is about 5.4 percent, its large population means that more than 7 million people are HIV positive. Access to AIDS drugs improved more than 500 percent between 2001 and 2005, but UNAids said that even with that increase, only one in five people around the world who needs the drugs get them.

Write: Only 20 percent of people in developing nations who need drugs for HIV and AIDS gets them. Do you think that drug companies have a moral responsibility to lower prices so more people can have access to drugs?

As you write your paper, remember to
- clearly state your position.
- give three reasons and explain your ideas fully.
- give examples to support your reasons.
- write in complete sentences and paragraph form.
- organize your ideas and include an introduction and a conclusion.
- use good grammar, spelling, punctuation, and capitalization.

CHAPTER 5

Africa and the World

"Independence," said Congo freedom fighter Patrice Lumumba, "is not a gift, but a right." In the 1950s, Lumumba was demanding an end to a centuries-old era of European domination. Europeans had brought Africans death and destruction. Slave traders had shipped millions of Africans into bondage in the Americas. Almost all of Africa had enriched Europe's great powers as colonies.

Lumumba and other African independence leaders wanted an end to colonial rule. They wanted Africans to build nations on foundations laid by the continent's ancient civilizations. Freedom came, but many African nations have not found an easy road to independence and prosperity.

Chapter Preview

LESSON 1
Africa and the Slave Trade
Slavery was an ancient practice. The Atlantic slave trade, which began after the European conquest of the Americas, cost millions of Africans their lives or freedom.

LESSON 2
European Imperialism in Africa
European imperialism brought almost all of Africa under European rule in the late 1800s.

LESSON 3
Independence and After
African countries won independence after World War II. Many still struggle with the effects of imperialism.

Black Star Arch, Independence Square, Acrra, Ghana

AD 1957

FREEDOM AND JUS...

Patrice Lumumba

Chapter 5

8

Chapter Resources

Print Resources
Fiction
Fox, Paula. *The Slave Dancer*. Atheneum, 2001. ISBN 0689845057.

McKissack, Pat. *Nzingha, Warrior Queen of the Matamba*. Scholastic, 2000. ISBN 0439112109.

Nonfiction
Bailey, C. *African Voices of the Atlantic Slave Trade: Beyond the Silence and the Shame*. Beacon Press, 2006. ISBN 100807055131.

Dugard, Martin. *Into Africa: The Epic Adventures of Stanley and Livingstone*. Broadway, 2004. ISBN 100767910745.

Hochschild, Adam. *King Leopold's Ghost: A Story of Greed, Terror and Heroism in Colonial Africa*. Mariner Books, 2006. ISBN 100618711678.

Kleinman, Joseph. *Life on an African Ship*. Lucent, 2001. ISBN 1560066539.

Meltzer, Milton. *They Came in Chains: The Story of the Slave Ships*. Benchmark Books, 2000. ISBN 076140967X.

Pakenham, Thomas. *The Scramble for Africa: White Man's Conquest of the Dark Continent from 1876 to 1912*. Avon Books, 1992.

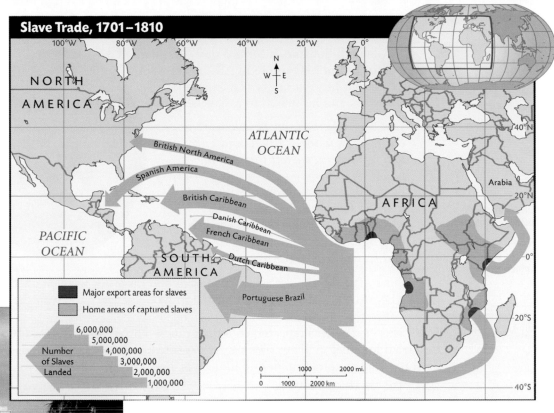

Slave Trade, 1701–1810

NORTH AMERICA

ATLANTIC OCEAN

PACIFIC OCEAN

SOUTH AMERICA

AFRICA

Arabia

British North America

Spanish America

British Caribbean

Danish Caribbean

French Caribbean

Dutch Caribbean

Portuguese Brazil

■ Major export areas for slaves
■ Home areas of captured slaves

Number of Slaves Landed
6,000,000
5,000,000
4,000,000
3,000,000
2,000,000
1,000,000

An independence parade in Accra, Ghana

Africa and the World   81

ISBN 100380719991.
Thornton, John. *Africa and Africans in the Making of the Atlantic World, 1400–1800.* Studies in Comparative World History Series. Cambridge University Press, 1998. ISBN 100521627249.
Worth, Richard. *Stanley and Livingstone and the Exploration of Africa in World History.* Enslow, 2000. ISBN 0766014002.

Audiovisual
Amistad. 1997. ISBN 0451195167.

Web Sites
Links to the following Web sites are found at **NCJourneys.com.**
• Africans in America: the Terrible Transformation
• Atlantic Slavery Timeline
• Exploring *Amistad*
• Slavery's Affects in West Africa, NPR Radio Expedition
• The Story of Africa, BBC (profiles on slavery, colonization, and independence in Africa)

Discussion Questions

1 Which countries took the largest number of enslaved people to the Americas? Why do you think this occurred?

Teacher Notes

Slave Trade
The map shows the initial destination of the transatlantic slave trade only. Millions of Africans were shipped from the Caribbean to North America. This movement is not shown on the map.

Map Activity

What Is a Flow-Line Map?

NATIONAL GEOGRAPHY STANDARDS: 1, 6, 9, 12, 17
GEOGRAPHIC THEMES: Location, Place, Movement, Region
OBJECTIVES: 1.02

Discuss with students what they notice about arrows on this map (note that widths of arrow shafts are different sizes). Explain that this type of flow-line map uses arrows to note the origin and destination of a type of movement. It uses the width of the arrow's shafts to note the size or quantity of the movement. Examining origins of the transatlantic movement of enslaved people, have students identify where, including major export areas by current city names, enslaved Africans lived before being taken into the middle passage. Next, have students identify the three major areas (South America, Caribbean, eastern/southeastern-Atlantic North America) that were the destinations of most enslaved Africans in the triangle of trade. Third, have students identify the five European countries that dominated the transatlantic slave trade from 1701 until 1810. Although the middle passage/triangle trade is only about 110 years of an extensive African history, note the significant impact it had and continues to have on Africans. In small groups, have students estimate how many Africans were captured and brought to the Americas by the Portuguese, British, Spanish, French, and Dutch.

 **OBJECTIVES:** 4.02, 4.03, 7.02

Discussion Questions

1 How would you have felt if you had been Olaudah or his sister? What would you miss most? What would you be most afraid of?

2 How did life in African villages change once the slave traders came?

3 How would you feel if you were suddenly torn from your family and carried away to a strange and cruel land? What would be the worst part of this for you?

 Caption Answer

Before the slave trade ended in the 1800s, millions of people from African villages had been captured and sent to the Americas.

Activity

What is the Legacy of European Imperialism?

 **OBJECTIVES:** 7.02

After reading Lesson 1, have students create a graphic organizer on "Slavery: Cause and Effect." Using the information in their organizer, have them write a histo-poem on slavery, the Triangular Trade, or imperialism, using the format outline below.

Include in the poem:
- the event
- when it happened
- where it happened
- causes
- prior historical events before it (three or four)
- historical events that followed (three or four)
- Important people or countries involved
- Other events going on in the world at that time (three or four)
- Important inventions of the time
- Effects

Extension ELL students should do this with a partner. The "lines" of the poem could be one or two words in length.

LESSON **1** Africa and the Slave Trade

KEY IDEAS

- Slavery was an ancient practice of taking captives in war.
- Muslims traded with East Africans for slaves.
- The transatlantic slave trade began after Europeans set up colonies in the Americas.
- Slavery devastated those parts of Africa from which slaves were taken.

KEY TERMS

racism

Gorée Island in Senegal was a holding and transfer point for slaves heading to the Americas. **How did the transatlantic slave trade affect african villages?**

Olaudah Equiano, a former slave, left a vivid record of his capture in Africa. He wrote about his first hours as a captive of slave traders and his march to a slave ship.

One day, when all our people were gone out to their work as usual, and only I and my sister were left to mind the house, two men and a woman got over our walls and ... seized us both; and without giving us time to cry out ... they stopped our mouths and ran off with us into the ... woods. Here they tied our hands, and [carried] us as far as they could.

Olaudah Equiano

For the trip to the slave ship, Olaudah and his sister were chained together. At the coast they were locked in wooden cages to await the arrival of trading ships.

This cruelty was repeated countless times. The African slave trade started long before these slaves were captured. Before the trade ended in the 1800s, untold millions had died or been transported to the Americas. The African slave trade ended more than a century ago. The trade was a devastating tragedy to those caught in it. African villages suffered terribly from the capture of their young men and women.

82   Chapter 5

Teacher Notes

Engand v. Great Britain v. United Kingdom

Students may notice that the references to England (and the English), Great Britain, and the United Kingdom change as different time periods are discussed in the textbook.

In the Act of Union of 1707, the kingdoms of England and Scotland merged to form the Kingdom of Great Britain. The English people became the British people when referring to the people of the nation as a whole (as opposed to ethnic Scots or ethnic English per se). The Act of Union of 1800 merged the Kingdom of Ireland and the Kingdom of Great Britain to create the United Kingdom of Great Britain and Ireland, effective January 1, 1801. This is now the United Kingdom of Great Britain and Northern Ireland.

This Elmina, Ghana, fort held Africans captive before they were forced onto slave ships. **How would you have felt if you were locked here?**

Slavery in African History

The slave trade did not begin with slave ships crossing the Atlantic. Capturing enemies and forcing them into slavery was an ancient practice and not limited to Africa. The slave trade was worldwide.

In ancient times, Africa probably suffered no more—and no less—from slavery than most other places in the world. From the time of the Egyptian pharaohs, Africans were captured in wars and taken as slaves by the victors. Other early civilizations in Southwest Asia, South Asia, and China took slaves after winning battles.

Africa became a major source of slaves in the 1200s. Muslim traders from Arabia bought slaves from rulers of East African city-states. Captives—most of them women—were exported in large numbers, especially to Southwest Asian kingdoms. At its height, this trade may have forced as many as 10,000 people into slavery every year. This trade lasted until the late 1800s.

The export of female slaves from East Africa became a serious problem. It

disrupted village life. Marriage patterns changed as fewer young women were available to start families. Birthrates fell. These difficulties were small in comparison with the terrors of a booming slave trade across the Atlantic Ocean.

Europeans and Slavery

Slave trade from Africa's Atlantic coast began after European nations launched voyages of trade and exploration. In the 1400s, Portugal began explorations along Africa's western coast. The Portuguese searched for ways to sail around the African continent to Asia. By rounding Africa's southern tip, the Portuguese opened trade with Asia.

Portuguese ships had stopped along Africa's west coast to build small forts and trading posts. The Portuguese were at first interested in gold that came from mines near the coast of modern-day Ghana. As trade developed, they decided to buy and sell slaves.

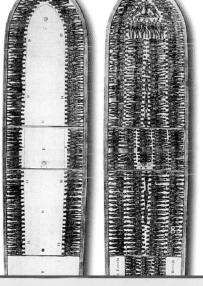

Africans were horribly crammed below deck aboard slave ships that sailed from West Africa. **Where were the ships heading?**

Africa and the World

Discussion Questions

1 How did the practice of slavery originate?

2 How did the exportation of enslaved females from East Africa impact village life?

Caption Answer

Answers will vary. Have students think of their loss of freedom and their homes.

Caption Answer

They were going to the Americas.

Research Activity

Middle Passage

 OBJECTIVES: 7.02

Have your students research the Middle Passage. Put students in groups of six and have each student draw a slip of paper that will say either African Trader, Slave Ship Captain, Plantation Owner, or Slave (at least three of the latter). Each person needs to research his or her part in the slave trade. The group must present their findings to the class.

As an extension: Have all students prepare a set of questions that they would ask each of the role players. When a group presents, they respond to the questions of the listeners. Students must be prepared to back up their answers. Students may also feel free to express their dislike of their character. They should explain what they dislike and why.

Background Information

Middle Passage

From about 1518 to the mid-1800s, millions of enslaved African men, women, and children made the terrible transatlantic crossing from freedom in Africa to enslavement in North or South America. Called the Middle Passage, the voyage took anywhere from 21 days to three months. Aboard horribly overcrowded sailing ships, the captives were wedged onto low-lying

platforms. Chains held them to these prison beds. The platforms were stacked in tiers. Each slave inhabited an average living space no more than 6 feet by 16 inches wide. For much of this time they could neither stand upright nor turn over. African men were often kept shackled to each other or to the deck to prevent uprisings.

Discussion Questions

1 How did Spain become involved in the slave trade?

2 What role did Christopher Columbus have in Spain's involvement in the slave trade?

3 How were enslaved people dehumanized and treated as commodities?

Caption Answer

Neighboring countries fought over the goods and profits offered by slave traders.

Map Activity

Triangle Trade

NATIONAL GEOGRAPHY STANDARDS: 00

GEOGRAPHIC THEMES: Movement

OBJECTIVES: 1.01, 4.02

Assign students to research the Triangular Trade using the Internet. Have students make a map to illustrate the trade that developed because of transatlantic slavery. Have them draw in each "leg" of the trade, labeling origins, destinations, and products carried. Students should include a map key and legend and title their maps.

The Transatlantic Slave Trade

Spain's involvement in the transatlantic slave trade came soon after Christopher Columbus's voyage to the Americas in 1492. Spain began immediately to explore the Americas. They claimed and conquered large parts of these continents. Spanish colonists opened gold and silver mines in South America and started sugar plantations on Caribbean islands. Portugal followed Spain into South America, where it opened sugar plantations along Brazil's coast.

The Spanish and Portuguese decided the hard jobs in the Americas would be done by others. At first, the Spanish thought Native Americans could be forced to do the work. Instead, millions of Native Americans died from diseases brought by Europeans. Soon Europeans looked to Africa for slaves to provide the labor that they needed in the Americas.

The first enslaved Africans crossed the Atlantic in 1532. For the next 100 years, the transatlantic slave trade grew slowly. Then, in the 1630s, demand for slave labor began to rise. Within a few years,

This Masai shield was used in battles with other groups of people in Africa. **How did the slave trade cause wars within Africa?**

the transatlantic slave trade had become much larger than the one in East Africa (see map, page 81).

The rapid expansion of agriculture in the Americas produced this demand. The French and British opened plantations in the Caribbean. In Brazil, enslaved people grew sugar or coffee. The Caribbean islands also had sugar plantations. Plantation owners in the southern part of North America wanted slaves to raise tobacco and cotton. Europeans wanted all of these products, and this demand made slavery profitable. In exchange for slaves, Africans received such goods as textiles, guns, and tobacco from America and Europe.

European countries began outlawing the slave trade in the early 1800s. The United Kingdom was the first to do so in 1807, followed by the United States in 1808, then France, Germany, Portugal, and Spain. The trade continued long after it became illegal. The last slaving ships crossed the Atlantic in the 1880s.

Slavery's Impact on Africa

People sold as slaves to the Americas came chiefly from coastal areas of western, central, and southeastern Africa, harming these areas. Families were torn apart; villages lost their strongest and brightest young people. Raids interrupted food production. Some Africans became wealthy from slavery and the goods for which slaves were traded. This wealth sometimes caused conflict.

The slave trade also spread *racism*, the belief that one race is superior to another. For some 300 years, many white Europeans and Americans viewed Africans as property rather than people. Such beliefs made it easier for Europeans to rule Africa in the 1900s.

84

Slavery—The Experience of Millions of Africans

Huge numbers of African villagers became trapped in the cruel transatlantic slave trade (see map, page 81). British North America received many more slaves from a part of the slave trade not shown on the map. A large number of Africans who ended up in North America were first sent to the Caribbean.

Many of the unlucky captives were people taken prisoner in local wars. European offers of guns, cotton cloth, and other trade goods for war captives made slavery profitable and appealing to local rulers.

Once captured, enslaved Africans were no longer treated as human beings but as property. For trying to escape, they were beaten or killed. At the coast they were locked in jails (above) or herded into shacks to await the arrival of slave ships.

Aboard ship, slavers chained their captives together and crammed them into dark, crowded spaces below deck. Captives received just enough food and water to survive. During the six-to ten-week voyage, unclean conditions caused disease. Illness spread quickly, sometimes killing all on board.

By the 1700s, slave trade had become part of an international network. Cotton cloth, rum, and firearms from Europe were traded in West Africa for slaves shipped to the Americas. In the Americas, cotton, sugar, molasses, and tobacco grown by slaves were sold to Europe.

The slave trade and slavery took an awful toll of human lives. No exact count exists of the millions who died on the way to the coast or during the voyage to the Americas. At journey's end, the captives faced equally harsh conditions. One-third died within the first three years of captivity.

Discussion Questions

1 Why would the rapid expansion of agriculture in the Americas cause an increased demand for slaves?

2 Why did the Atlantic slave trade last as long as it did?

3 How did trading in slaves cause conflict among the people of Africa?

4 What impact did the slave trade have on African society?

5 What role did Africans themselves play in the continuation of the Atlantic trade of enslaved people?

LESSON 1 REVIEW

Fact Follow-Up

1. Describe the early African slave trade.
2. How did the transatlantic slave trade begin, and why did it continue for as long as it did?
3. How were African societies affected by the Atlantic slave trade?
4. Describe the relative location of African areas most affected by the transatlantic slave trade.

Talk About It

1. Why was the transatlantic slave trade more damaging for African societies than earlier trading in slaves?
2. Were African people helpless to stop the transatlantic slave trade? Explain.
3. What is racism, and how did the transatlantic slave trade encourage it?

LESSON 1 REVIEW

Fact Follow-Up Answers

1. In the 1200s, Muslim traders from Arabia bought slaves from the rulers of East African city-states. Most of the captives were women, forced into slavery in Southwest Asian kingdoms.
2. Soon after Spain and Portugal began to explore the Americas, colonists opened large plantations. At first, they forced Native Americans to work on the plantations, but they died in large numbers. The Europeans replaced the Native Americans with Africans brought as slaves across the Atlantic. The rapid expansion of agriculture in the Americas produced a large demand for African slaves. The production of crops like tobacco and cotton made slavery profitable for plantation owners.
3. Great harm came to African societies. Neighbors fought one another over goods offered by slave traders, families were torn apart, villages lost their young men and women, and food production dropped.
4. Slaves in the transatlantic trade came chiefly from coastal areas of western and central Africa.

Talk About It Answers

1. The Atlantic slave trade was much, much larger than earlier trading.
2. Important points: Students should choose a position and support it with reasons. Note: European technology, including weaponry, was superior; Europeans were determined to acquire slaves for plantations in the Americas; the numbers of slaves taken weakened African societies; wars and chaos preceded and accompanied the trade.
3. Racism is the belief that one race is superior to another. The Atlantic slave trade encouraged Europeans to believe that whites were superior to blacks because they were successful in forcing Africans into slavery, transporting them to another continent, and possessing them like property.

 OBJECTIVES: 6.02, 7.01, 9.01

Discussion Questions

1 What were the factors that prevented inland exploration of Africa?

2 How did the exploration of the major river systems of Africa benefit Europeans?

3 What could be some possible consequences for dividing Africa the way Europeans did?

4 During the nineteenth century, Europe had a race for control of Africa. Give some examples of similar struggles in the twentieth century.

 Caption Answer

Europeans did not think Africans should have control.

LESSON 2 European Imperialism in Africa

KEY IDEAS

- Europeans began exploring Africa in the 1800s.

- Africa became a target of European imperialism in the late 1800s when European leaders divided Africa into colonies for their countries.

- Imperialism forced Africans to grow crops that benefited Europe, not themselves, thus harming the agricultural economy of Africa.

KEY TERMS

cash crops
civil war
genocide
imperialism

The Berlin Conference held in 1884 carved up Africa among European countries. **Why do you think no Africans were invited to the meeting?**

In 1884, European leaders met in Berlin, Germany, to divide Africa. Both Great Britain and Germany claimed adjoining portions of East Africa. Each wanted one of the high volcanic mountains of the East African highlands. To resolve the problem, the British and German ministers reportedly took out a ruler and drew a line on the map of Africa between Mount Kenya and Mount Kilimanjaro. Kilimanjaro became a part of the German colony of Tanganyika, and the British got Mount Kenya.

None of the officials thought about what this might mean to the people living in these places. No Africans attended this conference. They had not been invited. An era of European domination over Africa began at the Berlin Conference.

Europeans Explore Africa

Until the 1800s, few Europeans had explored Africa. Almost all travel to Africa had stopped along the coast. The lack of natural harbors, dense forests, vast deserts, the hot climate, and the threat of deadly diseases were barriers to inland exploration. In the 1800s, however, steamships made travel from Europe to Africa easier and new medicines reduced the risk of disease.

Throughout the century, Europeans explored the major river systems of Africa: the Niger, Nile, Zambezi, and Congo. Their searches sometimes turned into heated competition. Belgian, French, British, and German explorers joined the race to find the source of the Nile River.

European exploration of the continent had few benefits for Africans. Exploration had many rewards for Europeans eager to gain African resources and to know more about African lands. From the explorers, Europeans learned the locations of Africa's raw materials and natural resources. They also learned which of its rivers might be used for trade and transportation.

Scrambling for Empire

By the late 1800s, many Europeans believed their countries had a role to play in Africa. There were several reasons for their interest.

Christian churches had begun to focus attention on Africa. Missionary groups wanted to convert Africans to Christianity. Some groups wanted their governments to provide protection and support for their African mission stations.

Some merchants dreamed of fortunes to be made in the trading of African ivory, gold, and tropical trees.

Leaders of Europe's new industries also were attracted to Africa. The factories of Britain, France, and Germany were making so many cheap goods so quickly

86

Chapter 5

✔ It's a Fact

Imperialism

■ During Africa's colonial period, the United Kingdom gave local chiefs or sultans the right to tax and to use the local population for labor and military service in exchange for enforcing British laws. This helped the United Kingdom rule territories with fewer military troops.

■ While each European country built railroads crisscrossing their territories, each country used a different size track. Consequently, it is difficult to travel across Africa without switching trains at each border.

that they were running out of buyers. Manufacturers needed raw materials for the goods they made and new markets for their finished goods. Africa offered both.

Within African colonies, each European nation could make its own trade policies. Their rules prevented colonists from selling raw materials or buying goods from anyone but the home country.

Finally, Europe's political leaders saw the building of overseas empires as a way to increase their popularity at home. Their people became excited by stories of their nations' overseas conquests. British schoolchildren, for example, were taught that the "sun never sets on the British Empire."

Imperialism

By 1880, an age of *imperialism* had begun. Imperialism is the control by one country of another through economic, political, or military means.

One of the first to make a grab for Africa was King Leopold II of Belgium. He claimed the Congo as his personal property. Between 1880 and 1914, the United Kingdom, France, Germany, Portugal, Italy, Spain, and Belgium divided up the continent.

New technology aided the European nations in their land grab. In the 1880s, an American invented the Maxim gun, the first type of machine gun. This weapon made it very hard for Africans to fight back successfully. The opposition largely failed.

New Borders

Recall that European nations decided Africa's boundaries. No Africans were present to advise Europe's leaders. The maps Europeans used to draw boundary lines did not accurately depict the landforms and ethnic groups of Africa. They were not concerned about separating these ethnic groups. Fighting among these groups made it easier for Europeans to gain control.

The results created problems for years to come. Europeans created colonial boundaries that divided some ethnic groups and brought together other competing groups.

For example, the cattle herding Masai were split between German-ruled Tanganyika and British-ruled Kenya. In Kenya, the Kikuyu people lost their land to British settlers. Upon Kenyan independence, President Kenyatta favored his own Kikuyu group. During President Moi's rule, the Kikuyu became targets of ethnic violence. Between 1991 and 1994, the country was torn apart by ethnic violence pitting Moi's Kalenjin (KAH·len·jeen) group with the Masai against the Kikuyu and other groups. More than 300,000 persons were displaced by the fighting. Ethnic violence still rises up occasionally.

A Belgian decision put the Hutus and Tutsis—groups that had been enemies for centuries—together in Rwanda-Urandi (today's Rwanda). Because of this, the country has been the site of *civil war,* (a conflict between groups within a country), assassinations, and *genocide.* Genocide is when one group of people tries to eliminate another ethnic, racial, or political group entirely.

King Leopold II of Belgium claimed the Congo for himself during the period of European imperialism. **What is imperialism?**

What would YOU do?

In the 1860s, Europeans came to Africa to find the source of the Nile River. Entering villages, they traded cloth and beads for information and food. They also told people back home that African villagers were strange because they were different. Would you describe these villagers as strange? Why or why not?

WORD ORIGINS

Who named **Africa**? No one knows for sure, but the ancient Romans called the continent on the Equator *aprica,* which means "sunny." The name may have come from the Greek word *aphrike,* which means "without cold."

Africa and the World

87

Discussion Questions

1 What European countries were involved in African imperialism? During what time period was Africa under European rule?

2 What role did the Industrial Revolution play in events that occurred in Africa?

3 Why do you think missionary work and missionary schools were important in Africa?

4 How does the phrase "divide and conquer" apply to the European conquest of Africa?

5 Why do you think Europeans thought they had a right to rule Africa? How does this compare to what happened to Native Americans?

6 According to the text, what was one of the most devastating effects of European rule in Africa? What problems resulted from this decision?

7 Which areas in Africa fought against European rule?

Caption Answer

Control by one country of another through economic, political, or military means.

Writing Activity

Help Wanted

OBJECTIVES: 2.02, 4.01

Create an advertisement promoting colonization in Africa. Be sure to include which European country is advertising, which territory in Africa is being colonized, and which raw material or natural resource is being exploited. The advertisements should be colorful and visually represent the colony.

Have students give at least three other good reasons that would convince someone in Europe to leave home to live in Africa. Use natural resources and crops found in atlases. Display format of columns on bulletin in classified ads. Divide into the section headings European Powers or African Countries.

Extension Novice ELL students should create a collage of an African territory.

Background Information

King Leopold's Congo

In the 1890s, the spread of bicycles and motorcars in Europe and the United States sparked a boom in the world market for rubber. In King Leopold's Congo Free State, European traders ruthlessly exploited the people and the tropical forests of the region as they harvested wild rubber. With the king's consent, European companies took private armies of ex-slaves into the Zaire basin and forced local people to collect rubber. Resisters were killed or had their hands cut off. Missionaries' accounts of these abuses in European papers did little to stop them. A decade passed before African resistance, the international outcry against Leopold, and falling rubber prices ended Leopold's private kingdom in 1908.

"Dr. Livingstone, I Presume?"

NATIONAL GEOGRAPHY STANDARDS: 1, 4, 7, 14

GEOGRAPHIC THEMES: Location, Place, Movement, Human-Environmental Interaction

OBJECTIVES: 8.01, 1.02

Use one or more of the activities below to enhance students understanding of the journeys and impact of Livingstone and Stanley.

- Using pieces of string, assign students to overlay purple and orange paths David Livingstone and Henry Stanley traveled across East Africa from 1866 to1873 (Livingstone) and from 1871 to 1872 (Stanley). Have each string laid out on a flat surface side by side to note which length was shorter/longer.
- Ask students to analyze why the area around Bagamoyo would have been a good place for each explorer to begin his travels. Have students speculate why Stanley had success in finding the source of the Nile while Livingstone did not.
- Assign students to research *The New York Herald*'s accounts from Stanley.
- Assign groups of students to research if/how Livingstone's and Stanley's explorations influenced the end of the slave trade; the age of imperialism/Belgium's colonizing parts of Africa; publications describing African animals, resources, and vegetation from the nineteenth century; and maps published after 1873. Have students present their findings to the class.

Extension ELL students should use an ELL-friendly Web site for research.

Stanley and Livingstone

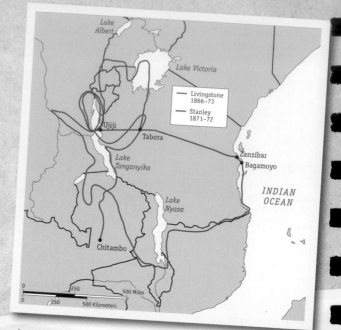

Africa beckoned European explorers. Africa had been traded with, explored, and developed by its native peoples and other nations. Phoenician traders of ancient times and Portuguese traders in the early 1600s had found their way to Africa. The British were latecomers. They arrived in the nineteenth century during the age of imperialism.

David Livingstone (above), a doctor and Scottish missionary, gained notice by his trips to Africa. Newspapers published long articles about his trips. His books sold well to a public curious about Africa's animals, rich resources, and unfamiliar vegetation. As a missionary, Livingstone's purpose in Africa was to help end the slave trade.

Fishing from the shores of Lake Victoria today

Chapter 5

Map compiled from Livingstone's exploration

Livingstone had been deep in Africa for two years (compare the map on page 88 to the map on page 90). No one back in Europe had heard from him. Many believed he was dead. But a reporter from *The New York Herald*, Henry Stanley (below), searched ten months for Livingstone in 1871. He later wrote about finding him: "I walked deliberately to him, took off my hat, and said, 'Dr. Livingstone, I presume?'"

Livingstone had hoped to find the White Nile's source. Stanley did find it. He showed how it flowed from Lake Victoria (left) to Lake Albert before joining the Blue Nile and flowing into Egypt. In 1874, Stanley explored the Congo River. The account of his travels attracted the attention of King Leopold II of Belgium. Four years later, Stanley returned to the Congo to claim this area for the king.

Africa and the World

89

Writing Activity

Stanley and Livingstone

OBJECTIVES: 8.01

Here are three writing-related activities about Stanley and Livingstone.

- After completing additional research on Stanley and Livingstone, write an obituary for either of them highlighting their work. For students who prefer art, they can design a tombstone for one of the explorers using construction paper.
- Ask students to pretend to be either Stanley or Livingstone. Then instruct them to write a journal entry for a day spent in Africa.
- Give students a graphic organizer to help them understand the significance of Stanley's and Livingstone's explorations. Using the graphic organizer, have them research the explorers and their legacy on the Internet.

Extension Assign ELL students the tombstone only.

Caption Answer

Most of Africa was controlled by other countries. Belgium, Britain, France, Germany, Portugal, Italy, and Spain controlled Africa.

ELL Teaching Tips

Give Clear, Simple Directions to ELL Students

Complex directions should be broken down into smaller steps. Ask students to explain in their own words what you are asking them to do before they do it.

Map Activity

Who Owns What?

NATIONAL GEOGRAPHY STANDARDS: 1, 5, 12, 14, 17

GEOGRAPHIC THEMES: Location, Place, Human-Environmental Interaction, Movement, Region

OBJECTIVES: 1.02, 7.02

Discuss with students why the Untied Kingdom possessed certain areas of Africa in 1850 and why their territory expanded so greatly until World War I began. Have students identify which areas remained under British, French, Portuguese, and Spanish control from 1850 until 1914. Students must then identify which European nations gained possessions in Africa by 1880 that they did not have in 1850. Have students speculate why Ethiopia and Liberia were never colonized by any European nation. Finally, have students identify all areas of Africa that maintained their name-identities from 1914 until today. The Berlin Conference of 1884 essentially established the boundaries of the current states of Africa. A comparison chart can be designed noting past African name-identities with current country's names. Use the Africa—Political map in the atlas as a reference.

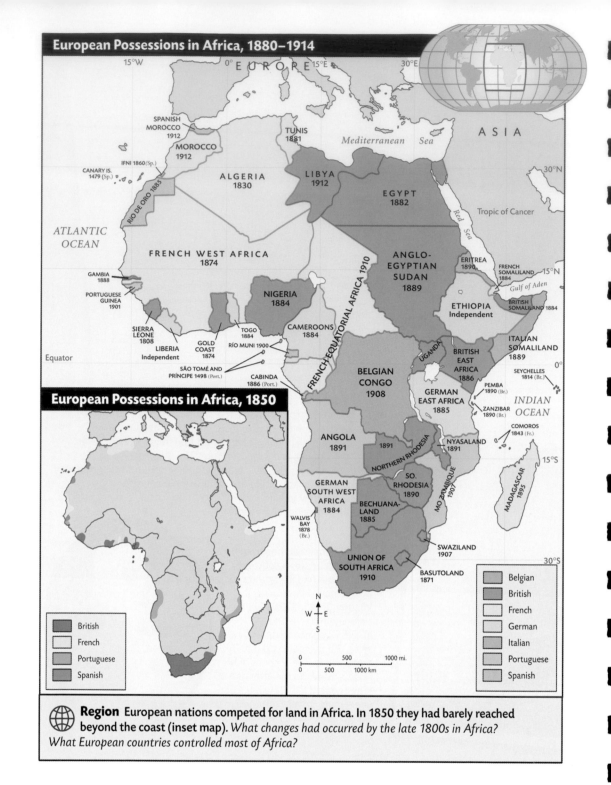

Region European nations competed for land in Africa. In 1850 they had barely reached beyond the coast (inset map). *What changes had occurred by the late 1800s in Africa? What European countries controlled most of Africa?*

Resisting European Control

Almost all of Africa fell under European control (see map, page 90). By 1914, only two countries, Liberia and Ethiopia, remained independent. Liberia—established by the United States in 1822 as a home for former slaves—gained freedom in 1847. Ethiopia remained free of European control until 1935, when it was taken by the Italians.

Many Africans forcefully resisted European control. For example, in the Sudan, well-organized but poorly armed armies fought back against the British until the late 1880s. Dahomey, a kingdom in present-day Benin, held out against the French until 1894. The Herero and Nama peoples battled the Germans in German South West Africa until 1907.

Impact of Imperialism

Africa spent less than a century under colonial rule yet great changes occurred. European nations had no interest in their colonies becoming self-supporting and independent, so Africans were not trained for industrial jobs or leadership.

African economies were changed to benefit colonial powers. Mining and **cash crops,** crops grown for sale or export, became the two most important economic activities. African farmers had to grow cash crops instead of crops to feed their families. Grains, yams, and other food crops were replaced by coffee, tea, peanuts, palm oil, rubber, cotton, cocoa, and other export crops. Colonial laws did not allow Africans to sell raw materials for their own benefit.

European rulers imposed heavy taxes. If Africans could not grow crops to pay their taxes, they took jobs as miners or laborers far from their homes to earn wages.

Such changes hastened the destruction of Africa's traditional farm economy and weakened families. Particularly in southern Africa, men spent many months away from home each year working in mines. Villages lost workers and leaders, and families lost husbands, fathers, and sons.

European colonists in Nyasaland (nigh·ᴀʜᴢ·ah·land) watch African farmers load tobacco. Today the country is called Malawi (ma·ʟᴀʜ·wee). **Why did African farmers grow cash crops instead of food crops?**

Discussion Questions

1 What changes took place in Africa under colonial rule?

2 What crops do you think would be regarded as cash crops in North Carolina?

3 What happens to a country when a country changes its economy from food production to cash crops?

4 What can you infer about the situation in Africa based on the picture?

Caption Answer

Controlling countries insisted that they grow cash crops.

Writing Activity

OBJECTIVES: 7.01

Europeans made a lasting impact on Africa. Some of these effects include a vacuum in leadership, an emphasis on cash crops, and a weakened family structure. Europeans did, however, improve the infrastructure, thereby increasing medical care and education.

Write: Would Africa be better off today if Europeans had never been involved in Africa?

As you write, remember to

- tell whether Africa would be better off.
- give three reasons explaining why Africa would or would not be better off.
- write in paragraph form.
- check to be sure you are writing good sentences.

LESSON 2 REVIEW

Fact Follow-Up

1. How did Africa's physical characteristics of place discourage European exploration of Africa?
2. What caused European imperialism in Africa?
3. What economic changes did European imperialism cause in Africa?
4. What parts of Africa remained independent after European colonization?

Talk About It

1. Which argument for imperialism do you think was most powerful? Explain why.
2. Why did competition in Europe result in imperialism in Africa?
3. Why was imperialism so devastating for Africa?
4. Predict what some lasting effects of imperialism could be.

Africa and the World   91

LESSON 2 REVIEW

Fact Follow-Up Answers

1. The lack of natural harbors, dense forests, vast deserts, the hot climate, and the threat of deadly diseases were barriers to inland exploration by Europeans.
2. European exploration of Africa's river systems acquainted Europeans with African resources and raw materials. Merchants were interested in tapping the resources, manufacturers wanted raw materials and markets for their products, Christian churches wanted to convert Africans, and rulers saw the building of an overseas empire as a way to increase their power at home.
3. African economies were changed to benefit the European colonial rulers, not Africans. European trade policies forced African farmers to switch from farming that would feed their families to the production of crops grown for sale or export. European rulers also imposed heavy taxes on African subjects. If farmers could not grow enough cash crops

to pay the taxes, they were forced to take jobs as miners or laborers far from home.
4. Liberia and Ethiopia remained independent.

Talk About It Answers

1. Note the following arguments: spreading Christianity, the desire for African resources and raw materials, competition for empires among European leaders.
2. Africa represented a new source of raw materials and markets for industrializing European nations. Owning colonies in Africa was also a source of national pride in Europe.
3. Imperialism took away the possibility for self-government and economic growth. It also destroyed the traditional economy and weakened families.
4. Students should support their predictions with facts from the text.

OBJECTIVES: 6.02, 7.02, 9.01

Discussion Questions

1 How did World War II give African leaders a renewed chance to fight for independence?

2 Why do you think it was so difficult for African nations to gain their independence? How does their fight compare with the American colonies' desire to gain independence?

Caption Answer

Independence movements started in Egypt, Nigeria, and the Gold Coast.

Writing Activity

African Leaders

OBJECTIVES: 8.01

Have students research the leaders of two African independence movements. Based upon their research, students will write a mock conversation between the two leaders in which each explains why they think their nation should be free, the steps they plan on taking to make their nation free, and what they envision their nation will be like after independence.

KEY IDEAS

- African countries began winning independence after World War II.

- Regions where there was little European control, such as West Africa, more easily won independence.

- By 1970, most African countries had won independence. African leaders took power.

- Many African governments have been authoritarian.

- African economies suffered from the effects of slavery, colonialism, and foreign domination.

KEY TERMS

authoritarian
corrupt
diversify
free trade
global economy

LESSON 3 Independence and After

In 1961, Kwame Nkrumah of Ghana issued a defiant warning to European colonial powers. "Africa wants her freedom," he said. "Africans must be free. For years Africa has been the footstool of colonialism and imperialism. These days are gone forever."

Nkrumah's cry for freedom echoed throughout Africa. In 1950, five years after World War II, there were only four independent nations in all of Africa. By 1968, 38 nations were free. Africa was swept by independence movements that few could have imagined before the world went to war.

Roots of Independence

Africa's independence movements did not take shape overnight. Despite their inability to stop Europe's conquests, Africans resented European rule. Independence movements started in Egypt, Nigeria, and the Gold Coast, renamed Ghana, almost as soon as the Europeans took control. Freedom movements multiplied and spread during the 1920s and 1930s. Few Europeans believed that these movements threatened their rule.

Kwame Nkrumah spoke to the United Nations in 1960. He had led Ghana to independence in 1957. **What were the roots of independence movements in Africa?**

Africa's chance for gaining independence appeared suddenly after World War II. Europe's once powerful nations were badly weakened by the war. They no longer could afford to govern colonies, especially if they had to fight to hold them.

African leaders recognized that the postwar world had presented them with opportunities. They demanded independence and prepared to take control of their homelands. That is why so many new African nations appeared in the 1950s and 1960s.

Paths to Independence

African men and women who had gone abroad for education became leaders in campaigns for independence. They had returned to their countries to become doctors, lawyers, teachers, and to serve as lower-level officials in colonial government. They worked to end colonial rule. Calls for independence met little resistance in West Africa.

African leaders met stiff opposition to independence in some parts of the continent, especially in the East African Highlands and Southern Africa, where there were many Europeans.

Algeria, with a million French settlers, broke free from France in 1962 only after a bloody eight-year war. In much of the remainder of North Africa, however, the

Background Information

Help for Africa from Rock Stars and Computer Nerds

The lead singer of the rock band U2, Bono, and the foundations set up by Bill Gates (the co-founder of Microsoft) and his wife, Melinda, have led efforts in the 2000s to eradicate poverty in Africa. They have worked to bring attention to critical issues facing Africa including healthcare, access to vaccinations, poverty, HIV/AIDS, agriculture, and debt relief.

Bono is a co-founder of the DATA (Debt, AIDS, Trade, Africa) organization, from which later came the ONE Campaign to Make Poverty History. He successfully worked with world leaders, including President George W. Bush and Prime Minister Tony Blair of the United Kingdom, to have the world's richest industrial nations forgive the debts of African governments.

The Bill and Melinda Gates Foundation is the world's wealthiest charitable

foundation. In 2005, the Bill and Melinda Gates Foundation committed $750 million to improving access to child immunizations, speeding the introduction of new vaccines, and improving the ways vaccines get to people who need them. In 2006, they gave grants to improve the agricultural output of Africa's farmers.

path to independence was peaceful. Libya, Tunisia, and Morocco gained independence without a fight.

Independence came to most of Africa south of the Sahara starting in the late 1950s. The Gold Coast led the way in 1957 when it was granted independence from British rule. In 1960, 17 new nations, including Nigeria, became independent.

The transfer of power was mostly peaceful in Africa south of the Sahara. The British East Africa colony, Kenya, was a notable exception. European settlers were determined not to submit to African rule. British military forces fought Kikuyu guerrilla fighers known as the Mau Mau. Although the guerillas were defeated, this bloody conflict helped convince the United Kingdom to decolonize. Kenya was granted independence in 1963.

By 1970, most African nations had won independence. White-controlled minority governments were replaced by African-born black leaders during the next 25 years. The places that remained colonies became independent by the mid-1990s.

Rhodesia (ro·DEE·zhah) remained a white-minority-ruled government until 1980. After black Africans came to power there, they named the nation Zimbabwe after the Great Zimbabwe civilization. With the support of the United Nations, Namibia (na·MIB·ih·ah) gained its independence from South African control in 1990.

South Africa remained under white rule until 1994, when Nelson Mandela was elected president of that country. He had been jailed almost 30 years for his role in leading opposition to white rule.

Explosions damaged Algiers during the long Algerian war for independence against France. **Where else in Africa did conflict arise over independence?**

Africa and the World

93

Discussion Questions

1 Independence came peacefully to most countries in Africa. What were the exceptions?

2 How successful were the various African nations in gaining their independence?

3 Can you see any similarities between Africa's struggle for independence and the struggle of the former Soviet states against the Soviet Union?

4 What role did Nelson Mandela play in the independence and leadership of South Africa?

Caption Answer

Kenya had great difficulty. South Africa saw great conflict.

Map Activity

The Past and the Present

NATIONAL GEOGRAPHY STANDARDS:
GEOGRAPHIC THEMES: Location, Place
OBJECTIVES: 1.01

Have students label a map of colonial Africa, indicating the colonial names, for example, Rhodesia. Using an atlas of modern Africa, on a piece of notebook paper write the name of each European possession in Africa and the name/names of the modern African nations formed from each.

Discussion Questions

1 What conflicts could arise by merging two rival nations together under one government?

2 Why was it so important to build schools when the African leaders gained power?

3 Who do you think would teach the students in these new schools?

4 Why are African nations changing their names to more traditional names?

5 How could the competition between the United States and the Soviet Union during the Cold War be advantageous to Africa?

Caption Answer

The colonizing countries had used authoritarian power to govern African countries. After independence, African leaders continued to follow this model of government.

Writing Activity

African Nation Advisor

 OBJECTIVES: 5.03

Give students the following prompt: Pretend you are an advisor to an African nation. Select three areas, such as education, infrastructure, or medical care, that should be the focus of development, and explain how each would help the African leader to develop the natural and human resources of the nation. Prepare a speech that you will present at a government meeting.

Ellen Johnson-Sirleaf was elected president of Liberia in 2005. She is Africa's first elected female head of state.
Why has it been hard to build democratic governments in Africa?

Building Unified Nations

Soon after the British withdrew from Northern Rhodesia, the new leaders named the country Zambia. Compare maps of colonial and present-day Africa on pages 90 and 20. You will quickly see that this practice of renaming newly independent nations was common throughout Africa. In giving their countries African names, governments were announcing their determination to be truly free of European domination.

African leaders found that new names would not eliminate the problems left behind by years of European domination. As you have read, Europeans once redrew the map of Africa. They separated members of some ethnic groups from one another and put long-time enemies together.

This meant that in Nigeria two rival groups, the Hausas and the Ibos, came under a single government. Shortly after Nigeria gained independence, the Ibos

announced that they would separate from Nigeria to form the nation of Biafra. This set off a three-year civil war.

Political Instability

When European nations turned over power to African leaders, they often did so in a hurry. Few African countries were prepared for the challenges they faced. Before the late 1940s, colonial rulers did not offer anything beyond elementary school education to most Africans. Few nations had enough college-educated workers to fill all the government positions suddenly left open when the Europeans left. One of the first actions taken by leaders of many new African nations was to build schools.

The Cold War struggle between the Western democracies and the Communist countries also caused instability in Africa. In the Cold War, both superpowers, the United States and the Soviet Union, competed for influence around the world. Both worked to win the support of African leaders. Each offered military or economic aid and sometimes backed *corrupt* government leaders in exchange for guarantees of support. Political corruption is when government officials use public property or betray the public's trust to benefit themselves or their families.

Seeking Stability

By the early twentieth century, most European powers holding African colonies were democracies at home. They ran their colonies, however, in *authoritarian* ways. This meant that colonial leaders exercised authority under the direction of their home governments. The African people, and even Europeans living in the colony, had little voice in governmental affairs. After independence, when African leaders took power, many followed this model. Few new nations encouraged the development of democracies.

Authoritarian rule did not guarantee that African people would live in peace or enjoy good government. Rival ethnic

---

 Background Information

Kofi Annan

Ghana's Kofi Annan, the seventh Secretary General of the United Nations, has been a role model to many Africans. He is the first black African to hold the post. Before taking the United Nations' top job, the soft-spoken diplomat spent most of his career at the United Nations serving in a variety of administrative posts. Born in Kumasi, Ghana, Annan is the son of a politician who was elected governor of the Ashanti

province. He is descended from tribal chiefs on both sides of his family. Annan grew up knowing both traditional customs as well as the modern world. At age twenty, he won a Ford Foundation scholarship to attend college in the United States, graduating from Macalester College in St. Paul, Minnesota. In 2001, he was awarded the Nobel Peace Prize, which he shares with the United Nations.

groups often engaged in bloody wars. Corrupt officials sometimes built personal fortunes from their countries' wealth.

Yet in many countries today, corruption has been greatly reduced. Africans have organized to gain free elections, a free press, and governments that are responsible to their people. In 1989, 35 nations were governed under the authority of a single political party. By 1994, the only one-party state authorized by its constitution was Eritrea. However, a number of nations, such as Zimbabwe, function mainly as one-party states with little opposition allowed. But many African nations are making real progress in building good governments.

Economic Independence

Building a nation requires more than political unity. To be independent, nations must have ways for their people to earn money.

A strong economy is important. Africa's leaders still wrestle with the results of imperialism. Both the slave trade and colonialism affected Africa's economy. Slavery took millions of productive people from villages. Colonial rulers forced villagers to grow cash crops for export.

Yet Europeans also left behind some foundations of modern economies. They opened mines and equipped them with machinery. They installed docks and cargo handling equipment in seaports and highways, railways, and airports.

Improved agricultural practices increased crop yields. Hospitals and schools were opened.

Now, many African nations want to create *free trade* zones. Free trade means nations will place few or no taxes on imported goods. This encourages the growth of trade.

Nigerians elected Olusegun Obasanjo president in 1999 after many years of military rule. He served two terms. **What were some of the problems created by Africa's authoritarian governments?**

Discussion Questions

1 How do you think the citizens of the United States would respond to an authoritarian ruler?

2 What are some ways that African nations can improve their economy?

3 How did the presence of the Europeans in Africa lay a foundation for economic growth?

Caption Answer

Authoritarian governments were sometimes led by corrupt officials out to build personal fortunes at the expense of their country. Conflicts between rival ethnic groups were common.

Africa and the World

95

Activity

African Challenges

OBJECTIVES: 5.01, 6.01, 10.01

African nations today face a number of challenges, including:

- authoritarian governments
- different currencies
- poor transportation and communication
- unstable governments

- export of raw materials instead of finished products
- ethnic loyalties
- lack of skilled workers
- dependence on one main export, one-crop economy
- civil war

Have students rank these problems from the most serious (1) to the least serious (9) as they relate to Africa's future development. Follow with a class discussion. Next, have students make three columns on a sheet of paper with the headings Political, Economic, and

Social, and then categorize each problem into the appropriate column. Discuss as a class how students classified certain problems. Ask students to pick one problem that, if solved, would most benefit African development. Have students offer solutions to the problem.

Extension Have students write a persuasive essay to support their points of view.

For ELL students, model and provide additional explanations.

Caption Answer

Most African nations are part of a global economy. Coffee crops in Africa can cause fluctuations in coffee prices in the world market. Oil prices worldwide affect African oil-producing nations.

Activity

Modern Trade Flow Chart

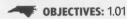 **OBJECTIVES:** 1.01

Select an African country. Using an almanac or the *CIA World Factbook* (visit **NCJourneys.com** for a link), have students create a flow chart showing the countries with which it trades and the imports and exports involved in the trading. Ask: Does this country maintain ties with the European country that formerly controlled it?

Extension Assign novice and intermediate ELL students to work with a peer tutor.

The Nairobi, Kenya, Kenyatta Conference Center is the site of international meetings. **How is Africa part of the global economy?**

96

Chapter 5

Global Economy

African nations are now affected by foreign involvement of another kind. The economies of nations throughout the world are so closely related that all nations are now part of a *global economy.* African nations are looking for ways to *diversify,* or broaden, their economies so that they will be less affected by changes in the global economy. Until this happens, many face an uncertain economic future.

The economic prospects are not the same for every African nation. Some are favored by climate and fertile soil for agricultural development. Others contain vast resources.

Today, the richest African nations—Libya, Gabon, South Africa, Algeria, and Botswana—depend heavily on the export of their oil or other minerals. As you have read, nations that depend on income from the export of minerals or cash crops face uncertain futures. Demand for these minerals and crops goes up and down. Also, minerals and fossil fuels are nonrenewable natural resources that will someday run out.

Raw materials exported by African nations may benefit the buyers more than the sellers. Raw materials cost less than the products made from them. Larger profits go to manufacturers. Some countries with oil and mineral wealth have used their wealth to broaden their economies. They have built factories where they can make goods from their raw materials themselves. This keeps profits at home and provides more jobs for a nation's own workers.

Other countries have spent their wealth on lavish or poorly planned building projects or on consumer goods to please their supporters. They have little to show for the sale of their nations' natural resources.

Africans today are searching for new ways to develop the continent's natural and human resources. Some nations hope to find new trading partners and markets for their products within their own and neighboring countries.

Africa's circumstances are difficult, but the years since independence have brought progress as well as challenges. The goals of independence have not been abandoned. It is a continent of many resources, the greatest of which is its people. Although some states have suffered major setbacks, Africa's strong family and social structures have allowed its people to overcome many of their problems and build the foundations for a strong future.

A Nigerian cuts pipe on an offshore oil rig near Port Harcourt, Nigeria. **What are the advantages and disadvantages of exporting minerals?**

LESSON 3 REVIEW

Fact Follow-Up

1. What world events encouraged African independence movements?
2. What were some problems faced by newly independent African nations?
3. How did authoritarian governments arise in some areas of Africa?
4. What does diversify mean?

Talk About It

1. Which areas of Africa gained independence quickly. Why? Which areas were late?
2. Colonialism in Africa lasted only about 100 years. Why did it have such a strong impact?
3. How can African nations improve their economies?

Africa and the World

Discussion Questions

1 How can building more factories in Africa help ensure economic stability and a secure future?

2 What are some ways African nations can become more a part of the global economy?

3 How do we develop and conserve our natural and human resources in the United States?

4 How can Africa improve their communication and transportation systems?

5 Do you know of any trade barriers between the United States and other countries?

 Caption Answer

Exports, including minerals, often favor the buyer not the seller. There is money to be made by demand, but if demand falters, then the economy will falter.

 **Teacher Notes**

Discussing Infrastructure

This is a good time to describe and assess the concept of infrastructure as a vital part of an economic development plan. Discuss what a country's infrastructure is and how it relates to the economy. Have students give examples of infrastructure in North Carolina and the United States.

LESSON 3 REVIEW

Fact Follow-Up Answers

1. After World War II, European nations were weakened and could no longer afford to govern colonies, especially if colonies were resistent.
2. Ethnic rivalries, lack of education and training, and instability caused by the Cold War were problems for newly independent African nations.
3. Some leaders of authoritarian governments were men who had led the country's independence movement. Others were military leaders who took power by force. Since European imperial powers had not encouraged the development of democracy in their African colonies, there had been little opportunity for the development of democratic leadership.
4. To diversity means to broaden.

Talk About It Answers

1. West Africa gained independence quickly because there were relatively few Europeans who lived there. Kenya in East Africa and South Africa were late because many Europeans and their descendants who lived there refused to accept African rule. In North Africa only those areas with large European populations (e.g., Algeria) had long battles for independence.
2. Under colonialism, Africans could not control their own political or economic life. African traditions, economies, and family systems were disrupted. During this time, Europe industrialized and increased in power and wealth. African labor and raw materials went to promote European, and not African, interests. Europeans did not encourage the education and training of Africans for leadership.
3. Improvements in communication, transportation, and education, as well as regional cooperation in trade, could improve the economies of African nations.

Teaching This Skill Lesson

Materials Needed textbooks, paper, pencils

Classroom Organization students working individually or in pairs

Beginning the Lesson Refer students to the photographs (see page 99). Ask them what movements they can observe, listing their responses on the chalkboard. Encourage students to challenge each other for evidence of these observations. Focus on the photograph of the Congo River ferry. What can be *inferred* about the movement of people, goods, and ideas from this photograph? Again, welcome students' challenges.

Developing the Lesson Direct students to sketch a data retrieval chart like the one on page 98. Monitor as they begin to complete the chart using information from Chapter 5. Make a homework assignment for students to complete data retrieval charts for Chapters 2, 3, and 4. Assign one third of the class to each chapter. Students should be able to answer the questions posed in this skill lesson when they have completed the homework assignment.

Conclusion Follow the homework assignment by discussing the questions in the last two paragraphs. Talk with students about the importance of learning to make inferences based on information.

Extension For intermediate ELL students, model and provide additional explanations. Assign students to work with a partner.

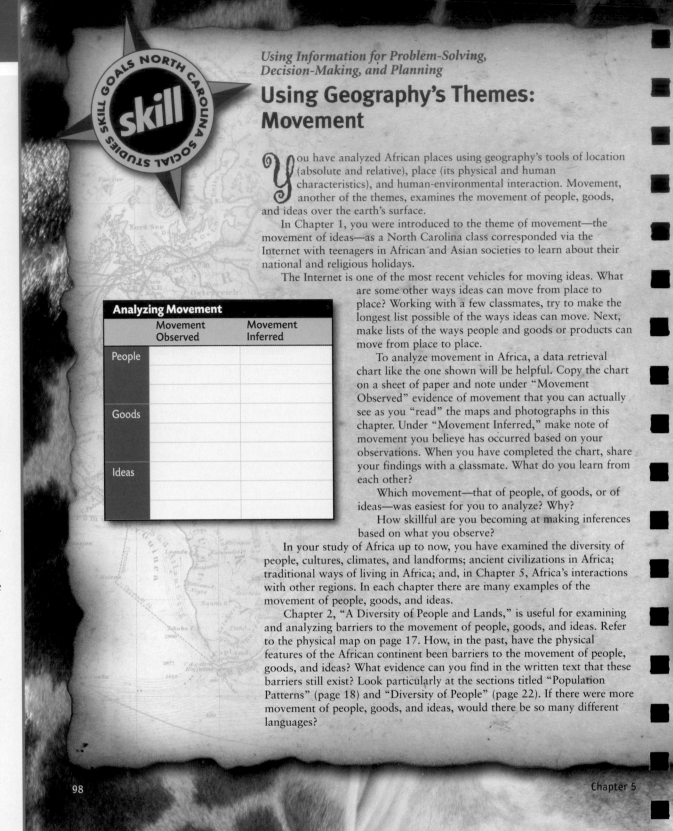

Using Information for Problem-Solving, Decision-Making, and Planning

Using Geography's Themes: Movement

SKILL GOALS NORTH CAROLINA SOCIAL STUDIES

skill

You have analyzed African places using geography's tools of location (absolute and relative), place (its physical and human characteristics), and human-environmental interaction. Movement, another of the themes, examines the movement of people, goods, and ideas over the earth's surface.

In Chapter 1, you were introduced to the theme of movement—the movement of ideas—as a North Carolina class corresponded via the Internet with teenagers in African and Asian societies to learn about their national and religious holidays.

The Internet is one of the most recent vehicles for moving ideas. What are some other ways ideas can move from place to place? Working with a few classmates, try to make the longest list possible of the ways ideas can move. Next, make lists of the ways people and goods or products can move from place to place.

To analyze movement in Africa, a data retrieval chart like the one shown will be helpful. Copy the chart on a sheet of paper and note under "Movement Observed" evidence of movement that you can actually see as you "read" the maps and photographs in this chapter. Under "Movement Inferred," make note of movement you believe has occurred based on your observations. When you have completed the chart, share your findings with a classmate. What do you learn from each other?

Which movement—that of people, of goods, or of ideas—was easiest for you to analyze? Why?

How skillful are you becoming at making inferences based on what you observe?

In your study of Africa up to now, you have examined the diversity of people, cultures, climates, and landforms; ancient civilizations in Africa; traditional ways of living in Africa; and, in Chapter 5, Africa's interactions with other regions. In each chapter there are many examples of the movement of people, goods, and ideas.

Chapter 2, "A Diversity of People and Lands," is useful for examining and analyzing barriers to the movement of people, goods, and ideas. Refer to the physical map on page 17. How, in the past, have the physical features of the African continent been barriers to the movement of people, goods, and ideas? What evidence can you find in the written text that these barriers still exist? Look particularly at the sections titled "Population Patterns" (page 18) and "Diversity of People" (page 22). If there were more movement of people, goods, and ideas, would there be so many different languages?

Analyzing Movement

	Movement Observed	Movement Inferred
People		
Goods		
Ideas		

98

Chapter 5

The photographs used in this skill lesson show both movement and barriers to movement. How can rivers both aid and hinder movement? Can waterfalls or cataracts ever help the movement of ideas?

Chapter 3, "Historical Foundations of Africa," describes ancient Africa's great civilizations. The chapter is useful for examining both relatively isolated civilizations (ancient Egypt, for one) and civilizations built on movement (Ghana and Songhai, for example).

Try using the data retrieval chart again to chart the geographic concept of movement in one of the ancient African civilizations described in Chapter 3. When you have finished, discuss your findings with a classmate.

Are you becoming more skilled in using the theme of movement? Is it becoming easier to make valid inferences? (A valid inference is one that turns out to be a correct guess.)

This chapter describes Africa and other regions of the world, in particular its relationships with Europe. Look now at the two maps illustrating this chapter. The map of the Atlantic slave trade shows movement between Africa and other world areas. What people, goods, and ideas entered Africa during the era of the Atlantic slave trade? What people, goods, and ideas moved from Africa to other world areas? Be careful to review Lesson 1 in this chapter for additional information on this particular example of movement.

The second map, that of European colonies in Africa, can be read as well. What people, goods, and ideas moved from Europe to Africa during Europe's "rush for empire"? What people, goods, and ideas moved from Africa to Europe? Did people, goods, and ideas pass from one colony to another? Finally, what were the consequences of these movements for Africans? for Europeans?

Nile steamer, Sudan

Marchison Falls, Nile River

Africa and the World

99

 Skill Lesson Review

1. Which of the three kinds of movement—of people, goods, or ideas—is easiest to observe? Why? *People or goods: because they are usually the most visible sign of movement.*

2. How would knowledge of the theme of movement be useful to an expert trying to persuade African farmers to adopt new farming methods? *Answers will vary. This is an example of the movement of ideas. An expert should know that his new ideas might not be immediately accepted. Barriers to movement have sometimes prevented the spread of ideas in Africa.*

3. In what ways can movement be a benefit? In what ways can it be a burden? *It can promote understanding and prosperity. If movement is forced, as in the slave trade, it can be a tragedy.*

4. Can any society avoid the theme of movement? Explain. *No. Even the most remote society experiences some movement.*

5. How can the movement of ideas be traced? *It can be traced through the printed page, the arts, television, radio, film, telephones, and computers.*

Talk About It

1. Important points: Students should choose one of the two and support their choice. Note: The strongest young people were taken as slaves. Families and economies collapsed in some areas as a result. It is possible that this collapse contributed to the relatively easy conquests of the imperialists.

2. Important points: Students should describe the results of the Atlantic slave trade for African societies. Africa might have developed economically and begun trade with Europe and Asia.

3. Important points: Students should choose one legacy and give reasons for the choice. Political instability is partly the result of boundaries imposed by Europeans. Raising cash crops and limited trade within Africa are legacies of colonialism as well.

4. Important points: Students should mention the following: they promise stability; there is no recent tradition of democracy.

5. Important points: Encourage students to suggest as many rational actions as they can and decide which one would benefit Africa most. Possible actions: aid for economic development, health programs, housing, or education. Focus on which actions would be most effective in benefiting Africa in the future.

6. Important points: Encourage students to consider a variety of reasons. Independent nations inherited political borders imposed by European powers in the nineteenth century. Many new nations included rival ethnic groups or separated members of the same ethnic group.

7. Positive consequences include having goods from all over the world available for consumption in Africa and having world markets open to African goods. Negative consequences include the fact that many of Africa's most valuable products are raw materials. World prices for raw materials tend to go up and down, and African countries are thus vulnerable to these changes. Raw materials exported by African countries may benefit buyers more than sellers since raw materials have less value than the finished products made from them.

CHAPTER 5 REVIEW

Lessons Learned

LESSON 1
Africa and the Slave Trade
Africa became a major source of slaves from the 1200s onward. The number of Africans seized as slaves skyrocketed, however, after the Americas were opened to European colonization in the 1500s. Over a 350-year period, millions of men and women were shipped across the Atlantic as slaves. Large regions of Africa suffered from this cruel trade.

LESSON 2
European Imperialism in Africa
Explorers and merchants from emerging European countries appeared along Africa's coast in the 1400s. By the 1800s, several European nations were strong enough to seize and divide almost all of Africa. For the next 100 years or more, Africans lived under foreign rule.

LESSON 3
Independence and After
Africans gained independence from European rule in the 1900s. Freedom has opened opportunities for Africans to build once again on traditions of their own, but independence also has brought economic and political challenges.

Talk About It

1. Which was more devastating for Africa: the Atlantic slave trade or European imperialism? Explain your answer.
2. Suppose there had been no Atlantic slave trade. How do you think Africa would have been different today?
3. What is the most important legacy of imperialism in Africa? Give reasons for your answer.
4. Why do you think authoritarian rulers have come to power in so many recently independent African nations?
5. Imagine that you are an advisor to the president of the United States. What one action would you urge him to take that would benefit Africa most? Give reasons for your answer.
6. Why has it been so difficult for independent African countries to build unified nations?
7. Explain how participating in a global economy has both positive and negative consequences for African countries.

Mastering Mapwork

MOVEMENT
Use the map on page 81 to answer these questions:

1. Which kind of movement (of people, goods, or ideas) is presented on this map?
2. To what area of the Western Hemisphere was there the greatest movement of people?
3. To what area of the Western Hemisphere was there the least movement of people?
4. Which area(s) of Africa appear from this map to have been most affected by the movement of people in the Transatlantic slave trade?

Mastering Mapwork

1. The movement of people is presented on this map.
2. Portuguese Brazil received the greatest number of people.
3. British North America experienced the least number of people.

4. An area stretching down the west coast of the continent from the southern coast of the bulge of West Africa to the desert areas of Southern Africa was most affected by the movement of people during the Transatlantic slave trade.

Go to the Source

Reading Slave Narratives

Read the excerpt from the former slave Olaudah Equiano's autobiography below. Answer the questions using specific references from the text.

The first object which saluted my eyes when I arrived on the coast, was the sea, and a slave ship . . . waiting for its cargo. These filled me with astonishment, which was soon converted into terror, when I was carried on board. I was immediately handled, and tossed up . . . by some of the crew; and I was now persuaded that I had gotten into a world of bad spirits, and that they were going to kill me. Their complexions, too, differing so much from ours, their long hair, and the language they spoke, (which was very different from any I had ever heard) united to confirm me in this belief . . . When I looked round the ship . . . [and saw] a multitude of black people of every description chained together, every one of their . . . [faces] expressing dejection and sorrow, I no longer doubted of my fate; and, quite overpowered with horror and anguish, I fell motionless on the deck and fainted. When I recovered a little, I found some black people about me, who I believed were some of those who had brought me on board, and had been receiving their pay; they talked to me in order to cheer me, but all in vain . . . Soon after this, the blacks who brought me on board went off, and left me abandoned to despair.

. . . I was soon put down under the decks . . . amongst the poor chained men, I found some of my own nation, which in a small degree gave ease to my mind. I inquired of these what was to be done with us? They gave me to understand, we were to be carried to these white people's country to work for them. . . . I could not help expressing my fears and apprehensions to some of my countrymen.

Every circumstance I met with, served only to render my state more painful, and heightened my apprehensions, and my opinion of the cruelty of the whites.

Go to the Source

Questions

1. Once on board the ship, Equiano's first impression was that he would be:
   - a. killed
   - b. released
   - c. forced to work
   - d. thrown overboard

2. Equiano writes: the "blacks who brought him on board and went off." The reader can conclude these blacks were:
   - a. not strong enough for the sea voyage
   - b. to be placed on another slave ship
   - c. involved in the slave trade
   - d. from the same village as Gustavo

3. Why might today's historians value Equiano's narrative?
   - a. His family back in Africa wanted to know what happened to him
   - b. He represents the experience of many people of African descent whose stories were not written down.
   - c. He became an important civil rights leader in the United States.
   - d. The slave traders wanted to keep a record of all of their passengers.

Go to the Source

OBJECTIVES: 4.01; Skills 1.01, 3.05, 4.06

Lesson 1 of this chapter opens with a passage from Olaudah Equiano's autobiography that describes his kidnapping. The excerpt here describes his first impressions and emotions when he is taken to the slavers' ship.

When Equiano wrote his autobiography, *The Life of Gustavus Vassa,* he titled it using his "slave" name, given to him in slavery. Historians today prefer to use his African name, which is his original name, given before he was kidnapped and enslaved.

The entire text is available on line for additional research. Visit NCJourneys.com for a link.

ANSWERS

1. a
2. c
3. b

How to Use the Chapter Review

There are three sections in the Chapter Review: Talk About It, Mastering Mapwork, and Go to the Source. Use the Vocabulary Worksheets and the Chapter Review Worksheet in the Teacher's Resource Guide for additional reinforcement and preparation for the Chapter Assessments. The chapter and lesson reviews and the Chapter Review Worksheets are the basis of the assessment for each chapter.

Talk About It questions encourage students to speculate about the content of the chapter and are suitable for class or small-group discussion. They are not intended to be assigned for homework.

Mastering Mapwork has students apply one or more of the Five Themes of Geography to maps within the chapter.

Go to the Source activities allow students to analyze a primary source that relates to the content of the chapter. The questions and activities familiarize students with different types of primary sources and also build content-reading skills.

Unit 2 Africa Today: Regions

This unit begins with a picture of the West African Yam Harvest Festival, which is also featured in *Things Fall Apart*, Chinua Achebe's novel about an Ibo village. The unit introduces your students to the regions of Africa today—the geography and customs, history and traditions, of this diverse continent.

In North Africa, your students will discover a shared history and common culture. West Africa offers a mixture of ancient traditions from the old African empires and the shaping influence of European colonialism. The rain forests and the Congo River dominate Central Africa, a region of only partly developed resources. In East Africa, some countries border the Red Sea and the Indian Ocean, four are island nations, and others stretch through the Eastern Highlands. South Africa contains vast resources, but its progress has been slowed by policies of racial separation that have only recently been abandoned.

UNIT LESSON PLAN

	LESSON 1	LESSON 2	LESSON 3
CHAPTER 6 North Africa	North African nations share a physical environment of coastlines and interior desert. Most people live in coastal cities that are gaining population. **Essential Question:** How does the physical environment of North Africa affect the people of North Africa? **Suggested Time:** 1 day	North African nations have focused on building independent governments and strong economies since independence in the 1950s and 1960s. **Essential Question:** In what ways have North African countries worked to build strong central governments and economies? **Suggested Time:** 2 days	North Africa is becoming increasingly urban. Islam is the religious faith embraced by nearly all North Africans. **Essential Question:** What influence has Islam had on the culture of North Africa? **Suggested Time:** 2 days
CHAPTER 7 West Africa	The region provides three environments—desert, grassland, and rain forest. Most people live in the well-watered south. **Essential Question:** What are the characteristics of the different environmental regions of West Africa, and how does the physical environment affect the culture? **Suggested Time:** 2 days	Different groups mix in West African nations, making national unity difficult. People live by subsistence farming and exports. **Essential Question:** What obstacles must West African countries overcome in order to build national unity? **Suggested Time:** 2 days	The region remains heavily rural, and daily life continues in many traditional ways. But cities are growing rapidly. **Essential Question:** How does the traditional daily routine of West African villages compare to the daily routine of the rapidly growing urban centers of West Africa? **Suggested Time:** 1 days
CHAPTER 8 Central Africa	Rain forests and the Congo River and its tributaries dominate the land. Population is scattered throughout the region. **Essential Question:** What is the connection between population patterns and physical environment in Central Africa? **Suggested Time:** 1 day	Transition from colonial rule has been difficult. The region's water, forest, and mineral resources are only partly developed. **Essential Question:** What factors have prevented Central Africa from fully developing their economic resources? **Suggested Time:** 1 day	Life in forests, on farms, and in cities creates different customs among the region's many ethnic groups. **Essential Question:** How are customs different among the various ethnic groups in Central Africa? **Suggested Time:** 1 day
CHAPTER 9 East Africa	East Africa's environment offers desert in the North and areas with vegetation in the South. The region is unevenly populated. **Essential Question:** How does the physical environment affect population patterns in East Africa? **Suggested Time:** 1 day	The years since independence have been marred by civil wars. Agriculture is the region's major industry. **Essential Question:** Why has civil war plagued East Africa since gaining independence in the region, and what are the effects of civil war on the regions's stability and economy? **Suggested Time:** 2 days	The people's diverse heritages and ways of farming create many ways of life in East Africa. **Essential Question:** How is culture different for the various ethnic groups who live in East Africa? **Suggested Time:** 1 day
CHAPTER 10 Southern Africa	Southern Africa is located on a plateau with a steep escarpment and narrow coastal plain. It has mountains, deserts, the Zambezi River, and a wealth of mineral resources. Its diverse people are from Africa, Europe, and Asia. **Essential Question:** What impact does geo-graphy have on the lives of the people living in Southern Africa? **Suggested Time:** 1 day	Southern Africa has been a region of violent conflict. Its countries have suffered through civil wars and struggles of blacks to achieve rights under white-minority-ruled governments. **Essential Question:** Why has Southern Africa been a region of violent conflict? **Suggested Time:** 2 days	Blacks and whites are beginning to share their cultures. Religion in the region often mixes Christianity and traditional African beliefs. **Essential Question:** How are blacks and whites in Southern Africa overcoming cultural differences and past conflicts? **Suggested Time:** 2 days

Preparing the Unit

- Worksheets, assessments, and reproducibles for this unit are found in the Teacher's Resource Guide.
- See the list of Cultural Resources in the Teacher's Edition.
- Display the student work produced in Unit 1 to decorate your room.
- Review the resource list and collect as many of the suggested resources as possible for a classroom resource center, including North Carolina State University Humanities Extension/Publications videos.
- Share the suggested art and music activities with your cultural arts teachers so that they may help you integrate the curriculum.
- Review the suggested activities and select the ones that are most appropriate for your classroom. Plan ahead by collecting the materials for the activities.
- As you prepare your daily lessons, refer to the suggested goals listed in the chapter plan for selecting the specific objective(s) that you plan to cover in each lesson. Refer to the North Carolina Standard Course of Study for the specific objectives covered.
- Refer to the resource list for suggested titles of novels related to Africa for students to read during the study of Unit 2. Coordinate with the English language arts teacher to integrate the curriculum.

Unit Teaching Strategies

- If you feel like you spent too much time on Unit 1, implement the unit project ideas as a strategy for quickly covering the material in Unit 2. You can share the projects by inviting administrators and parents to the presentations or you can videotape the presentations. As a culminating project, allow students to bring in foods for a buffet luncheon highlighting the foods of Africa. Speakers may also be invited to participate in the Culminating Project Day.
- Check NCJourneys.com for updates and materials.

Divide the class into collaborative pairs or groups of three. Assign each group a country in Africa and ask them to complete a research project. Make sure that you assign countries from the different regions so that each region is represented. Once assigned with a country, each group is responsible for reading the chapter that correlates with their country. For example, if a group is assigned to research the country of Egypt, they should read the information in Chapter 6 to help them with their research. As the teacher, you should assign the research projects based on the amount of time available, resources, and ability of students. These choices allow you to differentiate instruction for your students. One or more of the projects below can be assigned to each group.

PROJECT CHOICES

OBJECTIVES: 1.01, 2.02, 9.04

Students will have seven days to complete their project. Suggested report format: two pages in length, typed, and double-spaced.

Making a Regional Map of Africa

Students will select one of the five regions of Africa and create a three-dimensional map—it could be a salt map, a clay map, or a cookie map. The map must include the following items: land and water forms, bordering countries, and capitals.

Music in Africa

Students will research music found in the different regions of Africa. They will then either make a musical instrument found in Africa and perform for the class or will learn dances found in Africa. Students will explain the importance of the dance in African culture and perform it for the class.

You Are There

Students will research apartheid in South Africa. They will pretend to be news reporters in Soweto on the day of elections for Nelson Mandela, and will interview a black South African who is voting for the first time. Included in the news report: a brief history of apartheid, information about Nelson Mandela's qualifications, and how the lives of the voters will change because of the election. They will prepare a list of at least ten questions that would be asked of a first time voter and give their responses.

AIDS in Africa

Students will research the spread of the AIDS epidemic in Africa over the last decade. Present the information in a graph using Excel or Works. Students might research AIDS in a specific region or compare regions. After the graph has been created, analyze the data and predict the impact of AIDS in Africa over the next ten years.

Board Game of Africa

Students will create a board game in which players travel across Africa. All questions, answers, and squares in the game must be based on facts studied throughout the unit.

Bulletin Board Ideas

African Regions

Have a map of Africa as the centerpiece of the bulletin board. Color each region a different color. Label each region on the map and have items available that represent each region. Have students place items (can be pictures, names of items on paper slips) in the proper region as you study each one.

African Deserts

Have students create a desert mural on the bulletin board. Have a map of Africa with its desert areas labeled on one side of the mural. Students might draw the mural scenes or use available pictures for a collage effect.

Extension For ELL students, model and provide additional explanations.

"To the Shores of Tripoli"

Have students research Tripoli and report back on the facts they found. Create a Tripoli and United States involvement time line from their facts. You could place the verse of the Marine Hymn at the top of the board.

Extension For Intermediate ELL students, model and provide additional explanations.

Introductory Activity

Regions

 OBJECTIVES: 1.03

To introduce students to the regions of Africa, provide each student with a blank political map of Africa. After students label the map with the names of the countries, use five different colored pencils to shade in the different regions of Africa. This activity can be done independently by referring students to the maps on pages 105, 127, 147, 165, and 185, or you may model on the overhead using a transparency.

Teacher preparation: Find as many different pictures of different scenes from Africa (*National Geographic* is an excellent source) as possible so that you have enough pictures to give several to a group of two or three students in a team. Give each team of students a blank map of Africa with the regions identified and a set of the pictures. Ask the teams to predict where they might see the different scenes on the pictures that were provided. Give each team a few minutes to complete the task, then ask students to select one or two of their pictures and explain why they predicted that it would occur in the region that they chose.

Extension ELL students should use an ELL-friendly Web site for research. Have them make a timeline or collage with minimum words.

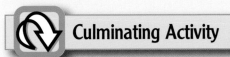
Culminating Activity

Building a Newspaper

OBJECTIVES: 1.01

Students will create a newspaper about a country from the region studied in this unit, as they did in Unit 1. This will be issue number two of their newspaper.

Since there are many countries in Africa, assign students the African nations that were not assigned in Unit 1. Try to assign students a nation from a region different from the region of the nation they wrote about for Unit 1. For example, if a student wrote about Algeria in Unit 1, have him or her write about Mozambique in Unit 2.

Refer to the Unit 1 Culminating Activity on page 14C in the Teacher's Edition for specific directions and references on how to create and organize the newspaper. Remind students that the newspaper should feature two articles on the front. The back of the newspaper should include a map, a box displaying vital statistics, an article about something special or current events, and a puzzle. The students should use their newspapers from the previous unit as a model, and thus the students should be able to complete it in similar or slightly less time.

Share the newspapers with others in the class. Have the students keep each of their newspapers. At the end of the year, bind each student's newspapers together so he or she will have their own volume of newspapers covering the regions studied throughout the year. Use copies of all students' newspapers to organize a class volume according to region.

Math Activity

Made to Order: Flags of Africa

 OBJECTIVES: 10.02

Assign each student a different African nation. They will construct a flag from construction paper that they must "order" from the teacher. The finished product will be based on a 9-inch by 12-inch piece of construction paper. Most students should be able to use their observation skills and rules of proportions to determine the dimensions of each piece. The base color is an integral part of the flag. If the flag design has a triangle, the student should consider it an upper layer after laying down the stripes.

Circles and stars should be estimated as a square with the diameter being the measurement of the side. Supply compasses for making the circles and templates to help with the stars. Triangles in flags are generally of two types:

Those with 9-inch bases have their height estimated as a fraction of the 12-inch length of the flag.

Those with a right angle are measured by the length of the two legs that are estimated as a fraction of the length and width of the finished flag.

Use the worksheet in the Teacher's Resource Guide.

Extension For ELL students, assign peer tutors to help with measurements.

Science Activity

Sickle-Cell Anemia and Malaria

OBJECTIVES: 2.03, 3.01

Sickle-cell anemia is a genetic disorder found most commonly in individuals of African ancestry. The disorder is caused by a gene mutation that causes the shape of the red blood cells to form in a "sickle" shape. The sickle-shaped cells reduces the amount of oxygen carried by the blood cells. Scientists believe that the sickle-cell allele in African people is related to another disease that affects the people of this continent, malaria. Malaria is a disease, which also affects the red blood cells. Carriers of the sickle-cell disease are resistant to malaria. Have one group of students research current findings of how many people in Africa have both malaria and the sickle-cell allele. Malaria occurs in South America and areas of Asia. Have another group of students research the populations of people having sickle-cell allele verses malaria in these areas of the world also. Students can graph this information and compare graphs.

Extension For ELL students, assign peer tutors to help with the graph if needed.

Technology Activity

Economies of Africa

OBJECTIVES: 3.02, 5.01

Have students use the Internet and almanacs to research the economies of Africa's regions. Students will create a spreadsheet or database to track such information for the nations in each region as: major natural resources, industries, transportation, exports, and imports. Students will then sort data and compare regions. Which region is most industrial? the least industrial? Which region has the most resources? Is that the same region that is the most industrial? Which region has the best transportation network? Does that have any relation to the economy of that region? Students should word process a paragraph that uses the data to support their findings to these questions.

Extension For ELL students, assign peer tutors to help. Do not assign the writing portion of this activity.

Unit Resources

Print Resources

Nonfiction

Burckhardt, Ann. *The People of Africa and their Food.* Capstone Press, 1996. ISBN 1560654341. Discusses food preparation and customs in Africa, regional dishes. Includes 12 recipes.

Castle, Caroline. *The Rights of the Children in Words and Pictures.* Phyllis Fogelman Books, 2001. ISBN 0803726503. This book can be used as a follow-up for the Paideia on Unit 2 or Unit 3. It is based on the United Nations Convention on the Rights of the Child. Archbishop Desmond Tutu wrote the introduction to the book. An extending activity could be to have students write what they think are the five most fundamental rights of children.

Maier, Karl. *Into the House of the Ancestors: Inside the New Africa.* John Willey & Sons, 1999. ISBN 100471295833.

Scholes, Katherine. *Peace Begins With You.* Little, Brown and Company, 1994. ISBN 0316774405. Can be used as an alternative to "The Faithful Elephants" Paideia.

Audiovisual

Music available at national music stores

Ali Farka Toure: musician from Timbuktu, Mali

Ladysmith Black Mambazo: vocal group from South Africa

Web Sites

Go to **NCJourneys.com** for links to the following Web sites:

- Africana: Resources on Africa
- Africa Guide, Facts and Figures
- African Population Database Documentation
- Africa Resource
- Africa Resources: Folktales, Biography, Poetry, Nonfiction
- African Studies Internet Resources, Columbia University
- Africa South of the Sahara Resources, Stanford University
- Art and Life in Africa, University of Iowa
- The Center for Sustainable Urban Development, Columbia University
- Exploring Africa, Africa in the Classroom, Michigan State University
- History for Kids, Africa
- K-12 Electronic Guide for African Resources on the Internet, African Studies at the University of Pennsylvania
- Peace Corps Educator Lesson Plans, Africa

Paideia Seminar

Nelson Mandela Paideia

OBJECTIVES: 7.02, 8.01

Nelson Mandela joined the African National Congress (ANC) in 1944 to aid in its struggle against apartheid. During more than 25 years in prison he became the world's most famous political prisoner. After a long campaign of resistance within South Africa and political and economic pressure from without, President F. W. de Klerk ended the government ban on the ANC and freed Mandela in 1990, whereupon he assumed leadership of the organization. He worked to end apartheid and minority rule, gaining widespread respect and support in the process. On May 10, 1994, Nelson Mandela was inaugurated as the first black president of South Africa. Visit **NCJourneys.com** for a link to the text of his inaugural address.

Opening Questions

- If you were going to write a newspaper headline for an article about this speech, what would it be?
- What catches your attention in his speech?
- What can you infer about the past from this speech?

Core Questions

- Why would Mandela refer to South Africa as the former "skunk of the world" in the closing line?
- Human dignity seems to be one of Mandela's major themes. What lines can you point to support this view?
- Does the line "Let freedom reign" remind you of other texts?

Closing Questions

- What values (besides dignity) does Mandela advance in this speech?
- How do think you would feel if you were living in South Africa when this speech was given?
- What do you imagine people might say about this speech in 2100?

Extension Instead of participating in a discussion, ELL students could read the speech online (using the **WorldLingo** translator, link found at **NCJourneys.com**) and listen to discussion in class.

Map Activity

Transparent Africa

NATIONAL GEOGRAPHY STANDARDS: 1, 5, 9

GEOGRAPHIC THEMES: Region

 **OBJECTIVES:** 1.01, 2.03

Distribute copies of the outline map of Africa from the Teacher's Resource Guide. Students should bring in five clear plastic sheet-protectors to place in their notebooks—one for each region of Africa. As students study each region, they should place their blank map of Africa inside each of the sheet protectors. Using crayons, colored pencils, or wipe-off pens, have students draw in physical features, economic and natural resources, and the major cities of each region.

Extension For ELL students, model and provide additional explanations.

Unit 2

How would you like to go back in time? You could visit Umuofia, a West African Ibo village of the late 1800s. Chinua Achebe, a famous African novelist, will take you there. You will meet Okonkwo, a village hero. He will show you his village. You can join in the celebration of the Feast of the New Yam and watch villagers compete in wrestling matches. You may even see a stranger from Britain pedal his bicycle into the village. To discover what happens next, read Achebe's book Things Fall Apart.

102

Unit 2

Social Studies at Work

Horticulturist

A horticulturist is a scientist who specializes in growing and cultivating fruit, vegetables, flowers, or ornamental plants.

Meet Bill Stoffregen

Co-owner of Homewood Nursery and Garden Center and international agricultural volunteer.

In 1967, Raleigh's Bill Stoffregen and his wife, Peggy, built a greenhouse to grow plants for themselves and to sell to friends. That enterprise has grown to include an amazing 80,000 square feet of greenhouses, a garden center, and a nursery featuring winding paths, bridges, and display gardens. It is located in the Stoffregen's 33-acre "backyard" in north Raleigh.

Stoffregen's love of growing things started early when, as a boy, his father let him have one row of the family garden all for himself. When he was a bit older, he was given a pony—and had to grow enough corn to feed it. Stoffregen attended North Carolina State University to study forestry. He worked as a forest ranger in Wake County before his gardening hobby grew into a full-time enterprise.

Stoffregen spends several weeks each year sharing his expertise all over the world. He is especially excited about his involvement in Mauritania, located in northern Africa.

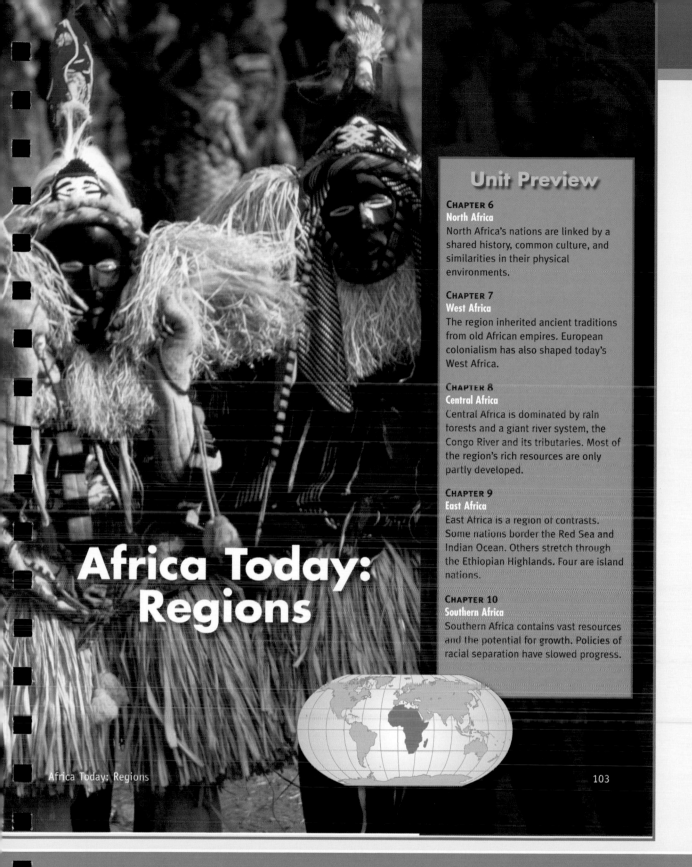

Africa Today: Regions

Unit Preview

CHAPTER 6
North Africa
North Africa's nations are linked by a shared history, common culture, and similarities in their physical environments.

CHAPTER 7
West Africa
The region inherited ancient traditions from old African empires. European colonialism has also shaped today's West Africa.

CHAPTER 8
Central Africa
Central Africa is dominated by rain forests and a giant river system, the Congo River and its tributaries. Most of the region's rich resources are only partly developed.

CHAPTER 9
East Africa
East Africa is a region of contrasts. Some nations border the Red Sea and Indian Ocean. Others stretch through the Ethiopian Highlands. Four are island nations.

CHAPTER 10
Southern Africa
Southern Africa contains vast resources and the potential for growth. Policies of racial separation have slowed progress.

Africa Today: Regions 103

In 2000, Stoffregen went with a group of experts to explore ways to use agriculture to improve the standard of living for the Mauritanian people. The first phase of the project involved helping villagers establish a mint crop that they can grow and sell locally.

While in Mauritania, Stoffregen came across an even more useful agricultural resource. He noticed some small, well-shaped trees that his translator identified as neem trees. Stoffregen says "bells went off in my mind" because he remembered that at home he used a popular, environmentally safe, neem-based insecticide to protect plants.

Stoffregen suspected he was on to something big. Upon his return to North Carolina he used the Internet to find out all he could about the neem. He discovered that it was used in many useful medicines, insecticides, and other products.

Stoffregen is working with officials in Mauritania to determine how these trees can be used to provide jobs and opportunities for the people there.

Horticulturalist for-a-Day Activity
Visit **NCJourneys.com** for a link to the Neem Foundation and see how many uses you can find for the neem tree. Don't quit looking until you've listed at least a dozen.

CHAPTER 6

North Africa

Social Studies Strands

Geographic Relationship
Physical features
Climate and vegetation
Population

Government and Active Citizenship

Economics and Development

Cultures and Diversity
Ethnic traits
Language
Religion

Global Connections

North Carolina Standard Course of Study

Goal 2 The learner will assess the relationship between physical environment and cultural characteristics of selected societies and regions of Africa, Asia, and Australia.

Goal 5 The learner will evaluate the varied ways people of Africa, Asia, and Australia make decisions about the allocation and use of economic resources.

Goal 6 The learner will recognize the relationship between economic activity and the quality of life in Africa, Asia, and Australia.

Goal 11 The learner will recognize the common characteristics of different cultures in Africa, Asia, and Australia.

Teaching & Assessment

• English Language Learner Modified Lesson Plans for this chapter are found in the Teacher Resource Guide.

• *ExamView® Assessment Suite* is provided at **NCJourneys.com.** It includes customizable assessments for all chapters. Paper tests are also available in the Teacher Resource Guide. See pages T16–T17 for information about how to use the assessments and the Scoring Guide.

Worksheets

Worksheets and answer keys are found both in the Teacher Resource Guide and at **NCJourneys.com**, including Reading Guides, Reading Strategies, Chapter Reviews, English Language Learner and others.

ACTIVITIES AND INTEGRATIONS

SOCIAL STUDIES

Activator: North African Food, p. 104
● What's in a Name? p. 105
▲ ■ Population Distribution, p. 109
▲ ■ Using an Almanac, p. 110
★ Western Sahara Time Line, p. 114
● Governments of North Africa, p. 113
★ Suez Canal, p. 118
Skill Lesson: Using Geography's Themes: Region, p. 123

READING/LANGUAGE ARTS

	READING/LANGUAGE ARTS OBJECTIVES
Analogies, p. 104B	2.01
Writing Prompt: Living in a City or Rural Area? p. 104	3.03
Letter to Your Family, p. 108	2.01, 6.02
Peer Mediation Activity, p. 112	2.01
★ Canals, p. 119	2.01, 2.02
★ Be a Planner, p. 120	
Go to the Source: Understanding Government Documents, p. 125	1.02, 2.01, 4.01

SCIENCE

	SCIENCE OBJECTIVES
Rain Shadow Effect, p. 109	3.05

MATHEMATICS

	MATHEMATICS OBJECTIVES
● Population Math Problem, p. 107	4.01, 4.02
★ Suez Canal Word Problem, p. 118	1.02, 2.02

TECHNOLOGY

	TECHNOLOGY OBJECTIVES
▲ Planning a Souk, p. 104B	3.10, 3.11
North Africa's Five Themes, p. 104B	3.01, 3.03, 3.10
Eid! p. 106	3.01, 3.03 , 3.10
● Governments of North Africa, p. 113	3.01, 3.03, 3.11

VISUAL ARTS

	VISUAL ARTS OBJECTIVES
Morrocan Radial Mosaic, p. 104B	2.04, 5.01, 5.02
★ ▲ ■ The Building of Egypt as a Nation, p. 111	2.04, 4.01
Illustrations of North Africa, p. 116	4.01, 4.03
▲ ■ Morrocan Sconce, p. 117	2.04, 5.01

CHARACTER AND VALUES EDUCATION

	TRAITS
Writing Prompt: Living in a City or Rural Area?, 104	good judgment
Peer Mediation, p. 112	good citizenship, respect
What Would You Do?, p. 114	good judgment

● Basic Activities ★ Challenging Activities ▲ English Language Learner Novice ■ English Language Learner Intermediate

Introductory Activity

Planning a Souk

OBJECTIVES: 3.01, 3.02, 4.02

Have students brainstorm a list of products that might be available in a village souk. Examples might include textiles, jewelry, perfume, clothing, spices/herbs, food shops, bread, coffee, sweets, farm produce, meat, fish, leather goods. Assign students (in groups) to develop one of these village souks. They will need to research specific products (vegetables, fruit, flowers, and so forth), design a shop sign or logo, and plan the layout of the shop as well as the specific goods sold. Have students present their finished product on large construction paper so that shops can be arranged as a souk on the bulletin board or wall.

Extension For novice ELL students, model and provide additional explanations. Assign students to work with a partner or group.

 **Culminating Activity**

North Africa's Five Themes

OBJECTIVES: 1.02, 2.01, 3.01

Divide students into five groups. Assign each group one of the five countries in North Africa.

Each group will design a poster or Web page about its country. Have students put the nation's flag in the center and illustrate around the flag each of the Five Themes of Geography as it pertains to that country. Students should be able to explain the flag's symbolism. Display the posters or show the Web pages to the class.

Extension For novice ELL students, model and provide additional explanations.

 Art Activity

Moroccan Radial Mosaic

OBJECTIVES: 4.03, 7.01, 8.02

Materials many colors of construction paper, scissors, glue, pencils, drawing paper, compass, colored pencils; optional: tempera paint and brushes, paper to paint on

To make the design, use a compass and draw a large circle. Draw or create a geometric and symmetrical design radiating out from center. Lightly color design. Use colors that match the paper you will be using.

To make the mosaic, create a large (18 inches is recommended) circle on black construction paper. Lightly pencil out design (no need to color). Cut colored construction paper into 1-inch squares. Begin gluing down colored squares to match design. Trim squares that do not fit in the tiny spots. Optional activity, use tempera paint to create unique colors. Paint 9-inch by 12-inch sheets of paper one color. Repeat different colors for different sheets of paper. Cut into 1-inch squares and repeat above.

 Analogies

OBJECTIVES: 1.02

Analogies are useful to help students make associations with prior knowledge. Read the analogies aloud and ask students to identify the relationship between the terms. As an extension, ask students to write their own analogies using key terms or places discussed in the chapter.

Aswan High Dam : Egypt :: Hoover Dam : United States of America (is located in)

fellaheen : Egypt :: farmers : United States of America (work the land in)

Tunisia : France :: Libya : Italy (once was ruled by/colonized by)

muezzin : mosque :: bell : church (calls the faithful to prayer at a)

steeple : church :: minaret : mosque (is a tower in a)

mud bricks : dry climates :: concrete blocks : wet climates (are used in buildings in)

Friday : Islam :: Sunday : Christianity (is the Sabbath/holy day in)

Teaching Strategies

Because of the importance of Islam in North Africa, this chapter may be used in conjunction with Unit 3 after an introduction of Islam found in Chapter 12. Using this format, teachers may find that students understand the information on North Africa much better if they have a comprehensive study of Islam beforehand.

Activator

OBJECTIVES: 5.02, 6.02, 12.03

To introduce the chapter on North Africa, put together a platter of North African foods such as dates, olives, and apricots for the students to sample. Sampling these foods will immediately capture the students' attention.

OR

Ask students if they have ever shopped at a flea market or farmer's market. If so, what did they see and what items were available to buy? Explain that in North Africa, almost every rural village has its mosque (Islamic house of worship) and a souk (market). Ask students to look at the pictures in the chapter and to decide what items might be bought and sold at a souk. For an extension, you might bring in some items to illustrate North African goods.

Extension Use an ELL parent as a possible resource to come and speak to the class.

Writing Prompt

OBJECTIVES: 3.02

Evaluative

If you had the choice, would you rather live in the city or in a rural area? Write or word process an essay to convince your classmates that either the city or a rural area is the best place to live. State your position and explain your reasons fully.

As you write your essay, remember to
- clearly state your preference.
- give at least three reasons and explain your reasons fully.
- give examples to support your reasons.
- write in complete sentences and paragraph form.
- organize your ideas and include an introduction and a conclusion.
- use good grammar, spelling, punctuation, and capitalization.

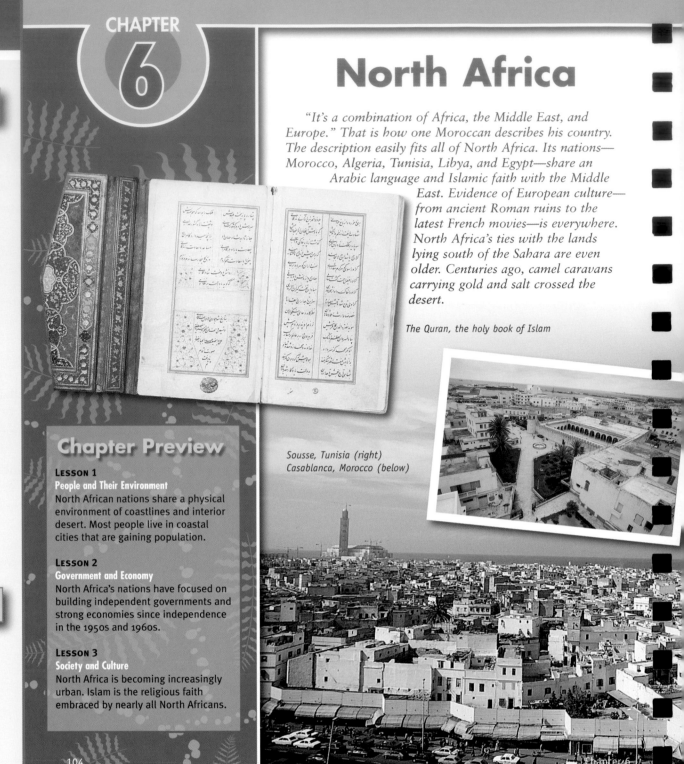

CHAPTER

6

North Africa

"It's a combination of Africa, the Middle East, and Europe." That is how one Moroccan describes his country. The description easily fits all of North Africa. Its nations— Morocco, Algeria, Tunisia, Libya, and Egypt—share an Arabic language and Islamic faith with the Middle East. Evidence of European culture— from ancient Roman ruins to the latest French movies—is everywhere. North Africa's ties with the lands lying south of the Sahara are even older. Centuries ago, camel caravans carrying gold and salt crossed the desert.

The Quran, the holy book of Islam

Sousse, Tunisia (right)
Casablanca, Morocco (below)

Chapter Preview

LESSON 1
People and Their Environment
North African nations share a physical environment of coastlines and interior desert. Most people live in coastal cities that are gaining population.

LESSON 2
Government and Economy
North Africa's nations have focused on building independent governments and strong economies since independence in the 1950s and 1960s.

LESSON 3
Society and Culture
North Africa is becoming increasingly urban. Islam is the religious faith embraced by nearly all North Africans.

104

Chapter 6

Chapter Resources

Print Resources

Nonfiction

Abbas, Jailan. *Festivals of Egypt.* Hoopoe Books (AMIDEST) ISBN 9775325471.

Barghusen, Joan. *Daily Life in Ancient and Modern Cairo.* Runestone Press, 2001. ISBN 0822532212.

Blauer, Ettagale. *Morocco* (Enchantment of the World series). Children's Press, 1999. ISBN 051621053X.

de Villiers, Marq, and Sheila Hirtle. Sahara: The Extraordinary History of the World's Largest Desert. Walker & Company, 2003.

ISBN 0802776787.

Kagda, Falaq. *Algeria* (Enchantment of the World Series). Children's Press, 1997. ISBN 0761406808.

Kalman, Bobbie. *Egypt: The Culture.* Crabtree, 2000. ISBN 0865052344.

—. *Egypt: The Land.* Crabtree, 2000. ISBN 0865052328.

—. *Egypt: The People.* Crabtree, 2000. ISBN 0865052336.

Sanders, Renfield. *Libya* (Modern World Nation series). Chelsea House Pub., 2000. ISBN 0791053881.

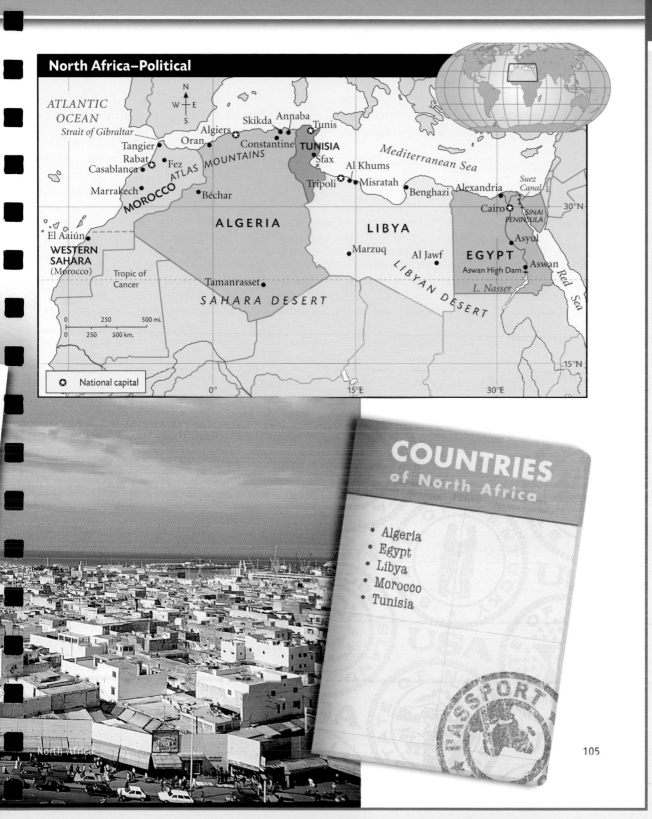

North Africa–Political

ATLANTIC OCEAN
Strait of Gibraltar
Tangier
Rabat
Casablanca
Marrakech
MOROCCO
WESTERN SAHARA (Morocco)
El Aaiún

Oran
Algiers
Skikda
Annaba
Constantine
TUNISIA
Tunis
Sfax
ATLAS MOUNTAINS
Fez
Béchar

Mediterranean Sea
Al Khums
Tripoli
Misratah
Benghazi

ALGERIA
LIBYA
Marzuq
Al Jawf

Alexandria
Cairo
SINAI PENINSULA
Suez Canal
30°N
Asyut
EGYPT
Aswan
Aswan High Dam
L. Nasser
Red Sea
15°N

Tropic of Cancer
Tamanrasset
SAHARA DESERT
LIBYAN DESERT

0   250   500 mi.
0   250   500 km.

✪ National capital

0°   15°E   30°E

North Africa

COUNTRIES of North Africa

- Algeria
- Egypt
- Libya
- Morocco
- Tunisia

105

Map Activity

What's in a Name?

NATIONAL GEOGRAPHY STANDARDS: 1, 4, 10, 16, 18

GEOGRAPHIC THEMES: Location, Place, Human-Environmental Interaction, Movement, Region

OBJECTIVES: 1.02, 1.03

One mnemonic to help some students recall the five North African nations: **A**ll (Algeria) **E**ager (Egypt) **L**izards (Libya) **M**ake (Morocco) **T**racks (Tunisia)

Discuss with students why North Africa is often studied with Southwest Asia. Discuss why various nicknames (Maghreb, Middle East, Barbary Coast) are often used for North Africa.

Using world insert map, assign students to clarify why the quote "It's a combination of Africa, the Middle East, and Europe" accurately describes North Africa to individuals like the Moroccan who made this statement.

Divide students into five groups and assign each group one North African country. Each group will compose three truths and one lie about their country that they have gleaned only from the map (page 105). For example, "Egypt is west of Libya" is a lie; "Egypt includes the Sinai Peninsula" is a truth; "Egypt includes the city of Aswan" is a truth; "Egypt has its northern coastline along the Mediterranean Sea" is a truth. Several sets of four statements (three accurate and one incorrect) can be designed to extend challenges for students to solve in a game. Each country-group quickly states their three truths and one lie for remaining students to quickly decide (within 10 seconds) which is the erroneous statement.

Stewart, Gail. *The Suez Canal*. Lucent Books, 2001. ISBN 150068426.

Seligman, Thomas K., Kristyne Loughran, and Edmond Bernus (Eds.). Art of Being Tuareg: Sahara Nomads in a Modern World. UCLA Fowler Museum, 2006. ISBN 100974872946.

Fiction

Lewin, Ted. The Storytellers. Lothrop, Lee and Shepard Books, 1998. ISBN 0688151787.

Back issues of magazines

Berbers. Cobblestone Publishing

Company. ISBN 0382445279.

Morocco. Cobblestone Publishing Company. ISBN 0382445910.

Web Sites

- The Middle East North Africa Internet Resource Guide
- North Africa by Region and Country
- International Development Resource Center: Middle East and North Africa
- The Maghreb Center
- United Nations Educational, Scientific and Cultural Organization, Rabat

OBJECTIVES: 2.03, 3.04, 6.02

Discussion Questions

1 Why do most people of the Maghreb live near the coast?

2 What are the advantages and disadvantages of living between the mountains?

3 What physical features do all of the North African nations share?

 Caption Answer

It causes most people to live on the coast because the mountains block moisture-bearing winds.

Research Activity

Eid!

 OBJECTIVES: 6.01, 8.03, 11.02, 11.03

Eid is the Arabic word for festival or feast. Have students research foods that are typical in North African countries. Have students compile lists of foods. Ask for volunteers to help locate and prepare foods. Those who do not plan the food should plan the rest of the day's activities.

Suggested Foods dates, figs, citrus fruit, olives, yogurt, pilaf, couscous, tabouli, pita bread, lentils, goat milk, and goat cheese.

Additional Activities Design and display travel posters, design and wear North African clothing, or locate and play recorded North African music.
Resources include international cookbooks and the book *Festivals of Egypt* by Jailan Abbas, illustrated by Abdel W. Bilal (Hoopoe Books, 1995. ISBN 9775325471.).

Extension See if an ELL parent would be willing to be a guest speaker.

LESSON 1 People and Their Environment

KEY IDEAS

- The people of North Africa share an Islamic faith, the Arabic language, and a similar history.
- The physical environment encourages people to settle along the region's coast or in the Nile River valley.
- Cities in North Africa are growing rapidly.
- Some differences distinguish Egypt from its western neighbors.

KEY TERMS

fellaheen
Maghreb
oases

All the countries of North Africa have coastlines that open on the Atlantic Ocean or Mediterranean Sea. Much of the interior of these countries is a vast stretch of desert.

The Maghreb and Libya

In Africa's northwest are nations—Morocco (including Western Sahara, a land that Morocco claims), Algeria, and Tunisia—that are often known as the Maghreb (MAGH·reb). *Maghreb* comes from an Arabic term meaning the "west." The name came into use long ago when these lands were on the western edge of an Islamic empire centered in Southwest Asia. Today, these nations, along with Libya, share similar cultural and physical characteristics.

Most people speak Arabic and follow Islam. They mainly live in crowded coastal lands along the Mediterranean Sea and Atlantic Ocean. As you have read, these people share much of the same history. Daily lives do not vary much from country to country.

Most people of the Maghreb live near the coast because the high Atlas Mountains block the path of moisture-bearing winds moving inland from the Atlantic and Mediterranean. The mountains stretch from southern Morocco to northwestern Tunisia. Some of the valleys between the mountains receive as much as 40 to 50 inches (102 to 127 cm) of rain and snow each year. Moisture

The buildings of a Moroccan village seem to climb up a side of the Atlas Mountains. **What effect does the mountain range have on climate to its south?**

106   Chapter 6

Name Origin

Algeria Takes its name from the British mispronunciation of the Arabic capital city Al Djazair (Algiers).

Egypt The Greek name for this region was Aigyptos, named for the first pharaoh, Menes, who united Upper and Lower Egypt.

Cairo, Egypt Named by Arabs who conquered the city calling it Al Qahirah, "the victorious."

Libya An ancient Greek name for North Africa, excluding Egypt.

Morocco A mispronunciation by early explorers for those who lived in Marrakech. Later thought to mean "Land of the Moors."

Marrakech, Morocco Arabic for "the adorned."

Tunisia Taken from the name of the capital city—Tunis—giving a French twist to the pronunciation.

combined with good soil has made this area fertile. South of the Atlas Mountains, the land is desert.

Libya has only a few miles of mountains on the coast near Egypt (see map on page 17). Winds from the sea carry moisture and drop rain into the area. But Libya receives less rain than the Maghreb.

Distribution of Population

People living in the Maghreb and Libya live mostly within 200 miles (322 km) of either the Mediterranean Sea or, in the case of Morocco, the Atlantic Ocean. In Egypt, the population is concentrated along the Nile River.

It is not surprising that the population is so unevenly distributed. Most people live where the climate is milder and water is available. The hot, dry desert climate means that large parts of the region are sparsely populated or uninhabited.

Almost all of Libya lies within the Sahara or Libyan deserts (see map, page 15). The only places where people can live in the Sahara are the desert *oases,* places watered by underground wells or springs. More than 85 percent of Libya's 5.2 million people live in cities along the Mediterranean coast.

The mountains and deserts of the Maghreb are not highly populated. The mountains have slightly more people than the desert because highland areas have reliable, though seasonal, rainfall.

In Morocco, such coastal cities as Casablanca (kas·ah·BLAN·kah), Tangier (tan·JEER), and Rabat (ra·BAHT) have expanded rapidly as rural dwellers have moved to the cities. Rural families leave their villages because the population in rural areas is growing much faster than the availability of land. Cities offer the promise of jobs, education, better medical care, and an exciting daily life. For most,

the promise fades quickly because cities cannot offer the jobs and housing that villagers expect. Many new arrivals end up in crowded slums on the outskirts of the cities.

WORD ORIGINS

The name **Morocco** originated as an English translation of Marrakech, the city founded in A.D. 1070 by the Berbers. The skill of Morocco's tanners and bookbinders have made the word "morocco" synonymous with fine leather.

Residents of Fez, Morocco, live inland, about 100 miles (161 km) east of the Atlantic Ocean. **Why do most people in North Africa live in cities?**

North Africa

107

Chapter 6, Lesson 1

Discussion Questions

1 Why is the population of North Africa so unevenly distributed?

2 What are some of the problems facing rural families as they leave their villages and move to the cities?

3 What impact will this have on the rural areas? urban areas?

 Caption Answer

Many people live in cities along the coast because the climate offers milder weather and more rainfall. The soil is more fertile. The seacoast is a more hospitable place to live than the desert.

 Math Activity

Population Math Problem

OBJECTIVES: 2.01, 2.02

Find the population of each country in North Africa. Create a bar graph to show this data. Use a spreadsheet or database to create this graph. As an technology activity, students could also create a database of the population of the top five cities in each country of the region. Students should create a field for city name, nation, absolute location, relative location, and population. Then have students sort the data by the different criteria (fields) and compare the results.

Extension For novice ELL students, model and provide additional explanations.

✔ It's a Fact

North Africa

■ Algeria has no significant rivers, thus depends on oases fed by underground springs. Shallow salt lakes called chotts form during rainy periods in the plateaus, but these lakes are useless for irrigation or drinking water.
■ Hot windstorms blow throughout Egypt during the spring. Called khamsin, these winds create sand and dust storms that damage crops and raise

temperatures by many degrees in just a few hours.
■ About 95 percent of Libya is uninhabited. More than 70 percent of its population lives in coastal cities.
■ The shanty towns or slums on the outskirts of large cities in Morocco cities are called bidonvilles, meaning "tin can towns."
■ Tunisia has only one year-round river, the Majardah.

Discussion Questions

1 Although Egypt receives little precipitation, it has some of the most fertile lands in Africa. Why is this so?

Caption Answer

Engineers closed thousands of small river channels and dried out swampy plains.

Writing Activity

Letter to Your Family

OBJECTIVES: 3.02, 4.01, 5.03

With a population of more than 74 million, Egypt is the most populous nation in the Arab world. Almost 99 percent of Egypt's population lives along the narrow strip of land bordering the Nile River. Although Egypt has increased agricultural and industrial production, the annual per capita GNP in 2006 was $4,200. Many of the fellaheen, Egyptian farmers, live in poverty. In order to try to find a job and a better future, many young people are moving to Cairo.

Give students the following instructions: Imagine you are a young fellah who has moved to Cairo. Write a letter to your family back home describing your new life. Students may search Internet sites about Egypt and Cairo for additional information.

Extension For intermediate ELL students, model and provide additional explanations. Assign students to work with a partner.

This fertile farmland along the Nile River was once too dry to plant crops. **What technology has created fertile soil along the Nile where none existed before?**

Egypt

Egypt's coast receives little rainfall. It is the Nile River that has set Egypt apart from other North African lands. If you flew over the Nile Valley from the Aswan High Dam northward to Cairo, you would see a ribbon of intensely green land. These are farms irrigated by the Nile. They extend about 5 to 10 miles (8 to 16 km) on either side of the river. Beyond the reach of irrigation the land is barren, except where several oases supply moisture.

You might imagine that Egypt has looked this way since ancient times, but there is more vegetation today. Modern technology enables Egyptians to irrigate more land along the banks of the river today than they could in years past.

CONNECTIONS • GEOGRAPHY & SCIENCE •

Desert Wildlife

A bird that nests in a well? Locusts that look like rocks? A two-week trek across a desert without water?

Desert species survive by adapting to their desert environment. Desert animals face months without water, little cover from plants, and scarce food. Yet if you could look about carefully, you would find life in the desert.

Camels live in the desert. People once believed that a camel's hump stored water. The hump actually stores fat. This nourishment keeps camels alive as they search for food.

The camel can make a two-week trek without water. Camels can drink 525 pints (247 liters) of water. The water is stored in their blood cells. These cells swell 240 times their normal size to hold the water.

A camel's feet help it navigate the desert floor. The foot pads grow to the size of dinner plates. The broad feet keep the animal from sinking into the sand.

Rock doves, pigeonlike birds, find a way to take care of their young and stay cool. These blue-gray doves have been found inside ancient irrigation systems. Deep underground, they nest and hatch their young. Safe from falcons, the young are fed and practice their flights in underground canals. Then they make their flight to the outside—straight up the well.

Locusts have been on the earth for millions of years. They appear to be one of its most adaptable creatures. In the desert, locusts take on a rocklike sheen, flatten themselves, and stay still. If one moves, you might think a rock had legs. This way the locust (inset) protects itself from birds and lizards (below).

Plated lizard, Sudan

Background Information

Crowded Cairo

Because of Egypt's uneven population distribution, the banks of the Nile River are among the most densely populated in the world. Egypt's populated areas are packed with more than 1,700 persons per square mile. Nowhere is the population crunch more apparent than in Cairo, one of Africa's largest cities. This city of more than 7.9 million people has nonstop traffic jams. It is the country's major banking and finance center as well as the home of its major universities. Cairo is home to most of Egypt's major banks, shipping companies, and airlines. About one third of all sports and amusement centers, cafés, restaurants, and hotels are in Cairo. With a third of Egypt's population under the age of fifteen, population pressures in Cairo and all along the Nile will not end soon.

Even more farmland has been opened in the Nile Delta, where the river empties into the sea. Here engineers found ways of drying out a swampy plain dotted with lagoons. They closed thousands of small river channels and forced the river water through a few large channels. Larger river channels lose less water through evaporation. The project provided Egypt with a large area of the most fertile land in Africa.

In the 1960s, Egypt built the Aswan High Dam in the Upper Nile Valley. The dam trapped the yearly Nile floods, creating behind it a huge body of water, Lake Nasser. This lake provides water for millions of acres of new farmland. The Aswan High Dam provides power to run electric generators.

The dam increases production in yet another way. The water stored behind the dam can be released whenever it is needed. Farmers downstream no longer have to wait for the yearly flood season to start their cycle of planting and harvesting. Engineers can create artificially more than one flood a year. Farmers in turn can plant more than a single crop.

The Aswan High Dam also has created some environmental problems. The water released from the dam for irrigation downstream does not carry rich soil. So farmers must buy fertilizers. In the delta region, the shoreline is eroding, because no soil is deposited to replace what the Mediterranean Sea is washing away. Elsewhere, weeds have filled irrigation canals and ditches because floods no longer flush out the channels. Still, most Egyptians look on the Aswan High Dam with pride.

Lake Nasser provides water for millions of acres of farmland. **How was Lake Nassar formed?**

Desert locust

North Africa

109

Discussion Questions

1 How is it possible to make use of the waters of the Nile year-round?

2 In what ways has the Aswan Dam helped the Nile River Valley? Are there any negative consequences? Explain.

Caption Answer

The lake was formed behind the Aswan High Dam as a result of the water the dam collected from yearly Nile floods.

Activity

Population Distribution

OBJECTIVES: 1.01, 1.02, 3.01

Materials space for students to walk around, squares of different colored paper, county maps or state maps, map of Africa that shows population density (see map page 20)

Mark off an area on the floor large enough for 25 to 30 students. Give each student a colored chip or square of paper. Place several obstructions in the area in random fashion: a chair, some books, a trash can. Have students mill around in the area for a minute. Then tell them to stop, place their colored paper or chip on the floor, and move out of the area. Note the position of markers; remove the obstructions and note that there are "holes" in the distribution pattern. Discuss why they occurred. Next take a North Carolina county map. Have students look at the map and mark the areas where most people live. Mark cities and towns with populations of more than 75,000. Then mark towns and villages with less than 75,000. Look at where these areas of habitation occur. Ask students to look for resources near the larger populated areas. Can they find a pattern of settlement? Then have students look at the map of North Africa. Have them choose one country and study its population distribution. Ask students to write a paragraph explaining why the population distribution is the way it is.

Extension Novice ELL students should draw a picture instead of paragraph. Intermediate ELL students should use simple sentences.

Science Activity

The Rain Shadow Effect

OBJECTIVES: 2.02, 3.02, 3.05

Have students research adiabatic heating and cooling, which is the rate of temperature change as air rises and falls. Discuss with students that air cools as it rises and warms as it falls due to changes in pressure. Air is made of molecules of a number of different gases, and those molecules are always moving. When the air molecules are close together (higher pressure) there is a lot of friction between molecules. Thus, the air will be warm. When the air molecules spread out (lower pressure), there is less friction between them and the air will be cool.

The farther up from the earth's surface (elevation/sea level), the more spread out the molecules of the atmosphere become. Since the molecules are more spread out, and there is therefore less friction between them, the air gets cooler as you move upward in elevation.

Students should work in groups to create a model to explain how adiabatic heating and cooling creates the rain shadow effect in North Africa. How does the rain shadow effect contribute to the expansion of the Sahara Desert?

Discussion Questions

1 What are some of the problems that have come about as a result of rapid population growth?

2 What will the future hold for Egypt if young farmers continue to leave their land and move to the city?

3 What are some ways the Egyptians can slow down their population growth?

 Caption Answer

They move to Alexandria or Cairo looking for jobs.

 Research Activity

Using an Almanac

OBJECTIVES: 5.01, 5.02, 5.03, 6.01

Students will look up the following facts for the countries of North Africa in the most recent almanac: total population, population density, percent arable land, percent in agriculture, percent urban, per capita GNP, literacy, life expectancy, and percent of natural increase. Ask students to answer this question: Based on the above information, which country do you think will be an economic power in the region by the year 2025?

Extension ELL students should define terms in their native language and then look up the items in an almanac with a partner's help. Do not assign the written explanation.

Technology Extension Have students prepare a spreadsheet or database with this information.

Population Pressures

Egypt has enjoyed remarkable success in its efforts to use the Nile River effectively. The nation has increased its agricultural and industrial production. Increased production has encouraged rapid population growth. Every year, more than 1.4 million Egyptian children are born. Egypt today, with a population of 74 million, is the largest nation in the Arab world.

Such rapid expansion has brought problems that Egypt has not been able to solve. Because most of the nation is desert, farmland and cities are increasingly crowded. Almost everyone (95 percent of the population) lives within 12 miles (19 km) of the Nile. In Cairo, many of the poorest families have built shelters in the City of the Dead, a large cemetery. Every year, Egypt needs more food, housing, schooling, and jobs. These needs alarm government planners. The *fellaheen,* the Egyptian name for peasant farmers, have increased food production, but they cannot keep pace with demand. Egypt must import food.

Meanwhile, the fellaheen, along with millions of other Egyptians, continue to live in poverty. Young farm people try to escape poverty by moving to Alexandria or Cairo. Both cities offer some opportunities, but there are not enough jobs.

Efforts to create more jobs are continuing. The government has tried with some success to slow the population growth rate by encouraging families to have fewer children. Thirty-three percent of Egyptians are younger than fifteen years old. They will marry and have children. The population will continue to grow.

An Egyptian fellah raises crops on tiny plots of land, using old-fashioned hand tools. **How do many young farmers try to escape poverty in Egypt?**

LESSON ① REVIEW

Fact Follow-Up

1. What are the Maghreb nations? What does their name mean?
2. How is population distributed in the Maghreb?
3. How is population distributed in Egypt?
4. What is the Aswan High Dam? How does it affect life in Egypt?

Talk About It

1. How has Egypt dealt with population growth? Explain your answer.
2. Why is population growth a great challenge in the nations of the Maghreb?
3. In Egypt, 33 percent of the people are fifteen years old or younger. How will this fact change life in Egypt? Why?

110

LESSON ① REVIEW

Fact Follow-Up Answers

1. The Maghreb nations are Morocco (including Western Sahara), Algeria, and Tunisia. Maghreb comes from an Arabic term meaning the "west."
2. Population is unevenly distributed with clusters of heavily populated areas along the Mediterranean Sea and Atlantic Ocean coastlines.
3. Population is unevenly distributed; the Nile River valley is the area of densest population.
4. The Aswan High Dam, built in the 1960s in the Upper Nile Valley, provides irrigation and electric power for Egypt. Because it provides year-round water for agriculture, farm production and acreage have increased. Environmental problems such as erosion and pollution from agricultural fertilizers have also been caused by the dam.

Talk About It Answers

1. The Egyptian government has tried to deal with the growing population by creating more jobs and encouraging families to have fewer children.
2. The Maghreb nations face the challenges of rapidly expanding cities and little water.
3. The fact that Egypt has a large and youthful population means that the population will continue to grow. More jobs, housing, and other services will be needed.

LESSON 2 Government and Economy

Have you ever sung the opening lines of the United States Marine Corps Hymn?

From the Halls of Montezuma
To the shores of Tripoli

These lines recall battles fought by the United States Marine Corps early in the 1800s. The shores of Tripoli refers to the state of Tripoli, one of the Barbary States in North Africa, where Libya is today. These states were part of the Ottoman Empire. The Barbary States supported pirates, who often attacked American ships.

Ships from the United States were safe again after marines and other Arab forces marched from Egypt across 500 miles (805 km) of desert. Led by William Eaton, an American diplomat, they captured the Tripolitan port of Derna. During the aftermath, Eaton learned a peace treaty had been signed.

American and European attacks on North Africa led to the decline of piracy, leaving much of North Africa in economic chaos and vulnerable to attacks from outside forces. The French invaded several North African cities and conquered Algeria in 1830. France used Algeria's agricultural resources to its benefit. Spain and France ruled different parts of Morocco. In 1882, the British gained control of Egypt. Italy took over Libya in 1912. North Africa remained under European control until the 1950s and 1960s.

KEY IDEAS

- North African nations won freedom from European rule in the 1950s and 1960s.
- Egypt's plans to expand and diversify its economy are closely related to its foreign relations.
- Nations in the Maghreb have followed different paths in efforts to expand their economies.

KEY TERMS

protectorate
redistribution of wealth

The 1804 capture of the U.S.S. Philadelphia was one of many incidents that led to a U.S. invasion of Tripoli. **What effect did such raids have on European nations? on North Africa?**

North Africa

 **Caption Answer**

It caused those nations to fight back. It encouraged other nations to invade Africa, which eventually led to colonialism.

OBJECTIVES: 5.03, 6.02, 11.04

Discussion Questions

1 What is the relative location of Tripoli in respect to Cairo?

2 What European nations invaded and took control of North Africa?

3 When did North African nations regain their independence?

 Activity

The Building of Egypt as a Nation

OBJECTIVES: 7.01, 8.03, 9.03

Students will design a human timeline using sandwich boards. To make the sandwich boards, write one of the historical events listed below on one piece of paper and the date written on a second sheet of paper. Punch holes in the top corners of both pages. With the pages back to back, place string or yarn through the holes of each sheet to hang on a student's shoulders (or write information on the front and back of index cards and have students hold the cards and show classmates the information).

Students will arrange themselves in chronological order standing in open classroom area without speaking. Students may use Lessons 1 and 2 as a reference.

- lacked funds and skills to increase industrial and agricultural production
- decided to seek lasting peace with Israel
- joined Arab nations and Soviet Union against Israel
- tied economic programs to foreign policy
- built the Aswan High Dam in the Upper Nile River valley
- Became a protectorate of the United Kingdom
- suffered from destruction of its air force by Israel that also claimed Sinai Peninsula oil fields
- gained independence
- received aid from the Soviet Union and the United States
- joined the United Nations to help expel Iraq from Kuwait
- signed formal peace treaty with Israel negotiated by United States President Jimmy Carter

Extension ELL students can participate but may need the assistance of peer tutors.

111

Caption Answer

After independence, Egypt looked to both the United States and Soviet Union for help. The Cold War and other issues strained Egypt's relations with the United States. Egypt turned to the Soviet Union, which had supported Egypt in 1956 when it took control of the Suez Canal.

 Activity

Peer Mediation

OBJECTIVES: 10.02

Discuss with the class issues that have been a problem either at the community, school, grade, or class level. Further discuss some solutions to those issues. Divide the class into small groups of three or four. Have each group select one of the issues and write a peace treaty that could be ratified by each party in the dispute.

Extension For intermediate ELL students, model and provide additional explanations. Novice ELL students will observe.

Egypt and the Soviet Union worked together to build the Aswan High Dam. **Why did the Soviet Union give money and assistance to Egypt?**

112

Nation Building— Egypt

Egypt was never a true British colony. But the United Kingdom did gain control of Egypt in World War I. From 1914 to 1922, Egypt was a *protectorate* of the United Kingdom. A protectorate is a state or territory partly controlled by another country, but not a possession of that country. After much opposition to the British, Egypt became independent. The British, however, continued to direct Egypt's affairs until 1954. Only then was Egypt free.

The Cold War

After independence, Egypt looked to both the United States and Soviet Union for help to improve its agriculture and industry. However, Egypt's requests for aid were complicated by Cold War rivalries. Egypt's relations with the United States were also strained by America's support of the newly created state of Israel.

The United States offered aid but required Egypt in return to support American policies. Egypt, for example, would be expected to join an alliance of powers opposed to the expansion of communism in the Middle East. Egypt agreed that communism ought to be stopped—it had outlawed the Communist Party within its own borders—but it refused to join the alliance. It feared the United States, the United Kingdom, and other nations would use the alliance to bring Egypt under foreign control.

At this point, Egypt turned to the Soviet Union. The Soviets supported Egypt in 1956 when it took control of the Suez Canal from the Israelis, British, and French. The Soviets also helped build the Aswan High Dam and backed Egypt in the June 1967 Arab–Israeli War.

Six years later, after the United States helped negotiate an end to another Israeli-Egyptian war, Egypt's foreign policy took a dramatic turn. Egypt decided to seek a permanent peace with Israel.

Peace with Israel

In 1979, Egypt and Israel signed a formal peace treaty. Egypt became the first Arab nation to recognize Israel's right to exist. Israel agreed that Egypt could reclaim the Sinai (SIGH·nigh) Peninsula.

Egypt's foreign policies have been criticized by other Arab states. In 1990, Egypt joined the United Nations forces, led by American troops, that drove Iraqi troops out of Kuwait (ku·WAYT).

The ties between Egypt and Russia have weakened. The United States has given Egypt a great deal of economic help, especially for its industry and military.

Egypt has technology to expand irrigated land along the Nile. More farms promise two major benefits—food and jobs. Building more irrigation systems will be expensive, but it is necessary. Egypt is a net importer of food, meaning it imports more food than it exports. About one-third of Egyptians live below the poverty line.

Egypt's educational system does not meet its needs. Only about 58 percent of Egyptians can read. There is still a shortage of educational opportunities, although the number increased greatly in the 1990s. Egypt has many well-educated professional people, but it lacks skilled industrial workers.

Anwar Sadat of Egypt (left) and Menachem Begin of Israel (right) began a period of cooperation between their nations when they signed a peace treaty negotiated by United States President Jimmy Carter (center). **What did the countries agree upon in the treaty?**

Discussion Questions

1 How and when did Egypt win true independence from the British?

2 What problems faced Egypt as they became an independent nation?

3 Why has there been such strong conflict between Israel and Egypt?

4 Why is it important to build more irrigation systems along the Nile?

Caption Answer

Israel agreed that Egypt could reclaim the Sinai Peninsula.

Writing Activity

Governments of North Africa

OBJECTIVES: 9.01, 9.03, 10.02

Have students research and complete the chart below.

Based on the information in the chart, have them write or word process a paragraph describing which country they would prefer to live in and why.

Extension For ELL students, model and provide additional explanations. Assign students to work with a partner.

Technology Extension Have students set up this chart as a spreadsheet or database and complete it online.

Country	Colonial Power	Date of Independence	Type of Government Today	Current Events or Challenges
Algeria				
Morocco				
Libya				
Tunisia				
Egypt				

Discussion Questions

1 Why did it take Algeria so much longer to win independence?

2 How do most people of Morocco make their livelihood?

3 What is a monarch?

4 Why did it take so long for Tunisia to move toward democracy?

Caption Answer

Wheat, maize, citrus fruit, and olives along with phosphates

Research Activity

Western Sahara Timeline

OBJECTIVES: 7.01, 1.02, 8.02

Assign students to research Western Sahara. They should answer the following questions: Why does Morocco claim Western Sahara? What other nation (Mauritania) also would like to have Western Sahara's territory? Why? Who colonized this area of North Africa? What have Western Sahara's names been since 1880 (see map page 90). Students should prepare a time line showing this information.

Extension ELL students should create the time line by using only ELL-friendly Web sites for research.

Nation Building—The Maghreb and Libya

Well over 1 million Europeans—mostly French—immigrated to the Maghreb after the French conquest. Many became involved in trade in Casablanca, Algiers, and Tunis. Others saw the possibilities of developing farms in the areas around the Atlas Mountains.

The French colonists prospered, but native North Africans often suffered. North African independence movements gained force after World War II. Tunisia and Morocco gained freedom from France. Algeria, where oil had been discovered, won independence after an eight-year war. Libya became independent after Italy was defeated in World War II.

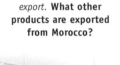

What would YOU do?

Your family has a decision to make. Your parents have always lived in villages. Their life has been hard, and the family is poor. So now your parents are considering a move to a city. If your father finds work, you may go to school. Yet the family will live in a slum if your parents do not find good jobs. Everyone will have to earn money to stay alive. What do you hope that your family will do?

A Moroccan tannery in Fez makes leather goods for export. **What other products are exported from Morocco?**

Morocco

"Ours is a small operation by Detroit standards," says Khalifa Terraf, a manager at an automobile factory in Casablanca, Morocco. "Only 90 cars a day." Moroccan workers assemble the cars from parts made in Europe. Terraf's plant is just one of a growing number of small industries in this city of 3.7 million people. Other factories make glass, leather goods, carpets, and wines. In 2004, the United States and Morocco signed a free trade agreement, which took effect in 2005. Both nations hope it will strengthen their economies.

Forty percent of all Moroccans are farmers. They raise wheat, maize, citrus fruit, and olives. These crops and minerals, especially phosphates, are exported. Income is also earned from tourism. About 5 million people visit Morocco each year because of its crafts, souks, and ancient architecture.

Efforts to improve Morocco's economy were encouraged by King Hassan II, who died in 1999. Morocco is North Africa's last remaining monarchy. King Hassan II was succeeded by his son King Mohammed VI.

Tunisia

Tunisia has oil, but there is not enough for export. Like Morocco, Tunisia's economy has been built partly on sales of its phosphates to foreign buyers. The export of farm products—a business started by the French when Tunisia was a

114

Chapter 6

Background Information

A New Qaddafi?

When Ghana became the first black African state to win independence in 1957, its leader Kwame Nkrumah exclaimed, "Africa must unite!" Over the decades, other African leaders have echoed his call for unity. Libyan leader Muammar Qaddafi has become the latest champion of an African Union, or what he calls a "United States of Africa." In the 1970s and 1980s Qaddafi's support for terrorism led to his international isolation. More recently he has sought a new role for himself in African affairs as a regional peacekeeper. He served as a mediator in civil wars in neighboring Sudan and Congo and has hosted summits of African leaders.

The United States announced in 2006 that it is restoring full diplomatic relations with Libya and will soon open an embassy in Tripoli.

colony—has been revived. It has become another valuable source of income.

For 30 years after independence, Habib Bourguiba ruled Tunisia. In 1987, Tunisians grew tired of single-party rule. Public demonstrations forced the aging leader from office. Since then, Tunisia has followed a path toward democracy. Several political parties take part in elections.

Algeria

The French invested heavily in Algeria, developing mines, power stations, railroads, highways, and port facilities that would benefit France. French exploration teams found rich pools of oil under the sands of the Sahara in 1956. Roads soon crossed the Sahara, and networks of pipelines carried oil and natural gas northward to harbors on the Mediterranean coast.

After independence, the Algerian government took over the oil exploration and production facilities owned by private businesses. The government increased production. The Algerians used their oil revenues to build new oil refineries and to enlarge iron and steel plants that the French had built. The Algerians also constructed factories for making cement, paper, and other products.

Algeria's riches in oil at first seemed to solve the country's problems. The nation's economy boomed in the 1970s when global oil prices rose, but many workers lost their jobs when oil prices fell in the 1980s.

During the 1980s and 1990s, Algerians struggled to reform their government and increase democratic participation. The military and militant Islamic fundamentalists sometimes clash violently. Algeria's oil-based economy has provided the government with significant money, but it has not been used to address Algeria's economic or social challenges.

Libya

Muammar Qaddafi has headed a military dictatorship in Libya since 1969. Upon taking power, he began eliminating Western influences. Everyone had to obey Islamic law in every detail of their daily lives.

A second rule called for the *redistribution of wealth.* His government established limits on the amount of property that an individual might own and the savings that an individual could hold. The government would seize any holdings in excess of the amount allowed.

Libya has more oil than any other country in Africa. Before oil was discovered in 1961, Libya was one of the poorest nations in Africa. Over the next 20 years it grew to become one of the richest. However, because of Qaddafi's support of international terrorism, Libya was sanctioned by the United Nations in 1992. Sanctions were lifted in 2003.

Muammar Qaddafi is the dictator of Libya. **What are some changes he forced upon the country?**

Discussion Questions

1 Why did the French invest so heavily in Algeria?

2 How did Algerians become prosperous after they won their independence?

3 What natural resource has drastically changed Libya since 1961? How?

4 What are some changes that Qaddafi introduced after taking power?

Caption Answer

He eliminated Western influences and redistributed wealth.

LESSON 2 REVIEW

Fact Follow-Up

1. Describe Egypt's relations with the United States, the former Soviet Union, Israel, and other Arab nations.
2. How and when did the Maghreb nations and Libya gain independence from European colonial powers?
3. How has oil affected the economy of Algeria and Libya?

Talk About It

1. Which North African nation has had the most stable government? Explain why.
2. What do you think is the greatest economic or political challenge facing nations of North Africa? Explain your choice.
3. Which North African nation do you think has the best chance of successfully meeting its economic and political challenges? Explain.

LESSON 2 REVIEW

Fact Follow-Up Answers

1. During the Cold War, the United States and the Soviet Union both offered aid to Egypt. Since the fall of the Soviet Union, Egypt has moved closer to the United States. Egypt and Israel fought wars in 1967 and 1973, but Egypt signed a peace agreement with Israel in 1979 and became the first Arab country to recognize Israel. Other Arab nations have criticized Egypt's policies, particularly those toward Israel. Egypt joined the United Nations in the 1990 Gulf War against Iraq.
2. All have become independent since World War II, Libya gaining independence as Italy was defeated in that war. Morocco and Tunisia gained independence from France rather easily, but Algeria fought an eight-year war of independence against France.
3. Algeria's oil at first seemed to solve the country's problems. The nation's economy boomed in the 1970s when global oil prices rose, but many workers lost their jobs when oil prices fell in the 1980s. Before oil was discovered in 1961, Libya was one of the poorest nations in Africa. Over the next twenty years, it grew to become one of the richest.

Talk About It Answers

1. Important points: Students should choose one nation and support their choice with reasons. Note: Morocco has had a stable and relatively popular monarchy.
2. Important points: Students should choose one challenge and support their choice with reasons. Note: Rapid population growth, little water, and the need to develop industry are all challenges.
3. Important points: Students should choose one nation and give reasons to support their choice. Note: Egypt has hydroelectric power, agriculture, and a good chance for industrial growth.

OBJECTIVES: 2.03, 6.02, 11.01

Discussion Questions

1 Islam influences everyday life in North Africa. Explain how.

2 In what ways did rural farmers, nomadic herders, and urban dwellers depend on one another?

 Caption Answer

The traders of the cities and towns needed the desert transportation that the nomads provided. The latter also provided guides across the desert. Farmers provided food for all groups.

Art Activity

Illustrations of North Africa

 OBJECTIVES: 5.04, 6.01

Divide the class into groups of three. Give each student in the group a large piece of paper and have each student illustrate one North African lifestyle—nomad, village, or city dweller based upon the descriptions in the textbook. Have the groups draw arrows and other illustrations to show the relationships, such as trading goods, between the people. Each group should list and report their observations to the class.

LESSON Society and Culture

Hajii Ammar Baccar climbs the 101 steps to the top of the minaret, or tower, of the Great Mosque in Kairouan (ker·WAHN), Tunisia. Baccar is the *muezzin* (mu·EH·zin), the person who calls the Muslim faithful to prayer. Baccar has made this climb every day for more than 30 years. At the top he begins: *"Allah akbar"*—"God is most great." These are the first words said to a Muslim baby when it is born and the last words said before a Muslim is buried.

Throughout North Africa, this same call to prayer echoes daily from the minarets of thousands of mosques. Not every mosque today has a muezzin like Baccar to call the faithful to prayer. Some play a recorded message over a loudspeaker. Whatever form the call takes, the religion of Islam is central to the cultural life of North Africa.

Ways of Living

In earlier times, three distinctive ways of life mingled in North Africa. The lives of the rural farmer, the nomadic herder, and the urban dweller depended on one another. Traders and merchants in coastal cities and towns bought and sold goods. They organized the camel caravans that crossed the Sahara. Desert nomads provided the camels that carried goods and supplies and guided the traders safely to their destinations. Farmers raised the food that both city dwellers and desert nomads depended on.

Today, new patterns are replacing old ones. Nomadic herders and camel caravans are disappearing. Rural villagers no longer make up the majority of the population. Most people live in cities.

Tuareg people camp at a settlement near the Sahara Desert. **How were the lives of rural dwellers tied to the cities of North Africa?**

Nomads of the Sahara

At one time, nomadic herders could be found throughout North Africa, living in or along the edges of the desert. The few who still practice this way of life survive by raising livestock and carrying goods along Saharan trade routes. They raise goats, sheep, and camels. The goats provide milk and meat, and the sheep furnish wool for making tents and blankets. Camels, the practical ships of the desert, supply food and carry heavy loads.

Women add to the family income by weaving blankets and carpets that the men sell in towns and cities. At desert oases, the men trade animal meat and milk with farmers for dates, barley, and other foods. From townspeople, they buy tea, sugar, cloth, and goods they cannot make themselves. Living in tents, these groups move seasonally to winter and summer pasture lands.

This way of life is dying. A long period of drought in the 1970s and 1980s limited grazing land and water for animals. At the same time, roads across the desert reduced the need for camel caravans. A single big truck can haul as much as a hundred camels. Some desert nomads have become truckers, the modern-day camel drivers.

Rural Villages

The people of Rommani, Morocco, are celebrating. Women and children sing and shout. All around them on horseback, men in long, hooded robes called *jellabas* (jel·LAH·bahs) ride through the streets shooting rifles into the air. This is not an everyday event in this quiet village. Usually this celebration, called a *fantasia*, takes place before a wedding or during a visit of government officials. On this occasion, the villagers are celebrating the opening of a new hospital.

Villagers make their houses out of mud or brick covered with a whitewash. Mud makes an excellent building material in warm, dry climates. Houses stay cool in the hottest part of the day but absorb enough heat to warm the house during the night when temperatures drop.

Many houses are surrounded by high walls. The house itself is built around a central courtyard where the family gathers in good weather. Rural villages in Libya once consisted of stone houses grouped together. After Libya became an oil producer, the government used some money to give farmers more modern houses with electricity and water. Most are connected to the world by radio or television.

Almost every rural village has its mosque and its *souk* (SOOK), or market, where farmers bring their vegetables and fruit for sale and trade livestock. At the larger markets, craftspeople display leather goods and carpets.

Rabat, the capital of Morocco, is a modern city surrounded by ancient walls. **Why have many North African cities expanded rapidly?**

Horsemen celebrate a fantasia in a Moroccan village. **What is a fantasia?**

Customs

Blue is the favored color of the Tuareg (TWAH·reg) desert people of Northwest Africa. They dye their clothes varying shades of this color. They do not mind when the dye runs and turns their skin a shade of blue. Sometimes the Tuareg are called the "blue men."

Discussion Questions

1 Describe the life of a nomadic herder.

2 Why is this lifestyle dying out?

3 How does the life of a nomadic herder differ from traditional village life?

4 What materials do villagers use to build their houses? Why is it a good building material?

5 How did the average Libyan benefit after the discovery of oil?

6 What in the United States can you compare to the souk in North Africa?

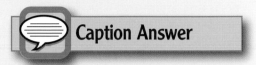
Caption Answer

Nomadic herders and rural villagers have moved to the cities.

Caption Answer

A celebration of a wedding or a special visit by an official. The men ride through the town on horseback shooting pistols into the air and children and women sing.

Art Activity

Moroccan Sconce

OBJECTIVES: 4.03, 7.01, 12.02

Materials black or dark-colored construction paper, scissors, pencil, drawing paper; optional: X-acto knife, needle-nose pliers, and wire

To make the design, fold a sheet of 9-inch by 12-inch black construction paper in half longways. Cut geometric designs starting from the folded side. They should get smaller and smaller as they get nearer the bottom of the page. Unfold and roll construction paper into a broad conical shape. Lightly glue or tape where the two bottom corners meet. Advanced option: More elaborate designs can be cut with X-acto knives. More elaborate forms can be created with stiff wire as a frame.

If you have enough sconces, they look lovely with Christmas lights attached to the bottom where the cone comes to a point. If you do not have lights, tape them to the window to illuminate.

Background Information

Changing Marriage Laws

Throughout the Muslim world, family law is generally based on Sharia, the Islamic legal code. Under this code, a Muslim man can divorce his wife automatically, but for a woman to divorce her husband she must first prove to a court that he has beaten her, is a drug addict, or has failed to support the family. Even when a woman is granted a divorce, the husband may appeal the decree indefinitely. With the support of moderate Muslim clerics, women's advocates, and civil court judges, Egypt is changing its divorce laws. In 2000, Egypt passed new laws that allow a woman to divorce her husband with or without his consent. To win the support of Muslim authorities, the law states that wives who want a divorce over the objections of their husbands must return all money or property paid to them by their husbands when they married.

Eyewitness Activity

Suez Canal

OBJECTIVES: 3.03, 5.04, 13.03

Using a graphic organizer of their choosing, have students research the Suez Canal and its impact on trade within the global community. Research should include the history of the canal, who built the canal, and who owns the canal. Students can visually display reports on posterboard with drawings of the canal or create a PowerPoint presentation or digital story. Students should also include how the canal works. Students can include who uses the canal the most, problems with the canal, and consequences if the canal were to be closed. They must answer the question: Why is the Suez Canal considered vital to trade between the West and Southwest Asia?

Extension For ELL students, model and provide additional explanations. Assign students to work with a partner. Use ELL-friendly Web site for research.

Math Activity

Suez Canal Word Problem

OBJECTIVES: 3.03, 5.04, 13.03

The Suez Canal is about 230 feet wide, 101 miles long, and about 26 feet deep. How much dirt was removed from the Suez Canal? (Use the formula for volume: volume = length x width x height. Each unit must be in feet.)

Answer 3,189,014,400 cubic feet

Extension Assist ELL students by setting up the problem for them.

The Suez Canal

The Suez (SOO·EHZ) Canal connects the Mediterranean and Red Seas. It opened in 1869. Ships traveling between Europe and Asia no longer had to sail around the southern tip of Africa. The voyage between Great Britain and India was cut by 6,000 miles (9,660 km).

Ferdinand de Lesseps, a French diplomat and engineer (above), designed the canal. He could not claim credit for the idea of connecting the Red and Mediterranean Seas. Canals had been dug between the Nile River and the Red Sea thousands of years earlier. British merchants who traded with Asia benefited more than others from the Suez Canal. The French and Egyptians did the actual construction.

118

Chapter 6

An international agreement signed in the 1880s allowed ships of all nations to use the canal (right). British troops closed the canal to enemy shipping in World Wars I and II (below). Egypt regained control of the canal in 1956 and again closed the canal during wars that Egypt fought with Israel.

At first, the canal was about 230 feet (69 m) wide and 101 miles (163 km) long. The main channel was 26 feet (7.8 m) deep and 72 feet (21.6 m) wide . Because sea levels at both ends of the canal were about the same, no locks had to be built. The Suez Canal has been widened and deepened several times. It now can handle most of the large ships (above) that sail the ocean. It is one of the world's busiest waterways.

Research Activity

Canals

OBJECTIVES: 1.01, 3.01, 5.03

Have students research canals around the world (Panama, Erie, North Sea Canal in the Netherlands, St. lawrence Seaway, Great Dismal Swamp Canal in North Carolina, and so on). Each student should choose one canal and determine what the impact of the canal has been in the region(s) it serves. Students should consider the economic, environmental, and regional or international significance of the canal.

Students will write or word process a report describing the location of the canal, who built the canal and who operates it now, how the canal works, basic facts about the canal (length; whether it is still in operation; the type of transportation it serves—barges, ocean-going ships, or pleasure craft; and how much traffic the canal handles now or at its historic peak), and the significance of the canal to the region. Students should include a map showing the location of the canal with their report, and present their findings to the class.

Extension For ELL students, model and provide additional explanations. Assign students to work with a partner.

Discussion Questions

1 What are the two largest cities in North Africa?

2 Why are they known as two cities in one?

3 How do the newer sections of the cities differ from the older sections?

Writing Activity

Be a Planner

OBJECTIVES: 3.02, 4.03, 5.03

Students are to assume the roles of Egyptian government planners. Have them answer the question: What is the greatest problem facing Egypt? Students must write three or four paragraphs stating the problem, identifying its causes, and suggesting possible solutions.

Old City and New

"What do you think?" asks Muhammad Makram as he surveys the site. "Just like California, eh?" Makram is proud of the modern theme park recently built near Cairo. Amid the desert landscape, Crazy Water, as the theme park is called, offers tourists "sun and fun."

Cairo and Alexandria, the two largest cities in North Africa, offer a variety of entertainment that villagers might have difficulty imagining. As in other North African cities, each is actually two cities in one. A part of the city is new and looks like a modern city in Europe or the Americas. Construction of the newer parts of North African cities began during colonial rule.

Today, these newer sections consist of high-rise apartments, factories, and office buildings. They are centers of finance, banking, and government. In cities such as Algiers, Tunis, and Tangier, as well as Cairo and Alexandria, the newer districts have skyscrapers, supermarkets, modern hotels, fancy shops and restaurants, and department stores. These sections also have mosques where the faithful pray. Streets are jammed with traffic.

The older city sections may date back hundreds of years. Tangles of narrow streets are lined with two-story and three-story houses and shops. Here in their small one-room shops, barbers give haircuts, dentists pull teeth, workers weave carpets or hammer intricate designs onto brass trays. Shoppers can leaf through booksellers' stacks of novels and poetry or buy medicinal herbs.

In Tunis, the capital of Tunisia, the old market has a special area for sellers of bath oil, body lotion, incense, and candle wax. It is called the Souk el Attarine, the market of the perfumeries. A few streets over are meat and fish markets and tables of crafted leather.

120

LESSON **3** REVIEW

Fact Follow-Up Answers

1. The Suez Canal connects the Mediterranean Sea to the north with the Red Sea to the south.

2. The rural farmer, the nomadic herder, and the urban dweller all lived side by side in cooperation. Rural farmers provided food for urban dwellers and nomadic herders; urban dwellers organized the trade that used camel caravans to transport products; and the nomadic herders provided meat and hides for consumption and camels and guides for trading caravans.

3. Nomadic herders survive today by raising livestock and carrying goods along Saharan trade routes. They raise sheep, goats, and camels. Women weave blankets and carpets to sell in the towns and cities. Herders trade meat and milk at oases for dates, barley, and other foods. In towns, they buy tea, sugar, cloth, and goods they cannot make themselves. They live in tents and move often to find grazing land for their animals. Theirs is a vanishing way of life.

4. Villagers make their houses out of mud or brick covered with a whitewash to keep the houses cool during the day and warm at night. Many houses have a central courtyard where the family gathers in good

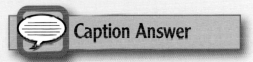

Boats owned by Alexandrians have changed over time (right), but life remains focused on the water surrounding the city (left). **What is the importance of the Mediterranean Sea to this region?**

with a prayer leader. Men go to mosques for Friday prayer. Women may pray at a mosque in a section set aside for them or in their homes.

Some religious leaders in North Africa—and throughout the Islamic world—are calling for a religious revival. They point to widespread poverty, women dressed in Western styles, or the popularity of Western TV programs. These changes, they say, are bringing ruin. Some Islamic religious leaders are calling for more than a voluntary religious revival. They insist that every government should require its people to follow the strictest of Islamic traditions. Not all Muslims agree with these changes. We will learn more about this movement in Unit 3.

In Tunis, the religious center of the old section is the Great Mosque built almost 1,300 years ago. During most of the week, Muslims can pray wherever they are. On Friday, Islam requires Muslim men to pray

LESSON ❸ REVIEW

Fact Follow-Up

1. Which bodies of water does the Suez Canal connect?
2. What three distinctive ways of life once existed side by side in North Africa? How were they related?
3. Describe the life of nomadic herders in North Africa.
4. Describe traditional village life in North Africa.

Talk About It

1. How can the presence of Islam be observed in North Africa?
2. How does life differ in traditional and modern neighborhoods of North African cities? Explain the reasons for the differences.
3. If you were to visit North Africa, would you prefer to visit a city or a rural area? Why?

North Africa

121

1 How do the prayer rituals differ for men and women in the Muslim religion?

2 Why are religious leaders in North Africa asking for a religious revival? How are they demanding it?

ELL Teaching Tips

Be Positive

The more comfortable new ELL students feel in your classroom, the faster they will learn. Find the positive things about your students' work and praise them. Put away the red pen for a little while. Instead, create frequent opportunities for their success in your class.

Caption Answer

Most people live in cities along the Mediterranean coast. These cities offer recreational opportunities such as boating, beaches, and theme parks.

---

weather. The village has a souk, or market, where farmers bring their vegetables and fruit for sale and trade livestock. Larger markets might include leather goods and carpets. Most villages also have a mosque. Village life is changing as more people move into the cities.

Talk About It Answers

1. Even small villages have mosques where prayers are said five times daily and men attend Friday prayers. In many areas women wear traditional clothing.

2. The traditional neighborhoods date back hundreds of years. Narrow streets are lined with two-story and three-story houses and shops. The modern neighborhoods include high-rise apartments and office buildings, and sometimes modern hotels, fancy shops, and restaurants. This part of the city serves as a center for finance, banking, and government.

3. Important points: Students should choose either city or rural area and support that choice with detailed reasons.

Teaching This Skill Lesson

Materials Needed textbooks, references such as atlases, encyclopedias, paper, pencils

Classroom Organization individual work

Introducing the Lesson Review the theme of region with students, asking such questions as "Is a shopping mall a region? Why/why not?" or "Is a school zone a region? is a cemetery? is a state? is the Atlantic Coast Conference?" Tell students that regions can be cultural (example: the Atlantic Coast Conference or a cemetery), physical (the coastal plains or Piedmont or mountain regions in North Carolina), political (a school zone, a state), or economic (a shopping mall). Elicit other examples of each kind of region. Tell students they will be analyzing information about North Africa to determine whether it is a region and—if it is a region—what type of region it is.

Lesson Development Make sure students understand how to complete the data retrieval chart and monitor them as they begin it. The chart can be completed as a homework assignment.

Conclusion Again, ask the question "Is North Africa a region?" Students should support any answers with information from their charts. If they conclude that North Africa is a region, they should then come to agreement as to what type of region North Africa is.

Analyzing, Interpreting, Creating, and Using Resources and Materials

skill

NORTH CAROLINA SKILL GOALS SOCIAL STUDIES

Using Geography's Themes: Region

Region is geography's fifth theme. Beginning with North Carolina in fourth grade, you have made a concentrated study of regions in world areas. As you study Africa, Asia, and the Pacific Realm this year, you will be encountering world areas with the longest histories, largest populations, and some of the richest natural resources on the face of the earth. Understanding the theme of region can help you organize this massive study.

Geographers define a region as "a large area with common features that set it apart from other regions." The "common features" that set one region apart from another can vary. There are regions defined by physical features—mountainous regions, desert regions, lowland regions, and rain forest regions. North Carolina's three regions—Mountains, Piedmont, and Coastal Plain—are physical regions. Regions also can be political, economic, or cultural.

North Africa consists of five nations: Morocco (including its claim to Western Sahara), Algeria, Tunisia, Libya, and Egypt. The first question geographers must answer in analyzing the region is to ask the simple question "Do these five nations make up a region?" One Moroccan described his own country in this way: "It's a combination of Africa, the Middle East, and Europe." The same perhaps could be said of the four other nations. All these nations may combine features from those parts of the world. Together, do these features make up a region different from all others in any important respect?

To answer this question, you will need to locate, organize, and analyze information. In the process, you may want to use a graphic organizer like the one in this lesson.

Examine the map on page 17. What information from the map would lead you to believe that these nations form a region?

Physical features such as mountains and other landforms, deserts, coastlines, rivers, and lakes can define a physical region. What physical features do the five nations of North Africa share? To answer this question you may want to consult the vegetation map on page 35 as well as the physical map on page 17. Does North Africa share any of these physical features with nations outside the region?

There are *political* regions within North Africa. A political region can be defined as an area set off from all others by political beliefs or boundaries. Each of the five nations is a political region using this definition since each has its own national boundaries. Does the map on page 105 show any

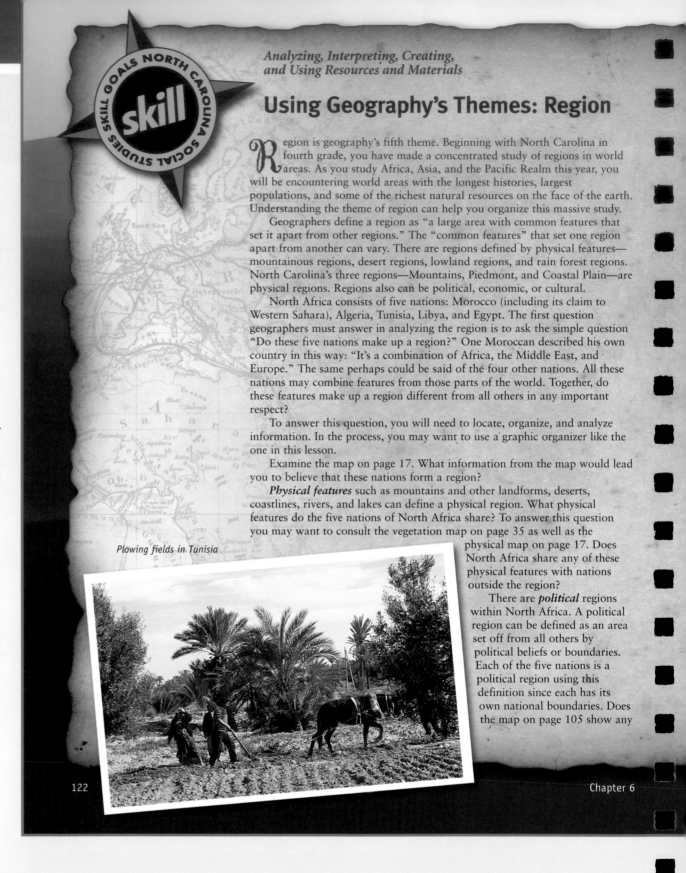

Plowing fields in Tunisia

Graphic Organizer–Defining Region

	Morocco	Algeria	Tunisia	Libya	Egypt
Physical Features					
Political Features					
Economic Conditions					
Cultural Features					

other political regions in North Africa? Skim Chapter 6, especially the information in Lesson 2. Could the five nations of North Africa be described as a political region?

Places having similar economic activities might constitute an *economic* region. Consult the map of economic activities on page 61 to learn what economic activities are shared by the five nations of North Africa. What are they? Do these five nations share more than one economic activity? The vegetation map on page 35 may help answer these questions. Is North Africa an economic region?

Finally, *cultural* regions—areas defined by a common language, tradition, set of religious beliefs, or other cultural phenomena—can be identified.

Look again at the chapter. Can you determine whether North Africa is a cultural region? Try re-examining Lessons 1 and 3. What clues do you find to lead you to believe that North Africa is a cultural region?

As you have answered all the questions in this skill lesson, you have been constructing a data retrieval chart. Your chart should be complete. You are now ready to answer the following questions:

1. Is North Africa a physical region?
2. Is North Africa a political region?
3. Is North Africa an economic region?
4. Is North Africa a cultural region?
5. Is North Africa a region or just five separate nations?

If you have done your work carefully, you should be able to summarize your answers to the questions in a brief paragraph that will include specific reasons to back up your answers.

Finally, you will be able to answer this question: Is North Africa a region or is it a "combination of Africa, the Middle East, and Europe"?

 Skill Lesson Review

1. Which information was easier to "read" and use: information from maps or readings from the text? *Important points: Students should state a preference and explain it.*

2. Which region was easier to define: political or physical? *Important points: Students should choose either political or physical and explain why. Political and physical features both can be shown on a map.*

3. Did you find that North Africa was a part of other regions? If so, which ones? If not, why not? *Important points: Students should be specific*

in answers and should explain their answers clearly.

4. After examining the various maps you used, would you be willing to include other nations in the region known as North Africa? Explain your answer. *Important points: If physical features are important, nations located just to the south of these could be included. Students should be specific about their reasons.*

Talk About It

1. Important points: Students should state whether the description is accurate or not and give detailed reasons. Note: Europe, Africa, and Southwest Asia all influence life in the region.

2. All have a high population density near their coasts and nearly empty desert regions in the interior. They are united in language and religion but very different in economies and governments.

3. Important points: Students should choose one challenge and give detailed reasons for their choice. Note: Rapid population growth puts stresses on limited resources such as water.

4. Colonial powers tapped the resources of the region, and international rivalries have led to wars. However, the rivalry of the Cold War did help produce Egypt's Aswan High Dam.

5. Important points: Students should choose one nation and explain why they chose it, giving detailed reasons.

6. Mosques, minarets, and the call to prayer are evident in all parts of North Africa.

7. The nations of North Africa share a common faith, language, and history. Like the rest of Africa, North Africa was colonized by European nations. Like Southwest Asia, it has deserts.

CHAPTER 6 REVIEW

Lessons Learned

LESSON 1
People and Their Environment
The region of North Africa consists of Morocco (Western Sahara, claimed by Morocco), Algeria, Tunisia, Libya, and Egypt. All border either the Mediterranean Sea or the Atlantic Ocean. They also share much desert land and crowded areas along the Nile River and the coasts. North African culture includes the Islamic faith and the Arabic language.

LESSON 2
Government and Economy
European colonialism ended in North Africa in the 1950s and 1960s. As independent nations, their political development has been influenced by the United States-Soviet Union rivalry and the Arab-Israeli conflict. Farming and the mining of phosphates are important to the economies of Morocco and Tunisia. Algeria and Libya depend on oil. Egypt must import most of its food.

LESSON 3
Society and Culture
The rural farmer, the nomadic herder, and the urban dweller once depended on one another in North Africa. Now they lead very different lives. Cities are growing rapidly, especially Cairo and Alexandria. Those cities, plus Tunis, Algiers, and Tripoli, have old and new sections. Islam is important to the culture of North Africa.

Talk About It

1. "It's a combination of Africa, the Middle East, and Europe" is one description of North Africa. Do you think the description is accurate? Explain your answer.
2. In what ways are the nations of North Africa alike and different?
3. What do you think is the greatest challenge facing the region of North Africa? Explain.
4. Have colonialism and involvement in international rivalry slowed or speeded the development of North Africa's nations? Explain.
5. If you could visit only one nation of the region, which would it be? Explain why.
6. How has Islam influenced the cultural characteristics of place in North Africa?
7. In what ways is North Africa a region, and how is it a part of other regions?

Activity

REGIONS
Use the maps on page 61 and 105 to answer these questions:

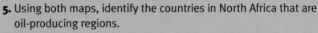

1. What is the largest political region (country) shown on the map on page 105?
2. What is the smallest political region (country) shown on the map on page 105?
3. How many political regions are shown on the map on 105.
4. What additional map features would be needed to display a language region or an economic region on the map on page 105?
5. Using both maps, identify the countries in North Africa that are oil-producing regions.
6. Using the map found on page 61, describe the relative location of the major phosphate-producing region in North Africa.
7. Using both maps, describe the relative location of the commercial fishing region of North Africa.

Mastering Mapwork

1. Algeria is the largest political region.
2. Tunisia is the smallest political region.
3. Six political regions, including Western Sahara, are shown.
4. Symbols or color coding could be used to display language regions; similar methods could show economic regions.
5. Algeria, Tunisia, Libya, and Egypt are oil-producing regions.

6. The major phosphate-producing region is found in an arc stretching along the Atlantic coastline of Morocco and along the Mediterranean coast of Algeria and Tunisia.
7. The region of commercial fishing is located along the Atlantic and Mediterranean coasts of Morocco and along the Mediterranean coast of Algeria and Tunisia.

Go to the Source

Understanding Government Documents

A preamble to a constitution is an introduction that usually explains its purpose. It may also identify how the government is formed. For example the United States Constitution begins "We the people," meaning that the government is a democratic one formed by the citizens of the United States.

Read the Preamble to the Tunisian Constitution below. Answer the questions using specific references from the text.

In the name of God, the Compassionate and Merciful, We, the representatives of the Tunisian people, meeting as members of the National Constituent Assembly, Proclaim the will of this people, set free from foreign domination thanks to its powerful cohesion and to its struggle against tyranny, exploitation, and regression;

- to consolidate national unity and to remain faithful to human values which constitute the common heritage of peoples attached to human dignity, justice, and liberty, and working for peace, progress, and free cooperation between nations;
- to remain faithful to the teachings of Islam, to the unity of the Greater Maghreb, to its membership of the Arab family, to cooperation with the African peoples in building a better future, and with all peoples who are struggling for justice and liberty;
- to install a democracy founded on the sovereignty of the people, characterized by a stable political system, and based on the principle of the separation of powers.

We proclaim that the republican regime constitutes:
- the best guarantee for the respect of rights and duties of all citizens;
- the most effective means for assuring the prosperity of the nation through economic development of the country and the utilization of its riches for the benefit of the people;
- the most certain way for assuring the protection of the family and guaranteeing to each citizen work, health, and education

We, the representatives of the Tunisian people, free and sovereign, proclaim, by the Grace of God, the present Constitution.

Questions

1. What principle is Tunisia's democracy based upon:

a. republicanism
b. separation of powers
c. Islam
d. human dignity

2. According to this Preamble, Tunisia's resources are to benefit

a. the government
b. the people of the Magreb
c. the Tunisian people
d. the Arabs

3. The Preamble places greatest importance on which of the following:

a. modernization
b. international cooperation
c. freedom from foreign domination
d. women's rights

Go to the Source

Go to the Source

OBJECTIVES: 5.03, 10.02; Skills 1.08, 3.05

Tunisia is a republic. The Tunisian Constitution was adopted on June 1, 1959, and amended in 1988 and 2002.

Have students compare this to the United States Constitution. What principals are the same? What are some differences?

A link to Tunisia's constitution is found at **NCJourneys.com.**

ANSWERS

1. b
2. c
3. b

How to Use the Chapter Review

There are three sections in the Chapter Review: Talk About It, Mastering Mapwork, and Go to the Source. Use the Vocabulary Worksheets and the Chapter Review Worksheet in the Teacher's Resource Guide for additional reinforcement and preparation for the Chapter Assessments. The chapter and lesson reviews and the Chapter Review Worksheets are the basis of the assessment for each chapter.

Talk About It questions encourage students to speculate about the content of the chapter and are suitable for class or small-group discussion. They are not intended to be assigned for homework.

Mastering Mapwork has students apply one or more of the Five Themes of Geography to maps within the chapter.

Go to the Source activities allow students to analyze a primary source that relates to the content of the chapter. The questions and activities familiarize students with different types of primary sources and also build content-reading skills.

CHAPTER 7

West Africa

Social Studies Strands

Geographic Relationships
Physical features
Climate and vegetation
Population

Government and Active Citizenship

Economics and Development

Society and Culture
Ethnic traits
Language
Religion

Global Connections

Cultures and Diversity

North Carolina Standard Course of Study

Goal 2 The learner will assess the relationship between physical environment and cultural characteristics of selected societies and regions of Africa, Asia, and Australia.

Goal 5 The learner will evaluate the varied ways people of Africa, Asia, and Australia make decisions about the allocation and use of economic resources.

Goal 11 The learner will recognize the common characteristics of different cultures in Africa, Asia, and Australia.

Goal 12 The learner will assess the influence of major religions, ethical beliefs, and values on cultures in Africa, Asia, and Australia.

Teaching & Assessment

• English Language Learner Modified Lesson Plans for this chapter are found in the Teacher Resource Guide.

• *ExamView® Assessment Suite* is provided at **NCJourneys.com.** It includes customizable assessments for all chapters. Paper tests are also available in the Teacher Resource Guide. See pages T16–T17 for information about how to use the assessments and the Scoring Guide.

Worksheets

Worksheets and answer keys are found both in the Teacher Resource Guide and at **NCJourneys.com**, including Reading Guides, Reading Strategies, Chapter Reviews, English Language Learner and others.

ACTIVITIES AND INTEGRATIONS

SOCIAL STUDIES

● ▲ Baobab Tree, p. 126B
Activator: *Why Mosquitoes Buzz in People's Ears,* p. 126
■ Environmental Concerns, p. 130
Population Density Map, p. 131
Colonial Fingerprints, p. 132
"Who Has . . . I Have . . . ?" p. 133
Why Migration? p. 136
● West Africa Peanut Butter Stew, p. 139
Skill Lesson: Making Economic Plans to Improve a Country, p. 143

READING/LANGUAGE ARTS	READING/LANGUAGE ARTS OBJECTIVES
Analogies, p. 126B	2.01
Writing Prompt: Rain Forests, p. 126	3.02
Why is West Africa So Special? p. 127	3.02
Writing Activity: Planning a School, p. 128	3.01
▲ ■ Mangroves, p. 130	2.01
★ "The Sun Never Sets", p. 133	1.01
★ Ivory Trade Research, p. 135	4.01
★ "Name That Role," p. 138	5.02
● Creative Coffins, p. 141	2.01
Go to the Source: Using Letters as Primary Sources, p. 145	2.01, 4.01, 4.02

MATHEMATICS	MATHEMATICS OBJECTIVES
Village Math Problem, p. 129	5.01, 5.04
★ Oil v. the Economy, p. 137	4.01, 4.05

SCIENCE	SCIENCE OBJECTIVES
Drought and Desertification, p. 135	3.05

TECHNOLOGY	TECHNOLOGY OBJECTIVES
▲ West African Mural, p. 126B	3.01, 3.10
▲ ■ Mangroves, p. 130	3.01, 3.10
★ Oil v. the Economy, p. 131	3.01, 3.10
★ Ivory Trade Research, p. 135	3.01, 3.10, 3.11

VISUAL ARTS	VISUAL ARTS OBJECTIVES
▲ Kente Cloth, p. 126B	2.04, 3.02, 5.02
● ▲ Soap Sculpting, p. 134	2.04, 5.03
Design Adinka Cloth Activity, p. 140	1.04, 2.04, 4.02
● Creative Coffins, p. 141	2.04, 4.02

CHARACTER AND VALUES EDUCATION	TRAITS
Writing Prompt: Rain Forests, p. 126	good citizenship/civic virtue, respect

● Basic Activities   ★ Challenging Activities   ▲ English Language Learner Novice   ■ English Language Learner Intermediate

 **Introductory Activity**

Baobab Tree

OBJECTIVES: 1.02, 2.01

Show students a picture of the baobab tree and discuss how this plant adapts to its environment by being shaped like a bottle, having a moist pulp, being 30 feet in diameter, being pollinated by bats, and so forth. As a class, make a chart of different plants in the world that have adapted to their environment (examples: cactus, bald cypress). Students can create a chart like the following:

Plant	Environment	Adaptation
Baobab tree	Poor soil	large diameter
	lack of moisture	bottle shaped
	sparse vegetation	pollinated by bats
	no leaves in dry season	

Extension ELL students should work with a partner on this activity.

 **Culminating Activity**

A West African Mural

OBJECTIVES: 1.01, 1.02, 1.03, 2.01

Materials large bulletin board paper, rulers, markers, meter sticks, construction paper (assorted colors), pencils, colored chalk

Preparation Begin by dividing the into three large groups. Assign each large group one lesson from Chapter 7 to reread and discuss for ideas. Each group should brainstorm various displays of the contents of each lesson. Examples for "Environment" may include landforms, simple maps, plants, animals, and panorama. Examples for "Government/Economy" may include colonial flags, country flags, natural resources, and cash crops. Examples for "Society and Culture" may include city life, village life, works of art, and sports.

Each group will complete three panels. Each sheet of paper is approximately 3 feet by 3 feet. The size of the finished panel will be 27 feet by 3 feet. If using colored chalk, lightly spray with hair spray before hanging the mural.

Extension For novice ELL students, model and provide additional explanations.

 **Art Activity**

Kente Cloth

OBJECTIVES: 12.02, 13.02

The Ashanti people live in Ghana in Western Africa. They are famous for the colorful kente cloth that they weave. Fine strips of silk are sewn together in marvelous patterns.

Using construction paper students can make a wall hanging in the traditional colors of kente. Each student will need one 12-inch by 18-inch sheet of black construction paper, three 12-inch by 1-inch red strips of construction paper, and three yellow and six green strips of the same size. They will also need glue, a wooden rod about 16 inches long, and a 20-inch piece of yarn in any color.

Fold the black construction paper in half. Starting at the fold, make cuts 1 inch apart, stopping 2 inches from the top. Open the paper. Roll the top over and glue its edge to the back so that the rod can pass through. Cut a fringe 1 inch long at the bottom. Then weave in the colored strips. Start row one under, row two over, and so forth. Follow a yellow, green, red, green pattern until you reach the bottom. Then pass the rod through the space at the top. Tie the yarn to each end and hang.

Extension For novice ELL students, model and provide additional explanations.

 Analogies

OBJECTIVES: 1.03, 5.01, 13.03

Analogies are useful to help students make associations with prior knowledge. They can be used as an instructional strategy to help students better understand new materials. Read the analogies aloud and ask students to identify the relationship between the terms. As an extension, ask students to write their own analogies using key terms or places discussed in the chapter.

Niger River : West Africa :: Nile River : North Africa (is located in)

Sahel : West Africa :: Equator : earth (bisects)

gold : Ghana :: petroleum : Nigeria (is the major resource of)

Union Army : Confederate Army :: Yoruba and Fulani : Ibo (was on the opposite side in a civil war with the)

ECOWAS : West Africa :: NAFTA : North America (is a trade agreement among countries in)

Teaching Strategies

This chapter enables students to learn about the desert, the Sahel, and the rain forest. Use the suggested activities to help emphasize the cultures in these three different environments so that students will gain a greater understanding of how environment can influence culture.

Activator

OBJECTIVES: 12.02, 12.03

Activators are great tools to use in order to "hook" the attention of the students.

Why Mosquitoes Buzz in People's Ears by Verna Aardema (Penguin Putnam, 1975. ISBN 0140549056.)

Chinye: A West African Folktale, retold by Obi Onyefulu (Penguin Putnam. ISBN 0140557601 (out of print).)

Extension For ELL students, model and provide additional explanations.

OR

Find pictures of West African art or samples of the variety of art forms in Africa. There are many Web sites that specialize in African Art with online exhibits that may also be useful in showing the examples of West African art. Once you have collected a variety of these art samples, have some fun with "Show and Tell."

Writing Prompt

OBJECTIVES: 2.01, 2.02, 2.03, 3.01

Problem-Solution

Have students research the importance of rain forests. After they complete their research, students must address the following prompt: Write a letter to the president of the United States in which you explain why rain forests should or should not be preserved.

As you write your letter, remember to
- clearly state your position.
- give at least three reasons and explain your reasons fully.
- give examples to support your reasons.
- write in complete sentences and paragraph form.
- organize your ideas and include an introduction and a conclusion.
- use good grammar, spelling, punctuation, and capitalization.

Extension Have students write about ways in which they or their community can conserve water.

CHAPTER 7

West Africa

People exploring dry caves north of Ghana and Toga discovered several narrow strips of a remarkably fine blue and white cloth. These proved to be about 1,000 years old, the oldest known examples of a fabric—Kente cloth—that is still woven by Asante and Ewe people in West Africa.

There are more designs today. The art of weaving Kente cloth, however, remains much as it was centuries ago. This skilled craft is one of many ways Africa's ancient past continues to influence life today.

Village women of Niger

Kente cloth

Chapter Preview

LESSON 1
People and Their Environment
The region provides three environments—desert, grassland, and rain forest. Most people live in the well-watered South.

LESSON 2
Government and Economy
Different groups mix in West African nations, making national unity difficult. People live by subsistence farming and exports.

LESSON 3
Society and Culture
The region remains heavily rural, and daily life continues in many traditional ways. But cities are growing rapidly.

126

Chapter 7

Chapter Resources

Print Resources

Fiction

Aardema Verna. *Why Mosquitoes Buzz in People's Ears.* Penguin Putnam, 1975. ISBN 0140549056.

Musgrove, Margaret. *The Spider Weaver: A Legend of Kente Cloth.* Blue Sky Press, 2001. ISBN 0590987879. In this retelling of a tale from Ghana, a wondrous spider shows two Ashanti weavers how to make intricate, colorful patterns in the cloth that they weave.

Onyefulu, Obi. *Chinye: A West African Folktale.*

Penguin Putnam. ISBN 0140557601 (out of print).

Nonfiction

Ahiagble, Gilbert Bobbo. *Master Weaver from Ghana.* Open Hand Publishing, 1998. ISBN 094088061X.

Blauer, Ettagale. *Ghana* (Enchantment of the World series). Children's Press, 1999. ISBN 051621053X.

Brook, Larry. *Daily Life in Ancient and Modern Timbucktu.* Runestone Press, 1999. ISBN 0822532158.

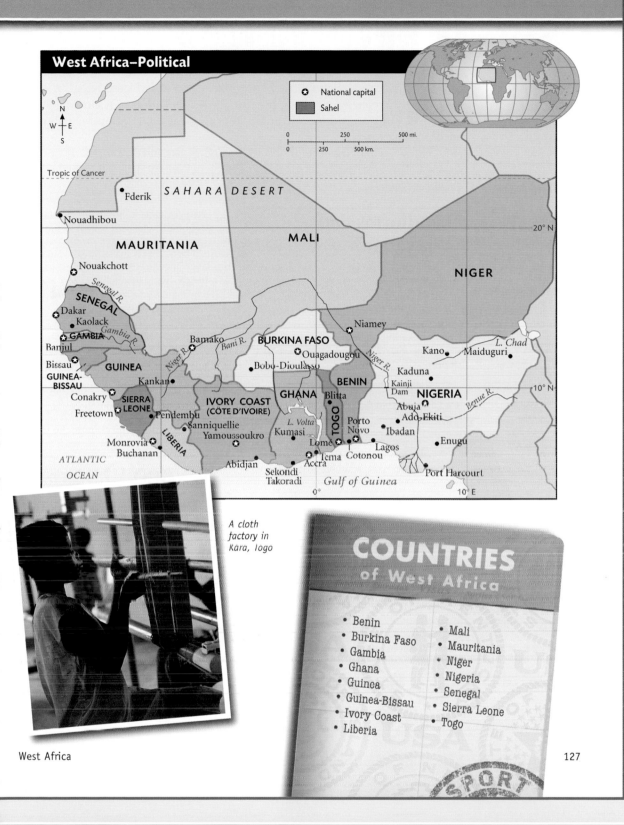

West Africa–Political

National capital

Sahel

SAHARA DESERT

Tropic of Cancer

MAURITANIA

MALI

NIGER

SENEGAL

Dakar
Kaolack
GAMBIA
Banjul
Bissau
GUINEA-
BISSAU
GUINEA
Kankan
Conakry
SIERRA
LEONE
Freetown
Pendembu
Sanniquellie
Monrovia
Buchanan
LIBERIA

Nouakchott

Fderik

Nouadhibou

Senegal R.
Gambia R.
Bamako
Bani R.
Niger R.
BURKINA FASO
Ouagadougou
Bobo-Dioulasso

Niamey

Niger R.
Kano
Maiduguri
L. Chad

Kaduna
Kainji
Dam
NIGERIA
Abuja
Ado-Ekiti
Benue R.
Enugu

IVORY COAST
(CÔTE D'IVOIRE)
GHANA
Blitta
TOGO
BENIN
Porto
Novo
Ibadan
Lagos
Cotonou
Kumasi
Lomé
Tema
Accra
Abidjan
Sekondi
Takoradi
L. Volta

ATLANTIC
OCEAN

Gulf of Guinea

Port Harcourt

A cloth
factory in
Kara, Togo

COUNTRIES
of West Africa

- Benin
- Burkina Faso
- Gambia
- Ghana
- Guinea
- Guinea-Bissau
- Ivory Coast
- Liberia
- Mali
- Mauritania
- Niger
- Nigeria
- Senegal
- Sierra Leone
- Togo

West Africa

127

Map Activity

Why Is West Africa So Special?

NATIONAL GEOGRAPHY STANDARDS: 1, 4, 5, 9, 14, 17, 18

GEOGRAPHIC THEMES: Location, Place, Human-Environmental Interaction, Movement, Region

OBJECTIVES: 1.02, 1.03, 2.01

Language Arts-Writing Assign students to identify which of the 15 West African nations are landlocked and which have a coastline *(landlocked: Burkina Faso, Mali, Niger).* Have students identify the alternate name—often preferred—of the Ivory Coast *(Côte d' Ivoire).* Have students identify the countries crossed by the prime meridian *(Mali, Burkina Faso, and Ghana).* Have students speculate where the prime meridian intersects the Equator *(Gulf of Guinea).* Have students speculate why the Sahel is included on this map *(significance of desertification impacting several nations).*

Research Topics

- What is happening to Lake Chad? Why?
- Why are Abidjan (Ivory Coast) and Lagos (Nigeria) often thought to be capital cities?
- Why does Mauritania want to control Western Sahara?
- Which West African nations changed their names after gaining independence? What is the significance of each name change?

Using the map key and scale bar, have students estimate how much of West Africa is covered by the Sahel.

Extension For novice ELL students, model and provide additional explanations.

Goodsmith, Lauren. *The Children of Mauritania: Days in the Desert and at the River Shore.* Carolrhoda Books, 1993. ISBN 0876147821. Follows the lives of two children from two of Mauritania's cultural groups: a Moorish girl and a Halpoular boy.

Heinrichs, Ann. *Niger* (Enchantment of the World series). Children's Press, 2001. ISBN 0516216333.

Kerr, Esther, Yinka Ismail and Dorothy L. Gibbs (Ed.), *Welcome to Nigeria* (Welcome to My Country Series), Gareth Stevens Publishing, 2002. ISBN 0836825373.

Levy, Patricia. *Liberia* (Cultures of the World series). Marshall Cavendish, 1998. ISBN 076140810X.

Mari, Carlo. *The Serengeti's Great Migration.* Abbeville Press, 2000. ISBN 100789206692.

Rosenberg, Anne. *Nigeria: The Culture.* Crabtree, 2001. ISBN 0865052492.

—. *Nigeria: The Land.* Crabtree, 2001. ISBN 0865052476.

—. *Nigeria: The People.* Crabtree, 2001. ISBN 0865052484.

Continued on page 135

Discussion Questions

1 What would be the positive and negative reasons why someone might live in the Sahel region?

2 What is the relationship between population and water supply in the Sahel region?

Caption Answer

Framers learned to cope with the limited rainfall this area receives by growing crops during the short rainy season. They moved to new areas when the soil wore out. Herders raised animals that fed on grasses and leaves. The herders moved south during dry spells. Since the 1960s, however, things have been more difficult because people and animals have worn out the land.

Writing Activity

Planning a School

OBJECTIVES: 5.01, 6.01, 6.02

Explain to the students that each of them has been chosen to travel to Mali to help the children there learn how to read. Have each student write a paragraph explaining how they would plan to teach students in Mali. Students should consider what their village will be able to provide toward the school and the types and ages of the students. Students should identify what they will need to bring and how they will physically set up their school as well as how they will organize and run their class.

LESSON 1 People and Their Environment

KEY IDEAS

- West Africa offers two contrasting environments—desert and arid areas in the North and well-watered areas in the South.

- West Africa is the continent's most heavily populated region. People are unevenly distributed through the region.

KEY TERMS

desertification

"**N**ow we navigated trackless valleys and sailed sand seas," a traveler wrote about his trip across the Sahara Desert in 1993. Only an old bicycle pump kept the leaking tires on his pickup from going flat.

The worried young man described one of the hard realities of desert travel: "In some parts of the Sahara, a camel is still a better vehicle than a truck."

Landforms and Vegetation

The Sahara Desert (see map, page 17) extends from North Africa into West Africa. The region of West Africa is located in the "great bulge" that extends into the Atlantic Ocean. Three of this region's nations—Mauritania (mawr·ih·TAY·nee·ah), Mali, and Niger—lie mostly in the Sahara.

Southern areas of these three countries are in the Sahel, a broad borderland between the desert and the savanna farther south. The Sahel receives enough rain to support some vegetation (see maps, page 35). People living there grow a few hardy crops or herd animals across the land in search of grass.

The map on page 20 illustrates the close connection between population density and water. Some of the desert areas of Mauritania, Mali, and Niger are uninhabited. Even the Sahel borderlands are thinly populated. West Africa's people live mostly south of the Sahel in 12 countries surrounding the southern coastline of Africa's "great bulge."

Sahel and **Swahili** (see page 22) share the same origin. Both come from an Arabic word, *sahil*, that means "border" or "shore." The Sahel forms the southern shore of the Sahara, the sand sea that covers part of North Africa. The Sahel is between desert North Africa and West and Central Africa's rain forest.

This young girl belongs to a nomadic tribe in Niger. **How does the environment of the Sahel affect its inhabitants?**

Name Origin

Benin Once known as Dahomey (site of the last slave-trading country), this name means "Blessed" in Latin.

Burkina Faso Once called Upper Volta. Thomas Sankora, one of the early leaders after independence who called for all officials to open their financial records for public scrutiny, renamed the country. It translates as "land of incorruptible people."

Gambia Named after the river that runs through the country.

Ghana Upon independence, it was renamed after the ancient empire of the region.

Guinea "Land of many rivers."

Guinea-Bissau Same as Guinea, above, but with Bissau to help differentiate from Guinea.

Ivory Coast English version of the French name "Coite d'Ivoire," reflecting the ivory trade.

Liberia "Land of the free."

The Sahel

The Sahel crosses northern Senegal and Burkina Faso (buhr·KEY·nah FAH·so) and the southern portions of Mauritania, Mali, and Niger. The Sahel is a transitional area between desert and savanna. It receives anywhere from 6 to 24 inches (15 to 61 cm) of rain yearly. The Sahel experienced a catastrophic drought in the 1990s. The rains have returned, however. Scientists closely study changes in the Atlantic and Indian Oceans and how these changes affect Africa's rainfall. The rainy season in the Sahel is from July to September.

Before the drought, the Sahel's nomadic herders and farmers had learned to cope with limited rainfall. Farmers grew crops during the short rainy season. When soil wore out, farmers moved to new areas.

Herders raised camels, cattle, and sheep. The herds grazed on short grasses and the leaves of the baobab and acacia trees during the rainy season. The herders then moved south during dry spells. By migrating, animals and people did well until the 1960s. Since then, increased animal and human populations have worn out the land. Sahel grasslands are turning to desert, a process called *desertification.*

The Spreading Desert

In less than 50 years, 250,000 square miles (650,000 sq km) of the Sahel has turned to desert. Lack of rainfall is not the only cause. The soil has worn out because of overgrazing in some areas. Nomadic herders move more often in search of food for their animals. Livestock watered at wells trample the soil and destroy grasses and shrubs. Sometimes, herders set grass on fire to promote new growth.

As the Sahel's already sparse trees and vegetation disappeared, there was little to hold the soil in place. When severe droughts came to the Sahel in the 1970s and 1980s, the dry soil turned to a fine dust and simply blew away.

Herders from Niger stop at a well to water their cattle. **How have cattle contributed to the change of the Sahel from grasslands to desert? What is that process called?**

West Africa 129

Discussion Questions

1 The desert is spreading. In less than 50 years, 250,000 square miles of the Sahel has turned to desert. The rain forests are also disappearing. Imagine you are a governmental official in West Africa. What are some ways you could help the environment? Explain.

2 Discuss how the process of desertification is affecting the Sahel's nomadic herders and how it is changing their lifestyle.

 Caption Answer

Increased cattle population has led to overgrazing. This is called desertification.

 Map Activity

Village Math Problem

OBJECTIVES: 2.01, 2.02, 2.03

If the people in a village use 1,250 gallons of water in one day, how much is the average use per person if there are 125 people in the village? Write an algebraic equation.

Answer
$125x = 1,250$ gallons $x = 10$ gallons

Extension Assist ELL students by setting up the problem for them.

Mali Colonial name was French Sudan. Upon independence, the name was changed to Mali, meaning hippopotamus, a symbol of power and strength.

Mauritania Latin for "land of the dark," named because so little was known about the area.

Niger and Nigeria Named after the Niger River. Niger is the Latin word for black.

Senegal Named after the river running through the country.

Sierra Leone Spanish for "mountains of the lions."

Togo Named after the low mountain range and river of the same name.

Monrovia, Liberia Named after James Monroe, fourth president of the United States, who helped secure land for settlement.

Tombouctou (Timbuktu), Mali Named for a legendary woman, Buktu.

Discussion Questions

1 What are the benefits of living near a delta?

2 Rain forests are disappearing throughout coastal West Africa. Explain why they are disappearing and suggest some ways to prevent this from happening.

Caption Answer

Forests are being cut for income and land use is changing.

Research Activity

Mangroves

 OBJECTIVES: 2.01, 2.02, 2.03

Using the Internet, research the importance of mangrove swamps. With a partner, students should create a poster, poem, or song trying to convince people to preserve them. You can also have students study the issue of desertification in this manner.

Extension ELL students should use an ELL-friendly Web site for research. They may create a diorama or poster to show important concepts from their research.

Activity

Environmental Concerns

 OBJECTIVES: 2.01, 2.02, 2.03

The increase of desert areas and the depletion of the rain forest are concerns for Africans and the global community. Have students reread the section on the rain forest and desertification in Chapter 7. Have students make two flow charts that suggest the cause/effect relationships for the rain forest and desertification. Model the creation of the flow chart on the rain forest with the students. Have them prepare a second flow chart with a partner on desertification. Possible elements of the flow chart are listed as follows:

Rain forests in Ghana and throughout coastal West Africa are disappearing. **Why?**

South of the Sahel

Countries along the coast are the most heavily populated in West Africa (see maps, page 20 and 127). These countries have ample water and other natural resources.

Heavy rains and high temperatures produce mangrove swamps and salt marshes. A variety of birds, reptiles, and fish live there.

Until a few years ago, rain forests spread across much of Liberia, Sierra Leone (see·EHR·ah lee·OWN), and the south-western Ivory Coast. The forests are now being cut, especially in the Ivory Coast. Ships loaded with mahogany and other tropical woods sail from Abidjan (ab·ih·JAHN), the capital and chief port of the Ivory Coast. These exports provide income, and farmers move into the cleared land.

Rivers

The Niger River flows 2,590 miles (4,170 km) through five countries to the Gulf of Guinea. The Niger runs down the mountains of Guinea (GIH·nee) about 150 miles (242 km) from the Atlantic Ocean, then turns northeastward into the Sahel before bending in a great arc to the south. Yawning hippopotamuses and snapping crocodiles dwell in the river.

As it nears the sea, the Niger forms a delta 150 miles (242 km) long and 200 miles (322 km) wide. People who live nearby depend upon the Niger for transportation and trade. Others fish or grow sorghum, millet, or rice along its banks.

Since 1968, the Niger River has provided electricity for Nigeria through the Kainji Dam. The Gambia, Senegal, and Volta are also important rivers for travel, trade, and irrigation. Some West African countries have begun projects together to harness these rivers for hydroelectric power.

Depletion of the rain forest
heavily cut for timber
rain forests have not grown again
farmers move into cleared areas
crops do not grow well
less fertile soil through leaching

Desertification
drought
overgrazing
farm practices of burning off grass
livestock trample soil at water areas
more wood cut and erosion occurs

Have students pick either the depletion of the rain forest or desertification. They will create a poster or digital story/PowerPoint presentation that depicts the causes and effects of their topic. They can use slogans, drawings, or lists of facts to help emphasize the seriousness of their topic.

Extension Have students research environmental organizations on the Internet that persuade for their cause. Students should identify the arguments used by the organization(s) to convince visitors on their Web sites. Students should then determine if these arguments are persuasive. Why or why not?

Extension Have ELL students use the Wordlingo Web site to research this topic. Students should make a poster illustrating why this is bad or should stop.

Mineral Resources

Minerals are important natural resources in parts of West Africa. Deposits of bauxite, the raw material for aluminum, are found in Guinea, Ghana, and Sierra Leone. Liberia, Senegal, and Mauritania have iron ore deposits. Togo and Senegal contain phosphates (see map, page 61).

Nigeria holds some of the largest deposits of oil and natural gas in Africa. Tin, iron ore, and coal also are mined there. Oil was discovered off the coasts of Ghana and Senegal, but it has been too costly to drill for it. Gold is Ghana's principal mineral. Nigeria and the Ivory Coast also have natural gas fields that are not yet fully developed. A new offshore natural gas pipeline is planned for the coast of Africa between Ghana and Nigeria.

Population Patterns

West Africa is the most heavily populated region south of the Sahara. With more than 131.5 million people, Nigeria has the largest population in Africa. Ghana, with almost 22.1 million, also ranks high in population among African countries.

The majority of West Africa's people still live in villages. Migration to cities is

occurring rapidly. More than a dozen cities in the region have a population of a million or more. Abidjan, Ivory Coast, and Ibandan, Nigeria, have populations of more than 3 million. At the current rate of urbanization, the movement of people to cities, half of all West Africa's people will live in cities by 2015.

Iron ore is mined in Zouérate, Mauritania. Mining is a key economic activity in parts of West Africa. **What other mineral resources are found in West Africa?**

Discussion Questions

1 What factors might explain why Nigeria has the largest population in Africa?

2 Explain how rapid population growth will affect West Africa in the future.

3 The Niger River flows through five countries in West Africa. Talk about some of the things you may see on a journey down the Niger.

 **Caption Answer**

Iron ore and coal are found there. Gold is found as well.

 Map Activity

Population Density Map

NATIONAL GEOGRAPHY STANDARDS: 1, 2, 9

GEOGRAPHIC THEMES: Human-Environmental Interaction, Movement

OBJECTIVES: 1.01, 2.02

Have students use the World Almanac to look up the population density of each country. As a class, using a blank map of West Africa, make a key to show that one symbol equals ten people per square mile. In each country of West Africa, draw the correct number of symbols to show the population density. Students should study the map and write three conclusions about population patterns in West Africa, giving reasons explaining the patterns.

Extension Do not assign novice and intermediate ELL students the writing.

LESSON 1 REVIEW

Fact Follow-Up
1. What is the Sahel? What nations of West Africa include the Sahel?
2. What factors cause or contribute to desertification?
3. What is the relative location of the most densely populated nations in West Africa? the least densely populated?
4. What are the major rivers of West Africa?

Talk About It
1. How can West Africans stop or reduce desertification?
2. In North Africa, more people live in cities than in rural areas. In West Africa, more people live in rural areas. Why do these differences exist?
3. Which do you think is more important in the Sahel: the physical or cultural characteristics of a place? Explain.

West Africa

LESSON 1 REVIEW

Fact Follow-Up Answers
1. The Sahel is a dry borderland between the desert and the savanna. It crosses northern Senegal and Burkina Faso and the southern portions of Mauritania, Mali, and Niger.
2. Lack of rainfall, increased animal and human populations, and the practice of setting grass on fire to promote new growth have all contributed to desertification.
3. The most densely populated nations are along the Atlantic coast. The Sahel and the Sahara are the locations of the least densely populated nations.
4. The major rivers of the region are the Niger, the Gambia, the Senegal, and the Volta.

Talk About It Answers
1. Strategies for stopping or reducing desertification include the following: reducing human and animal populations in threatened areas, irrigation, replanting grasslands, and placing limits on herding.
2. West Africa offers more farmland to work. Most of North Africa includes the Sahara. The fertile areas are along the highly populated coast.
3. Important points: Students should choose a position and support it with reasons; they should also distinguish between physical and cultural characteristics of place.

OBJECTIVES: 4.01, 5.01, 6.03, 7.01, 9.01

Discussion Questions

1 Explain how the quote in the first sentence relates to the government and economy of West Africa.

2 Why do you think it has been so difficult to bring unity to West Africa?

3 What characteristics of colonial times are reflected in West Africa today?

4 What hardships did West Africans face in the 1800s as a result of farmers being forced to grow cash crops rather than food crops?

 Caption Answer

Colonial governments forced subsistence farmers to grow such cash crops instead of food crops.

 Map Activity

Colonial Fingerprints

NATIONAL GEOGRAPHY STANDARDS: 1, 11, 13, 17

GEOGRAPHIC THEMES: Movement, Human-Environment Interaction

OBJECTIVES: 1.02, 2.01, 5.01

Have students examine political, physical, and transportation maps to determine "fingerprints" left on the regional landscape by European powers. Points to consider include locations of capital cities, locations of major cities/population centers, transportation patterns, and political boundaries/physical barriers. Next have students develop statements generalizing about the impact of European colonialism on the region and how the region is dealing with this legacy.

From this, each student can make a poster using his/her own hand as a model, labeling an example of the impact on each finger. These can then be assembled for a bulletin board or display around a map of the region. See below the kinds of information that could appear on a hand.

LESSON 2 Government and Economy

KEY IDEAS

- West Africa's national borders—inherited from a colonial past—enclose diverse people. Achieving unity among these people has been difficult.

- Most people are subsistence farmers. Others export oil and agricultural products.

KEY TERMS

ECOWAS

"Little by little the hunter catches the monkey in the forest." That saying of the Wolof people of Senegal and Gambia describes how West African nations, like the hunter, have steadily worked for an improved government and economy. The right mix, they hope, will bring prosperity.

European Legacies

Contacts between Europeans and West African kingdoms have a long history. As early as the 1500s, European merchants traded for gold, ivory, slaves, and palm oil. Many West Africans were caught in the transatlantic slave trade.

In the 1800s, the region was drawn more closely to Europe. Europe divided almost all of Africa into colonies. The national boundaries of West African countries today reflect how Europeans drew lines between their colonies.

Most of West Africa fell under British or French colonial rule. One exception was Liberia, a nation founded as a homeland for freed slaves from the United States. Cape Verde (vehrd) and Guinea-Bissau (GIH·nee-bis·ow) came under Portugal's control. British colonies became today's Nigeria, Ghana, Sierra Leone, and Gambia. They maintain ties to the United Kingdom and other former British colonies.

The rest of the region made up colonial French West Africa. In 1960, these French colonies became today's Benin, Burkina Faso, Guinea, Ivory Coast, Mali, Mauritania, Niger, Senegal, and Togo.

Colonial governments forced subsistence farmers to grow such cash crops as coffee, cocoa, peanuts, cotton, and palm oil. The change to cash crops took place mainly in the coastal areas near ports. These products chiefly benefited Europeans and a few African merchants. West Africans suffered from the shift away from food crops. In the years they did not make money from cash crops, farmers faced starvation.

Villagers harvest cocoa in Ivory Coast.
How are cocoa and other cash crops a legacy of European capitalism?

Names: Porto-Novo, Côte d'Ivoire
Location of capitals and major cities: Lagos
Boundaries following natural features: rivers
Transportation links: interior to coast; few between countries
Government forms: parliament
Other: cash crop farming, plantations, export raw materials

Extension ELL students could do this activity with a peer tutor's help.

Post-Colonial Trade

West African colonies, much like those in North Africa, gained independence between 1957 and 1960. Freedom from colonial rule did not break economic ties with Europe. Along the coast, African merchants continued to promote trade. Their governments encouraged this trade with Europe as a way of gaining badly needed income. Many West African countries continued to have more contacts with the United Kingdom or France than with their nearby neighbors.

Away from the coast, some West Africans had never raised crops for export markets. Today, inland villagers live on whatever crops they grow. They trade in village markets, after walking, riding bicycles, or traveling by other means. Village markets provide farm families with a way of acquiring a pot, a basket, cloth, or other objects they cannot make at home. In the Sahel, farmers trade a little millet or an animal. Farther south, farmers exchange yams, corn, or palm oil. No one buys or sells much.

The Search for National Unity

Since independence, West African nations have had political problems. Their borders—drawn by their former colonial powers—often brought together people from different ethnic groups. Often those groups did not work together in support of a new nation. Sometimes these differences threatened a nation's survival.

Nigeria's population, for example, consists of three main groups. The Yoruba people live in southwest Nigeria. For centuries, they had lived in walled cities and farmed the land around them. The Yoruba began growing cash crops and became involved in international trade after the

British arrived. The Yoruba helped build the port of Lagos, a city today of more than 1.5 million people.

The Ibo people live in Nigeria's southeast. Unlike the Yoruba, they reside in small communities in the countryside. They also differ from the Yoruba in their traditional ways of life.

Far to the north, the Hausa and Fulani people live in an area that stretches across all of Nigeria. The Hausa/Fulani follow Islam and have little in common with either the Ibo or Yoruba.

Tensions among these three groups reached a breaking point in the 1960s when the Ibo proclaimed independence from Nigeria. They wanted to establish a new nation to be called Biafra. The Yoruba and Hausa/Fulani felt threatened by this proposed change. They united in attacking the Ibo. Thousands were killed and even more died of starvation during the Biafran War.

The Biafra War in Nigeria was a failed movement for independence by the Ibo against the Yoruba and Hausa/Fulani. **How was the war a legacy of colonialism?**

West Africa

Discussion Questions

1 Even after independence, what tied the new African nations to their former European rulers?

2 How did the economy inland differ from that closer to the coast?

3 Explain the tensions that existed between the Yoruba, Fulani, and Ibo people. What was the end result?

Caption Answer

The borders of these countries were drawn by colonial rulers who did not care if rival groups were united within one nation.

Activity

"Who Has ... I Have ... ?"

OBJECTIVES: 1.02, 1.03, 2.01

Design "Who has... I have...?" facts on each West African nation to review aloud with students. Hand out the cards to the class. They can use their books as a refer-ece.

For example, you could begin with, "Who has the West African nation that has Banjul as its capital?" The student with Gambia would respond, "I have Gambia. Who has the West African country located between Benin and Ghana?" The next student, who has Togo, would respond, "I have Togo. Who has the West African nation crossed by both the Benue and Niger Rivers?" Another student, who has Nigeria, would respond, "I have Nigeria." "Who has the West African country that surrounds Gambia on three sides?" The next student, who has Senegal, would respond, "I have Senegal. Who has ..." Responses and questions continue until all students have responded or until all review items have been covered (students can be given more than one response/questions to accommodate number of facts to be orally reviewed).

Research Activity

"The Sun Never Sets"

OBJECTIVES: 1.02, 1.03

The United Kingdom was only one of the imperial powers in Africa. However, British colonies covered so much of the world that the saying "the sun never sets on the British Empire" was coined. Have students research the location of British colonies throughout the world at the peak of the British empire. Students should locate the colonies on a map of today, noting any changes in names (see map, page 90, to compare for post-colonial name changes). After locating the colonies, have students study the time zones of the colonies to determine whether the sun ever set on the British Empire.

Eyewitness Activity

Soap Sculpting

➤ **OBJECTIVES:** 5.04, 7.02, 12.02

Centuries ago carved ivory decorated the palaces of African kings. Ivory scepters were held by kings as symbols of power. Elephants tusks were carved and used as horns to sound the arrival of rulers. Have students use bars of soap, plastic knives, toothpicks, or art utensils from the art specialist to carve miniature artifacts such as animals, scepters, horns, shields, small statues, and/or masks. Display.

Extension For novice ELL students, model and provide additional explanations.

EYEWITNESS TO HISTORY
The Ivory Trade

Centuries ago, carved ivory decorated the palaces of African kings. Ivory scepters were held by kings as symbols of power. Elephant tusks were carved and used as horns to sound the arrival of rulers. The appeal of ivory all over the world since then has threatened the existence of elephants.

In 1930, the African elephant population was estimated at between 5 to 10 million. In 1989, that estimate had fallen to less than 600,000. The elephant, both African and Asian, is on the endangered species list. One reason is the profitable ivory trade.

The elephant's ivory tusks came to be highly valued for many purposes. Traders took the ivory brought from the interior of Central and West Africa and shipped it to Europe and, later, to the United States. West Africa came to be known as the Ivory Coast.

Ivory pendant mask from the Democratic Republic of Congo

What would YOU do?

Ivory chess pieces feel cool to the touch. Ivory can be beautifully carved into jewelry. With laws forbidding ivory trade, would you buy such a piece of jewelry? What if someone wanted to give you a present of an ivory chess set or a necklace of carved ivory? What would you do?

134   Chapter 7

 Background Information

Poverty in Nigeria's Oil-Rich Delta

The Niger Delta has been a source of both wealth and conflict for Nigeria. The oil-rich delta yields more than $10 billion in profits yearly for Nigeria. Yet the region has little to show for this oil wealth. Its schools are run-down. Potholes mar the roads. Equally serious has been the loss of life and the environmental damage caused by oil spills and explosions of fuel leaking from broken pipelines. The government has done little to end the desperate poverty or to clean up the environment. Analysts say that most of the money has gone to northern Nigeria, the power base for Nigeria's former military rulers, who hoped to keep the oil-rich area weak and poor. Anger and frustration have fueled discontent in the delta.

In the 1970s, elephant tusks became a cash crop for farmers and governments. At $100 a pound, the few dollars a family earned as farmers seemed worthless. One elephant's tusks earned a year's income.

Carving ivory

In 1989, the ivory trade was banned internationally. Elephants are still threatened by habitat loss and conflicts with humans—including ivory poachers and hunters who want the elephants' meat. Prices have fallen and poaching has slowed down. But by 2001, the elephant population had fallen to 301,000.

An elephant pack in Lake Manyara, Tanzania

West Africa

135

Research Activity

Ivory Trade Research

OBJECTIVES: 5.03, 5.04, 6.03

Using the Internet, have students research the global ivory trade. Students should determine which countries have banned trade in ivory, which countries have widespread illegal ivory trade, how smugglers trade in ivory, and what African, Asian, and other nations are doing to stop the ivory trade. Students should write a letter to the president of the United States or to the leader of an African or Asian nation suggesting ways in which that country can help stop the illegal trade of ivory.

Extension ELL students should use a partner or an ELL-friendly Web site to assist with research. They should create a poster showing why this was bad and should be stopped.

Science Activity

Drought and Desertification

OBJECTIVES: 2.02, 3.02, 3.05

Divide the class into cooperative learning groups. Have students explore the relationship between periods of drought and land use in West Africa in the process of desertification. The fragility of the ecosystem combined with the need to support a large population has combined to destroy the grasslands of the Sahel region. Using at least three blackline maps of Africa, students should illustrate the changes in the Sahel and the deserts over the past 50+ years. Students will need to research these changes on Web sites such as NASA's Earth Observatory: Defining Desertification and the USGS International Program Sahel Land Use site. Students should use one final map to project what they think will happen to the Sahel in 20 years based on climate changes and human factors

Chapter Resources (continued)

Continued from page 125

Back issues of magazines

Asante World. Cobblestone Publishing Company. ISBN 0382404785.

Elephant and Ivory. Cobblestone Publishing Company. ISBN 0382405528.

Mali. Cobblestone Publishing Company. ISBN 0382407873.

Senegal. Cobblestone Publishing Company. ISBN 0382405676.

Yoruba of West Africa. Cobblestone Publishing Company. ISBN 0382408985.

Audiovisual

Destination: Senegal. Peace Corps,1996. Introduces the culture and geography of Senegal, Africa. Video (16 min.). ISBN 0160633958.

Web Sites

Go to **NCJourneys.com** for links to the following Web sites:

- Panafrican Film and Television Festival of Ouagadoudou, Burkina Faso
- Ancient West African City of Benin A.D. 1300–1897, Smithsonian Institution
- History for Kids, Africa West Africa and the Bantu
- West Africa (ECOWAS) Energy Data, Statistics and Analysis - Oil, Gas, Electricity, Coal

Discussion Questions

1 What effect did the drop in world oil prices have on Nigeria's economy? How did it recover?

2 What factors have contributed to Nigeria becoming the leading economy in West Africa?

3 Think of a crop or a product from North Carolina that has experienced a sudden drop in price. What effect did it have on the local economy?

 Caption Answer

Nigeria borrowed money to pay for improvements based on oil income. It gave people jobs. Drops in world prices hurt the oil export business.

 Activity

Why Migration?

OBJECTIVES: 4.01, 4.02, 4.03

Discuss with students the geographic theme of movement and the way the concept of migration relates to it. Describe this scenario to students: A man in a village in Nigeria is considering moving to the city of Lagos, on the coast of Nigeria. Based on their reading of this chapter, have students brainstorm the "push" and "pull" factors that might influence him to migrate to the city. Which factors are stronger?

Building Stronger Economies

"I want Nigeria to become a country that makes the things we now have to import," said a Nigerian boy. Government leaders and planners throughout West Africa share the youth's dream. They are working to export products instead of raw materials.

The problem is that the cost of factories and equipment for processing metals and minerals is high. Most West African countries, especially those in the Sahel, lack the money to build such plants and train workers.

Foreign-owned companies have set up factories. They provide jobs for West Africans. Yet West Africa may not receive other benefits. Most of the profit leaves the region, returning to the companies' home country.

West African nations do have some small factories. Food processors make peanut oil from locally grown peanuts. Textile mills spin, weave, and dye locally grown cotton.

Nigeria is a leading oil producer. **How has it gained from that export? What are some drawbacks of depending on oil?**

Nigeria's Economy

The oil-rich Nigerian economy (see map, page 61) was hurt by a long period of political instability, corruption, and mismanagement. Nigeria's former military rulers did not diversify the oil-based economy. Farmers have not been able to produce enough food to keep up with the population. Nigeria must import more than 50 percent of its food.

In 1999, after almost 16 years of military rule, a new constitution was adopted. Nigeria has made a peaceful transition to a civilian-led government. President Olusegun Obasanjo's government is trying to bring democracy to Nigeria. To bring stability to the country, Nigeria must also rebuild the economy and unite many different ethnic groups.

 Background Information

ECOWAS and Trade

In 2005, the combined Gross Domestic Product (GDP) for ECOWAS was estimated at $139 billion. Economies within the Community are at varying stages of development. Nigeria's economy is larger than the combined GDP of all other ECOWAS countries, with a GDP of $78 billion. The region's major export commodities were energy products (crude oil and refined petroleum products), minerals (gold, diamonds, and bauxite) and agricultural products (cocoa, coffee, groundnuts, and cotton). The primary United States import from the region was Nigerian crude oil. As of January 1, 2006, President Bush designated 37 sub-Saharan African countries as eligible for tariff preferences under the African Growth and Opportunity Act (AGOA). The AGOA requires that each year countries make specific progress toward a market-based economy, the rule of law, free trade, and economic policies that will reduce poverty, and protection of worker's rights. The Ivory Coast, Liberia, and Togo were the only countries in the region not approved for the AGOA.

Working Together

During colonial rule, the French and British created roads and rail lines to link inland areas of their West African colonies with the coast. Little happened to encourage trade among West African countries.

Today the Economic Community of West African States, *ECOWAS,* an organization of West African nations, hopes to increase trade among themselves.

It has already made progress in the construction of regional roads and telecommunication links. It now hopes to eventually have one currency among all of its member nations similar to the European Union's Euro.

ECOWAS also plans to improve energy services for its members. They hope this will improve economic development. They have set a goal to decrease poverty by 50 percent by 2015.

Ghana still earns money from gold mining. **What prevents areas of West Africa from building mines and factories?**

LESSON 2 REVIEW

Fact Follow-Up

1. What are some important economic results of European rule in West Africa?
2. What European nations were the colonial rulers of present-day nations of West Africa?
3. Describe difficulties of unification in the present-day Nigeria.
4. What is ECOWAS? What are its aims?

Talk About It

1. In what ways did European colonialism both help and hurt modern-day West African nations' efforts to become economically and politically independent?
2. Which challenge facing nations of West Africa do you think will be most difficult to overcome? Explain.

West Africa

137

 **Caption Answer**

Countries often lack money to build plants and often lack trained workers.

 Math Activity

Oil v. the Economy

 OBJECTIVES: 5.04, 6.03, 13.03

Using almanacs or the Internet, students can track the price of oil per barrel for selected years and make a bar graph of the information. Students can then research the per capita GNP of Nigeria for those same years. On the same graph, record the information in the form of a line graph.

OR

Students could track the price of oil over the past year and make a line graph. They can then research the rate of inflation in the United States quarterly and see if there is a connection between the price of oil and the United States economy.

Extension ELL students should use an ELL-friendly Web site for research.

LESSON 2 REVIEW

Fact Follow-Up Answers

1. Many West African nations continue to trade more with European countries than with their neighbors. Many also continue to trade cash crops.
2. Most of West Africa fell under the colonial rule of Great Britain or France. Portugal controlled Cape Verde and Guinea-Bissau. Liberia remained free during the period of colonial rule in Africa.
3. Nigeria is still suffering from the effects of a civil war that occurred in the 1960s. The Ibo people wanted their own nation, separate from the Fulani and Yoruba who also live in Nigeria. The war that followed the Ibo proclamation of independence was bloody and caused starvation. Nigeria is unified, but the people's loyalties toward the Ibo, Fulani, and Yoruba remain.
4. It is the Economic Community of West African States. The organization hopes to increase trade among the nations of West Africa and make it easier to move goods within the region.

Talk About It Answers

1. European colonialists did build the African roads, railroads, port facilities, and European-style factories and other structures. These remained after independence, though the roads, railroads, and port facilities were built for the purpose of extracting resources (raw materials) from West Africa. Europeans left West Africa dependent on cash crops rather than on crops that might have benefited West African families and communities. European colonial borders were drawn by Europeans with little regard for African ethnic groups, and independent nations in West Africa inherited these borders, which often put rival ethnic groups in the same nation or separated ethnic groups.
2. Important points: Students should select one challenge and explain the choice in detail. Note: national unity, industrial growth, government stability.

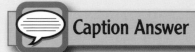

OBJECTIVES: 2.02, 11.01, 12.02

Discussion Questions

1 Explain the dual personality of Dakar.

2 What is a major contributor to the development of shanty towns?

Caption Answer

There are now skyscrapers and high-rise apartments. There are expensive houses and luxury cars. There are also more and more shanty towns, where poor people live on the outskirts of the cities.

Activity

"Name That Role"

OBJECTIVES: 8.01, 9.03, 10.02

Using the first name of the student, have each student write an acrostic in which they explain what they see as their role in their own family. Have students share with the class (if student has a short name, include last name).

Extension Have ELL students write one word for each letter of their name in the acrostic.

LESSON **3** Society and Culture

KEY IDEAS

- West Africans leave rural areas to look for jobs in the city.
- West Africans try to keep village life alive.
- West Africans try to hold on to their culture while making progress.

KEY TERMS

shanty towns

The University of Ghana at Legon, near Accra (below), and Cheikh Anta Diop University in Dakar, Senegal (bottom), are both signs of modern life in their countries. **How are West African cities changing?**

Kwasi Oduro teaches at the University of Ghana near Accra. He is the only member of his family with a university degree, a job, and a house. Oduro has left his village, but he has followed the tradition of helping his relatives. His house has been home to as many as 18 extra people whom he describes as "cousins of a sort." These distant relatives did not pay rent or pay for the meals they ate at his house each day.

City Life

Dakar (da·KAR), Senegal's capital city, typifies today's modern West African city. Its skyscrapers and high-rise apartments show the changes of the region. Dakar's street markets and grand mosques reflect West Africa's history.

Downtown city streets are paved and well lighted. Shops beckon to tourists and the few wealthy locals who can afford to buy goods there. There are expensive houses with Mercedes Benzes or other luxury cars in driveways. High gates and electric fences or barbed wire surround these houses.

Villagers and young people hear of a better life and leave rural Africa looking for jobs. A lucky few find work in government offices or foreign-owned businesses. Demands for decent housing, clean water, and more roads exceed government ability to provide them.

Each day people move into the city, but most cannot find or afford housing. Cities overwhelmed by rapid growth soon develop *shanty towns,* or slum settlements on the outskirts of the city. New arrivals make shelter out of whatever materials they can find: cardboard, tree branches, plywood, sheets of corrugated iron, or plastic. Most of these makeshift homes lack running water and electricity.

West Africa and countries throughout Africa are overwhelmed by rapid growth. People in cities experience power failures, poor sanitation service, and traffic jams called "go slows."

138

Chapter 7

Background Information

Education in the Sahara

The arid, sparsely settled Sahel and Sahara cover much of Mali. Its residents are mainly nomadic herders. In one windswept patch of the Sahara, children from Tuareg families are attending school for the first time. At the Tindjambane community school, they sit on carpets in shelters with thatched roofs. They have no books or paper, just chalk and chalkboards. The community school is part of a program by the Mali government to encourage villagers to build their own primary schools. Its ambitious goal is to educate 75 percent of Mali's children by 2008. Right now only 44 percent of boys and 34 percent of girls can read. In the past many Tuareg refused to send their children to public schools. The teachers spoke French, a language few understood. In addition, some Tuareg feared that the teachers would try to convert from Islam to Christianity.

Family Responsibilities

When rural villagers first come to the city, many stay with members of their extended family. Helping members of this large group has been considered an important responsibility of kinship. Kwasi Oduro of Accra is only one of many city dwellers who supported newcomers from home villages.

Some traditional ties of kinships are beginning to break down in cities. More and more people in cities are refusing to house family from the country. Fewer young people rely on their parents or elders back in the village to make arranged marriages. They choose their own partners and use their own wages to pay any bridewealth. Some choose to marry people from different ethnic groups.

Village Life

Round village huts, muddy paths, and 10-mile (16-km) walks for water contrast vividly with large cities, skyscrapers, and traffic jams. Both are Africa today.

Far away from bustling coastal cities is the village of M'bagne (mm·BAHN·y). Located in southern Mauritania on the Senegal River, M'bagne contains many extended families. Grandparents, married and single children, and grandchildren live there together. Almost all the villagers belong to the Halpular ethnic group. Villagers build mud and thatch or concrete houses around an open yard.

Families keep their belongings inside the houses. During the day everyone stays outdoors. Although there is often no electricity, most families have a radio and many also have a bicycle.

The villagers' main source of livelihood is small-scale farming. M'bagne villagers share fields along the banks of the Senegal River. Everyone in the village helps tend this farmland. Villagers grow potatoes, onions, beans, tomatoes, and okra. Water from the river irrigates the fields.

West Africa

A family gathers on their apartment balcony in Abidjan, Ivory coast.

Villagers crowd a riverside market in Niger.

Villagers in Senegal live in round huts (above). This woman and her child (right) are from a remote Bedik village in eastern Senegal. **How do many people in cities remain connected with villages?**

Discussion Questions

1 What are some expected responsibilities of kinship when family members of rural villagers move to the cities?

Caption Answer

They return home for harvests and other celebrations. Some family members move to the city.

Activity

West African Peanut Butter Stew

OBJECTIVES: 2.01, 6.01, 12.01

Ingredients
peanut oil
4–5 pound chicken, cut in small pieces
3 medium chopped onions
2 14½-ounce cans of diced tomatoes
2 chopped green peppers
¼ cup tomato sauce
hot sauce
1 cup peanut butter
6 cups chicken broth
1 cup sliced okra
2 cubed sweet potatoes
½ teaspoon of thyme
salt
cinnamon
paprika

Preparation In a large pot, heat 3 or 4 tablespoons of peanut oil. Add the chicken to the hot oil and cook until browned and then remove. Cook the onions, tomatoes, and green peppers in the remaining oil until softened. Add the chicken to the cooked vegetables. Heat the chicken broth and then mix the peanut butter in the hot broth. Pour into the chicken and vegetables. Add tomato sauce and season with a few drops of the hot sauce and simmer over low heat for approximately 45 minutes. After simmering, add the okra and sweet potatoes and season with a pinch of salt, cinnamon, and paprika. Continue to cook over low heat until the stew is fully cooked and the sauce is thickened. Serve over rice.

Teacher Notes

Peanuts and Goobers

In the American South, "goober" and "goober pea" are other names for the peanut. Goober is related to Kongo or Kimbundu *n-guba*, meaning peanut. This word was brought over by enslaved Africans. Peanuts were brought from Africa for the slaves to eat on the Voyage across the Atlantic.

Peanuts are a common food in Africa. They were first brought to Africa by the Portuguese. The Portuguese discovered the peanut in South America in the 1500s.

Discussion Questions

1 Compare and contrast life in the larger cities of Africa to life in M'bagne.

2 Describe a typical day in the life of a teenage boy or girl living in M'bagne.

3 What importance do art and music hold in West African society?

Caption Answer

Important points: Students should speculate that African music came with Africans brought as slaves to America.

Caption Answer

They express their culture in art, film, and music.

Art Activity

Design Adinka Cloth

OBJECTIVES: 12.02, 13.02

Have students design symbols that represent themselves. They should then sketch the designs on clean metal trays or sponges and cut out the designs. Give a large piece of paper or piece of an old sheet to each student. Using poster or fabric paint, students can stamp a row of one symbol on the paper or cloth. Repeat for each of the symbols. Play African music during this activity.

ELL Teaching Tips

Be Aware of Culture Shock

The new ELL students in your classroom are probably suffering from culture shock. Imagine how you would feel if you were in their shoes! Make sure you create an environment where the ELL students feel safe. This will lessen the intensity and duration of culture shock

---

The M'bagne farmers also plant some fields farther from the river. Crops in these fields rely entirely on rainfall for survival. Sometimes there is no rain in the Sahel. Plants wither and die.

Children in the village attend primary school, where they learn French, once the official language in Mauritania. At home villagers speak Pular, the language of their ethnic group. After finishing primary school, a few of the brightest boys may go on to a high school. They must leave the village for a larger town such as Bogue or a city such as Nouakchott (noo·AHK·shat).

A day off from school finds boys playing soccer or swimming in the river. Most boys will become farmers or fishermen along the Senegal River.

Girls have few chances for education beyond the village school. After completing primary school, girls perform such daily chores as taking care of younger children, carrying water from one of the public faucets in the village square, or washing clothes in the river. They must gather firewood for cooking and shop at the village marketplace for fish, grains, and other food. They also work in the fields planting, weeding, and harvesting crops.

West African drumming, dance, and traditional music have influenced music and dance all over the world. **How did African music come to the Americas?**

Sculptures made from teak and ebony wood are common in West African markets. **How do many West Africans express their culture?**

Art and Music

More than 500 years ago, craftsmen in Benin and Ife made stunningly beautiful wood and ivory carvings and bronze statues. Art lovers still admire traditional West African art. Culture also finds expression in lively music and good movies.

Ouagadougou (wah·guh·DOO·goo), the capital of Burkina Faso, has hosted an African film festival every other year since 1969. The competition of only African-made films promotes both the film industry and film as an African art form.

West Africa is also the place to hear some amazing guitar playing. West African musicians are known worldwide for the excitement and variety of their musical styles.

140

Background Information

Musical Fusion and Protest

A synthesis of African musical styles is creating devoted fans for West African music worldwide. In Senegal gifted musicians merge griot storytelling traditions with musical elements from Cuba and other parts of the world. In Nigeria the style known as Afrobeat, made popular by Fela Anikulapo Kuti, merged defiant political statements against Nigeria's leaders with West African drumming and American jazz. During the rule of one of Nigeria's military leaders, Fela's songs landed him in jail. Soldiers burned down his house, but his songs helped end the dictatorship.

Customs

Burial traditions change over time. In West Africa, a more recent change has been the shape of coffins. Bright and colorful special coffins were once reserved for chiefs.

Today, coffin makers honor requests for unusual designs that reflect a person's life. They may build a coffin that looks like a loaf of bread for a baker, a bird for a cook, or an airplane for a traveler.

A coffin builder in Ghana has carved two coffins in animal shapes.

A Journey to  BURKINA FASO

The Panafrican Film and Television Festival

Burkina Faso is internationally known as the host of the Panafrican Film and Television Festival of Ouagadougou. The festival started in 1969, and runs for one week in February every other year.

People fly in from all over the world to see films in indoor and outdoor theaters. African films are shown with an African language and English or French subtitles. It is the largest African film festival. The organization that sponsors the festival publishes newsletters about African cinema. The festival also presents awards for television and new media productions.

Visitors may think that today's grim poverty makes the city an unlikely spot for a film festival. Yet Ouagadougou is an ancient city with a distinguished past. It once was the capital of the Mossi Kingdom of Wagadugu. It came under French colonial rule in the late 1800s and won

independence in the early 1960s. Factories produce textiles, matches, and footwear. Villagers move to Ouagadougou looking for work.

Residents of Burkina Faso recognized the value of their African heritage and looked for ways to honor it. The film festival's value goes beyond the income earned from tourists. It is one way the people of the continent are drawn together. Audiences see films based on folktales that cross cultural boundaries. The festival hosts screenings throughout the world. All show films that portray Africa.

Attendee at the Panafrican film festival

LESSON 3 REVIEW

Fact Follow-Up
1. Describe city life in West Africa.
2. What are shanty towns? Why do they exist in West African cities?
3. Describe the variety of art and musical forms in West Africa.

Talk About It
1. Would you prefer to live in an African city or in a rural area? Explain.
2. Do young West Africans have too much family responsibility? Explain your answer.
3. What West African tradition would you like to see adopted in the United States? Why?

West Africa   141

Art Activity

Creative Coffins

OBJECTIVES: 11.02, 12.02

Materials white photo-copier paper, fine line black pens, colored pencils or markers, construction paper for mounting

Assignment Students have read that people in West Africa will spend their life savings to have a custom-made coffin made to reflect something special about their life. Students should think about things that are special in their life or that they really like to do: hobbies, daily or special activities, animals or pets, sports, or something they hope to do in the future. Students should fold the "coffin-cut" paper in half. A horizontal or vertical fold is acceptable. On the outside of the "coffin-cut" paper, each student should draw a picture of the coffin design reflecting his or her life, using colored pencils to enhance the appearance of the coffin. On the bottom of the inside fold of the coffin-cut paper, students should write a paragraph explaining how the coffin reflects their life.

Extension Do not assign novice and intermediate ELL students the paragraph. Intermediate students should write simple sentences. Novices should draw pictures only.

LESSON 3 REVIEW

Fact Follow-Up Answers
1. Some sections of the city are paved and well lighted, with expensive houses, skyscrapers, and high-rise apartments. But the rapid growth in cities has outrun the supply of houses and clean water. Cities also experience power failures, poor sanitation service, and traffic jams.
2. Shanty towns are slum settlements on the outside of the city. They exist because people moving into the cities often cannot find affordable housing. People build makeshift houses out of cardboard, plywood, branches, or sheets of corrugated iron or plastic.
3. Traditional West African art includes wood and ivory carvings and bronze statues. Film is an important cultural expression, and guitar music is also popular.

Talk About It Answers
1. Important points: Students should choose either and support the choice with reasons.
2. Important points: Students should take a position and explain it. Note: West Africans can also rely on their families when necessary; the family responsibility system has both benefits and burdens for everyone.
3. Important points: Students should choose one tradition and explain the choice with detailed reasons. Note: The closeness of family life in West Africa might be attractive to students.

Teaching This Skill Lesson

Materials Needed textbooks, paper, pencils

Classroom Organization individual student work

Introducing the Lesson Talk with the class about a school or local issue on which a decision is to be made. Examples: how to improve test scores, how to stop graffiti at school, where to build a new superhighway. It is important that the issue you choose be one on which citizens really disagree. Ask how students think the issue will be decided, what is the best way for it to be decided. Talk about what people will think about as they decide on the issue, leading students to list some of the criteria people are using (if needed, refer students to the discussion of criteria by sketching a decision-making grid on the chalkboard listing options and criteria.

Recall that students have been studying about nations in West Africa, all of which must make decisions about the best way to improve their economies. Tell students that the skill lesson presents three proposed projects aimed at increasing economic independence.

Lesson Development Monitor students as they work on decision-making models. If necessary, this activity can be completed as a homework assignment.

Conclusion Have each student report recommendations to the class and tally results. Ask what criteria were used and if one criterion was more important than the others.

Extension If desired, have students apply this decision-making model to the issue used to introduce the lesson, make a decision, and write letters supporting their chosen proposal(s) to policy makers.

Applying Decision-Making and Problem-Solving Techniques to World Issues

Making Economic Plans to Improve a Country

"I want Nigeria to become a country that makes the things we now have to import," said a young Nigerian interviewed by a reporter about his hopes for his country. The youth of other nations in West Africa would probably agree with him.

Governments in West Africa have to make tough decisions about policies that will bring economic independence to the region. Money is scarce, and there are many needs. Every time they decide to spend public money on a project, these governments must ask which projects will do most to help their nation gain economic independence.

Imagine that you are an economic advisor to the government of a West African nation. Three proposals lie on your desk. Each will cost about the same amount of money to implement. You must recommend just one of them. Here are the proposals:

1. Build a rail line linking an inland city with the largest port.
2. Provide clean drinking water to 500 villages.
3. Build and equip 250 schools in villages that have no schools.

Which project will you recommend that the government fund? To help you decide, draw and use a decision-making model like the one below. Notice that the proposed projects are written along the top line. Down the left side are spaces for the criteria you will use in deciding. (Turn to the Skill Lesson for Chapter 18 on page 368 to learn more about what criteria are.) Here are some questions that will help you in stating the criteria you will use:

• Does this project address the goal of economic independence?
• How many people would benefit?
• Would benefits be short-term or long-term?
• Would this project be popular with many people or just a few?
• Must this project be implemented right now or can it wait until later?

Are there other questions you should ask when you are stating criteria? Once you have stated the criteria or standards for choosing which project to recommend, complete the decision-making model.

Which project will you recommend? Why? Have an explanation ready.

Decision Making—Improving the Economy of a West African Nation			
	Proposed Projects		
Criteria	Project No. 1	Project No. 2	Project No. 3

A young student in Burkina Faso

West Africa

143

 Skill Lesson Review

1. Which project did you recommend? Why? *Answers will vary. Ask students to share their ideas.*

2. What criteria did you establish to help you make your decision? Did the criteria help you? Which criterion was most important to you? *Answers will vary. The balance between health concerns and trade expansion is the issue here.*

3. Did you consider recommending parts of proposed projects—providing clean drinking water to 250 villages and building 125 schools, for example? *Answers will vary. The class could discuss this possibility and create a combination of its own.*

4. What other projects could you suggest to help West African nations become economically independent? *Answers will vary. Loans to small businesses and farms would help, and so would building a communications system.*

143

CHAPTER 7 REVIEW

Talk About It

1. There is more farmland and water to support a rural population in West Africa.

2. Important points: Students should choose one nation and explain the choice in detail. Nigeria has the leading economy in West Africa today.

3. Important points: Students should choose one challenge and explain why. Notes: tradition of trade with European countries rather than African countries, transportation routes and limitations, nations trade in order to get manufactured goods from Europe.

4. People from the country are moving to the cities for opportunities in government and businesses. Many of the businesses are foreign-owned. Cities offer a link to the world economy.

5. Overuse of the Sahel by people is destroying the land that once supported herders.

Lessons Learned

LESSON 1
People and Their Environment
West Africa has desert, savanna, and rain forests. The region of dry grassland is called the Sahel. Most people live in the well-watered area of the South along the Atlantic Ocean. Population is unevenly distributed. Migration to cities is occurring quickly, but most people still live in villages.

LESSON 2
Government and Economy
The borders drawn by colonial powers created problems for countries after independence. Larger colonies were split up into several smaller nations by the British. These are today's Ghana, Nigeria, Sierra Leone, and Gambia. The French occupied a huge area called French West Africa. After independence, the countries of Benin, Burkina Faso, Guinea, Ivory Coast, Mali, Mauritania, Niger, Senegal, and Togo were created. Cape Verde and Guinea-Bissau were Portuguese colonies. Liberia was never an European colony.

LESSON 3
Society and Culture
Villagers are reluctantly leaving village life behind to find work in large cities. They can often only afford to live in shanty towns on the outskirts of the cities. Those who move to the city sometimes feel responsible for their extended family in the home village. Village life is centered around small farming. Often villagers belong to the same ethnic group.

144

Talk About It

1. Why is the population of West Africa largely rural while that of North Africa is largely urban?
2. Which West African nation do you think has the best chance of economic and political success? Explain why.
3. What is the most important challenge faced by ECOWAS? Explain why.
4. How do rapidly growing cities in West Africa show the geographic theme of movement?
5. How does the Sahel illustrate the geographic theme of human-environmental interaction?

Mastering Mapwork

PLACE
Use the map on page 127 to answer these questions:

1. What physical characteristics are shared by Mauritania and Mali?
2. What physical characteristics are shared by Freetown, Sierra Leone, and Monrovia, Liberia?
3. What physical characteristics are shared by Niger and Mali? Do they share any cultural characteristics?
4. What physical and cultural characteristics are shared by Accra, Ghana, and Dakar, Senegal?

Mastering Mapwork

1. The Sahara Desert and the Sahel are present in both nations; both lie mostly within the Tropics.

2. Both are located on the Atlantic Ocean; both are in tropical areas, being located south of 10ºN latitude. Both are national capitals, a cultural characteristic of place.

3. The Sahel crosses both nations; neither has an outlet to the sea; the Niger River passes through both; and both lie almost entirely in the Tropics. The only cultural characteristics shown on this map are national capitals.

4. Both Accra and Dakar are located in the Tropics and on the Atlantic Ocean sharing these physical characteristics of place. Both are also national capitals, a cultural characteristic of place.

Go to the Source

Using Letters as Primary Sources

The nation of Liberia was founded as a homeland for freed slaves from the United States. The [sic] indicates that the error is in the original document. Read the letter below from a freed slave who has resettled in Liberia. Answer the questions using specific references from the text.

Careysburg, Jan. 28, 1858

My dear Miss.

I now write in answer to your two letters I received this year, I was glad to hear from you and all the freinds [sic] in that part of the Country. I and children are well, and may this find you and all well and enjoying the blessings of kind heaven. I now tells you something about Careysburg. This is a fine place and fine country indeed, the custom of the natives is very good they are docile and friendly people, I have not seen one hostile one as yet. Those persons that came out with us, most all living except those you [have] heard death. [sic] If you pleased to send me 1 Keg of nails, 1 Barrel of Pork, and children shoes and pair for myself, and two axes, pantaloons stuff 1 piece, 1 piece Calico, 1 grumbling 1 hoes and some [of] the cheapest of Cloths which is different kinds of Calico piece of each, 1 Box of soap and two B [unclear: ridle] B [unclear: labes] and 1 sett [sic] of knives and forks and half dozen of water pails. We have meetings every Sunday and the Baptist Association have appointed a young man from Grand Bassa Country by the name of [unclear: F.] Roberts to teach us all little and big who wished to go to school

My love to sister Jinny tell her I like this country very well and I cannot find no faults now as we cannot gets everything wished in this new country, and tell all the friends howdy for me. Pray for us

To Lizze Lewis
Yours Respectfully
Dick Barrett

P.S. If you pleased to tell Mr. J. H. Minor to send me a gun I means a American musket
D.B.

Go to the Source

Questions

1. What evidence is given in this letter that the writer, Mr. Barrett, maintains customs from the United States?
2. Using this letter from Liberia and your knowledge of the United States after the Civil War, evaluate whether a freed slave should stay in America or move to Liberia. Justify your choice with reasons and supporting details. Your response should have an introduction, body, and conclusion.

 Go to the Source

🏴 **OBJECTIVES:** 4.01; Skills 1.03, 4.03

Review with students what a primary source is. Explain the meaning of "[sic]" to indicate errors in original documents. Discuss that "[ ]" may also be used to supply a word that may be missing in the original document or to define a word that the reader may be unfamiliar with.

To view more letters from Liberian settlers, visit **NCJourneys.com** for a link to the collection of "Letters from former slaves of James Hunter Terrell settled in Liberia."

ANSWERS

1. Possible answers would include the need to import items such as knives and forks and clothing or American fashions. This would imply that the author has not accepted the local customs and is trying to maintain his American ways in Liberia.

2. Students will need additional resources to create a response. Important points: free African Americans and former slaves were American in culture. They usually had been separated by at least a generation from living in Africa. Therefore, the new settlers had to adapt to life in the new colony. The new settlers were also leaving behind their family in America. On the other hand, these new settlers had an opportunity to create a new life for their families.

How to Use the Chapter Review

There are three sections in the Chapter Review: Talk About It, Mastering Mapwork, and Go to the Source. Use the Vocabulary Worksheets and the Chapter Review Worksheet in the Teacher's Resource Guide for additional reinforcement and preparation for the Chapter Assessments. The chapter and lesson reviews and the Chapter Review Worksheets are the basis of the assessment for each chapter.

Talk About It questions encourage students to speculate about the content of the chapter and are suitable for class or small-group discussion. They are not intended to be assigned for homework.

Mastering Mapwork has students apply one or more of the Five Themes of Geography to maps within the chapter.

Go to the Source activities allow students to analyze a primary source that relates to the content of the chapter. The questions and activities familiarize students with different types of primary sources and also build content-reading skills.

CHAPTER 8

Central Africa

Social Studies Strands

Geographic Relationships
Physical features
Climate and vegetation
Population

Government and Active Citizenship

Economics and Development

Society and Culture
Ethnic traits
Language
Religion

Global Connections

Cultures and Diversity

North Carolina Standard Course of Study

Goal 2 The learner will assess the relationship between physical environment and cultural characteristics of selected societies and regions of Africa, Asia, and Australia.

Goal 3 The learner will analyze the impact of interactions between humans and their physical environments in Africa, Asia, and Australia.

Goal 5 The learner will evaluate the varied ways of people of Africa, Asia, and Australia make decisions about the allocation and use of economic resources.

Goal 11 The learner will recognize the common characteristics of different cultures in Africa, Asia, and Australia.

Teaching & Assessment

• English Language Learner Modified Lesson Plans for this chapter are found in the Teacher Resource Guide.

• *ExamView® Assessment Suite* is provided at **NCJourneys.com.** It includes customizable assessments for all chapters. Paper tests are also available in the Teacher Resource Guide. See pages T16–T17 for information about how to use the assessments and the Scoring Guide.

Worksheets

Worksheets and answer keys are found both in the Teacher Resource Guide and at **NCJourneys.com**, including Reading Guides, Reading Strategies, Chapter Reviews, English Language Learner and others.

ACTIVITIES AND INTEGRATIONS

SOCIAL STUDIES	
● ▲ ■ What Makes Central Africa Unique, p. 147	
★ Count the Features, p. 150	
● To Farm or Not to Farm: That Is the Question! p. 154	
Create an Economic Mobile, p. 156	
Skill Lesson: Obstacles to Development, p. 161	

READING/LANGUAGE ARTS	READING/LANGUAGE ARTS OBJECTIVES
★ Finding Out, p. 146B	3.01
Letter to the Editor of the *Belgian Times*, p. 146B	3.03, 4.03
Analogies, p. 146B	2.01
Writing Prompt: Improving the Standard of Living, p. 146	3.02, 3.03
★ ▲ My Life Story, p. 155	1.01, 1.04
Dr. Livingstone, I Presume, p. 160	1.01
Go to the Source: Analyzing Historic Speeches, p. 163	2.01, 4.01, 4.02

SCIENCE	SCIENCE OBJECTIVES
Rain Forests, p. 148	3.05

MATHEMATICS	MATHEMATICS OBJECTIVES
★ Activator: Rain Forests, p. 146	1.02, 1.03
▲ Stanley Math Word Problem, p. 151	1.01, 1.02, 1.03

TECHNOLOGY	TECHNOLOGY OBJECTIVES
★ Finding Out, p. 146B	1.06, 3.01, 3.03

VISUAL ARTS	VISUAL ARTS OBJECTIVES
▲ Namchi Doll with Rattle, Cameroon, p. 146B	2.04, 5.01
Create an Economic Mobile, p. 156	2.04, 4.01
● ▲ Making a Mankala Board, p. 159	2.04, 3.01

CHARACTER AND VALUES EDUCATION	TRAITS
Writing Prompt: Improving the Standard of Living, p. 146	good citizenship
What Would You Do?, p. 149	responsibility, good judgment

● Basic Activities   ★ Challenging Activities   ▲ English Language Learner Novice   ■ English Language Learner Intermediate

146A

Introductory Activity

Finding Out

🔺 **OBJECTIVES:** 5.03, 6.01, 6.02

Divide the class into groups. Have students choose a country in Central Africa and research several facts about each country, such as life expectancy, literacy rate, infant mortality rate, number of physicians per 100 people, or GNP. Students may use a database to compile their data and do this research on the Internet. Have students compose a letter to the country's leader asking polite questions about a problem or issue in the country. Have students exchange letters and answer them. The letter writer and recipient should then meet and determine whether their country could be considered developed or developing, and explain why.

Extension ELL students should use an ELL-friendly Web site for research. Assign a peer tutor to help with the database. Do not assign novice and intermediate ELL students the paragraph.

 Culminating Activity

Letter to the Editor of the *Belgian Times*

🔺 **OBJECTIVES:** 7.01, 7.02, 8.01

Have students write or word process a letter to the editor of the *Belgian Times* as if they were citizens of the Belgian Congo and opposed to King Leopold's rule. Have students support their opinion with facts from the chapter. Students should make suggestions for solutions to problems caused by colonialism in the Belgian Congo.

 Art Activity

Namchi Doll with Rattle, Cameroon

🔺 **OBJECTIVES:** 3.01, 12.02

Namchi dolls were made of hardwood. They consisted of cylinders for the body, the arms, and the legs. There is a large hollow section at the base of the body to house the noise-making contents.

Materials: newspaper, wheat paste (papier mâché paste), paper towel tubes or longer cardboard tubes, beads, string, masking tape, hard beans, beads (or other items to make noise in the rattle), tempera paint or brown construction paper, small round balloons, small yogurt containers.

To construct the doll, use a 12-inch piece of cardboard tubing for the body. Use 4-inch tubing for arms and legs, and attach each piece with masking tape. Fill a small yogurt container one-quarter to one-third full with small, hard, noisy items. Attach the small yogurt container to the base of the body with masking tape. Attach a small balloon for the head (1½ to 2 inches in diameter).

Cover everything with at least two layers of papier-mâchéd newspaper or brown construction paper. Make sure the paper is torn into small strips 2 inches long by 1 inch wide. If you use newspaper, then paint the Namchi brown. These dolls are traditionally adorned with beads. These can be glued on or strung, then tied on.

Extension For novice ELL students, model and provide additional explanations.

 Analogies

🔺 **OBJECTIVES:** 1.03, 2.03

Analogies are useful to help students make associations with prior knowledge. They can be used as an instructional strategy to help students better understand new materials.

Read the analogies aloud and ask students to identify the relationship between the terms. As an extension, ask students to write their own analogies using key terms or places discussed in the chapter.

rain forest : Central Africa :: desert : North Africa (is primary vegetation of)

coastal : Cameroon :: landlocked : Chad (continental location)

cobalt : Democratic Republic of Congo :: diamonds : Republic of South Africa (is the major resource of)

Mbuti : short stature :: NBA players : tall stature (are)

Mbuti : hunter gatherers :: Bantu : farmers (are an example of)

Teaching Strategies

Since much of the material in Chapter 8 will be familiar due to the information found in Unit 1, this chapter will be easy to cover quickly. In fact, you might want to assign it as a "Student Teach" activity, where you assign segments to collaborative pairs and they teach that section to the rest of the class.

Activator

 OBJECTIVES: 3.02

It is estimated that rain forests around the world are depleted at the rate of 192 square miles each day. Using that figure, have students calculate how much forest disappears in a week, a month, a year, five years, and ten years. Have them calculate in reverse the amount of forest that disappears in the course of a class period.

Answers

1 month:
192 x 30 = 5,760 square miles
1 year:
5,760 x 12 = 69,120 square miles
5 years:
69,120 x 5 = 345,600 square miles
10 years:
69,120 x 10 = 691,200 square miles

1 hour:
192 ÷ 24 = 8 square miles
class period:
number of minutes x .13 square miles= _____
1 minute:
8 ÷ 60 = .13 square miles

Writing Prompt

 OBJECTIVES: 5.03, 5.04

Problem-Solution

Although the countries of Central Africa are resource-rich, they have a low per capita incomes. After studying Chapter 8, write or word process an editorial for a newspaper in one of the Central African countries explaining the changes that need to be made for the country to improve the standard of living. Explain your answer fully.

As you write your editorial, remember to
- clearly state your position.
- give at least three reasons and explain your reasons fully.
- give examples to support your reasons.
- write in complete sentences and paragraph form.
- organize your ideas and include an introduction and a conclusion.
- use good grammar, spelling, punctuation, and capitalization.

CHAPTER 8

Central Africa

Throughout Africa, the end of colonial rule brought demonstrations against colonial rule and joyful celebrations. People wanted to show the world that they were African, not European. Celebrations everywhere featured traditional dances, music, and art.

In today's Democratic Republic of the Congo—once the Belgian Congo—people cheered as workers pulled down the statues of explorer Henry Morton Stanley and Belgian's King Leopold II. In Kinshasa, the capital of the country, dancers in ethnic dress celebrated African traditions that everyone hoped would guide their new nation.

Celebrating independence in Kinshasa

A tribal mask from Cameroon

Chapter Preview

LESSON 1
People and Their Environment
Rain forests and the Congo River and its tributaries dominate the land. Population is scattered throughout the region.

LESSON 2
Government and Economy
Transition from colonial rule has been difficult. The region's water, forest, and mineral resources are only partly developed.

LESSON 3
Society and Culture
Life in forests, on farms, and in cities creates different customs among the region's many ethnic groups.

146

Chapter 8

Chapter Resources

Print Resources

Nonfiction

Adinoyi-Ojo, Onukaba. *Mbuti*. Rosen Pub. Group, 1996. ISBN 0823919986.

Burnham, P.C. *Gbaya*. Rosen Pub. Group, 1997. ISBN 0823919951.

Nzongola-NtalajaZed, Georges. *The Congo: From Leopold to Kabila: A People's History*. Zed Books, 2002. ISBN 1842770535.

Okeke, Chika. *Kongo*. Rosen Pub. Group, 1997. ISBN 0823920011.

Roberts, Mary Nooter. *Luba*. Rosen Pub. Group, 1997. ISBN 082392002X.

Wynaden, Jo, and Nina Kushner, *Welcome to the Democratic Republic of the Congo* (Welcome to My Country Series), Gareth Stevens Publishing, 2001. ISBN 0836825306.

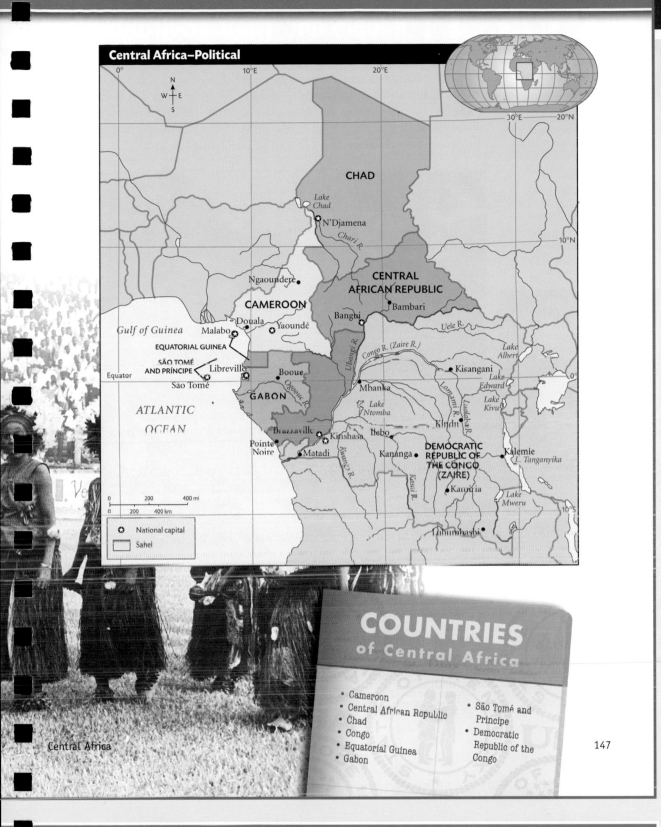

Central Africa–Political

Central Africa

COUNTRIES
of Central Africa

- Cameroon
- Central African Republic
- Chad
- Congo
- Equatorial Guinea
- Gabon
- São Tomé and Príncipe
- Democratic Republic of the Congo

147

Audiovisual

Destination: Cameroon. Peace Corps. 1996. 20 minutes. ISBN 0160634083.
Lumumba. Zeitgeist Films, 2001. 115 minutes. French with English subtitles. Includes excerpts 1991 documentary Lumumba: Death of a Prophet, historical timeline and background on the Congo. ASIN: B00006LPHK.

Web Sites

Go to **NCJourneys.com** for links to the following Web sites:
- Congo River
- Congotrek 360, National Geographic
- Democratic Republic of Congo, Diamond Mining and Conflict
- Elephants of Cameroon
- International Rivers Network; Grand Inga Hydroelectric Power System, Democratic Republic of Congo
- USAID Congo Forest Basin Partnership

Map Activity

What Makes Central Africa Unique?

NATIONAL GEOGRAPHY STANDARDS: 1, 4, 7, 13, 15, 17, 18

GEOGRAPHIC THEMES: Location, Place, Human-Environmental Interaction, Movement, Region

OBJECTIVES: 1.01, 1,02, 1.03, 2.01

Assign students to identify which of the Central African nations are landlocked and which have a coastline *(landlocked: Central African Republic and Chad; have a coastline: Cameron, Equatorial Guinea, Gabon, Congo, Democratic Republic of the Congo, São Tomé and Principe).* Also have students note the following: that this small coastal strip is the only area that prevents Democratic Republic of the Congo from being landlocked; that Equatorial Guinea does not touch the Equator (being located totally north of the Equator); that Equatorial Guinea, one of three "Guineas" in Africa (Guinea and Guinea-Bissau are covered in Chapter 7), is partly on the African continent (called Rio Muni), but its capital territory is on an island, Bioko; that Equatorial Guinea's capital is actually closer to Cameroon to the northwest than the remainder of Equatorial Guinea.

Research Topics
- What has been/is happening that causes Democratic Republic of Congo to keep changing its name?
- Why is Cameroon often referred to as "the hinge of Africa"?
- What is the Aozou Strip, where is it located, who claims it, and why?
- Where does the country of São Tomé and Príncipe get its name?
- Who was the famous Nobel Prize–winning physician and philosopher who lived in Gabon in the early 1900s? What did he find near Lambarene?

Extension Assign ELL students an alternate activity (this alternate can be used with similar activities in the following chapters as well). They should make a collage or poster highlighting what is important about these countries.

147

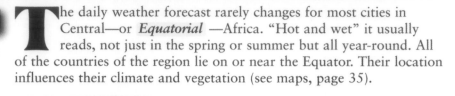

LESSON 1 People and Their Environment

Discussion Questions

1 What regions in North Carolina have a climate that changes little throughout the year? Do any parts of North Carolina have a climate that resembles that of Central Africa? Why?

2 What would be some jobs people would have in this type of climate?

Caption Answer

Most are near the Equator. The Sahel crosses Chad. Northern Chad is mostly desert.

Science Activity

 OBJECTIVES: 2.02, 2.03, 3.02

Rain Forests

Rain forests have been described as the global heat and water pumps because of their influence on climate.

Have students research the effect of rain forests on the world's climate. As rain forests are cut down, have students predict what will happen to the earth's climate? What might be the effects on global warming? Have students write a paragraph summarizing their analysis.

KEY IDEAS

- The Equator cuts through Central Africa. Heat and abundant rain have created a rain forest that dominates the region.

- Central Africa is the continent's most lightly populated region.

- The region's water, forest, and mineral resources are not yet well developed.

KEY TERMS

Equatorial

The daily weather forecast rarely changes for most cities in Central—or *Equatorial* —Africa. "Hot and wet" it usually reads, not just in the spring or summer but all year-round. All of the countries of the region lie on or near the Equator. Their location influences their climate and vegetation (see maps, page 35).

Central Africa varies from the wet rain forests of Gabon (above) to dry areas of Chad (right). Mandrills (left) thrive in rain forests. **Where are most rain forests in Central Africa? Where is the Sahel? the desert?**

Chapter 8

Climate and Vegetation

The average annual temperature is near 80° Fahrenheit (27° Centigrade) and varies only a few degrees from month to month. Most of the region has more than 80 inches (203 cm) of rainfall a year. Some areas have as much as 150 inches (381 cm)—more than the Sahel receives in ten years. Except for Chad and southern Democratic Republic of the Congo, no nation in the region has a dry season.

Rain forests in Central Africa cover an area four times the size of France. Few forests have been cut because many are difficult to reach. Roads and rails are costly to build and maintain in a region with such heavy rains.

Heavy year-round rain coupled with the hot tropical sun creates an environment in which plants and animals thrive. Scientists estimate that 4 square miles (10.4 sq km) of rain forest hold more than 750 different kinds of trees, 1,500 species of flowering plants, 400 species of birds, and tens of thousands of insect varieties.

Despite having rich plant and animal life, rain forest soils are poor. Heavy rains wash away nutrients in the soil. When the soil is cleared of trees, underbrush, and vines, leaching removes more nutrients. The soil becomes unsuitable for farming.

Moving away from the Equator to the north and south, rain forests disappear. The Sahel crosses Chad. Here, where the rainy season is shorter and the climate is drier, are grasslands and savanna. Southern Chad has grasslands. Northern Chad stretches into the desert. In such desert and grassland areas, most soils are also poor.

What would YOU do?

If Central Africa is to overcome its poverty, the government and people must use its resources more wisely. Some say the rain forests could be cut down to increase land use. Would you cut down rain forests to build towns and villages? Would you try to make rain forests into farmland? What would you do?

Landforms

The mountains of Central Africa rise on the western edge of the region along the Atlantic coast of Cameroon. In the Democratic Republic of the Congo, the Ruwenzori (ru·en·ZOR·ih) Mountains (see map, page 17) tower above the central African plateau.

The plateau drops sharply to narrow coastal plains. Such sharp drops create cataracts in the Congo and other rivers that flow into the Atlantic.

Two nations of the region, Chad and the Central African Republic, are landlocked. The Democratic Republic of the Congo has only 25 miles (40 km) of coastline.

Tiny São Tomé (sow·tow·MAY) and Príncipe (PREEN·si·pay), is one nation located on two islands in the Gulf of Guinea. It is one of the smallest nations in the world. Equatorial Guinea is not much larger. It consists of two islands and a mainland.

Discussion Questions

1 Compare the rain forest with the region known as the Sahel.

2 How would life be different if there were a drought that affected our region for several years?

3 If you lived in a landlocked country, why would it be necessary to have positive relationships with neighboring countries?

4 What regions in North Carolina best replicate the landforms in Central Africa?

ELL Teaching Tips

Compile a List of Translators

Compile a list of the people in your building who speak another language so that teachers will have a resource when they need someone to translate information. Make sure that the office has a copy of this list.

Background Information

Democratic Republic of the Congo's Transportation Woes

The Democratic Republic of the Congo, formerly Zaire, may someday be one of the world's richest nations. It holds a treasure chest of natural resources–diamonds, oil, uranium, gold. Yet today its roads are among the world's worst. Giant craterlike potholes, many filled with muddy water, make many roads impassable. Other roads are littered with abandoned trucks and vehicle parts. Lack of roads prevents goods from getting to market and sick children from reaching clinics. In 1960, when the nation gained independence from Belgium, it had 88,000 miles of usable roads. Today less than 10 percent of its roads are paved. Dictator Mobutu Sese Seko neglected all aspects of infrastructure. Few roads were built or repaired. After Mobutu's death, the country became a battlefield in a war that only added to the Democratic Republic of the Congo's transportation woes.

Discussion Questions

1 What are some verbs and adjectives you would use to describe the Congo River?

2 Why is the Congo River called the lifeline of the region?

3 Why would river transportation be less expensive than highway transportation?

4 With so much hydroelectric power potential, what do you think accounts for the lack of development in the Democratic Republic of the Congo?

5 Does North Carolina have any rivers that are used for transportation?

Eyewitness Activity

Count the Features

◀ **OBJECTIVES:** 1.02, 2.01, 2.02

Have students research and locate on a map of Central Africa rivers, plains, mountains, and plateaus. Ask them to determine which features have the greatest effect on the development of the region. Have students use the questions below to help them find their answers: What is the feature? Why is it there? How is it being used? What difference does it make?

Working independently or in groups, have students prepare a visual and written product (poster, giant book, brochure, PowerPoint presentation, digital story, Web page) focusing on the importance of physical features on life in Central Africa. Share them with the class.

Extension ELL students should use an ELL-friendly Web site for research. They should produce a visual product to demonstrate the importance of only physical features, focusing on one assigned by teacher.

Rivers Through Time

The River traffic has been part of the African scene since humans first hollowed out a hardwood tree. With carved canoes, villagers used the navigable parts of the river to paddle from one village to another.

The Congo River (below) opens into the Atlantic. To Europeans it seemed to disappear into interior Africa. Waterfalls and a 75-mile (121-km) stretch of rapids made the 2,700-mile (4,347-km) river impossible to navigate its entire length. It took Henry Stanley 999 days to survey the river between 1874 and 1877.

150

The pirogue (pee·ROWG), made from hollowed out hardwood trees (right), is still found on the river. Used for fishing, it also provides a means of rowing short distances.

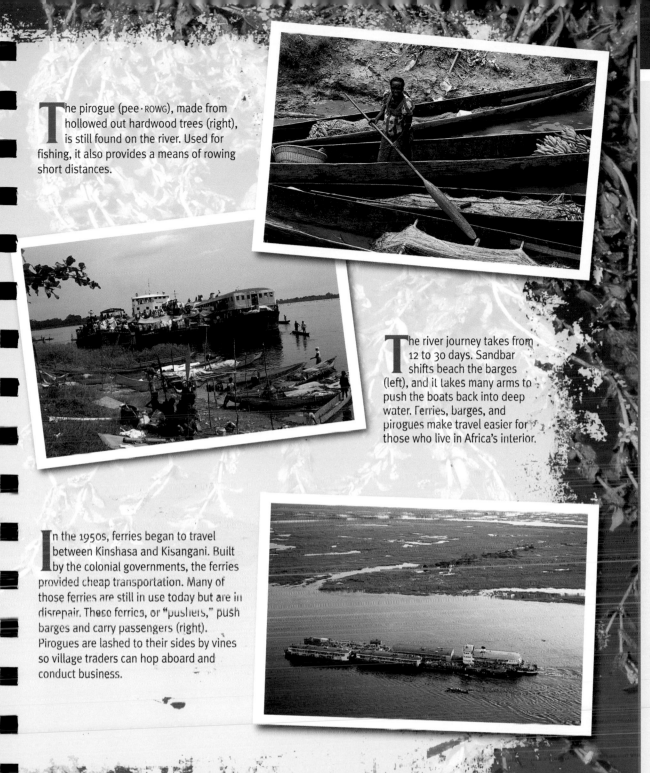

The river journey takes from 12 to 30 days. Sandbar shifts beach the barges (left), and it takes many arms to push the boats back into deep water. Ferries, barges, and pirogues make travel easier for those who live in Africa's interior.

In the 1950s, ferries began to travel between Kinshasa and Kisangani. Built by the colonial governments, the ferries provided cheap transportation. Many of those ferries are still in use today but are in disrepair. These ferries, or "pushers," push barges and carry passengers (right). Pirogues are lashed to their sides by vines so village traders can hop aboard and conduct business.

Math Activity

Stanley Math Word Problem

OBJECTIVES: 3.01, 8.01

It took Henry Stanley 999 days to survey the 2,700-mile (4,347-km) Congo River. How many years is 999 days? Round to tenths. How many miles did Stanley average traveling each day? Round to whole miles.

Answer 2.7 years, 3 miles/day

Extension Assist ELL students by setting up the problem for them.

Caption Answer

The river and its tributaries provide an excellent transportation network.

Name Origin

Cameroon Portuguese word for "shrimp," which were found in the Wouri River.

Central African Republic Named for its geographic location on the continent.

Chad Named after the large shallow Lake Chad (Tsade), which means "water."

Gabon Portuguese for "cabin," which is also the name of a local river.

Congo and Democratic Republic of the Congo Mandingo word (Kongo) meaning "mountains."

São Tomé and Príncipe São Tomé was named for the Portuguese Saint Thome. Príncipe (Prince Island) was named for Prince Henry the Navigator.

Congo River: Lifeline for a Region

The Congo River is the most important river in Central Africa. It flows entirely within the Democratic Republic of the Congo. Its 2,700-mile (4,347-km) route makes it the world's fifth longest river. On its way to the Atlantic Ocean, the Congo crosses the Equator twice, collecting water from tributaries throughout Central Africa. The Congo sends 10 million gallons (38 million liters) of water every second into the ocean. Only the Amazon River in South America carries more water.

The Congo has been called the lifeline of the region. The river and its tributaries provide miles of navigable water running through the region's interior. These connecting rivers provide an excellent transportation network within Central

Africa. Unlike roads that crumble in soggy soil, the river highway never needs repair.

This watery highway, however, has limitations. Kinshasa and Matadi (ma·TAHD·ih), cities on the river in western Democratic Republic of the Congo, are about 125 miles (201 km) apart (see map, page 147). In that distance, the river drops more than 1,000 feet (300 m) through cataracts. These rapids kept Europeans from exploring the region in the 1800s. Waterfalls made it difficult to move goods by water from the interior to coastal ports. Even today, goods have to be transported overland.

Someday the churning water of the Congo might be the source of electric power. Engineers estimate that half of Africa's hydroelectric power needs could be met by the river. Dams and power plants would have to be built to create that level of hydroelectricity.

The Ubangi (oo·BANG·ih) and the Ogooue (oh·goh·WAY) Rivers also are important to the region. The landlocked countries of Chad and the Central African Republic ship mineral resources to Brazzaville, Congo, on the Ubangi and Congo Rivers. The Ogooue River system provides transportation for Gabon.

The Congo River flows through much the Democratic Republic of Congo. **Why is the Congo called the lifeline of the region?**

Word Origins

The name **Congo** comes from the name of the kingdom of the Kongo people, who live near the river's mouth.

Chapter 8

A Sparsely Populated Region

Central Africa has fewer people living in it than other parts of Africa. This is especially true of rain forests. Those who do live in rain forests often live along riverbanks or near rail lines. Poor soils and the difficulties of clearing land have kept more people from moving into these areas.

Equatorial Guinea, Gabon, and the Central African Republic have some of the smallest populations in Africa. Gabon, a country the size of Colorado, has about 1.4 million people. Gabon must hire workers from other African countries to fill jobs there.

The Democratic Republic of the Congo is the third largest country in Africa. It covers an area the size of the United States east of the Mississippi River—905,354 square miles (2,353,920 sq km). Only Sudan and Algeria contain more land.

Central Africa has few large cities. Most people live in rural areas, but cities are growing. In about 50 years, Kinshasa, Democratic Republic of the Congo, has grown from 500,000 people to more than 5 million, making it the largest city in the region. Kinshasa and its sister city just across the Congo River, Brazzaville, Congo, have drawn people because they are capitals and have rail connections with the coast.

Boats on the Congo River provide vital links for river settlers. **Besides transportation, how is the river used?**

Discussion Questions

1 What has accounted for the tremendous population growth in the Democratic Republic of the Congo? What pressures would this growth put on the government?

2 What are some of the more sparsely populated regions of North Carolina? How can you explain the reason for this?

3 How does North Carolina meet its needs for workers? What impact would this have on a region?

Caption Answer

For fishing, bathing, and washing clothes.

LESSON 1 REVIEW

Fact Follow-Up
1. Describe the physical characteristics of Central Africa.
2. How do landforms affect possibilities for trade in Central Africa?
3. What important rivers are found in Central Africa?
4. Describe the size of the Democratic Republic of the Congo.

Talk About It
1. Should the Congo River be called the "lifeline" of Central Africa? Explain your answer.
2. Is the Central African rain forest an economic benefit for the region? Why or why not?
3. Why is Central Africa so sparsely populated?

Central Africa

153

LESSON 1 REVIEW

Fact Follow-Up Answers
1. Rain forests and the Congo River and its tributaries dominate the region. Beyond the rain forest lie the Sahel and the desert. The east and west are mountainous. Near the coast, the plateau drops sharply, creating cataracts in the rivers.
2. The mountains, rain forests, and desert hinder movement over land. The Congo offers transportation within the region, but the cataracts of the river make transportation inland from the coast difficult.
3. The important rivers are the Congo, Ubangi, and Ogooue.
4. It is the third largest country in Africa, after Sudan and Algeria. It covers an area the size of the United States east of the Mississippi River.

Talk About It Answers
1. Important points: Students should choose a position and support it with explanations. Note: The Congo and its tributaries provide miles of navigable water running through the region's interior despite cataracts as the Congo falls over the high escarpment near the Atlantic Coast. Unlike roads that crumble in soggy soil, the river highway never needs repair.
2. Important points: Students should take a position and support it with reasons. Note: The rain forest has valuable timber, but rainfall leaches nutrients from the soil; transportation through forested areas can be difficult.
3. Among the reasons for Central Africa's sparse population are few resources, infertile soil, difficult transportation, and large rain forest areas.

 **OBJECTIVES:** 5.01, 5.04, 9.01

Discussion Questions

1 What European countries were once colonial powers in Central Africa?

2 Why do you think Portugal was so slow in giving up its colonies?

3 Which countries were colonial powers in North America? Why would they want to retain control of the region?

 **Caption Answer**

France, the United Kingdom, Spain, Portugal, Germany, and Belgium were all powers.

Activity

To Farm or Not to Farm: That Is the Question!

 **OBJECTIVES:** 2.01, 3.01, 4.01, 5.01

Give students two squares of construction paper or tag board. Working independently or in small groups, have them imagine that one of their squares represents four square miles of rain forest. In this square they are to list or illustrate the diversity of plant and animal life and uses for the rain forest.

Have them use the other square to represent four square miles of land cleared and converted to farming. They should list or illustrate the plant and animal life found there now as well as its potential uses.

After some discussion of pros and cons of farming and forest, have students decide which way they would go. Allow each individual or group to place one of their illustrated squares on opposite sides of a bulletin board, chalk board, or suspended towel rod. Have students discuss the significance of the resulting balance or imbalance.

Have students use the Internet to research the possibility of rain forest plants being used to find cures for diseases. Many are opposed to the cutting of the rain forest because potential cures could be lost.

Extension ELL students should use an ELL-friendly Web site to research items for both squares. They should choose one to put on board.

LESSON **2** Government and Economy

KEY IDEAS

- The transition from colonial rule by six European colonial governments has been difficult.
- Most people are small farmers. The region does not have much prospect of agricultural development.
- The region does have rich water, forest, and mineral resources awaiting development.

KEY TERMS

export economies
International Monetary Fund (IMF)
World Bank

In 1908, news of King Leopold II's savage treatment of workers in Belgium's colony attracted international attention (see page 87). The Belgian government took control of the colony from the king. The Belgian Congo remained a colony until 1960. Several years after coming to power, President Mobutu Sese Seko changed the country's name to Zaire (now Democratic Republic of the Congo).

France, the United Kingdom, Spain, Portugal, and Germany had joined Belgium as colonial powers in Central Africa. Four present-day nations—the Central African Republic, the Congo, Chad, and Gabon—were once French colonies. Parts of present-day Cameroon were claimed by France, the United Kingdom, and Germany. Germany lost its portion to France and the United Kingdom after World War I. After independence, the French and British colonies reunited as modern Cameroon. Equatorial Guinea is a former Spanish colony.

All of the nations of the region became independent in the 1960s, except the island nation of São Tomé and Príncipe. This nation had been ruled by Portugal, a country that was slow to give up its colonies. São Tomé and Príncipe was refused independence until the 1970s.

Public buildings in Africa often show European influence. This cinema in the Belgian Congo, now the Democratic Republic of the Congo, has European architecture and signs in French. **What European nations were powers in Central Africa?**

 It's a Fact

Central Africa

■ Cameroon has been the site of human habitation for thousands of years. Rock carvings and stone tools have been found that date back to the Old Stone age.

■ In 1986 the bottom of Lake Nyos was stirred up by seismic activity, causing a cloud of toxic gas to be released, killing more than 3,000 people as they slept in shoreline villages.

■ Lake Chad, in Chad, varies in size between the rainy and dry seasons. Over the past 25 to 30 years, nearly 90 percent of the lake has dried up.

■ Whereas the Central African Republic is nearly as large as Texas, only 3 percent of the land is suitable for farming.

■ Seventy-seven percent of Gabon's export earnings come from oil. Earnings have been spent wisely on development programs, especially on education.

■ Early European settlers of São Tomé and Príncipe included Portuguese convicts and Jewish refugees. The tiny country is about the size of New York City. Equatorial Guinea's official language is Spanish.

Government Today

In recent years, Gabon, the Central African Republic, and São Tomé and Príncipe have begun moving toward democracy and multiparty elections. Their struggles for political reform are typical of a region where government has been mostly one-man or single-party rule.

The dictator of Zaire, Mobutu Sese Seko, was overthrown in 1997. Laurent Kabila, the new president, renamed the country the Democratic Republic of the Congo and promised democracy. The citizens welcomed him. In 1998, Kabila announced that elections would be postponed until all foreign military forces withdrew from his country. He was assassinated in 2001 and succeeded by his son Joseph. The transitional government he heads held elections in 2006.

Regional Economies

Central Africa is resource-rich (see map, page 61). Most nations in this region have forest resources or mineral resources or both. Yet their resources have not been used to their full potential. Businesses cannot operate well when governments are inefficient or corrupt. Central African governments have been unable to provide essential services that businesses need.

Natural Resources

The rain forests offer lumber and such forest products as rubber and palm oil. Mahogany and other hardwood trees provide fine woods for furniture making and building materials. However, in many areas forest products are not easily harvested. Logging companies look for areas along rivers or where railroads can be built.

The greatest potential source of wealth for many Central African nations is minerals. High heat and heavy rains make road and track maintenance difficult. Business operations are likely to fail when transportation is so uncertain.

Despite such problems, the Democratic Republic of the Congo has

Joseph Kabila of the Democratic Republic of Congo was confirmed as president in free elections in 2006. He led negotiations to remove foreign troops from his country. **Why is stability important in this region?**

large copper and diamond mines. The country also holds 60 percent of the world's cobalt reserves. Cobalt is a rare metal used in jet engines to resist heat and wear.

Three Central African countries have oil—Cameroon, Gabon, and the Congo. These nations also have diamonds, copper, gold, manganese, and uranium. Chad has oil and some mineral resources, but these resources have yet to be developed. As you have read, the region's many rapids and waterfalls may become a resource for hydroelectric power.

The Democratic Republic of the Congo exports copper from mines in the Katanga Province. **What are some of the region's other resources?**

Central Africa

155

Discussion Questions

1 Would it be to the advantage of a country to fully develop its resources? Why have the countries in Central Africa not done so?

2 Why have African governments been unable to provide the essential services that are needed in the country?

3 Although Central Africa has not done an efficient job in developing its natural resources, how has the Democratic Republic of the Congo been able to lead the world in mining copper and diamonds?

 Caption Answer

Stability is necessary for the governments and the people to prosper.

 Caption Answer

Lumber, rummber, palm oil, minerals, and oil.

 Writing Activity

My Life Story

OBJECTIVES: 2.03, 3.01, 3.02

Write resources of Central Africa on slips of paper. Ask each student to select a name of a resource, research information, and develop "My Life Story" for that resource. Resources include mahogany, rubber, palm oil, copper, industrial diamonds, cobalt, petroleum oil, coffee, cacao, tea, manganese, uranium, and gold. Students can make an accordion-style book to write and/or draw a story or create a digital story.

Include:
- Location in Central Africa.
- How is resource grown/formed?
- How is it harvested/mined?
- How is it transported? to where?
- How is it processed?
- How is it used as finished products?

Extension ELL students should use an ELL-friendly Web site for research. They should draw pictures and write simple explanations in the book.

Background Information

Equatorial Guinea and Oil Wealth

In 1996 the tiny nation of Equatorial Guinea, population 466,000, got a welcome surprise. United States companies had discovered oil there. Soon it ranked just behind South Africa and oil giants Nigeria and Angola in American investments in sub-Sahara Africa. By late 2000, American oil companies were pumping thousands of barrels a day. In the nation's capital, Malabo, hopes are high that the country will become a "Kuwait" of Africa. So far only Malabo has benefited. It has new paved roads, traffic lights, and a power plant that provides reliable electricity. Residents hope their country will not repeat the experience of neighboring Gabon. Today Gabon, despite a small population and huge oil reserves, remains dependent on foreign aid. Experts blame government mismanagement and corruption.

Discussion Questions

1 What problems would the dependence on a cash crop create in a country?

2 How does the location of a people determine their livelihood?

Caption Answer

Most are subsistence farmers who grow cash crops.

Activity

Create an Economic Mobile

OBJECTIVES: 1.01, 1.02, 1.03

Allow students to work with a partner or in small groups. Assign each group a country from Central Africa and have them research the economy of that country. They are to look for economic activities, natural resources, mineral resources, and how each are distributed within their country.

To assemble the mobile, students should have a card with the name of the country. On the back they should draw a map of the country and locate the regions of that country. They should then create a card for each of the regions. On one side draw a map of the region with important cities or landforms noted. On the other side, students are to illustrate a type of economic activity carried out; draw pictures of products produced, farmed or mined; or glue on pictures of products. The region cards should be hung from the name card.

Note: An alternative to a mobile is a stabile, which is a small mobile hung from a stand on a desk (similar to an ornament display stand). Students can make stands using wire coat hangers and tape.

Extension ELL students should use an ELL-friendly Web site for research. Assign peer tutors for help as needed.

Agriculture

Throughout Central Africa, most people are small farmers who raise food for their own use or for sale in local markets. Farming takes place in the grassland areas north and south of the rain forest. In Equatorial Guinea, which has few minerals, farming is the main source of income.

People living in or near a rain forest depend on its products for their livelihood. Fruit and roots add to a diet that includes such forest animals as antelope and wild pig. Small farmers also depend heavily on fishing. They eat some of their catch and sell the rest for cash income.

In Central Africa, growing cash crops for export is not as important an economic activity as in other parts of Africa. One exception is Cameroon. Farmers in Cameroon grow such cash crops as bananas, coffee, cocoa, oil palm products, natural rubber, and tea. These crops grow mostly on small plots of land. Cotton is the main cash crop in the Central African Republic and in Chad.

Coffee is raised in Central Africa (above). Fishing (right) is a key economic activity in Central Africa. **How do most Central Africans earn a living?**

156

Export Economies

Central Africa's chances for growth in agriculture seem limited. Some of its nations, however, could build wealth from mineral resources. For such countries as the Democratic Republic of the Congo, Gabon, Congo, and Cameroon, the export of oil, timber, and minerals is already their most important economic activity. These nations have more work to do to enjoy the greatest benefit from their resources.

Central African nations know many of the problems associated with **export economies,** an economy based upon the sale of raw materials abroad. Congo was a nation with little to sell in world markets. It built its economy soon after independence almost entirely on oil exports. At first oil prices were high, and Congo's leaders borrowed money to build schools and food processing factories. When oil prices fell sharply in 1986, the government could not pay its debts.

Government leaders had to work with such international agencies as the *International Monetary Fund (IMF)* and the *World Bank* to cut back on spending. Now Congo no longer wants to depend on oil exports. It has a plan to broaden its economy, producing such cash crops as cocoa, coffee, sugar, and palm oil.

Some Central African nations are trying to increase the value of their raw materials by processing them before they are exported. African engineers have worked with companies from France, Belgium, and other countries to build processing plants and to develop a skilled work force.

In the Democratic Republic of the Congo, minerals are mined and smelted (separated from rock) before being shipped to factories outside of Africa for further processing. Once all the processing can be done in the region, nations will be able to sell their minerals at higher prices and keep more profits for themselves.

Bulldozers and cranes shovel copper in the Democratic Republic of the Congo.
Why does it benefit a nation to process its own minerals?

Discussion Questions

1 What problems might a country that exports its products encounter in a global economy?

2 What transitions will the people of the Congo have to make as they move away from an economy primarily dependent on oil exports?

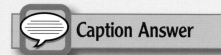 **Caption Answer**

It can make more of a profit selling processed minerals.

LESSON ② REVIEW

Fact Follow-Up
1. What European powers held colonies in Central Africa? Which was the largest landholder?
2. What are some economic and political challenges facing Central African nations today?
3. What mineral resources do Central African nations possess?

Talk About It
1. How is the Democratic Republic of the Congo's colonial history representative of nations in Africa you have already studied? Explain.
2. Why can Central Africa be described as a resource-rich yet economically poor region?

LESSON ② REVIEW

Fact Follow-Up Answers
1. Belgium, Great Britain, Spain, Portugal, and Germany held colonies in Central Africa. Belgium was the largest landholder.
2. Among the challenges are single-party governments, political instability and corruption, slow economic growth, and limited government services.
3. The Democratic Republic of the Congo leads the world in copper production and industrial diamonds. The nation also has cobalt. Cameroon, Gabon, and the Congo have diamonds, copper, gold, manganese, and uranium.

Talk About It Answers
1. Its minerals and forests were used by Belgium in the same way that the nations of West Africa produced cash crops for European markets. Also, its history of authoritarian government is partly a legacy of colonialism.
2. The region has many mineral and forest resources, but when exported as raw materials, these resources do not bring as much money into the country as finished goods would.

OBJECTIVES: 3.01, 4.03, 11.01

Discussion Questions

1 Would you rather live in the Congo River basin or in Brazzaville, Congo? What would be your reasons?

2 What challenges are presented by ethnic and language diversity?

3 According to the most recent census, Hispanics are the fastest-growing minority group in the United States. What changes would you expect to see in United States culture as a result?

Caption Answer

Their many ethnic groups, plus people from other nations have moved there.

LESSON **3** Society and Culture

For families in the Ituri Forest in the Congo River basin, the search for food is the most important daily activity. They hunt rain forest animals with nets or bows and poison dart arrows, and gather plants in the forest. In a rural village in Gabon, women prepare vegetables raised in their gardens or bought at the local market. Villagers celebrate births, weddings, and religious observances with song and dance.

Brazzaville, Congo, is the largest city in Congo and the home of almost one third of its people. Well-paid workers can spend their paychecks dining at one of the city's many French restaurants and then dance late into the night at popular spots such as Le Millionaire Nightclub. Contrasts between forest and farm, city and countryside make Central African society and culture distinctive and fascinating.

KEY IDEAS

- Central Africa is home to diverse people speaking many languages and following different customs.

- The region's diversity is heightened by different ways of life in forests, on farms, and in cities.

KEY TERMS

abeng

Central Africa is a region of diversity, especially in its large cities, such as Kinshasa, Democratic Republic of the Congo. **What makes Kinshasa and the rest of Central Africa diverse?**

A Diverse Region

Central Africa, like West Africa, has great ethnic and language diversity. The Democratic Republic of the Congo's 200 ethnic groups speak at least that many languages. In Gabon, people speak 43 different languages or dialects. Each of the 200 ethnic groups in Cameroon speaks its own language.

In former colonies of France, French is an important second language for government and business. It is the official language in many countries.

Many of the region's nations still have close cultural ties with France. Central Africa's best-known authors write in French. In Gabon, for example, movie theaters show French films. Radio and television stations broadcast in French, with some programs coming from France.

Between 2,000 and 4,000 years ago, large numbers of Bantu-speaking people migrated into Central Africa from other regions. One of the largest groups of Bantu descendants are the Fang people of Gabon, Cameroon, and Equatorial Guinea. Most Fang once had been farmers, but today many live in cities. Others own coffee and cocoa plantations.

Religion

Most people in Central Africa are Christians or followers of traditional African religions. Chad is the exception. The northern half of Chad is largely Muslim, like many other nations of the Sahel. In southern Chad, the population is evenly divided between Christians and believers in traditional religions.

Coming Together Through Soccer

Soccer is a popular sport throughout Africa. National teams unite people from many backgrounds. Africans take pride in one national soccer team, the Indomitable Lions of Cameroon. The Lions qualified for the World Cup Finals of 1990, 1994, 1998, and 2000. They won the gold medal at the 2000 Olympic Games in Sydney, Australia.

Chapter 8

ℹ️ Background Information

Changes Coming for Cameroon's Rain forest People

Like the Mbuti in Congo, Jean Bikanda lives in a Pygmy village in the rain forest of Cameroon. Each day he hunts in the forest for rats, porcupines, rabbits, boars, and antelopes. He wonders how a proposed pipeline carrying oil from Chad through the Central African rain forest to the Atlantic coast will affect his life. Will it disturb the animals he relies on for food? Bikanda's people make up a tiny percentage of Cameroon's 17 million people. They have no formal schooling and few speak

French, the language of Cameroon's colonial rulers. In the past logging companies have forced them out of their forest homes, but this time many hope to get pipeline jobs and compensation for their land loss. International aid agencies worry about how oil revenues will be spent and about the pipeline's environmental effects. In many oil-rich African countries little has gone into education, health, rural development, or infrastructure.

CONNECTIONS • GEOGRAPHY & THE ARTS •

Central African Art

People in every culture make their art from materials available to them. The raffia palm, bone, ivory, wood, pigment from clay, and plants are handy materials for artists in Central Africa. The raffia palm grows well in the region. Fibers from the fronds become the fabric of raffia cloth. This cloth becomes a work of art in the hands of weavers in Central Africa.

The length of the fibers, from 3 to 5 feet (0.9 to 1.5 m), determines the size of the piece to be woven. For a large piece, several small pieces are sewn together.

Raffia cloth decorates carved figures. The people of the Luba culture in Central Africa carved large statues called singiti to represent their ancestors. The 23-inch (59-cm) statue (right) is dressed in a raffia cloth wrap. The Western Pande people carve masks of wood. The initiation mask (called mbuya) shown at far left is framed by a collar and top piece of raffia cloth. The artist carved eyes, ears, and a nose, and then used red, white, and black paint to give the mask's face depth and emotion.

Some masks are decorated with feathers, seed pods, and the talons of a bird of prey. The symbols on the mask have meaning known only to the maker.

Settlers on the Congo River use reeds and leaves to make homes. **Why do many Central Africans live along the river?**

Village Life

Most Fang who live in rural villages are small farmers. They make their homes out of wood and clay bricks or concrete with metal roofs. Rectangular houses are divided into many rooms for cooking and sleeping.

The village is likely to have an *abeng*, or traveler's house, for visitors. There might be a church. A community meeting house, usually a long building made of wooden poles that support a roof, sits in the central square. Villagers use this building as a dining room, meeting place, courtroom, and dance hall.

In the fields near the village, farmers raise manioc, a starchy root, and bananas. Most families also keep chickens or goats. Men hunt for deer or monkey to add to the family meals.

Central Africa

Customs

A favorite game of Central Africa played by young and old is mankala. A counting game similar to backgammon, mankala is played on a carved board with 12 shallow cups and 48 peas. The object of the game is to capture the most peas. The game originated in Egypt more than 8,000 years ago.

159

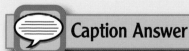

Caption Answer

Important points: Students should speculate that the river is the lifeline of the region. The river provides transportation.

Discussion Questions

1 What could you tell about a society that uses such products as metal for roofing?

Activity

Making a Mankala Board

OBJECTIVES: 12.02, 12.03, 13.02

The Customs Feature on page 159 describes the *mankala* game. To make the mankala game board, cut the lid off two cardboard egg cartons (not Styrofoam). Paste one of the lids underneath the egg-holder portion of one of the cartons. Retain only the egg-holder portion of the other carton. Cut two separate egg sections from the second egg-holder and staple one on each end of the carton. Paint the game board brown.

The mankala game is played in many parts of Africa. East Africa has given this game its name of mankala. In the west they call it *oware* or *ayo*. In South Africa it is called *ohoro*. To play mankala you need 48 stones or dried peas/beans. These stones or beans are called *hasa*. Place four beans in each of the 12 cups of the bottom of the egg carton. Player A picks up all the hasa from any cup and starting with the next cup to the right, drops one hasa at a time into each successive cup. After he drops his last hasa in the cup, he picks up all the hasa contained in that cup and continues dropping one in each successive cup. Player A's turn ends when he puts his last seed in an empty cup (the first player has the longest turn). Player B then chooses any cup of hasa and begins his turn exactly like Player A. A player scores when he drops his last seed in a cup with three others, making four seeds in a cup. He puts all four seeds in his bank. If he puts a seed in a cup, his partner puts the four seeds in his bank. The player who gets the next to the last four seeds gets the remaining seeds in the board. The player who has accumulated the most seeds in his bank wins.

Discussion Questions

1 Why would the Mbuti consider the term "jungle" disrespectful?

2 Would you be able to survive in the forests as well as the Mbuti have? What determines if one is educated? What role does location play in our definition of "educated"?

3 How would the human-environmental interaction theme be applicable to the Mbuti?

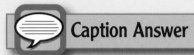

Caption Answer

The Mbuti help clear land, help plant and harvest, and supply farmers with meat and honey. The Bantu give them vegetables, salt, soap, and cloth.

Writing Activity

Dr. Livingstone, I Presume

OBJECTIVES: 1.01, 2.01, 5.01, 8.01

Have students research the exploration of Africa by David Livingstone and the efforts of Henry Stanley to locate David Livingstone when he was "lost" in Africa. Have students pretend they are Henry Stanley. Write a news article for the *New York Herald* describing efforts to find David Livingstone and information learned concerning Livingstone's exploration.

The Mbuti in the Rain Forest

"Do not call the forest that shelters you a jungle." This saying shows the respect the Mbuti (mu·BOOT·ih) people of the Democratic Republic of the Congo have for their forest home. The Mbuti are one of many related groups who live in the rain forests of Central Africa. They are descendants of the earliest inhabitants of Central Africa's rain forests. The Mbuti are recognized by their short stature. Most adults are between 4 feet (1.2 m) and 5 feet (1.5 m) tall.

All of these forest people have a close and respectful relationship with their forest home. The Mbuti live within the forest in small camps of about 100 people. They build their houses around a common space where a community fire always burns. They depend on the forest to meet their needs for food, shelter, and clothing. They build their homes of leaves and branches and eat meals of roots, birds, fruit, and fish gathered from the forests and its streams.

Honey is a prized food for the Mbuti and other forest groups. To gather it, the Mbuti climb tall forest trees carrying a basket of smoking leaves. The basket is placed near the beehive until the smoke drives the bees away. Then the hunter grabs the honey.

The Mbuti men are hunters as well as food gatherers. They capture their prey with bows and arrows tipped with poison from forest plants or with nets made from knotted vines. The men arrange their nets in a circle and hide behind trees as the women make noise and beat the brush with sticks. Monkeys, antelope, and smaller game run into the nets, where they are captured by the men. Women gather plants for food and medicine, cook meals, and care for children.

Most Mbuti live near the villages of Bantu farmers. For hundreds of years, the Mbuti have had close economic and social ties with Bantu farmers. The Mbuti help the Bantu clear forest land for fields and assist them in planting, weeding, and harvesting their crops. They also supply the farmers with such forest products as animal meat, wild plants used as medicine, and honey.

In return, the Mbuti take home bananas, maize, and tobacco grown by the Bantu. The Mbuti also swap for salt, soap, cloth, and other goods the farmers buy in the local markets. Both the Bantu and Mbuti gain from the trade connection.

The Mbuti people live in the rain forest of Central Africa. **How do they cooperate with Bantu villagers to make a living?**

LESSON **3** REVIEW

Fact Follow-Up
1. Describe ethnic and language diversity in Central Africa.
2. If you were to visit a village in Central Africa, what would you expect to find?
3. How do the art forms of Central Africa make use of available resources?
4. Describe how the connections between the Mbuti and Bantu benefit both groups.

Talk About It
1. Apply the geographic theme of human-environmental interaction to the life of the forest people of Central Africa.
2. Apply the geographic theme of movement to the Fang people.
3. In what ways might the ethnic and language diversity of Central Africa have both positive and negative effects? Explain.

LESSON **3** REVIEW

Fact Follow-Up Answers
1. Central Africa is a region of great language and ethnic diversity, with 43 different languages or dialects in Gabon alone and more than 200 ethnic groups in both Cameroon and the Democratic Republic of the Congo. Because of the many and diverse African languages in the region, French is a key second language for business and trade.
2. You might find homes made out of wood and clay bricks or concrete with metal roofs. The village is likely to have an *abeng*, or traveler's house for visitors, as well as a church and a community meeting house. Near the village would be farm fields.
3. The raffia palm, bone, ivory, wood, pigment from clay and plants, all readily available materials, are used by artists in Central Africa.
4. The Mbuti help the Bantu clear the forest land for fields and assist them in raising their crops. They also supply farmers with animal meat, wild plants used as medicine, and honey. In return, the Mbuti take home bananas, maize, and tobacco grown by the Bantu. They also trade for salt, soap, cloth, and

other goods the farmers buy in the market. Both the Mbuti and Bantu gain from the trade.

Talk About It Answers
1. The Mbuti use the forest land for hunting and gathering, taking from the forest honey, animals, and medicinal plants. The Bantu farmers clear and use forest land for farming, changing the physical environment more than do the Mbuti.
2. The Fang people who migrated to Central Africa from other regions between 2,000 and 4,000 years ago now are moving from the forests to the city, illustrating the geography theme of the movement of people.
3. Ethnic and language diversity contribute to the cultural richness of the region and encourage a variety of ethnic traditions. On the other hand, such diversity may be a barrier to creating national economies rather than those based on tradition.

Analyzing, Interpreting, Creating,
and Using Resources and Materials

Obstacles to Development

One paragraph in Chapter 8 tells you that

...Central Africa is resource-rich.
Yet its resources have not been used to their full potential.

The same is true of other regions in Africa. In this lesson, you will focus on physical obstacles to development. Begin with the obstacles in Central Africa. Then move on to other regions.

To start, bookmark the physical/political maps for each African region in Chapters 6–10. In Chapter 2, also bookmark the physical map of all of Africa (page 17), the population density map (page 20), and the vegetation map (page 35).

Draw a diagram like the one below. To complete the diagram, ask the questions below and record the answers. Use the maps and text to discover the information. The questions focus on the physical features that may encourage and discourage economic development.

1. Which Central African nations border a seacoast? Do these coastal cities seem to have ports?
2. Which Central African nations are landlocked? Do any of these nations contain rivers that connect them to an ocean or another country?
3. What are the natural barriers to transportation of goods between nations?
4. What are the natural transportation routes?
5. What information on the population density and vegetation maps suggests environmental obstacles to development? What are these obstacles? Where are they?

Once you have completed the Central African portion of the diagram, record the information for the regions of North Africa, West Africa, East Africa, and Southern Africa.

Now, ask yourself this question: Do physical and environmental characteristics appear to slow African development? In which region have you found the greatest obstacles? the least? Explain your answers.

Physical and Environmental Obstacles to Development					
	Coastal Nations	Landlocked Nations	Natural Barriers	Natural Routes	Environment Obstacles
Central Africa					
North Africa					
West Africa					
East Africa					
Southern Africa					

Central Africa

161

Teaching This Skill Lesson

Materials Needed textbooks, paper, pencils

Classroom Organization students working individually

Beginning the Lesson Remind students that they used a decision-making model in the skill lesson in Chapter 7. Examine the graphic organizer on page 161, asking how this graphic is similar to and different from the one on page 142. Lead them to realize that the organizer on page 161 is used for organizing and storing information, not for making decisions, and that they will use this graphic organizer for making some decisions later.

Lesson Development Direct students to complete the graphic organizer—fill in the information—for the three regions of Africa they have already studied (North, Central, and West Africa) as a homework assignment.

Conclusion In a class discussion, have students use their organizers to answer the three questions in the last paragraph on page 161. Seek agreement among students during the discussion.

Extension Direct students to save the organizers in their notebooks. When you have completed Chapters 9 and 10, the organizers can be completed and the three questions asked again.

Skill Lesson Review

1. How many landlocked nations are there in Central Africa? in other regions? in all of Africa? How does this affect movement? *There are two landlocked nations in Central Africa, three in West Africa, three in East Africa, and five in Southern Africa. There are 13 landlocked nations in all of Africa. Coastal nations have a distinct advantage in movement because of access to the sea. Nations that must move goods and people overland are frequently slowed or blocked by landforms, such as desert, rain forest, or river cataracts.*

2. Based on your analysis, what should Central African nations do to make the movement of people and goods easier? *Rail and road systems would help the movement of people and goods.*

3. Should Central African nations concentrate on building transportation routes to the coast? Should they build more inland routes? Explain. *Answers will vary. Roads to the ports would increase trade, which would generate income that could be used for building more roads inland.*

161

Talk About It

1. The rain forest, which is spread widely over the interior of the region, is hard to cut down. It is also hard to maintain roads in the interior.

2. Important points: Students should state policies and explain why they chose them. improving transportation and communication would increase productivity.

3. Important points: Students should choose one theme and explain why they chose it. Note: Human-environmental interaction: Life in the rain forest depends on the wise use of resources. Movement: Forest people are dependent on the Congo River for mobility. The rain forest hinders movement away from the rivers.

4. The economic resources of the region are plentiful, but they must be developed. Political stability in the region has not yet been achieved in all the countries.

5. Important points: Students should choose just one area to visit and give reasons for the choice.

CHAPTER 8 REVIEW

Lessons Learned

LESSON 1
People and Their Environment
The Equator, rain forests, and the Congo River are the key features of Central Africa. The Equator creates a climate of heat and moisture. The rain forests are the habitats for a large variety of plants and animals. The Congo River and its tributaries unite the region by providing transportation. Central Africa's resources of forests, minerals, and water have barely been developed.

LESSON 2
Government and Economy
Central African countries are living through the legacies of European colonial rule. A few countries are developing democracies, but others are ruled by military-backed single-party governments. Resources of lumber and minerals are difficult to reach because of the rain forests and hot climate. Most Central Africans are subsistence farmers.

LESSON 3
Society and Culture
Central Africa has many ethnic groups, each with different languages and customs. A unifying factor is the French language, spoken and read in the former French colonies. Most Central Africans live in villages, but cities are growing.

162

Talk About It

1. Why do you think Central Africa has few large cities?
2. What policies could you suggest to promote greater economic productivity in Central Africa? Why would you suggest these policies?
3. Which geographic theme is more useful in analyzing the life of forest people: movement or human-environmental interaction? Explain why.
4. Which is the greater strength of nations of Central Africa: economic resources or political stability? Explain why.
5. If you could visit just one area described in this chapter, which would it be? Why?

Mastering Mapwork

LOCATION
Use the map on page 147 answer these questions:

1. Describe the absolute location of Libreville, Gabon.
2. Describe the relative location of Kinshasa in the Democratic Republic of the Congo.
3. Which national capital in the region is located nearest 10°N latitude?
4. Which two national capitals are closes to one another in terms of relative location?
5. Describe the relative location of the Congo River.
6. Which nation is made entirely of islands?

Chapter 8

Mastering Mapwork

1. Libreville is located just north of the Equator and just east of 10°E latitude.

2. Kinshasa is located along the Congo (Zaire) River in the far western area of the Democratic Republic of the Congo.

3. N'Djamena, Chad

4. Brazzaville, Congo, and Kinshasa, Democratic Republic of the Congo, are located on opposite banks of the Congo (Zaire) River.

5. The Congo River flows through the Democratic Republic of the Congo, crossing the equator twice, to the Atlantic Ocean.

6. São Tomé and Príncipe

Go to the Source

Analyzing Historic Speeches

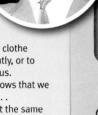

Patrice Lumumba helped win the Congo's (today's Democratic Republic of the Congo) independence from Belgium in June 1960. He became its first prime minister. Only ten weeks later, his government was overthrown in a coup. Lumumba was assassinated in January 1961. He is still an inspiration to Africans today.

Read the excerpt from Lumumba's Independence Day speech below. Answer the questions using specific references from the text.

Men and women of the Congo, victorious fighters for independence, today victorious, I greet you in the name of the Congolese Government. All of you, my friends, who have fought tirelessly at our sides, I ask you to make this June 30, 1960, an illustrious [important] date that you will keep indelibly [permanently] engraved in your hearts, a date of significance of which you will teach to your children, so that they will make known to their sons and to their grandchildren the glorious history of our fight for liberty.

For this independence of the Congo, even as it is celebrated today with Belgium, a friendly country with whom we deal as equal to equal, no Congolese worthy of the name will ever be able to forget that is was by fighting that it has been won, a day-to-day fight . . . for which we gave our strength and our blood.

We are proud of this struggle, of tears, of fire, and of blood, to the depths of our being, for it was a noble and just struggle, and indispensable to put an end to the humiliating slavery which was imposed upon us by force.

This was our fate for 80 years of a colonial regime . . . We have known harassing work, exacted in exchange for salaries which did not permit us to eat enough to drive away hunger, or to clothe ourselves, or to house ourselves decently, or to raise our children as creatures dear to us.

We have known ironies, insults, blows that we endured . . . because we are Negroes. . .

We have seen that the law was not the same for a white and for a black, accommodating for the first, cruel and inhuman for the other. . .

We have seen that in the towns there were magnificent houses for the whites and crumbling shanties for the blacks, that a black was not admitted in the motion-picture houses, in the restaurants, in the stores of the Europeans . . .

Who will ever forget the massacres where so many of our brothers perished, the cells into which those who refused to submit to a regime of oppression and exploitation were thrown?

All that, my brothers, we have endured.

But we, whom the vote of your elected representatives have given the right to direct our dear country, we who have suffered in our body and in our heart from colonial oppression, we tell you very loud, all that is henceforth ended.

The Republic of the Congo has been proclaimed, and our country is now in the hands of its own children.

Go to the Source

Questions

1. Who is the speaker? Who is the intended audience?
2. What is the occasion? What is the subject of the document?
3. What is the purpose of the document?
4. What is the significance of the document?
5. What is the tone of the document?

Central Africa

163

 Go to the Source

OBJECTIVES: 4.03, 7.01, 7.02, 8.01; Skills 3.05

The link to the entire text of Lumumba's Independence Day Speech can be found at **NCJourneys.com**.

Today some feel it was this speech, in part, that led to Lumumba's downfall. His tone in this speech angered the Belgium government. Lumumba demanded that Belgian troops withdraw, but they did not. Therefore, Lumumba expelled Belgian diplomats and called on the United Nations to defend the newly-independent state. He hinted that it might be necessary to ask the Soviet Union to assist unilaterally. That set alarm bells ringing in the West. Lumumba was overthrown 67 days after taking office and was killed by his enemies several weeks later. Belgium admitted to a portion of responsibility of his assassination in 2001.

POSSIBLE ANSWERS:

1. Speaker: Patrice Lumumba; Audience: The people of the Congo many of whom had suffered under Belgium colonial rule

2. Occasion: June 30, 1960 on the occasion of the Congo's independence from Belgium; Subject: Lumumba uses examples of sacrifice, suffering, and inequalities to fire up the audience in order to demonstrate that the elected officials are now ready to lead an independent Congo.

3. Purpose: To inspire unity, to recognize the sacrifice and suffering of the Congolese under colonial rule and to let Belgium know that Congo is its equal

4. Significance: He was only the prime minister for a short time and was then assassinated.

5. Tone: shows anger towards the past cruelties of the colonial power (Belgium)

 How to Use the Chapter Review

There are three sections in the Chapter Review: Talk About It, Mastering Mapwork, and Go to the Source. Use the Vocabulary Worksheets and the Chapter Review Worksheet in the Teacher's Resource Guide for additional reinforcement and preparation for the Chapter Assessments. The chapter and lesson reviews and the Chapter Review Worksheets are the basis of the assessment for each chapter.

Talk About It questions encourage students to speculate about the content of the chapter and are suitable for class or small-group discussion. They are not intended to be assigned for homework.

Mastering Mapwork has students apply one or more of the Five Themes of Geography to maps within the chapter.

Go to the Source activities allow students to analyze a primary source that relates to the content of the chapter. The questions and activities familiarize students with different types of primary sources and also build content-reading skills.

East Africa

Social Studies Strands

Geographic Relationships
Physical features
Climate and vegetation
Population

Government and Active Citizenship

Economics and Development

Society and Culture
Ethnic traits
Language
Religion

Global Connections

Cultures and Diversity

North Carolina Standard Course of Study

Goal 4 The learner will identify significant patterns in the movement of people, goods, and ideas over time and place in Africa, Asia, and Australia.

Goal 6 The learner will recognize the relationship between economic activity and the quality of life in Africa, Asia, and Australia.

Goal 7 The learner will assess the connections between historical events and contemporary issues in Africa, Asia, and Australia.

Goal 11 The learner will recognize the common characteristics of different cultures in Africa, Asia, and Australia.

Teaching & Assessment

• English Language Learner Modified Lesson Plans for this chapter are found in the Teacher Resource Guide.

• *ExamView® Assessment Suite* is provided at **NCJourneys.com.** It includes customizable assessments for all chapters. Paper tests are also available in the Teacher Resource Guide. See pages T16–T17 for information about how to use the assessments and the Scoring Guide.

Worksheets

Worksheets and answer keys are found both in the Teacher Resource Guide and at **NCJourneys.com**, including Reading Guides, Reading Strategies, Chapter Reviews, English Language Learner and others.

ACTIVITIES AND INTEGRATIONS

SOCIAL STUDIES

● Each One Teach One, p. 164B
Activator: *Moja Means One,* p. 164
● Earth as a Blue Marble Satellite Image, p. 166
▲ ■ Economic Products Map of Eastern Africa, p. 171
● ▲ ■ United Nations: A Peace Keeping Organization?, p. 172
● Recipe: Lasary Voatabia, p. 174
Skill Lesson: Preserving Wildlife, p. 181

READING/LANGUAGE ARTS	READING/LANGUAGE ARTS OBJECTIVES
Safari Brochure, p. 164B	1.01, 2.02, 6.01
Analogies, p. 164B	2.01
Writing Prompt: Endangered East African Animals, p. 164	2.01, 3.03
★ What Is There to Consider in East Africa?, p. 165	2.02, 6.01
Language Poster, p. 178	2.01
Go to the Source: Analyzing Speeches as Primary Sources, p. 183	2.01, 4.01, 4.02

SCIENCE	SCIENCE OBJECTIVES
Effects of Urbanization, p. 180	3.05

MATHEMATICS	MATHEMATICS OBJECTIVES
Story Problems, p. 168	1.02, 1.03
★ Coffee Math Word Problem, p. 173	1.02, 1.03
▲ ■ Graphs, p. 176	4.01, 4.05

TECHNOLOGY	TECHNOLOGY OBJECTIVES
★ Safari Brochure, p. 164B	1.01, 1.13
What Is There to Consider in East Africa?, p. 165	3.01, 3.03
The United Nations: Peace Keep Organization?, p. 172	3.0, 3.11

VISUAL ARTS	VISUAL ARTS OBJECTIVES
★ Regional Symbols, p. 164B	2.04, 5.01, 5.02
★ Safari Brochure, p. 164B	2.04, 4.01, 6.01
What Is There to Consider in East Africa?, p. 165	4.01, 4.03
Matatu, p. 169	2.01, 4.01

CHARACTER AND VALUES EDUCATION	TRAITS
Writing Prompt: Endangered East African Animals, p. 164	good citizenship responsibility
What Would You Do?, p. 168	responsibility, good judgment

● Basic Activities   ★ Challenging Activities   ▲ English Language Learner Novice   ■ English Language Learner Intermediate

Introductory Activity

Each One Teach One

 OBJECTIVES: 2.01, 2.02, 3.01, 3.02

Using a list of statements from the chapter material you think important for the students to know, copy and cut so each statement is on a separate strip of paper. Distribute one strip to each student, and have students pair up to teach other students by saying, for example, "Did you know that . . .?" The second student then teaches the first about his/her own fact. Students are to continue to move about the room until each student has had several opportunities to teach and be taught. As a class discuss the facts that the students learned.

 **Culminating Activity**

Regional Symbols

 OBJECTIVES: 2.01, 3.01, 5.01

Create a symbol to use as a logo on a flag or shield that reflects the region's human, physical, political, and economic characteristics. To prepare for this activity, have students discuss the symbols and their meanings. These could include colors, designs, or pictures. Flags are good examples. Look at the flags of the individual countries for their significance.

Assign students to work in groups of four to design a suitable symbol for the region. Tell them it must reflect human, physical, economic, and political characteristics.

 **Art Activity**

Safari Brochure

 OBJECTIVES: 1.01, 2.01, 3.01

Ask students to plan a safari for tourists and design a brochure. The tour should start in Tanzania and end up in Kenya. The brochure should explain about travel, food, other supplies, and communication with a medical team. It should show the animals that the safari might see and the landforms that will have to be negotiated. It should also include information about towns and villages where tourists might lodge.

Technology Extension Students may use the Internet to conduct the research for their brochure. They may also use graphic design software to create their brochure. Instead of a brochure, students may design a Web page featuring the same information.

Alternate Activity for ELLs Collage that will include travel, food, animals, landforms, and villages of East Africa; use ELL-friendly Web site to do research.

Analogies

 OBJECTIVES: 1.01

Analogies are useful to help students make associations with prior knowledge. They can be used as an instructional strategy to help students better understand new materials. They are not intended to be definitions or test items.

Read the analogies aloud and ask students to identify the relationship between the terms. As an extension, ask students to write their own analogies using key terms or places discussed in the chapter.

Sudan : Djibouti :: Alaska : Rhode Island (largest to smallest)

plate tectonics : Great Rift Valley :: glaciers : the Great Lakes (formed)

tsetse fly : sleeping sickness :: mosquito : yellow fever (causes)

herder : livestock :: caretaker : children (looks after)

wildlife : Tanzania :: Outback : Australia (is a major attraction of)

Gabbra : East Africa :: nomads : Sahara (live in)

Teaching Strategies

Because many students are familiar with African Safaris, treat this chapter as a "Student Safari." Be creative by decorating the room, making passports and travel itineraries, and by pretending to be the "tour guide" through the chapter.

Activator

OBJECTIVES: 11.01, 12.01, 12.02

Activators are great tools to use in order to "hook" the attention of the students. Reading picture books or stories is an excellent way to build interest in the subject and is also a great way to integrate language arts into the social studies curriculum.

Moja Means One: Swahili Counting Book by Muriel L. Feelings (Smith Peter, 1992. ISBN 0844669008.)

The Orphan Boy: Masai Tale by Tolulwa M. Mollel, (Houghton Mifflin, 1995. ISBN 0395720796.)

Bringing the Rain to Kapiti Plain by Verna Aardema (Dial, 1981. ISBN 0803708092.). Use as a choral reading with students taking different parts and adding sound effects.

Writing Prompt

OBJECTIVES: 3.01, 5.01, 5.03, 6.01

Problem-Solution

East Africa is famous for its wildlife. Unfortunately, many animals are endangered because of poaching. One possible solution is to put the rhinoceros and the elephant to sleep and surgically remove the horn or tusks. Without them, the value of the rhinoceros and elephant would be worthless to the poacher. Pretend that your are going to give a speech to the World Wildlife Fund and write a presentation explaining why you think this would or would not be a good solution to the problem of endangered animals. As you write your presentation, remember to:

- clearly state your position.
- give at least three reasons and explain your reasons fully.
- give examples to support your reasons.
- write in complete sentences and paragraph form.
- organize your ideas and include an introduction and a conclusion.
- use good grammar, spelling, punctuation, and capitalization.

Extension Allow students to present their speeches to the class and take a vote on the issue.

CHAPTER **9**

Giraffe

Chapter Preview

LESSON 1
People and Their Environment
East Africa's environment offers desert in the north and areas with vegetation in the south. The region is unevenly populated.

LESSON 2
Government and Economy
The years since independence have been marred by civil wars. Agriculture is the region's major industry.

LESSON 3
Society and Culture
The people's diverse heritages and ways of farming create many ways of life in East Africa.

164

East Africa

"If I know a song of Africa—I thought of the giraffe, and the African new moon lying on her back, of the plows in the fields—does Africa know a song of me?"

In these few lines Isak Dinesen expresses her deep affection for Africa. Dinesen had left her home in Denmark to operate a coffee plantation in East Africa. She was part of Europe's conquest of the continent. Yet as her internationally acclaimed book Out of Africa *shows, Africa really conquered her. Few European writers offer readers such a vivid sense of Africa's lands and people.*

Coffee workers in Kenya

Chapter 7

Chapter Resources

Audio Visual

The Last King of Scotland, 2006 (movie about Idi Adim, rated R)
Out of Africa, 1985

Print Resources
Fiction
Kurtz, Jane. *The Storyteller's Beads.* Gulliver Books 1998. ISBN 0152010742.

Nonfiction
Blauer, Ettagale. *Madagascar.* Children's Press, 2000. ISBN 051621053X.
Gourevitch, Philip. *We Wish to Inform You That Tomorrow We Will Be Killed with Our Families: Stories from Rwanda.* Picador, 1999. ISBN 0312243359.
Moorehead., Alan. *The Blue Nile.* Harperperennial Library, 2000. ISBN 100060956402.
---. *The White Nile.* Harperperennial Library,

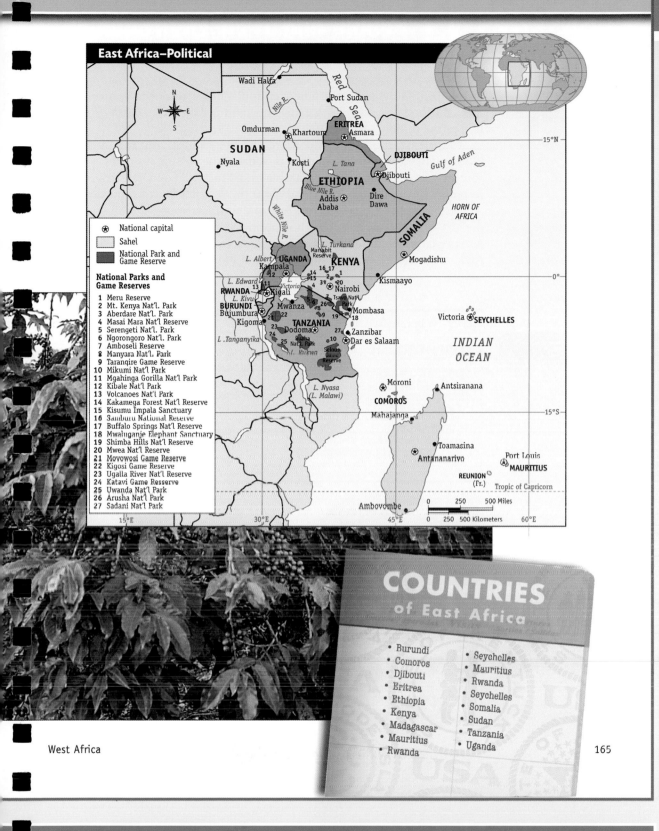

East Africa–Political

West Africa

COUNTRIES
of East Africa

- Burundi
- Comoros
- Djibouti
- Eritrea
- Ethiopia
- Kenya
- Madagascar
- Mauritius
- Rwanda

- Seychelles
- Mauritius
- Rwanda
- Seychelles
- Somalia
- Sudan
- Tanzania
- Uganda

165

Map Activity

What Is There to Consider in East Africa?

NATIONAL GEOGRAPHY STANDARDS: 1, 4, 5, 6, 7, 8, 10, 13, 15, 17;

GEOGRAPHIC THEMES: Location, Place, Human-Environmental Interaction, Movement, Region

OBJECTIVES: 1.02, 1.03, 6.01

Assign students to identify which East African countries are landlocked (*Burundi, Ethiopia, Rwanda, Uganda*). Also have students identify which of these 14 East African nations are island nations (*Comoros, Madagascar, Mauritius, Seychelles*). Discuss with students why Mauritius and Seychelles are connected with this African region instead of an Asian subregion (*proximity to African continent, cultural similarities, past history of colonization*). Discuss why Sudan is sometimes included with North Africa's study of Egypt, Libya, and Chad instead of with East Africa (*proximity, cultural similarities, Islamic and Arab influences*). Also, discuss the significance of the creation of Eritrea making Ethiopia landlocked and why this is still a volatile issue in East Africa.

Assign students to identify the six East African nations impacted by the Sahel (*Djibouti, Eritrea, Ethiopia, Kenya, Somalia, and Sudan*).

Research Topics

- The uniqueness of Madagascar's climates, flora, and fauna
- The quantity of national parks and games reserves in East Africa
- Identify the ways in which the lakes in East Africa contribute to this region's characteristics.
- Explain the nickname the Horn of Africa.

Have students design a mobile/stabile giving the official names of each of the East African countries, emphasizing to students how many nations consider themselves to be republics. The design can include flags for illustrations or boundary outline shapes of nations.

2000. ISBN 100060956399.
Roddis, Ingrid. *Sudan.* Chelsea House Pub., 2000. ISBN 0791053989.
Welcome to Ethiopia. Franklin Watts Ltd., 2005. ISBN 0749660120.
Western, David. *In the Dust of Kilimanjaro.* Island Press, 1997. ISBN 1559635347.

Back Issues of Magazines
Cobblestone Publishing titles:

Ethiopia. ISBN 0382405757.
Kenya. ISBN 0382443829.
Madagascar. ISBN 038240520X.
Swahili. ISBN 0382409051.

Web Sites

Links to these at **NCJourneys.com:**
- Kenya's Game Parks
- Lake Victoria
- Madagascar
- Save Darfur

OBJECTIVES: 2.03, 3.04, 4.03

Discussion Questions

1 What is the nickname of the area in the center of East Africa, and why is it called this?

2 Name five East African countries that comprise the Sahel.

3 What determines the climate near the Equator?

4 What crops can be grown by highland farmers? What key conditions enable the crops to be grown?

 Caption Answer

The Red Sea and the Indian Ocean rim East Africa.

Activity

Earth as Blue Marble Satellite Image

OBJECTIVES: 1.02, 2.02

Using this satellite image of earth from space, have students describe the white swirls (clouds). Knowing that a large portion of Africa and the Arabian Peninsula are visible beneath the cloud cover in this image, assign students to explain why astronauts and cosmonauts often refer to earth as a big, blue marble when seen from outer space.

If possible, obtain this image as a ball or actual marble for students to use.

LESSON 1 People and Their Environment

KEY IDEAS

- Desert land and the Sahel occupy northern East Africa. In southern East Africa, rainfall is moderate. Highland areas keep temperatures moderate.

- The region has few mineral resources. Most people are farmers.

- The region's people are remarkable diverse. Although growing, the region is unevenly populated.

KEY TERMS

Horn of Africa
tsetse fly

The characteristic shape of the Horn of Africa can been seen from space. **What bodies of water rim East Africa?**

E ast Africa is easy to spot. Check the east edge of the map on page 165. Do you see the land that looks like a rhinoceros horn jutting out into the ocean? This land is called the *Horn of Africa*. It is in the middle of East Africa.

To the east, the region is bordered by the Red Sea and the Indian Ocean. The northernmost nation is Sudan. The region stretches southward to the borders of Zambia and Malawi. The Democratic Republic of the Congo and Chad form the region's western borders.

East Africa is a huge region. Just one of its nations—Sudan—is about the size of New Mexico, Oklahoma, and Texas combined. Sudan is Africa's largest nation. Another East African country, Djibouti, is one of Africa's smallest nations. Only the island nations of West Africa are smaller.

East Africa's Environment

East Africa shares the desert, savanna, and the Sahel with West Africa. Northern Sudan is a desert, nearly as dry as Mauritania, Mali, Niger, and Chad. The Nile River provides Sudan with moisture along its narrow path. Southern Sudan has the hot and wet climate of equatorial areas.

The Sahel sweeps through central Sudan, northern Ethiopia, and Eritrea, and then bends southward through Somalia to the Kenyan border. As you have read, the Sahel is a broad band of semiarid land. In West Africa, the Sahel lies between desert and savanna areas. Highlands border the southern Sahel in East Africa.

Elevation and Climate

The Equator crosses parts of East Africa. The equatorial climate is changed by elevation in the highlands of Ethiopia and Kenya.

Because of their higher elevations, the Ethiopian and Kenyan highlands are cooler and wetter than surrounding lowlands. Unless there is a drought, the Ethiopian Highlands are fertile lands. Parts of Kenya, Uganda (oo·GAHN·dah), and Tanzania also lie on or near the Equator, but at higher elevations than neighboring Democratic Republic of the Congo. This means that in their highlands farmers can grow wheat, apples, and strawberries. Such crops normally can be grown only in lands farther away from the Equator.

166

Chapter 9

Teacher Notes

Tanzania's Capital

The national capital of Tanzania is being moved from Dar es Salaam to Dodoma. Dedoma has been planned as the new capital. The National Assembly meets there on a regular basis and the legislative offices have been moved there.

The Great Rift Valley

The most distinctive landform in East Africa is the Great Rift Valley, which you read about in Chapter 2. The Great Rift Valley stretches for a total of 6,000 miles (9,660 km) across East Africa from the Red Sea into Ethiopia and Kenya and as far south as Malawi.

The rift is actually a valley with steep sides, some as much as a mile high. The valley floor contains many lakes, such as Lake Nyasa and Lake Tanganyika (tan·gan·YEE·ka).

Close by the valleys are mountains with extinct volcanoes. Ash from volcanic explosions that took place many millions of years ago have helped make the valley floors fertile. Wind and rain have mixed the ash with dirt from the steepsided cliffs to make rich soil. East Africa's most productive farmlands are found in these volcanic areas.

Lakes and Rivers

Most of the lakes in Africa are found in East Africa's Great Rift Valley. Lake Nyasa and Lake Tanganyika are long and narrow. Each is more than 12,000 square miles (31,200 sq km) in size. Lake Tanganyika serves as a border for four nations. East Africans use it as a transportation waterway and a food source. Its fish feed millions.

Lake Victoria and other East African lakes formed in shallow basins, like saucers in the earth's crust. Lake Victoria is about half the size of North Carolina. It is the largest lake in Africa and the third

Over time, water has filled parts of the Great Rift Valley, forming lakes. **Why does the valley contain productive farmland?**

largest on earth. Only the Caspian Sea and Lake Superior are bigger. Three countries claim parts of Lake Victoria.

Both branches of the Nile have their sources in the highlands of East Africa. The White Nile starts in Uganda and the Blue Nile has its source in Ethiopia. The two join in Khartoum (kar·TOOM), Sudan, before flowing into Egypt.

Lake Victoria, the largest lake in Africa, provides transportation for the three nations that border it. **What are those nations?**

East Africa   167

Discussion Questions

1 What countries comprise the Great Rift Valley?

2 Describe the Great Rift Valley. How was it formed?

3 In what ways is Lake Tanganyika beneficial to people in the region?

4 How many countries claim Lake Victoria?

Caption Answer

Old volcanic explosions millions of years ago left behind fertile soil.

Caption Answer

Kenya, Tanzania, and Uganda

Background Information

The Island of Ethiopia?

Most of the breaks in the earth's tectonic plates lie below the surface of the ocean. The 5,400-mile crack that includes the Great Rift Valley is an exception. It runs from the Jordan River valley in the north through the Red Sea and into the Ethiopian plains and then through Kenya and Tanzania to the coast of the Indian Ocean in Mozambique.

This rift has been forming for 30 million years, and it is not finished yet. Geologists believe the fault line will continue to open up causing a wider and wider separation between the Horn of Africa and all land to the east of the Rift. Over time the gap between the Horn and the land to the east will flood with seawater, causing further erosion of the land until the Horn becomes an island somewhat larger than Madagascar.

Discussion Questions

1 What is one of the largest industries in East Africa, and from what countries does it draw customers?

2 Evaluate the effect of the tsetse fly in East Africa.

3 What country in East Africa has to import food to feed its citizens?

 **Caption Answer**

Students should support their answer with facts from the text.

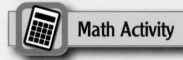 **Math Activity**

Story Problems

OBJECTIVES: 11.01

Eastern Africa has great ethnic and language diversity. Tanzania's and Kenya's ethnic groups speak many languages. There are about 1,700 languages spoken on the African continent. Swahili is a common language of East Africa. Most people know Swahili along with their own ethnic language. The word "Swahili" originally came from the Arabic word meaning coast. Have students write four story problems about animals using the Swahili counting words below. For larger numbers, combine counting words.

Counting words

1: nne (N nay)
2: tatu (TA tu)
3: mbili (m BEE lee)
4: moja (MO jah)
5: tano (TAH no)
6: sita (SEE tah)
7: saba (SAH bah)
8: nane (NAH nay)
9: tisa (TEE sah)
10: kumi (KOO mee)

Extension For ELL students, model and provide additional explanations.

Tsetse fly

Natural Resources

Unlike other regions of the continent, East Africa has few mineral resources. Sudan might have untapped oil reserves, but no nations of the region are oil rich.

Some East African nations have built major businesses based on the region's extraordinary scenic beauty and the diversity of its animal life. Each year, many thousands of tourists from the United States, Canada, France, the United Kingdom, Australia, and Japan fly to Kenya or Tanzania for picture-taking safaris. Tourism creates many jobs for the region's people.

What would YOU do?

Grazing elephants can destroy a village's crops. A pride of lions can kill a farmer's goats. How are villagers to survive? They can join a cooperative that collects money from the tourists to pay for protection from wildlife. This may provide some income. Or they can refuse to join and kill the animals that eat their crops or livestock. What would you do if you were an East African farmer?

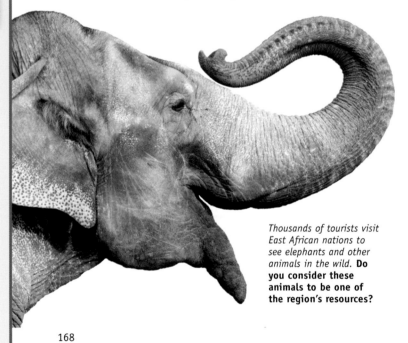

Thousands of tourists visit East African nations to see elephants and other animals in the wild. **Do you consider these animals to be one of the region's resources?**

Population

East Africa is unevenly populated. In some areas, the *tsetse fly* keeps the population low. The tsetse (TET·see) fly spreads a deadly sleeping sickness among people and cattle. Tanzania has large areas where tsetse flies breed. The country is larger than Kenya, Uganda, Rwanda, and Burundi combined. Yet its population is only slightly larger than Kenya's. In other places, population is limited by such inadequate rainfall that farming or herding is difficult.

The most heavily populated areas of East Africa are the highlands encircling Lake Victoria in Kenya, Tanzania, and Uganda. Large areas of Rwanda and Burundi are also heavily settled. People have moved there because of rich, volcanic soils and plentiful rainfall.

Most East Africans live in rural areas. Burundi is densely settled, yet fewer than one in ten people live in cities. In Sudan, Somalia, Kenya, and Tanzania, city dwellers make up only one fourth of the population. Khartoum, Sudan, and Addis Ababa (AD·is AH·bah·bah, Ethiopia, are East Africa's largest cities.

Kenya has one of the fastest rates of population growth in the world. Between 1970 and 2005, its population tripled to more than 34.3 million people. If that growth rate continues, Kenya's population will exceed 83 million by 2050.

In Kenya, and many other countries where populations are growing rapidly, food production has not been able to keep up with the demand. Kenya imports food to feed its citizens. The Kenyan Highlands, however, are one of the most productive agricultural regions in Africa.

168

Chapter 9

A Mosaic of Peoples

East Africans, especially along the Indian Ocean, blend heritages of Asia and Africa. The region's African ethnic groups are highly diverse. The region is also home to Asians and Arabic-speaking peoples.

The northern areas of East Africa are populated—as are the northern areas of West Africa—by followers of Islam. Muslim traders came up the Nile, crossed the desert in camel caravans, or sailed to East Africa. As a result, modern-day Sudan, Eritrea, and Somalia are Muslim nations.

The Sahel is a cultural as well as a physical boundary. As in West African countries and Chad, Islam is not common south of the Sahel in East Africa.

Asians, especially from India, came to the East Coast of Africa. Many came to help build the first railroad from Kenya to Uganda. After the railroad was completed, many stayed. Asians often have become successful merchants in East Africa.

Others came to work on sugar plantations on the islands in the Indian Ocean. Their descendants remain. Today, nearly half of all the people living on the island nations of Madagascar and Mauritius (located in the Indian Ocean 500 miles—805 km—east of Madagascar—see map, page 165) are descendants of people who came originally from Southeast Asia or India.

Most people in northern Sudan are Muslims and attend mosques, such as this one in Khartoum.
How did Islam spread to East Africa?

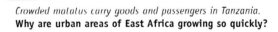
Crowded matatus carry goods and passengers in Tanzania.
Why are urban areas of East Africa growing so quickly?

Customs

In East Africa there are bad roads and few privately owned vehicles. Brightly painted minibuses serve as transportation. These matatus (a Swahili term that roughly translates to "cooperatives") have names like "Banana Peel" and "Wing Commander." For 30 cents, a city dweller jams into the minibus and holds on for dear life as the matatus speed from stop to stop. It is the only way to move around town.

Discussion Questions

1 In what way is East Africa a "mosaic of peoples"?

2 What is the major religion in East Africa, and where is it practiced?

3 What drew Asians to East Africa? What mode of transportation did they help build? In recent years in the United States, what ethnic groups have migrated to work with agricultural industries?

 Activity

Matatu

 OBJECTIVES: 1.02, 1.03

Using the "Travel by Bus" pattern from the Teacher's Resource Guide, students are to identify two East African cities by name and absolute location. These are to be put inside rectangles on side of the bus. On the bottom they are to put a description of these two cities (population, climate, etc.) and a brief analysis why matatus would be useful and necessary in these cities. Students may want to show a person driving a bus and some passenger's heads through the windows. The bus must be cut out (including around wheels so bus will stand when slots are cut and tabs slipped through these slots so wheels touch pavement), grill, bumper, doors, and windows added even passengers holding onto bus. Students can then display and present their matatu with locations, descriptions, and analysis.

Extension For novice ELL students, model and provide additional explanations.

 **Caption Answer**

Muslim missionaries came up the Nile and crossed the desert.

Caption Answer

Populations are living longer, and younger people go to cities to look for new opportunities.

Caption Answer

Genocide is the killing of a group of people because of their race, culture, or political ideas.

 Background Information

Genocide in Sudan

As of January 2007, the non-profit group SaveDarfur.org presented the following information:

Darfur has been embroiled in a deadly conflict for over three years. At least 400,000 people have been killed; more than 2 million innocent civilians have been forced to flee their homes and now live in displaced-persons camps in Sudan or in refugee camps in neighboring Chad; and more than 3.5 million men, women, and children are completely reliant on international aid for survival. Not since the Rwandan genocide of 1994 has the world seen such a calculated campaign of displacement, starvation, rape, and mass slaughter.

Since early 2003, Sudanese armed forces and Sudanese government-backed militia known as "Janjaweed" have been fighting two rebel groups in Darfur, the Sudanese Liberation Army/Movement (SLA/SLM) and the Justice and Equality Movement (JEM). The stated political aim of the rebels has been to compel the government of Sudan to address underdevelopment and the political marginalization of the region.

Ethnic Violence

The countries of the Horn have fewer ethnic groups than those farther south. Somalia is one of the few countries in all of Africa where everyone is a Muslim and speaks the same language. Sadly, this ethnic unity has not kept Somalians from fighting with one another. Conflicts in Somalia, Ethiopia, Eritrea, and Sudan have threatened the stability of the entire region, due to increased violence, weapons, refugees, and lawlessness.

In the early 1990s—after several years of war with Ethiopia over disputed territory—Somalia's government collapsed. Fighting among rival Somalian groups threatened the lives of its people.

By 2007, a transitional government was in place, but struggling. Other local and regional governments control parts of the country.

Beginning in 2003, an ethnic conflict broke out in the Darfur region of western Sudan. The United States government has called the conflict a genocide. More than 400,000 people have been killed. About 2.5 million have lost their homes.

This woman fled the conflict in Darfur, Sudan. She is in a refugee camp along with 120,000 others. **What is genocide?**

LESSON 1 REVIEW

Fact Follow-Up

1. What is the relative location of East Africa?
2. Describe the Great Rift Valley.
3. Name the rivers and lakes of East Africa.
4. What problems are caused by the tsetse fly?
5. Describe the groups of people who have settled in East Africa.
6. Where have ethnic conflicts been a problem?

Talk About It

1. How do equatorial areas in East Africa differ from equatorial areas in West and Central Africa? Why?
2. How do the physical characteristics of place contribute to the tourism industry in East Africa?
3. How is the Sahel both a cultural and physical transition zone in East Africa?

LESSON 1 REVIEW

Fact Follow-Up Answers

1. To the east, the region is bordered by the Red Sea and the Indian Ocean. Egypt lies to the north. The south is bordered by Zambia and Malawi. The Democratic Republic of the Congo and Chad are on the west.
2. The Great Rift Valley has steep sides, some as much as a mile high. It stretches more than 6,000 miles through East Africa from the Red Sea into Ethiopia and Kenya and as far south as Malawi. The valley floor contains many lakes, such as Lake Nyasa (Malawi) and Lake Tanganyika.
3. The rivers are the White Nile and the Blue Nile, which join to form the Nile River. The lakes are Lake Nyasa, Lake Tanganyika, and Lake Victoria, the largest lake in Africa.
4. The tsetse fly spreads sleeping sickness among the people and cattle, which keeps the population low.

5. Many diverse African groups have settled in the region. In addition, East Africa is home to Asians and Arabic-speaking people.
6. Somalia, Ethiopia, Eritrea, and Sudan

Talk About It Answers

1. Equatorial land is much higher in East Africa, so the climate is cooler.
2. The cool climate, the beauty of the highlands, and the animals of the region all draw tourists.
3. The Sahel is a physical transition zone from desert to savannas. It is also a cultural transition zone because it marks the southernmost extent of Islam as the dominant religion in the region.

LESSON 2 Government and Economy

A rebel leader in Kenya's struggle for independence more than 40 years ago remembered his experience. "I remember the past, but I do not carry it with me," said Frederick Ndirangu. Looking back, he does not regret fighting against the British to reclaim his country. Today, he owns land, his younger children attend good schools, and his older sons have become skilled electricians.

In East Africa, the United Kingdom and France were the main colonial powers. Kenya and Uganda became British colonies in the late 1800s. Germany claimed Tanganyika (modern-day Tanzania), but it became a British colony after Germany's defeat in World War I. Ethiopia remained independent for much of its history. Most colonies in East Africa gained independence in the late 1950s and 1960s.

Conflict in the Horn and Sudan

"In the Horn people shift like sands," goes a saying that has been true for decades. Refugees flee from one country to another in search of safety. Since independence, nations of the Horn have been torn apart by conflict. You read of the recent ethnic violence in Lesson 2.

The Horn occupies a strategic position near the oil fields of Southwest Asia and alongside the shipping lanes of the Suez Canal. Its location has long made it important to world powers. During the Cold War era, the Soviet Union and the United States gave money and arms to local forces fighting one another.

Sudan, Ethiopia, and Somalia each suffered through long civil wars. In Sudan, fighting erupted as the mostly Arab-Muslim north and Christian south battled for control of the newly independent country. Warfare, drought, and floods have caused great suffering. At least a million people died when constant warfare prevented the distribution of food to starving people. Fighting continues today. United Nations peacekeepers have struggled to keep the region stable.

East Africa

From 1974 to 1991, there was civil war in Ethiopia. The mostly Muslim province of Eritrea wanted to secede and become independent. On May 24, 1993, Eritrea became a nation. Ethiopia held its first multiparty election in 1995. Eritrea and Ethiopia fought border wars from 1998 until they signed a treaty in 2000.

Somalia has suffered from civil war since 1977. In 1991, the northern portion declared independence but was not recognized internationally. As the war continued, a drought threatened mass starvation. As part of a United Nations effort to stop the famine and bring peace, the United States sent troops to Somalia. Although the famine was ended, peace did not return. First American troops and then United Nations peacekeepers left. The instability has also provided a haven for global terrorists.

Haile Selassie was the leader of Independent Ethiopia when Italy invaded in 1935.
What European nations ruled other parts of East Africa?

171

Discussion Questions

1 What three main colonial powers were involved in East Africa?

2 What countries in East Africa have been involved in long civil wars? Compare that to the dates of the United States independence and our Civil War. Compare and contrast civil wars in Africa to the United States Civil War.

3 Why do you think the Soviet Union and the United States gave money and arms to African nations involved in civil wars?

4 What problems exist in Somalia, and what two countries sent troops to try and keep peace in Somalia?

Caption Answer

Britain and France

Map Activity

Economic Products Map of Eastern Africa

NATIONAL GEOGRAPHY STANDARDS: 0
GEOGRAPHIC THEMES:

OBJECTIVES: 1.01, 1.02, 5.01

Farming is the most important economic activity in East Africa. Farmers practice both subsistence farming and production of cash crops. Using an outline map of Africa, identify the following countries: Burundi, Kenya, Mauritius, Rwanda, Tanzania, and Uganda. Label each country on the outline map. Make a key/legend for this map. Use a symbol to represent the following:

coffee	cassava	goats
cotton	bananas	sheep
cocoa	pyrethrum	sugar
tea	sisal	tobacco
corn	flowers	onions
sorghum	long-horned cows	

Place each symbol in the countries where each agricultural product can be found.

Extension For novice ELL students, model and provide additional explanations. Assign students to work with partners. They may need to define products in native language before labeling on map.

Discussion Questions

1 In what two countries south of the Horn of Africa were rival ethnic groups battling for power?

2 Which African ruler led Kenya through its independence movement?

3 Name the most important economic activity in East Africa and what cash crops are produced. Name a cash crop in North Carolina.

4 Many agricultural products from Africa are imported to Europe during the winter months of the Northern Hemisphere. From where does the United State import fruits, vegetables, and flowers during the winter?

Caption Answer

To safeguard the distribution of food while the United Nations tried peace-keeping efforts. United Nations peace-keeping efforts failed.

Caption Answer

He built loyalty in the country and united the people.

Activity

The United Nations: A Peacekeeping Organization?

OBJECTIVES: 1.02, 8.01, 9.01

Using a world outline map and the United Nations Web site (**un.org**), have students identify the places throughout the world that the United Nations has sent peacekeeping forces. Color those locations on the map. Follow up for class discussion: In how many of these places are the United Nations troops still deployed? Is the United Nations successful as a peacekeeping organization?

Extension For intermediate ELL students, model and provide additional explanations. Assign students to work with partners. Access the United Nations Web site through the **worldLingo.com** url translator; do map only.

This United States-French convoy was part of a United Nations peacekeeping force in Somalia in 1992. **Why was the force in Somalia? Did it accomplish its mission?**

Conflict and Stability Outside the Horn

South of the Horn of Africa, warfare frequently has followed independence. In Burundi and Rwanda, rival ethnic groups battled for power. Civil war in Uganda led to several dictatorships. Idi Amin came to power in 1971. He expelled more than 50,000 skilled Asian workers and tried to rid Uganda of any opposition. In 1979, Amin was driven from power. In 1996, Uganda held its first election in 16 years.

Julius Nyerere led Tanzania through independence in 1961 until 1985. **Why was he a respected leader?**

Two nations can boast of secure governments after independence. For decades, strong leaders in Kenya and Tanzania have brought stability to these countries. Jomo Kenyatta led Kenya's independence movement. Then he ruled Kenya for years. In 1992, Kenya held its first multiparty election.

In Tanzania, Julius Nyerere led the country from its independence in 1961 until 1985, when he stepped down. Nyerere helped build loyalty to the nation and united its people. World leaders respected Tanzania for its peaceful changes in government. Tanzania held its third peaceful multiparty elections in 2005.

Regional Economies

During the years after independence, East African nations experimented with different types of economic systems. Today, however, most nations have market based systems.

Agriculture

Farming is the region's most important economic activity. In Tanzania, Uganda, Rwanda, and Burundi, eight out of ten people are small farmers or raise such cash

172   Chapter 9

It's a Fact

Mainland Nations of East Africa

■ Burundi has been the site of years of ethnic fighting between the Hutus, who are mostly farmers, and the Tutsi, who raise cattle. The fighting over government and military control began almost as soon as Burundi became independent.

■ Djibouti has one of Africa's highest unemployment rates. It has no known natural resources and little arable land. Its main source of income is derived from being

the location of port cities leading to the Suez Canal.

■ Eritrea took Ethiopia's coastline when it received independence. Ethiopia must now pay the new nation to use its old ports for foreign trade. Ethiopia is nearly as large as Alaska, but it has more than 40 ethnic groups and more than 70 languages. Most people are subsistence farmers who are still using wooden plows pulled by oxen. Drought and

crops as coffee, cotton, cocoa, and tea.

Heavy dependence on a single cash crop has sometimes hurt the nations of East Africa. At times, prices on world markets for these crops have fallen. The economies of East Africa have suffered.

Many Kenyans, especially in the highlands near Nairobi, are farmers. After independence in 1963, Jomo Kenyatta encouraged all workers to join him in building the economy. In asking for their cooperation he often used the Swahili word *harambee,* which means "let us all pull together." Many British settlers had left the country. Kenyans took over the farming. Kenyatta urged farmers to continue growing such cash crops as coffee and tea that had been raised by the British. Solid economic growth followed.

Coffee and tea remain key cash crops for export. Pyrethrum, used to make insecticides, and sisal, a fiber that can be made into rope, are also exported. Farmers also grow corn, sorghum, cassava, and bananas as major food crops.

The mild highland climate is also well suited to growing flowers, fruit, and vegetables sent by air to Europe and Southwest Asia for sale. During colonial rule, the British built an excellent rail and road system that has helped Kenya develop its agriculture.

In the years after independence, the Tanzanian government took control of most businesses and industries in the country. The government-controlled economy enjoyed only modest success in economic development. Experiments in moving city people into the countryside to work on farms failed. Food production did not increase.

WORD ORIGINS

The word **coffee** comes from the name *Kaffa,* a province in southwest Ethiopia that is believed to be the birthplace of coffee.

Coffee beans

By the late 1980s, many government controls over the economy were removed. More private businesses were allowed. The economy continues to improve today.

Herding

The long-horned cow might make a good symbol for East Africa. Herding is an important way of making a living. Before the wars began in Somalia, livestock was Somalia's main export. Herders sold most of their goats, cattle, and sheep to buyers in Southwest Asia, mainly in Saudi Arabia. In Kenya and Tanzania, the Masai also depend on their cattle, goats, and sheep to survive.

The East African climate and vegetation usually are well suited to herding. With fewer tsetse flies, the wild short grasses of the savanna are ideal for grazing.

Few herders in the Horn depend completely on their livestock to support their families. Most also grow a few crops. In northern Uganda, the Karamojong people cultivate small plots of land near their villages and take herds of cattle, sheep, and goats in search of pasture.

A woman hoes corn in Tanzania. East African farmers raise cash crops like coffee or food crops for their families. **What crops are exported from East Africa?**

Long-horned cattle (below) are raised in this region. **Why would this animal make a good symbol for East Africa?**

East Africa

173

Discussion Questions

1 Who buys most of the livestock from East Africa?

2 Why do you think Tanzania's economy improved with less government control?

 Caption Answer

Coffee, tea, cotton, and cocoa

Caption Answer

Herding is an important way of making a living. People also depend on the cattle for food.

 Math Activity

Coffee Math Word Problem

OBJECTIVES: 5.02, 5.04, 6.02

A buyer for a coffee company arrives in East Africa. She contacts the coffee broker. She finds that raw beans cost $180 per 1,000 pounds. If she buys 12 tons of coffee beans, how much will her company pay for the beans? If the beans are put into 100-pound sacks, how many sacks will be needed to hold the beans?

Answer $4,320, 240 sacks

Extension Assist ELL students by setting up the problem for them.

years of civil war here made Somalia, which surrounds Ethiopia to the east, dependent upon food donations from the rest of the world.

■ In rural areas of Kenya where the government has not yet established schools, residents have created "self-help" classes called Harambee Schools. Approximately 80 percent of Kenyans have an elementary education.

■ The Virunga Mountains in Rwanda are one of the last refuges of the mountain gorillas. With the highest population density in Sub-Saharan Africa, the great apes habitat is severely threatened.

■ The Sudanese proverb "When Allah created the Sudan, Allah laughed" reflects the environment of this large country: deserts in the north, junglelike swamps in the south, and frequent droughts, floods, and mile-wide locust swarms. The Sudan is home to the world's largest irrigated farm (2.1 million acres) that produces cotton.

■ Tanzania is home to the world's largest animal reserve. The Selous Game Reserve covers more than 21,000 square miles (54,600 sq km). Lake Tanganyika is the world's longest freshwater lake at 420 miles (676.2 km) long and is larger than Belgium. More than two thirds of the country cannot be farmed due to the tsetse fly infestation and lack of water.

■ Uganda is smaller than the state of Oregon. The British settlers called this colony "the pearl of Africa" because of its mild climate due to high elevation, plentiful rainfall, and rich volcanic soil.

Eyewitness Activity

Recipe: Lasary Voatabia

OBJECTIVES: 2.01, 11.03

A side salad is often enjoyed in the East African island nation of Madagascar.

Ingredients
2 large tomatoes
2 scallions
2 tablespoons water
1 tablespoon lemon juice
½ teaspoon salt
pepper to taste
1 drop hot sauce (optional)

Wash vegetables in cold water. Carefully chop tomatoes and scallions into bite-size pieces. Place chopped vegetables in large bowl. Add water, lemon juice, salt, pepper, and hot sauce. Use spoon to mix ingredients. Place in refrigerator and chill one hour.

EYEWITNESS TO HISTORY

Madagascar

Madagascar was once part of Africa. It became an island 165 million years ago when it broke away from the continent. Located 250 miles off the African coast, it is often considered an African nation. Its people, however, do not think of themselves as African.

Chameleon

Most of the population descended from people who sailed 3,000 miles (8,050 km) from the islands of modern-day Indonesia. Some Africans and Arabic people arrived later. Together they developed a language and culture unlike any in Africa.

Cut off for millions of years from Africa, thousands of Madagascar's plants and hundreds of animals developed into species unlike any others in the world. Today scientists from around the world are fighting hard to protect these rare forms of life.

Children in a Toamasina schoolyard

Lemur

174

Chapter 9

Some women in Madagascar like to paint their faces with elaborate geometric patterns.

European influences were added later. France ruled the island as a colony from the late 1800s until 1960. Today the island has two official languages: Malagasy—a language similar to some used in Southeast Asia—and French. More than half the people follow traditional religions. Others are Christians and Muslims.

Madagascar is poverty-striken. Even the hardest labor does not produce good crops. The soil is poor, and farmers have few good tools. People are trying to find enough land for food by cutting down rain forests. As the rain forests disappear, so do the rare plants and animals that scientists are trying to save.

A man pushes a cart of wood past a sisal plantation.

East Africa

175

 It's a Fact

Island Nations of East Africa

■ Nearly 80 percent of Madagascar has been subjected to slash-and-burn farming techniques, leaving much of the former rain forest barren. Scientists believe that as many as 150,000 plant and animal species found nowhere else in the world are threatened. Major exports include cloves and vanilla.
■ Mauritius is about the size of Rhode Island. Most of the arable land is covered with sugarcane and more than one third of

its workforce is employed in the sugar industry: growing, harvesting, or processing.
■ Comoros has been the site of the only coelacanth found. The "living fossil fish" was thought to have been extinct for 70 million years. This island nation is the world's leading producer of "ylang-ylang," the oil of a fragrant flower used in perfumes.

■ The Seychelles is composed of 92 coral atolls and granite islands, many that are inhabitable. Some geologists believe that granite islands are the remains of an ancient small continent because they form a continental shelf.

Caption Answer

Tourists come to see the animals.

Math Activity

Graphs

OBJECTIVES: 5.03, 6.01, 6.02

Have students choose one set of statistics to research about each East African country. For example, students can look up the life expectancies, literacy rates, religion percentages, or the GDP of all the countries in the region. Students will make a bar graph, pie graph, or pictograph to display their statistics and illustrate the graph by choosing a symbol to represent each country. They will then present their graphs to the class and draw conclusions about the standard of living of the countries in this region and whether their country is developed or developing. You may want to provide a graph of these statistics for the United States to contrast the statistics of their country.

Technology Extension Students can create a spreadsheet or database for their statistics and use the software program to generate their graphs. For ELL students, model graph and have them prepare only the graph.

Extension Research using ELL-friendly Web sites; assign a peer tutor to help with the graphing and technology components of this project. No presentations or drawing conclusions for ELL students

Rhinoceroses, lions, zebras, and other wildlife draw visitors to a game park in Kenya. **What benefits do game parks bring to East Africa?**

176

Chapter 9

Background Information

Game Parks

East Africa is home to some of Africa's most spectacular game parks. The open savannas of Kenya and Tanzania are ideal for camera safaris. Twenty-five percent of Tanzania's land is designated as a national park or game reserve. Selous Reserve, Tanzania's biggest park, is larger than Denmark. Almost every African country has one or more national parks. These parks represent a significant part of total land use. They protect wildlife and support tourism and recreational activities, and are important in other ways. For example, in some Kenyan game parks, the Masai and other groups are allowed to cull game for food. Other carefully controlled uses include timber extraction, herding, and fishing. In this way the parks benefit the nation as well as help local people survive.

Tourism

Wildlife and natural beauty are economic resources for East Africa. Tourism is big business in Kenya and Tanzania. Game parks in both countries attract tourists who want to see wild animals in their natural environment (see map, page 165). Kenya has 20 of them. One is in Nairobi, Kenya's capital.

Tanzania has 15 national parks and 23 game reserves. One of its best known is the Ngorongoro (en·gor·own·GOR·oh) Crater, a 12.5-mile (20-km)-wide volcanic crater where African animals from antelope to zebra live. Wildlife flock here because a large shallow lake in the crater offers a permanent watering hole surrounded by good grazing land. The animals share the crater with cattle belonging to local Masai herders who graze their animals in the crater.

Tourists come prepared to spend money. Taking care of them provides jobs for thousands of people in hotels, restaurants, and transportation. Some also work as tour guides and game scouts. These service industry jobs make up a growing sector of the economy.

Industrial Growth

Kenya has more industries than other countries of the region. Most Kenyan factories, however, rely on imported raw materials. The center of manufacturing is in Nairobi. Workers there process local food crops and make soft drinks; assemble radios, cars, and trucks with imported parts; and make cloth.

Mauritius has few natural resources aside from fertile soil. Yet the tiny island country has one of Africa's highest incomes per person. Until the 1970s, the nation's main source of income was sugar. Now its economic growth comes from the environment created by its stable government and from the exports produced at textile mills owned by local and Asian investors. Farmers plant sugarcane, tea, tobacco, onions, and flowers. Tourism also has helped the island's economy soar.

East African Cooperation

In 1999, Tanzania, Kenya, and Uganda re-established the **East African Community** (EAC). Rwanda and Burundi are interesting in joining the EAC also. This organization has been designed to assist in developing mutual trade, investment, and security in the region. It is modeled on the European Union, and it is hoped that it will eventually allow the free movement of goods and services within the region, promote economic growth and development, and attract needed foreign investment to these nations.

Tourists on safari use binoculars to get a closer look at animals. **Are Kenya's national parks an economic resource or an environmental resource?**

Discussion Questions

1 What economic resource is big business for Kenya and Tanzania?

2 Name three areas in which tourism thrives in East Africa. What areas in North Carolina draw a lot of tourists? areas in the United States?

3 If you were to visit East Africa, which country would you like to visit, and what would you like to see and do there?

4 Name businesses that benefit from the tourism traffic.

5 Which country in East Africa is most industrialized? What commodity does it import?

6 What exports have assisted Mauritius in having an economic boom?

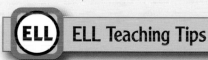

Caption Answer

They are both an economic resource and an environmental resource.

ELL Teaching Tips

When students answer the discussion questions above, have them point to a map in the classroom to show that they know the location of the countries in their answers.

LESSON 2 REVIEW

Fact Follow-Up

1. What European nations held colonial possessions in East Africa?
2. Which East African nations have had stable governments since independence? Which have had continual conflicts?
3. Name the main economic activities of East Africa. What products are exported?

Talk About It

1. Why have some East African governments been stable since independence while others have experienced difficulties?
2. What does *harambee* mean? How does this idea show the spirit of Kenyans?
3. Why are cash crops important in this region?

East Africa

177

LESSON 2 REVIEW

Fact Follow-Up Answers

1. Great Britain, France, and Germany held colonies in East Africa. Ethiopia remained independent.
2. Kenya and Tanzania have had stable governments. Sudan, Ethiopia, and Somalia have suffered through long civil wars. In Burundi and Rwanda, rival ethnic groups have battled for power. Civil war in Uganda has led to several dictatorships.
3. The economic activities are farming, herding, and tourism. East Africa exports coffee, tea, flowers, fruit and vegetables, pyrethrum, and sisal.

Talk About It Answers

1. Strong leaders in Kenya and Tanzania have brought stability by uniting people. Other nations have experienced difficulties because of rival ethnic groups fighting for power.
2. *Harambee* means "let us pull together." Students should discuss how this idea shows that the Kenyans have cooperated to strengthen their country.
3. Cash crops are exported, which in turn provides an economic benefit to this region.

OBJECTIVES: 11.01, 11.02, 12.01

Discussion Questions

1 What two religions are found in Kenya, Uganda, and Tanzania?

2 Why do most Muslims live along the coast of East Africa?

3 What peoples occupy the Seychelles?

4 Analyze the blend of ethnic heritages that make the East African islands unique. What are the benefits of cultural diversity, and what problems could cultural diversity produce?

Activity

Language Poster

OBJECTIVES: 11.01, 12.02, 12.03

Four major languages spoken in East Africa are Arabic, Swahili, English, and French. Students will choose ten commonly used words in English and research and find their equivalent in Arabic, Swahili, and French. They will then make a language poster displaying their information.

Extension ELLs could add some terms in their native language to the poster. Pictures would enhance this project as well, and make it more comprehensible for ELLs.

Caption Answer

Asians as well as other Europeans

Name Origin

Burundi Once part of Ruwanda-Urundi Belgian Trusteeship, it took its name from the chief language.

Comoros Named after the largest island in the nation—Grand Comore.

Djibouti Named for the capital city.

Eritrea Taken from ancient Greek name for Red Sea, "Erythros."

Ethiopia Greek for "land of the people with sunburned faces."

LESSON ③ Society and Culture

KEY IDEAS

- The rich mix of ethnic heritages—different religious faiths, national origins, and ancient African traditions—remains a major influence on ways of life.

- Farming, animal herding, and plantation agri-culture also influence where and how people live.

KEY TERMS

poaching

People from Europe, Africa, India, and China meet on the mainland and islands of East Africa. The result is a rich heritage of many cultures.

Religion

In Ethiopia and Eritrea, many people belong to the Ethiopian Orthodox Church, a branch of Christianity. Throughout most of the Horn and coastal East Africa, the influence of Islam is strong. As you learned in Chapter 3, Muslim Arabs helped build the trading states that grew up along the east coast of the continent. Sudan and the countries of the Horn have been influenced from at least the tenth century by Muslim culture coming from the Arabian Peninsula.

In Kenya, Uganda, and Tanzania, the population is divided among Muslims, Christians, and followers of traditional African religions. Most Muslims live along the East Coast.

The government house in Port Louis, Mauritius, shows the influence of French culture on the island. **What other groups settled there?**

Island Diversity

All the island nations have been influenced both by contact with Asia, Europe, and the African mainland. In Mauritius, Hindus, Christians, Muslims, and Buddhists live side by side and celebrate one another's religious holidays and festivals. The islands of the Seychelles (say·SHELZ) are populated by Europeans, East Africans, and Asians, mostly from India and China.

Workers from India and other parts of South Asia came to work on sugar plantations in Mauritius. Their descendants now make up about two thirds of the island's population. Although English is the official language, most people speak French or the Creole language, a mixture of French and African languages.

Many of the settlers of Madagascar and the Comoros Islands came originally from throughout Asia. Many speak Arabic or Southeast Asian languages.

All four island nations have been strongly influenced by France. French settlers built plantations on Madagascar and Comoros. France still has some island colonies in the Indian Ocean.

Kenya Named after Mount Kenya.

Madagascar Named for the descendants (98 percent of the population) who came from the Malay Peninsula.

Mauritius Named for Prince Maurice, son of King William of the Netherlands.

Rwanda See Burundi—named for the chief language spoken in the country.

Seychelles Named for Morau de Seychelles, France's finance minister to Louis XV.

Somalia Named for the Somali ethnic group who settled the region in the thirteenth century.

Sudan Formerly the southern part of the ancient Kush empire. Sudan is Arabic for "black."

Tanzania Formerly Tanganyika, the Bantu expression "to gather water chestnuts," an abundant plant and food source growing along Lake Tanganyika's shoreline.

Uganda "Land of Ganda," a powerful ethnic group in the area.

Ways of Living in East Africa

As you have read, East Africa has few large cities. Those who have moved away from villages work in banking, trade, and tourism. Such businesses, however, are not major forces in giving the region its character. Life in the villages is more important.

Village life changes with varying climates. In dry northern areas, cattle are raised and herded. In wetter areas, farmers tend crops and keep some livestock.

The Gabbra people of northern Kenya live along the eastern shore of Lake Turkana. Their lives as herders are one example of how people exist in East Africa.

Rainfall in this part of Kenya is scattered and uncertain, so water sources and grazing lands are uncertain. The Gabbra must move often to find grazing land for their herds of camels, cattle, sheep, and goats.

The Gabbra women are skilled at packing up an entire settlement. In just a few hours they can load tents, food, aluminum cooking pots, wooden and woven containers for storing food, bed poles, and sleeping skins onto camels. This skill is needed, because the Gabbra must move quickly when they learn that rain has fallen nearby. Fully loaded, a camel can travel 50 miles (81 km) a day.

The Gabbra might move as often as ten times a year, depending on grazing conditions. During dry times, they live in small groups, putting up their tents around a lake, well, or other watering hole. When the rains come, they spread out across the grasslands. Three times a year, related families gather for a sorio, a ceremony to bless the community and the livestock and to pray for rain.

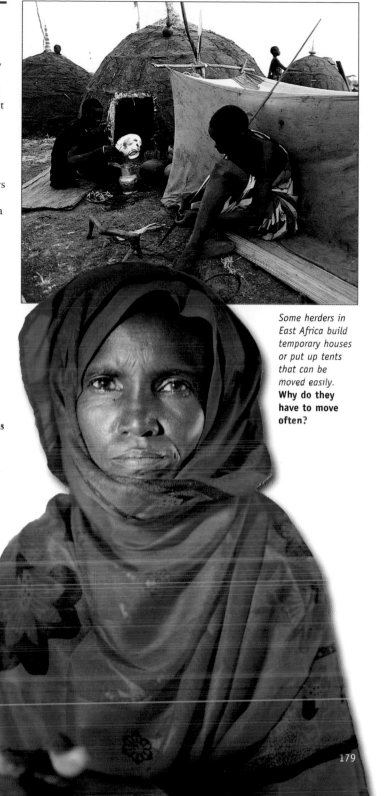

This Gabbra woman lost most of her goat herd during a drought. **How does the environment affect the ways the Gabbra live?**

East Africa

179

Some herders in East Africa build temporary houses or put up tents that can be moved easily. **Why do they have to move often?**

Discussion Questions

1 In what way does climate affect economic activities in villages of East Africa?

2 Explain how the Gabbra people have adapted to their environment.

3 Describe your life if you were a male member of the Gabbra group. If you were female.

4 What problems would you have in adapting to life among the Gabbra people?

Caption Answer

In their dry climate, they must move often to find water and grazing land for their herds.

Caption Answer

Since rainfall is uncertain and scattered, the Gabbra move frequently to find grazing land for their animals.

Background Information

Entertainment—East African Style

In Kenya's major urban centers such as Nairobi and Mombasa, the movies are a popular form of entertainment. Martial arts and action films are crowd pleasers as are movies from India. In recent years entrepreneurs have taken the movies to rural areas through makeshift movie houses in living rooms or market stalls. A television and VCR serve as a movie screen. In rural areas many of these "movie houses" are in or near village markets. Throughout Uganda traveling theater troupes draw audiences. Often their plays focus on such issues as politics, health, or family problems. These plays educate as well as entertain. In Uganda, where more than a third of the people cannot read, theater is playing a key role in teaching Ugandans about HIV/AIDS and its prevention.

Science Activity

Effects of Urbanization

OBJECTIVES: 2.02, 2.03, 3.02

Scientists today are engaged in studying effects of urbanization in Addis Ababa. For example, some scientists study the rising levels of air pollution in the Ethiopian city. Divide your class into cooperative learning groups. Instruct each group to write a paragraph, design a poster, or create a presentation that outlines how a scientist might identify and study the effects of urbanization in Addis Ababa.

A Journey to ADDIS ABABA

Linking Village to City

Joseph Kariango works as a file clerk in a government office in Addis Ababa, Ethiopia, the capital and largest city. Joseph feels very lucky to have this job. He and his wife, Jane, and their two daughters came to Addis Ababa from a village about 25 miles (40 km) from the capital. His parents are farmers, but their land is too small to support Joseph and his family as well as Joseph's four sisters and brothers back home.

Joseph also decided to come to the city because he had eight years of schooling and believed he might be able to make a better living in the city. He chose Addis Ababa because his cousin lives there and has a job as a government office worker. After months of looking, Joseph got a job as a file clerk at the office where Joseph's cousin works.

Six months ago, Joseph and his family moved to their own apartment. Their new home consists of two small bedrooms, a living room, and a very small kitchen.

Most mornings Joseph goes to work on one of the small, crowded privately owned buses that streak through city streets. At the end of the day, he might share a taxi home if he is in a big hurry. Otherwise he walks.

Children of Addis Ababa

The family carefully watches its spending, putting aside a little money each month. Jane has a part-time job, helping a friend who has a stall at the market, where she sells clothes and homemade snacks.

Almost all of the money the family makes pays for the monthly bus tickets Joseph buys to return to his home village. He visits his parents and helps them tend their fields and make repairs on their house. He takes food back to the city for his family.

One day in the distant future, after his daughters have finished school, Joseph hopes he and Jane can return to their village. He misses the warmth and friendliness of his family and neighbors, and likes to be outdoors and surrounded by plants and trees. But for now, he is glad to have a job in Addis Ababa.

LESSON ③ REVIEW

Fact Follow-Up

1. What are some cultural characteristics of the island nations of East Africa?
2. In East Africa, How do physical characteristics of place influence ways of living?
3. Describe the religious diversity of East Africa.
4. Why do city dwellers in East Africa keep in touch with their rural families?

Talk About It

1. Compare the diversity of island nations with other areas of East Africa.
2. If you were a young East African living in a city, how would you feel about your obligations to family members? Explain.
3. Why would a family like the Kariangos live in the city but prefer the country?

LESSON ③ REVIEW

Fact Follow-Up Answers

1. All the island nations have been influenced by contact with Asia, Europe, and the African mainland. They are diverse in culture, language, and religion.
2. People farm in the areas with rich soil and plentiful rainfall. In dry northern areas, cattle are raised and herded. People there move constantly to find water and grazing land.
3. In Ethiopia and Eritrea, many belong to the Ethiopian Orthodox Christian Church. In the Horn and on the coast, Islam is strong. Farther south the population is divided among Muslims, Christians, and followers of traditional African religions. In the island nations, there are Hindus, Christians, Muslims, and Buddhists.
4. Many city dwellers hope one day to return to the country. They visit and support their families in the meantime.

Talk About It Answers

1. Mauritius includes many people who came from India to work on the sugar plantations. The Seychelles is home to Europeans, East Africans, and Asians, mostly from India and China. Many of the settlers of Madagascar and the Comoros Islands came originally from Asia and speak Arabic or Southeast Asian languages. In contrast, people living in the northern part of the East Coast and Sudan are mostly African in origin and are largely Muslim.
2. Students should show an understanding of the responsibilities of housing and supporting family members moving to cities.
3. Students should convey an understanding of the economic opportunities available in cities.

*Applying Decision-Making and
Problem-Solving Techniques to World Issues*

Preserving Wildlife

East Africa is home to some of the world's most exotic and beautiful wildlife reserves. People travel from all over the world to the region to observe and photograph animals and birds. Kenya and Tanzania have built a successful tourism industry based on the local wildlife.

Yet both the wildlife and the tourist industry are threatened. The threat comes not from the guns of big-game hunters, because hunting is strictly limited. Rather, it comes from the people who live on the borders of the great game reserves.

Often, animals such as lions will stray off the game reserves and attack livestock that African people depend on for food. The people whose animals are killed are understandably angry.

Other Africans threaten the game by *poaching*, or killing animals illegally. Animals such as elephants are killed for their meat and ivory tusks. Selling the ivory of elephant tusks is illegal. Still, there is such a demand for ivory, the tusks bring high prices. If a poacher can sell two tusks, he may have more money than he could earn in a year from farming. Other animals are hunted on the reserve for food.

Game wardens stand between the threatened animals and the neighboring African people. How do you think they feel? They are torn between the needs of people and the needs of animals and the wealth they attract.

To help you view the issues from the game wardens' perspectives, make two lists: one of all the arguments for protecting the animals and the other of all the arguments people living on the borders of the wildlife reserves might have. When you have finished your list, compare it with a classmate's and refine your list based on what you learn.

Now, pair with a classmate to do a simple role play. One of you will be a game warden, the other a person living on the border of the game reserve. The game warden will try to explain why the animals should be protected, and the other person will argue that the needs of African people are more important than animals or wealthy foreigners. After two minutes, switch roles and argue for the opposite side.

Which perspective was easier to express? After arguing from both sides, do you understand the issues more fully?

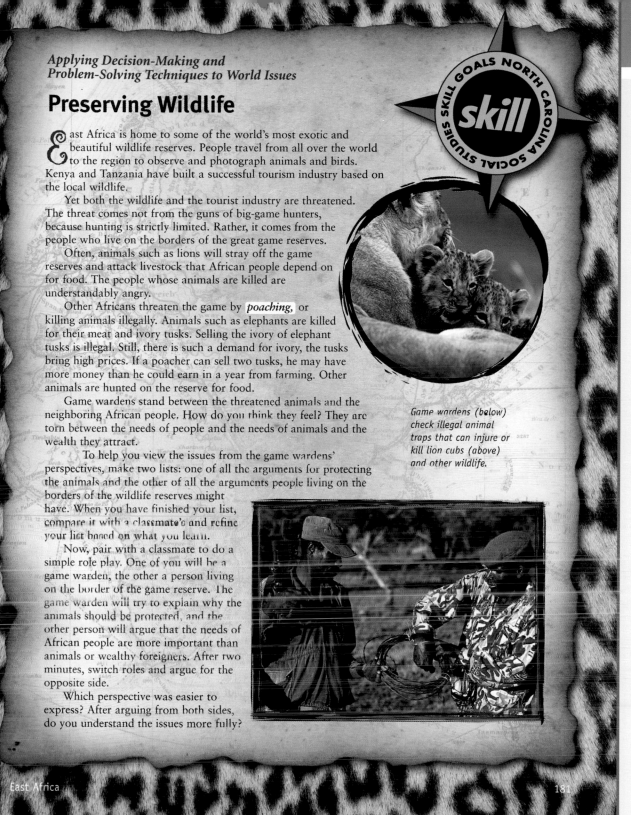

Game wardens (below) check illegal animal traps that can injure or kill lion cubs (above) and other wildlife.

East Africa

181

Teaching This Skill Lesson

Materials Needed textbook, paper, pencils

Classroom Organization Individual work and working in pairs. (If desired, you may have students work in trios with one student serving as an observer-reporter.)

Beginning the Lesson Have students read the first five paragraphs on page 181. Check for understanding. Ask students to divide a sheet of paper lengthwise, then label one side "protecting animals" and the other "needs of people." They are to make lists based on the reading *or* you may want to make these lists on the chalkboard instead.

Lesson Development Tell students they will be playing the roles of game wardens and people living on the borders of wildlife reserves. Assign roles, assigning observer-reporters if you wish. Direct students to assume their assigned roles and try to convince one another what should be done. After no more than five minutes, direct students to switch roles and argue from the other perspective.

Conclusion If observer-reporters were assigned, have them report on how well roles were played, whether important issues were brought out. Ask students who played the roles how easy or difficult it was to play each role. Did playing the roles help them understand the issues better? Tell students that governments in Kenya and Tanzania are now using community policing, hiring people living around the game preserves to stop poaching. This policy puts money into African communities and protects endangered animals.

Extension You may wish to give a writing assignment, directing students to write letters to friends from the perspectives above, laying out arguments.

Extension For ELL students, model and provide additional explanations. ELL students observe.

Skill Lesson Review

1. What do you think were the best arguments for each side of the issue in this skill lesson? *Answers will vary. Choices may be between people's right to a livelihood and animals' right to live.*

2. Which role was easier to play? Why do you think so? *Important points: Students should state a preference and explain it. Some students might be more familiar than others with animals' rights arguments.*

3. What are some other situations in which playing a role and then switching roles can help you understand a problem better? *Important*

points: Students should be encouraged to mention a variety of situations. Seeing the other person's side of the issue is helpful in any conflict.

4. What are some other ways of getting a good understanding of both sides of an issue? *Answers will vary. Research, creating charts, and writing letters from another person's perspective are possibilities.*

181

Talk About It

1. Important points: Students should choose one resource and explain why. Note: The location, climate, and natural beauty of many parts of the region draw visitors and encourage business.

2. Important points: Students should choose one policy and explain why. Note: It is important to have a varied economy in case the tourism industry becomes less profitable.

3. Important points: Students should state how important religious belief is and explain why. Note: Belief in the same religion will not guarantee a peaceable society. Sudan and Somalia are largely Muslim, but both suffered from civil wars.

4. Important points: Students should give specific reasons for their answers and choose one of the geography themes.

5. Important points: Students should state an opinion and explain it. Note: This is a strong tradition, coming out of the traditional importance of the extended family.

6. Because of its strategic location near the oil fields of Southwest Asia and alongside the shipping lanes of the Suez Canal, the Horn of Africa was important to world powers. Both the United States and the Soviet Union during the Cold War era gave money and arms to local forces fighting each other.

7. Important points: Students should make a decision and explain it. Note that Madagascar's people are mostly descended from South Asians, that there is great population and religious diversity, that they speak non-African languages, and that the plant and animal life is unique to Madagascar.

CHAPTER 9 REVIEW

Lessons Learned

LESSON 1
People and Their Environment
Unevenly populated East Africa has a variety of landforms: desert and semiarid land, the Great Rift Valley, and highlands. Most people farm or herd animals. There is diversity in population—African ethnic groups and various Asian groups.

LESSON 2
Government and Economy
Outside of Kenya and Tanzania, the region of East Africa has been torn by violent conflict since the countries' independence. The Horn of Africa has seen a series of civil wars. South of the Horn, ethnic groups have battled for control of the new countries. Kenya and Tanzania have enjoyed stable leadership which have built economic strength by encouraging farming. Tourism has added income to both countries.

LESSON 3
Society and Culture
Because of East Africa's location on the Indian Ocean and its nearness to Southwest Asia and South Asia, the region is a mix of many cultures. There is a diversity of religion, especially on the island nations of East Africa. Traditional ways, such as nomadic herding and farm village life, remain strong.

182

Talk About It

1. What do you think is East Africa's most important resource for the future? Explain why you think this.
2. Should East African nations concentrate more on tourism, or should they develop other resources? Why?
3. In your opinion, how important is a homogenous religious belief in guaranteeing a peaceable society? Explain your answer with examples from East Africa.
4. Which of the Five Themes of Geography do you think is most important in describing life in East Africa? Why?
5. Should city dwellers in East Africa be obligated to their families in rural areas? Explain.
6. How has relative location contributed to long years of unrest and bloodshed in the Horn of Africa?
7. Do you think Madagascar should be considered an African nation? Explain.

Mastering Mapwork

REGION

Use the map on page 165 to answer these questions:

1. In the region of East Africa, which national capitals are located on or near coastlines?
2. Through which political regions in East Africa do the White and Blue Nile flow?
3. Where in East Africa are the regions of national parks and game reserves located?
4. Which countries of East Africa are located in the region called the Horn of Africa?
5. Which national capitals of East Africa are located in the region known as the Sahel?
6. Which countries of East Africa are also island nations?

Mastering Mapwork

1. Dar es Salaam (Tanzania), Mogadishu (Somalia), Djibouti (Djibouti), and Asmara (Eritrea) are located on or near coastlines.

2. The White Nile and Blue Nile flow through Uganda, Ethiopia, and Sudan.

3. All national parks and game reserves are located in Kenya and Tanzania.

4. Sudan, Eritrea, Ethiopia, and Djibouti lie in the Horn of Africa.

5. Khartoum (Sudan), Asmara (Eritrea), and Djibouti (Djibouti) are located in the Sahel.

6. Comoros, Seychelles, Madagascar, and Mauritius are island regions.

Go to the Source

Analyzing Speeches as Primary Sources

The movement the British called the Mau Mau wanted the white settlers out of Kenya. In this speech, Kenyetta, the leader of the Kenyan African Union (K.A.U.) tries to distance the K.A.U. from the Mau Mau.

Read the excerpt from Kenyatta's 1952 speech "The Kenyan African Union is Not the Mau Mau" below. Answer the questions using specific references from the text.

... I want you to know the purpose of K.A.U. [Kenya African Union]. It is the biggest purpose the African has. It involves every African in Kenya and it is their mouthpiece which asks for freedom. K.A.U. is you and you are the K.A.U. If we unite now, each and every one of us, and each tribe to another, we will cause the implementation in this country of that which the European calls democracy. True democracy has no colour distinction. It does not choose between black and white. We are here in this tremendous gathering under the K.A.U. flag to find which road leads us from darkness into democracy.

In order to find it we Africans must first achieve the right to elect our own representatives. That is surely the first principle of democracy. We are the only race in Kenya which does not elect its own representatives in the Legislature and we are going to set about to rectify this situation. We feel we are dominated by a handful of others who refuse to be just. . . . we insist that we are the leaders here, and what we want we insist we get.

We want our cattle to get fat on our land so that our children grow up in prosperity; we do not want that fat removed to feed others. . . . [the] K.A.U. speaks in daylight. He who calls us the Mau Mau is not truthful. We do not know this thing Mau Mau. We want to prosper as a nation, and as a nation we demand equality, that is equal pay for equal work. Whether it is a chief, headman or labourer be needs in these days increased salary. He needs a salary that compares with a salary of a European who does equal work.

We will never get our freedom unless we succeed in this issue. We do not want equal pay for equal work tomorrow-we want it right now. Those who profess to be just must realize that this is the foundation of justice. It has never been known in history that a country prospers without equality. We despise bribery and corruption, those two words that the European repeatedly refers to. Bribery and corruption is prevalent in this country, but I am not surprised. As long as a people are held down, corruption is sure to rise and the only answer to this is a policy of equality. If we work together as one, we must succeed.

Go to the Source

Questions

1. Document type and date:
2. Author of document and author's position:
3. Who is the audience of the document?
4. List three things the author said that you think are important.
5. Why was this document written?
6. What evidence helps you know why it was written? Quote from the document.
7. List two things the document tells you about life in Kenya at the time it was written.
8. Write a question to the author that is left unanswered by the document.

East Africa   1

How to Use the Chapter Review

There are three sections in the Chapter Review: Talk About It, Mastering Mapwork, and Go to the Source. Use the Vocabulary Worksheets and the Chapter Review Worksheet in the Teacher's Resource Guide for additional reinforcement and preparation for the Chapter Assessments. The chapter and lesson reviews and the Chapter Review Worksheets are the basis of the assessment for each chapter.

Talk About It questions encourage students to speculate about the content of the chapter and are suitable for class or small-group discussion. They are not intended to be assigned for homework.

Mastering Mapwork has students apply one or more of the Five Themes of Geography to maps within the chapter.

Go to the Source activities allow students to analyze a primary source that relates to the content of the chapter. The questions and activities familiarize students with different types of primary sources and also build content-reading skills.

Go to the Source

OBJECTIVES: 4.03, 7.02, 9.01; Skills 3.05

The Mau Mau were a militant African nationalist movement active in Kenya during the 1950s. Their purpose was to remove British rule and European settlers from the Kenya. A few months after this speech, Jomo Kenyatta was arrested and found guilty of helping the Mau Mau by the colonial government in 1952. He lived in exile from 1952 to 1959.

For a link to the complete text of Jomo Kenyatta's "The Kenyan African Union is not the Mau Mau" speech visit **NCJourneys.com.**

ANSWERS:

1. Type: Speech; Date: July 26, 1952

2. Author: Jomo Kenyatta; Position: President of the Kenya Africa Union

3. The members of the Kenya Africa Union (Kenyetta might also have wanted the British to see that the K.A.U. was separate from the Mau Mau movement.)

4. Possible answers:

   a. Kenyans want to be a democracy with equality between races; b. There is bribery and corruption in Kenya; c. K.A.U. should not fight with fists but through discussion.

5. To persuade people to unite behind the K.A.U. whose purpose was to ask for freedom from the British.

6. Possible answer: Kenyetta asked several times for people to unite to improve the life of Kenyan. He said, "If we unite now, each and every one of us, and each tribe to another, we will cause implementation in this country of that which the European calls democracy." He closed the first paragraph with, "If we work together as one, we will succeed."

7. Important points: Black Kenyans did not get a fair wage when compared to other groups. Kenya had problems with criminal activity such as bribery, corruption, thieving, robbery, and murder.

8. Possible question: If the British Royal Commission doesn't listen to the requests for land reform, what will the K.A.U. do to get back the land you say God gave the Kenyans?

CHAPTER 10

Southern Africa

Social Studies Strands

Geographic Relationships
Physical features
Climate and vegetation
Population

Government and Active Citizenship

Economics and Development

Society and Culture
Ethnic traits
Language
Religion

Global Connections

Cultures and Diversity

Individual Development and Identity

North Carolina Standard Course of Study

Goal 2 The learner will assess the relationship between physical environment and cultural characteristics of selected societies and regions of Africa, Asia, and Australia.

Goal 5 The learner will evaluate the varied ways people of Africa, Asia, and Australia make decisions about the allocation and use of economic resources.

Goal 10 The learner will compare the rights and civic responsibilities of individuals in political structures in Africa, Asia, and Australia.

Goal 12 The learner will assess the influence of major religions, ethical beliefs, and values on cultures in Africa, Asia, and Australia.

Teaching & Assessment

• English Language Learner Modified Lesson Plans for this chapter are found in the Teacher Resource Guide.

• *ExamView® Assessment Suite* is provided at **NCJourneys.com.** It includes customizable assessments for all chapters. Paper tests are also available in the Teacher Resource Guide. See pages T16–T17 for information about how to use the assessments and the Scoring Guide.

Worksheets

Worksheets and answer keys are found both in the Teacher Resource Guide and at **NCJourneys.com**, including Reading Guides, Reading Strategies, Chapter Reviews, English Language Learner and others.

ACTIVITIES AND INTEGRATIONS

SOCIAL STUDIES

Activator: *The Problem We All Live With*, p. 184
★ In What Shape Is Southern Africa, p. 185
● Vegetation and Climate, p. 187
★ How it Happened, p. 192
▲ Famous South African Fold-a-Person, p. 196
Skill Lesson: Defeating Apartheid, p. 199

READING/LANGUAGE ARTS	READING/LANGUAGE ARTS OBJECTIVES
A Matter of Development, p. 184B	2.01, 2.02, 6.01
● ▲ Concentration, p. 184B	2.01
Analogies, p. 184B	2.01
Writing Prompt: Civil War in Zimbabwe, p. 184	3.01, 3.03
■ Travel Brochure of South Africa, p. 189	1.01, 2.02, 6.01
Writing Activity: "Free At Last," p. 191	1.01, 1.02
★ The Struggle Against Apartheid, p. 193	1.02, 2.01
Writing Activity: Paul Simon and South Africa, p. 198	1.02, 3.01, 6.01
● Rights of Children, p. 197	1.02, 2.01, 4.02, 5.01
Go to the Source: Analyzing National Symbols, p. 201	1.02, 2.01, 4.01

MATHEMATICS	MATHEMATICS OBJECTIVES
● Diamond Math Word Problem, p. 188	1.02, 1.03

SCIENCE	SCIENCE OBJECTIVES
Air Pollution Debate, p. 197	3.05

TECHNOLOGY	TECHNOLOGY OBJECTIVES
A Matter of Development, p. 184B	1.01, 3.01, 3.03
Ethnic Groups in Southern Africa, p. 190	3.01, 3.03, 3.11
★ Economic Development, p. 194	3.01, 3.03, 3.11

VISUAL ARTS	VISUAL ARTS OBJECTIVES
▲ Botswana Basket Design, p. 180B	2.04, 5.02, 6.01
■ Travel Brochure or Web Site of South Africa, p. 189	1.01, 6.01

CHARACTER AND VALUES EDUCATION	TRAITS
Writing Prompt: Civil War in Zimbabwe, p. 184	good citizenship good judgment
What Would You Do?, p. 188	responsibility, good judgment, good citizenship

● Basic Activities ★ Challenging Activities ▲ English Language Learner Novice ■ English Language Learner Intermediate

 **Introductory Activity**

A Matter of Development

OBJECTIVES: 5.01, 5.03, 6.01, 6.02

This activity is designed to help students understand the effect of economic development on the lives of people throughout Africa and to understand the significance of the Botswana miracle.

Use an almanac or the Internet to research data on developed and developing countries. Give students data sets for three developed nations—for example, the United States, Germany, and Japan—and data sets from the Republic of South Africa, Mozambique, and Angola. The sets should include data pertaining to such demographics as life expectancy, birth and infant mortality rates, literacy rates, GDP, trade (imports and exports), percent of arable land, percent of population engaged in manufacturing, and health care. Have students examine the data sets to determine similarities and differences in living standards among these countries. Discuss as a class what might be the relationships between economic development and governmental stability.

Extension Have students hypothesize levels of development from highest to lowest and compare their hypotheses to the HDI (Human Development Index) for each country.

For ELL students, model and provide additional explanations. ELL students will observe.

 **Culminating Activity**

Concentration

OBJECTIVES: 2.01, 7.01, 8.01

Put students in pairs. Give each pair ten "green" index cards and ten white index cards. Assign each pair ten terms from the chapter. On each green card, write a term; on each white card, write the definition and other information about the term. Do this with all the words. Now students are ready to

play the game. Each pair of students will mix up their cards and arrange them in rows, face down, with the green cards on the left and the white cards on the right. Students then take turns trying to match a term with its important information by turning cards over, two at a time, one of each color. Students go again each time they get a correct match. The student with the most correct matches wins the game. After students have had a chance to play with those cards, allow pairs to pass their sets around to different teams so that all students have a chance to play using all the important terms.

Extension ELLs should translate the words or important terms into their native language.

 **Art Activity**

Botswana Basket Design

OBJECTIVES: 4.03, 12.02

Materials big sheets of newspaper, drawing paper, tempera paint, paint brushes, pencils, glue, compass

These pieces will not function as baskets. Yet they will have a similar texture and display well. Consult your art specialist for basket weaving techniques.

Lay out a large sheet of newspaper. Beginning at one corner, tightly roll the entire sheet of newspaper diagonally. Glue the corner down (to look like a giant straw). Roll the "giant straw" tightly into a spiral. Leave no space in the center. Glue the end down.

Continue to form giant straws and adhering the corners with glue. Add each one onto your big spiraled basket design. Continue until your design is about 12 inches in diameter or larger.

To paint the designs, paint the scrolls white to keep the newsprint from showing through. Draw a 12-inch circle on drawing paper. Create geometric designs radiating out from the center. Lightly pencil out designs on basket. Fill in designs with a small brush. Note: Be patient painting this surface. Expect to paint multiple layers.

 **Analogies**

OBJECTIVES: 1.01, 2.01, 9.01

Analogies are useful to help students make associations with prior knowledge. Read the analogies aloud. Ask students to identify the relationship between the terms. As an extension, ask students to write their own analogies using key terms or places discussed in the chapter.

Kalahari : Southern Africa :: Sahara : Northern Africa (is located in)

Southern Africa : minerals :: Japan : industries (is known for)

apartheid : Republic of South Africa :: segregation : United States (was practiced in, example of racism in)

United States : Canada :: Ghana : Namibia (sequence of independence)

Lesotho : Republic of South Africa :: Vatican City : Italy (is surrounded by)

Teaching Strategies

- In this chapter, attention should be focused on the concept of apartheid and independence in the country of South Africa.

- Help prevent student confusion by carefully introducing the difference between South Africa the nation and Southern Africa the Region.

Discussion Questions

1 How long was Nelson Mandela a prisoner in South Africa? Who was elected president after him?

2 Compare and contrast the pictures at the bottom of pages 184 and 185. Relate them to similar situations in the United States.

Activator

OBJECTIVES: 8.01, 9.01, 9.03

Lead a discussion of the American civil rights movement. Ask for student input about what they know of the movement. If possible find pictures depicting segregation and integration, such as Norman Rockwell's 1964 painting *The Problem We All Live With* or a picture of Martin Luther King, Jr.'s March on Washington, and show to the students. Use this discussion as a springboard into their study of apartheid in South Africa.

Writing Prompt

OBJECTIVES: 9.01, 9.02, 9.03

Evaluative

Zimbabwe, once considered one of the more stable countries in Africa, is in the middle of civil war under a repressive regime. Zimbabwe also has one of the most famous game reserves in the world. Many people are concerned about the safety of the animals on the reserve as the civil war continues and the threat of starvation among the people heightens. Should the United States and other countries buy these animals, knowing that the money will go to this government that eliminates people who speak out against the president?

As you write or word process your paper, remember to
- clearly state your position.
- give at least three reasons and explain your reasons fully.
- give examples to support your reasons.
- write in complete sentences and paragraph form.
- organize your ideas and include an introduction and a conclusion.
- use good grammar, spelling, punctuation, and capitalization.

184

CHAPTER 10

Chapter Preview

LESSON 1
People and Their Environment
The region of Southern Africa is located on a plateau with a steep escarpment and narrow coastal plain. It has mountains, deserts, the powerful Zambezi River, and a wealth of mineral resources. Its diverse people are from Africa, Europe, and Asia.

LESSON 2
Economy and Government
Southern Africa has been a region of violent conflict. Its countries have suffered through civil wars and struggles of blacks to achieve rights under white-minority-ruled governments.

LESSON 3
Society and Culture
Blacks and whites are beginning to share their cultures. Religion in the region often mixes Christianity and traditional African beliefs.

184

Southern Africa

Nelson Mandela was prisoner number 466/64 for 27 years. Mandela spent those years in South African jails as punishment for fighting for equal treatment for black South Africans. In 1994 he became president of South Africa, Southern Africa's largest and most prosperous nation.

Though few nations of the region have experienced such remarkable changes as South Africa, others are also opening up in new ways. Southern Africa can be called the region of possibilities. Although it has been Africa's most politically troubled area for many decades, today its people are putting differences aside and planning for the future.

Nelson Mandela

Soweto Township near Johannesburg

Chapter 10

Chapter Resources

Print Resources

Nonfiction

Clark, Domini. *South Africa: The Culture.* Crabtree, 2000. ISBN 0865052379.

—. *South Africa: The Land.* Crabtree, 2000. ISBN 0865052352.

—. *South Africa. The People.* Crabtree, 2000. ISBN 0865052360.

Cooper, Floyd. *Mandela: From the Life of the South African Statesman.* Putnam Publishing Group, 1999. ISBN 0698118162.

James, R.S. *Mozambique* (Modern World Nation series). Chelsea House, 1999. ISBN 079104744X.

Klopper, Sandra. *The Zulu Kingdom* (African Civilization series). Franklin Watts, 1998. ISBN 0531202860.

Sheehan, Sean. *Zimbabwe* (Culture of the World series). Marshall Cavendish, 1996. ISBN 1854355775.

Fiction

Farmer, Nancy. *A Girl Named Disaster.* Orchard Books, 1996. ISBN 0531095398.

Gordon, Sheila. *Waiting for the Rain.* Bantam Doubleday, 1996. ISBN 0440226988.

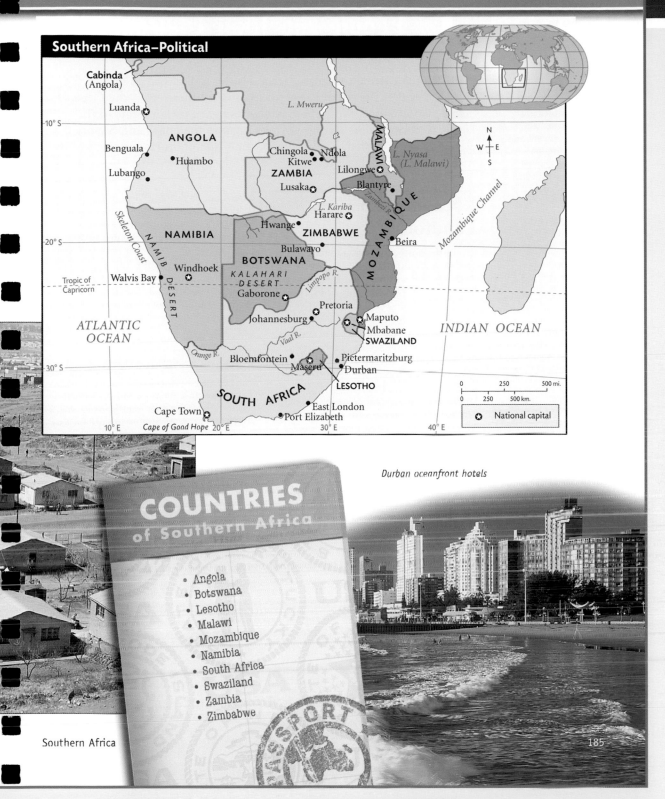

Southern Africa–Political

Cabinda
(Angola)

Luanda

L. Mweru

-10° S

ANGOLA

Benguala
Huambo

Chingola • Ndola
Kitwe
ZAMBIA
Lilongwe
Lusaka
Blantyre
L. Nyasa
(L. Malawi)

MALAWI

Lubango

Skeleton Coast

NAMIBIA
NAMIB DESERT

Windhoek

Tropic of
Capricorn
Walvis Bay

L. Kariba
Harare
Hwange
ZIMBABWE
Bulawayo

BOTSWANA
KALAHARI
DESERT
Gaborone

Zambezi R.

MOZAMBIQUE

Beira

Mozambique Channel

-20° S

ATLANTIC
OCEAN

Johannesburg

Limpopo R.
Pretoria

Maputo
Mbabane
SWAZILAND

INDIAN OCEAN

Vaal R.

Orange R.
Bloemfontein
Maseru
Pietermaritzburg
Durban

SOUTH AFRICA

LESOTHO

-30° S

Cape Town
Cape of Good Hope

East London
Port Elizabeth

10° E   20° E   30° E   40° E

0   250   500 mi.
0   250   500 km.

✪ National capital

N
W E
S

Durban oceanfront hotels

COUNTRIES
of Southern Africa

• Angola
• Botswana
• Lesotho
• Malawi
• Mozambique
• Namibia
• South Africa
• Swaziland
• Zambia
• Zimbabwe

PASSPORT

Southern Africa

185

 Map Activity

In What Shape Is Southern Africa?

NATIONAL GEOGRAPHY STANDARDS: 1, 4, 5, 7, 11, 15, 17, 18

GEOGRAPHIC THEMES: Location, Place, Human-Environmental Interaction, Movement, Region

OBJECTIVES: 1.02, 3.01

Review the Teacher Notes on page 186. Have students identify which countries of Southern Africa are landlocked: Botswana, Lesotho, Malawi, Swaziland, Zambia, and Zimbabwe. Discuss with students the five basic shapes of states (see Teacher Notes, page 186): compact, elongated, fragmented, perforated, and prorupted. Have students identify the shape of each Southern Africa nation: Angola–prorupted, Botswana–compact, Lesotho–compact, Malawi–elongated, Mozambique–elongated and prorupted, Namibia–prorupted, South Africa–perforated, Swaziland –compact, Zambia–prorupted, and Zimbabwe–compact.

Students will want to note otherwise that the only shape not found in Southern Africa is fragmented, but often when Comoros is studied with the Southern Africa subregion it is an example of fragmented. If Southern Africa is the last region emphasized on this continent, it is a good opportunity to identify the shapes of all African nations. Have students analyze dominant shapes, strengths and weakness, as well as opportunities and problems African nations face knowing these shapes of states.

Research Topics

- The difference between arbitrary boundaries and natural boundaries in Southern Africa.
- The locations and significance of the great Southern Africa deserts.
- The important Southern Africa rivers and the reasons why most have their mouths at the Indian Ocean.
- The uniqueness of these physical characteristics of South Africa: Cape Agulhas, Cape of Good Hope, Drakensberg Mountains, Great Karroo, Namib Desert, Kalahari Desert, Orange River, and Bloemfontein/Cape Town/Pretoria.

Naidoo, Beverley. *Chain of Fire.* Harper-Collins, 1990. ISBN 0064404684. protest.

Naidoo, Beverly. *Journey to Jo'Burg.* HarperCollins, 1988. ISBN 0064402371.

Naidoo, Beverley. *No Turning Back: A Novel of South Africa.* HarperTrophy, 1999. ISBN 0064407497.

Rochman, Hazel, ed. *Somehow Tenderness Survives: Stories of Southern Africa.* HarperCollins, 1990. ISBN 0064470636.

Magazine Back Issues

South Africa. Cobblestone Publishing Company (new issue of FACES magazine in 2001–02).

Audiovisual

Destination: Lesotho. Peace Corps, 1996. (22 min.) ISBN 0160634032.

Web Sites

Go to **NCJourneys.com** for links to the following Web sites:

OBJECTIVES: 2.01, 2.03, 5.01

Discussion Questions

1 What is ironic about the name the Cape of Good Hope? What name did sailors give to the same cape?

2 What is a landlocked country? What would be some special problems for a country that is landlocked? What kinds of relationships would it need to have with its neighbors? Why? Name a landlocked country studied last year.

3 What would happen in your community if it had to depend on another community for the import and export of all of its goods?

4 Why has Africa been nicknamed the Plateau Continent? What term is used to describe a plateau in South Africa and Zimbabwe?

5 Describe the Great Escarpment. What mountains are included in it?

Caption Answer

Much of the region is landlocked. Mozambique has a long coastline. The Namib Desert is on the western coast and the Kalahari is farther inland.

Teacher Notes

State Shapes

Shape is a characteristic of a state that can affect its well-being. In geographic terms, ideally a state should be a circle with the capital located in the center so that all areas can be reached with the least effort (assuming a flat topography). Several examples of a *compact* state—closest to this ideal—are Poland, Uruguay, Cambodia, and Zimbabwe.

A *prorupted* state is often compact with one or two extensions of territory that give the state access to a river or sea, or, in the case of Afghanistan, serves to separate two competing powers. Other examples are Myanmar (Burma), Thailand, and Namibia—its Caprivi Strip gave the German colonial power access to the Zambezi River.

The least efficient shape is an *elongated* state because many areas are

KEY IDEAS

- Southern Africa is a plateau region with a steep escarpment and several mountain ranges. The climate is dry on the west coast. On the east coast it is mild to hot and moist.

- Southern Africa is rich in water and mineral resources.

- Southern Africa is populated with many native African ethnic groups, as well as people descended from the Dutch, British, and Asians. Many people are moving to the large cities of the region.

KEY TERMS

Afrikaners
Great Escarpment

To the east of Southern Africa lies the Indian Ocean and to the west lies the Atlantic Ocean. At the southern tip is the Cape of Good Hope. Portuguese navigators gave it that name in the 1400s to cheer sailors during voyages around the continent. Sailors were not easily fooled. They called it the Cape of Storms because of its strong winds and slashing rains.

Location and Landforms

To the north, the region shares borders with Tanzania and the Democratic Republic of the Congo. Southern Africa has two countries with unusual locations. Lesotho, a country slightly larger than the state of Connecticut, is located entirely inside South Africa. Swaziland is almost completely surrounded by South Africa. On a map, they look like small islands in a sea of South Africa.

Six nations of the region are landlocked and depend on railroads and ports in other countries for trade. Mozambique has a long coastline on the Indian Ocean. Malawi and Zimbabwe export goods through Mozambique's ports (see map, page 185).

Africa has been called the Plateau Continent, and much of Southern Africa is plateau, mainly covered by grassland (see map, page 17). In South Africa and Zimbabwe, plateaus are called velds. Lesotho is located on the highest part of the plateau, up against the Drakensberg Mountains. Some peaks are above 10,000 feet (3,000 m).

Plateaus and Mountains

The plateau is rimmed by the **Great Escarpment,** a steep wall of rock often thousands of feet high that drops to the coastal plain. Some mountains are part of the escarpment. They include the Drakensbergs in South Africa.

Plateaus of sparse grassland and dry mountains are the major landforms of Southern Africa. **What are other land features of Southern Africa?**

Chapter 10

isolated and remote from the capital. It costs more money to keep all areas in touch with the core political area. Mozambique, Norway, and Chile are good examples of this type of state.

A *fragmented* state can be an island nation such as Indonesia, the Philippines, or Malaysia, or a combination of a mainland and island nation, such as Equatorial Guinea. Fragmentation makes it harder to impose centralized control.

A *perforated* state completely surrounds a territory it does not rule. South Africa is the best example—it completely surrounds Lesotho. The surrounded territory is called an *enclave.* San Marino and Vatican City are two enclaves that perforate Italy. An *exclave* is a territory of a state located outside of the state's borders. An example of this is Cabinda, which is an exclave of Angola.

The Namib Desert is one of two in the region.
Why is Namibia called the Skeleton Coast?

A Mostly Dry Region

Southern Africa has two deserts—the Namib, on the western coast in Namibia, and the Kalahari, which is farther inland and covers most of Botswana. Although not as fiery hot as the Sahara, the Namib is just as dry. The Kalahari is a scrub desert.

Namibia's dry western coast has a ghostly name. It is called the Skeleton Coast because of the the skulls and bones of humans and animals that sometimes surface when the sands of the Namib Desert shift. Long ago, storms at sea and dangerous currents caused sailing ships to run aground. Unlucky shipwreck survivors soon died from lack of water.

The eastern coast of the region has a mild to hot subtropical climate with high rainfall (see map, page 35). On this coast, altitude affects climate. In the Drakensberg Mountains, temperatures are lower and rainfall is higher than on the plateau. West of these mountains, the climate becomes much drier, with savanna giving way to desert.

The southern tip of the continent has a mild Mediterranean climate like that of the northwestern coast of Africa. It has cool, wet winters and warm, dry summers.

Southern Africa

These areas are two of the cooler places in a generally hot climate.

The region's northern countries have a tropical climate similar to the climate in parts of West Africa and all of Central Africa. Winters on the savanna in Southern Africa can be cool. North of Namibia, closer to the Equator, Angola (an·GOHL·ah) contains rain forests.

Rivers

Southern Africa has several river systems. The Zambezi River forms the border between Zambia (ZAHM·bih·ah) and Zimbabwe. Five countries—Angola, Mozambique, Zimbabwe, Zambia, and Malawi—have rivers that flow into the Zambezi.

The Zambezi is Southern Africa's longest river at 1,643 miles (2,645 km). It flows down the escarpment with enormous power. Two huge dams, the Kariba (ka·REE·ba) and Cahora Bassa, use that power to supply electricity for Zambia, Zimbabwe, Mozambique, and South Africa. In building the Kariba Dam, engineers created Lake Kariba, which is 175 miles (282 km) long.

The Limpopo River winds along the northern border of South Africa. The Limpopo and Zambezi Rivers flow into the Indian Ocean. The Orange River on the border between Namibia and South Africa empties into the Atlantic Ocean. South Africa receives electricity from several large dams along the Orange River.

The Zambezi River is the region's longest river. **What are the region's climates?**

187

Discussion Questions

1 Name and describe the two Southern Africa deserts.

2 How do mountains affect the climate of Southern Africa?

3 Where would you predict that most of the agriculture in the region would occur?

4 What might explain the similar climate of the northwest region and the southern tip of Africa?

5 What are some ways that the Zambezi River benefits Zambia and Zimbabwe?

6 Dams provide electricity for power. In what other ways are dams useful? What are some famous dams around the world?

Caption Answer

Skulls and bones of humans and animals sometimes surface when the sands of the desert shift.

Caption Answer

A dry western coast, an eastern coast with mild to hot subtropical climate with rainfall, cooler temperatures in the Drakensberg Mountains. Temperatures are lower and rainfall is higher on the plateau. The southern tip has a mild Mediterranean climate. Northern countries have tropical climates.

Writing Activity

Vegetation and Climate

OBJECTIVES: 1.01, 1.02, 1.03

Using an atlas or the Internet, have students make their own vegetation map of Southern Africa. Select two or three cities in different parts of Southern Africa and make climographs comparing the cities.

Extension For ELL students, model and provide additional explanations.

Background Information

Botswana's Wildlife

In Botswana it is the cattle ranchers' fences, not the poachers, that threaten the zebras and other wildlife. Although almost 40 percent of Botswana's land is set aside for national parks, the threat to wildlife results from the harsh, dry lands on which the animals live. Animals here must migrate long distances to reach food and water. During the dry season, they move close to rivers and other water sources. When the wet season starts, they return to fresh grazing areas created by the rains. Cattle fences have disrupted migration patterns. Officials say the fences are needed to protect cattle from diseases carried by animals coming from neighboring Namibia. Cattle are one of Botswana's major exports, and they must be disease-free for sale in Europe. Opponents of the fences warn that if wildlife cannot survive, tourism will dry up.

Discussion Questions

1 Discuss the natural resources of Southern Africa. How do they compare to the resources in other regions of Africa?

2 What factors contributed to the large settlement of Europeans in this region?

3 What factors determine where people settle? What nation in Southern Africa is the only one to have a highly urban society?

Gold, platinum, chromium, and other gems

 Map Activity

Diamond Math Word Problem

OBJECTIVES: 3.01, 13.03

A diamond merchant purchases diamonds weighing 20 carats. If diamonds sell for $250 per carat, how much will the broker be paid?

Answer $5,000

Extension Assist ELL students by setting up the problem for them.

Minerals and Other Natural Resources

Southern Africa is rich in mineral resources. Its mineral wealth includes gold, platinum, chromium, and precious gems, especially diamonds. The Copper Belt straddles the border of the Democratic Republic of the Congo and Zambia (see map, page 61).

South Africa has the world's largest reserves of gold, platinum, and chromium. Zimbabwe has huge reserves of platinum, chrome, and asbestos. Namibia's mineral wealth includes uranium, lead, and zinc. The region also has major energy sources. Angola contains oil. South Africa, Zambia, and Zimbabwe have coal.

What would YOU do?

You are a zookeeper. You need African animals for your exhibits. A hunter in Southern Africa wants to supply you with animals from the wild. Another zoo can supply you with the same species, but they are not wild. What would you do? Why?

Africa's Largest Population Centers

Slightly smaller in size than Angola, South Africa, in terms of population, wealth, and influence, is the giant of the region. It has most of the region's richest farmland, the best weather, the largest treasure chest of minerals, the biggest cities, the finest roads and railroads, and the most factories (see map, page 20).

Cape Town, Johannesburg, Durban, and Pretoria (pre·TOR·ee·ah) all have more than 1 million people. Johannesburg grew after the discovery of nearby goldfields. Another heavily settled area is Zambia's Copper Belt.

A little more than half of Southern Africa's population now lives in cities. The region's urban growth rate is twice that of the world. In South Africa, almost three out of every five people live in cities. Most people migrate to the cities due to drought or in search of work.

A miner uses heavy equipment to dig for diamonds in Namibia. **What other natural resources are found in Southern Africa?**

188

Chapter 10

LESSON 1 REVIEW

Fact Follow-Up Answers

1. Southern Africa lies west of the Indian Ocean and east of the Atlantic Ocean. At the southern tip is the Cape of Good Hope. To the north, the region borders Tanzania and the Democratic Republic of the Congo.

2. Much of Southern Africa is plateau, but at the Great Escarpment the plateau drops thousands of feet to a narrow coastal plain. The Great Escarpment also includes mountains, such as the Drakensberg Mountains. Important rivers in the region are the Zambezi, the Limpopo, and the Orange.

3. The Great Escarpment is a steep wall that divides the plateau from the coastal plain. The rivers of the region, the Zambezi, the Limpopo, and the Orange, flow down the escarpment with enormous power and produce electricity. It is important for that reason, although it hinders movement to the interior.

4. Southern Africa contains many ethnic groups, many with their own languages. For example, 27 different languages are spoken among the 1.5 million people of Namibia.

People from Many Continents

Three small nations—Lesotho, Swaziland, and Botswana—were established as homelands for distinctive ethnic groups. Each of these countries claims one language of its own. Other Southern Africa nations have a variety of ethnic groups. Many languages are spoken in those countries. For example, 27 different languages are spoken among the 2 million people of Namibia.

The San and the Khoikhoi (KOI·koi) peoples live in the deserts of Namibia and Botswana. They speak languages of the Khoisan (KOI·sahn) group, which uses distinctive clicking sounds.

South Africa is home to many people of European descent. Its white population is larger than the total of all the other nations south of the Sahara combined. Some of these white settlers, known as *Afrikaners,* are descendants of Dutch settlers who came to the continent in the 1600s. Many of them speak a language called Afrikaans, which also comes from Dutch.

Others are British settlers who came in the early 1800s. Later, South Africa became a British colony. Zimbabwe, another former British colony, also has many settlers of British descent. Namibia, a German colony before World War I, today has many people of German descent.

Many Asians, especially from India, also live in Southern Africa. Most are descendants of people who came in the late 1800s to work on British sugar plantations. Many came as contract workers, and stayed after their contracts ended, becoming traders and shopkeepers. Mohandas K. Gandhi, an Indian you will read about, lived in South Africa. His experience there defending Asians against abuse helped him lead India to freedom.

South Africa describes itself as the "rainbow nation" because of its ethnic diversity.

Young Afrikaners in Pretoria, South Africa, are descendants of Dutch settlers. **What other Europeans have settled in the region?**

LESSON 1 REVIEW

Fact Follow-Up
1. What is the relative location of Southern Africa?
2. Describe the landforms of Southern Africa.
3. What is the Great Escarpment? Why is it important?
4. Describe the language and ethnic diversity of Southern Africa.

Talk About It
1. What are some disadvantages for Southern Africa in having large populations that speak a variety of languages?
2. How would Southern Africa be affected if the Zambezi River dried up? Explain.

Talk About It Answers
1. The language variety makes it difficult to communicate and cooperate within and among different nations in the region.
2. Important points: Students should describe any effects in detail. Note: The Zambezi River offers access to the Indian Ocean and provides hydro-electric power. Transportation and electricity would be lost.

Discussion Questions

1 What feature unifies the small nations of Lesotho, Swaziland, and Botswana? Does it compare to newly formed nations in central Europe?

2 What is a click dialect, and where is it found?

3 How does the ethnic composition of South Africa differ from the rest of Southern Africa?

4 People from what two European nations settled in South Africa? Which group came first?

5 What European country once ruled Namibia? Why do you think its rule ended after World War I?

6 What other group of people live in South Africa, and who was a legal defender for them? Can you determine why Gandhi was living in South Africa?

Caption Answer

British settlers, German settlers, and some Asians, mostly from India

Activity

Travel Brochure or Web Site of South Africa

OBJECTIVES: 2.01, 3.03, 5.01

Have students design a travel brochure or Web site emphasizing South Africa. Tell them to use bright colors and creative ideas. The project should include a map of Southern Africa with a key with color codes for the countries. Label the capitals for each country. List the major lakes and rivers. Identify two deserts—the Namib and the Kalahari. Include the Drakensberg Mountains on the map, and a list of natural resources. The front should feature an eye-catching image that is appropriate for this region. On the back section of the travel brochure, write a brief report inviting visitors to see the sites and people of Southern Africa. Emphasize what has changed and what ancient traditions people might want to see.

Extension For novice ELL students, model and provide additional explanations. Good activity for ELLs without the report.

OBJECTIVES: 5.01, 10.01, 10.04

Discussion Questions

1 What was significant about May 1994 in Soweto, South Africa?

2 Why do you think black South Africans waited so long for the privilege to vote? Would you be willing to do that? Do we take voting for granted in our country? What suggestions do you have to change the attitudes of people in the United States?

3 What additional problems would there be for African nations that gained their independence through war?

4 Name three nations in Southern Africa that have stable and well-established democracies?

5 What two countries were Portuguese colonies until 1974.

6 Under what circumstances or for what cause would you be willing to stand in line for hours? (Discuss whether Americans are superficial in what we value.)

Caption Answer

White leaders did not want to grant independence. Africans wanted it enough to fight for it.

Math Activity

Ethnic Groups in Southern Africa

OBJECTIVES: 2.01, 3.01, 5.01

Students will research the following ethnic groups: Mbuti people of Central Africa and San or Khoikhoi Bushmen of the Kalahari Desert. Students may work in pairs or small groups. After they have gathered enough information, have them construct a poster chart or database to compare the ways each group has adapted to its "harsh" environments.

Extension Use ELL-friendly Web site for research and peer tutor as needed to complete this activity.

	Mbuti	Khoikhoi
Environment		
Shelters		
Clothing		
Foods(what) (how)		
Tools		
Beliefs/ Values		

KEY IDEAS

- Southern Africa was a region of violent conflict. Winning independence has taken some countries many years and many lives.

- South Africa's policy of apartheid segregated the races until 1991.

- South Africa has great mineral wealth, but it is paying the costs of apartheid because so many black Africans live in poverty.

KEY TERMS

apartheid

Soldiers cross a repaired bridge during the Angola Civil War. **Why did violence come before independence for several nations in Southern Africa?**

LESSON 2 Economy and Government

In May 1994, at 4:00 A.M. in the former black township of Soweto, South Africa, lines were already forming at voting sites. For millions of black South Africans, it was the first time they had ever voted. Those too sick or weak to walk were carried to vote by relatives or friends.

At some polling places, lines stretched for more than a mile, and voters waited for three or four hours to cast their ballots. When reporters asked one voter if he was tired of waiting, he replied "I've waited all these years, I'm ready to wait a few more hours for this incredible thing to happen."

Moving Toward Stability

Many nations in Southern Africa—including Botswana and Namibia—have stable and well-established democracies. In 1994, Malawi ousted Africa's longest-serving dictator and returned to multiparty elections. Throughout the rest of the region, peace is replacing war. There is the promise of more democratic governments.

Many British colonies in Southern Africa gained their independence in the 1960s, but others had to fight hard for their freedom into the 1990s. Five Southern African countries have similar histories. Angola, Mozambique, Zimbabwe, Namibia, and South Africa all had large populations of white settlers from Europe who resisted majority rule by black Africans. In all of these countries, civil war or violent conflict came before independence.

Angola and Mozambique

Angola and Mozambique were Portuguese colonies until 1974. Rebels fought Portuguese soldiers for many years to gain their freedom. Independence finally came after a military takeover in Portugal brought new leaders to power. Soon after, civil wars broke out in both countries. The wars lasted more than 15 years. Thousands of citizens fled the countries. Angola and Mozambique are slowly rebuilding.

190

Zimbabwe

Zimbabwe was originally Rhodesia, a British colony named after British imperialist Cecil Rhodes. He thought colonies would bring greater glory for the British. By 1964, the United Kingdom was willing to let go of Rhodesia, but white settlers resisted.

The British demanded that the white-led government give black Rhodesians political rights. The government refused. It declared Rhodesia independent. Rebel groups fought to overthrow Rhodesia's white government until 1980, when white government leaders stepped down.

A black majority government was formed. Rhodesia was renamed Zimbabwe. Today, it is a parliamentary democracy in name only. Robert Mugabe has ruled since 1980 and dominates the political system. Although both blacks and whites worked together to build the nation during the two decades after independence, tensions have resurged.

In 2000, President Mugabe put into place a new land redistribution system. This caused an economic collapse. Many white farmers fled the country. Chaos and violence continue today.

Namibia

Namibia was first a German colony. After Germany's defeat in World War I, it was given to South Africa. The white-ruled government treated Namibia as its own colony. It squashed any efforts by Namibians to become independent.

After World War II, the United Nations took Namibia from South African control. South Africa continued to fight with Namibians for more than 30 years. Finally, South Africa agreed to Namibia's freedom. In 1990, Namibia was the last African colony to become independent.

South Africa

The road to majority rule in South Africa has been long and hard. The Dutch were the first settlers in South Africa, founding Cape Town in 1652. Their descendants were called Boers (meaning "farmers" in Dutch). Later, they were known as Afrikaners.

The British arrived about 150 years later. They and the Boers fought two wars—the Boer Wars—to gain control of the land and rule the African majority. The last war ended in 1902 with a British victory. They worked out an agreement to allow both groups of white settlers to share control of the government.

Eight years later, the British formed the Union of South Africa, a self-governing territory (part of the British empire). It became independent in 1931.

Black South Africans had no voice in government. They could not vote or run for office. South Africa's political races were mostly contests between whites of British descent and Afrikaners. The Afrikaner population grew. In 1948, they established an Afrikaner-only government.

Apartheid At this point, Afrikaner leaders made *apartheid* (segregation of the races) law. All South Africans were assigned to one of four racial groups: black Africans; whites or Europeans; "coloreds," or people of mixed race; and Asians.

Apartheid ensured white-minority control. The government assigned each group its own homeland, or area to live. Whites, although only 13 percent of the population, controlled almost all of the most fertile land and mineral resources.

Thousands of apartheid laws banned blacks or mixed-race South Africans from sharing the same churches, buses, beaches, or park benches with whites. They could not vote or join political parties. Their children went to separate and inferior schools and hospitals.

Apartheid ended in 1993. The white minority party and black African parties, led by the African National Congress, agreed to write a new constitution. Under it, members of all races could vote and all segregated homelands were abolished.

These workers are pulling down a "whites only" sign at a Durban, South Africa, beach in 1989. The city's council had voted to open all of its beaches to all race groups. **What was apartheid?**

WORD ORIGINS

Apartheid literally means "apartness." It is used to refer to the body of laws and policies that once segregated the races in South Africa.

Southern Africa   191

Discussion Questions

1 Describe the changes Rhodesia made after independence.

2 What effects do you think colonialism had on racism?

3 Which South African countries did not get their freedom until the 1990s?

4 How did the British and the Boers resolve their conflict?

5 How did the colony change after the Boer War ended?

6 How did the policy of apartheid compare with the situation of African Americans in this country, especially before the Civil Rights Act of 1964?

7 Do you think it would be easier to overcome a social custom of segregation or a legal system of apartheid? Why?

Caption Answer

Segregation of the races

Writing Activity

"Free at Last"

 **OBJECTIVES:** 9.02, 9.03, 9.04

Have students write or word process a paragraph in the first person in which they express the feelings black South Africans must have felt when they were given the right to vote in the election of 1994.

Alternate ELL Activity Draw or create a collage or poster depicting the 1994 vote in South Africa. Can find pictures on internet using ELL-friendly Web sites.

It's a Fact

Southern Africa

■ More than 3 million slaves were shipped from Angola, once called Portuguese West Africa, to Brazil, Portugal's South American colony, during the days of slave trading.

■ Nearly half of Swaziland's territory is owned by nonresident Europeans.

■ Botswana is now the leading producer of quality diamonds. It has set aside 20 percent of the land as national parks or game reserves.

■ Most of Lesotho is mountainous. Its lowest elevation is only slightly less than one mile high.

■ Malawi established the first freshwater national park in an effort to protect cichlids (a tropical fish).

■ Mozambique is one of the world's leading producers of cashews.

■ Namibia's constitution was written under the supervision of United Nations monitors. Namibians consider it their most precious possession.

■ South Africa is the only African country with coastlines on two oceans. While South Africa possesses an abundance of most vital minerals, it does not have any oil.

■ Zambia is the leading producer of copper, but its reserves are being depleted at an alarming rate.

■ Some Biblical scholars believe Zimbabwe is the location of Ophir, the site of King Solomon's mines.

Activity

How It Happened

OBJECTIVES: 7.01, 8.01, 9.01, 9.03

Put students into cooperative groups. Have them research the injustices against African Americans before the civil rights movement and against black South Africans before apartheid was abolished in 1993. Information should be discussed, listed, and displayed. Have groups brainstorm changes in the way African Americans have been treated since the civil rights movement. Have groups present their opinions for discussion. Cooperative groups then are to predict changes in the manner black South Africans will be treated in the future. Based on the research and class discussions, have students write a five-paragraph essay about the outcome of the abolishment of apartheid.

ELL Teaching Tips

Encourage Participation

Encourage ELLs to participate in class. Most ELL students are hesitant to speak even when they know the correct answer. Give them nonverbal opportunities to respond to the questions.

The Struggle Against Apartheid

EYEWITNESS TO HISTORY

Steven Biko, Desmond Tutu, and Nelson Mandela peacefully tried for years to end South Africa's apartheid—the segregation of the races. When the white government refused, violent protests followed. The government killed, jailed, or banned almost all black leaders and their followers.

By 1986, more than 600 anti-apartheid groups in South Africa had joined together to work for change. The world's nations also put heavy pressure on the white government of South Africa to change.

In 1989, F.W. de Klerk (right) was selected as the country's leader. Although de Klerk was an Afrikaner, he let the white minority know that the time had come to end apartheid and to work with the black majority. One of his first acts was to release from prison black national leader Nelson Mandela.

Nelson Mandela before he was jailed for 27 years

192

Chapter 10

Name Origin

Angola Portuguese pronunciation of the Bantu word that means region.

Botswana "The people who speak Tswana," the official language.

Lesotho Named after the major language, "sesotho."

Malawi Local name meaning "flaming waters." Refers to the sun's reflection on Lake Nyassa.

Mozambique Mispronunciation of a local word meaning "boats together in the harbor."

Namibia Named for the Namib (Desert) a Khoikhoi word meaning desert or "land of no people."

South Africa Dutch name for the location.

Swaziland Named for the ethnic group who settled there.

Zambia Formerly Northern Rhodesia, named for the Zambezi River, or "Great Water."

Zimbabwe Formerly Southern Rhodesia, named after the ancient civilization, "dwelling place of the chief."

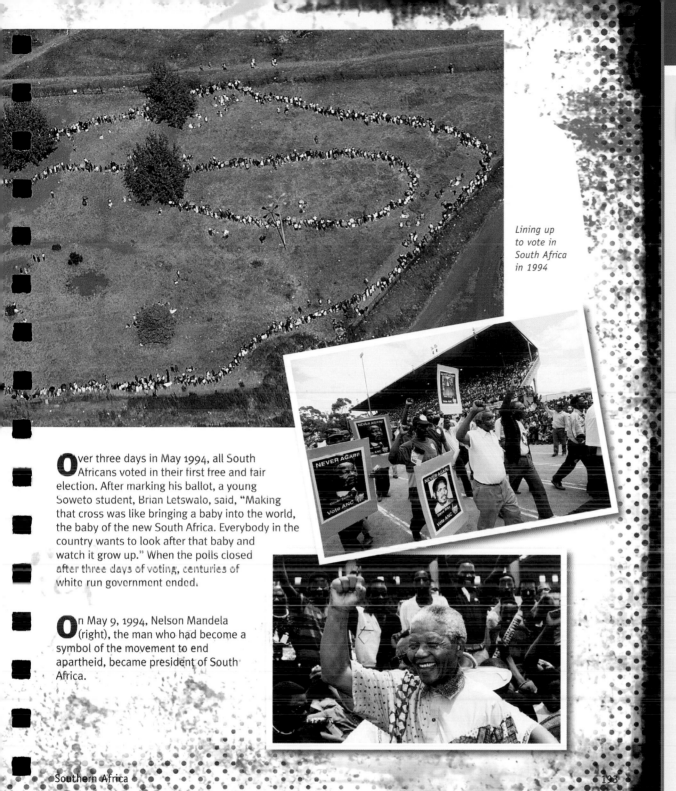

Lining up to vote in South Africa in 1994

The Struggle Against Apartheid

OBJECTIVES: 8.01, 9.03, 10.01, 10.04

To give students a personal glimpse of the life of Nelson Mandela, read *Mandela from the Life of the South African Statesman* by Floyd Cooper (Putnam, 1996. ISBN 0399229426.).

After reading the eyewitness account and hearing the story, ask students to make a list of obstacles that were overcome by Nelson Mandela and to brainstorm attributes that they think enabled him to succeed and overcome his obstacles. Ask students to write about their own personal obstacles and if they could employ some of Nelson Mandela's attributes to help them. Because of the privacy of this assignment, it shouldn't be shared unless students are willing to share.

Over three days in May 1994, all South Africans voted in their first free and fair election. After marking his ballot, a young Soweto student, Brian Letswalo, said, "Making that cross was like bringing a baby into the world, the baby of the new South Africa. Everybody in the country wants to look after that baby and watch it grow up." When the polls closed after three days of voting, centuries of white run government ended.

On May 9, 1994, Nelson Mandela (right), the man who had become a symbol of the movement to end apartheid, became president of South Africa.

Southern Africa

193

 Background Information

South Africa

More than ten years after the end of apartheid, South Africans are still facing the challenges of remaking a society in which a majority of the people were kept poor and uneducated for most of its history. South Africa's political leaders already have many achievements to point to. Political violence has greatly declined. Millions more people now have access to clean water, electricity, and telephones.

The country has a new constitution, and its legislators have tackled such difficult issues as women's rights, smoking and tobacco advertising, and racial inequalities. Serious problems remain. The most pressing are crime and unemployment. The country's economy has grown slowly, and its crime rate is among the highest in the world.

Teacher Notes

Homelands

Beginning in the 1950s, South Africa's government divided the black population into ethnic groups and assigned each group to a "homeland," also referred to as a bantustan. Ten of these territories were eventually established: Bophuthatswana, Ciskei, Gazankulu, KaNgwane, KwaNde-bele, KwaZulu, Lebowa, Qwaqwa, Transkei, and Venda. By the end of the 1970s, all of the homelands had become nominally self-governing. In actuality, they were entirely dependent on the national government and incapable of sustaining the 75 percent of the country's population assigned to live there. Most blacks continued to live outside of homelands in segregated townships. The vast majority of those who lived in homelands commuted to white areas as part of an enormous migrant labor force.

Caption Answer

It was peaceful.

Caption Answer

Many have low-paying jobs with many family members to support. There is still a gap between whites and blacks in job skills, education, and opportunity. The nation must bring more opportunity to all its citizens to stay stable and strong.

Activity

Economic Development

OBJECTIVES: 5.01, 5.03, 6.01, 6.02

Have students research and complete the chart (right) on countries in Southern Africa.

Using the information from the chapter and resources like almanacs on the Internet, students should put the countries into two categories: developed and developing. Students should support their answers in a class discussion.

Technology Extension

Students can create a database with their information and sort the countries based on the results of their research.

Extension Assign a peer tutor to assist ELL students. Have novice and intermediate define developed and developing in their native language using a native language dictionary. Do not expect ELL students to participate in the class discussion.

Regional Economies

For many decades most countries of the region were united by their hatred of apartheid in South Africa. Now that apartheid has ended, many hope that all the nations of the region can work together to reduce barriers to trade.

Africa's Economic Giant

South Africa has the region's strongest economy. More than one-fourth of all the goods and services and more than half of all electricity produced in Africa comes from South Africa. South Africa also has the continent's most varied economy.

Mining of metals, minerals, and precious gems provides thousands of jobs for South Africans and workers from other parts of the region. Most of the jobs are low paying. Working and living conditions are poor, but workers send home enough money to support their families. In a tiny country like Lesotho, money sent home by workers is a large part of the country's overall income.

Most of the world's gold and many of its diamonds come from South Africa. These and other minerals make up more than two-thirds of its earnings.

The outlook for South Africa's economic future is bright. It has good transportation and communication systems, skilled workers, and a varied economy with farms, factories, and a growing tourist industry. Most important, it also has peace and a stable government. Many foreign companies are returning to South Africa. Most had left the country as a protest against apartheid.

In 1999, South Africa peacefully transferred power to President Thabo Mbeki in its second national election. The biggest challenge that South Africa's leaders face is finding ways to reduce the gap between whites and blacks in education, income, and opportunity. After being denied basic rights for so long, many South Africans today are still very poor. Despite being the region's strongest economy, South Africa's unemployment rate is almost 26 percent. Some black townships lack clean water, good roads, housing, and schools.

When he took office, President Mbeki vowed to promote economic growth and foreign investment. South Africa is slowly making progress in spite of challenges.

Other nations of the region are hoping that South Africa will succeed. Foreign sanctions against the former apartheid regime prevented most South African companies from investing their profits outside the country. Now South Africa's stable government and strong economy are influencing investing in neighboring nations again. However, the future is still fragile. Huge inequalities of wealth,

Thabo Mbeki became president of South Africa in 1999 and was re-elected in 2004. **Why was the transfer of power from Mandela to Mbeki significant?**

The poor of South Africa build shelters near large cities, such as this camp near Durban. **Why are so many South Africans poor? How is this a challenge to the nation?**

Country	Economic Activities	Type of Gov't/Leader	GNP	Literacy Rate	Life Expectancy
South Africa					
Lesotho					
Swaziland					
Namibia					
Botswana					
Malawi					
Zambia					
Mozambique					
Angola					
Zimbabwe					

dwindling resources, rapid population growth, high rates of illiteracy and disease, and political and ethnic divisions continue to plague Southern Africa.

Other Economies

Some of South Africa's neighbors also have many resources and enjoy prosperity. The coast of Namibia is occupied by the Namib Desert. Southern Namibia has huge sheep ranches. These stand in sharp contrast to the villages and small farms that are found everywhere in the northern part of the country. Between the lands of these two agricultural regions are copper, zinc, and lead mines. Diamonds are dug from southern mines.

Angola suffered from a civil war backed by the former Soviet Union and the United States. United Nations peacekeepers occupied Angola from 1994 until 1999. The war ended in 2002, and Angola is now slowly rebuilding. Oil provides much income.

Zimbabwe exports a variety of minerals—copper, asbestos, and chromium—that are dug from large deposits found in its territory. It also has tobacco, cotton, tea, and sugar to sell. Some nations, such as Lesotho and Swaziland, have few resources. Workers from these countries seek employment in South Africa.

Building Regional Ties

As in Africa's other regions, Southern Africa's nations are building their economies by trading more with one another. A regional agency, the Southern African Development Community, encourages economic cooperation in everything from electricity to tourism. Southern African nations hope to have created a free trade area by 2008.

These people are cleaning fish caught along the Skeleton Coast of Namibia. **What are some of the region's other resources?**

Discussion Questions

1 What is the greatest challenge facing South Africa's future leaders? Does the United States have similar challenges within our society? Explain.

2 What is the outlook for the new government's success? Within South Africa, which economic group stands to gain the most from this success?

3 In order to have a higher standard of living, do you think it is important for a country to have natural resources? Why?

 **Caption Answer**

Minerals, oil, crops, and animals

LESSON 2 REVIEW

Fact Follow-Up

1. What are some political similarities and differences among the nations of Southern Africa?
2. Which countries were Portuguese colonies?
3. Who are Afrikaners?
4. Who are F.W. de Klerk and Nelson Mandela? Why is each important?
5. What are the economic foundations of South Africa? of other nations of Southern Africa?

Talk About It

1. Which nation of the region do you think has confronted the greatest political challenges? Explain your answer.
2. Which is more important in the nation of South Africa: the physical or the cultural characteristics of place? Explain.
3. Describe the apartheid policy and its effects on South Africa.
4. Could Nelson Mandela be appropriately called the "father of his country"? Explain your answer.

LESSON 2 REVIEW

Fact Follow-Up Answers

1. Many nations in Southern Africa, including Botswana and Namibia, have well-established democracies. Others working toward it. Many former British colonies gained independence in the 1960s. Others had to fight hard for freedom into the 1990s. Angola, Mozambique, Zimbabwe, Namibia, and South Africa had populations of white European settlers who resisted majority rule by black Africans. Civil war or violent conflict came before independence.
2. Angola and Mozambique were Portuguese colonies until 1974.
3. Afrikaners are descendants of the Dutch settlers of South Africa.
4. De Klerk was South Africa's appointed leader in 1989. He told the white minority that they must end apartheid. He freed Mandela, who had been in jail 27 years. Mandela became the first president of South Africa in an election in which all South Africans could vote.
5. South Africa's strong economy includes farming, industry, tourism, and mining. It still must close the economic gap between Africans and Europeans. Zimbabwe and Namibia export minerals. Angola's government and wars have crippled its economy. Lesotho and Swaziland have few resources.

Talk About It Answers

1. Important points: Students should focus on political challenges. South Africa sucessfully faced the challenge of ending apartheid.
2. Important points: Students should select one of the two. Note: The cultural characteristics have produced divisions in areas with common physical characteristics.
3. Apartheid was South Africa's official policy of separating the races. It ensured that the white minority would control the nation. Apartheid denied blacks or mixed-race South Africans the right to share the same churches, buses, movie theaters, beaches, and park benches with whites. Their children went to separate and inferior schools, hospitals, and health clinics. They could not vote or join political parties.
4. Important points: Mandela's leadership made possible the end of apartheid, which led to democratic majority rule in South Africa. He was the first black African president of the nation.

OBJECTIVES: 10.04, 12.01

Discussion Questions

1 How have the people of South Africa managed to combine Christianity with the indigenous religions?

2 How has the church adapted to the needs of the people in South Africa? Why do you think the church did this?

Caption Answer

Christianity

Activity

Famous South African Fold-a-Person

OBJECTIVES: 8.01

Materials blank 8½-inch by 11-inch sheets of paper; scissors; glue or transparent tape

Give students a sheet of paper to fold into sixteenths. Students will label the squares "A" through "P" (see diagram, below). Cut on the vertical right and left side fold line between B and C and between F and G. Fold sections A and B together toward center vertical fold line. Fold sections E and F toward the center vertical fold line, forming a coat on this person. The upper edges of A and E fold down diagonally to form collar on this person's coat. Cut out sections C and D to be one arm and cut out sections G and H to be another arm. Cut on fold between I and J to form pants/legs of this person. Glue arms (C/D and G/H) onto person's back at an angle. Cut a circle for the head from another piece of paper and glue onto top of fold-a-person. Have students write a brief description of Nelson Mandela, Desmond Tutu, Steven Biko, or F.W. de Klerk inside the coat of this person. Write the person's name on the head. Present to the class.

A	B	C	D
E	F	G	H
I	J	K	L
M	N	O	P

Extension May need a peer tutor to complete all the steps accurately.

LESSON ③ Society and Culture

KEY IDEAS

- Major religions in Southern Africa are Christianity, traditional African religions, and a mixture of both.

- Botswana is an example of an African success story through its unique form of democracy.

- South Africans can compete again in international sporting events.

KEY TERMS

censor
kgotla

Until 1997, South Africa had two national anthems. The official one was the Afrikaner hymn "The Call of South Africa." The unofficial one was "God Bless Africa," the anthem of the anti-apartheid movement known to millions throughout Africa. They have been combined into one new anthem with lyrics from five of South Africa's most spoken languages.

Today, blacks and whites are not only sitting together in the stands but also playing on the field together. In spite of the years of racial tension that divided communities, South Africans now share social events and cultural life.

Religions in Southern Africa

Christianity today is the major religion throughout most of Southern Africa. Yet many people practice traditional religious beliefs along with their Christian faith. In rural villages, some gather on Saturday nights to make offerings to the spirit of the chief or to their ancestors, and then go on Sunday mornings to Catholic worship services.

Throughout Southern Africa, thousands of Christians belong to the African Independent Churches, or AIC. This movement of churches, which broke off from European Catholic and Protestant groups, began in South Africa in the early 1900s. Since then it has spread to other nations.

Founders of these churches wanted a place where Christians could express their faith by using African symbols and sounds and feel comfortable doing so. Also, after early missionaries translated the Bible into African languages, many African church leaders began to interpret the Bible for themselves. They wanted to speak about what they learned from their studies to their congregations.

Some independent churches combine traditional African religious practices with Christian beliefs. Others strictly forbid their members to take part in services honoring ancestors or other traditional practices.

Archbishop Desmond Tutu is a religious leader in the major religion in South Africa. **What is that religion?**

Customs

In Namibia, a special ceremony reflects the mix of traditional customs and Christian beliefs. At sunrise and sunset, a fire is lighted to communicate with ancestors and with God. A person thought to have great spirituality is chosen to light the fires. A young person often is recognized for this honor.

Activity

Rights of Children

OBJECTIVES: 10.01, 10.04

As an extension, read the book *For Every Child: Based on the United Nations Convention on the Rights of the Child*, in words and pictures with a forward written by Archbishop Desmond M. Tutu (published in association with Unicef by Phyllis Fogelman Books in New York. ISBN 0803726503.) Afterward, the book can be a springboard into a discussion of the rights of children. Students can further their study by locating examples of places where the rights of children have been denied. This activity will enable students to engage in thoughtful reflection as well as meaningful research by utilizing a variety of sources such as newspapers, magazines, and the Internet.

Because South Africa has such a diverse population from Europe and Asia as well as other parts of Africa, worshippers can find Hindu temples, Muslim mosques, and Jewish synagogues in the larger cities.

The Botswana Miracle

At independence, one writer called the country of Botswana a "recipe for disaster." Botswana was largely covered by desert and had no known mineral resources. It had no paved roads and only one public secondary school. Botswana was one of the five poorest nations in the world.

Thirty years later, it is one of the richest nations in Africa. What went right?

The discovery of diamonds in the 1960s helped, but many other poorer countries also have mineral riches. Experts say it was diamonds, democracy, and wise leadership.

Botswana is the home of the Tswana people, who have a saying: "The chief is only the chief by the will of the tribe." Long before their lands became a nation, the Tswana leaders listened to their people before making decisions. Many say that this democratic tradition is the reason for Botswana's success.

A *kgotla* (GOAT·lah) is a public discussion in which everyone can give their views on issues. The *kgotla*, also called a freedom square, is a key part of Botswanan democracy. Members of the country's many political parties gather in freedom squares throughout the country

CONNECTIONS
• GEOGRAPHY & LANGUAGE ARTS •

South Africa Protest Theater

In South Africa, artists have used the stage as a weapon in the fight against apartheid. They follow a tradition of African storytelling.

Long before the coming of Europeans, people throughout Africa had a strong tradition of playmaking. In telling the history of their people or in religious ceremonies, villagers often combined storytelling with music, dance, and song to produce lively and exciting dramas.

Apartheid's problems became the focus of South Africa's modern storytellers. In Johannesburg and other major South African cities, local writers, directors, and actors pooled their dramatic skills in a unique and daring way to fight apartheid.

Writers such as Athol Fugard created works speaking to the tragedies of the separation of the races in South Africa. Fugard's *Master Harold and the Boys* tells the story of two men, one black and one white, who grew up as friends but were forced apart as adults by apartheid. Fugard uses humor to make serious points about prejudice.

Directors often had to fight government attempts to stop or **censor** (remove certain parts)

Whoopi Goldberg in Sarafina!

their works. Many South African plays became popular in New York and London before audiences saw them at home.

Mbongeni Ngema's hit musical *Sarafina!* tells the story of life in all-black Soweto township. Written in 1987 about an uprising in which teenagers rebelled against apartheid, *Sarafina!* played in the United States before it ever went to South Africa.

Sarafina! played on Broadway to standing-room-only audiences for almost a year. The musical also made it to Chicago and other stages before it became a popular film. By that time, South Africa's apartheid policy had been repealed. Six years after it was written, *Sarafina!* could be shown in South Africa.

Background Information

New Rights for Zulu Brides

Nompumelelo Mkhwanazi wore two dresses for her wedding celebrations. One was a white wedding gown with a 20-foot train. The other was a traditional Zulu beaded skirt with a leopard skin collar. First the bride wore her wedding gown to the service at the Baptist church that her family belongs to. Later she was welcomed into the groom's family's home in more traditional dress. Educated, urban South African women not only want modern wedding dresses but also the stronger legal

rights that state-sanctioned weddings guarantee. Under Zulu tribal law, wives are wards of their husbands. They cannot own property and if divorced have no claim on the couple's assets. Under laws the parliament passed in 1998, women are guaranteed equal rights in tribal marriages. Experts agree, however, that despite the reforms the status of married women will change slowly in rural areas.

Discussion Questions

1 What does the saying "the chief is only the chief by the will of the tribe" mean? What does that say about the type of government the people have? Does that saying hold true for the government in the United States?

2 Is Botswana really a miracle? Why?

3 How does the local government in Botswana differ from the type of government you have in your community? How is it similar?

Science Activity

Air Pollution Debate

OBJECTIVES: 2.02, 2.03, 3.02

Using some of the following information about South Africa's air pollution from the Energy Information Administration of the U.S. Department of Energy and additional sources, have students debate South Africa's use of coal to create electricity. Students should predict the future problems of air pollution facing South Africa, it's effect of people living in South Africa, and it contributions to global warming.

"More than 90% of South Africa's electricity is generated from the combustion of coal, which contains approximately 1.2% sulfur and up to 45% ash. Coal combustion can lead to particulate matter in the air, as well as contribute to acid rain. Despite harmful environmental effects, coal-fired power stations are not required to use coal scrubbers to remove sulfur, as use of clean-coal technology would significantly raise the cost of electricity for consumers. In addition to power generation, coal combustion in stoves and coal-heated boilers in hospitals and factories contribute to of low-level coal-related atmospheric pollution.

...According to UNICEF, in 2000, respiratory infections from air pollution were the fourth-largest cause of death in children under five in South Africa (more than 6,000 deaths per year). The effects of air pollution on children are often compounded by poverty, including lack of access to potable water, sanitary facilities, and health care."

Writing Activity

Paul Simon and South Africa

OBJECTIVES: 9.01, 9.03, 10.03

Give students the following prompt: The CD *Graceland* by Paul Simon is an example of South African township music, which is a blend of traditional African and Western music. Before apartheid was ended in South Africa, there was a boycott against South Africa that included cultural as well as economic exchanges. Paul Simon violated the boycott when he went to South Africa to produce the music, believing it was important for the world to learn about African culture. Do you think Paul Simon was right in violating the boycott the world had initiated in an attempt to end the practice of apartheid?

Remember to

- tell whether you think he was right or wrong.
- give at least three reasons why you think he was right or wrong.
- write in paragraph form.
- check to be sure you are writing good sentences.
- use correct grammar, spelling, capitalization, and punctuation.

Caption Answer

South Africa's apartheid policy had kept it out of international competition.

to speak about their party's beliefs and attack those running against them for office. Members of other parties argue with the speakers. Listeners freely speak their minds. In Botswana, *kgotlas* are the way most voters learn about the different political parties. In larger cities, newspapers print stories about the meetings on their front pages.

Botswana also has a long tradition of respecting human rights. Freedom of speech, press, and religion are the law in Botswana. The country also has had effective leaders. Forty years of civilian leadership and sound social policies have helped it become a strong nation.

Leaders have used the nation's diamonds and other resources wisely. They have built schools and improved health

Mbulaenia Mulaudzi won the silver medal in the 800m race at the 2004 Olympics in Athens, Greece. **Why was South Africa kept from sending a team to the Olympics until 1992?**

care. In the 1980s, when a drought hit Southern Africa, Botswana farmers lost most of their crops five years in a row. Yet no famine occurred and few people went hungry. Once the drought began, the government planned ahead and worked quickly to find and distribute food to those in need.

Return to the Sports World

At the 1992 Summer Olympics in Barcelona, Spain, runner Abel Mokibe competed for South Africa. Although he won no medals, he made history. It was the first time in 32 years that South African teams were allowed to take part in the Olympics, and the first time in South Africa's history that these teams included black South Africans.

South Africa's apartheid policy had kept it out of international sporting events for three decades. The country's all-white teams had been barred from most international athletic competitions. The ban was lifted in 1992 after South Africa's white-led government ended apartheid.

Almost all of the black competitors on South Africa's 1992 Olympic team were runners. By the 1996 Summer Olympics in Atlanta, there were many more black athletes on South Africa's teams. They competed in many different sports events and were even more committed to winning for the nation that is now truly theirs.

LESSON 3 REVIEW

Fact Follow-Up

1. Describe how Southern Africans have adapted Christian practices.
2. What is the economic miracle of Botswana? How did it happen?
3. How did the drama and music aid in the fight against apartheid in South Africa?
4. What is a kgotla? What is its importance in Botswana?

Talk About It

1. Why does South Africa have two national anthems? Do you think the nation will always have two? Explain.
2. Could the economic miracle of Botswana have happened somewhere else in Africa? Why or why not?
3. Why were the 1996 Olympic Games particularly important for South Africa?

198

LESSON 3 REVIEW

Fact Follow-Up Answers

1. In rural villages, some people gather on Saturday nights to make offerings to the spirit of the chief or to their ancestors, and then they go to church on Sunday. Others have formed their own independent churches to combine traditional African religious practices with Christian beliefs.
2. At independence, Botswana appeared to have no known mineral resources and was one of the poorest nations in the world. Diamonds were discovered, and now Botswana is one of the richest nations in Africa. Experts say the economic miracle occurred because of diamonds, democracy, and wise leadership.
3. South African artists used the stage as a weapon in the fight against apartheid. Dramatists used tragedy and comedy to make points about the injustice of apartheid and of all prejudice.
4. A *kgotla* is a public discussion in which everyone can give their views on issues. It is also called a freedom square, because it is a key part of Botswana democracy.

Talk About It Answers

1. One is an Afrikaner hymn; the other is the anthem of the anti-apartheid movement. They were given equal importance at the end of the apartheid era. Probably the time will come when there will be just one anthem. Having two anthems at the present time might prevent conflicts between Africans and Afrikaners.
2. Answers will vary. Botswana's economic miracle was the result of resources and a strong democratic tradition. Many resource-rich nations, like South Africa, did not have a democratic tradition.
3. South Africa's apartheid policies kept the nation out of international sporting events for many years. In 1992 the ban was lifted, and South Africa competed, mostly with runners. In 1996 South Africa fielded a large contingent of athletes in many different sports.

*Applying Decision-Making
and Problem-Solving Techniques to World Issues*

Defeating Apartheid

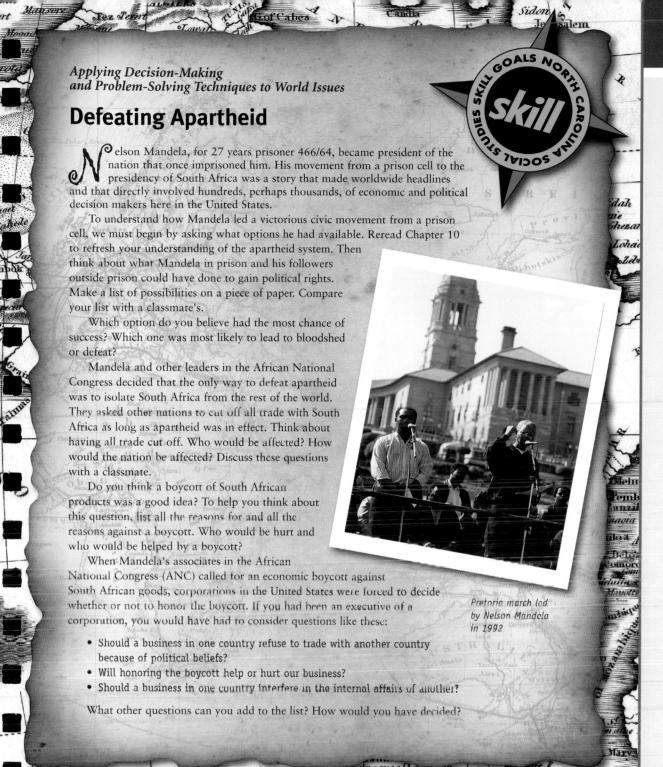

Nelson Mandela, for 27 years prisoner 466/64, became president of the nation that once imprisoned him. His movement from a prison cell to the presidency of South Africa was a story that made worldwide headlines and that directly involved hundreds, perhaps thousands, of economic and political decision makers here in the United States.

To understand how Mandela led a victorious civic movement from a prison cell, we must begin by asking what options he had available. Reread Chapter 10 to refresh your understanding of the apartheid system. Then think about what Mandela in prison and his followers outside prison could have done to gain political rights. Make a list of possibilities on a piece of paper. Compare your list with a classmate's.

Which option do you believe had the most chance of success? Which one was most likely to lead to bloodshed or defeat?

Mandela and other leaders in the African National Congress decided that the only way to defeat apartheid was to isolate South Africa from the rest of the world. They asked other nations to cut off all trade with South Africa as long as apartheid was in effect. Think about having all trade cut off. Who would be affected? How would the nation be affected? Discuss these questions with a classmate.

Do you think a boycott of South African products was a good idea? To help you think about this question, list all the reasons for and all the reasons against a boycott. Who would be hurt and who would be helped by a boycott?

When Mandela's associates in the African National Congress (ANC) called for an economic boycott against South African goods, corporations in the United States were forced to decide whether or not to honor the boycott. If you had been an executive of a corporation, you would have had to consider questions like these:

- Should a business in one country refuse to trade with another country because of political beliefs?
- Will honoring the boycott help or hurt our business?
- Should a business in one country interfere in the internal affairs of another?

What other questions can you add to the list? How would you have decided?

*Pretoria march led
by Nelson Mandela
in 1992*

Southern Africa

199

Teaching This Skill Lesson

Materials Needed textbook, paper, pencils

Classroom Organization individual, working in pairs

Beginning the Lesson Review facts about Nelson Mandela and apartheid from Chapter 10, paying particular attention to the feature on pages 192–93. Ask what Mandela and his followers could have done to defeat apartheid. Emphasize that Mandela, in prison, could do nothing himself, that his options were limited. Have students list some options for Mandela and his followers.

Lesson Development Tell students that Mandela chose an economic boycott as the major strategy. Make sure they understand what a boycott is and how an economic boycott works. As a homework assignment, have students list arguments for and against an economic boycott and bring the lists to class.

Conclusion Discuss the three questions on page 199 with students. Add other questions if they come up.

Extension Assign students to write a press release or a letter to the editor from a corporate executive supporting or opposing the economic boycott and giving persuasive reasons.

Skill Lesson Review

1. How many African nations are located on coastlines? *Thirty. Three others are islands.*
2. How many capital cities are located on coastlines? *Twenty-two. Ten more are on lakes or rivers.*
3. What are the relative and absolute locations of the following places?
   a. Addis Ababa, Ethiopia—*south of Eritrea, west of Somalia, east of Sudan, and north of Kenya; 9°N, 38°E.*
   b. Kalahari Desert—*south Africa; between 22° and 25°S latitude, between 15° and 25°E.*
   c. Nile River—*northeast Africa.; between 32°N and the Equator, between 30° and 32°E.*

   d. Luanda, Angola—*southwest Africa, on the Atlantic coast; 8°S, 12°E.*
   e. Bamako, Mali—*on the Niger River, northeast of Guinea, south of Mauritania, west of Burkina Faso; 13°N, 8°W.*
4. Which of the places above was easiest to describe relatively? absolutely? *The Nile is easiest to describe relatively. The easiest to describe absolutely were the cities.*
5. When do you think it is more useful to use absolute location? relative location? Why? *Absolute location is useful in identifying a city or other precise location. Relative location works better for large, sprawling landforms.*

Talk About It

1. It is more diverse than Northern Africa, but less diverse than East Africa.

2. Important points: Encourage students to suggest challenges and choose the one they think most important. Among other challenges, South Africa faces the challenge of closing the economic gap between blacks and whites.

3. Important points: Students should choose one region and explain why they think it is the wealthiest. Note: Southern Africa is rich in gold and diamonds, but so is Central Africa. North Africa has oil.

4. The nation would need overland access to ports. This might require building roads and a railroad, which are expensive projects. Your nation would also need the cooperation of the nations that lie between your country and the ports.

5. Important points: Students should choose a position and support it with reasons. Note: Botswana went from being a very poor to a very rich nation while preserving democracy.

Mastering Mapwork

1. The Zambezi River borders or flows through Angola, Zambia, Zimbabwe, Malawi, and Mozambique.

2. Angola, Namibia, South Africa, and Mozambique are located on seacoasts.

3. Windhoek, Namibia; Lusaka, Zambia; Harare, Zimbabwe; Lilongwe, Malawi; and Pretoria, South Africa would have most difficulty if they had to depend on nearby rivers.

4. Zambia, Malawi, Botswana, Zimbabwe, Lesotho, and Swaziland are landlocked nations.

5. Because the Vaal and Orange Rivers run through significant portions of the country and the Limpopo forms a part of its northern border, South Africa should find the movement of people, goods, and ideas easiest.

6. The fact that the Atlantic coastline of

CHAPTER 10 REVIEW

Lessons Learned

LESSON 1
People and Their Environment
Southern Africa's plateau is crossed by deserts, grasslands, mountains, and rivers. The Great Escarpment gives power to the Zambezi River. Climates differ on each coast. People in the region are diverse, coming from many ethnic groups in Africa, Asia, and Europe.

LESSON 2
Economy and Government
Five countries in Southern Africa lived under white minority rule that did not end until independence or violent demonstrations. Other countries in the region have suffered through civil wars. South Africa's policy of apartheid—segregation of the races—ended in 1991. Nelson Mandela—a leader in the struggle against apartheid—became the first South African president elected by all South Africans.

LESSON 3
Society and Culture
South Africa is now a racially mixed society. Religious practices have always reflected a mixture of Christianity and traditional practices. Botswana has a strong economy and democratic government.

Talk About It

1. Is the population of Southern Africa more or less diverse than that of other African regions? Explain.
2. What do you think is the greatest challenge facing South Africa? Explain why.
3. South Africa is the wealthiest nation in Africa. Do you think that Southern Africa may be the wealthiest region? Explain.
4. Imagine that you are a citizen of a Southern African nation that is landlocked. What problems might your nation face? Why would you have these problems?
5. Why should Botswana be described as an "economic miracle"? Explain.

Mastering Mapwork

MOVEMENT

Use the map on page 185 to answer these questions:

1. Rivers are often used for the movement of goods and people. Which river in this region passes through the most countries? Through which countries does it pass?
2. Countries located on seacoasts often find it convenient to move people, goods, and ideas by water. Which countries in this region are located on seacoasts?
3. Which national capitals do you think would find it most difficult to move goods and people? Why?
4. Landlocked nations often find the movement of people, goods, and ideas difficult. Which nations of Southern Africa are landlocked?
5. Rivers, if they are navigable, contribute to the movement of people, goods, and ideas. Given this, which nation in Southern Africa would find the movement of people, goods, and ideas easiest?
6. How might the movement of people, goods, and ideas be easier in Angola than in Namibia?
7. Under what circumstances might nations such as Lesotho and Swaziland find the movement of people, goods, and ideas difficult?

Namibia is a desert might make the movement of people, goods, and ideas more difficult there than in Angola.

7. Lesotho is completely surrounded by South Africa, and Swaziland has borders with Mozambique and South Africa. If these small nations did not get along with their much larger neighbors, the movement of people, goods, and ideas between them and other world areas would be difficult.

Go to the Source

Analyzing National Symbols

Use the chart below to analyze these examples of African currencies. What features on the currency show an identity with Africa? What features remind you of its colonial past?

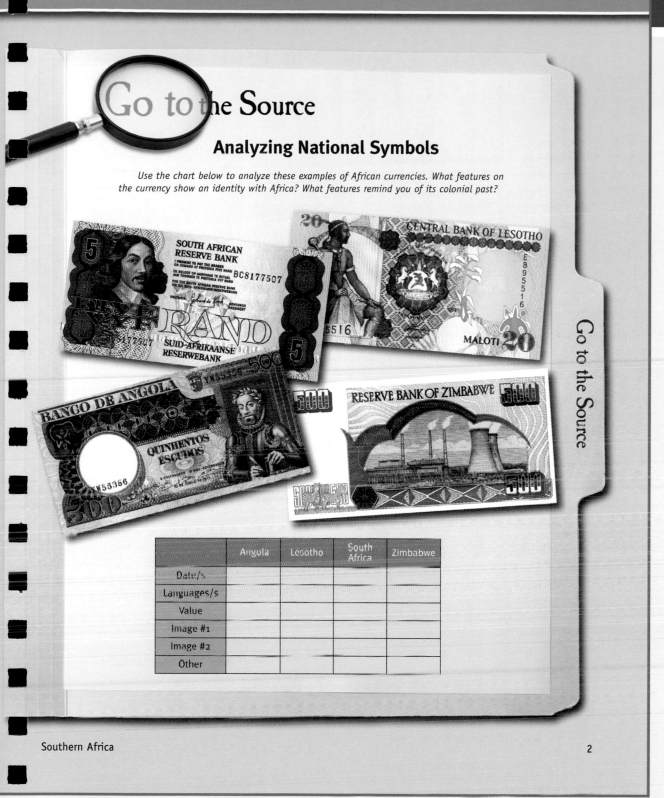

	Angola	Lesotho	South Africa	Zimbabwe
Date/s				
Languages/s				
Value				
Image #1				
Image #2				
Other				

Southern Africa

Go to the Source

2

OBJECTIVES: 11.04 Skills 3.05, 4.06

Currency is a primary source. Paper money and coins are official government documents. The dates, symbols, and signatures of government officials all can tell historians information about that nation at the time the money was printed.

Explore the symbolism on the currencies on this page. If students cannot find all the answers for the chart in the currency, challenge them to use other sources, such as the Internet.

ANSWERS

Angola

Date: 1973

Language: Portuguese

Value: 500 Quinhentos

Image #1: Colonial man (Luiz de Camoes, considered Portugal's greatest poet)

Image #2: Shield

Other: Answers will vary.

Lesotho

Date: 1994

Language: English

Value: 20 Maloti

Image #1: Coat-of-arms with crocodile

Image #2: Ruler (King Moshoeshoe)

Other: Answers will vary.

South Africa

Date: (not shown)

Language: English and Afrikaans

Value: 5

Image #1: Colonial man (Jan van Riebeeck, founder of Capetown)

Image #2: Diamond

Other: Answers will vary.

Zimbabwe:

Date: 2001 (not shown)

Language: English

Value: 500 dollars

Image #1: Nuclear power plant

Image #2: Zebras

Other: Answers will vary.

How to Use the Chapter Review

There are three sections in the Chapter Review: Talk About It, Mastering Mapwork, and Go to the Source. Use the Vocabulary Worksheets and the Chapter Review Worksheet in the Teacher's Resource Guide for additional reinforcement and preparation for the Chapter Assessments. The chapter and lesson reviews and the Chapter Review Worksheets are the basis of the assessment for each chapter.

Talk About It questions encourage students to speculate about the content of the chapter and are suitable for class or small-group discussion. They are not intended to be assigned for homework.

Mastering Mapwork has students apply one or more of the Five Themes of Geography to maps within the chapter.

Go to the Source activities allow students to analyze a primary source that relates to the content of the chapter. The questions and activities familiarize students with different types of primary sources and also build content-reading skills.

Unit 3 Southwest Asia

This unit opens with a view of pilgrims visiting the Kaaba, or Black Stone, in Mecca. Every Muslim has a sacred duty to make this pilgrimage at least once in a lifetime. The photograph illustrates the importance of faith in Southwest Asia, a region that is the birthplace of three great world religions—Judaism, Islam, and Christianity.

The 15 nations of Southwest Asia are influenced by a lack of water and plentiful oil resources. The region has also been shaped by ancient civilizations, three world religions, the Arab Empire, and European imperialism. Muslim culture also influences much of the region. In this region known for religious conflicts, Israel, Syria, Jordan, Iraq, and Lebanon share similar landforms and climate but have different national goals. Turkey and Iran in the Northern Tier and Saudi Arabia on the Arabian Peninsula have created different kinds of societies based on their resources and traditions.

UNIT LESSON PLAN

	LESSON 1	LESSON 2	LESSON 3
CHAPTER 11 Lands and People of Southwest Asia	Southwest Asia contains three regions—the Middle East, the Northern Tier, and the Arabian Peninsula. **Essential Question:** What are the regions of Southwest Asia? **Suggested Time:** 1 day	The region is dry except for fertile valleys of Turkey and the Middle East. Oil is a major resource. Water is scarce. **Essential Question:** How does the physical environment influence life in Southwest Asia? **Suggested Time:** 1 day	Arabs, Iranians, Turks, and Jews live in Southwest Asia. Its arid environment is home to farmers and herders. **Essential Question:** What groups of people live in Southwest Asia, and how have they adapted to the arid environment? **Suggested Time:** 1 day
CHAPTER 12 Southwest Asia's Enduring Traditions	Early civilizations of Sumeria, Mesopotamia, Babylon, and Phoenicia rose in Southwest Asia. Islam later contributed to the region's progress in law, architecture, learning, and the arts. **Essential Question:** How did the early civilizations affect Southwest Asia? **Suggested Time:** 2 days	Three major world religions began in Southwest Asia: Judaism, Christianity, and Islam. The common element in each religion is a belief in one God. **Essential Question:** What impact did the development of these three major world religions have on Southwest Asia, and what characteristics do these religions have in common? **Suggested Time:** 2-3 days	Islam spread through Southwest Asia, North Africa, and southern Europe. **Essential Question:** What impact has the spread of Islam had on Southwest Asia, North Africa, and southern Europe? **Suggested Time:** 1 day
CHAPTER 13 Economy and Government	Oil is important to many countries in Southwest Asia. Nations without this resource have different industries. **Essential Question:** How have the nations of Southwest Asia with oil resources and those without oil resources developed their economies? **Suggested Time:** 1 day	Middle East governments range from dictatorships to democracy. Conflicts over land and resources have fueled violence and wars. **Essential Question:** How have differing points of view between people in Southwest Asia and people in Israel and the West led to violence and terrorism in region and beyond? **Suggested Time:** 2 days	The governments of Turkey, Iran, and Saudi Arabia have different forms of government. **Essential Question:** How have the revolutions in Iran and Turkey influenced them as modern nations? **Suggested Time:** 1 day
CHAPTER 14 Society and Culture	The environments of the Middle East, the Northern Tier, and the Arabian Peninsula have influenced the societies that have flourished there for centuries. **Essential Question:** What non-religious aspects of culture can be found in Southwest Asia? **Suggested Time:** 1 day	Desert Traditions are strong on the Arabian Peninsula. Islam influences much of daily life. Islamists are conservative Muslims who want their nations to be governed by traditional Islamic principles. **Essential Question:** How have Arab-Islamic societies preserved their traditional ways of life while seeking to modernize? **Suggested Time:** 2 days	Jerusalem is a sacred city to Jews, Christians, and Muslims. Although Israel is a Jewish nation, Arabs and Christians also live there. **Essential Question:** What impact does religion have on the culture of Israel? **Suggested Time:** 1 day

Preparing the Unit

- Worksheets, assessments, and reproducibles for this unit are found in the Teacher's Resource Guide.
- See the list of Cultural Resources in the Teacher's Edition.
- Capture the interest of the students by showing a video on the Middle East and ask students to pay attention to the different scenes or ask students to flip through the pages of Unit 3.

Unit Teaching Strategies

- Essential Question for the Unit: Why and how is our foreign policy determined by events taking place in Southwest Asia?
- Explain that United States foreign policy is the topic for the unit and that there will be several concepts that students will study including geography, cultural beliefs, and economic policies to help them answer the question at the end of the unit.
- Explain that Southwest Asia is the correct geographical term for the region but that they will also hear the term "Middle East," which is a political term (used by journalist). You can also point out that the culture and geography of Southwest Asia are very similar to North Africa and that in some books they are studied together.
- Use the Unit 3 Introductory Activity to have the students complete a KWHL chart on Southwest Asia.
- Complete the *Angel in the East* map activity.
- Prepare a feast of traditional Southwest Asian foods for your students to sample. To give your feast more authenticity, spread your meal on a cloth on the floor and invite your students to join you for the taste test. Your feast can be a simple collection of mezze (appetizers) including falafel, hummus, pita bread, yogurt, olives, dates, celery, radishes, feta cheese, white cheese, and nuts. Most of these items are readily available at grocery stores and can be purchased premade or easily prepared with a mix.
- Check NCJourneys.com for updates and materials.

Students will have seven days to complete their project. Students have the option of choosing from five different projects and should only choose one of the five projects. The five choices offer a variety because students can select the project that best suits their taste. Suggested report format: reports should be two pages in length, typed, and double-spaced.

UNIT PROJECT CHOICES

OBJECTIVES: 3.01, 6.01, 12.01

Religion Paper

Students will research Judaism, Christianity, and Islam. In an expository paper, students will show three ways the religions are similar. Ways could include the importance of Abraham, Jerusalem, and the Old Testament in each of the holy books.

Way of Life Diorama

Students will create two dioramas, one portraying the life of a Bedouin and the other the life of a village farmer. The dioramas must include evidence of housing, animals, clothing, and transportation.

Extension ELL students should use an ELL-friendly Web site for research.

Follow That Oil

Students will locate information about petroleum and the process in which it is refined. Present the information in the form of a flow chart or other graphic organizer and explain it to the class.

Letters to a Friend

Students will imagine they are a middle school student from Saudi Arabia who has lived in the United States for five years. After returning to Saudi Arabia, e-mail friends back in the United States describing how the life they knew has changed. Include at least five detailed e-mails.

Maps and Flags

Students will prepare a booklet of maps and flags of all of the countries of Southwest Asia. Include information on per capita income, life expectancy, literacy rate, and other important information of these countries.

Extension ELL students should use an ELL-friendly Web site for research.

Bulletin Board Ideas

Religions of Southwest Asia

Use a physical map of Southwest Asia as a backdrop. Point a large arrow to the area where the Dead Sea Scrolls were found. Use another to point out the city of Jerusalem. Use a third large arrow to point to Mecca. Label each region with the proper name of the religion in that region.

Cultures of Southwest Asia

Put up pictures of Southwest Asia. Focus the pictures around the cultural aspects of the region. Use the appropriate parts of Chapter 1 to help students begin their search for cultural information.

Introductory Activity

KWHL

OBJECTIVES: 1.02, 2.01

Before starting the unit on Southwest Asia, have students complete a KWHL chart on the area. This identifies what they know or have heard about the region, and what misconceptions they have about the region.

K (Know)	W (Want to know)	H (How will I Learn)	L (Learned)

Under the K, students will write or tell the teacher what they know about Southwest Asia. Under the W, the students can state what they would like to know about the area, and it is also a place where teachers can direct the students by suggesting things that they will learn about the area. Under H, students can tell how they will learn this about Southwest Asia. Under L they should write what they have learned. After the unit, students can refer back to the chart to explain what they learned about Southwest Asia.

Culminating Activity

Building a Newspaper

OBJECTIVES: 1.01

Students will create a newspaper about a country from the region studied in this unit, as they did in Unit 1. This will be issue number three of their newspaper.

Refer to the Unit 1 Culminating Activity on page 14C in the Teacher's Edition for specific directions and references on how to create and organize the newspaper. Remind students that the newspaper should feature two articles on the front. The back of the newspaper should include a map, a box displaying vital statistics, an article about something special or current events, and a puzzle. The students should use their

newspapers from the previous unit as a model, and thus the students should be able to complete it in similar or slightly less time.

Share the newspapers with others in the class. Have the students keep each of their newspapers. At the end of the year, bind each student's newspapers together so he or she will have their own volume of newspapers covering the regions studied throughout the year. Use copies of all students' newspapers to organize a class volume according to region.

Technology Activity

Spreadsheet

OBJECTIVES: 5.01

Using an almanac, have students make a spreadsheet in which they identify the countries of the region, the oil production of each, and the per capita GDP of each. Students should be able to determine which country produces the most oil and which nation has the highest GDP per capita. Are they the same country? Why or why not?

Extension For ELL students, assign peer tutors to help.

Science Activity

Climate

OBJECTIVES: 2.01, 2.02

Altitude, latitude, ocean currents, nearness to the sea, and wind patterns affect climate. Trace a map of Southwest Asia. Shade the high-altitude areas of the Anatolian Plateau, Taurus Mountains, Zagros Mountains, Lebanon Mountains, and Yemen. Draw red arrows representing the hot, dry summer winds from the south. Draw blue arrows representing the winds from the west bringing moisture and cooler temperatures. Predict the climates of the higher altitude areas and the land beyond them. Why are the deserts located where they are? *(the moisture is blocked by the higher altitudes and mountains)* What is this called? *(rain shadow effect)*

Math Activity

Vedic Squares and Elements of Design Math Integration

OBJECTIVES: 12.02

One component common to math and design is patterns. The Vedic Square is based on ancient principles revealed in the Vedas, early Hindu sacred writings. It was used as a basis for many Islamic designs. To make a Vedic Square have your students first create a basic multiplication table. Refer to the Teacher's Resource Guide for a template for a completed Vedic Square.

Next create the same template with the numbers 1 through 9 on the upper and left row and column. Refer back to the first chart and convert any two-digit number into a one-digit number following this rule: If the product is a two-digit number, find the sum of the two digits. If the sum is still a two-digit number, find the sum of those two digits. For example: The product of 2 times 5 equals 10. The sum of 1 and 0 is 1. The product of 7 times 8 is 56. The sum of the two digits (5 and 6) is 11. The sum of those two digits is 2.

Next have the students pick a different color marker for each number and color in the squares. Have them analyze the patterns that emerge. Another method would be to have different students in the class color one square at a time and then connect the colored squares with straight lines.

Unit Resources

Print Resources

Arab—Fiction

Cohen, Barbara. *Seven Daughters & Seven Sons.* Beech Tree Books, 1994. ISBN 0688135633.

Kurds—Fiction

Laird, Elizabeth. *Kiss the Dust.* Puffin, 1994. ISBN 0140368558.

Palestine—Fiction

Nye, Naomi Shihab. *Habibi.* Aladdin Paperback, 1999. ISBN 0689825234.

Syria—Fiction

Schami, Rafik. *A Hand Full of Stars.* Translated from German by Rika Lesser. Puffin, 1992. ISBN 0140360735.

Nonfiction

El-Said, Issam. *Geometric Concepts in Islamic Art.* Dale Seymour Publishers, 1976. ISBN 086651421X.

Godlas, Sylvia. *Doorways to Islamic Art: A Curriculum for Interdisciplinary Studies.* Berkeley, CA: AWAIR, 1997. $49.95 Kit: 34 slides/spiralbound book

Shabbas, Audrey, editor, *The Arab World Studies Notebook.* Berkeley, CA: AWAIR, 1998. ISBN 1889993034.

The Middle East in Transition. Southern Center for International Studies, 1994. ISBN 0935082190.

Maps

National Geographic Society. Each is available as an uncirculated back issue with supplement map, many double-sided. Contact: *National Geographic* Back Issues, 800-777-2800, Fax: 813-979-6685. Cost: ranges between $5 and $10 (shipping included).

- July 1972—The Cultural Map of the Middle East (Peoples of Southwest Asia and Egypt and Libya/Peoples of the Magreb, historic maps)
- September 1978—Early civilizations in the Middle East
- December 1982—The Historic Mediterranean 800 B.C. to A.D. 1500
- December 1989—The Holy Land
- February 1991—The Middle East: States in Turmoil (political map/comparison of population, oil reserves, and military, historical maps)
- April 1996—Jerusalem

Magazine

Free bimonthly magazine focused primarily on Southwest Asia but often includes articles about other areas of the world influenced by Arabs or Islam. Request a subscription for your school: Saudi Aramco World, Box 469008, Escondido, CA 92046-9008.

Audiovisual

The 50 Years War: Israel and the Arabs, PBS Videos 800-344-3337.

The Arab World. Knowledge Unlimited, 1988 (18 minutes). Good introduction.

The Birth of Civilization 6000 B.C.–2000 B.C. From *The World,* a television series based on Hammond Concise Atlas of World History. Available at Social Studies School Services, (800) 421-4246. 26 minutes.

Web Sites

Go to **NCJourneys.com** for links to the following Web sites:

- ArabNet
- The British Museum, Learning and Information Department, Islam
- Culture and Art center for Islamic cultures
- The Different Aspects of Islamic Culture, UNESCO
- Encyclopedia of the Orient (North Africa/Middle East info)
- Islamic Art, Met Museum
- Islamic Culture and the Medical Arts, NIH
- Islamic Educational, Scientific and Cultural Organization -ISESCO
- Salaam Means Peace: An Introduction to Arab Americans

Paideia Seminar

Preamble to the Charter of the United Nations Paideia

Have students read the Preamble to the Charter of the United Nations (links are found at **NCJourneys.com**).

Issues to be discussed: human rights, what do all people deserve?

Opening Questions

- What can you infer about the United Nations as an organization from this preamble?
- How would you describe the language of this text?

Core Questions

- To what does the text refer in the second line where it says: "which twice in our lifetime has brought untold sorrow to mankind?"
- What does it mean to say "armed force shall not be used, save in the common interest?"
- What does this text suggest to be the long term goal of the United Nations?

Closing Questions

- To what extent do you feel that the United Nations has fulfilled its charter thus far?
- If the Secretary General of the United Nations came to you for ideas on amending this preamble, would you change anything?

A Paideia seminar is a formal discussion based on a text. The teacher only asks open-ended questions. Students must read and study the text, listen to other students' comments, think critically, and respond with their thoughts and with responses to the thoughts of others. Higher order thinking is evident, because students are required to summarize, analyze, synthesize, compare and contrast, and use logic to defend and challenge ideas.

Map Activity

Angel in the East

NATIONAL GEOGRAPHY STANDARDS: 2

GEOGRAPHIC THEMES: Location

OBJECTIVES: 1.02

Using Robinson world map projection with Southwest Asia in red, ask students to see if they notice an image represented by the red shape of Southwest Asia. Read "The Angel of the East" to the students. Identify features of the angel found in the shapes of Southwest Asian nations' boundaries and outline shape(s)—students can do this on individual paper maps while you outline the transparency.

Extension—for ELL students, model and provide additional explanations. Students should focus on the map only.

"The Angel of the East" by Rebecca Scott

If you could look east
across the United States,
over the Atlantic Ocean and
the Mediterranean Sea
to a place between
Asia, Africa and Europe.
You might see an angel—
an angel in the east—
resting on a sea of blue.
Her head hangs heavily,
bowed towards her chest
as she holds her hands
together in prayer
facing west.
A tear has fallen
from her cheek.
Her heart aches;
the heart of three religions.
She would like to be

Continued on page 203

Unit 3

"Oh ye men! Listen to my words and take them to heart! Know that every Muslim is brother to every other Muslim, and that you are now one brotherhood."

For more than a thousand years, Muslims have acted on Muhammad's words. They have traveled to Islam's holiest city, Mecca, to pray before the Kaaba, or cube. Every Muslim has a sacred duty to make the pilgrimage, or hajj, at least once in a lifetime if physically or financially possible.

Three great world religions—Judaism, Islam, and Christianity—came from Southwest Asia. They are part of the rich heritage that has made the region important to the world throughout history.

202

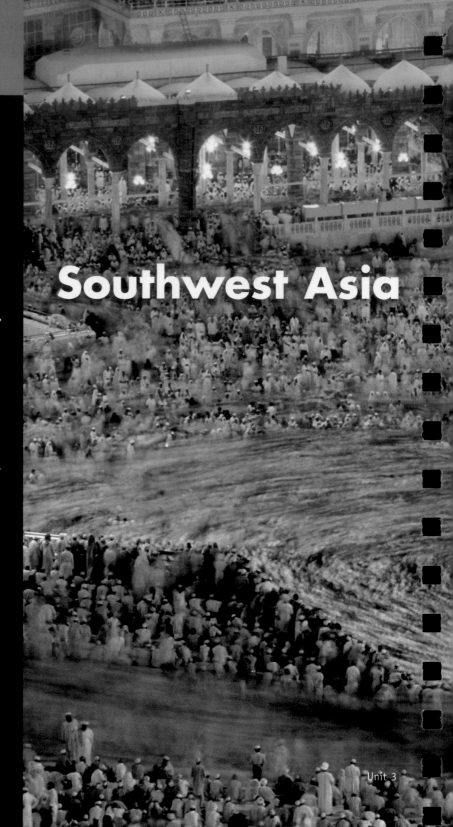

Southwest Asia

Unit 3

Social Studies at Work

Social Studies at Work: International Trade Specialist

An international trade specialist is a businessperson who advises other businesspeople about importing and exporting products and services to other countries.

Meet Young Oh

International Trade Specialist for the Carolinas Export Assistance Center

Young Oh was born and raised in Korea. She came to the United States as an adult to get an education. She majored in business administration at Oregon State College with the idea that she would someday work in international business.

Working for a company that made dietary supplements to sell in 20 different countries, including countries in Asia and the Pacific Realm, was Oh's first job in international business. Now she uses all that she learned about international trade to help North and South Carolina companies market and sell their products all over the world.

According to Oh, textile machinery, high-tech equipment, and building materials are particularly popular Carolina export products.

Sometimes her job is help companies work through all the

Southwest Asia

203

the angel for all people,
but it seems remote
on this southwest peninsula.
She is battle-worn
and war-torn,
this angel in the east—
praying someday for
a new world order and peace.

Use the following to define the countries that make up the angel of the Middle East. Have the students label their maps as you talk them through it.

Angel's Head	Turkey (her face, looking down, is the Taurus Mountains); the Northern Coast is her hair flowing back.
Her Tear	The Island of Cyprus
Chest	Syria
Right Shoulder	Lebanon
Right Arm	Israel
Left Shoulder	Iraq
Left Arm	Jordan
Hands in Prayer	Sinai Peninsula
Flowing Gown	Saudi Arabia (Arabian Peninsula)
Bottom of Gown Trimmed in Lace	Yemen, Oman, United Arab Emirates, Qatar
Two Buttons at Back of Gown	Kuwait (At the Upper Part) ; Bahrain (Loose Button)
Wings	Iran
Her Heart	Jerusalem

Unit Preview

CHAPTER 11
Lands and People of Southwest Asia
The 15 nations of Southwest Asia are influenced by a lack of water, plentiful oil resources, monotheistic culture, and ancient civilizations.

CHAPTER 12
Southwest Asia's Enduring Traditions
Southwest Asia has been shaped by ancient civilizations, three world religions, the strong Arab Empire, and by European Imperialism.

CHAPTER 13
Economy and Government
Israel, Syria, Jordan, Iraq, and Lebanon share similar landforms and climate, but they have different national goals. Conflicts over land have led to trouble.

CHAPTER 14
Society and Culture
Turkey, Iran, and Saudi Arabia have created different societies based on resources and traditions.

documents and paperwork associated with international trade; other times it's playing "matchmaker," trying to find buyers in foreign countries that need the products America is selling. Once a deal is made, Oh often helps companies make the financial arrangements that move payments from one side of the world to another.

Oh says that international business was a good choice for her. She thrives on the diversity and excitement of her work. Any given day may find her working on projects involving almost any nation. Since English is the universal business language Oh is able to communicate with colleagues all over the world.

International Trade Specialist for a Day
Let's say you want to start a company importing goods from Southwest Asia but you aren't exactly sure what kinds of products those countries produce. First make a chart with columns for Saudi Arabia, Jordan, Israel, and Syria. Then look up each country profile using the CIA World Factbook (link found at **NCJourneys.com**). Click on the country's name and then click on economy to find a list of the country's major exports. List each product on your chart. Can you find any products that might be good imports for your company?

Find Out More
Go to **NCJourneys.com** to find information and link about the International Trade Administration, U.S. Department of Commerce.

CHAPTER 11
Lands and People of Southwest Asia

Social Studies Strands

Geographic Relationships
Physical features
Climate and vegetation

Cultures and Diversity
Ethnic traits
Language
Religion

North Carolina Standard Course of Study

Goal 2 The learner will assess the relationship between physical environment and cultural characteristics of selected societies and regions of Africa, Asia, and Australia.

Goal 3 The learner will analyze the impact of interactions between humans and their physical environments in Africa, Asia, and Australia.

Goal 6 The learner will recognize the relationship between economic activity and the quality of life in Africa, Asia, and Australia.

Goal 11 The learner will recognize the common characteristics of different cultures in Africa, Asia, and Australia.

Teaching & Assessment

• English Language Learner Modified Lesson Plans for this chapter are found in the Teacher's Resource Guide.

• *ExamView® Assessment Suite* is provided at **NCJourneys.com.** It includes customizable assessments for all chapters. Paper tests are also available in the Teacher's Resource Guide. See pages T16–T17 for information about how to use the assessments and the Scoring Guide.

Worksheets

Worksheets and answer keys are found both in the Teacher's Resource Guide and at **NCJourneys.com**, including Reading Guides, Reading Strategies, Chapter Reviews, English Language Learner and others.

ACTIVITIES AND INTEGRATIONS

SOCIAL STUDIES

★ Name That Geographical Term, p. 204B
Activator: World Religions, p. 204
Map Activity: Southwest Asia, p. 203
● The Glow in Southwest Asia- Satellite View of Southwest Asia, p. 206
Map Inferences, p. 208
★ Vegetation and Biomes, p. 212
● Locate!, p. 213
Building an Aquifer, p. 214
Renewable v. Nonrenewable Resources, p. 215
▲ Population Tic-Tac-Toe, p. 219
Fertile Crescent and Its Importance, p. 220
Human-Environmental Interaction, p. 222
Skill Lesson: Using Maps to Understand Southwest Asia, p. 222

READING/LANGUAGE ARTS	READING/LANGUAGE ARTS OBJECTIVES
● Perceptions, p. 204B	2.01
▲ ■ Our Dymaxion World, p. 204B	
Analogies, p. 204B	2.01
Writing Prompt: Water Allocation, p. 204	3.01, 3.03
Create a Brochure, p. 215	2.02
★ Share the Water, p. 216	3.03
Go to the Source: Using Evidence to Make Predictions, p. 225	1.02, 2.01, 4.01

MATHEMATICS	MATHEMATICS OBJECTIVES
★ Shared Resources, p. 216	1.01, 1.03
▲ ■ Oil Math Word Problem, p. 217	1.02, 1.03
Standard of Living, p. 218	4.01

VISUAL ARTS	VISUAL ARTS OBJECTIVES
▲ ■ Our Dymaxion World, p. 204B	2.04, 4.01
Regional Clay Map, p. 208	2.04, 4.01
▲ ■ Building an Aquifer, p. 214	2.04, 3.01, 4.01

SCIENCE	SCIENCE OBJECTIVES
Vegetation and Biomes, p. 212	3.05

CHARACTER AND VALUES EDUCATION	TRAITS
Writing Prompt: Water Allocation, p. 204	good judgment, citizenship, fairness/justice
What Would You Do?, p. 213	fairness/justice

● Basic Activities ★ Challenging Activities ▲ English Language Learner Novice ■ English Language Learner Intermediate

Introductory Activity

Perceptions

OBJECTIVES: 2.01

To introduce Chapter 11, have students list ten characteristics they associate with the physical geography of Southwest Asia and the subregion of the Middle East and ten characteristics they associate with the people of that region. In groups of four or five have them share their lists and form a group list. Have one person from each group present their list to the class. Keep these lists until the end of Unit 3. At that time have the class discuss the accuracy of their lists.

Extension Allow ELL students to write some words on the list in their native language.

Culminating Activity

Name That Geographical Term

OBJECTIVES: 2.01

Divide the class into groups of three. Within each group there will be two players and a master of ceremonies. The materials needed are a map, a score sheet, and an envelope of terms. The envelope will contain slips of paper with the names of countries, cities, bodies of water, and landforms of Southwest Asia. The master of ceremonies will draw a term from the envelope. The emcee announces the category of the term to the two players. Example: if the term is "Persian Gulf," then the category will be bodies of water. Next, the two players will state how many clues they need to make a correct answer. Player number one might say, "I will answer correctly after five clues." The second player might say, "I will answer correctly after four clues." Each player may continue to choose the number of clues (lower than his opponent), until one player challenges the other to "name that term."

To receive a clue about the term, the challenged player must ask a question of the emcee and will be answered only by yes or no. For example a player can ask, "Is it an ocean?" The player continues asking yes or no questions until all his clues are used. If the player guesses incorrectly, the points are awarded to the other player. After 20 points are won, switch roles to let the emcee take a turn as a player.

Points are awarded on the following scale:
5 clues = 1 point
4 clues = 2 points
3 clues = 3 points
2 clues = 4 points
1 clue = 5 points

Art Activity

Our Dymaxion World

OBJECTIVES: 1.02, 1.03

Materials handouts of the dymaxion world map projection from the Teacher's Resource Guide; colored pencils, marker, crayons; scissors; glue/glue stick; optional: string

Give students copy of octahedron with dymaxion world map projection on it. Our location in the United States is indicated with "YOU ARE HERE"; have students find this position on the map projection. As students color this world map projection have them distinguish the lands of Southwest Asia in a different color from the remainder of Asia and Europe. When coloring is complete, students are to cut out their octahedron and fold tabs with letters on them and each triangular section. Tabs are matched by letter and glued together (can have string put into North Pole area with "A" tabs to hang this geometric shape).

Have students note how the location of the United States and Southwest Asia share similarities (Northern Hemisphere). Discuss with students that an octahedron is an eight-sided polyhedra with 12 edges and six vertices. Many call this three-dimensional shape a diamond.

Analogies

OBJECTIVES: 2.01, 12.01

Read the analogies aloud and ask students to identify the relationship between the terms. As an extension, ask students to write their own analogies using key terms or places discussed in the chapter.

strait : bodies of water :: isthmus : bodies of land (connects)

Tigris-Euphrates Rivers : Persian Gulf :: Mississippi River : Gulf of Mexico (empties into)

Ataturk Dam : Euphrates River :: Aswan Dam : Nile River (is built on the)

desalination : salt :: dehydration : water (removes)

sect : religion :: Catholic or Protestant : Christianity :: Sunni or Shiite : Islam (is a division of)

Teaching Strategies

In this chapter, students should gain an understanding of Southwest Asia's geography and the importance of its resources.

Activator

OBJECTIVES: 12.01

Locate pictures or objects from the three major religions of Christianity, Judaism, and Islam. Examples to bring include a menorah, dreidle, Bible, Quran, or
pictures of churches, synagogues, and temples.

After showing the pictures and objects to the students, ask them to brainstorm what they know about world religions and to predict what the religions have in common. After a brief discussion, explain that you will be studying the region where these three world religions originated.

OR

Using the information that students gained from their reading assignment the previous night, have them list five words that come to mind when they think of Southwest Asia. Discuss the words. Take only about 5 minutes for this activity.

Writing Prompt

OBJECTIVES: 5.03

Evaluative

Clean water is a precious commodity for every region of the world. Imagine that you are have been appointed to present a report to the area Water Resources Board on who should have first claim to the water: farmers, businesses, or residents? Explain your decision fully.

As you write your report, remember to
- clearly state your position.
- give at least three reasons and explain your reasons fully.
- give examples to support your reasons.
- write in complete sentences and paragraph form.
- organize your ideas and include an introduction and a conclusion.
- use good grammar, spelling, punctuation, and capitalization.

CHAPTER 11

Lands and People of Southwest Asia

In 1947, young Bedouin shepherds searching for a stray goat in Wadi Qumran near the Dead Sea entered a long-untouched cave. There they found jars filled with ancient scrolls. The discovery of these seven scrolls began a search that yielded thousands of scroll fragments over the next ten years.

The Dead Sea Scrolls reveal much about two great world religions—Judaism and Christianity. They shed new light on how Southwest Asia shaped civilizations 2,000 years ago.

Chapter Preview

LESSON 1
Location and Landforms
Southwest Asia contains three regions—the Middle East, the Northern Tier, and the Arabian Peninsula.

LESSON 2
Climates and Resources
The region is dry except for the fertile valleys of Turkey and the Middle East. Oil is a major resource. Water is scarce.

LESSON 3
People and Their Environment
Arabs, Iranians, Turks, Kurds, Armenians, and Jews live in Southwest Asia. Its arid environment is home to modern cities, farmers, and herders.

The Qumran Caves where the Dead Sea Scrolls (top left) were found.

Chapter Resources

Print Resources
Nonfiction

Heide, Florence Parry and Judith Heide Gilliland. *The Day of Ahmed's Secret.* Mulberry Books, 1995. ISBN 0688140238.
—. *Sami and the Time of Troubles.* Clarion, 1992. ISBN 0395720850.
Iran (Welcome to My Country). Franklin Watts Ltd., 2005. ISBN 0749660147.

National Geographic Atlas of the Middle East, 2003. ISBN 0792250664.
Nye, Naomi Shihab. *Sitti's Secret.* Simon & Shuster, 1997. ISBN 0689817061.
Pundyk, Grace. Welcome to Jordan (Welcome to My Country). Gareth Stevens Publishing, 2004. ISBN 0836825659.
Sabbah, Ann Carey. *Kurds.* Smart Apple Media, 2000. ISBN 1887068929.

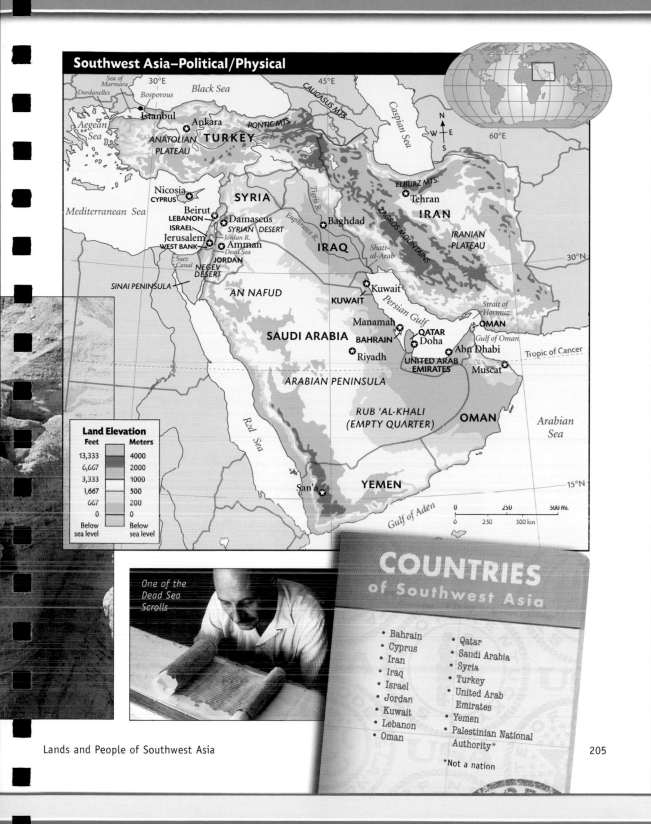

Southwest Asia–Political/Physical

Land Elevation

Feet	Meters
13,333	4000
6,667	2000
3,333	1000
1,667	500
667	200
0	0
Below sea level	Below sea level

One of the Dead Sea Scrolls

COUNTRIES of Southwest Asia

- Bahrain
- Cyprus
- Iran
- Iraq
- Israel
- Jordan
- Kuwait
- Lebanon
- Oman
- Qatar
- Saudi Arabia
- Syria
- Turkey
- United Arab Emirates
- Yemen
- Palestinian National Authority*

*Not a nation

Lands and People of Southwest Asia   205

Welcome to Turkey (Welcome to My Country). Gareth Stevens Publishing, 2002. ISBN 0836825411.

Whitcraft, Melissa. *The Tigris and Euphrates Rivers.* F. Watts, 1999. ISBN 0531117413.

Web Sites

Go to **NCJourneys.com** for links to the following Web sites:

- Interactive Map of Middle East
- MidEast Web - Middle East Conflict and Peace Process Source Documents
- Middle East Seismological Forum
- MuslimHeritage.Com
- World Seismicity Maps, Middle East

Map Activity

Southwest Asia

NATIONAL GEOGRAPHY STANDARDS: 1, 4, 17, 18

GEOGRAPHIC THEMES: Location, Place, Human-Environmental Interaction, Movement, Region

OBJECTIVES: 1.02, 1.03

First, note with students the important geographic features of Southwest Asia. Offer some mnemonics—for example, the image that the Arabian Peninsula is shaped like a large boot. Six countries follow the alphabet—I, J, I, K, I, L (with the first, Israel, coming to a point and the other five in alphabetical order from west to east, left to right): Israel, Jordan, Iraq, Kuwait, Iran, Lebanon getting from Iran to Lebanon by running from Iran back toward Israel.

Saudi Arabia is immediately south of the alphabetical states—Saudi and south begin with the letter "S." Bahrain is the island in the Persian Gulf between Saudi Arabia and Qatar—Bahrain and between begin with the letter "B." Syria is shaped like a triangle. Describe the divisions that have occurred in Yemen's history (creating North and South Yemen at times). Yemen forms the shape of the top part of the letter "Y."

Review the following features: Elbruz, Pontic, Taurus, and Zagros Mountains; Rub' al-Khali and Negev Deserts; Euphrates, Jordan, and Tigris Rivers; Aegean, Arabian, Black, Caspian, Dead, Marmara, Mediterranean, and Red Seas; Aden, Oman, and Persian Gulfs; and Strait of Hormuz.

Note which countries are crossed by the Tropic of Cancer (Saudi Arabia, United Arab Emirates, and Oman).

Briefly discuss Israel, Syria, and the Palestinian National Authority, including the conflicts over the Gaza Strip, Golan Heights, and the West Bank of the Jordan, including Jerusalem.

Remind students, too, that a commonly accepted division between Asia and Europe that impacts Southwest Asia is formed by the Ural Mountains, Ural River, Caspian Sea, Caucasus Mountains, and the Black Sea with its outlets, the Bosporus and Dardanelles.

Discussion Questions

1 What three continents cross to give Southwest Asia its relative location? Can you recall any other places that are considered crossroads?

2 What has contributed to the diverse cultures of Southwest Asia?

3 How has Southwest Asia's relative location helped shape its history?

4 Explain why Southeast Asia is considered to be a crossroads of world trade.

 Caption Answer

The region is bordered by the Mediterranean, Black, Caspian, Arabian, and Red Seas.

 Activity

The Glow in Southwest Asia—Satellite View of Southwest Asia

🔺 **OBJECTIVES:** 1.02, 2.01

Have students compare the satellite view on page 206 with the one on page 166. Have students point out Southwest Asia on the page 166 image. Using the map on page 205, assign students to identify the elevations and physical features that create the glow from golden yellow to reddish orange and brown on the Southwest Asia satellite view.

0 to 3,333 feet/1,000 meters is deserts and plains in golden yellow; 3,333 feet/1,000 meters to 13,333 feet/4,000 meters is high plateaus, hills, and mountains in reddish orange and brown

LESSON ① Location and Landforms

- Southwest Asia is described as 15 nations surrounded by the Mediterranean, Black, Caspian, Arabian, and Red Seas.

- The region has several landforms. Its rivers are a vital resource. Surrounding seas serve as transportation routes.

- The Middle East, Northern Tier, and Arabian Peninsula are key subregions of Southwest Asia.

KEY TERMS

relief
strait

Today, as in ancient times, Southwest Asia is an important region. It is the crossroad of three continents—Europe, Africa, and Asia. It is the birthplace of Judaism, Christianity, and Islam. Parts of the region are rich in one of the world's key resources—oil. It has the largest oil reserves in the world. Sadly, the region has been the focus of conflicts over land, resources, and religion.

What is Southwest Asia?

Unlike Africa, Southwest Asia is not a separate continent. It is a corner of the enormous Asian continent. Its nations may be easily located if you look for land almost surrounded by five bodies of water—the Mediterranean, Black, Caspian, Arabian, and Red Seas. Iran is the region's easternmost nation.

The region is not easy to define. Some speak of Southwest Asia as a place where Muslim people live in an "Arab world." Such a description, however, leaves out Turkey and Iran (ih·RAHN), whose people are Muslim but not Arab. Also, Arabs inhabit North Africa—a vast area outside of Southwest Asia. Christians and Jews have also always lived here.

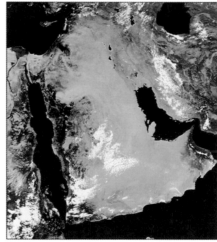

A satellite view from space of Southwest Asia shows the region is almost surrounded by water. **What bodies of water border the region?**

Geographers include 15 nations in the region of Southwest Asia—Turkey, Iran, Iraq (ih·RAK), Israel, Jordan, Lebanon, Saudi Arabia (SOWD·ih ah·RAY·bih·ah), Syria (SIHR·ee·ah), Yemen (YEM·en), Bahrain (bah·RAYN), Kuwait, Oman (oh·MAHN), Qatar (KAHT·er), the United Arab Emirates (EM·ih·rayts), and the Republic of Cyprus.

Southwest Asian Crossroads

Southwest Asia links Europe, Africa, and Asia. The photograph on the left covers the same area as the map on page 205. Note how Southwest Asia is southeast of Europe, east of Africa, and southwest of Asia. This crossroads location has shaped the region through history. In ancient times, many people migrated there. Traders crossed the region, spreading goods and ideas. Invaders from all directions conquered it. Each group left its cultural "footprints." Southwest Asia has become a region of complex and diverse cultures.

Modern Southwest Asia is still a crossroads of world trade. It controls vital sea and land routes. Turkey, for example, controls the Bosporus (BAHS·pruss) and Dardanelles (dard·en·ELZ) Straits. These straits link the Black Sea to the Mediterranean. A *strait* is a narrow waterway that connects two larger bodies of water.

 Background Information

Southwest Asia Geography

■ United Arab Emirates is composed of seven small Trucial states (formerly known as the Trucial States, Trucial Coast, or Trucial Oman). The seven constituent emirates were bound to the United Kingdom by truce in 1820 and agreement later (1892).

■ Turkey bridges Europe and Asia. The smaller European part (Thrace) is separated from the larger Asian Anatolia Peninsula by the Bosporus and Dardanelles Straits and the Sea of Marmara.

■ Cyprus is fragmented by Turkish Cypriots who want the northern third of this island to be the Turkish Republic of Northern Cyprus.

The Red Sea and Suez Canal, lying between Africa and Southwest Asia, are also important sea lanes. Ships use these waterways to avoid the long voyage around Africa on trips between Europe and Asia (see map, page 205).

Landforms

Many Americans think of Southwest Asia as one large desert. In fact, the region has a variety of landforms.

Turkey and Iran have the highest mountains. Find the Pontic (PAHN·tik), Taurus (TAWR·us), Elburz (el·BURZ), and Zagros (ZAG·ros) Mountains on the map on page 205.

Mountains affect movement and communication. Traders, invaders, and modern-day road builders had to find a way around or through the mountains.

Mountains also influence Southwest Asia's environment. The region's high peaks affect rainfall. The western and northern slopes of Southwest Asia generally receive more moisture and block precipitation from reaching the east and south. Long ago, major shifts in the earth's crust created the mountains. Shifts still occur in the mountains of Turkey and northern Iran, causing severe earthquakes. Some of these quakes have killed thousands of people.

North of the Taurus Mountains in Turkey lies the Anatolian (an·ah·TOH·lih·an) Plateau. It has a continental climate that makes it suitable for growing grain.

The Iranian Plateau lies east of Iran's Zagros Mountains. It is much dryer than the Anatolian Plateau because a great salt desert lies at its center. The Iranian Plateau has little plant life.

The Syrian Desert and the Rub' al-Khali (rub·al KAHL·ih)(meaning "Empty Quarter") and An Nafud (ahn nah·FUHD) in Saudi Arabia (see map, page 205) are mostly areas of low-lying rocky terrain. These deserts have little *relief*. There are few hills and valleys that create differences in height.

Some deserts are like seas of sand. Winds create dunes and patterns. Like mountains, deserts discourage the movement of people because they have little or no water. So in earlier times, most traders and invaders avoided them. Instead, they took routes where water was available.

WORD ORIGINS

Iran once appeared on European and United States maps as Persia. This name came from the word Persis, the Greek name for the area. The Persians, preferred the name "land of the Aryans." Iran comes from "Aryans," and it has been the country's name in modern times.

Saudi Arabia's Rub' al-Khali Desert is called the Empty Quarter. **What are other major landforms of Southwest Asia?**

Lands and People of Southwest Asia

207

Name Origin

Asia A Greek word meaning "east."

Euphrates River The Greek adaptation of a Semitic word meaning "great water."

Tigris An ancient word meaning "arrow," reflecting swiftness of the river's current.

Baghdad is a Persian word meaning "gift of God."

The Black Sea Named for the heavy fogs that form during winter, making the water look dark.

Bethlehem Hebrew for "house of bread." Jerusalem is Hebrew for "City of Peace."

Discussion Questions

1 Describe the different landforms of Southwest Asia and the climates associated with them.

Caption Answer

There are mountains in Turkey and Iran, the Anatolian Plateau, the Syrian Desert, and the An Nafud Desert.

Teacher Notes

Illustrating Relief

You can illustrate the key term of relief by taking a piece of notebook paper and demonstrating that it has no relief; it has all the same elevations. Next crumble the paper and then slightly unfold to demonstrate a relief surface. Students can also make a fist and see relief in that their knuckles are raised higher than the back of their hand.

Afghanistan and Southwest Asia

Briefly describe how some anthropologists, geographers, and historians often consider Afghanistan part of Southwest Asia, in part because of its cultural and linguistic ties to the Persian Empire (centered in today's Iran) and religious ties to Islam.

Earthquakes

Parts of Southwest Asia have a long history of earthquake activity. In the last 20 years, several large earthquakes in Turkey and Iran have resulted in huge disasters with thousands of deaths. The December 2003 Bam earthquake in southeast Iran killed more than 40,000 people. The region has high death rates due both to a dense population and also to a lack of coodinated earthquake building codes. The table in Chapter 19, page 379, will help illustrate this point for students.

Discussion Questions

1 What was the role of the Tigris and the Euphrates Rivers in the development of Mesopotamia? How have they continued to be important?

2 What is the relative location of the five major bodies of water that border Southwest Asia?

3 Why is the Persian Gulf important to this region? the Red Sea?

4 Describe the relationship between the Suez Canal and world trade. What canal in the Americas serves a similar purpose?

Caption Answer

Africa

Map Activity

Regional Clay Map

OBJECTIVES: 1.01, 2.01

Have students make a clay relief map of the region, including the parts of Europe and Africa that border Southwest Asia. Include surrounding bodies of water, mountains, plateaus, and the desert. It would be helpful if students had a different color of clay for each of the continents.

Clay Recipe

1 cup water
1 cup flour
½ cup salt
2 teaspoons cream of tartar
1 tablespoon cooking oil
food coloring

Students must use liquid cooking oil and cream of tartar. Do not use sugar! Combine dry ingredients in a saucepan and combine liquid ingredients in a cup. Stir the liquids into the dry ingredients. Cook over medium heat for approximately 3 minutes, stirring. When the mixture has the texture of play dough or cookie dough, remove from the heat. Knead until smooth (this does not take long), and store in airtight container. Clay should not be sticky at all.

Bodies of Water

Lack of moisture has made fresh water, especially from rivers, enormously important to Southwest Asia. Israel and Jordan, for example, struggle over control of the precious waters of the Jordan River.

The Tigris (TIGH·gris) and Euphrates (yoo·FRAYT·eez) Rivers rise in the mountains of Turkey and flow through Syria and Iraq before emptying into the Persian Gulf. The two rivers embrace a region that the ancient Greeks called Mesopotamia, meaning "land between the rivers."

These rivers played a key role in the birth of some of the world's earliest civilizations. Mesopotamia is part of the Fertile Crescent, an arc of green land stretching from the Mediterranean Sea to the Persian Gulf. Because of the availability of water, it remains a key agricultural region.

Turkey dammed the Euphrates and created a huge reservoir. Downstream, Syria and Iraq worry that Turkey will use the water their people need.

Southwest Asia is bordered by five major bodies of water. The Mediterranean Sea washes against Turkey, Syria, Lebanon, and Israel, and surrounds the island of Cyprus. The Black Sea borders Turkey to the north and separates it from Russia and Ukraine. The Caspian Sea is an inland lake bordering northern Iran. All but the Caspian Sea connect Southwest Asia to the world's oceans (see map, page 205).

Today, as in thousands of years past, the Persian Gulf is one of the region's most important bodies of water. It is a shallow, warm-water sea that separates Iran from the Arabian Peninsula to the south. The Tigris and Euphrates Rivers empty into it. The gulf is important to the world's economy. It has much oil below its surface and is a busy shipping route.

The Red Sea, another major sea route, separates Southwest Asia from Africa. Deserts line both its shores. The sea fills part of a huge valley that stretches from the Jordan Valley in Southwest Asia to the Great Rift Valley in East Africa.

The Red Sea has carried merchants between Arab lands and African shores for centuries. With the opening of the Suez Canal (see pages 118–119), the sea became a key link in world trade routes running between Europe and Asia.

The Red Sea, shown near Bir Ali, Yemen, is a major route between the Mediterranean Sea and the Indian Ocean. **What continent is separated from Southwest Asia by the Red Sea?**

208

Background Information

The Tigris and Euphrates Rivers

The Euphrates River begins high in the mountains of eastern Turkey, where rainfall accounts for four fifths of its volume. It is the largest river in western Asia and flows more than 1,700 miles across Syria and southern Iraq. The 1,180-mile-long Tigris River has its source within 50 miles of the Euphrates, although the two do not join until almost to the Persian Gulf. The Tigris-Euphrates river system may one day lead to conflict between Iraq, Syria, and Turkey. In 1975 Iraq threatened war with Syria over the scanty flow of the Euphrates below Syria's Tabaqa Dam. This dam diverted water to farmlands for Syrian irrigation projects. In Turkey, the Ataturk and other dams have also reduced the Euphrates River's flow, causing increased friction with Turkey's neighbors.

LESSON 2 Climates and Resources

What is the most important resource of Southwest Asia? If you asked Americans, many might say oil. If you asked people in the region the same question, most would say water. Oil is plentiful in parts of Southwest Asia. Water is scarce almost everywhere. The abundance of oil and scarcity of water have been powerful forces shaping the region.

Varied Climates

We often picture Southwest Asia as a hot, dry region. Large areas are indeed dry, yet climates in the region vary greatly.

Rainfall is partly controlled by wind patterns. In summer months, hot, dry air blows in from the south. Westward winds arrive in winter months, carrying moisture from the sea. These shifting winds provide parts of Southwest Asia with a Mediterranean climate. People who live in these areas experience warm, wet winters and hot, dry summers. Lebanon's location on the Mediterranean coast makes its climate patterns predictable. Winter rains provide moisture at lower altitudes for semitropical flowers, banana trees, and palms. Snow glistens on higher mountains.

Deeper in Southwest Asia's interior, the amount of moisture that will be carried by the winter winds is harder to predict. Good rains one year help farmers produce crop surpluses. The next few years may bring only a little rain and poor harvests. So farming is an uncertain occupation.

The arid climate and its effects are important to remember as you study Southwest Asia. You will learn how the scarcity of water has affected governments and economies in the region, and the daily life of many people there.

Elevation, nearness to the sea, and wind patterns also affect climate. Turkey's Anatolian Plateau, for example, is surrounded by mountains and lies high above sea level. Summer temperatures are hot and dry. Winters are cold with a moderate amount of rain and snow. Frequent winter storms bring heavy rains to the eastern Mediterranean coast. After a storm passes, the days are often sunny and the nights cool.

KEY IDEAS

- Southwest Asia's climates vary. Much of the region is arid.
- Climate has affected where people live in Southwest Asia.
- Oil and water are unevenly distributed in the region.

KEY TERMS

aquifers
deforestation
depleted
wadis

A camel and its rider have stopped in a dry streambed in Jordan.
What effect does unpredictable rain have on Southwest Asia?

Discussion Questions

1 What two natural resources have been major forces in shaping Southwest Asia? How?

2 Describe the varied climates of Southwest Asia. What are the reasons for these differences?

 Caption Answer

It makes agriculture more difficult and the scarcity of water affects economics, governments, and people.

 ELL Teaching Tips

Avoid Singling ELL Students Out
If you have some important information to convey, speak to the student one-on-one rather than in front of the class. When put on the spot, it is more difficult for them to understand what you expect.

 Name Origin

Lebanon Arabic for "White Mountain." The Lebanon Mountain is snow-covered most of the year. Iraq is the ancient Persian name, like Iran, but from a later dialect. Other theories say the word is Arabic for "origins."

Israel From the ancient Hebrew phrase meaning "people of God." Jordan was named for the river, a Hebrew word

meaning "descender." The Jordan River flows into the lowest site on the earth's surface.

Cyprus Greek meaning "cuprum," copper. Cyprus was where the ancient Greeks mined their copper. Turkey comes from the word Turk, which means "strong."

United Arab Emirates Seven small emirates that banded together in 1971. Each emirate is under the rule of an emir, Arabic for "ruler."

Yemen Arabic for "south," meaning the end of the peninsula.

Bahrain Arabic meaning "sea" or "water," indicating the islands' environment.

Kuwait Arabic for "Little Fort."

Iran The ancient Persian name from Babylonia.

Discussion Questions

1 How have the different climates affected the population and vegetation of the area?

2 What are some crops in your region that depend on predictable weather patterns? What effect does the weather have on the price of these goods?

3 What creative ideas have farmers initiated in order to produce crops in areas where little rain falls?

Caption Answer

Deciduous forest and mixed forest. Winds off the Mediterranean carry moisture during the winter. Areas farther east do not receive these moisture-bearing winds.

Science Activity

Vegetation and Biomes

NATIONAL GEOGRAPHY STANDARDS: 1, 4, 8

GEOGRAPHIC THEMES: Location, Place

OBJECTIVES: 2.01, 2.02

Discuss with students the definitions for deciduous, coniferous, and scrub. Generally the earth's biomes (mature ecosystems) consists of four categories: forest, grassland, desert, and tundra. Assign students to identify which of these categories are found in Southwest Asia (*forest, grassland, and desert*). Lead students to notice there are two forest biomes in Southwest Asia (*mid-latitude deciduous and mixed*) and that mixed is more widespread in this region than mid-latitude deciduous being located north of 30°N latitude. Ask students to identify which two vegetation areas are most prevalent (*temperate grassland and desert scrub*). Introduce xerophytic plants as those that are capable of growing in deserts and tolerating annual precipitation levels below 10

Climate and Agriculture

Today, and throughout history, rainfall has affected where people settled in Southwest Asia. Civilizations arose in river valleys that had ample supplies of water. Agriculture thrived in moist areas along the rainy Mediterranean coast.

Southwest Asia was home to the world's first farmers. Early farmers learned to plant the seeds of grains they had found growing in the wild. Today, grains are still the most important food crops grown in the region. Turkey and Iran receive enough rain for widespread farming. They produce much of the region's wheat, barley, and corn.

Even though many people are farmers, the region has to import food because of the lack of enough fertile land and moisture. Without adequate rain, most countries can grow only a limited number of agricultural products. Even land that is suitable for crops must often be irrigated. The small Persian Gulf nations must irrigate all of their farmland. Canals, pumps, and pipelines carry water to farm fields. Israel irrigates about half of its cropland.

This limits what farmers can grow. So farmers concentrate on raising vegetables that will grow with a little water running between the crop rows.

Other farmers produce fruit, especially olives, grapes, and dates. Such fruit can be sown on the lower slopes of mountains where rain falls. Farmers often dig terraced fields there. These small, flat fields are efficient uses of hilly or mountainous land. They more easily trap the moisture that crops need than do hills or rugged mountain slopes.

Oil Wealth

Our cars run on it; homes and schools are heated by it. Industry depends on it. "It" is oil. Much of the world's supply is from Southwest Asia.

This one region is thought to have about 60 percent of the world's entire supply of oil. Yet only a few nations in Southwest Asia have large oil reserves. Most of these nations are located in the desert lands around the Persian Gulf. The countries with this "black gold" generally

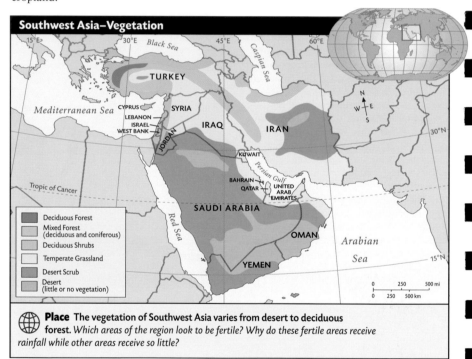

Place The vegetation of Southwest Asia varies from desert to deciduous forest. *Which areas of the region look to be fertile? Why do these fertile areas receive rainfall while other areas receive so little?*

Chapter 11

inches. Guide students to understand that the scattered vegetation is usually small, grows slowly, and many types have a life cycle that follows the rare rainfalls and includes months or years of dormancy between weeks of blooming (see photograph, page 209, for an example).

Have students create a graphic organizer of specific examples—words and illustrations—of vegetation types found in Southwest Asia.

have small populations. They include Iraq, Saudi Arabia, Kuwait, Qatar, Oman, and the United Arab Emirates. Among the richest oil-producing nations, only Iran has a very large population (see map, page 219).

Modern Southwest Asia is largely divided between nations with and without oil. Most nations with oil are wealthier than nations without it. But Dubai, one of the United Arab Emirates, is successful without oil. In contrast, Saudi Arabia's leaders do not fully share their oil wealth.

Oil wealth has permitted oil-producing nations to build new cities and offer such services as education, transportation, and medical care to their people. But some nations do not try to diversify their economies, and so become dependent on oil. Southwest Asian nations that do not contain oil are not able to provide as many benefits to their people. These poorer nations are still affected by oil. Workers from Egypt and Jordan as well as India, Pakistan, Bangladesh, and the Philippines have taken jobs in the oil-rich countries. They send most of their

earnings home to help their families.

Another energy source—natural gas—is often found alongside oil. Gas is also pumped from underground reservoirs. Along the Persian Gulf, valuable reservoirs of natural gas have been estimated to be about 45 percent of the world's reserves.

*Oil is a major resource throughout Southwest Asia. **What nations in the region are oil-rich?***

 What would YOU do?

Sheep and goats provide food and materials for shelters everywhere in Southwest Asia. But they are destructive to the environment. They eat grasses that hold moisture. Goats also devour young trees. Efforts to replant forests run into problems because herders want to let their animals graze freely. What would be a solution?

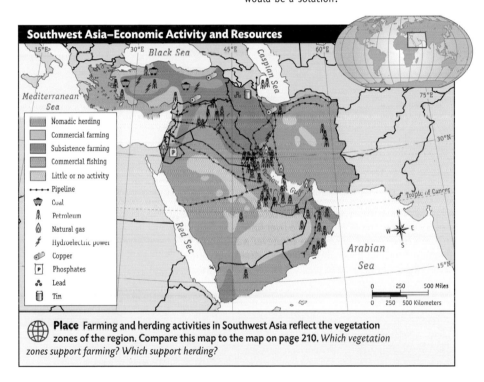

Southwest Asia—Economic Activity and Resources

- Nomadic herding
- Commercial farming
- Subsistence farming
- Commercial fishing
- Little or no activity
- ⊷ Pipeline
- Coal
- Petroleum
- Natural gas
- Hydroelectric power
- Copper
- Phosphates
- Lead
- Tin

Mediterranean Sea · Black Sea · Caspian Sea · Red Sea · Arabian Sea · Tropic of Cancer

15°E · 30°E · 45°E · 60°E · 75°E · 30°N · 15°N

0   250   500 Miles
0   250   500 Kilometers

Place Farming and herding activities in Southwest Asia reflect the vegetation zones of the region. Compare this map to the map on page 210. *Which vegetation zones support farming? Which support herding?*

Lands and People of Southwest Asia

213

Discussion Questions

1 Some of the richest oil reserves are located in nations with very small populations. How would this affect their per capita income?

2 Nations of this region are classified as the haves and the have-nots based on their income from oil. Can you think of other places in the world where there is a division of the haves and the have-nots?

3 What is the relative location of Iran? Why does it have such a large population?

4 Would you classify these countries as developed or developing? Explain why.

5 Although the poorer nations do not have oil reserves, they are still affected by oil. Explain.

6 Why do you think natural gas is often found alongside oil in underground reservoirs?

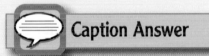 **Caption Answer**

Iraq, Iran, Saudi Arabia, Kuwait, Qatar, Oman, and the United Arab Emirates are oil-rich.

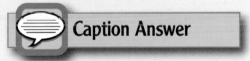 **Caption Answer**

Deciduous forest, mixed forest. Temperate grassland.

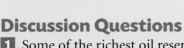 **Map Activity**

Locate!

NATIONAL GEOGRAPHY STANDARDS: 0

GEOGRAPHIC THEMES: Region, Place, Human-Environmental Interaction

OBJECTIVES: 1.02, 1.03

Students should use this map, and the maps in Unit 4 to find the following facts about Southwest Asia. Write additional facts for the class, or have the class write facts. In

pairs or as a class, have students ask each other to locate where they are. Students should round to the absolute location to whole numbers.

"I am at the northernmost point. Where am I?" *North coast of Turkey.* "What is it in degrees?" *42°N*

"I am at the southernmost point. Where am I?" *South coast of Yemen.* "What is it in degrees?" *14°N*

"I am at the easternmost point? Where am I?" *Iranian border with Pakistan.* "What is it in degrees?" *64°E*

"I am at the westernmost point? Where am I?" *West coast of Turkey.* "What is it in degrees?" *26°E*

"How far does Southwest Asia extend from east to west?" *Approximately 1,700 miles.* "North to south?" *Approximately 1,800 miles.*

"Which countries does the Tropic of Cancer pass through?" *Saudi Arabia, United Arab Emirates, Oman.*

"I have a pipeline to the Red Sea. What country am I?" *Saudi Arabia*

Eyewitness Activity

Building an Aquifer

OBJECTIVES: 2.03, 3.01

Materials one 6-inch by 8-inch clear plastic container that is at least 6 to 8 inches deep (shoe box or small aquarium); one pound of modeling clay or floral clay; two pounds of white play sand; two pounds of aquarium gravel (natural color if possible) or small pebbles (small rocks may have a powdery residue on them, you may wish to rinse them and dry on a clean towel prior to use; it is best if they do not add cloudiness to water); 1 drinking water straw; 1 plastic spray bottle (be sure the stem that extends into the bottle is clear); 1 small piece (3-inch by 5-inch) of green felt; ¼ cup of powered cocoa; red food coloring; 1 bucket of clean water and small cup to dip water from bucket; transparent tape

To one side of the container place the small drinking water straw, allowing approximately one eighth of an inch clearance with the bottom of the container. Fasten the straw directly against the long side of the container with a piece of tape. Explain to the students that this will represent two separate well functions later in presentation (if not placed at this time, sand will clog the opening).

Pour a layer of white sand completely covering the bottom of the clear plastic container, making it approximately 1 inch deep. Pour water into the sand, wetting it completely, but there should be no standing water on top of sand. Let students see how the water is absorbed in the sand but remains around the sand particles, as it is stored in the ground and ultimately in the aquifer.

Flatten the modeling clay (like a pancake) and cover the sand with the clay (try to press the clay into the three sides of the container in the area covered). The clay represents a "confining layer" that keeps water from passing through it. Pour a small amount of water onto the clay. Let the students see how the water remains on top of the clay, only flowing into the sand below in

EYEWITNESS TO HISTORY

Sources of Water Through History

The deserts were green forests 25,000 years ago. Rains that kept the forests green penetrated the earth's surface and collected in **aquifers,** geological formations that hold water. These aquifers continue to supply fresh water, even though heavy rains have not fallen for centuries.

Harvesting wheat along the Euphrates River (above); an irrigation canal in Jordan (above right)

Israel and Jordan share the Jordan River. The river is about 200 miles (322 km) long. The river flows from Lebanon south through the Sea of Galilee into the Dead Sea. The river forms the boundary between Jordan and Israel. Jordan uses whatever water comes downstream, but this supply is always limited. Israel, not Jordan, controls the amount of water that reaches Jordan. Jordan does not have access to any other major river.

areas not covered by the clay.

Use the aquarium rocks to form the next layer of earth. Place the rocks over the sand and clay, covering the entire container. To one side of our container, slope the rocks, forming a high hill and a valley. Now pour water into your aquifer until the water in the valley is even with your hill. Let students see the water around the rocks that is stored within the aquifer. They will all notice that a "surface" supply of water (a small lake) has formed. This will give them a view of both the ground and surface water supplies that can be used for drinking water purposes.

Next, place the small piece of green felt on top of the hill. If possible, use a little clay to securely fasten it to the side of the container it reaches. Using the cocoa, sprinkle some on top of the hill while explaining to students that the cocoa represents improper use of fertilizers, lawn chemicals, etc.

Use the food coloring and put a few drops into the straw, explaining to students that often old wells are used to dispose of trash, chemicals, used motor oils, etc. They will see that it will color the sand in the bottom of the container. This is one way pollution can spread throughout the aquifer over time.

TURKEY
Ataturk Dam
(at·ah·TURK)

Euphrates River

Tigris River

IRAN

CYPRUS

SYRIA

LEBANON

Mediterranean Sea

Sea of Galilee

IRAQ

WEST BANK

Jordan River

Dead Sea

Lake Hammar

ISRAEL

JORDAN

Persian Gulf

The Tigris and Euphrates Rivers empty into the Persian Gulf.

Turkey controls the headwaters to the Euphrates. The Ataturk Dam (left), built across the river by Turkey, will hold more water than the Sea of Galilee. Iraq and Syria—downstream from the dam—fear that Turkey can use its control of the water to threaten them. These fears show how water becomes the source of serious conflict. Diplomats have urged the nations to agree to share water.

nds and People of Southwest Asia   215

Art Activity

Create a Brochure

OBJECTIVES: 1.01

Use the Internet to research a location in Southwest Asia. Download photographs and design and create a brochure describing that location. Topics might include Jerusalem, Mecca, Dead Sea, Rub' al-Khali, Persian Gulf, or Istanbul. Display the brochures.

Extension Expect more pictures than writing from novice and intermediate ELL students.

Activity

Renewable v. Nonrenewable Resources

OBJECTIVES: 5.04, 11.01

The concept of renewable and nonrenewable resources is important for students' understanding of the United States' interest in Southwest Asia. Have students compose a list of renewable and nonrenewable resources. Discuss oil's importance as a natural resource and alternate solutions to using oil.

Give each group of students 15 M&M's of different colors in a cup. Tell the students that they are members of two countries that are in a border dispute. The two countries are fighting over the rights to natural resources located along the border. Without talking, the students have 30 seconds to look at the resources placed in their cup and decide how there are going to divide the resources fairly. After 30 seconds, the two sides of the group can verbally negotiate to decide who gets the resources for 4 minutes. After the activity, have each group report to the class how they felt when they were first looking at the resources. This may symbolize two countries not being able to communicate because of language barriers. Ask the groups how they finally decided to divide the resources. Many groups will say they assigned different colors to be different resources such as water, coal, oil, and so forth.

215

Discussion Questions

1 Water, like oil, is a valuable commodity. Which do you think is more valuable to the people of Southwest Asia? Why?

2 Describe the direct relationship between water and settlement of people in an area?

3 What are some problems caused by deforestation? What resources have been depleted as a result? What can be done to replenish these resources?

Caption Answer

An aquifer is a geological formation that holds water. A wadi is a dry streambed found throughout desert regions.

Activity

Share the Water

OBJECTIVES: 1.02, 2.01

Water is an important resource in Southwest Asia. Using an atlas, have students make a list of cities in Southwest Asia that are located on bodies of water. Have the students divide the list into cities on freshwater and those on saltwater. Now list cities that don't appear to be on a river, lake, or sea.

Answers

Freshwater: *Baghdad—Tigris*

Sea/Saltwater: *Jiddah, Saudi Arabia—Red Sea; Tel Aviv, Israel—Mediterranean; Beirut, Lebanon—Mediterranean; Istanbul, Turkey—Sea of Marman*

No water source: *Damascus, Syria; Tehran, Iran; Ankara, Turkey; Jerusalem*

Discuss the following: What are the advantages of a location on freshwater? of a location on saltwater? Are there disadvantages? How do you explain the location of cities in areas away from bodies of water?

The Key Resource

Because of the arid climate, water is a scarce and valuable resource in Southwest Asia. Many rivers slow to mere trickles in the long, dry season.

There are few lakes. Fewer still provide fresh water. Most, like the Dead Sea, are loaded with mineral salts. The waters of the Dead Sea are unfit for humans, animals, or plants to drink.

Fresh water springs are found in many places. In Lebanon, water gushes from mountains. Water is often found only a few feet below the surface of wadis. *Wadis* are dry streambeds found throughout desert regions. Water flows beneath parts of the Arabian deserts and the Iranian Plateau. Long ago, nomads tapped this water by digging wells.

As population grows, demands for water increase. People need water for drinking and washing, for animals and crops, and for industry. Today, there is often tension among nations that share water supplies.

Other Resources

People have lived in Southwest Asia for thousands of years. Many natural resources have been *depleted*, or exhausted, over the centuries. Forests, for example, have been cut down to provide fuel for cooking and heating, and for smelting, or refining, metals. Today, few forests remain. The removal of forests is called *deforestation*. The treeless mountains of present-day Iran and the Anatolian Plateau were once covered with forests.

We know from ancient stories that Southwest Asia was not as dry 2,000 years ago as it is today. Scientists are not certain about the reasons for the climate change. Many believe that deforestation has contributed to erosion and the loss of soil. Without roots to hold the soil, wind and water have stripped the ground of fertile earth.

Minerals, too, have been depleted. Long ago, Southwest Asia produced copper, gold, iron, zinc, and lead.

A water reservoir in Jordan is filled from an underground aquifer that flows into a wadi.
What is an aquifer? What is a wadi?

Activity

Shared Resources

OBJECTIVES: 3.01, 5.03

After students understand that water is a scarce resource, have students pretend to be the mayor of a Southwest Asian city of 20,000 people. They have to allot amounts of water to various groups. Below are the four groups:

city dwellers who need water for everyday living (60 percent of the population)

Bedouins who come to your city to trade and water animals (20 percent of the population)

local farmers who need large amounts of water to irrigate crops (10 percent of the population)

the city's elite who have such luxuries as pools and baths (10 percent of the population)

Students should allocate the water using percentages to show the amounts each group receives, based upon a total of 100 percent. Students must justify their decisions as to who has a priority for water and how much they should receive.

Mountains near Bashir, Iran, show the effects of deforestation. **What other resources have been depleted in Southwest Asia?**

Discussion Questions

1 Why has this region not become a major manufacturing center?

Caption Answer

Gold, iron, zinc, and lead have been depleted.

Math Activity

Oil Math Word Problem

OBJECTIVES: 5.01, 5.04

Oil is a key resource in this region. A barrel (the unit for selling oil) holds 32 gallons. If a barrel sells for $55, what is the cost per gallon? Look in the newspaper/Internet for the current oil price per barrel. What is the current price per gallon (round to the hundredths place)?

Answer Approximately $1.71/gallon

Extension Using a newspaper's auto section, students will identify the gas mileage of a hybrid car, a compact car, and a sport utility vehicle. Next, they should determine the average cost of a gallon of gas in their community (they may also take a survey and find the average themselves) and calculate how much it would cost to operate each type of vehicle for a year based upon an average annual distance traveled of 12,000 miles. Create a bar graph to compare results.

Extension Assist ELL students by setting up the problem for them.

Constant mining used up these resources. Some copper mines have been reopened using up-to-date mining methods. Turkey has coal and chrome, two valuable industrial minerals. Iran has found some copper deposits. Jordan and Israel possess quantities of phosphate, an essential ingredient of chemical fertilizers (see map, page 213).

Industries, however, do not operate on such scattered resources. A few of Southwest Asia's wealthier nations import raw materials and use them to support a few industries. Despite such efforts, the region as a whole is not a major manufacturing center.

LESSON 2 REVIEW

Fact Follow-Up

1. Describe the different climates in Southwest Asia.
2. What crops are grown in the region?
3. What Southwest Asian nations are oil producers?
4. What mineral resources are found in Southwest Asia?

Talk About It

1. What has happened to the climate and earth resources of Southwest Asia over its long history?
2. How has water or its absence influenced how people live in Southwest Asia?
3. What is the relation between water and settlement in the region?

LESSON 2 REVIEW

Fact Follow-Up Answers

1. Climates in the region vary from Mediterranean (with hot, dry summers and warm, wet winters) on the coasts of Turkey, Lebanon, and Israel to desert in the interior. The high Anatolian Plateau has hot and dry summers and cold and moderately wet winters. Southwest Asian climates are affected by elevation, nearness to the sea, and prevailing winds. Interior areas have arid climates.
2. Wetter areas such as Turkey and Iran grow wheat, barley, and corn. In drier nations with irrigation, farmers grow olives, grapes, dates, and other fruit and vegetables.
3. Iraq, Iran, Saudi Arabia, Kuwait, Qatar, Oman, and the United Arab Emirates are oil-rich.
4. Mineral resources include copper, phosphate, chrome, and coal in addition to oil.

Talk About It Answers

1. Long years of human habitation have depleted resources and deforested the region. The region has become drier over time, and fertile soil has been blown or washed away.
2. Agriculture has developed in well-watered areas. In some areas, farmers use terraced fields on the lower slopes of mountains to catch rain. Even with new irrigation methods, food must still be imported into the region. Near or in the deserts, people herd animals, moving constantly in search of water and food. The presence or absence of water in the region contributes to the uneven distribution of its population.
3. The first civilizations arose in the fertile area between the Tigris and Euphrates Rivers and along the rainy Mediterranean coast.

OBJECTIVES: 3.01, 6.02, 11.01

Discussion Questions

1 Why is there so much confusion about how to define the word "Arab"? How would you define it? How has the meaning of the word "Arab" changed over the years?

2 "All Arabs are Muslims. All Muslims are Arabs." Prove or disprove this statement.

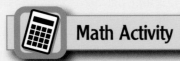

Caption Answer

Arabs are people in different countries who share a common culture and language.

Math Activity

Standard of Living

OBJECTIVES: 6.01

Have the students use the almanac or the Internet (the CIA World Factbook and the United Nation's Cyber Schoolbus iare good sources) to determine the standard of living of the fourteen Southwest Asia countries by comparing literacy rate, life expectancy, and per capita income. Assign countries so that all will be covered. Students should all graph their findings using the same type of graph to facilitate comparing the information. Have students enter the data into a spreadsheet and sort to create their graphs.

LESSON 3 People and Their Environment

KEY IDEAS

- Southwest Asia is home to many different people and religions.

- The arid environment has shaped different ways of life—settled farming, nomadic herding, and cities.

- Various technologies have helped people adapt to an arid environment.

KEY TERMS

desalination
fertigation
Holocaust
sects

If you meet people in Arab Southwest Asia, they will greet you: "As-Salaam alaykum" ("Peace be upon you"). Your reply should be "Wa alaykum as-salaam" ("And upon you peace").

This is Arabic, the most important language in Southwest Asia. Still, it is far from the only language spoken in the region. Arabs make up the great majority of the people in Southwest Asia. There also are many smaller ethnic groups with their own languages.

Who Is an Arab?

Almost 75 percent of the people in Southwest Asia are Arabs. Yet it is often hard to define the word Arab. Does it mean all people who speak Arabic? Or are Arabs just the people living in the Arabian Peninsula?

The confusion begins with events in history. Arabs were once few in number and lived only in the Arabian Peninsula. In the A.D. 600s and 700s, the Arabs built a huge empire. They spread a new religion, Islam, and their language, Arabic, from Egypt westward to Spain and eastward into India. "Arab" then came to mean not just the original Arabs but also the Arab-speaking peoples of their empire.

Today, Arabs are people in different countries who share a common culture and language. For example, people living in Algeria or Tunisia in North Africa consider themselves Arabs. As Arab-speaking Muslims, they share similar beliefs with many others living in Southwest Asia. They are also loyal to their own countries.

There are other confusions. Some Westerners think that all Arabs are Muslim and all Muslims are Arabs. That is simply not so. Some Arabs are Christian or Jewish. Also, only about a quarter of the world's Muslims live in Southwest Asia. The rest live around the world.

Diversity

Migration and conquest contributed to the diversity of Southwest Asia. Persians, Greeks, Romans, Arabs, Turks, and Mongols left their mark on the languages and customs of the region.

Iran and Turkey have the largest populations in the region with around 70 million people each. Iranians and Turks are not Arabs. They each belong to separate ethnic groups. Both also have many minority groups within their borders.

Most Iranians are Persian, and most are Muslim. They speak their own language, Farsi (FAR·see), but use Arabic script to write it. Long ago, Turks migrated to Southwest Asia from Central Asia and became Muslim. They, too, have their own language. They have used the Roman alphabet for writing since World War I.

Arabs walk down a street in Hama, Syria. **Who are the Arabs?**

Chapter 11

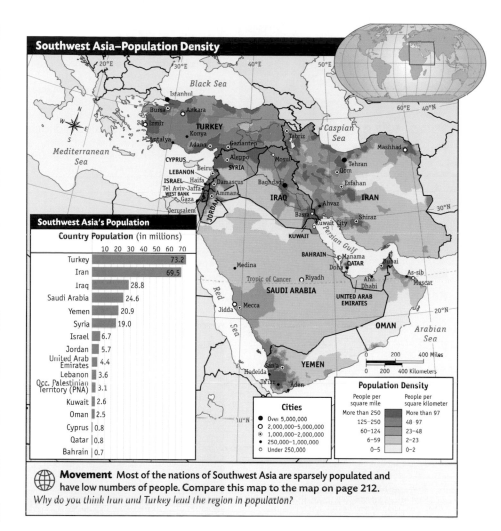

Southwest Asia–Population Density

Southwest Asia's Population

Country Population (in millions)

Country	Population
Turkey	73.2
Iran	69.5
Iraq	28.8
Saudi Arabia	24.6
Yemen	20.9
Syria	19.0
Israel	6.7
Jordan	5.7
United Arab Emirates	4.4
Lebanon	3.6
Occ. Palestinian Territory (PNA)	3.1
Kuwait	2.6
Oman	2.5
Cyprus	0.8
Qatar	0.8
Bahrain	0.7

Cities
- ● Over 5,000,000
- ◉ 2,000,000–5,000,000
- ◉ 1,000,000–2,000,000
- ⊙ 250,000–1,000,000
- ○ Under 250,000

Population Density

People per square mile	People per square kilometer
More than 250	More than 97
125–250	48–97
60–124	23–48
6–59	2–23
0–5	0–2

Movement Most of the nations of Southwest Asia are sparsely populated and have low numbers of people. Compare this map to the map on page 212. *Why do you think Iran and Turkey lead the region in population?*

Among the many smaller ethnic groups of the region are Armenians, Greeks, Jews, Kurds, and various African peoples.

Armenians, Kurds, and Jews have suffered persecution. Armenians were massacred by Turks early in the 1900s. Today, some live in Turkey, Syria, and Iran. Millions of Kurds live in Turkey, Syria, Iraq, and Iran. They are Muslim but also have their own language and customs.

Southwest Asia has fewer languages than Africa. Yet you can hear more than 25 languages including Arabic, Persian, Turkish, Hebrew, Armenian, Greek, Kurdish, and Aramaic. In some cities, English and French are widely spoken.

Customs

Arabs serve coffee to honor guests. Refusing it is a refusal of generosity. The Al Murrah bedouins of the Arabian desert make a fresh pot when guests arrive. While grinding the beans in a brass bowl, the host hits the bowl to make a loud ringing sound—inviting anyone nearby to join them. After flavoring and brewing the coffee, the host tastes it first then serves his guests. Upon finishing the coffee, guests say, "to your health."

Lands and People of Southwest Asia

219

Discussion Questions

1 How are the language and customs of the people of Southwest Asia a gift from other civilizations?

2 If you met a person from this region, is it more likely that you would be meeting an Arab or a non-Arab? Support your choice.

Caption Answer

Those areas have less desert.

Map Activity

Population Tic-Tac-Toe

NATIONAL GEOGRAPHY STANDARDS: 1, 4, 9, 12
GEOGRAPHIC THEMES: Location, Place, Movement
OBJECTIVES: 1.02, 2.02

Using the map and graph on page 219, have students compose true-false statements about Southwest Asia's population density. Review these for accuracy. Tape large tic-tac-toe pattern onto classroom floor. Prepare five each of large X's and O's (to fit the squares) for students to hold/place in game pattern on the floor. Divide class into two teams, X and O. Displaying a transparency of Southwest Asia on overhead projector, read aloud the opposing team's true/false statements to each team. The person who identifies the truth or falsity of a statement can mark a space with their X or O. The winning team can be given a small reward.

Background Information

Salt Free

Although the Red Sea and Persian Gulf have a very high salt content, the oil-exporting Gulf states lead the world in commercial desalinization. Saudi Arabia transforms more than 1 billion cubic meters of water from salty to fresh each year, accounting for almost one third of world capacity. The process requires several steps that include heating the water to boiling, capturing the steam, and condensing it. Because of the high fuel costs, the desalinization process is expensive. The importance of this process to the oil states became clear during the 1990–91 Gulf War. Saudi Arabia and other smaller states were alarmed when a massive oil slick seemed about to clog desalinization equipment.

Discussion Questions

1 Most of the population of Southwest Asia is Muslim. Although they are of the same religion, they are divided. Explain.

Caption Answer

Persians, Turks, Armenians, Greeks, Jews, Kurds, and various African peoples also live in Southwest Asia.

Caption Answer

They use desalination to meet the demand for freshwater, and they employ fertigation to grow crops in dry places.

Activity

Fertile Crescent and Its Importance

 OBJECTIVES: 8.02, 12.3

The Fertile Crescent is entirely in the continent of Asia, but it serves as a bridge between Asia and its neighbors Africa and Europe. Throughout its history, the Fertile Crescent has played a role in many civilizations. Divide the class into eleven groups and have them research and present a poster to the class. Each poster should include a map showing the limits of that civilization/empire, a time line, and the influence of that civilization in the Middle East today. Projects should cover the Egyptian, Assyrian, Babylonian, Phoenician, Persian, Greek, Roman, Byzantine, Islamic, Ottoman Empires, and Hebrew Kingdoms of David and Solomon.

Extension ELL students should use an ELL-friendly Web site for research.

Kurds from Iraq carry belongings into a refugee camp near the Iraqi border. **What other ethnic groups live in Southwest Asia?**

Religions

About 90 percent of the people in Southwest Asia are Muslim. They are divided into two main *sects,* or groups, Sunni (soo·nee) and Shiite (SHEE·ite), as well as many smaller ones (see page 239). Some countries, however, have a large population of Christians. They, too, belong to different churches, including Greek Orthodox, Roman Catholic, and various Protestant groups. Half of Lebanon's population is Christian. Israel is mostly Jewish, but small groups of Jews also live in Egypt, Turkey, and elsewhere.

For centuries, Jews were persecuted in Europe. During World War II, millions were killed in a mass murder, or *Holocaust,* carried out by Nazi Germany. In 1948, Israel was formally established as a Jewish homeland in Palestine.

Adapting to the Land

Early on, the people of Southwest Asia adapted to the varying climates and landforms. Some land was not fit for humans. It has remained uninhabited. Southwest Asians speak of two other kinds of land, sown land and desert land. Different ways of life have developed on each. There are also transition zones, where sown land merges into desert.

Village Farmers

Sown land is found mostly in plains and river valleys, on mountainsides and uplands, and where some rain falls. Ancient people learned to farm in these places and created villages. They developed technologies and skills to irrigate the land with canals and ditches.

Modern scientists invented other methods to help people adapt to an arid climate. Saudi Arabia, for example, has built desalination plants to provide fresh water. *Desalination* involves changing salty sea water into fresh water that can be used for drinking and irrigation.

Israel pioneered *fertigation,* feeding water and fertilizer directly to the roots of crops. This way water is not lost to evaporation. Agricultural scientists breed plants that can survive arid conditions.

A village farmer in Syria releases water into a canal to irrigate a field near the Euphrates River. **How else have the people of Southwest Asia adapted to living in an arid climate?**

Desert Herders

A different way of life developed in desert and near-desert lands. Nomadic herders also had to adapt to arid conditions. Mostly, they lived in small groups. At certain seasons, they moved with their herds of goats, sheep, or camels. They followed well-planned routes to places where the animals could graze.

Nomadic peoples were skilled in finding their way across large areas. They could find water in the most desolate landscapes. To survive, they used all parts of their animals. Hides were made into tent homes that could be folded and moved easily. Animals provided food and milk.

Nomads were not completely isolated. They often traded with settled people. Some sold camels to farmers and town dwellers. Others arranged to carry goods across the desert.

Today, only a few people are nomadic herders. Technology has replaced camel caravans with trucks and planes.

Ancient Cities

Damascus, located in present-day Syria, claims to be the oldest continuously occupied city in the world. Its roots go back at least 7,000 years.

Southwest Asia is home to many other ancient cities. Among these are Jericho, Baghdad, Istanbul, and Jerusalem. Long

ago, people settled where there was enough rainfall for crops. Cities grew nearby. Drier lands had smaller populations.

Ancient cities, like those today, played important roles. They were centers of business, trade, and culture. Today, the majority of people in Lebanon, Iraq, Jordan, and Israel are city dwellers.

As in Africa, population growth in Southwest Asia's cities is outrunning growth in rural areas. Economic opportunities are few in rural areas. Where water is scarce, farmland is limited. Cities attract families with promises of jobs, educational opportunities, and exciting daily activities.

Damascus, Syria, has a population of more than 1.5 million people. **Why are people attracted to the city?**

Discussion Questions

1 How have scientists of today helped people adapt to living in an arid climate? Can you suggest other ideas that might help these people?

2 How does the theme of movement apply to nomads?

3 Why do you think Damascus has thrived for so many years?

4 Southwest Asia has become increasingly urbanized. Why?

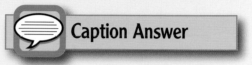

Caption Answer

It is a center of business, trade, and culture.

LESSON 3 REVIEW

Fact Follow-Up
1. Define the word Arab.
2. What people other than Arabs live in Southwest Asia?
3. What are the two main sects of Islam?
4. What religious groups, other than Muslims, are found in the region?
5. What is desalination?
6. Describe fertigation.

Talk About It
1. How does the theme of movement explain why the meaning of the word Arab has changed so much throughout history?
2. Diversity is an important characteristic of life in Southwest Asia. Explain why.
3. Which life is easier: that of a nomadic herder or a village farmer? Explain.
4. Why has Southwest Asia become so urbanized?

Lands and People of Southwest Asia

221

LESSON 3 REVIEW

Fact Follow-Up Answers
1. Arabs are people in different countries who originated in Saudi Arabia and who share a common culture and language.
2. Persians, Turks, Armenians, Greeks, Jews, Kurds, Europeans, and various African peoples also live in Southwest Asia.
3. The two main sects are Sunni and Shiite.
4. Christians, including Greek Orthodox, Roman Catholic, and various Protestant groups, and Jews also are found in the region.
5. Desalination is the process by which salty sea water is changed to fresh water that can be used for drinking and irrigation.
6. Fertigation is feeding water and fertilizer directly to the roots of crops so water is not lost by evaporation.

Talk About It Answers
1. Arabs once lived only in the Arabian Peninsula, but with the growth and spread of the Arab Empire, Arab came to mean Arab language and culture.
2. Important points: Student responses should mention diversity of peoples, religious beliefs, and ways of living. Their explanations should include reasons for such diversity.
3. Important points: Students should choose one way of life and explain why. Notes: Both lives are difficult. Farmers can be helped by technology (desalination, fertigation) and engineering skills (irrigation). Nomads are disappearing as trucks and airplanes replace camel caravans.
4. Cities originally developed in areas of sufficient rainfall. Economic opportunities are limited in rural areas. Families are attracted to cities by the promise of jobs, educational opportunities, and a desire for other benefits of city life.

Activity

Human-Environmental Interaction

 OBJECTIVES: 3.01

Create a fishbone graphic organizer with the facts below showing how Southwest Asian farmers and herders have changed the landscape over time. Have students use this for review. The fish head should be titled "Landscape." Possible bones for the fish:

Farmers
1. Negev irrigation with control of Jordan River
2. Turkey's dams on Euphrates River
3. Lebanon and Yemen with terraces

Herders
1. Desertification with grazing lands destroyed
2. Some reforestation
3. Water demands with depletion

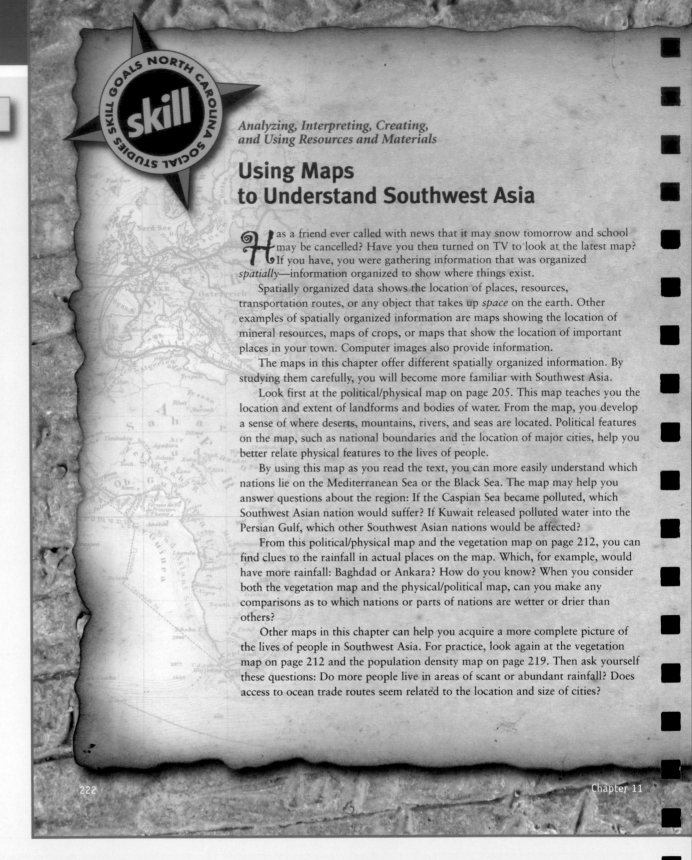

Analyzing, Interpreting, Creating, and Using Resources and Materials

Using Maps to Understand Southwest Asia

Has a friend ever called with news that it may snow tomorrow and school may be cancelled? Have you then turned on TV to look at the latest map? If you have, you were gathering information that was organized *spatially*—information organized to show where things exist.

Spatially organized data shows the location of places, resources, transportation routes, or any object that takes up *space* on the earth. Other examples of spatially organized information are maps showing the location of mineral resources, maps of crops, or maps that show the location of important places in your town. Computer images also provide information.

The maps in this chapter offer different spatially organized information. By studying them carefully, you will become more familiar with Southwest Asia.

Look first at the political/physical map on page 205. This map teaches you the location and extent of landforms and bodies of water. From the map, you develop a sense of where deserts, mountains, rivers, and seas are located. Political features on the map, such as national boundaries and the location of major cities, help you better relate physical features to the lives of people.

By using this map as you read the text, you can more easily understand which nations lie on the Mediterranean Sea or the Black Sea. The map may help you answer questions about the region: If the Caspian Sea became polluted, which Southwest Asian nation would suffer? If Kuwait released polluted water into the Persian Gulf, which other Southwest Asian nations would be affected?

From this political/physical map and the vegetation map on page 212, you can find clues to the rainfall in actual places on the map. Which, for example, would have more rainfall: Baghdad or Ankara? How do you know? When you consider both the vegetation map and the physical/political map, can you make any comparisons as to which nations or parts of nations are wetter or drier than others?

Other maps in this chapter can help you acquire a more complete picture of the lives of people in Southwest Asia. For practice, look again at the vegetation map on page 212 and the population density map on page 219. Then ask yourself these questions: Do more people live in areas of scant or abundant rainfall? Does access to ocean trade routes seem related to the location and size of cities?

Relief map of southwest Asia

You have now examined Southwest Asia from the perspective of physical/political features, vegetation, and population density. Finally, look again at the map of economic activity and resources on page 213. It shows the location of mineral resources such as petroleum. With this added information, how can you more fully describe living in Southwest Asia?

To practice organizing information from maps, attack this problem: You have been assigned by your employer, a company that sells oil drilling equipment, the task of suggesting the three best locations in Southwest Asia for a manufacturing plant. Use the maps in this chapter to help you select the three best locations. Discuss with a classmate the requirements such a company would have in each location. It might be helpful to use a data retrieval chart similar to the one on page 123.

Teaching This Skill Lesson

Materials Needed textbooks, paper, pencils

Classroom Organization whole class, small groups

Beginning the Lesson Have students use strips of paper to mark pages 205, 212, 213, and 219. Tell them they will be using five different maps in this skill lesson. Direct students to study the maps on pages 212 and 213 and have them locate Oman on the map. Where in Oman would they expect most people to live? Why? Next, have them turn to the map on page 219 to check their answer.

Developing the lesson: Have students work individually or in pairs to read the skill lesson on page 222 (up to the last paragraph). As they read the lesson, circulate to see that students are using the various maps indicated. When they have completed the reading, divide the class into small groups of three to five students. Direct students to read the final paragraph and suggest the three best locations for the plant manufacturing oil drilling equipment.

Conclusion Use a wall map of the region or one on an overhead projector. As each group reports its three locations, indicate them on the map. Is there a clear favorite? Why or why not?

Skill Lesson Review

1. What kinds of maps would you need to describe the economy of a nation? *Maps of economic activities and resources.*
2. What maps would you need in order to plan a vacation in an area? *A political and a physical map might help in deciding where to go. A map showing transportation routes, such as a state or national highway map, would be most helpful in planning how to get there.*
3. Which information would you prefer to read on maps, and which would you find easier to use if it were in chart or table form? Why? *Important points: This is a matter of personal preference; students should state and explain their preferences.*
4. What, other than the map information, would help you decide which nation is economically most powerful? *Important points: The maps should provide sufficient information. Other sources would be information such as gross domestic product, average income, imports and exports.*

Talk About It

1. The deserts were green forests 25,000 years ago. After forests were cut down, erosion robbed the area of much of its fertile soil.

2. The Middle East was a term used by Europeans to describe this area that lay, for them, midway between Europe and East Asia. Southwest Asia is the more accurate geographic term.

3. Three continents meet in the region. It is the location of important land and sea trade routes.

4. Important points: Students should take a position and explain it. Note: The description is not entirely accurate. Many Arabs live in the region, but so do other ethnic groups. Arabs also live elsewhere in the world.

CHAPTER 11 REVIEW

Lessons Learned

LESSON 1
Location and Landforms
The 15 nations of Southwest Asia are divided among three subregions—the Middle East, the Northern Tier, and the Arabian Peninsula. Each contains contrasting landforms, resources, and people.

LESSON 2
Climate and Resources
Varying climates and resources have affected patterns of settlement in Southwest Asia. Agriculture thrives in parts of the Middle East and in fertile valleys of Turkey. Oil is a major resource of the Arabian Peninsula and Iran. Water is unevenly distributed in the region.

LESSON 3
People and Their Environment
Southwest Asia is home to a variety of people and religions. The majority of this region's population is Arab and Muslim. Iranians and Turks are not Arabs, but are mainly Muslim. Israel is mainly Jewish. The arid environment encouraged two very different ways of life—settled farming and nomadic herders.

Talk About It

1. How have the physical characteristics of place in Southwest Asia changed over time?
2. Explain why geographers call this region Southwest Asia instead of the Middle East.
3. Why might Southwest Asia be described as a crossroads?
4. Would it be accurate to describe this region as "the Arab World"? Explain your answer.

Mastering Mapwork

HUMAN-ENVIRONMENTAL INTERACTION
Use the map on page 205 to answer these questions:

1. What physical characteristics of place in the Rub' al-Khali, located in Saudi Arabia, would influence human-environmental interaction?
2. In the Empty Quarter of Saudi Arabia, do you think there is greater human influence on the environment or greater environmental influence on humans? Why?
3. In which of the areas shown on the maps on pages 213 and 219 do you think there is the most human-environmental interaction?
4. Using this map and those on pages 212 and 213, compare the evidences of human-environmental interaction one would expect to observe in Yemen and Turkey.

Southwest Asia–Political/Physical

Mastering Mapwork

1. The absence of water and most vegetation influence human-environmental interaction in the Rub' al-Khali.

2. Important points: Students should state a position and explain reasons. Note: In the Empty Quarter there is little vegetation and little or no economic activity; there is likely to be little human influence on the environment.

3. Important points: Students should use information from the two maps to select an area of great human-environmental interaction.

4. Yemen is an area of nomadic herding and subsistence farming. Turkey does have nomadic herding and subsistence farming, but it also has commercial farming, fishing, coal and copper mines, and hydroelectric plants. One would expect to observe less evidence of human-environmental action in Yemen than in Turkey.

Go to the Source

Using Evidence to Make Predictions

Read the excerpt from the Draft of the Palestinian Constitution (Chapter 1, Section 1: "General Foundations of the State") below. Complete the activity using specific references to the document.

Article 1
This constitution is based on the will of the Arab Palestinian people. It shall be approved democratically.

Article 2
The Arab Palestinian people believe in the principles of justice, liberty, equality, human dignity, and their right to practice self-determination and sovereignty over their land.

Article 3
The Palestinian people are a part of the Arab and Islamic nations.

Article 4
Palestine is an independent state with complete sovereignty that cannot be conceded. Its system shall be republican and its lands are unitary and indivisible.

Article 5
Arabic shall be the official language.

Article 6
Islam shall be the official religion of the state. The monotheistic religions shall be respected.

Article 7
The principles of the Islamic Shari`a are a primary source for legislation. The legislative branch shall determine personal status law under the authority of the monotheistic religions according to their denominations, in keeping with the provisions of the constitution and the preservation of unity, stability, and advancement of the Palestinian people.

Article 8
Jerusalem shall be the capital of Palestine and its seat of government.

Article 9
Palestine's flag, motto, seals, emblems, and national anthem shall be determined by law.

Article 10
Sovereignty belongs to the Palestinian Arab people. Its prerogatives shall be exercised by the people directly, by means of elected representatives, by referendum, and through their constitutional institutions.

Article 11
The Palestinian political system shall be a representative democracy based on political pluralism. It shall guarantee the rights and freedoms of minorities without discrimination in their rights and obligations. It shall guarantee their protection and their respect for legitimacy in that which insures the supreme

Go to the Source

Activity

The representatives of the Palestinian people have drafted their first constitution. The first 11 articles are shown here. Your task is to evaluate all of these articles and then pick the three that you believe are most critical to make Palestine a secure and prosperous nation. Justify your choices with reasons and supporting details.

CRITERIA FOR EVALUATION	OPINION	SUPPORTING EVIDENCE

Go to the Source

OBJECTIVES: 9.03; Skills 4.03

Draft of the Palestinian Constitution, Chapter 1, Section 1.

This draft is the work of the Palestinian Constitution Committee. Yassar Arafat established the Committee in November 1999.

ANSWERS

Important points: Students may include criteria that create stability, economic growth, and peace. Students should cite specific passages to support their criteria.

How to Use the Chapter Review

There are three sections in the Chapter Review: Talk About It, Mastering Mapwork, and Go to the Source. Use the Vocabulary Worksheets and the Chapter Review Worksheet in the Teacher's Resource Guide for additional reinforcement and preparation for the Chapter Assessments. The chapter and lesson reviews and the Chapter Review Worksheets are the basis of the assessment for each chapter.

Talk About It questions encourage students to speculate about the content of the chapter and are suitable for class or small-group discussion. They are not intended to be assigned for homework.

Mastering Mapwork has students apply one or more of the Five Themes of Geography to maps within the chapter.

Go to the Source activities allow students to analyze a primary source that relates to the content of the chapter. The questions and activities familiarize students with different types of primary sources and also build content-reading skills.

Southwest Asia's Enduring Traditions

Social Studies Strands

Historic Perspectives
The development and importance of monotheistic religions
Judaism
Christianity
Islam
  Five Pillars of Faith
  Sunnis and Shiites

Cultures and Diversity

Individual Development and Identity

Global Connections

North Carolina Standard Course of Study

Goal 4 The learner will identify significant patterns in the movement of people, goods, and ideas over time and place in Africa, Asia, and Australia.

Goal 8 The learner will assess the influence and contributions of individuals and cultural groups in Africa, Asia, and Australia.

Goal 10 The learner will compare the rights and civic responsibilities of individuals in political structures in Africa, Asia, and Australia.

Goal 12 The learner will assess the influence of major religions, ethical beliefs, and values on cultures in Africa, Asia, and Australia.

Teaching & Assessment

- English Language Learner Modified Lesson Plans for this chapter are found in the Teacher Resource Guide.

- *ExamView® Assessment Suite* is provided at **NCJourneys.com.** It includes customizable assessments for all chapters. Paper tests are also available in the Teacher Resource Guide. See pages T16–T17 for information about how to use the assessments and the Scoring Guide.

Worksheets

Worksheets and answer keys are found both in the Teacher Resource Guide and at **NCJourneys.com**, including Reading Guides, Reading Strategies, Chapter Reviews, English Language Learner and others.

ACTIVITIES AND INTEGRATIONS

SOCIAL STUDIES	
Activator: Hammurabi's Code, p. 226	
● ▲ The Fertile Crescent, p. 227	
● ▲ Civilizations, p. 231	
Islamic Visual, p. 231	
Birthplace of Three World Religions, p. 233	
Where Have All the Muslims Gone, p. 238	
Skill Lesson: Organizing Information Using a Time Line, p. 243	

READING/LANGUAGE ARTS	READING/LANGUAGE ARTS OBJECTIVES
Analogies, p. 226B	2.01
● Alphabets, p. 230	3.01
Writing Prompt: Similarities Among Three Major Religions, p. 226	3.01
Comparing Religions, p. 228	2.01
Old Laws, p. 230	3.01
● Get Up and Move, p. 234	2.02
★ Journey, p. 235	6.01
★ Three World Religions Symbolization, p. 236	2.02
People of Islam, p. 237	2.02
Word Salad, p. 239	1.03
Go to the Source: Comparing Documents and Statistics, p. 245	1.02, 2.01, 4.01

MATHEMATICS	MATHEMATICS OBJECTIVES
★ Religion What Is It and How Many Are There?, p. 226B	1.01, 4.01
▲ ■ Time Math Word Problem, p. 229	1.02, 1.03

TECHNOLOGY	TECHNOLOGY OBJECTIVES
Houses of Worship, p. 226B	3.01, 3.11
● Civilizations, p. 231	3.01, 3.11
■ People of Islam, p. 237	3.01, 3.11
T-Chart, p. 240	3.01, 3.05, 3.11

VISUAL ARTS	VISUAL ARTS OBJECTIVES
▲ ■ The Beads of Ur, p. 226B	2.04, 5.01

CHARACTER AND VALUES EDUCATION	TRAITS
Writing Prompt: Similarities Among Three Major Religions, p. 226	respect
What Would You Do?, p. 229	self-discipline

● Basic Activities   ★ Challenging Activities   ▲ English Language Learner Novice   ■ English Language Learner Intermediate

Introductory Activity

Religion—What Is It and How Many Are There?

 OBJECTIVES: 2.02, 11.03

Ask the students to record all the different faith groups represented in the community. They may consult the telephone directory or a city Web page. After the list is developed, ask the students to place the information into categories, based upon a common characteristic. Once the information is in categories have the students look at fractions of a whole (the whole community), decimals, and percentages. The students can then take the information and develop bar graphs, line graphs, and pie graphs. Finally, the students are able to analyze the data. When the students look at the data have them hypothesize reasons why or why not these particular denominations are found in this area of the United States. Consider the differences between your community and a village in Southwest Asia. If the same exercise were conducted in a Southwest Asian city or village, would the same results be found? Why or why not? What would an Israeli, Saudi Arabian, or Lebanese seventh grader likely find if they did the same activity? Discuss this as a whole class and discuss the impact religion has on culture here and in Southwest Asia.

 **Culminating Activity**

Houses of Worship

OBJECTIVES: 4.03, 12.01

After studying Judaism, Islam, and Christianity, give students the opportunity to compare and contrast the different houses of worship from these three religions. Provide a variety of materials that show the different houses of worship (magazines, art prints, slides, pictures). Then instruct students to make a poster illustrating the three different houses of worship with labels on distinguishing features.

Extension ELL students may need to consult an ELL-friendly Web site for research before labeling the poster.

 Art Activity

The Beads of Ur

OBJECTIVES: 12.02

Materials magazines, glue, round toothpicks, glue, elastic string, and polyurethane or clear-gloss fingernail polish.

The beads in the jewelry of Ur were made primarily of gold, agate, silver, carnelian, and lapis lazuli. To create paper beads: find magazine pages with the desired colors. Fashion magazines are best. Cut out triangular strips that are the height of the page and ¾-inch wide at the base (it is wise to measure and draw lines prior to cutting, or use a template that fits the dimensions of the magazine). Place the ¾-inch side of the paper strip on the tooth pick and roll it up. Keep it tight while rolling. When you get to the end with the point, add a tiny bit of glue, hold until it sticks, and remove it from the toothpick (this will require a little practice, be patient). You will need about 75 or 80 beads to make a nice necklace.

String the beads on the elastic string until the desired length is achieved. Option: beads can be coated with polyurethane to make them shiny and to increase their life span.

Consult the art specialist for advanced stringing techniques. Research *The Royal Tombs of Ur* for more jewelry examples.

Analogies

OBJECTIVES: 2.01, 9.04, 12.01

Analogies are useful to help students make associations with prior knowledge. They can be used as an instructional strategy to help students better understand new materials. They are not intended to be definitions or test items.

Read the analogies aloud and ask students to identify the relationship between the terms. As an extension, ask students to write their own analogies using key terms or places discussed in the chapter.

Code of Hammurabi : Mesopotamia :: Constitution : United States of America (is the basis for law in)

Muslim : mosque :: Christian : church :: Jew : synagogue (worships in)

Quran : Islam :: Bible : Christianity :: Torah : Judaism (is the holy text of)

monotheism : polytheism :: monogamy : polygamy :: monochromatic : polychromatic (singular to multiples)

Five Pillars of Islam : Muslim :: Ten Commandments : Christians (are guidelines for)

imam : Islam :: pastor : Christianity (is leader in)

Suez Canal : Red Sea and Mediterranean Sea :: Panama Canal : Atlantic and Pacific Oceans (joins)

Teaching Strategies

Because religion is a major concept for understanding seventh grade curriculum, you should focus a great deal of time to this concept to ensure students have a working knowledge of the major world religions and their characteristics. See the Teacher's Note on page 234 for guidance on learning about religions.

Activator

OBJECTIVES: 9.01, 10.02

On a piece of posterboard, write some of the rules from the Code of Hammurabi, an ancient ruler from Babylon. Ask students to identify the conditions that may have existed to cause a society to have laws such as these.

Writing Prompt

OBJECTIVES: 11.01, 12.01

Evaluative

Too often people focus on the differences among the three religions of the Middle East. After studying Chapter 12, write an essay arguing that these three religions are more alike than they are different.

As you write your report, remember to

• clearly state your position.
• give at least three reasons and explain your reasons fully.
• give examples to support your reasons.
• write in complete sentences and paragraph form.
• organize your ideas and include an introduction and a conclusion.
• use good grammar, spelling, punctuation, and capitalization.

CHAPTER

12

Southwest Asia's Enduring Traditions

"Where did you go?" a father asks his son.

"I did not go anywhere," replies the boy.

"If you did not go anywhere, why do you idle about? Go to school. Be humble and show fear before your teacher. When you show terror, the teacher will like you."

Does this conversation sound like one that you might have heard? The father and son in this story lived 5,000 years ago in a Southwest Asian city called Sumer.

Chapter Preview

LESSON 1
Roots of Southwest Asian Societies
Early civilizations of Sumeria, Mesopotamia, Babylon, and Phoenicia rose in Southwest Asia. Islam later contributed to the region's progress in law, architecture, learning, and the arts.

LESSON 2
Three World Religions
Three major world religions began in Southwest Asia: Judaism, Christianity, and Islam. The common element in each religion is a belief in one God.

LESSON 3
Shaping Modern Southwest Asia
Islam spread through Southwest Asia, North Africa, and southern Europe.

226

Chapter 12

Chapter Resources

Print Resources

Nonfiction

Fine, Doreen. *What Do We Know About Judaism?* Peter Bedrick Books, 1995. ISBN 087226386X.

George, Linda S. *The Golden Age of Islam* (Cultures of the Past series). Bench-mark Books, 1998. ISBN 076140273X.

Landau, Elaine. *The Sumerians* (Cradle of Civilization series). Millbrook Press, 1997. ISBN 0761302158.

Macdonald, Fiona. *A 16th Century Mosque* (Inside Story series). Peter Bedrick

Books, 1994. ISBN 087226310X.

Malam, John. *Mesopotamia and the Fertile Crescent,* 10,000 to 539 B.C. Raintree Steck-Vaughn, 1999. ISBN 081725434X.

Marchant, Kerena. *Id-ul-Fitr.* Millbrook Press. ISBN 0761309632.

Martell, Hazel. *The World of Islam Before 1700.* Raintree Steck-Vaughn, 1999. ISBN 0817254307.

Nardo, Don. *Empires of Mesopotamia* (Lost Civilization series). Lucent Books, 2001. ISBN 1560068205.

Oakes, Lorna. *Assyria & Mesopotamia* (Step Into series). Arness Publishing, 2001.

ISBN 0754806561.

Penney, Sue. *Christianity* (World beliefs and cultures series). Heinemann Library, 2001. ISBN 1575723557.

—. *Islam* (World Beliefs and Cultures series). Heinemann Library, 2001. ISBN 1575723573.

—. *Judaism* (World Beliefs and Cultures series) Heinemann Library, 2001. ISBN 1575723581.

Service, Pamela F. *Mesopotamia* (Cultures of the Past series). Bench-mark Books, 1999. ISBN 0761403019.

Shahrukh, Husain. *What Do We Know*

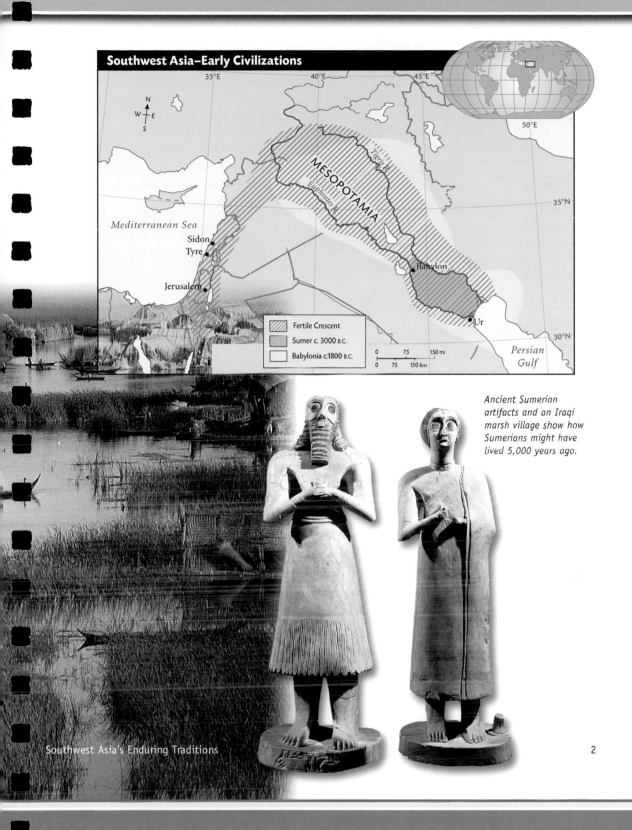

Southwest Asia–Early Civilizations

- Fertile Crescent
- Sumer c. 3000 B.C.
- Babylonia c.1800 B.C.

Ancient Sumerian artifacts and an Iraqi marsh village show how Sumerians might have lived 5,000 years ago.

Southwest Asia's Enduring Traditions

2

Discussion Questions

1 Identify the three main areas included in Southwest Asia's early civilizations.

2 What are some of the defining characteristics of the artifacts from Sumer?

3 What do you see in the photograph of the Iraqi marsh village?

Map Activity

The Fertile Crescent

NATIONAL GEOGRAPHY STANDARDS: 1, 3, 12, 17
GEOGRAPHIC THEMES: Location, Place
OBJECTIVES: 1.02, 2.01

Give each student a large-scale map of Southwest Asia showing the Fertile Crescent historic region, including the Sinai Peninsula and the regions comprised of modern-day Israel, Jordan, Syria, Turkey, Iraq, and Saudi Arabia to the Persian Gulf. Give each student yarn/string to glue into place on map showing where Fertile Crescent was located. Supply small pieces of colored plastic wrap for each student to cut and glue onto maps showing where Babylonia was located. Also give each student one button (proportional to the map's size and the size of Sumer for that map) to glue onto map showing Sumer's location. Discuss with students the difference between the Fertile Crescent and Mesopotamia.

About Islam? Peter Bedrick Books, 1995. ISBN 0872263886.

Tubb, Jonathan N. *Bible Lands* (Eyewitness books series). Dorling Kindersley, 2000. ISBN 0789465795.

Watson, Carol. *What Do We Know About Christianity?* Peter Bedrick Books, 1997. ISBN 0872263908.

Language Arts: Writing Connections
Story Starters on Ancient Mesopotamia. Heinrich Enterprises.

Back issues of magazines
Cobblestone Publishing Company:

Babylonians. ISBN 0382445783.
Caliph of Baghdad, al-Ma'mun. ISBN 0382445163.
Early Christianity. ISBN 038240758X.
Ibn Battuta. ISBN 0382443969.
Islam. ISBN 0382407938.
Judaism. ISBN 038240601X.
Mesopotamia. ISBN 0382425986.
Suleiman the Magnificent. ISBN 0382407571.

Audiovisual
Islam: Empire of Faith. PBS Home Video [180 minutes].

Heritage Civilization and the Jews. PBS Video.
NOVA, *Lost Tribes of Israel.* PBS Video.

Web Sites
Go to **NCJourneys.com** for links to the following Web sites:
- Heritage Civilization and the Jews Companion Web Site
- The Jews of Lebanon Companion Web Site
- Heritage Civilization and the Jews
- Islam Empire of Faith

OBJECTIVES: 2.03, 4.03, 6.02

Discussion Questions

1 How do the civilizations of ancient times speak to us today?

2 How did the early Mesopotamian areas develop?

3 Why are the two great rivers important to ancient Mesopotamia?

4 What contributed to the rapid growth of towns?

5 Explain how the city-states progressed toward building a civilization.

Caption Answer

They show that ancient peoples of the region had domesticated animals to work for them. They also show people carrying goods, perhaps to trade at market.

Activity

Comparing Religions

OBJECTIVES: 11.01, 12.01

Have the students make a data retrieval chart, including such categories as importance of Abraham, importance of Jerusalem, and importance of the Old Testament in the holy books of these religions. After the data retrieval chart is completed, make a web. Students will use this data to write papers. Within each paragraph, students will elaborate a similarity by explaining how the topic applies to each religion (example: in the paragraph on Jerusalem, explain why Jerusalem is important to Judaism, to Christianity, and to Islam). These three similarities are the easiest for students to see connections and similarities.

KEY IDEAS

- Early civilizations rose in the fertile Tigris and Euphrates River valleys.

- The people of ancient Southwest Asia made advances in many areas—government, technology, the arts and sciences.

- Islam has been a major force in Southwest Asia for more than 1,300 years.

KEY TERMS

Code of Hammurabi
domesticate
mosques
Quran
Shariah

How do we know so much about the Sumerian father and son who lived so long ago? Their words were written on a clay tablet. Archaeologists in recent years dug up the tablet—along with thousands of others—from the earth. From such records we can learn about the ancient civilizations that grew in Southwest Asia.

Ancient Foundations

About 10,000 years ago—long before the father ordered his son to go to school—some people living north of the Tigris and Euphrates Rivers began building one of the world's first civilizations. Earlier, they had lived in small groups, moving about, hunting for animals, and gathering plants to eat. They gradually learned how to farm and how to *domesticate,* or tame and raise animals. With a steady food supply, they gave up hunting and gathering. They built homes and settled in small villages.

Years later, their descendants moved out of the mountains onto the plains along the Tigris and Euphrates Rivers. The Greeks later called this region Mesopotamia (mes·oh·pah·TAY·mih·ah) (see map, page 227). There, as in Egypt, farmers used river water to irrigate crops on fertile river soils. As their farming methods improved, they produced food surpluses. Populations grew, and towns became cities.

Farming spread throughout an area called the Fertile Crescent (see map, page 227). This well-watered area stretches from the eastern Mediterranean Sea through the Tigris and Euphrates River valleys (in modern-day Iraq) to the northern end of the Persian Gulf.

In Mesopotamia, cities became centers of government. Sumer (SOO·mer), where the father lectured his son, was a city-state. A city-state included a crowded urban area and lands that surrounded it. Each city-state had its own government. Government officials controlled irrigation canals, organized city defenses, and collected taxes.

Sumerian city-states also developed mathematics, science, the arts, and law. In all of these accomplishments, these city-states were beginning to build a civilization.

Sumerian city-states battled each other. In time, outsiders conquered Mesopotamia. They learned ideas from Sumerian civilization, blending them with their own traditions.

This royal mosaic was painted in 2750 B.C., north of the Tigris and Euphrates Rivers. **What do the images show of ancient life?**

Achievements of Early Empires

About 1750 B.C., Hammurabi (hahm·EH·rah·BEE), ruler of Babylon (BAB·ih·lon), created a huge empire that sprawled across Mesopotamia. His empire included many different people. To ensure order, Hammurabi had laws carved on stone slabs that were posted across the land. In this way everyone knew the king's law. One law said:

If a man has knocked out the eye of a noble, his eye shall be knocked out. If he has broken the limb of a noble, his limb shall be broken. If he has knocked out the eye of a commoner or broken the limb of a commoner, he shall pay one mina of silver.

The *Code of Hammurabi*, as his laws were called, also dealt with marriage, family, and business contracts. Many of these laws seem harsh today.

Laws of the Code of Hammurabi were carved into stone. **Who was Hammurabi? Do you think his laws would work today? Why?**

Southwest Asia's Enduring Traditions

What would YOU do?

Every summer some students from North Carolina join teams digging up and studying the remains of ancient civilizations in Southwest Asia. They get to visit another culture and may help discover new or important artifacts. The work is hard and hot. Students earn credit toward graduation but no pay. Would you join one of these teams?

A Phoenician chest ornament displays a falcon. **How did the ideas of Phoenicia spread?**

Continuing Accomplishments

Many civilizations, like Sumer, rose and fell in Mesopotamia. Each new conqueror built on the achievements of earlier people.

Some people, such as the Phoenicians (fuh·NEESH·uhnz) made important contributions through trade rather than conquest. The Phoenicians lived in today's Lebanon. About 3,000 years ago, these sea-going traders began to move throughout the Mediterranean. For several centuries they gained wealth as successful traders.

Phoenician merchants also absorbed ideas from Egypt and Mesopotamia. Through trade, the Phoenicians spread technology and ideas from these civilizations to less advanced societies. The Phoenicians improved the writing systems started by others. The Phoenician alphabet serves as the basis of our alphabet.

229

Discussion Questions

1 Why was it important for Hammurabi to write down his laws? How does that compare with our system today?

2 Why did many civilizations fall during this time in history?

3 Explain how trade became important in advancing societies.

Caption Answer

They spread through trade in the Mediterranean.

Caption Answer

Hammurabi was the ruler of Babylon who created a code of laws. They were accepted at the time, but they seem too harsh to us.

Math Activity

Time Math Word Problem

 OBJECTIVES: 5.02

The Babylonians used a base sixty system. We use it today to tell time and measure degrees. A bus travels for 6 hours, 24 minutes, 20 seconds and then travels an additional 3 hours, 52 minutes, 48 seconds. How long has the bus traveled?

Answer 10 hours, 17 minutes, 08 seconds

Extension Assist ELL students by setting up the problem for them.

Eyewitness Activity

Alphabets

OBJECTIVES: 8.03

Have students research the different types of alphabets and make a poster illustrating their findings.

To help students understand the different alphabets, share the books *Reading the Past: Ancient Writing from Cuneiform to the Alphabet* by J.T. Hooker (University of California Press, 1991. ISBN 076070726X.) and *Science in Ancient Mesopotamia* by Carol Moss (Franklin Watts, Inc., 1999. ISBN 0531159302.).

Extension For novice ELL students, model and provide additional explanations. Assign students to work with a partner.

Activity

Old Laws

OBJECTIVES: 9.01, 10.01

Below are examples of laws from the Code of Hammurabi. Read part of the code out loud to the class and discuss what it tells you about life in ancient Mesopotamia. Ask the students to think about these laws. Why are only men mentioned? Are the laws just or harsh? Would any be right for today or are any similar to laws we have today?

If a man has hired an ox and has caused its death, by carelessness or blows, then he shall restore ox for ox to the owner.

If a son has struck his father, his hands shall be cut off.

If a woman has not been discreet and has gone out, ruined her house and belittled her husband, she shall be drowned.

If a man steals a child, he shall be put to death.

If a man has borne [given] false witness [lied in court] in a trial or can not prove his statement, then if it is a capital trial, the man shall be put to death.

If a man has stolen goods from a temple, he shall be put to death.

If someone receives the stolen goods from that robbery, he shall be put to death.

If a man builds a house and the house is not sound and falls down and kills the owner, then the builder of the house will be put to death. If the owner's son is killed, then the son of the builder will be killed.

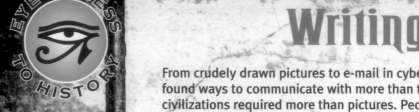

Writing

From crudely drawn pictures to e-mail in cyberspace, humans have found ways to communicate with more than the spoken word. Early civilizations required more than pictures. People needed records of trade, laws, and religion. In our complex societies today, we communicate billions of words and need quick ways to transmit them to one another.

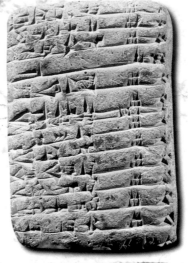

The word *cuneiform* (kyoo·NEE·ih·form) describes the Sumerian writing. It comes from the Latin cuneus, meaning "wedge."

Sumerian clay tablets

Writing first appeared only 5,000 years ago. Sumerians began the age of written history with their records on clay tablets. In Mesopotamia, Sumerians found reeds and clay readily available. They used the sharpened end of a reed, called a stylus, as a writing tool. The stylus made wedge-shaped marks in wet clay tablets. The clay then hardened, so the writing was preserved.

Alphabets Through History					
Phoenician	𐤀	𐤁	𐤂	𐤃	𐤄
Greek	Α	Β	Γ	Δ	Ε
Modern	A	B	C	D	E

About 1000 B.C., the Phoenicians began using 22 syllabic signs that stood for consonants. The first two symbols of their alphabet were aleph and beth, meaning "ox" and "house." Their system was adopted by the Greeks. The Greeks created an alphabet using vowels and consonants.

Phonecian inscription

Two alphabets came from Greek writing. One called Cyrillic is used today in some Balkan countries and Russia. The other, the Roman alphabet, was passed on to Europe and the Americas. Today, that alphabet appears in our books and on our blackboards and computer screens.

Ruins of an ancient Greek library in Ephesus, Turkey

Southwest Asia's Enduring Traditions

231

Art Activity

Islamic Visual

OBJECTIVES: 12.01

Make a visual using Islam as the theme. Examples include posters, mobiles, models, or other items. Students should remember that Islam forbids the use of images such as the human figure.

Research Activity

Civilizations

OBJECTIVES: 1.02, 1.03

Have students research facts from the textbook or from other sources to find the location of these early civilizations: 10,000 years ago; mountains near Tigris and Euphrates around 8000 B.C.; Mesopotamia and Fertile Crescent settled in 7000 B.C.; Sumeria circa 3100 B.C.; Babylon about 1750 B.C.; and Phoenicia in 1000 B.C. Students should use different colors or shade the area occupied by each of them on an outline map of the Middle East found in the Teacher's Resource Guide. On the key include the color, name, and date of each of the early civilizations.

It's a Fact

Southwest Asian Contributions

■ The umbrella was an early invention from the area of Mesopotamia. First used approximately 3,400 years ago as a sunshade. Umbra is a Latin word meaning "shade."

■ Mirrors were first created in Sumer around 3,500 B.C. They were made of polished bronze and set in handles made of wood, ivory, or gold.

■ The Middle East was home to early astronomers, especially Muslim scholars.

They improved on an early Greek invention, the astrolabe, an instrument used to determine the positions of the stars, thereby helping guide ships across the seas and caravans across the deserts. Early Muslim geographers created maps that depicted the world as round.

■ An early Persian, Avicenna, wrote a medical encyclopedia. Europeans returning from the Crusades had the encyclopedia translated into Latin. This encyclopedia served as a textbook in European medical schools until the 1700s.

Discussion Questions

1 Who were the peoples who inhibited Southwest Asia, and what were the contributions they made to this area?

2 How did the Islamic religion come to Southwest Asia?

3 Why is Islam an entire way of life?

4 Has there ever been a time in our history where law and religion had inseparable ties? Explain.

5 What do you think makes Islam a strong religion with such a wide group of followers?

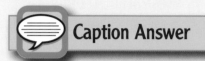

Caption Answer

Under Islamic empires, most people of the region became Muslim. Muslim architects developed building styles that blended old and new kinds of architecture. Many great mosques remain standing in the region. Islam also introduced new ways of life and a legal system based on the Shariah, law drawn from the Quran.

Pilgrims encircle Masjid al-Haram, The Sacred Mosque in Mecca, Saudi Arabia, the holiest city of Islam. The pilgrims enter the mosque to pray before the Kaaba (see pages 202-203). **How has Islam left its mark on Southwest Asia?**

Islamic Civilization

Many people left their mark on Southwest Asia. Jews built their own kingdom there. Persians, Greeks, and Romans conquered the region. Much later, various Islamic empires flourished. The Arabs, for example, ruled an empire that reached from Spain to India. Like earlier conquerors, they absorbed customs and ideas from the people they ruled. Out of these contacts grew a new and vital Islamic civilization.

Under Islamic empires, most Southwest Asian people became Muslim. Successful rulers supported new kinds of architecture. Muslim architects blended old and new building styles. They created splendid palaces and *mosques,* Muslim houses of worship. Their buildings reflected the power and wealth of Islamic civilization. Many great mosques remain standing in Turkey, Syria, and other countries.

A mosque differs in many ways from a Christian Church. Islam forbids the use of such images as the human figure. Muslim artists decorated with wonderful colors and geometric designs (see page 235).

Islam guides its followers. Islamic beliefs cover all areas of daily living including marriage, family matters, food, and dress. In some Muslim countries today, as in the past, legal systems are based on the Shariah. The *Shariah* (shah·ree·AH) is law drawn largely from Islam's holy scripture, the **Quran** and other Islamic sources. Other Southwest Asian nations have moved away from religious law codes to secular—nonreligious—legal systems.

By 2004, there were more than 1.3 billion Muslims throughout the world. You have read largely that North Africa is inhabited by people of this faith. Muslims also live in other parts of Asia. Southwest Asia remains the heart of the Islamic world. Wherever they live, all Muslims pray facing toward Mecca, the birthplace of Islam. Muslims everywhere share a faith that creates a community of believers. You will read about the origins and development of this faith in the next lesson.

LESSON 1 REVIEW

Fact Follow-Up
1. How was farming linked to the development of early civilizations?
2. What was the city-state?
3. What were some accomplishments of Hammurabi?
4. In what ways did the Phoenicians help with the development of civilization?
5. How did Islamic empires change Southwest Asia?

Talk About It
1. Why did early civilizations develop in Mesopotamia? Could they have developed in a drier area? Explain.
2. What do you think was the most important accomplishment of the Phoenicians? Explain your choice.
3. How does Islam guide its followers?

LESSON 1 REVIEW

Fact Follow-Up Answers
1. As farming developed and improved, increased food surpluses encouraged the growth of population and encouraged the development of other occupations.
2. In Mesopotamia, the city-state included a crowded urban area and lands that surrounded it. Each city-state had its own government.
3. He created a huge empire that sprawled across Mesopotamia. He also developed a code of law that united and ordered the empire.
4. In their trade throughout the Mediterranean, the Phoenicians spread technology and ideas from Egypt and Mesopotamia to less advanced societies. Their improved writing systems serve as the basis of our alphabet.
5. The huge Islamic Empire stretched from Pakistan into Portugal. Changes include the development of the mosque, changes in law and the arts; and a new religion, Islam.

Talk About It Answers
1. The Tigris and Euphrates River valleys provided fertile land and water to produce a surplus of food. Students should explain and support whether they believe the civilizations could have developed in a drier area.
2. Important points: Students should choose one accomplishment and give reasons for their choice. Note: The alphabet and development of writing, the creation of an empire were important.
3. Islamic beliefs and duties cover all areas of daily life such as marriage and family matters, food, and dress, in addition to government and law.

LESSON 2 Three World Religions

"*La ilaha illa'Llah*"—"There is no god but Allah (God)." Muslims recite these words as part of their daily prayers. This Muslim declaration of faith is similar to the First Commandment familiar to Jews and Christians—"You shall have no other gods before me."

Most people in Southwest Asia today are Muslims. Followers of two other world religions also live there. About 75 percent of Israelis are Jewish. About 6 percent of Southwest Asia's population are Christian. Lebanon has the largest number of Christians in the region, approximately 38 percent of its population. It is not surprising that there are large numbers of people in the region who belong to these faiths. Judaism, Christianity, and Islam were all born there.

KEY IDEAS

- Judaism is based on sacred laws given by God to the ancient Hebrews. Jews believe that God made a covenant, or sacred agreement, with their ancestors.

- Christianity is based on the belief that Jesus is the Messiah. Many Jewish beliefs are also shared by Christians.

- The Five Pillars of Islam are basic beliefs and duties of Muslims.

KEY TERMS

covenant
Diaspora
Five Pillars of Islam
Gospels
hajj
Messiah
monotheism
polytheism
Torah

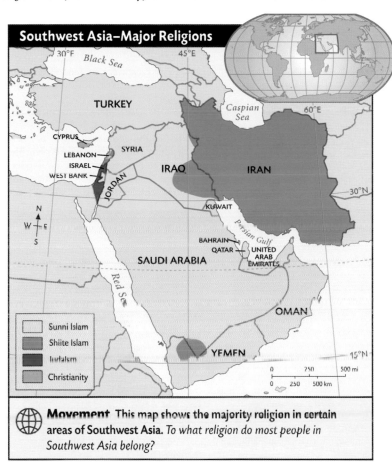

Southwest Asia–Major Religions

Legend:
- Sunni Islam
- Shiite Islam
- Judaism
- Christianity

Movement This map shows the majority religion in certain areas of Southwest Asia. *To what religion do most people in Southwest Asia belong?*

OBJECTIVES: 4.03, 12.01, 13.02

Discussion Questions

1 Why do you think there are so many Muslims in Southwest Asia today?

Caption Answer

Most people are Muslim.

Map Activity

Birthplace of Three World Religions

NATIONAL GEOGRAPHY STANDARDS: 1, 6, 10, 13, 17, 18

GEOGRAPHIC THEMES: Location, Place, Region

OBJECTIVES: 4.03, 12.01, 13.02

Divide the class into four groups to research Sunni Islam, Shiite Islam, Judaism, and Christianity. Each group is to provide brief informational facts or descriptions on the religion's name, the name of followers/denominations, the name of the founder, historical development (time and place), diety(ies), main text(s), its holy day of the week, major holidays, main beliefs/symbol(s), and present development (time and place).

Jigsaw student(s) from each religious group into new graphic-organizer groups. Assign each of these new groups to design a triple Venn diagram comparing and contrasting Judaism, Christianity, and Islam. Each group should present its triple Venn diagram using large chart paper, transparency, or hula hoops overlapping on the floor with sentence strips containing written facts and descriptions. Debrief students, clarifying any confusing and incomplete facts.

Caption Answer

The Torah records how God made a special covenant, or sacred agreement, with the Hebrew people. The Jews would be God's chosen people, but only if they obeyed his laws.

Caption Answer

Christians believe that Jesus was chosen by God to bring salvation to all people. They believe his life, teachings, death, and resurrection showed the way to eternal life in heaven.

Caption Answer

After Jesus died, his followers carried his teachings throughout the Roman Empire. After Roman authorities accepted the faith, missionaries spread it around the Mediterranean and into Europe. Still later, they carried the Christian message around the world.

Activity

Get Up and Move

 OBJECTIVES: 12.01, 13.02

Put on the board or wall the words "Islam", "Judaism", and "Christianity." Give students sentence strips with a fact or a symbol from one of the religions being studied. Students then will place the facts under the correct religion. Have students write a compare and contrast essay with the information.

Judaism

Judaism is the oldest of the three major religions of Southwest Asia. Jews were the first to base their faith on a single, all-powerful God. Belief in one god is called *monotheism*. Belief in more than one god is called *polytheism*. Five sacred texts record Judaism's beliefs. These are collected in a holy book, the *Torah*.

The Torah records how God made a special *covenant*, or sacred agreement, with the Hebrew (Jewish) people. The Jews would be God's chosen people, but only if they obeyed His laws. The Ten Commandments given by God to Moses on Mount Sinai contain the laws that Jews must obey. They demand belief in one God and a moral life. Among the Commandments are those that forbid killing, stealing, lying, and cheating.

Jews settled in Eretz Israel (the historic land of Israel). This area has also been known as Palestine for long periods of history. It lies at the eastern end of the Mediterranean Sea. The Jews had kingdoms of their own at various times. But for long periods they were ruled by others. They revolted against the Roman Empire in A.D. 68. They were defeated. The Romans forced Jews to leave their homeland. Jews were scattered throughout the world. This migration is called the *Diaspora*.

The Torah is the holy book of Judaism. **What is recorded in the Torah?**

An eleventh-century mosaic of Jesus Christ is set in the dome of a Greek church. **What do Christians believe about Jesus?**

Wherever Jews settled, they preserved their history and beliefs. Although their number remained small, Jews have had great influence on every field of human achievement. The story of Judaism's influence on Southwest Asia, however, does not end here. Judaism had great impact on two later religions, Christianity and Islam.

Christianity

Almost 2 billion people today are Christian. Most live in Europe and the Americas, but Christians also live on every continent.

For Christians, as for Jews, Palestine is a holy land because it is where ancient Jewish prophets spoke of the one Almighty God. For Christians it is special also as the place where Jesus of Nazareth was born and taught.

The teachings of Jesus were recorded. His message is contained in books known as the *Gospels*. The Gospels and other books of the New Testament contain Christian beliefs.

Jesus' teachings were rooted in Jewish religious traditions. Jesus believed in the Ten Commandments. Like ancient Jewish leaders, Jesus defended the poor, the weak, and the powerless. Jesus did depart from some Jewish traditions. Judaism demanded strict obedience to the letter of the law,

Jerusalem's Church of the Holy Sepulchre contains the Chapel of Calvary, depicting the crucifixion of Jesus. **How did his ideas spread beyond Southwest Asia?**

234

Teacher Notes

Teaching About Religion

For guidance in teaching about religion and religion-related subjects per North Carolina law, please see the Religious Expression in the Public Schools: Questions and Answers publication from the N.C. Attorney General's Office (link available at **NCJourneys.com**).

but Jesus stressed moral ideals over the law itself. He praised the virtues of charity, mercy, and justice.

Some Jews were drawn to Jesus' ideas. To them he appeared to be a new prophet or even the *Messiah,* the leader God had promised would save the Jews. According to the Gospels, Jesus made enemies among Jewish leaders and Roman officials, who ruled Palestine. Jesus was arrested, brought to trial, and condemned to die on a cross. Crucifixion was the Roman way of executing criminals.

After Jesus died, his followers carried his teachings throughout the Roman Empire. Christians believe that Jesus was the Messiah. In Greek, an important language of the time, Jesus became known as Christos (Christ), the anointed one. Leaders chosen by God were anointed or blessed with oil. Christians believe that Jesus was chosen by God to bring salvation to all people. They believe his life, teachings, death, and resurrection show the way to eternal life in heaven.

At first, Christians faced terrible persecution. Their beliefs challenged Judaism and the polytheistic religions of the Romans and others. Later, Roman leaders accepted the faith. Missionaries spread the faith throughout the Mediterranean and Europe. Later, they carried Christianity around the world. For centuries, Christianity was a powerful religion in Southwest Asia. In the A.D. 600s, it was challenged by the rise of Islam.

Islam

Muhammad often escaped from the busy streets of Mecca, a town on the Arabian Peninsula near the Red Sea. He retreated to the quiet of nearby hills, where he prayed and meditated on the evils he saw all around. One day, he heard a voice commanding him: "Recite in the name of your Lord who created…man…" Muhammad believed it was the angel Gabriel's voice speaking for God.

As Muhammad kept hearing the command, he finally obeyed. He founded Islam, the third world religion to come out of Southwest Asia.

Customs

Muslims believe that God commanded Muhammad to cleanse the Kaaba and dedicate it to the worship of God. Every year since Muhammad's first pilgrimage, faithful have come from distant places to pray and walk around the cubic structure they call "the holy House of God."

Muhammad was born in Mecca in A.D. 570. Orphaned at an early age, he was raised by an uncle. As a young man, he led camel caravans across the desert. At age twenty-five, he married Khadija, a wealthy widow. He was a kindly, helpful man, deeply troubled by the social and economic inequalities he saw.

The revelations, or words spoken by Gabriel, were recorded in the Quran, the holy book of Islam. At the heart of Islam is belief in one God. Islam means "submission to God." According to Islam, this God is the same God revealed to Jewish prophets and to Jesus. Muhammad accepted both the Torah and New Testament as God's word. He called Jews and Christians "People of the Book." Muhammad believed that he, like the Jewish prophets and Jesus, was proclaiming truths about the one God who had guided humankind throughout history.

Muhammad ascended to heaven from the rock at the center of this Islamic temple, called the Dome of the Rock. **The messages Muhammad heard from the angel Gabriel were recorded in what holy book of Islam?**

Discussion Questions

1 Compare and contrast Islam, Christianity, and Judaism.

2 Explain why Judaism, Christianity, and Islam are referred to as "world religions."

3 How does the Quran compare to the Torah and the Bible? How does it differ?

Caption Answer

The Quran

Activity

Journey

 OBJECTIVES: 11.01, 12.01

Have students pretend they are traveling from Saudi Arabia's capital, Riyadh, to Mecca. They are completing the Five Pillars of Faith by making the pilgrimage, or hajj, to Mecca. Have students write a series of three letters to their pen pal in the United States who is unfamiliar with Muslim customs. The letter should include prayer customs, the events leading up to the actual visit to Mecca, and things they might see along the way. Students should use resources to research Muslim traditions and in particular the hajj. They may also include photos of their trip.

Extension You may have an ELL student or their family member who has completed this journey. Ask them to come in and talk about it.

Teacher Notes

Allah and God

There is some debate about the appropriateness of using "Allah," rather than simply "God," when writing about Islam in English because of the fear that it creates a sense of otherness. For example, Westerners typically do not use Jehovah when referring to God in a discussion about Judaism. Some believe that this sense of otherness created by the use of the name "Allah" makes it easier to see what sets these religions and people apart rather than what Christians, Jews, and Muslims have in common.

Background Information

Prayer: The Second Pillar of Islam

A devout Muslim says the first of the five daily prayers at dawn. The second is at noon, the third in mid-afternoon, the fourth at sunset, and the fifth is said before going to bed. The muezzin, the official who proclaims the call to prayer, often does so from a minaret, or tower, in a larger mosque. At the mosque, the prayer is lead by the imam, or prayer leader, who stands in front of the worshipers facing in the direction of Mecca. The congregation stands behind him in rows. On Fridays a special prayer service replaces the prayer that normally would be said just after noon. This service includes a sermon.

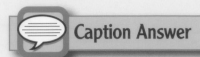

Caption Answer

They are summarized in the Five Pillars of Islam.

ELL Teaching Tips

Be Familiar with the "Silent Period"

Don't expect your new ELL students to speak before they are ready. ELLs will acquire language best when they can sit and listen instead of being forced to participate. Don't get discouraged by their silence. Embrace it!

Activity

Three World Religions Symbolization

OBJECTIVES: 12.01, 13.02

After reading and studying the information on pages 233–36 on the three world religions, students can create a brochure with pictures and symbols that represent each religion. Give students a piece of paper and instruct them to fold it into thirds. On each third, students should write the name of one of the three religions and then draw pictures or symbols that represent each religion. Explain the significance of the symbols. Note that Moses and Jesus are considered prophets of Islam.

Differentiation Ideas Provide ELL students pictures to glue under the appropriate heading. The pictures will help them visualize and distinguish important symbols for each religion. Examples: for Judaism—menorah, torah, Moses; for Christianity—Christmas tree, cross, Bible, Jesus; for Islam—Quran, Muhammad.

Advanced learners can draw or create their own symbols and can do further research to identify symbols that represent the religions.

A man in the Al Aqsa Mosque of Jerusalem reads the Quran. **How are the duties of Muslims summarized in the Quran?**

was welcomed. Muhammad later returned to Mecca and destroyed the old idols from near the Kaaba. He and his followers unified and converted the Arabian Peninsula before he died in A.D. 632.

Muslims believed the truths of Islam were for all people.

The Message of Islam

The duties of Muslims are summed up in the *Five Pillars of Islam:*

- faith, or belief in one God and Muhammad as the messenger of God;
- prayer, performed five times a day while facing in the direction of Mecca;
- acts or gifts of charity to those in need;
- fasting from dawn to dusk during the holy month of Ramadan;
- *hajj,* or pilgrimage to Mecca for every Muslim, at least once in his or her life.

Muhammad taught that Muslims were to respect Jews and Christians. To Muslims, however, Muhammad was God's last and final messenger. They believe that the faith Muhammad proclaimed should be heard by all the world. Today, as in its beginnings, Muslims believe that Islam is a faith for everyone. They hope people of every race and nation will embrace the Five Pillars of Islam.

Soon after Muhammad's death, Islam burst out of its Arabian Peninsula home. Islam spread throughout Southwest Asia into Europe, Africa, and Asia (see map, page 238). Today, Islam is a growing faith in the United States.

Islam Spreads

Muhammad first proclaimed his beliefs in Mecca. Arabs came there to trade and to worship many gods near the Kaaba, a black cube. His teachings angered local merchants. Worshippers visiting Mecca, they feared, would be outraged by Muhammad's message of one God and no other. Business might suffer if people stopped coming to the city.

Faced with persecution, Muhammad and his followers left Mecca in A.D. 622. They went to Medina, where Muhammad

LESSON 2 REVIEW

Fact Follow-Up
1. What are the basic beliefs of Judaism?
2. What are the basic beliefs of Christianity?
3. What are the basic beliefs of Islam?
4. What beliefs link these three religions?
5. Identify the following: Torah, Gospels, and Quran.
6. Why is Mecca important to Muslims?

Talk About It
1. In what ways are Judaism, Christianity, and Islam similar? How are they different?
2. Why did Muhammad call Jews and Christians People of the Book?
3. The phrase "world religions" has been used to describe Judaism, Christianity, and Islam. Is it an accurate description? Why?

LESSON 2 REVIEW

Fact Follow-Up Answers
1. Judaism is monotheistic; its basic beliefs are contained in the Torah. Jews believe they have a special covenant or sacred agreement with God and that God will honor this covenant if Jews live a moral life.
2. Christians believe that Jesus was chosen by God to bring salvation to all people. They believe his life, teachings, death, and resurrection showed the way to eternal life in heaven. The basic beliefs of Christianity are recorded in the Bible. Christianity stresses moral ideals such as charity, mercy, and justice.
3. Islam affirms one God. Muslims believe that Muhammad was the final messenger of Allah and that Allah revealed to him the duties of living a just life. These

duties are summed up in the Five Pillars of Islam. The Quran is the holy book of Islam.
4. Beliefs in monotheism (one god rather than many) and the necessity for a moral life link these three religions.
5. The Torah is composed of five sacred books that record Judaism's beliefs. The Gospels present the teachings of Jesus. They form part of the New Testament, the text that contains Christian beliefs. The Quran is the holy book of Islam. It contains the revelations, or words spoken by the angel Gabriel to Muhammad.
6. Muhammad was born in Mecca, first proclaimed his message there, and returned there from exile in Medina to remove the idols near the Kaaba, now the holiest place in Islam.

In 917, Christian visitors from Constantinople visited Baghdad, the capital of the Islamic caliphate (empire). They were greatly impressed by its splendor and wealth. Among the sights was the Palace of the Tree. It had a giant tree fashioned entirely of silver. Perched on its limbs were countless birds also made of silver and whistling with every movement of the wind.

Baghdad was indeed one of the richest and most sophisticated cities in the world. It was the center of Islamic learning and a storehouse of the world's knowledge. In just a few hundred years, Islam had grown from a small local religion into a faith guiding a major empire.

Ali ibn Abi Talib, fourth Caliph of Islam, holds the body of a dead holy man of Islam. **What is a caliph?**

Islamic Empires

Before Islam, Arabs had lived in small, independent groups. By the time of Muhammad's death in 632, Arabs had united under Islam. Over the next 200 years, Arab armies created a huge empire.

The Arab Empire

By the early 800s, the Islamic world extended westward in North Africa from Egypt to Morocco's shores on the Atlantic Ocean (see map, page 238). Islamic forces ruled regions that are now Spain and Portugal. Islam linked the Arabian Peninsula to Middle Eastern lands to the north and east. Islamic forces pushed through modern-day Iran, through the Hindu Kush Mountains, and into the area that is now Pakistan.

The Arab Empire was ruled by a *caliph* (KAY·lef), a leader claiming to be the successor of Muhammad. As the empire grew, caliphs moved the capital from Arabia to Damascus and then to Baghdad.

Religion unified the Arab Empire. Islamic rulers allowed Christians and Jews to practice their faiths. Many conquered people chose to convert to Islam. They were attracted by Islam's successes and its beliefs. Also, by converting, they escaped the tax imposed on non-Muslims.

KEY IDEAS

- After Muhammad's death, the Arabs built a huge empire.

- Muslim scholars studied earlier civilizations.

- Even as Islam expanded, different beliefs divided Muslims.

- During imperialism, European powers pushed into Southwest Asia. By the 1950s, nations had won independence.

KEY TERMS

caliph
imams
Shiite
Sunni

237

Discussion Questions

1 Do you think the Islamic rulers were wise in the way they treated people of other faiths? Why?

 **Caption Answer**

A caliph was the ruler of the Arab Empire. He claimed to be the successor of Muhammad.

🔆 Activity

People of Islam

OBJECTIVES: 1.02, 4.01

Materials the worksheet on "People of Islam," in the Teacher's Resource Guide; a transparency of a world political map (it may be useful to use a map that includes only Africa and Asia in order to make locating some of the smaller countries on the list easier).

Divide the class into groups A and B. Ask group A to locate the 21 countries on the table whose population is 95 to 100 percent Muslim. Ask group B to locate the 15 nations that have 15 million or more Muslims.

Upon completion, use a transparency map and have the student call out and mark in green those countries that are 95 to 100 percent Muslim. This is a good geographic place name activity. Next have the other group call out and mark in black those countries with a Muslim population of 15 million or more. Use black lines across the green in those countries that fit both search criteria.

Culmination Have the students research and write about the spread of Islam from the Arabian Peninsula to other parts of the world. This is a good example of cultural diffusion and represents the geographic theme of movement. Students should include those elements in their paper.

Technology Extension Using the chart, create a database on the computer. Then have students use the program to sort and rank the countries by percent of Muslim population and by total Muslim population.

Talk About It Answers

1. All three religions affirm the existence of one God (monotheism) and the necessity for a moral life. All three are practiced throughout the world. They differ in some of their other beliefs. Jews believe that they have a special covenant or relationship with God; Christians believe that Jesus is the Messiah; and Muslims believe that Muhammad is the final messenger of Allah.

2. Muhammad accepted the Torah and the New Testament, the sacred books of Judaism and Christianity, as coming from God. He believed that he, like the Jewish prophets and Jesus, was proclaiming truths about the one God.

3. Important points: Students should state whether the description is accurate or not and explain why. Note: All three religions have followers throughout the world, and each has had a great effect on world history.

Discussion Questions

1 What was it about Islam that enabled it to survive the invasions of the thirteenth and fourteenth centuries?

 **Caption Answer**

The Moguls were from Central Asia. The Ottomans were from Turkey.

 **Map Activity**

Where Have All the Muslims Gone?

NATIONAL GEOGRAPHY STANDARDS: 1, 6, 9, 13, 17

GEOGRAPHIC THEMES: Location, Place, Movement, Region

OBJECTIVES: 1.02, 1.03, 12.01

Using the map on page 238 and atlas map(s), have students brainstorm as a class to list the nations where Islam spread. These nations include Portugal, Spain, Bosnia and Herzegovina, Yugoslavia, Macedonia, Albania, Bulgaria, Turkey, Armenia, Azerbaijan, Kyrgyzstan, Uzbekistan, Kazakhstan, Turkmenistan, Tajikistan, Lebanon, Israel, Jordan, Syria, Iraq, Iran, Kuwait, Bahrain, Qatar, United Arab Emirates, Oman, Yemen, Saudi Arabia, Afghanistan, Pakistan, India, Bangladesh, China, Thailand, Malaysia, Brunei, Indonesia, Morocco/Western Sahara, Algeria, Tunisia, Libya, Egypt, Mauritania, Mali, Niger, Chad, Sudan, Ethiopia, Djibouti, Somalia, Senegal, Gambia, Guinea-Bissau, Burkina Faso, Guinea, Côte d'Ivoire, Ghana, Benin Nigeria, Cameroon, Central African Republic, Uganda, Kenya, Tanzania, and Mozambique. Divide the list equitably among students. Each student should look up in almanac his or her assigned nation to determine whether it is

Invaders

In time, the Arab Empire weakened and broke into rival states. New invaders pushed into Southwest Asia, including the Turks, Mongols from Central Asia, and Christian crusaders from Europe.

The Crusades were a series of military conflicts between 1095 and 1291. Europeans invaded Southwest Asia to recapture the Holy Land from the Muslims. These invasions scarred the region for centuries.

Between 1258 and 1400, the Mongols from Central Asia proved to be the most fearsome invaders of all. They leveled cities such as Baghdad. Yet Islam survived these disasters. The Turks and Mongols became Muslims.

The Ottoman Empire

In the 1300s and 1400s, a group of Muslim Turks, the Ottomans, built a huge empire. It extended from the Balkans in southeastern Europe through the Anatolian Plateau, into Egypt, and across North Africa.

Perhaps the greatest Ottoman leader was Suleiman, who ruled from 1520 to 1566. Suleiman had many mosques built. "I have built for you, O emperor," wrote his chief architect, "a mosque which will remain on the face of the earth till the day of judgment." This mosque, the Suleiman Mosque, still stands in Istanbul.

For centuries, the Ottoman Empire's great rival was the Safavid Empire centered in Persia (today's Iran). Between 1225 and 1269, a powerful ruler, Shah Abbas, united the empire. He promoted farming, trade, and manufacturing. Persia became a center of Islamic culture. Shah Abbas built a beautiful capital at Isfahan. The finest artists decorated its palaces, mosques, and gardens. Other Muslim rulers imitated Persian art and literature. Europeans began importing Persian silks, tapestries, ceramics, and carpets.

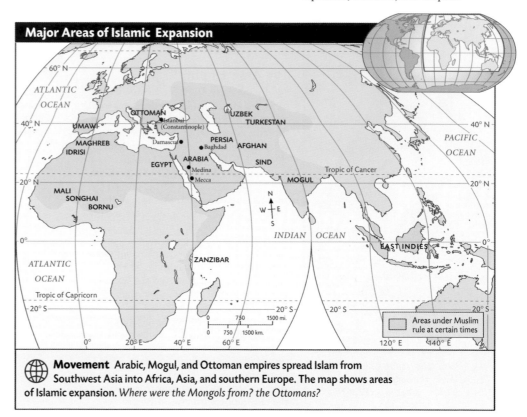

Major Areas of Islamic Expansion

Movement Arabic, Mogul, and Ottoman empires spread Islam from Southwest Asia into Africa, Asia, and southern Europe. The map shows areas of Islamic expansion. *Where were the Mongols from? the Ottomans?*

predominately Sunni or Shiite (Shiite includes Iran, Iraq, Afghanistan, Pakistan, Tajikistan, and Yemen, with Iran being the only nation where Shiites dominate). Debrief students on why and how Islam expanded. Also emphasize the possibilities why Shiite Muslims are concentrated in certain countries and how this impacts Iran, in particular, today. Briefly discuss how popular Islam is in the United States and how rapidly it is growing here.

An imam leads Friday prayer at a Baghdad mosque. **How do the two divisions of Islam differ in their view of imams?**

Divisions Within Islam

The Islamic faith has inspired millions of people. A shared belief in Muhammad's teaching helped unify empires. Yet even as Islam expanded, divisions grew within it.

After Muhammad died, a quarrel broke out about his successor. Two groups, **Sunni** (SOON·ee) and **Shiite** (SHEE·ite), had different ideas about who should lead them. Their differences over the *imams,* religious leaders, continue to divide Islam today.

The Sunnis believed that the Caliph should be picked by members of the community. They wanted a pious Muslim who also had leadership qualities. He should be able to bring Muslims together and give them direction.

Shiites placed more emphasis on religious qualities. They believed that Islam had expanded because people were inspired by Muhammad's spiritual qualities. Since Muhammad did not leave any male descendants, Shiites believed that leadership should pass to the sons of Muhammad's daughter. As descendants of Muhammad, they were believed to be divinely inspired.

Muhammad's death began a quarrel between Sunnis and Shiites that has lasted for more than 1,300 years. Sunnis and Shiites do agree on many basic religious matters. Both believe in one true God. Both look to the Quran for guidance and encourage Muslims to make the hajj.

Yet Sunnis and Shiites differ sharply on how Islam shall be applied in daily life. Both groups have more conservative, moderate, and liberal factions. Sunni Islam has strict conservative factions. Saudi Arabia is one example of a conservative Sunni state.

Traditionally, Shiites have been in the minority of Muslims. Shiites are a majority in Iran and Iraq. Others live in Lebanon and Yemen (see map, page 233). Shiites make up about 10 percent of Muslims. Thus, the vast majority of Muslims in the world are Sunni.

In Iran, religious conservatives have controlled the government since 1979. Officials do not allow people to read Western books, listen to Western music, and watch Western movies. Such steps are designed to create a Muslim nation and society. Some of the limited rights gained by women under the prior government were taken away, but some rights have been won back. For example, the right to attend men's sporting events, such as soccer, was granted in 2006. Women did not loose the right to vote, however.

WORD ORIGINS

Zero comes from the Arabic *sifr,* or *cipher,* meaning the "absence of quantity." Arab mathematicians introduced the concept of zero to European scholars.

Southwest Asia's Enduring Traditions   239

Discussion Questions

1 Describe the differences between the Sunni and Shiite Muslims.

2 How do these sects compare to the various sects in Christianity?

Caption Answer

The Sunnis believe that imams should be picked for leadership qualities by members of the Muslim community. The Shiites place more emphasis on religious qualities: only a descendant of Muhammad would be worthy of being an imam.

Activity

Word Salad

OBJECTIVES: 8.02, 12.01

Draw an outline of a bowl on a transparency. Then write the following terms in the bowl all tossed up as in a tossed salad. Tell students to read the words and then write them in the correct categories. If they have trouble determining the categories, you might want to list the categories underneath the bowl and then have them write the terms under the appropriate heading. In this activity students can work in collaborative pairs, independently, or as a whole group discussion with the teacher.

Below are the terms that can be used in the word salad. Make sure that you scramble them up in the bowl so that students are challenged to categorize them.

Mosques	Sharia
Quran	Muslims
Allah	Muhammad
Five Pillars of Faith	Sunni
Shiite	Torah
Jews	Star of David
Passover	*Moses
Diaspora	Gospels
*Ten Commandments	Bible
Christmas	Jesus
Easter	Messiah

*Note that some students may want to place these two terms under both Judaism and Christianity because they can be found in both religions.

Teacher Notes

Shiite

In newer translations, the term "Shiite" is being replaced by "Shica" or "Shi'a" in order that English speakers will more closely approximate the sound of the word in Arabic. These three terms are all referring to the same sect of Islam.

Islam and the Nation of Islam

In the United States, members of the Nation of Islam are primarily African Americans who profess Islam as their faith. The leaders of the Nation of Islam, founded in 1930, advocate economic cooperation and self-sufficiency, which are not part of traditional Islamic practice, and enjoin a strict Islamic code of behavior governing such matters as diet, dress, and interpersonal relations. Members follow some Islamic religious rituals and pray five times daily. With about 100,000 followers in the United States, the Nation of Islam is the most prominent organization within the Black Muslim movement. Not all Black Muslims are members of the Nation of Islam.

Teacher Notes

Astrolabes

An astrolabe is an instrument used for measuring the positions of the sun and the stars. It consists of a circle or section of a circle, marked off in degrees, with a movable arm pivoted at the center of the circle. The sky is drawn on the face, with marking so that positions in the sky at different times of day are easy to find. Islamic astronomers used them to calculate answers to astrological, calendrical, and meteorological questions.

Sometimes the backs of astrolabes had scales to calculate the qibla (the direction a Muslim should face when praying towards Mecca). Astrolabes provided a quick and easy way to make calculations.

Activity

T-Chart

OBJECTIVES: 11.01, 12.01

Make a T-chart comparing Sunni and Shiite Muslims. Have the students go into as much detail as they are able to from the textbook or assign this as a research activity using the library or Internet.

CONNECTIONS • GEOGRAPHY & MATH •

Ancient Mathematicians

Whether designing a rocket or baking a cake, you have to know some math. Early civilizations also needed math skills. Workers had to know how many bricks were needed to make a temple. They had to know how water could be measured. The weight of barley and the depth of a river were questions that had to be answered.

Both Egyptians and Sumerians developed systems of mathematics. The Egyptians chose the number 10 as the base number for computing mathematical problems. Why 10? Look at your fingers and toes. An easy tool to use since most of us have them. Much later, the word digits became a word for numbers. Digit is the Latin word for finger.

In Southwest Asia, the Sumerians and the Babylonians developed techniques for dealing with fractions and measurements for time. We still use their method for telling time. We use the base of 60 to divide hours and minutes. This system probably goes back to Babylonian times. Babylonians used the base of 60 in counting their money.

Arabic astrolabe

Much later, an Islamic scholar, al-Khwarizmi, who lived around A.D. 800, pulled together several mathematical concepts that became *al-jabr*, or algebra. We use algebra to calculate compound interest and distance-rate-time problems or to determine unknown quantities from a body of known data. Al-Khwarizmi also introduced Arabic numerals and methods of calculation by decimals. Al-Khwarizmi brought some of these ideas from India to Southwest Asia. Arab mathematicians later introduced them to Europe.

The links between the Europeans and the Ottomans continued the development of math and science well into the eighteenth century. Arab-Islamic civilizations made constributions in astronomy, physics, chemistry, medecine, and engineering.

Drawing of an ancient temple in Southwest Asia

Background Information

Ottoman Empire

The Ottoman Empire began around 1300. It lasted more than 600 years, ending after its defeat in World War I. The empire takes its name from its founder and first sultan, Osman, also called Othman. Expansion in the 1400s led to Sultan Muhammad II's capture of Constantinople in 1453. This conquest ended the Byzantine Empire. The Ottomans changed the city's name to Istanbul and made it their capital. By the 1600s, the Ottoman Empire was the world's largest, but 1683 marked the beginning of its slow decline, that lasted more than two centuries. In that year, Austrian and Polish troops turned back an Ottoman attack on Vienna. Military defeats, government corruption, inflation, and poor leadership all played a part in the empire's collapse.

Imperialism

The lands of Southwest Asia have been part of several empires. Arab and Ottoman rule predated European imperialism.

"The Ottomans may have been our rulers, but at least they did not take our lands," one Arab noted. The writer was pointing to European nations as thieves.

In the 1800s, European powers were growing in strength. They took territory from the Muslim-led Ottoman Empire just as the Ottomans had once expanded into Europe. Mainly the United Kingdom, France, Germany, and Russia competed for influence in Southwest Asia. European nations wanted markets for their products. They also created political boundaries that combined conflicting interests. This led to years of political violence.

As European influence spread, it brought changes to Southwest Asia. Europeans thought that they had a mission to "civilize" the region by introducing Western ways. As in Africa, such changes had benefits and costs. Western medical knowledge saved lives, but increased populations more quickly used scarce resources. Schools organized on Western models taught young people ideas about democracy and nationalism but did not teach them their own languages. Better farming methods improved output, but the improvements changed many local economies.

Many peoples of the region resisted changes that were foreign to their traditions. Some rulers did introduce new ideas, hoping to modernize their countries and compete with the West.

Nationalism began taking root in Southwest Asia in the late 1800s. Arabs, Turks, and other groups rallied behind national leaders who spoke of creating independent nations free of European control.

The Battle of Gallipoli was a battle in World War I between the Ottoman Empire and forces from Australia, New Zealand, and the United Kingdom. **How had the Ottoman Empire been weakened by Europeans?**

Discussion Questions

1 What has been the legacy of Western imperialism in Southwest Asia?

Caption Answer

European nations competed for territory and influence in the Ottoman Empire. As European cultural influence spread, it brought political and economic change to Southwest Asia. Local cultures became less powerful.

Teacher Notes

Arabic Words

It might be of interest to explain that several words from Arabic have come into the English language. These include algebra, algorithm, almanac, alkali, alcohol, atlas, baroque, candy, coffee, elixir, gauze, lemon, lime, magazine, magnet, orange, sofa, sugar, syrup, zenith, and zero.

LESSON 3 REVIEW

Fact Follow-Up

1. Describe the expansion of the Arab Empire.
2. What were caliphs? What did they do?
3. What differences divided the Islamic world?
4. Describe relations between Southwest Asia and the West in the 1800s.
5. What are some contributions of Arab-Islamic civilizations?

Talk About It

1. Why do you think the Arabs tolerated other religions in the areas they conquered?
2. What are similarities and differences in the beliefs of the Sunni and Shiite Muslims? Why are the differences important?
3. What was the most important effect of European imperialism in Southwest Asia?

LESSON 3 REVIEW

Fact Follow-Up Answers

1. Arabs united under Islam before Muhammad's death in 632. At its height, the Arab Empire included the entire Arabian Peninsula and extended westward as far as Morocco in North Africa and Portugal in Europe.
2. Caliphs claimed to be the successors to Muhammad. They ruled the Arab Empire.
3. The Islamic world was divided in its leadership between two sects, Sunni and Shiite. Sunni Muslims believed that the imam, or religious leader, should be picked for leadership qualities by the Muslim community. Shiites believed that only the descendants of Muhammad should be imams.
4. Europeans thought that they had a mission to "civilize" the world by introducing Western ideas. European influence brought political and economic change to the region.
5. Arab-Islamic civilizations made contributions to mathematics, including the pulling together of concepts that became known as algebra. Arabic numerals and methods of of calculation by decimals were also introduced. These civilizations developed techniques for telling time. Their contributions can also be seen in astronomy, physics, chemistry, medicine, and engineering.

Talk About It Answers

1. Muhammad taught that Muslims were to respect Jews and Christians because they were "People of the Book."
2. Both are monotheistic and believe in the revelations of Muhammad. They both look to the Quran for guidance and encourage followers to make a pilgrimage to Mecca. But they differ on ideas of leadership and how Islam should be applied in daily life.
3. Important points: Students should choose one effect and support the choice with reasons. Note: Possible effects include political changes, medical care, population growth, education, agricultural methods, nationalism in the region.

Teaching This Skill Lesson

Materials Needed chart paper, rulers, pencils, textbooks

Classroom Organization whole-class activity

Beginning the Lesson Draw both vertical and horizontal time lines on the chalkboard and, using the same information, fill them in. Suggested topics: your own life over a period of years; a time line of the school year with special activities such as sports, holidays, other events having to do with school. Once you have completed the time line, talk with students about whether you personally find a vertical or horizontal timeline easier to complete. Encourage their comments. Tell students they will be making a time line of some enduring traditions in Southwest Asia.

Developing the Lesson Have students read the skill lesson and, in class, complete the suggested time line on Islam. Circulate as they work on the time line, encouraging them to include as much additional information as possible. For instance, the time line on Islam should also reflect what was happening in politics. Tell students they will be completing a multidimensional time line on some period of the history described in Chapter 12. Ask students to think about what they might choose for their time line. Accept answers, encouraging students to be as specific as they can in their plans. Students are to complete their time lines as a homework assignment.

Conclusion Post students' time lines around the room. Ask students to reflect on what was easiest and most difficult about the assignment. If the time lines are sparse (for example, if there is little information) or are one-dimensional, return them to students for further work.

Extension For ELL students, assign peer tutors to help complete the activity.

Analyzing, Interpreting, Creating, and Using Resources and Materials

skill

NORTH CAROLINA SOCIAL STUDIES SKILL GOALS

Organizing Information Using a Timeline

This chapter covers a lot of human history! Roughly 10,000 years of it, as a matter of fact. How can you possibly keep it all in your memory or make sense of it? Organization is the key to success in this case.

Since history is chronological—meaning that it takes place through time and is measured by dates—some sort of timeline may be just what you need. There are two types of timelines: linear and comparative. Linear timelines deal with just one topic or theme, either vertically or horizontally. A horizontal timeline runs across a sheet of paper. A vertical timeline runs down from the top of the sheet.

Notice the examples of linear and comparative timelines below and on the opposite page. The comparative timeline organizes topics chronologically and can compare two or more of a variety of topics: political events, religious movements, economic and intellectual milestones, or major developments in the arts, for example. This timeline compares world events to regional events in Southwest Asia. To help you organize information from this chapter, you will make a comparative timeline of events relating to Southwest Asia.

Comparitive Timeline

World	Southwest Asia
1897 Zionist Congress meets in Switzerland, discusses future Jewish state	**1516** Ottoman Empire begins
1914–1918 World War I	**1917** British defeat Ottomans, occupy Palestine and Syria in World War I; The Balfour Declaration
	1918 Ottoman Empire ends
1919 Treaty of Versailles League of Nations formed	**1920** Treaty of Sèvres between World War I Allies and Ottomans (Turks)
	1923 League of Nations creates British Mandates for Palestine and Iraq and French Mandates for Syria, Lebanon, and part of Turkey
1939–1945 World War II and the Holocaust **1945** United Nations formed	**1936–1939** Arab Revolt
	1937 British Peel Commission recommends partition of Palestine into Jewish and Arab areas
	1939 British MacDonald White Paper recommends restricting Jewish immigration

Organizing Your Choices

How do you begin your timeline? First, you must decide which you will build: a vertical timeline or a horizontal one. Before deciding, ask yourself if it will be easier for you to make sense of information organized horizontally across the page. Or do you think you can remember information better if it is presented vertically?

Next, you must decide what you will record on the timeline. Chapter 12 offers almost unlimited possibilities. You decide what you will include. Do you wish to concentrate on only one period of history, or will you trace the history of roughly 10,000 years? Are you interested in organizing (and thereby helping yourself remember) political events, economic changes, or events in the histories of the three great religions described in Chapter 12?

Perhaps it might be wise to construct two brief timelines (one vertical, one horizontal) as a beginning point. Try making a timeline on Islam. Decide which format you prefer and discuss your choice with a classmate. Now you are ready to proceed to construct a multi-dimensional timeline.

Point-of-View

When you decide what information you want to place on your timeline, you are deciding what facts or events are most important. These choices can influence the person reading or using your timeline.

When historians make timelines or write about history, they also make choices. Their point of view influences what they decide to include and also to exclude.

When you are making your timeline think about why you have chosen the events and facts you have. What is your point of view? What does your timeline say about your point of view?

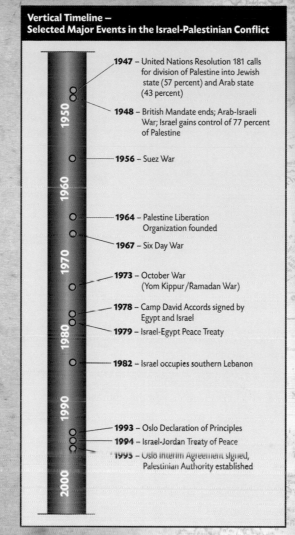

Vertical Timeline – Selected Major Events in the Israel-Palestinian Conflict

1947 – United Nations Resolution 181 calls for division of Palestine into Jewish state (57 percent) and Arab state (43 percent)

1948 – British Mandate ends; Arab-Israeli War; Israel gains control of 77 percent of Palestine

1956 – Suez War

1964 – Palestine Liberation Organization founded

1967 – Six Day War

1973 – October War (Yom Kippur/Ramadan War)

1978 – Camp David Accords signed by Egypt and Israel

1979 – Israel-Egypt Peace Treaty

1982 – Israel occupies southern Lebanon

1993 – Oslo Declaration of Principles

1994 – Israel-Jordan Treaty of Peace

1995 – Oslo Interim Agreement signed, Palestinian Authority established

 Skill Lesson Review

1. Which time line—horizontal or vertical—did you construct? Why was that choice the best for you? *Important points: Students should explain why their choice was best for them. Note: writing styles may influence the choice.*

2. Which step was easiest? Which was most difficult? Why? *Important points: Students should reflect on their experience in constructing the time line and explain. Note: Thinking of changes might be easiest, but deciding how they fit in an organization might be more challenging.*

3. What are some ways, other than using time lines, that might help you remember chronological information? *Answers will vary. Some people use rhyming memory tricks.*

4. What are some uses of time lines in your daily life? *Time lines students may use often include the school calendar, the daily class schedule, a schedule of athletic events, and a television schedule.*

Talk About It

1. Students should choose a civilization and support their choice with evidence from the text.

2. Important points: Both are monotheistic, have holy books, and have establish rules for good and moral lives. Christianity developed out of Judaism.

3. The teachings of Islam contained in the Quran and the Shariah, the law codes drawn from the Quran, cover all areas of daily living including food, dress, and marriage and family matters as well as government and law for the larger community.

4. The *hajj* affirms the holiness of the city of Mecca to Muslims. A pilgrimage honors it as the place of Muhammad's revelations.

5. Important points: Students should choose one way in which imperialism was beneficial and one way in which it was not. Note: Medical knowledge, education, farming methods, increased population.

CHAPTER 12 REVIEW

Lessons Learned

LESSON 1
Roots of Southwest Asian Societies
Early civilizations in Mesopotamia and Babylon were located near the Tigris and Euphrates Rivers. Farming advances helped these societies to make later progress in law, mathematics, and science. Phoenicians who lived in present-day Lebanon were seafaring people who spread these ideas throughout the Mediterranean.

LESSON 2
Three World Religions
Southwest Asia is the birthplace of three world religions—Judaism, Christianity, and Islam. Jews believe in a covenant with God that made them His chosen people. Christians believe in salvation through Jesus Christ. Muslims believe the Prophet Muhammad was a messenger of God.

LESSON 3
Shaping Modern Southwest Asia
An Arab Empire developed after the death of Muhammad, spreading Islam from Southwest Asia into North Africa, South Asia, and parts of southern Europe. Islam faced a conflict between Sunni and Shiite Muslims. Europeans pushed into Southwest Asia in the 1800s.

244

Talk About It

1. How did the ancient civilizations in Southwest Asia influence one another? Why was this more important?
2. Which religion do you think is more like Christianity: Judaism or Islam? Explain.
3. How does Islam guide the daily lives of Muslims?
4. Why do you think the *hajj* is so important in Islamic belief?
5. In what ways was European imperialism most and least beneficial to people living in Southwest Asia? Explain why.

Mastering Mapwork

LOCATION
Use the map on page 227 to answer these questions:

1. Describe the relative location of the Rub' al-Khali Desert.
2. Describe the relative location of Baghdad.
3. Describe the location of the Tigris River relative to the Euphrates River.
4. Through what countries does the Tropic of Cancer pass?
5. Describe the relative location of the Persian Gulf.

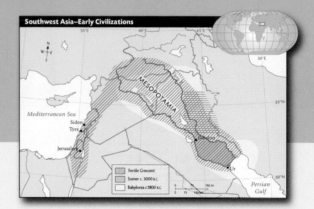

Southwest Asia–Early Civilizations

 Mastering Mapwork

1. The Rub' al-Khali is located on the Arabian Peninsula and stretches across southern Saudi Arabia from east to west.

2. Baghdad is located at about 35ºN and 45ºE.

3. For most of its length the Tigris is located to the northeast of the Euphrates and runs roughly parallel to the Euphrates.

4. The Tropic of Cancer passes through Saudi Arabia, the United Arab Emirates, and Oman.

5. The Persian Gulf is located northwest of the Arabian Sea. It is bounded on the east and northeast by Iran, on the north by Iran, on the northwest by Kuwait, and on the west by Saudi Arabia and Qatar. It is bordered on the south by the United Arab Emirates, and Oman.

Go to the Source

Comparing Documents and Statistics

Read the Balfour Declaration that established Palestine as a home for Jewish People. Then study the population chart below. Answer the questions using specific references to the materials. The Balfour Declaration has had a profound effect. One author wrote that in this short letter "one nation solemnly promised to a second nation the country of a third."

November 2nd, 1917

Dear Lord Rothschild,

I have much pleasure in conveying to you, on behalf of His Majesty's Government, the following declaration of sympathy with Jewish Zionist aspirations which has been submitted to, and approved by, the Cabinet.

"His Majesty's Government view with favour the establishment in Palestine of a national home for the Jewish people, and will use their best endeavours to facilitate the achievement of this object, it being clearly understood that nothing shall be done which may prejudice the civil and religious rights of existing non-Jewish communities in Palestine, or the rights and political status enjoyed by Jews in any other country."

I should be grateful if you would bring this declaration to the knowledge of the Zionist Federation.

Yours sincerely,
Arthur James Balfour

Questions

1. What was Balfour, the British Foreign Minister, promising Lord Rothschild and the Zionist movement?

2. Interpret the phrase "establishment in Palestine of a national home for the Jewish people"?

3. What is the impact of Arab and Jewish population growth in Palestine between 1927 and 1936? What trends do you notice?

YEAR	POPULATION				JEWISH LAND OWNERSHIP (CUMULATIVE)	
	ARABS		JEWS			
	#	%	#	%	DUNAMS	%
1880	300,000	94	24,000	6	N.A.	N.A.
1917	504,000	90	56,000	10	650,000	<3
1922	666,000	89	84,000	11	751,192	3
1931	850,000	83	174,094	17	1,171,529	4
1936	916,061	72	384,078	28	1,380,578	5
1945–1946	1,252,000	69	608,000	31	1,588,365	6
1947 UN PARTITION PLAN	1,300,000	67	640,298	33	1,900,000	7

Source: The Middle East in Transition
Southern Center for International Studies, 1994

Go to the Source

Go to the Source

Go to the Source

OBJECTIVES: 4.01, 7.02; Skills 3.05, 4.02

The Balfour Declaration was a classified document. In it, the British government, at a cabinet meeting on October 31, 1917, agreed that it would support Zionist plans for a Jewish "national home" in Palestine. The letter places the condition that nothing should be done which might prejudice the rights of existing communities there, meaning the Palestinians.

The "Balfour Declaration" became part of the Sèvres peace treaty with Turkey (Ottoman Empire) that ended World War I and established the League of Nation's British Mandate for Palestine.

ANSWERS

1. A national home for the Jewish people

2. Important points: Students should identify that some type of nation or homeland would be reserved for Jewish people.

3. Answers will vary. Important points: students should be directed to integrate some math skills to answer rate of change.

How to Use the Chapter Review

There are three sections in the Chapter Review: Talk About It, Mastering Mapwork, and Go to the Source. Use the Vocabulary Worksheets and the Chapter Review Worksheet in the Teacher's Resource Guide for additional reinforcement and preparation for the Chapter Assessments. The chapter and lesson reviews and the Chapter Review Worksheets are the basis of the assessment for each chapter.

Talk About It questions encourage students to speculate about the content of the chapter and are suitable for class or small-group discussion. They are not intended to be assigned for homework.

Mastering Mapwork has students apply one or more of the Five Themes of Geography to maps within the chapter.

Go to the Source activities allow students to analyze a primary source that relates to the content of the chapter. The questions and activities familiarize students with different types of primary sources and also build content-reading skills.

Economy and Government

Social Studies Strands

Government and Active Citizenship

Economics and Development

Global Connections

North Carolina Standard Course of Study

Goal 5 The learner will evaluate the varied ways people of Africa, Asia, and Australia make decisions about the allocation and use of economic resources.

Goal 6 The learner will recognize the relationship between economic activity and the quality of life in Africa, Asia, and Australia.

Goal 7 The learner will assess the connections between historical events and contemporary issues in Africa, Asia, and Australia.

Goal 9 The learner will analyze the different forms of government developed in Africa, Asia, and Australia.

Goal 10 The learner will compare the rights and civic responsibilities of individuals in political structures in Africa, Asia, and Australia

Teaching & Assessment

• English Language Learner Modified Lesson Plans for this chapter are found in the Teacher Resource Guide.

• *ExamView® Assessment Suite* is provided at **NCJourneys.com.** It includes customizable assessments for all chapters. Paper tests are also available in the Teacher Resource Guide. See pages T16–T17 for information about how to use the assessments and the Scoring Guide.

Worksheets

Worksheets and answer keys are found both in the Teacher Resource Guide and at **NCJourneys.com**, including Reading Guides, Reading Strategies, Chapter Reviews, English Language Learner and others.

ACTIVITIES AND INTEGRATIONS

SOCIAL STUDIES

- ● Million-Year Maps, p. 246B
- ● Activator: Oil, p. 246
- ★ Different Perception: Middle East, p. 247
- Oasis Chart, p. 249
- ▲ Active Lecture: Palestine Conflict, p. 256
- ■ Israel and Its Neighbors, p. 257
- Student Debate: Invasion of Iraq, p. 258
- Lebanon: Paris of the Middle East, p. 260
- S.W.O.T., p. 262
- The Northern Tier, p. 263
- Think It Through, p. 265
- Empires of the Northern Tier, p. 266
- Skill Lesson: Dealing with Change in Southwest Asia, p. 267

READING/LANGUAGE ARTS	READING/LANGUAGE ARTS OBJECTIVES
Analogies, p. 244B	2.01
■ Writing Prompt: Israel in Conflict, p. 244	3.03
Compare and Contrast, p. 254	2.02
The Al Jazeera Effect, p. 261	3.03
S.W.O.T., p. 262	1.03
■ Biographical Research, p. 264	1.02, 1.03
Go to the Source: Analyzing a Political Cartoon, p. 269	2.01, 4.01, 4.02

MATHEMATICS	MATHEMATICS OBJECTIVES
■ Government and Economy, p. 250	4.01
● ▲ Gas Time Line, p. 252	4.01
★ Oil Production Word Problem, p. 253	4.02
Aid to the Middle East, p. 259	1.03, 4.01

TECHNOLOGY	TECHNOLOGY OBJECTIVES
Leaders, p. 244B	3.01, 3.11
Fertile Crescent and Its Importance, p. 246	3.01, 3.11
Time Line, p. 247	3.01, 3.11
Aid to the Middle East, p. 250	1.06, 3.01
■ Biographical Research, p. 264	3.01, 3.09
★ ■ Ottoman Time Line, p. 264	3.01, 3.10

SCIENCE	SCIENCE OBJECTIVES
★ Hydroponics, p. 248	3.01, 3.11

VISUAL ARTS	VISUAL ARTS OBJECTIVES
● ▲ Design a Mosaic, p. 243	4.04, 5.02

CHARACTER AND VALUES EDUCATION	TRAITS
■ Writing Prompt: Israel in Conflict, p. 246	good judgment, fairness/justice
What Would You Do?, p. 265	self-discipline

● Basic Activities   ★ Challenging Activities   ▲ English Language Learner Novice   ■ English Language Learner Intermediate

Introductory Activity

Leaders

 OBJECTIVES: 8.01

Leaders of the Middle East are often in the news. Many have had a great impact on their nation. Have students research one of the following leaders of the Middle East and prepare a presentation for the class explaining why this person is/was important to the region.

Golda Meir
Saddam Hussein
Menachem Begin
Yasser Arafat
Hafez Assad
Anwar Sadat
Yitzhak Rabin
Ayatollah Khomeini
Ariel Sharon
King Hussein of Jordan
King Abddallah II of Jordan
Queen Noor of Jordan
Queen Rania of Jordan
Bashar al-Asad
Mustafa Kemal Ataturk

Extension ELL students should use an ELL-friendly Web site to research one of the leaders and make a time line of their life or a collage or mobile representing important events that occurred. Assign minimal writing (Novice—one or two words per item; Intermediate—one to two sentences per item).

 Culminating Activity

Million-Year Maps

OBJECTIVES: 3.04

Using present-day maps of Africa and Southwest Asia, have students draw what they think a map of the area looked like millions of years ago. Have them draw three more maps showing the changes over time. Your students will need paper, pencils, and atlases to complete this activity. As an extension, have students explore the idea of how different the world might be if this area were still green and had plenty of rainfall.

 Art Activity

Design a Mosaic

 OBJECTIVES: 12.02

After giving students a variety of mosaics to examine (pictures, prints, actual mosaics), ask them to design their own based on geometric designs. Students should choose three or four colors of construction paper. Have them cut the paper into small squares approximately the same size. Put squares aside. Have students draw a pattern and outline on a piece of posterboard. Have the pattern reflect something of Middle Eastern culture. Fill in the outline with the squares, glue each square to the board, and let dry. Students can work in cooperative groups to create a large mosaic or as individuals to make smaller ones. They can design their own or recreate a "copy" of one they study.

Extension Invite a weaver or rug specialist to give a presentation to your class.

 Analogies

 OBJECTIVES: 5.04, 9.02

Analogies are useful to help students make associations with prior knowledge. They can be used as an instructional strategy to help students better understand new materials. They are not intended to be definitions or test items.

Read the analogies aloud and ask students to identify the relationship between the terms. As an extension, ask students to write their own analogies using key terms or places discussed in the chapter.

constitutional monarchy : Jordan :: democracy : Israel (form of government in)

Arab League : Arab nations :: Organization of American States : nations of North and South America :: Organization of African Unity : African nations (whole to part of)

OPEC : petroleum :: cartel : commodity (limits production/distribution of)

Ataturk : Turkey :: George Washington : United States of America (soldier-hero, first president of)

Rub' al-Khali : Arabian Peninsula :: Sahara Desert : North Africa (is the largest desert in)

Northern Tier : plateaus and mountains :: Arabian Peninsula : desert (is characterized by)

theocracy : religious leaders :: democracy : people (is ruled by)

Teaching Strategies

Lead the class to an understanding of the conflict between the Israeli Jews and the Palestinian Arabs.

Use current events to highlight the issues discussed in this chapter that directly impact students' lives in North Carolina inlcuding oil prices, the war in Iraq and larger War on Terror, and terrorism.

This chapter is a excellent touchstone for reflection on how America's actions around the affect other nations' perceptions of the United States and what it means to be an American. Have students identify ways in which our government's actions may obscure the way the world sees Americans. How might the reverse be true; i.e., how might the way we view the people of Southwest Asia be colored by the actions of their governments?)

Discussion Questions

1 Using your geographic eye, note an example of each of the Five Themes of Geography seen in the two photographs from Baghdad.

Activator

 **OBJECTIVES: OBJECTIVES:** 8.03, 13.03

Discuss as a class the various uses for oil. Then divide students into small groups and ask each group to brainstorm a list of ways they would be affected if the world's supply of oil was depleted. After they have come up with their list, ask them to invent a solution or new item that would counteract the effect of no more oil.

Extension ELL students should be participant observers.

Writing Prompt

OBJECTIVES: 4.01

Problem-Solution

Israel, at times, has encouraged Jewish settlers to live in the territory it has claimed in the West Bank. This land was taken in war and has not been internationally recognized as belonging to Israel. This land is now in dispute because Palestinians, who lost their homes in Israel when the Jewish homeland was formed, would like to claim this area as their independent state. They would like the Jewish settlers to return to Israel. The Jewish settlers, however, want to stay in the West Bank and have it remain under Israeli control. How should the Palestinians and the Jewish settlers resolve this conflict?

As you write your paper, remember to
- clearly state your position.
- give at least three reasons and explain your reasons fully.
- give examples to support your reasons.
- write in complete sentences and paragraph form.
- organize your ideas and include an introduction and a conclusion.
- use good grammar, spelling, punctuation, and capitalization.

Jordanian money

CHAPTER 13

Economy and Government

Southwest Asia has long been a center of trade. The caliph Mansur built Baghdad more than 1,000 years ago as his capital. He proclaimed, "Here is the Tigris to put us in touch with lands as far as China and bring us all that the seas yield."

Today, leaders around the globe continue to focus attention on the Middle East. As the home to holy sites of three world religions, major trade routes, and large reserves of oil, these nations are important to the people and economies of many countries around the world.

It is also a land where peace is frequently difficult to maintain. The people of this region have lived for more than half a century dealing with the aftereffects of frequent conflicts and the threat of violence. However, their desire to live in this region remains strong despite many setbacks.

Merchant vessels anchor in the Gulf of Aqaba

Chapter Preview

LESSON 1
Economy
Oil is important to many countries in Southwest Asia. Nations without this resource have different industries.

LESSON 2
Governments of the Middle East
Middle East governments range from dictatorships to democracy. Conflicts over land and resources have fueled violence and wars.

LESSON 3
Other Governments of the Region
The governments of Turkey, Iran and Saudi Arabia have different forms of government.

246

Chapter 13

Chapter Resources

Print Resources
Nonfiction

Amari, Suad. *Cooking the Lebanese Way* (Easy menu and ethnic cookbooks). Lerner Publications Co.,1986. ISBN 082250913X.

Carter, Jimmy. *Palestine: Peace Not Apartheid.* Simon & Schuster, 2006. ISBN 0743285026.

Foster, Leila M. *Iraq* (Enchantment of the World series). Children's Press, 1998. ISBN 0516205846.

Kent, Zachary. *The Persian Gulf War: "The Mother of All Battles."* Enslow, 1994. ISBN 0894905287.

Kotapish, Dawn. *Daily Life in Ancient and Modern Baghdad.* Runestone Press, 2000. ISBN 0822532190.

Mulloy, Martin. *Syria* (Major World Nation series). Chelsea, 1999. ISBN 0791049833.

Sheehan, Sean. *Lebanon* (Cultures of the World series). Marshall Cavenish, 1997. ISBN 0761402837.

Slavik, Diane. *Daily Life in Ancient and Modern Jerusalem.* Runestone Press, 2000. ISBN 0822532182.

Smith, Debbie. *Israel: The Culture.* Crabtree, 1999. ISBN 086505231X.

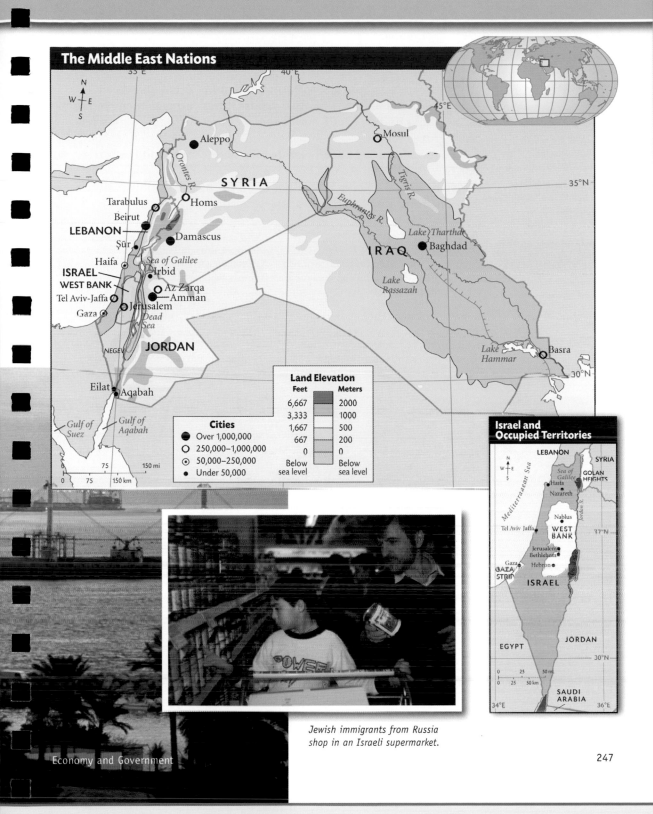

The Middle East Nations

SYRIA · Aleppo · Mosul · Tarabulus · Homs · Beirut · LEBANON · Damascus · Şūr · Haifa · *Sea of Galilee* · Irbid · ISRAEL · WEST BANK · Az Zarqa · Amman · Tel Aviv-Jaffa · Jerusalem · Gaza · *Dead Sea* · NEGEV · JORDAN · Eilat · Aqabah · *Gulf of Suez* · *Gulf of Aqabah* · *Orontes R.* · *Euphrates R.* · *Tigris R.* · *Lake Tharthar* · Baghdad · IRAQ · *Lake Rassazah* · *Lake Hammar* · Basra

0 75 150 mi
0 75 150 km

Cities
- ● Over 1,000,000
- ○ 250,000–1,000,000
- ◉ 50,000–250,000
- • Under 50,000

Land Elevation

Feet	Meters
6,667	2000
3,333	1000
1,667	500
667	200
0	0
Below sea level	Below sea level

Jewish immigrants from Russia shop in an Israeli supermarket.

Economy and Government

247

Israel and Occupied Territories

LEBANON · SYRIA · *Mediterranean Sea* · *Sea of Galilee* · Haifa · Nazareth · GOLAN HEIGHTS · Tel Aviv-Jaffa · Nablus · WEST BANK · Jerusalem · Bethlehem · GAZA STRIP · Gaza · Hebron · ISRAEL · EGYPT · JORDAN · SAUDI ARABIA

Map Activity

Different Perception: Middle East

NATIONAL GEOGRAPHY STANDARDS: 1, 5, 6
GEOGRAPHIC THEMES: Location, Region
OBJECTIVES: 1.02

Have students identify the five nations and one authority generally identified as the Middle East: Jordan, Lebanon, Iraq, Israel, Palestinian Authority, and Syria. Note with students that as many as 21 countries can be included in the Middle East.

Different scholars define the Middle East using different criteria. Some authors apply the term to the area extending from Morocco in the west to Pakistan in the east, with Turkey as the most northern point and Sudan as the most southern, including the island republic of Cyprus; others restrict it to the Arabic-speaking section of the region, and thus leave out Turkey, Cyprus, Iran, Afghanistan, and Pakistan. Still others narrow it further by excluding Arab North Africa—Egypt, Morocco, Tunisia, Algeria, and Libya—and Sudan.

Using the inset world map, explain that the term Middle East is a Euro-centric perspective of the Eastern Hemisphere (with the Far East being China, Japan, and Korea). The area is in the middle of Europe, Africa, and Asia. Three hoola-hoops, interlocking/overlapping yarn circles, or taped sections can be placed on the classroom floor representing Europe, Africa, and Asia, with each circle overlapping the other two. Write the names of the Middle Eastern nations and the Palestinian Authority on note cards or outline maps of each nation, and place them in the center of the three circles. Write the names of the other 16 countries on cards or outline maps to be placed in the European, African, and Asian portions of the circles:

Europe: western Turkey
Africa: Algeria, Egypt, Libya, Morocco, Tunisia
Asia: Afghanistan, Bahrain, Cyprus, Iran, Iraq, Israel, Palestinian Authority (West Bank and Gaza Strip), Jordan, Kuwait, Lebanon, Oman, Qatar, Saudi Arabia, Syria, eastern Turkey, United Arab Emirates, Yemen

—. *Israel: The Land.* Crabtree, 1999. ISBN 0865052298.
—. *Israel: The People.* Crabtree, 1999. ISBN 085052301.
South, Coleman. *Jordan* (Cultures of the World series). Marshall Cavendish, 1997. ISBN 076140287X.

Back issues of magazines
Jerusalem Today. Cobblestone Publishing Company. ISBN 0382443810

Audiovisual
The 50 Years War, Israel and the Arabs. PBS Home Video. 300 minutes. Formation of Israel through the Oslo Agreements.

Web Sites
Go to **NCJourneys.com** for links to the following Web sites:
- Country Resources, Future State, U.S. Department of State for Youth
- Global Issues, the Middle East
- Middle East Research and Information Project
- Photo Essay: A Vicious Circle in the Middle East, Time Magazine

Discussion Questions

1 What role does precipitation play in the region?

Caption Answer

Improved farm production will mean increased food output.

Research Activity

Hydroponics

OBJECTIVES: 3.01, 3.03

Using the Internet, have students research the ways in which technology has enabled farmers to grow crops in water, the agricultural practice of hydroponics. Students should determine what types of crops grow best with this technology and what resources are needed to support large-scale hydroponics operations. Discuss. Students may try to grow their own hydroponic plant from a cutting or seed.

Extension ELL students should use an ELL-friendly Web site for research so they can actively listen during the discussion.

LESSON 1 Economy

KEY IDEAS

- Water and mineral resources are scarce, although several nations contain oil.

- Middle Eastern nations have had to overcome many obstacles to economic progress.

KEY TERMS

fossil water
mixed economies
OPEC
socialism

Since ancient times, wood from Lebanon's cedars has been harvested and sent to other lands. It has furnished the pharaohs' tombs and palaces from Arabia to Europe. Today, only a few cedar groves remain.

Lebanon has tried to reforest its hills with cedars and other trees. The task is difficult. As you have read, the cedar is one of many depleted Middle Eastern resources. In all of the sub-regions, Southwest Asian nations now carefully use scarce resources.

Agriculture

Parts of the Fertile Crescent have rich soil. The moist Mediterranean coast and nearby hills produce such crops as grains, fruits, and vegetables.

Syria and Israel have increased food production by irrigating desert areas. Syria's wheat belt relies on water from the Orontes (aw·RAHN·teez) and Euphrates Rivers. Syria has created large-scale wheat and cotton farms, where machines increase output. Israel has irrigated parts of the Negev Desert. Israel exports farm goods such as fruit and vegetables.

Many crops, such as grapes, olives, and figs, thrive on Turkey's coastal plains, especially on the Black Sea coast. Turkey has more cropland than other nations in the region. It is a major grain producer and also exports cotton, tobacco, tea, and sugar beets.

Kuwaiti farmers must grow crops in a protected environment. **Why is it important for nations of the Arabian Peninsula to improve farm production?**

Chapter 13

Only about 10 percent of Iran's land can be cultivated. A few areas enjoy enough rain for farming. Irrigation allows a little more land to be used. Iranians are mostly herders and farmers who struggle to earn a living in a harsh, dry climate.

In Saudi Arabia, only about 2 percent of the land can be farmed. Irrigation makes farming expensive. Still, the government wants to increase food output. Water wells have been drilled. On irrigated lands, farmers grow wheat, barley, and millet. They also harvest dates and such fruits as grapes and tomatoes.

Resources

The Fertile Crescent lacks many useful mineral resources. Jordan and Israel take phosphates from the Dead Sea. Israel has copper and a little oil. Jordan has no oil. Lebanon has some iron. Syria and Iraq are fortunate to have oil reserves.

Turkey has some mineral resources and some oil. It hopes to find more oil fields under water in the Aegean Sea. Longtime tensions between Turkey and Greece could prevent oil exploration there.

Iran has vast oil fields. Refineries and pipelines dot the landscape. Iran earns billions of dollars from oil annually, which has helped it develop.

Oil changed Saudi Arabia's fortunes—it was no longer a poor desert kingdom. The royal family mixes self-indulgence with social support. It uses its oil wealth to build palaces and buy luxuries as well as to fund social and economic programs for Saudi Arabia and even other Arab countries.

Customs

A favorite treat in the Middle East for young and old is *falafel*. Street vendors sell ground and seasoned chickpeas, a vegetable, shaped into a ball and fried in a crunchy dough. It is sometimes served in pita bread. No knife or fork is necessary. The pita pocket makes an easy sandwich.

A few cedars still grow in Lebanon. **How are the cedars symbolic of the resources of the Middle East?**

The Power of Oil

In 1960, many major oil-producing nations set up the Organization of Petroleum Exporting Countries *(OPEC).* Its members include Arab and non-Arab nations from around the world.

In the 1970s, OPEC set out to control oil prices by limiting production. With less oil available, the members expected prices would rise. For a time oil prices soared. This affected the whole world. Developing nations were hard hit because they imported much of their oil. Industrial nations such as the United States and Japan looked for other forms of energy and ways to conserve energy.

OPEC's efforts eventually failed because it did not have absolute control over the oil market. Some major oil producers, like the Soviet Union (now Russia), were not members. Some members abandoned efforts to limit production. They needed income from oil exports.

Today, oil is more expensive than during the oil crisis of the 1970s. Instability in Southwest Asia, increased demand worldwide, and shrinking world resources are some reasons for record level prices.

Discussion Questions

1 Which do you think would be a more important resource: water or oil?

2 How has oil been a mixed blessing to the region?

3 What can the rest of the world do to cope with rising oil prices as a result of OPEC limiting production of oil?

 Caption Answer

They were plentiful in ancient times, but now they are depleted.

 Activity

Oasis Chart

OBJECTIVES: 2.01, 3.01

Have students research oases on the Internet and complete the chart below.

Oases

Definition	Importance
Crops	Draw a picture

Discuss as a class the relationship between oases and life in the Arabian Peninsula.

 Background Information

OPEC

In 1973, OPEC effectively used oil as a political weapon. In September 1973, OPEC members agreed to raise oil prices by 70 percent. Three months later, they increased oil prices by another 130 percent. The Middle Eastern members of OPEC used these price increases to retaliate against the United States and other Western nations for their support of Israel in the October 1973 Yom Kippur War. Further price increases over the next seven years sent the price of crude oil soaring from $3 a barrel in 1973 to $30 in 1980. In the 1980s many Western nations reduced their dependence on OPEC oil through conservation and by buying from North Sea wells and from Mexico and the Soviet Union.

CITY LIFE
in Southwest Asia

EYEWITNESS TO HISTORY

Southwest Asia has built a strong economy on more than just oil. Many countries have taken advantage of their locations to develop the transportation, tourism, and entertainment sectors of their economies. The region's large, modern cities offer all the conveniences of those in America.

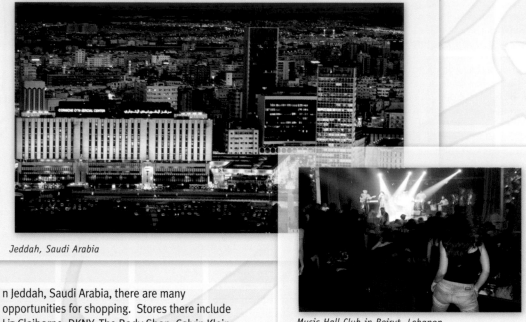

Jeddah, Saudi Arabia

Music Hall Club in Beirut, Lebanon

Research Activity

Government and Economy

OBJECTIVES: 1.03, 5.01, 9.02

Have students research governmental and economic facts about the countries of Southwest Asia. They should create and complete the database below using the most recent almanac available or information researched on the Internet. Below is an example of how a student's chart might look.

Questions
1. What might account for Iraq's low per capita income considering its high output of oil production?
2. Why might Israel spend a large portion of their GDP on defense?

Extension Assign a peer tutor to help intermediate ELL students with database and conclusion of this activity.

In Jeddah, Saudi Arabia, there are many opportunities for shopping. Stores there include Liz Claiborne, DKNY, The Body Shop, Calvin Klein, Emporio Armani, Tommy Hilfiger, Christian Dior, Boss, and IKEA. In addition to the modern shopping centers, Jeddah also has many traditional souks where all types of products can be purchased. There are also supermarkets in Jeddah where American and European products can be found. Although women cannot drive in Saudi Arabia, taxis are everywhere. They are inexpensive, too.

Dubai is a center of culture and luxury in the United Arab Emirates (U.A.E.). Major international music stars perform there, such as Mariah Carey, Enrique Iglesias, and Elton John. People may attend the ballet or the orchestra. This country has also built the world's first city devoted only to sports. It opened in 2007.

People enjoy dancing in nightclubs to Western pop tunes or traditional Arabian music all over the region.

250

Chapter 13

Country	Capital	Government Type	% Spent on Defense	Oil Resources (Billions of Barrels)	Arable Land (Percent)	$ per Capita Income
Israel	Jerusalem	Republic	10	-	17	3,500
Jordan	Amman	Constitutional Monarchy	65	-	4	3,000
Syria	Damascus	Autocracy	6	1.7	28	5,700
Iraq	Baghdad	Republic	75	100	12	2,000
Lebanon	Beirut	Republic	4.4	-	21	1,720

Young boy at a video arcade in Dubai

I n shopping malls in Iran, Saudi Arabia, Kuwait, and all over the region, families shop and relax. Young people play video games in arcades. Girlfriends enjoy chatting over coffee.

Women at a Starbucks in Kuwait City

T he Wafi City Mall in Dubai looks like an ancient Egyptian temple. It has more than 200 shops inside. It also houses the largest health spa in the emirates, two swimming pools, tennis courts, a climbing wall, a roller-blading rink, virtual reality simulators, a 3-D cinema, two adventure playgrounds, almost 30 restaurants, and a nightclub.

One of the many modern shopping malls in Dubai

Economy and Government

251

Eyewitness Activity

OBJECTIVES: 5.01

Using a KWL chart, have students identify what they know about the economies of Southwest Asia. Identify common stereotypes, such as all countries have oil, or everyone shops in open-air markets. Use the Eyewitness to History to help students understand through a discussion and research on the Internet that Southwest Asia's economy is varied. Not all nations have oil.

Break the class into groups of four students. Using the CIA World Factbook (link found at **NCJourneys.com**), have each group create pie charts showing the breakdown of the workforce for each country. Discuss how do these pie charts illustrate economic diversity of the region. Which nations have successfully diversified?

Extension Have students compare the sectors of the different nations using mean, median, and mode. For example, what is the region's mean percentage of employment in the service sector? agriculture? What nation has the median service sector employment percentage? for manufacturing or industry?

It's a Fact

Middle East

■ Iraq, according to many historians and biblical scholars, is the home of the "Garden of Eden."

■ Israel is about the size of Maryland. Surrounded by Arab nations, Israelis pay more than 50 percent taxes on their earnings to maintain a well-equipped and well-trained military.

■ Jordan's greatest source of income is from money sent home by Jordanians working in other countries.

■ Syria is a land of young people. More than half the population is under the age of twenty-five. Syria and Egypt attempted to unite in 1958. Called the United Arab Republic, the union lasted less than four years.

■ Lebanon's executive structure has a special custom. The president is Christian, the prime minister is Sunni Muslim, and the president of the legislature is Shiite Muslim.

1 Why do you think many governments around the world have moved towards a mixed economy? What might be the benefits of limited government ownership of industry?

2 Why would Southwest nations with oil want to diversify their economies?

Caption Answer

The Middle East has some fertile soil, copper, oil, and iron.

Activity

Gas Time Line

OBJECTIVES: 5.03

Using the library and the Internet, have students research the rise in gasoline prices from the 1960s to the present. Students should create a time line of the rise in prices, noting the times in which the nations of Southwest Asia or OPEC caused an increase or decrease in the price of gas. Have students discuss as a class the impact that these nations have on the daily lives of Americans.

Extension ELL students should use an ELL-friendly Web site for research. Expect that novice and intermediate students will participate minimally in the discussion.

Economic Modernization

Middle Eastern countries are building modern economies. They have worked to improve agriculture, increase food production, set up industries, and end foreign influence. Many experimented with *socialism,* a system that gives government ownership of at least some economic enterprises. Today, most have **mixed economies,** or a combination of government and private ownership.

Economic progress has come slowly. Many countries lack good farmland, water, and technical know-how. Diseases and drought constantly threaten crops. Often, a few wealthy landowners control most of the land. Political violence has taken a toll. Lebanon, for example, once had a thriving economy. Then political struggles plunged it into a 17-year civil war. Its capital, Beirut, and other cities were almost completely destroyed.

War slowed economic development. It drove millions of people into refugee camps and disrupted farming and industry.

Despite such problems, Middle Eastern countries have made gains. Through irrigation they have increased the number of acres farmed. New seeds and farming methods have paid off with higher crop yields. Industry has grown. Dams have been built to provide electricity. Governments have developed textile factories, mines, and steel mills. Jordan has signed a free trade agreement with the United States.

Israel

Like other Middle Eastern nations, Israel has a mixed economy, but during the last two decades the government has reduced its role in it. Today, many private companies operate alongside government-run industries. Israel has developed both agriculture and industry.

Israel benefits from an educated workforce. It has a strong electronics industry and a profitable diamond-cutting industry. Stones brought from Africa are polished and cut. The prized gems are then exported to world markets.

Saudi Arabia

Saudi Arabia's royal family's motto is "Progress without Change." They want to develop the economy but preserve their traditional culture. The Saudis also want to build an economy based on more than oil. They know that within this century the oil will run out. So the government is using oil money to diversify.

The Saudis have searched for natural gas, which can used for energy or for fertilizers, and built steel factories. It also supports small private factories that produce plastics, cement, and chemicals.

Phosphate from the Dead Sea is held in a loading facility in Aqaba, Jordan. **What are other natural and mineral resources of the Middle East?**

Chapter 13

Background Information

Water Worries

In the 1980s, greater energy use and improved technology led to increased water use in much of the Middle East. Residential use grew and carefully irrigated trees lined major streets in some desert cities. Many nations of the region rely on irrigation for the production of such export crops as tomatoes, oranges, and wheat. Today population increase, rising standards of living, and growing food production may one day force Israel, Jordan, and other nations of the region to choose between water conservation and economic development. Israel already recycles some 30 percent of its water and sewage for reuse in agriculture. Israel, Jordan, and Syria share the water of the Jordan River. Either through conflict or cooperation these nations will soon have to decide how its waters will be shared.

Oil wealth has allowed the Saudis to change their land in many ways. The government improved conditions for visiting Muslim pilgrims in Mecca. It built cities, airports, and roads.

They have drilled deep wells to tap underground water. Some underground pools have *fossil water,* water collected millions of years ago when the Arabian Peninsula received more rainfall. Pipelines carry this water to remote areas.

Desalination plants take the salt out of seawater so it can be used for irrigation and for drinking. Desalination is expensive, so its use is limited.

Schools and universities were opened, first for boys only, then schools for girls. Housing improved. In time, Saudis exchanged mud brick homes for ones made of concrete blocks. Hospitals were built. Today, Saudi medical care equals that in rich industrial countries.

Pipelines carry oil to waiting ships. **What are some of the benefits oil has brought to the region?**

LESSON ❶ REVIEW

Fact Follow-Up
1. What are some important crops grown in the region?
2. What natural and mineral resources are found in Southwest Asia?
3. What has the government of Saudi Arabia done to diversify the economy?
4. What is OPEC?

Talk About It
1. Why do you think many Southwest Asian nations have turned from socialism to mixed economies?
2. How much success will Middle Eastern nations have in building modern economies?
3. Southwest Asian oil might be gone in a number of years. Will the region continue to have importance in world affairs? Why?

Caption Answer

The oil wealth has given the people money to improve conditions in this region. Cities, schools, hospitals, airports, and roads have been built. Housing has improved.

Math Activity

Oil Production Word Problem

OBJECTIVES: 5.01

Find the mean, median, and mode of the following production statistics:

OPEC Crude Oil Production, 2000
(Thousand barrels per day)

Algeria	826
Indonesia	1,252
Iran	3,803
Kuwait	2,146
Libya	1,411
Nigeria	2,132
Qatar	713
Saudi Arabia	8,456
UAE	2,343
Venezuela	2,988
Iraq	2,266
Total OPEC Production	31,106

Extension Assist ELL students by setting up the problem for them.

LESSON ❶ REVIEW

Fact Follow-Up Answers
1. Crops grown in the region include grains, fruits, vegetables, cotton, tobacco, and tea.
2. The Middle East includes some fertile land, phosphates, copper, oil, and iron.
3. The government has searched for natural gas, which can be used for energy or fertilizers, and built factories. It has also supported small private factories that produce plastics, cement, and chemicals.
4. OPEC stands for the Organization of Petroleum Exporting Countries.

Talk About It Answers
1. Important points: Students should point out what a socialist economy is and what a mixed economy is.
2. Important points: Many nations lack good farmland, water, and technology. There are border disputes, unrest and violence, and religious and ethnic divisions. Scarce resources are spent on weapons.
3. Important points: Students should choose a position and explain their prediction. Note: Location at the center of sea and land routes will still be important.

OBJECTIVES: 7 (all), 8.01, 8.02, 9.02, 9.04, 10 (all)

Discussion Questions

1 Do you think the concept of a single Arab nation would work? Why or why not?

2 How can a republic not be a democracy?

Caption Answer

Constitutional monarchy

Activity

Compare and Contrast

OBJECTIVES: 1.01, 9.02, 11.02

Have students write "Israel" on the top line of the left side of a piece of lined paper (Concept One), and "Other Countries" on the right side of the same line (Concept Two). Centered on the page two lines down, write "Same" and list four ways these countries are alike directly underneath. Then have them skip two lines and write "Different." Under this heading in the center of the page students should list the following areas each on a separate line: Religion, Government, Economy, Language, Ties to the West. Have students write the ways in each subject area that Israel and other Southwest Asian countries differ on the appropriate side of the page. Use the graphic organizer to write a short essay comparing and contrasting countries of the Middle East.

KEY IDEAS

- Governments in the Middle East range from dictatorships to democracies.

- Most people in the Middle East desire peace, but violence continues to hinder progress.

- The Middle East has become a battle ground in the United States' War on terror

KEY TERMS

Arab nationalism
sanctions
terrorism
weapons of mass destruction
Zionists

Signs of ancient history are everywhere in modern Jordan. Ruins of cities lie along desert trade routes. According to the Bible, John the Baptist baptized Jesus in the Jordan River. The Hashemite Kingdom of Jordan was established in 1921.

Like Jordan, most Middle Eastern nations are relatively new. They were formed after World War II from lands colonized by the United Kingdom and France.

Diverse Governments

Governments in the Middle East range from authoritarian regimes to democratic republics. As elsewhere, many republics in the Middle East limit citizen participation. For example, Syria's president is approved by popular referendum for a seven-year term, but President Hafiz al-Asad ruled from 1967 until his death in 2000. His son, Bashar al-Asad has ruled since then.

Jordan is a constitutional monarchy. Its king shares some power with an elected legislature. Lebanon is returning to its tradition of democratic government. The United States and the United Kingdom are working to build a democratic republic in Iraq. The Palestinian National Authority has an elected council.

Israel governs itself as a democracy with many political parties. America and others have helped Israel become a Westernized state. Its parliamentary democracy reflects a society where people enjoy personal freedom. But religion—Judaism—also influences its government.

Israelis must serve two years in the armed forces (Arab citizens often serve in segregated units or are restricted from service). They then remain in the reserves for many years. Israel has spent huge sums on defense because it has believed that its existence is threatened. It also receives military aid from the United States. Thus Israel, though small, is a major military power.

Building stable governments in the region has been a challenge. Some countries have suffered from internal violence. Assassins have killed government leaders in Israel, Jordan, and Lebanon.

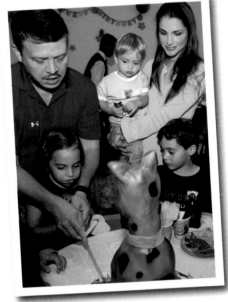

King Abdullah, Queen Rania, and their children are the ruling family of Jordan. **What type of government does Jordan have?**

Arab Nationalism

Several Arab leaders, including Egypt's Gamal Abdel Nasser, tried to unite the Arab world. The idea that Arabic-speaking people should be united into a single nation is called *Arab nationalism.* After World War II, Arab nationalism had widespread appeal. Arabs shared a common heritage and language.

However, the Arab world today remains divided into many countries.

Chapter 13

These divisions are unlikely to change in any major way. Within each country, people have developed their own national loyalties. They talk of "Arab brothers" outside their borders, but few want to share scarce resources with them.

The Arab League was set up in 1945. Its original goals were to gain independence for Arab states and hinder the establishment of a Jewish state in Palestine. Today, the League promotes political, economic, and cultural cooperation in the Arab world. The League has also been active in settling some disputes between Arab states, as well as limiting some conflicts.

The Imperial Legacy

Political divisions exist throughout Southwest Asia. Turkey and Iran see themselves as different from other Middle Eastern nations because they are not Arabic. Arab states, like nations elsewhere, have their differences. Islam, however, is one of the forces uniting much of the region. But there are divisions within Islam as well.

As in Africa, the legacy of imperialism meant that Middle Eastern states were not created because the people of that region shared similar beliefs or ethnicities or a shared desire to unite as a nation. Instead the land was divided up by European powers. In Iraq, for example, this meant that Sunni and Shiite Muslims, who are frequently distrustful of each other, as well as Kurds in the north, were brought together in one state. This posed a great challenge to creating a stable government.

European powers were not successful in bringing their democratic traditions to their Southwest Asian territories as well. The region still struggles to find ways to overcome differences peacefully and find ways to compromise.

Cold War tensions pitting Western European nations and the United States against the Soviet Union reached into Southwest Asia. On many issues, Western Europe and the United States supported Israel, Saudi Arabia, Lebanon, and Jordan. The Soviets backed Egypt, Syria, and Iraq.

This made regional rivalries more intense. After the collapse of the Soviet Union, however, the region began to change.

A Region in Conflict

Throughout the past 50 years, life in the Middle East has been marked by short periods of peace separated by wars and violence. Every nation has been affected.

Arab-Israeli Conflicts

A long, complex struggle has pitted Arab countries and Israel against each other. It is another legacy of imperialism.

This conflict has grown out of competing nationalisms—Arab and Jewish. In the 1890s, Jewish nationalists, called *Zionists,* desired a Jewish state in Palestine, homeland of the ancient Hebrews. They wanted a place where Jews could live without persecution. Many Jews moved there in the 1920s and 1930s. After World War II, survivors of the Nazi Holocaust in Europe moved to Palestine. They were supported by the United Kingdom, although the British did try to control the flow of Jews to Palestine.

Arabs who lived in Palestine opposed the newcomers. They did not want to be forced to move from the land where they had lived for hundreds of years. Violence broke out. As conflict grew, the United Nations voted to divide Palestine into an Arab state and a Jewish state.

Foreign ministers of Arab nations meet at the opening session of the Arab League in Cairo, Egypt, in March 2006. **What does the Arab League do today?**

Discussion Questions

1 Do you think mixed economies would be successful? What would be the advantages and disadvantages of mixed economies?

2 How do you think the region would be different if there had not been so much conflict in Southwest Asia?

3 Do you think Southwest Asia has the potential to be a highly developed area?

4 What would be the dangers of having a very conservative religious group create the government? Do we have any similar situations in the United States?

Caption Answer

The Arab League promotes political, economic, and cultural cooperation in the Arab world.

Research Activity

Timeline

OBJECTIVES: 7.02

Using the instructions on creating a timeline outlined in the skill lesson on pages 242 and 243, have students, individually or in small groups, research the origins of the Arab-Israeli conflict. Students should incorporate maps showing how Palestine and Israel have been formed over the years.

ELL Teaching Tips

Become an Active Listener

When listening to ELLs speak, give lots of nonverbal feedback and praise. Give students all of your attention while attempting to understand their comments. Be sure your body language is patient and inviting.

Discussion Questions

1 Why do you think Anwar Sadat's dialogue with Israel was so critical to the region?

Caption Answer

Many people in this region agree with the issues that terrorists identify as problems, though they do not agree with the terrorists' tactics. Others don't view these groups as terrorists, but rather as armed militias fighting for just causes.

Activity

Active Lecture

🔺 **OBJECTIVES:** 4.01

To help students understand the conflict between the Israeli Jews and the Palestinian Arabs and actively involve students in the process, try an active lecture.

Place tape or yarn on the floor in the approximate shape of Israel. Make it large enough for half of the students in the class to stand inside of it comfortably. Then, ask a little more than half of the students to move to the taped area on the floor and stand inside of "Israel." Place a poster on the floor labeled Ancient Israel and explain to the class that the people standing inside of Israel, the taped area on the floor, represent people who lived thousands of years ago in Israel until the Diaspora.

Have all but a few of the students scatter to other parts of the room. These students represent the Jews. The students remaining in the area are Arabs or Palestinians who stayed in Palestine. Explain that over time, other people moved into the area.

Have the other half of the students come to the taped area on the floor. Once they are standing inside of the area, remove the Israel sign and replace it with a poster labeled Palestine. Explain the colonial presence in the area. Describe the Holocaust and the United Nations creation of a Jewish state in the old homeland of Israel, which was now called Palestine.

In 1948, Jews proclaimed the state of Israel. Neighboring Arab nations attacked. In that war, and in three other conflicts, Israel defeated the attackers and took Arab land, including the Gaza Strip, the Golan Heights, and the West Bank. Palestinians fled their homes and ran to refugee camps. These camps became the homes of many Palestinians for decades. Any Arab-Israeli peace settlement must determine where Palestinians will live.

In 1979, Egypt's President Anwar Sadat bravely became the first Arab leader to make peace with Israel. In the 1990s, the outlook for peace improved. The Oslo Peace Accords acknowledged the right of the Palestinians to govern themselves in parts of the Gaza Strip and the West Bank. Violent conflicts frequently undermine progress towards peace in the region.

Thousands of Jordanians marched to protest terrorism in 2004. **What are the different points of view in the Middle East regarding terrorism?**

Motivations for Terrorism

Many people associate terrorism with the Middle East. However, what terrorism is and its relationship and identification with this region are complex issues.

Most people who live in Southwest Asia desire peace, stable governments, and prosperous economies. However, some extremists have different agendas. These small groups greatly disrupt life in the region and other parts of the world.

In the Middle East, one or more of the following factors motivate many terrorist groups. Primarily, they oppose Israel's occupation of Palestinian, Syrian, and Lebanese lands. A few groups want to eliminate Israel and establish a Palestinian state in its place. Second, some groups seek to establish a conservative form of Islam as a state religion all over the region and world. Third, groups may wish to drive Western influence from the region.

Terrorist groups often target Western citizens because Western democracies, such as the United States, tend to be supporters of Israel. Some groups view America, Israel, and other Western nations as powers that seek to dominate them and occupy their lands. The United Nations and human rights organizations have investigated Israel's treatment of Palestinians in the occupied territories and cite a number of human rights abuses. That, and images like those of American troops in Iraq fuel these views.

Point-of-View Many in the region do not view these groups as "terrorists" even if they disagree with their tactics. Understanding this different point-of-view is important. Some people in the Middle East fear that the United States, Israel, and other Western nations want to control their oil resources, take their lands, and destroy their way of life. They also resent past American support for oppressive authoritarian regimes. Although most Westerners would largely disagree with these opinions, it is still important to know they exist.

These different points-of-view help us decide whether these groups are armed resistance movements or terrorists. For example, Hezbollah is considered by the

After this explanation, tell all of the students to return to the taped area. They should immediately understand how crowded it is in the taped area on the floor and based on their particular perspective, they should have an opinion as to who deserves the land. Then tape off smaller areas to represent the Gaza Strip, Golan Heights, and West Bank. Instruct the "Palestinians" to move to those areas. Once students have participated in this reenactment, they can do a variety of follow-up activities.

• Based on their identity in the active lecture, have the students write a persuasive paper

explaining why their group deserves the land.
• Collect current events about the news in Israel.
• Pretend you are the president of the United States and propose a peace agreement between the two groups.

Extension Have ELL students follow up by collecting current events in their own language online at a Web site such as **Univision.com** about the events in Israel. Be aware that you may have a student from one or both of these areas—you do not want to offend them.

United States to be a terrorist group. But others see it as an armed militia fighting unjust Israeli occupation of Lebanese and Palestinian territory.

Although terrorist groups exist worldwide, the Middle East is connected to a number of the more active groups. A few have attacked citizens of Western nations over the last 25 years. But these groups do not only attack the West. Recently there have been attacks in Egypt, Jordan, Saudi Arabia, and Indonesia, all Islamic nations, as well as the United States, Spain, and the United Kingdom.

The War on Terror

In 1993, the Egyptian Islamic Jihad, led by Sheikh Omar Abdul Rahman and Ayman al-Zawahiri, set off a truck bomb at the World Trade Center in New York City. Al-Qaida (al-KIGH·dah), led by Osama Bin Laden (oh·SAH·mah BIN LAH·din), later bombed two United States embassies in East Africa and the USS *Cole*. Although al-Qaida is based in the mountains of Afghanistan, many people who carry out attacks are from Southwest Asia.

After al-Qaida's attacks on the United States on September 11, 2001, terrorist activities in Afghanistan and Southwest Asia became a top concern of the United States. President George W. Bush declared that America is fighting a "War on Terror." Some countries, like Jordan, are aiding the United States in this war. Others, like Iran, continue to be a source of concern. The top target of this fight is al-Qaida.

Discussion Questions

1 Do you believe terrorism is the gravest problem facing the United States today?

2 Why do many people assume all terrorists are from Southwest Asia? Is this stereotype correct?

3 How can the United States improve its image in Southwest Asia?

4 Why is point-of-view important to understand when discussing motivations for terrorism?

Activity

Israel and Its Neighbors

OBJECTIVES: 4.01, 6.02, 11.01

Have students work in cooperative groups to make lists of the ways Israel is different from and similar to its Arab neighbors. The list below is an example of what they might include.

Differences: religion, Jewish state, non-Arab population, many languages spoken, modern, Westernized, parliamentary democracy, women have equality, major military power, a developed agriculture and industry, private companies, skilled and educated workforce

Similarities: limited fertile land, few mineral resources, large imports, water scarcity, location

Have students consider the items on the list and then compare them with those of other groups. Have students develop a plan to bring about peace between Israel and its neighbors. Students must think through implementation.

What Is Terrorism?

The terrorist bombing of Sharm el-Sheikh, Egypt in 2005

There are numerous ways to define terrorism. The U.S. Army, in the late 1980s, developed more than 100 definitions. Terrorist acts take many forms and occur all over the world. They are not confined to one place, one religion, or one form.

For example, the 1995 bombing of Oklahoma City's Alfred P. Murrah Federal Building is considered by some to be domestic terrorism—done by an American on American soil for political reasons. Attacks on civilians by the Provisional Irish Republican Army and the loyalist paramilitary groups in Northern Ireland in the twentieth century are considered to be terrorism. Jewish groups have also used terrorism: in 1946, Zionists bombed Jerusalem's King David Hotel, killing 91 British, Jewish, and Palestinian people.

Generally, **terrorism** is considered to be the use, or threatened use, of violence, including killing or injuring people (usually civilians) or taking hostages, to intimidate a government in order to achieve a goal, usually political. Terrorist acts are intended to frighten and influence the societies where the victims live. Terrorism is a type of nontraditional war because terrorist groups are not usually part of a government, although several governments, such as Iran and Syria, do support terrorist groups.

Terrorists often target civilians. They want the media to cover the attack. They hope that seeing violence and death on TV will create fear in the general public so that the public, in turn, will pressure the government to meet the terrorist's demands. Western nations, such as the United States and the United Kingdom, have policies of not cooperating with terrorist groups. They believe that giving in to a terrorist's demands will only encourage more terrorism. This policy is sometimes selectively applied, however.

The hardest part of understanding terrorism is deciding when violence is legitimate and when it is not. In 1974, Yassar Arafat of the Palestinian Liberation Organization noted in a speech before the United Nations General Assembly that, "The difference between the revolutionary and the terrorist lies in the reason for which each fights." Terrorism is often the weapon of the powerless, marginalized, and dispossessed. Often, they believe that in order to be heard or to achieve their goals, they have no choice but violence. People accused of being terrorists usually do not agree with that label. Instead they may believe themselves to be "freedom fighters" or revolutionaries trying to overthrow a repressive government. Some are motivated by religion, believing that they will be rewarded in the afterlife for their sacrifice.

The United States believed that Saddam Hussein had built weapons of mass destruction.

They fought against Iraq to remove them from Kuwait.

Student Debate: Invasion of Iraq

OBJECTIVES: 7.01, 13.01

Divide the class into teams. Assign one team the affirmative position, and the other team the negative position. Have the teams select four speakers to conduct the debate. The other students will support the speakers with research and the preparation of arguments. Students will debate the following: Resolved: that the United States was justified in removing Saddam Hussein from power in 2003. See the Guide to Student Debates in the Teacher's Edition for format suggestions.

This statue of Saddam Hussein was pulled down by American troops in Baghdad on April 9, 2003. **Why did the United States invade Iraq?**

Iraq

The oil-rich nation of Iraq was ruled by the dictator Saddam Hussein from 1979 until 2003. He repressed ethnic and religious groups that threatened to weaken the state.

Iran-Iraq War In the 1980s, Iran and Iraq fought a bloody eight-year war. Iraq took advantage of the revolution in Iran to seize a disputed border area. Iraq was also concerned that the revolution in Iran would spill over into the Shiite population in southern Iraq. Both nations attacked oil tankers in the Persian Gulf, threatening world oil supplies.

Persian Gulf War In 1990, Hussein sent troops into Kuwait claiming that it was part of Iraq's lands. Iraq also disagreed with Kuwait on several issues, including Kuwait's oil sales. In 1991, the United States led United Nations forces and drove Iraq out of Kuwait. The United Nations imposed economic **sanctions,** or restrictions, banning Iraq from selling oil or trading with other nations until Iraq stopped developing **weapons of mass destruction** (chemical, biological, and nuclear weapons).

These sanctions hurt many civilians in Iraq. In late 1999, the United Nations allowed Iraq to export as much oil as needed to purchase food and medical supplies for its people. However, Hussein used this money instead to support his regime rather than help his citizens.

Soldiers from the United States fought in the Gulf War in 1991. **What country did they fight against? Why?**

Chapter 13

2003 Invasion The United States believed, based on faulty intelligence reports, that Hussein had built weapons of mass destruction. So in 2003, the Americans led an invasion of Iraq and called it part of the War on Terror. After the invasion and the ousting of Hussein, it was found that Iraq did not have any weapons of mass destruction. The removal of Hussein and the ruling Ba'ath party that supported him left much of the country in chaos. After being found guilty of crimes against humanity by an Iraqi court, he was executed by Iraqi officials in 2006.

Although the United States, with help from the United Kingdom and other nations, has been trying to rebuild Iraq, it has been a struggle. America has been working to replace the dictatorship with a democratic government. They have faced many challenges. The war damaged much of Iraq's infrastructure. Iraq's population is divided between Sunni and Shiite factions that have violently fought each other for control. Terrorist groups have attacked and kidnapped journalists, foreign workers, and Iraqi civilians.

The military troops stationed there to keep peace have often been violently attacked by a number of different terrorist groups within Iraq, including a branch of al-Qaida. By 2007, many Americans wanted their troops to come home, but United States leaders were concerned that terrorists might gain more control over Iraq and use that to launch more attacks against the West. There have been strong feelings on both sides.

Palestine

The Palestinian National Authority (PNA) is a transitional government that oversees parts of the West Bank and all of the Gaza Strip—part of the Palestinian Territories that had been occupied by Israel for about four decades. The PNA was established in 1994, by the Oslo Accords between the Palestinian Liberation Organization and the government of Israel. During the five years after the accords were signed, an agreement was supposed to be reached

Economy and Government

between the PNA and Israel, with the eventual goal of the territories becoming recognized as an independent state. This final agreement has not yet been reached. The PNA continues to operate as a quasi-independent council with limited powers.

In 2006, elections were held for the Palestinian Legislative Council, which is the PNA's legislative branch. Palestinians in the Gaza Strip and the West Bank voted in the first council election since 1996. The political arm of the organization Hamas won the election.

This complicated relationships in the region. For example, the United States supports the Palestinian elections because it is a movement toward a future democratic state of Palestine. However, the United States also believes that there should be no place in the political process for groups, like Hamas, and individuals who support terrorists, refuse to disarm, and do not recognize Israel's right to exist. This means that it is difficult for the United States to provide aid or work with the Hamas-led government toward independence.

Mahmoud Abbas (right) succeeded Yassar Arafat as the prime minster of the Palestinian National Authority. Here he meets with Ismail Haniyeh from Hamas (left). **Why do the Palestinians want to govern themselves?**

259

Discussion Questions

1 Was the United States justified in invading Iraq in 2003?

2 What is the difference between the Persian Gulf War of the early 1990s and the invasion of Iraq in 2003?

3 What role do you believe Iraq's oil wealth plays in the fighting between the Sunnis and Shiites there?

4 Why do you think there are so many factions within the Palestinian people?

Caption Answer

Palestinians want to make decisions about what will happen with the land in the West Bank and the Gaza Strip.

Activity

Aid to the Middle East

OBJECTIVES: 13.03

Using the CIA World Factbook Web site, have students research how much aid the United States gives to each of the nations in the Middle East and the GDP of each of these nations. Students should create a database to organize this information. After compiling the data, students should analyze the data to see if there is a correlation between the economy of a nation and the amount of aid they receive from the United States. Students should develop reasons to explain why this is or is not the case.

Extension Assign ELL students to access the CIA World Factbook through the **worldlingo.com** Web site. Assign a peer tutor to help with the database and conclusion of this activity.

Caption Answer

Hezbollah launched an attack on Israel from Lebanon. Hezbollah believed Israel was unfairly occupying Palestinian lands. Israel then retaliated against Hezbollah by launching airstrikes and sending ground troops to Lebanon.

Activity

Lebanon: Paris of the Middle East Time Line

OBJECTIVES: 7.01, 13.01

Divide the class into pairs. Each pair will create a time line of tracing the occupation of Lebanon by outside powers. Students should trace Lebanon's history from the Phonecians to the present day. Students will need to use the internet or the media center to complete their time lines. After students have finished, display the time lines. Compare as a class the amount of time Lebanon has been truly independent versus under control of another power. Discuss how these illustrate the challenges the nation faces today.

This Red Cross worker is searching for victims of the fighting in Lebanon in the summer of 2006. **Why did the fighting occur?**

Lebanon

During the spring of 2005 in Lebanon, a series of demonstrations demanded the end of Syrian influence in Lebanese politics. These protests, now called the Cedar Revolution, were triggered by the assassination of former Lebanese Prime Minister Rafik Hariri in February of that year. The citizens demanded the withdrawal of Syrian troops from Lebanon, an international investigation of Hariri's assassination, and the organization of free and fair elections. Syria, responding to international pressure and the demonstrations, completely withdrew its 14,000 troops from Lebanon in April 2005. The pro-Syrian government was also disbanded. Things looked positive for Lebanon's democratic future.

However, in July of 2006, Hezbollah launched an attack on Israel from Lebanon. Hezbollah was fighting against what they saw as Israeli occupation. The government of Lebanon was not part of the attack. First, Hezbollah kidnapped two Israeli soldiers and then killed eight others. Israel responded by launching airstrikes and sending ground troops into Lebanon. Hezbollah then shot rockets into Israeli cities. Some rocket launchers were located in Lebanese neighborhoods. The Israeli airstrikes destroyed many neighborhoods. The Lebanese call this the July War. It lasted 34 days. A United Nations-brokered ceasefire went into effect on August 14, 2006.

This war shows how small acts of violence quickly escalate. It left 1,500 dead and destroyed much of southern Lebanon. More than 1 million Lebanese and 500,000 Israelis fled their homes. It will take Lebanon several years to rebuild.

LESSON ② REVIEW

Fact Follow-Up

1. In what ways do governments of the Middle East differ?
2. What is Arab nationalism?
3. What has been the impact of imperialism in the Middle East?
4. What are the challenges that must be overcome to create an independent Palestinian nation?

Talk About It

1. Do you think democratic forms of governments can be successful in the Middle East? Why or why not?
2. What is terrorism? Why is it hard to define?
3. What do you think is the single greatest challenge facing the region? How would you address this challenge?

LESSON ② REVIEW

Fact Follow-Up Answers

1. Most Middle Eastern countries are republics, but many limit citizen participation. Iraq is a military dictatorship. Jordan is a constitutional monarchy. Israel is a democracy, and Lebanon is returning to democracy.
2. Arab nationalism is the idea that Arabic-speaking people throughout Southwest Asia should be united into a single nation.
3. The land was divided up based on the desires of the imperialist countries, not because the people in the regions shared similar beliefs, ethnicities, or desired to unite as a nation. This has led to instability in the region. The Arab-Israeli conflict is another legacy of imperialism. Jewish zionists desired a Jewish state in Palestine, homeland of the ancient Hebrews, where they could live without being presecuted.
4. Students should discuss the situation from the points of view of both the Palestinians and the Israelis. Long-held animosities on both sides about who is entitled to the land will need to be overcome in order for an independent Palestinian nation to be formed.

Talk About It Answers

1. Important points: Students should discuss the success and failure of democracies in the Middle East. For example, Israel is a functioning democracy. The estabilishment of a democratic government in Iraq is proving to be very difficult.
2. Important points: Students should discuss what their ideas about terrorism are. Terrorism is difficult to define because it depends on one's point of view as to whether the motivations of the people who engage in violence are justified or not.
3. Important points: Students should suggest challenges and choose the one they think is most important, then describe how they would address the challenge. Note: Relationships with neighboring states, the Palestine refugee question, and divisions between Ashkenazi and Sephardic groups are all challenges.

LESSON ③ Other Governments of the Region

A new TV channel may be coming to your home directly from the Arabian Peninsula. It is Al Jazeera International, an English-language 24-hour cable news network, and part of the Al Jazeera television network. Its headquarters are in Doha, Qatar.

The Arabic-language Al Jazeera was launched in 1996 with funding from Emir Sheikh Hamad bin Khalifa Al-Thani, the ruler of Qatar. His government does not try to censor the news. Al Jazeera was the first independent Arabic television station in the region.

But Al Jazeera is also controversial. Many Southwest Asian nations ban or limit the station's ability to report from inside the country. Many people in the West are concerned that Al Jazeera does not report objectively. But despite these issues, the changes Al Jazeera has brought to the region are visible. The growing influence of satellite television news on public opinion has been called the "Al Jazeera effect." Some experts believe that this effect could bring more democracy or openness to the region over the next decades. Al Jazeera represents some of the strides the nations of the Arabian Peninsula are making to balance practicing Islam with developing a modern nation.

KEY IDEAS

- Saudi Arabia is an absolute monarchy that honors conservative Islamic traditions.

- Saudi Arabia has improved both agriculture and industry.

- Ataturk began Turkey's modernization.

- Under the Shah, Iran modernized. These reforms created tensions in the nation.

- An Islamic revolution set Iran on a new course after 1979.

KEY IDEAS

diversity
Kurds
theocracy

Al Jazeera is an important source of information in Southwest Asia.
How does Al Jazeera and this image of anchorwoman Khadija Bengana reflect modern Southwest Asia?

💬 Caption Answer

Al Jazeera represents some of the strides the nations of the Arabian Peninsula are making to balance the practice of Islam with the development of a modern society. This anchorwoman represents how attitudes are changing about women's roles in society.

📔 Writing Activity

The Al Jazeera Effect

OBJECTIVES: 4.01, 4.03, 11.03, 11.04

Have students research the origins and effects of A Jazeera to answer the question: "What is the Al Jazeera effect?" Students should write a short essay explaining what the effect is in the region, and also addressing what the news channel's global effect has been. Students should also consider in their essays why Westerners often consider Al Jazeera's reporting to be biased.

As a conclusion, discuss the perception people in Southwest Asia may have of Western media sources. Might they believe that American media outlets are also biased?

Economy and Government   261

ℹ️ Background Information

Smaller Arab States on the Move

In recent years smaller Arab states such as Qatar, Bahrain, and Dubai have embraced change even as the larger ones have resisted it. Because they have limited oil resources, many have welcomed global links. "We diversified out of oil early," says Bahrain's Crown Prince Salman, "because we had to. We really concentrated on developing our human capital." Bahrain offers some of the region's best legal, insurance, and consulting services. Dubai has its own Internet City, where more than 200 multinational tech firms have regional headquarters. These states have also made political reforms. In 1999 Qatar held the first free municipal elections in the region and allowed women to vote and run for office. Its popular al-Jazeera satellite TV station beams uncensored news across the Arab world.

Discussion Questions

1 How would our lives be different if we lived under an absolute monarchy?

2 Do you think the government has the right to limit the consumption of alcohol and tobacco?

Caption Answer

Students should support their prediction. They should point out that Southwest Asia's economies are currently based largely on oil.

Activity

S.W.O.T.

OBJECTIVES: 1.02

S.W.O.T. is a strategy to analyze factual statements in four categories: Strength, Weakness, Opportunity, Threat. Strength is a fact that offers a nation an advantage. Example: a nation having the world's largest iron supply. Weakness is a negative fact that presents an obstacle to a nation. Example: a nation with a high death rate. Opportunity is a factual item that offers a nation some way to improve a situation. Example: a nation that designs an irrigation project to improve agriculture without drastically altering the existing environment. Threat is a fact that offers a nation the potential for a problem to occur. Example: a nation that suffers periodic droughts.

Have students decide which of the following facts is a strength, a weakness, an opportunity, or a threat. Some countries may be in two categories, but if that is the case, then students must justify the answer. Students should work in small groups and must reach consensus within their group.

Saudi Arabia

O Occupies about 80 percent of the Arabian Peninsula.

T Mostly desert, with mountains on eastern slope of the Red Sea.

W Average population density: fewer than 20 people per square mile.

S World's third-largest petroleum products producer.

Saudi Arabia

The Kingdom of Saudi Arabia is a young country. It was established in the 1920s. Saudi Arabia is the only country in the world named after its ruling family, the House of Saud. At first it was a poor desert kingdom. Today, Saudi Arabia is a major power because of its oil wealth.

Saudi Arabia is an absolute monarchy. It has a non-elected parliament. The king has absolute power, but he asks for advice from Sunni Islamic scholars. Islamic law serves as the kingdom's constitution.

Saudi Arabia's royal family has opened the nation to many innovations, especially modern technology. But the king's advisors are conservative. They weigh carefully the adoption of new technologies or ideas before approving them. They are aware, for example, that modern forms of communication—the radio, television, or movies—might be used to challenge Islamic beliefs.

Modernization, they say, could corrupt people and lead them to disobey the Quran. They have accepted some modern technologies such as cars. Yet there are no public movie theaters. Videos are allowed only in private homes. Alcohol and tobacco are forbidden.

All business must stop five times a day for Muslim prayer. In the workplace, schools, and other public areas, women and men are segregated, or separated. When women go out in public, they must wear the *abayah*, a long black robe that covers the entire body. Women have an inferior legal status to men. They may not drive cars.

Saudi Arabia's Shaybah oil field produces 550,000 barrels of oil per day, which is sent via pipeline to Abqaiq, about 373 miles (600 km) away. **What do you think will happen to Southwest Asia's economies when the oil runs out?**

Turkey

"Ne mutlu Türküm diyene." "What a joy it is to call oneself a Turk!" Kemal Ataturk, founder of modern Turkey, coined that slogan. It reflects his desire to build national pride. Today, his words are carved into hillsides and wave on banners at parades. Why is Kemal Ataturk still remembered?

Ataturk was a soldier-hero, reformer, and first president of the Republic of Turkey. During the 1920s and 1930s, he created the modern nation of Turkey out of the ruins of the Ottoman Empire.

Ataturk was determined to make Turkey into a strong nation along Western lines. He separated religion and state, ending the strong influence of Islamic leaders over government. Law based on the Quran was replaced with a nonreligious code based on Western law.

Public schools were founded to replace Islamic schools. Ataturk introduced the Latin (Western) alphabet and demanded that Turks use it instead of Arabic script.

Chapter 13

S Oil exports: 88 percent of the country's exports by value and about 60 percent of all government revenues.

O Deposits of natural gas, iron, gold, and copper.

W Agriculture affected by lack of arable land and water.

O Main crops: dates and grains.

W Not self-sufficient in food.

S Oil income has transformed society and ways of life within one generation.

O, T Adheres to a strict interpretation of Islamic law.

O, T Urbanization increasing rapidly.

T Nearly one third of population is composed of resident foreigners.

T Oil spills in the Persian Gulf.

W Severe damage to coastal wildlife and fisheries.

T Severe environmental damage from Gulf War.

T Desertification rate about 30 feet per year in some areas.

O Reforestation project at Al-Hasa, the largest oasis.

W Water for agricultural purposes is pumped from aquifers that cannot be replenished.

The Northern Tier

Land Elevation

Feet	Meters
13,333	4000
6,667	2000
3,333	1000
1,667	500
667	200
0	0
Below sea level	Below sea level

City Population
- Over 1,000,000
- 250,000–1,000,000
- 50,000–250,000
- Under 50,000

Movement and Location Both Turkey and Iran are located between two seas—Turkey between the Black Sea and the Mediterranean Sea and Iran between the Caspian Sea and the Persian Gulf. *Why is Turkey more fertile than Iran?*

Ataturk made Turks wear what he called "civilized," or Western, clothes. Women were told to give up the traditional Islamic veil. Ataturk urged women to go out in public. Women gained the right to vote.

Ataturk ordered the construction of a new capital at Ankara (AN·ker·rah) in the center of Turkey. He wanted this modern city to become a symbol for the new Turkey. However, Istanbul, capital of the old Ottoman Empire, remained a thriving financial and cultural center.

Modern Turkey

Ataturk turned Turkey toward the West. Today, Turkey is a member of NATO, the North Atlantic Treaty Organization, a defensive alliance of Western nations. It is also an associate member of the European Union. It is working hard to improve its economy in order to become a full member of that group.

Economy and Government

Turkey's economy is growing. It has built large industries, developed mining, and expanded transportation. Agriculture has improved. Its economy is less developed than those of other industrial nations, but it is far ahead of its neighbors.

Turkey has faced serious political problems. Ataturk himself ruled as a dictator, crushing opposition to his policies. Strongman rulers, often military officers, later followed him into office. Today, Turkey is a multiparty democracy. In the mid-1990s, Tansu Ciller held office as Turkey's first female prime minister.

Political tensions in Turkey are fed by three factors. The first comes from the Islamist movement, which wants to make Turkey more of an Islamic nation. Strong army generals who often violate human rights are a second challenge.

A third factor are the *Kurds,* a minority ethnic

Kemal Ataturk founded the modern nation of Turkey.
What changes did he make in the nation?

Background Information

Slowly Changing Saudi Arabia

In recent years, Saudi Arabia's rulers are trying to create a more diversified economy. Foreigners now are allowed to own property and open businesses without a Saudi citizen as a majority owner. The government has also begun looking for foreign investors in gas development, power industries, and desalination plants. Work has also started on reforming the nation's legal system and trade rules in hopes of

joining the World Trade Organization, but many Saudis oppose any changes in the Islamic laws and ancient tribal traditions that govern the nation. Officials censor foreign publications and the teaching of Western philosophy is banned. Only Muslims can be citizens. The royal family knows it must move slowly. Economic reforms may lead to demands for political change as well.

Discussion Questions

1 Does Turkey sound like a place in which you would like to live? Why or why not?

2 How are alliances such as NATO beneficial? What problems can they create?

Caption Answer

Iran is more mountainous.

Caption Answer

Ataturk remodeled Turkey along Western lines. He separated church and state, replaced Muslim law with a nonreligious code based on Western law, founded public schools, introduced the Western alphabet, required Western dress, encouraged women to go out in public and gave them the right to vote, and built of a new capital at Ankara.

Map Activity

The Northern Tier

NATIONAL GEOGRAPHY STANDARDS: 1, 9
GEOGRAPHIC THEMES: Location, Place
OBJECTIVES: 1.02, 1.03

Have students complete the following:
1. Which city bridges two continents? *Istanbul*
2. Identify the cities with a population of more than one million. *Istanbul, Izmir, Ankara, Tabriz, Tehran, Mashhad, Eshafan, Shiraz*
3. Which city is on an island? *Nicosia*
4. Which cities are located on the Persian Gulf? *Abadan, Bandar-e Abbas*
5. How many people live in Hamadan? *250,000–1,000,000*
6. Which cities are located on the coast of the Black Sea? *Istanbul, Zonguldak*
7. Which cities are located on the coast of the Caspian Sea? *Rasht*
8. In which body of water is Cyprus located? *Mediterranean Sea*
9. Which Iranian city is located closest to 30ºN? *Kerman*
10. Which city is located closest to the delta of the Tigris and Euphrates Rivers? *Abadan*

Discussion Questions

1 Do you think the Kurds are entitled to have their own homeland? Is there any similarity between the situation with the Kurds and that of the Palestinians?

2 Does a leader have the right to force changes that are for "the good of the people"?

3 If you were a leader and wanted to bring about changes in your country, what would be the best way to implement these changes?

4 If you were the executive of a company in a foreign country that had been nationalized, how would you respond?

Caption Answer

The Kurds are a minority group in Turkey. Most want a homeland of their own.

Research Activity

Biographical Research

 **OBJECTIVES:** 8.01

Use the material available in Lesson 2 of Chapter 14 or other sources to research the lives of Kemal Ataturk, Reza Shah Pahlavi, Muhammad Reza Pahlavi, the Saudi royal family, and Ayatollah Khomeini. Divide the class into one group for each of these leaders, and have the students research the goals of each. Have a panel discussion in which each person is represented and debates on whether each leader was correct in leading the country in the path it took. Include in the discussion a segment in which each leader includes what would be done differently if it could be done over again.

---

group of between 20 and 30 million people. The Kurds are scattered across Southwest Asia, from Turkey and Syria to northwestern Iran and northern Iraq. About 13 million Kurds live in southern Turkey. Most want a homeland of their own. Turkey has long placed restrictions on the Kurds. Under pressure from other nations, Turkey has eased some of its limitations on the Kurds' freedoms.

Iran

In Iran, an army officer also gained power over his nation in 1926. He called himself Reza Shah Pahlavi. He set up his own dynasty in Persia. Reza Shah also forcefully modernized his country. He renamed it Iran, introduced Western technology, and tried to build a secular state. He promoted Iranian nationalism as a way to unite Iran's ethnic groups.

In the cities especially, the Shah forced people to wear Western-style clothes. He banned the veil for women and urged men and women to appear together in public.

Reza Shah's son, Muhammad Reza Pahlavi, pushed reforms even further. With Iran's oil wealth, he built industries and expanded agriculture. He redistributed land to peasants, hoping to improve their lives. He set up health clinics and schools. In 1963, Iranian women won the right to vote (but the country and the elections were not democratic).

Thanks to its oil, Iran became a major world power. Its economy grew rapidly. Yet only a few Iranians profited from the Shah's modernization. Most people were still poor farmers. As Iran changed, many of these farmers moved to cities. There they lived in poverty while the wealthy lived comfortable lives. By the 1970s, many Iranians disapproved of the Shah's policies. Many were angered by the Shah's iron-handed rule and his government's corruption.

Kurds, a minority group of Southwest Asia, receive food from Iranian soldiers. **Why are Kurds a challenge to Turkey?**

Activity

Ottoman Time Line

OBJECTIVES: 8.02

Using the library or the Internet, have students research the Ottoman Empire. Students should create a time line identifying and illustrating the expansion and eventual collapse of the empire. Students should also write a paragraph explaining who the Ottomans were and how their legacy can be seen today.

Extension ELL students should use an ELL-friendly Web site for research. Do not assign novice and intermediate ELL students the paragraphs.

Unlike Turkey, where Ataturk had weakened the Muslim clergy's power, Iran's Shiite leaders remained a powerful force. They blamed social problems on the Shah's Western, secular policies. As unrest grew, the Shah's secret police brutally crushed critics.

Iran's Islamic Revolution

The Shah's police force failed to silence his critics. Many Iranians opposed his rule. People rallied behind the Ayatollah Ruhollah Khomeini. Ayatollah means "sign of God," and is used for high-ranking Shiite clerics. Revolutionaries seized power in 1979, creating an Islamic republic.

Iran became a *theocracy,* or a government that claims to rule with divine authority. The Ayatollah did not hold government office. He and other clergy did set out to reshape Iran. They wrote a new law code based on the Shariah and the Quran.

Revolutionary leaders banned Western music, movies, and other influences, which they saw as corrupt and evil. Women had to wear the chador, or head-to-foot covering. They could not attend school with men. Women could still vote, but they became less visible in public.

Meanwhile, Iraq took action in part to prevent Shiite revolution from spilling across the border. Iraqi troops occupied a disputed border territory. The destructive Iraqi-Iranian war followed. Fighting lasted from 1980 to 1988, when both sides accepted a United Nations cease-fire.

Ayatollah Khomeini died in 1989. In the late 1990s, younger Iranians helped elect new leaders who took steps to rebuild the economy, improve international relations, and allow their people new freedoms. However, new concerns were raised in 2005 about Iran's support of such groups such as Hezbollah, as well as its development of a nuclear weapons program. Iran has not convinced the international community that its nuclear power program was developed for peaceful purposes.

What would YOU do?

There are similarities between the Islamists' insistence that women return to traditional dress and arguments that students wear school uniforms. The changes are urged as a way of bringing about more order and modesty. Would you be willing to wear a uniform if it helped your school run more smoothly? What other reasons are given by those who think all students should wear uniforms?

Ayatollah Khomeini led the Islamic Revolution in Iran in 1979. **How did he change Iranian law?**

Discussion Questions

1 How would your lives be different if you lived in an area governed by a theocracy?

2 Many young people are currently protesting the changes brought in by the revolutionaries in 1979. What do you think has caused this change in feelings?

Caption Answer

The Ayatollah and other clergy wrote a new law code based on the Sharia and the Quran.

Activity

Think It Through

OBJECTIVES: 12.02

Iran's government and Saudi Arabia's Islamic law, the Quran and Sharia, seem harsh to many non-Muslims. Have students prepare to role-play a defense of their Muslim beliefs on one of the following scenarios:

1. You want to travel and study abroad. Your parents and family can financially afford for you to do so, but your arranged marriage is to take place in the next year.

2. You are a talented soccer player who has qualified to play on your country's World Cup soccer team. While competing in a large United States city, you are asked to make a television ad for a large company. What would your answer be?

Discussion Questions

1 How does Cyprus bridge Europe and Asia?

2 Do you think Turkey should remain in Cyprus? Why or Why not?

Research Activity

Empires of the Northern Tier

OBJECTIVES: 8.02, 9.01

Have pairs of students research the great empires of the Northern Tier. Students should include the Byzantine Empire, Ottoman Empire, and the Persian Empire. Students should compare their rulers, location, periods, and great achievements. Have them record their findings on a graphic organizer. Can the legacies of these empires be seen in the region today?

A Journey to CYPRUS

A Divided Island

Cyprus is an island located in the northeastern corner of the Mediterranean Sea. Because it is so close to Europe, Asia, and Africa, it is called a stepping stone to three continents. Cyprus has been invaded and claimed by many civilizations, all of which have shaped its culture and character. It has been controlled by each of the empires that have dominated the eastern Mediterranean.

Cyprus' recorded history begins with Egypt's occupation of part of the island about 1450 B.C. Later, seafaring and trading peoples from the Mediterranean basin set up scattered settlements along the coast. The first Greek colony is believed to have been founded by traders about 1400 B.C.

Turkey captured the island in A.D. 1571 and held it until 1878. Fearing greater expansion by Russia, Turkey asked Britain to administer Cyprus. Britain received complete control of Cyprus for a rental of about $500,000 yearly while Turkey retained nominal title. Independence was proclaimed in 1960. Turkey invaded part of the island in 1974.

Today, Cyprus consists of two states. The Republic of Cyprus occupies the southern two thirds of the country. Only Turkey has recognized the Turkish Republic of Northern Cyprus, which declared independence in 1983. The capital for both states is Nicosia.

Greek-speaking Cypriots make up about 85 percent of the population. About 12 percent of the population is Turkish. The remainder is made up of Armenians and other ethnic groups. Greek Cypriots occupy the southern two thirds of the island and Turkish Cypriots occupy the northern third. Both Greek and Turkish communities retain the customs and the national identity of their counterparts on the mainland.

A farm in Cyprus

LESSON 3 REVIEW

Fact Follow-Up

1. How does religion influence government and daily life in Saudi Arabia?
2. Who was Kemal Ataturk? How did he influence Turkey?
3. What are some challenges faced by Turkey today?
4. What have been some results of the Islamic Revolution in Iran?

Talk About It

1. In what ways were modernization efforts in Turkey and Iran similar? In what ways were they different? Give reasons for your answers.
2. In your opinion, is a theocracy a good form of government? Or do you prefer the separation of government and religion? Explain.

LESSON 3 REVIEW

Fact Follow-Up Answers

1. The absolute monarch abides by Islamic law and has Islamic advisors. Prayer five times daily stops all business. Women and men are segregated at work, in school, and in other public areas. Women who go out in public must wear the abayah, or *chador*, a long black robe that covers the entire body.
2. Kemal Ataturk was the founder of modern Turkey. As president, he reformed Turkey's government, law, education, writing, and social life along Western lines.
3. There is a challenge from Islamists who want to end Ataturk's reforms, restore the Shariah as the official law code, and make Turkey an Islamic nation. Strong army generals who often violate human rights are another problem. A challenge also comes from the Kurds, a minority ethnic group who want their own homeland.
4. After the Islamic Revolution, Iran became a theocracy, or government ruled by religious leaders claiming to rule with divine authority. The

Ayatollah Khomeini and other clergy wrote a new law code based on the Shariah and the Quran. Western music, movies, and non-Islamic influences were banned. Women had to wear the *chador* and could not attend school with men. Iraq seized the opportunity of turmoil to occupy a disputed border territory. The resulting Iraqi-Iranian war lasted eight years.

Talk About It Answers

1. In both Turkey and Iran, dictators forcefully modernized the countries, introducing Western ways of doing things. Both changed the countries into secular states in which government and religion were separated. Unlike in Turkey, Iran's Muslim leaders remained powerful and eventually seized power, creating an Islamic republic. Turkey is a democracy.
2. Important points: Students should understand that a theocracy is a government that claims to rule by divine authority. They should then take a position and support it. Theocracies often repress minorities. Separation of church and state means the government cannot favor any religion.

Analyzing, Interpreting, Creating,
and Using Resources and Materials

Dealing with Change in Southwest Asia

By now, you have learned a great deal about Southwest Asia, a region of great complexity and diversity. Southwest Asia is a region coping in one way or another with change. Some people of the region welcome change, and others resist it. Others welcome some changes but not other changes. Some people seek to undo change, to reverse it.

To understand how people respond to changes, think about yourself, your own life, and some changes you have faced. You might have moved; you have almost certainly changed schools; you might have had family changes; your body has changed and is still changing; and surely you have had changes in friendships. You have probably found some of these changes were more welcome or more difficult than others. Some of them you probably resisted while you adapted or accommodated yourself to others. People in Southwest Asia have had some of the same reactions as you have experienced.

What can people do when they are faced with change? For one thing, they can prepare for the change by learning as much about the proposed change as possible. They can also anticipate the possible effects of the change, imagining how the change will affect their own lives and the lives of others.

If people like some parts of the proposed change but not other parts, they might seek to amend or divert the course of the change. An example of this might be laws requiring that a new factory be equipped with effective pollution controls. If people think the proposed change will be good in the long run, they might adopt it or accommodate themselves to it. If they oppose the change, they might resist it.

How have the people and nations you learned about in Chapter 13 responded to the changes in their lives and in the lives of their nations? How do you think they might respond to changes in the future?

Dome of the Rock, Jerusalem

Economy and Government

2or

Teaching This Skill Lesson

Materials Needed textbooks, paper, pencils

Classroom Organization whole class

Beginning the Lesson Use a current example of change in the local community or a hypothetical such as: "Suppose you found out this morning that the price of gas had risen to $5 per gallon. How would you and your family deal with this change?" Accept all answers, recording them on the chalkboard.

Lesson Development Use the responses to change (prepare for change, anticipate the possible effects of change, seek to amend or divert the change, adopt or accommodate to change, resist change) from the student text to begin to categorize students' responses to the question used to begin the lesson. As you categorize, make certain that students understand what each response means.

Have students skim Chapter 13 for examples of how both people and nations have responded to recent changes. Use the responses to change (above) to establish how people and nations have responded to changes. Encourage students to find as many examples as they can in each category.

Conclusion Discuss with students the idea that change can benefit some and disadvantage others. Change is not a neutral event, nor does it take place in a vacuum. Change is shaped by power interests of particular groups and individuals. The challenge is how to bring about change in a manner than minimizes the negative aspects and maximizes the positive ones.

Ask students to make some judgments as to how people and/or nations have most generally responded to recent changes. Probe by asking if these are logical responses. What other responses might have been made? What have been the costs and benefits? have these nations successfully maximized the benefits to their people in their eyes?

Extension For ELL students, model and provide additional explanations. Novice students will observe and intermediate students should work with a partner.

Skill Lesson Review

1. What are some ways of resisting change? Are any of these being used in Southwest Asia? Which resistance movements do you think are most likely to succeed? to fail? Why? *Important points: Students should be encouraged to offer a number of ways of resisting change. The Islamists are mounting a resistance movement, and the revolution in Iran was a response to the changes brought by Westernization. Saudi Arabia's reliance on law and custom is another kind of resistance to change.*

2. Which changes have Southwest Asians found easiest to deal with? most difficult? Explain your answer. *Important points: Encourage students' answers. Oil wealth has brought both technology and Western social influences. The technology is easier to deal with than the social influences.*

3. In your own life, what are some changes you have adapted to and some you have resisted? Why do you think you responded to these changes as you did? *Important points: Encourage students' responses and explanations. The birth of a sibling or a move are possible changes for discussion.*

4. Someone has said, "The only people who welcome change are those whose idea it was to change." Do you think this is true? Explain. *Important points: Encourage student discussion. Note that the statement is not necessarily accurate. Sometimes people see advantages to change as it occurs.*

Talk About It

1. Important points: Strategic location and oil resources make the area strategic. Conflict in Southwest Asia can threaten the world economy.

2. Important points: Students should make a choice and support the choice with reasons. Note: Oil is important for prosperity, but water is necessary for life.

3. Important points: Students should choose one nation and give reasons for their choice.

4. Probably not, though Saudi influence would likely continue for a time. Saudi Arabia has few resources beyond oil, though the Saudis have developed their education system. An educated population might find ways to continue Saudi leadership in the region. Since Mecca and Medina are in Saudi Arabia, people from all over the world would continue to visit those holy sites.

5. Important points: Saudi Arabia has a well-developed oil industry, though its supply is limited. Turkey's location and climate are better suited for development. Turkey also has coal and hydroelectric power for industry.

6. Important points: Students should choose one way to resolve conflicts, explain why they made this choice, and give reasons why leaders have not chosen and followed this path. Note: Mutual respect and cooperation are of course essential; many nations, especially Israel, worry that compromise might lead to disaster; feelings of nationalism make compromise difficult; scarce resources encourage conflicts over those resources.

7. Important points: Students should offer support for their opinions by analyzing the possible outcomes of negotiating and not negotiating with terrorists. They should consider whether compromising with terrorists is a possiblity and whether terrorists would release hostages and stop the violence if compromises were reached.

8. Important points: Students should support their assertions with facts from the text and current events.

CHAPTER 13 REVIEW

Lessons Learned

LESSON 1
Economy
Water is scarce. Syria and Iraq produce oil. and one of the world's top oil producers. Iran also contains oil resources. OPEC and other factors influence the price of oil on the world market.

LESSON 2
Governments of the Middle East
The Middle East is filled with tension because of conflicting forms of government, boundary disputes, terrorism, and religious barriers. Israel has survived challenges to its existence from Arab nations, some of whom have signed peace agreements with Israel. The Palestinian National Authority faces many challenges to create an independent Palestinian nation. The United States' war on Terror is being fought in Iraq against several terrorists groups with strong ties to the region.

LESSON 3
Other Governments of the Region
Saudi Arabia is ruled by a monarchy that strictly follows Islamic traditions. The Saudi government uses its oil wealth to invest in agriculture and industry. Turkey is more Western-oriented than any other Islamic Southwest Asian country. Iran had begun to modernize under the Shah. Islamists shunned the changes in Iran as anti-Islamic and led a revolution there.

Mastering Mapwork

1. Jordan, Lebanon, and Israel.

2. The region surrounding the Tigris and Euphrates Rivers lies at an elevation of 0 to 667 feet (200 meters) above sea level.

3. Iraq is the largest political region shown on this map.

4. The most populous region lies on the eastern edge of the Mediterranean Sea in Israel, western Jordan, Lebanon, and western Syria.

Talk About It

1. The world's leaders pay close attention to events in Southwest Asia, especially to events in the nations of the Middle East. Explain why.
2. Which is more important to people living in the Middle East: oil or water? Explain why.
3. If you could choose to live in one nation of the region, which would it be? Why?
4. Without oil, would Saudi Arabia occupy the same position of leadership? Explain.
5. Which nation has the more important natural resources: Turkey or Saudi Arabia? Why?
6. What do you think is the single most important way to solve conflicts in the region? Why would you choose this one solution? Why do you think leaders have not committed their nations to this solution?
7. Should governments negotiate with terrorists? What might be some effects of negotiating for the release of hostages?
8. How does instability and religious fighting in Iraq affect the rest of the region?

Mastering Mapwork

REGION
Use the map on page 247 to answer these questions:

1. What political regions border the Jordan River?
2. What is the elevation of the region surrounding the Tigris and Euphrates Rivers?
3. What is the largest political region shown on this map?
4. Describe the relative location of the most populous region shown on this map.
5. In what ways is the low-lying area along the Tigris and Euphrates Rivers both a physical and a cultural region?
6. Describe the relative location of the political region of Jordan.
7. Which country in the Middle East has the most regions defined solely by the elevation of the land?
8. Which two political regions have land elevations below sea level?

5. The area along the river valleys is a physical region because of elevation, rainfall, and vegetation. It is a cultural region because of the long record of human habitation as well as being today a center of Islamic culture.

6. Jordan is bordered by the Jordan River and Dead Sea on the west, by Syria on the north, by Iraq on the east, and by Saudi Arabia on the south.

7. Syria has five elevation regions.

8. Jordan and Israel

Go to the Source

Analyzing a Political Cartoon

Study the political cartoon "Middle East Peace," by Malcolm Evans of New Zealand, from July 31, 2006. Answer the questions using specific references from the cartoon. This cartoon was a commentary on the conflict in Lebanon in the summer of 2006 (see pages 210 and 260).

Go to the Source

Questions

1. Identify the meaning of each image within this cartoon: coffin, bullets/bombs, bird/dove, and olive branch.
2. Based on what you read and the cartoon, what is the target of the attack and what group/s are represented by the bullets?
3. Why do you think the artist does not label the bullets?
4. List any other conflicts in the Middle East where this cartoon might be relevant.

Go to the Source

OBJECTIVES: 7.02; Skills 3.04

This cartoon can be symbolic of more than just the conflict between Israel and Hezbollah in Lebanon in the summer of 2006. Discuss with students the idea that peace in the Middle East is a process where some steps toward progress are made, symbolized by the dove, only to then suffer setbacks stemming from various quarters (symbolized by the bullets), including disagreements between Palestinian factions, Israel's reaction to the actions of its neighbors, and interference from a number of other nations on all sides.

ANSWERS

1. Answers will vary. Suggestions: coffin: death; bullet: bombs or forces that are preventing peace; bird/dove: peace

2. Based on Chapter 13, Lesson 2, the coffin could represent Lebanon or the wider conflict of the Middle East. The bullets are the attacks and counterattacks of Hezbollah and Israel.

3. The artist might have left the bullets unmarked to allow readers to make up their own minds about who was responsible.

4. Other conflicts: Palestine/Israel, Iraq, Iran

How to Use the Chapter Review

There are three sections in the Chapter Review: Talk About It, Mastering Mapwork, and Go to the Source. Use the Vocabulary Worksheets and the Chapter Review Worksheet in the Teacher's Resource Guide for additional reinforcement and preparation for the Chapter Assessments. The chapter and lesson reviews and the Chapter Review Worksheets are the basis of the assessment for each chapter.

Talk About It questions encourage students to speculate about the content of the chapter and are suitable for class or small-group discussion. They are not intended to be assigned for homework.

Mastering Mapwork has students apply one or more of the Five Themes of Geography to maps within the chapter.

Go to the Source activities allow students to analyze a primary source that relates to the content of the chapter. The questions and activities familiarize students with different types of primary sources and also build content-reading skills.

Society and Culture

Social Studies Strands

Global Connections

Cultures and Diversity
Islamic Revival and its effects on
the region

North Carolina Standard Course of Study

Goal 2 The learner will assess the relationship
between physical environment and cultural
characteristics of selected societies and regions of
Africa, Asia, and Australia.

Goal 11 The learner will recognize the common
characteristics of different cultures in Africa, Asia,
and Australia.

Goal 12 The learner will assess the influence of major
religions, ethical beliefs, and values on cultures in
Africa, Asia, and Australia.

Teaching & Assessment

• English Language Learner Modified
Lesson Plans for this chapter are found
in the Teacher Resource Guide.

• *ExamView® Assessment Suite* is provided
at **NCJourneys.com.** It includes
customizable assessments for all
chapters. Paper tests are also available in
the Teacher Resource Guide. See pages
T16–T17 for information about how to
use the assessments and the Scoring
Guide.

Worksheets

Worksheets and answer keys are found
both in the Teacher Resource Guide and
at **NCJourneys.com**, including Reading
Guides, Reading Strategies, Chapter
Reviews, English Language Learner and
others.

ACTIVITIES AND INTEGRATIONS

SOCIAL STUDIES

Foods from the Middle East, p. 270B
Activator: Tasting Dates, p. 270
Pyramid: Arabian Peninsula–Northern Tier, p. 271
Cultural Connection: Southwest Asian Feast, p. 274
● ▲ Clothing and Culture, p. 279
Falafel, p. 280
Potato Latkes for Hanukkah Recipe, p. 285
Skill Lesson: Diversity in the Middle East, p. 287

READING/LANGUAGE ARTS	READING/LANGUAGE ARTS OBJECTIVES
Analogies, p. 270B	2.01
Traditions: Compare and Contrast, p. 270B	2.02
Writing Prompt: Separation of Church and State, p. 270	3.03
Write a Song, p. 273	5.02
One Thousand and One Nights, p. 276	1.01, 1.02
Stories of Southwest Asian Culture, p. 278	3.03
Fishbowl, p. 282	1.03
Jerusalem: City of the Faithful, p. 283	1.02
Go to the Source: Following Recipes, p. 289	1.02, 2.01

VISUAL ARTS	VISUAL ARTS OBJECTIVES
● ▲ Turkish Marbling, p. 270B	2.04
Pyramid: Arabian Peninsula–Northern Tier, p. 271	2.04, 5.02

CHARACTER AND VALUES EDUCATION	TRAITS
Writing Prompt: Separation of Church and State, p. 270	good judgment, citizenship, justice
What Would You Do?, p. 285	respect

GO TO THE SOURCE	GTS OBJECTIVES
Following Recipes, p. 289	ELA 1.02, 2.01

● Basic Activities   ★ Challenging Activities   ▲ English Language Learner Novice   ■ English Language Learner Intermediate

Introductory Activity

Foods from the Middle East

OBJECTIVES: 11.01

Prepare a dish from the Middle East for a tasting party. Students may research different foods and recipes from the Middle East and then prepare a recipe for the class to sample. Students should research the different ingredients and be able to explain to the class how they relate to the Middle East. If time or resources are a factor, the teacher may choose to bring in a variety of Middle Eastern foods for students to try. Possible choices: hummus, pita bread, pita chips, olives, and dates. Play Southwest Asian music in the background.

 **Culminating Activity**

Traditions: Compare/Contrast

OBJECTIVES: 12.02, 12.03

Have students look back through Unit 3 to identify important traditions of Southwest Asia. They should make a poster or chart highlighting the traditions and write a paragraph comparing the traditions of the Middle East, Arabian Peninsula, and Northern Tier. What is the cultural significance of these traditions? Discuss as a class.

 Art Activity

Turkish Marbling

OBJECTIVES: 12.02

Materials large wide tub for water, oil-based paint (diluted) or model paint, paper that is smaller than your pan for water, skinny sticks for dipping paint out of jars.

Fill the tub with 1 inch of water. Dip out several drops of one color of paint with stick. Repeat with several other colors. Gently swirl paint with stick or multiple sticks until desired effect is achieved. Carefully place the paper paint-side down on the surface of the water. Lightly push down any spot where an air bubble may be trapped. In one smooth continuous motion, pull the paper up by one corner and place face up in a spot to dry.

This paper can be used as covers for books, pages to books, background for artwork, or artwork by itself.

 Analogies

OBJECTIVES: 2.01, 8.01

Analogies are useful to help students make associations with prior knowledge. They can be used as an instructional strategy to help students better understand new materials. They are not intended to be definitions or test items.

Read the analogies aloud and ask students to identify the relationship between the terms. As an extension, ask students to write their own analogies using key terms or places discussed in the chapter.

diversify : limit :: broaden : narrow (antonyms)

patriarch : matriarch :: male : female :: paternal : maternal (antonyms)

Sephardic Jew : Arab and Mediterranean origins :: Ashkenazi Jew : European origins (comes from)

Persian : Iran :: Ottoman : Turkey (former empires)

Ramadam : Islam :: Lent : Christianity (holy season)

Saturday : Judaism :: Friday :: Islam :: Sunday : Christianity (the Sabbath or holy day of rest and prayer)

The Book of One Thousand and One Nights . Persia :: The Odyssey : Greece (great work of literature of the empire)

Teaching Strategies

Help students to understand that, although understanding Islam is critical to understanding the region, Southwest Asia has a distinct and rich cultural heritage as well.

Discussion Questions

1 What are some regional expressions that we use?

Activator

 OBJECTIVES: 3.01

Bring in a box of dates and give each student a piece to taste. Explain that the date palm is about the only vegetation that can survive in the desert, as explained on page 273. Ask students to brainstorm ways that people can survive in the desert. Ask them to elaborate on their list.

Extension For ELL students, model and provide additional explanations.

Writing Prompt

 OBJECTIVES: 10.03, 11.03

Evaluative

Saudi Arabia has an absolute monarchy with Islamic Law as its constitution. Turkey established a republic and separated church and state. Which of these two countries do you believe will be most successful in both making economic progress and maintaining their traditions? Write an essay giving your opinion and explain your answer fully.

As you write your paper, remember to

• clearly state your position.
• give at least three reasons and explain your reasons fully.
• give examples to support your reasons.
• write in complete sentences and paragraph form.
• organize your ideas and include an introduction and a conclusion.
• use good grammar, spelling, punctuation, and capitalization.

14

Society and Culture

We sometimes speak of a "heartwarming experience." It means a moment of feeling especially good about something. In Saudi Arabia, people have a different expression for the same feeling.

They call it "heart-cooling." The cool, moist climate of the Northern Hemisphere has influenced our language and culture. In the same way, a hot, dry climate has affected the language and culture of Saudi Arabia.

Arab women in a Dubai shopping mall

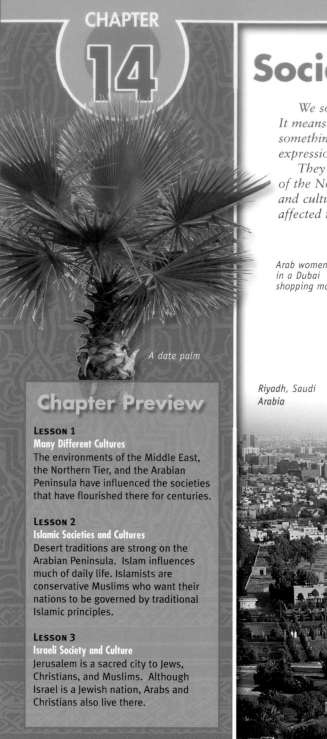

A date palm

Riyadh, Saudi Arabia

Chapter Preview

LESSON 1
Many Different Cultures
The environments of the Middle East, the Northern Tier, and the Arabian Peninsula have influenced the societies that have flourished there for centuries.

LESSON 2
Islamic Societies and Cultures
Desert traditions are strong on the Arabian Peninsula. Islam influences much of daily life. Islamists are conservative Muslims who want their nations to be governed by traditional Islamic principles.

LESSON 3
Israeli Society and Culture
Jerusalem is a sacred city to Jews, Christians, and Muslims. Although Israel is a Jewish nation, Arabs and Christians also live there.

270

Chapter 14

Chapter Resources

Print Resources

Nonfiction

Bator, Robert. *Daily Life in Ancient and Modern Istanbul.* Runestone Press, 2000. ISBN 0822532174.

Foster, Leila. *Kuwait* (Enchantment of the World series). Children's Press, 1998. ISBN 0516206044.

—. *Oman* (Enchantment of the World series). Children's Press, 1999. ISBN 0516209647.

Janin, Hunt. *Saudi Arabia* (Cultures of the World series). Marchall Cavenish, 1996. ISBN 1854355325.

Miller, Louise R. *Turkey: Between East and West* (Exploring Cultures of the World series). Benchmark, 1998. ISBN 0761403973.

Spencer, William. *Iran: Land of the Peacock Throne* (Exploring Cultures of the World series). Benchmark, 1997. ISBN 0761403361.

Spilling, Michael. *Cyprus* (Cultures of the World series). Marshall Cavendish, 2000.

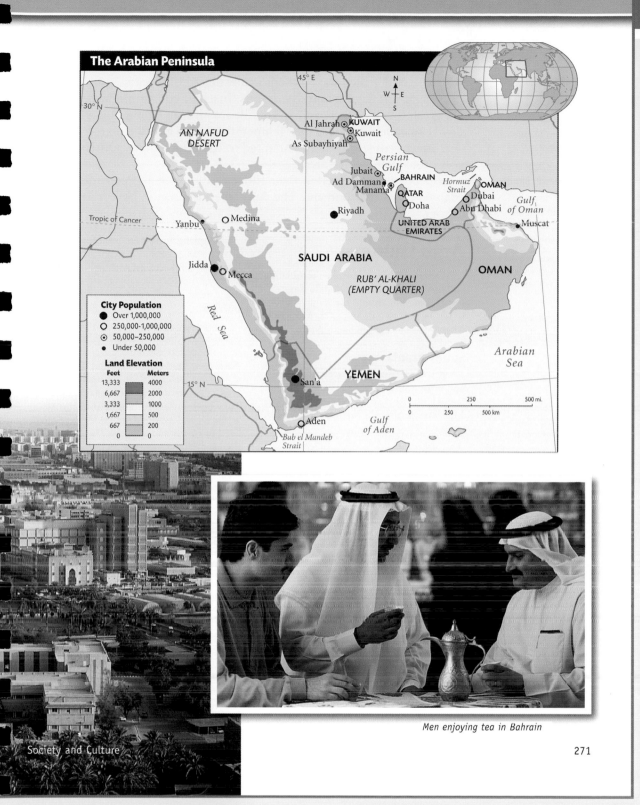

The Arabian Peninsula

AN NAFUD DESERT

Al Jahrah ⊙ **KUWAIT**
⊙ Kuwait
As Subayhiyah

Persian Gulf

Jubait ⊙
Ad Damman ⊙ **BAHRAIN**
Manama ⊙ *Hormuz Strait* ⊙**OMAN**
QATAR ⊙ Dubai
⊙ Doha ⊙ Abu Dhabi *Gulf of Oman*

Yanbu ⊙ Medina ● Riyadh **UNITED ARAB EMIRATES**
● Muscat

Tropic of Cancer

Jidda ●
Mecca ⊙ **SAUDI ARABIA**

RUB' AL-KHALI (EMPTY QUARTER) **OMAN**

Arabian Sea

Red Sea

● San'a **YEMEN**

⊙ Aden *Gulf of Aden*

Bab el Mandeb Strait

City Population
● Over 1,000,000
⊙ 250,000–1,000,000
⊙ 50,000–250,000
● Under 50,000

Land Elevation

Feet	Meters
13,333	4000
6,667	2000
3,333	1000
1,667	500
667	200
0	0

0 250 500 mi.
0 250 500 km

Society and Culture

Men enjoying tea in Bahrain

271

Discussion Questions

1 What can you tell about life in Riyadh by comparing and contrasting these two pictures?

Map Activity

Pyramid: Arabian Peninsula—Northern Tier

NATIONAL GEOGRAPHY STANDARDS: 1, 4, 10, 11, 16

GEOGRAPHIC THEMES: Location, Place, Human-Environmental Interaction, Region

OBJECTIVES: 9.02, 1.01, 11.01

Materials handout pyramid pattern in the Teacher's Resource Guide; colored pencils, markers, or crayons; rulers; scissors; glue/glue stick or transparent tape

Using the pyramid pattern, students should choose one nation from the Arabian Peninsula or Northern Tier and illustrate components from each lesson on their chosen country. The square base can be used for the student's identifying information. One triangular face must include the nation's identity with an illustration representing that country. A second triangular face must focus on an aspect of the people and their environment for the chosen country. The third triangular face must emphasize the government and economy of this nation. Finally, the fourth triangular face must focus on the culture and society in this country. Once the five faces are completed students should cut out the pyramid, fold on the lines, and glue the tabs on either side of the triangular faces together forming a pyramid shape.

ISBN 0761409785.
Back issues of magazines
Kurds. Cobblestone Publishing Company. ISBN 0382443845.
Saudi Arabia. Cobblestone Publishing Company. (issue of FACES magazine, 2001-02)
Turkey. Cobblestone Publishing Company. ISBN 0382405781.

Web Sites

Go to **NCJourneys.com** for links to the following Web sites:

- Exodus and Exile: The Spaces of Diaspora, Osher Map Library
- History, Geography, and Culture of the Middle East
- Iran Heritage
- Jeruselem 3000: Three Millenia of History, Osher Map Library, University of Southern Maine
- The Jews of Lebanon
- Kidscience: Deserts
- UAE Culture and Heritage: Dubai
- U.S. Army Training Materials on Arab Culture

LESSON 1 Many Different Cultures

OBJECTIVES: 11.01, 12.02, 12.03

Discussion Questions

1 Why do you think many Bedouins are clinging to their old ways of life rather than moving to cities where they would have more modern conveniences?

Caption Answer

Long ago, nomads moved with their herds of camels and flocks of sheep or goats in search of grazing land. The government has encouraged nomads to settle in cities and towns.

KEY IDEAS

- Arab cultures have adapted to the desert environment.
- The United Arab Emirates have a mainly foreign population.
- Turkey and Iran are non-Arab nations with their own identities.
- Persians are an ethnic group in Iran with a rich heritage. Not all Iranians are Persian.

KEY TERMS

Bedouin

Most of the Arabian Peninsula is desert. **How have people adapted to this environment?**

I f you had visited the Arabian Peninsula 25,000 years ago, you would not have found dry deserts. Instead, you would have seen green forests, lakes, and rivers filled with fish. Changes in climate slowly remade the landscape. Temperatures rose and the region dried out. Some people stayed and adapted to the arid climate. Others moved north to cooler, wetter areas.

The people who lived in the nations of the Arabian Peninsula adapted to its environment. The cultures of the region have a long history.

Arab Cultures

Culture on the Peninsula—especially Saudi Arabia, and in the Middle East revolves mainly around the religion of Islam. Islam's two holiest sites, Mecca and Medina, are located in Saudi Arabia.

Saudi Arabia

All Saudi citizens must be Muslim, and most follow the conservative Wahhabi Sunni sect. Around 15 percent of Muslims are Shiite. They live mostly in cities.

Adapting to the Environment

Imagine miles of gravel plains or sand dunes or wind-scarred rock or salt basins. Summer days are scorching and dry. At night, temperatures can drop to near freezing.

Long ago, Arabs adapted to this harsh environment. Some Arabs lived as desert nomads, called *Bedouin* (BEH·da·wen). With their herds of camels and flocks of sheep or goats, the Bedouin moved along regular routes in search of grazing land. They knew where to find natural springs, wells, or underground water. Other Arabs lived in towns and villages. They farmed the land around oases or in moist coastal areas.

New cities have grown in the desert. The government has encouraged nomads to settle in towns and cities. Many Bedouin now work in the oil industry.

Like other developing nations, Saudi Arabia's population is both growing and more urban. Yet its 24.6 million people are relatively few for a country of Saudi

WORD ORIGINS

Bedouin means "wanderer," which describes the way of life for these people. For centuries they roamed with their tents, camels, and goats. Today, you are likely to see Bedouin riding in jeeps.

It's a Fact

Southwest Asia

■ Iran must import more than 65 percent of its food. Seventy percent of its land is uninhabited. Ancient Persians built underground canals called qanats to bring water from the Zagros Mountains to farmlands. Built underground, the water would not evaporate on its journey to the fields. Some of the qanats are 40 miles long, 300 feet deep, and 2,500 years old.

■ Cyprus reflects its Greek influence in the name of its highest point: Mount Olympus, 6,403 feet in height.

■ Turkey is the home of some very old civilizations. A New Stone Age village was discovered in 1958. A large village dating back to approximately 7000 B.C., Catal Huyuk was home to more than 6,000 people. Evidence of specialization and trade have been found among the ruins.

■ Saudi Arabia has a very large royal family. The House of Saud has more than 5,000 princes and princesses. More than 2 million pilgrims visit Mecca each year during the annual hajj.

■ Yemen was two countries until 1990. North Yemen was better educated and wealthier; South Yemen was poorer and established a Communist government in an attempt to redirect its economy. Civil war and secessionist movements plagued the nation until a new constitution was written and parliamentary elections were held in 1997.

Arabia's size (larger than all of the United States east of the Mississippi). Some of the people are temporary immigrants. More than 7 million foreigners have come to work in the oil fields. Yet Saudi Arabia has a high unemployment rate among its youth. To address this, the government has created the "Saudi-ization" policy, meaning that businesses should fill jobs with Saudis instead of foreign workers.

Culture Around 90 percent of Saudis are ethnically Arab. There are also some citizens of Asian and African descent. About 100,000 Westerners live in Saudi Arabia, mostly in compounds. Christians, Hindus, and people of other faiths may enter the country as temporary workers, but are not allowed to practice their faiths.

But there are other aspects to life in Saudi Arabia. Al Ardha, the national dance, is based on ancient Bedouin tradition. Men with swords dance to the rhythm of drums while a poet chants.

The annual Jenadriyah Heritage and Cultural Festival has been held for more than 20 years. Today, more than 1 million Saudis attend the two-week festival, which begins with a camel race. Traditional music and dances, including the Ardha, are performed by people from across the kingdom. Visitors enjoy the national cake, carrot cake, which is handed out to all.

United Arab Emirates

Even before the discovery of oil in the region, people moved to the coastal cities of today's United Arab Emirates to dive for pearls in the Persian Gulf. Today, the oil industry attracts people from all over.

Since the mid-1980s, people from across Southwest and South Asia have settled in the United Arab Emirates. Noncitizens make up more than 80 percent of its population. The standard of living is similar to that in Western Europe.

Dubai is the largest city, with approximately 1.2 million people. About 88 percent of residents live in cities. The others live in tiny towns or in desert oilfield camps.

Date palms are an important symbol in Saudi culture. In addition to providing food and shade, they represent vitality and growth. **How does the date palm symbolize how Arabs have adapted to this environment?**

Spectators watch a soccer match in King Fahd II Stadium in Riyadh, Saudi Arabia. **What are some other cultural events Saudis enjoy?**

Discussion Questions

1 What would be some of the reasons why the governments would want the temporary immigrants to live apart from the citizens of the country?

2 Why do you think different Arab societies on the Arabian Peninsula have differing restrictions on Westerners and immigrants?

3 Compare freedom of religion in the United States with the restrictions on religious practice in Saudi Arabia.

 Caption Answer

Date palms have put down roots and learned how to find water and make the most out of their environment.

 Caption Answer

Saudis enjoy their national dance, the Al Ardha, and the Jenadriyah Heritage and Cultural Festival.

 Activity

Write a Song Activity

 OBJECTIVES: 2.01, 11.01

Using information you have learned in this chapter, write a song about Saudi Arabia, Turkey, or Iran. Use a familiar tune. In your song you must include the following:

description of the geography
characteristics of the people
resources
religion
a simile/metaphor
famous person/leader

Extension Novice students may draw pictures while intermediate ELL students should be assigned to work with a partner.

Discussion Questions

1 Why would conservative Muslim women swim at a women-only beach?

Caption Answer

Iranians ski and go to the beach. They also enjoy soccer, wrestling, and archery.

Activity

Cultural Connection: Southwest Asian Feast

OBJECTIVES: 2.02, 5.01

Prepare a feast of traditional Southwestern Asian foods for your students to sample. To give the feast more authenticity, spread the meal on a cloth on the floor and invite students to join you for the taste test. Your feast can be a simple collection of mezze (appetizers) including falafel (see page 280), hummus, pita bread, yogurt, olives, dates, celery, radishes, feta cheese, white cheese, and nuts. Most of these items are readily available at the grocery stores and can be purchased premade or easily prepared with a mix.

While eating, discuss with students the relationship between foods and the geography (including landforms, climate, vegetation) of Southwest Asia.

Rice with Saffron, Almonds and Raisins

2 cups long-grain rice
4 tablespoons vegetable oil
2 tablespoons vegetable oil
1 pinch saffron (or curry)
1 tablespoon rose water
¼ cup slivered, unsalted raw almonds
4 cups water
1 teaspoon salt
¼ cup raisins

In a 2-quart pan, mix water, saffron, salt, and oil. Bring to a boil on high heat. Add rice. Bring back to a boil then lower to medium heat. Let cook uncovered until most of the water is absorbed. Mix from the bottom up, lower heat to low,

cover, and let simmer for at least 15 minutes or until mealtime.

Meanwhile, heat the 2 tablespoons of vegetable oil in a small pan, then fry the almonds until slightly brown. Add the raisins to the almonds, stir for few seconds until fluffy. Remove from heat and set aside. Mix rice again, then serve in a platter. Garnish with the almonds and raisins.

Extension This is a good opportunity to get ELLs and families involved in the classroom with authentic food and items from the home.

These Iranian girls are hanging out with their friends. **What types of activities do Iranians enjoy?**

The Northern Tier

Turkey and Iran are giants in Southwest Asia. Both are Muslim nations, but their people are not Arabs. Ethnically, Turks and Iranians differ. So do their languages and traditions. Most Turks are Sunni Muslims. Most Iranians are Shiites.

Both Turkey and Iran offer recreational activities. Turkey welcomes Western tourists and their money, but Westerners may also travel in Iran. Both offer a wide range of activities, even skiing. Beaches in Turkey are open to both men and women. Women may wear Western-style bathing suits. Conservative Islamic women may choose suits that cover their bodies from neck to ankle. Iran has both women-only and foreigner-only beaches where these groups can wear what they like. Other popular activities in the region include soccer, wrestling, archery, and the traditional Turkish steam bath.

Turkey

Turkey has more than 73 million people, 66 percent of whom live in cities. The Anatolian Peninsula where Turkey is located was an ethnic mosaic for more than a thousand years, home to Greek-speaking Byzantines, Armenians, Kurds, and others. Modern Turkey has brought together several peoples, many of whom now reject certain ethnic or ancestral labels. "We Turks resemble ourselves," some modern Turks say. Due to this diversity, the word Turk or Turkish today refers to people living in Turkey and those who speak Turkish in places such as Cyprus and Central Asia.

This girl in Isparta, Turkey, wears traditional clothing. **Who are today's Turks?**

Sunbathers line the beach in Bodrum, Turkey, on the Aegean Sea. **What makes Turkish culture different from other Islamic cultures in the region?**

Discussion Questions

1 How is the use of the term "Turk" similar to the use of the term "American"?

2 What is an ethnic mosaic? To which other nations would this description apply?

3 Study the photo of the Iranian girl. What do you see that is similar to that of teenage girls in North Carolina?

 Caption Answer

Today's Turks are people living in Turkey and those who speak Turkish in places such as Cyprus and Central Asia.

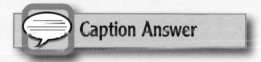 Caption Answer

Turkish culture is made up of various ethnic groups. It is also not as restrictive as some Islamic societies.

 Background Information

Busy Bosporus Waterway

The nation of Turkey sits on two continents—Asia and Europe, and the 19-mile-long Bosporus Strait separates them. The strait, known as the gateway to the West, is a busy waterway that cuts right through the city of Istanbul. Every day huge tankers travel through the strait carrying crude oil from the Caucasus and Central Asia to markets in the West. An average of 50,000 commercial ships pass through the Bosporus each year along with thousands of ferries and smaller passenger boats. The strait handles three times as much traffic as the Suez Canal and is four times as busy as the Panama Canal.

Discussion Questions

1 Why do you think many Arabs today do not remember or acknowledge the role of the Persian Empire in shaping modern Southwest Asia?

Caption Answer

Ethnic groups include Bedouin, Persians, Turks, Armenians, Byzantines, Arabs, Jewish people, and others.

Writing Activity

One Thousand and One Nights

🏁 **OBJECTIVES:** 12.02, 13.02

In the book, *One Thousand and One Nights*, the wives of Sultan Shariar only last one night. He cuts off their heads at dawn to prevent them from being unfaithful to him. His new wife, Sheherezade, believes that if she can get the sultan interested in a new story just before dawn each day, he will not cut off her head because he will want to hear the end of the story. This work of literature is a frame story, where many tales are told within the framework of an larger story.

Obtain a copy of this work in one of its many versions (*1001 Nights, 1001 Arabian Nights,* and so on.) Read a few of the stories aloud to your students. Discuss as a class what themes are important in each tale. What does this tell us about what the Persian and Arab cultures valued? Are there any morals?

Next have students write their own story for Sheherezade to tell. It can be set in modern-day North Carolina or in the time of Sheheredzade.

Beirut, Lebanon (above), is nicknamed the "Paris of the Middle East" because of its rich cultural heritage. Damascus, Syria (above left) is thought to be one of the oldest continuously inhabited cities in the world. Both cities are home to Muslims, Christians, and Jews. **What are some of the ethnic groups of Southwest Asia?**

Iran

Persians are the main ethnic group of Iran, but not all Iranians are Persian. The term Persia comes from Greek. Because Western nations called Iran "Persia" until the 1930s, many non-Persian Iranians have been labeled as Persians. Persians descend from Aryan tribes that migrated from Central Asia around 2000 B.C. and have their own language and culture.

The Persian Empire had a large sphere of influence: Iran, Tajikistan, Uzbekistan, Turkmenistan, Afghanistan, Azerbaijan, and Kyrgyzstan have a Persian-related culture. The empire was a center of learning and trade. The famous works of literature, *The Book of One Thousand and One Nights* (also know as *1001 Arabian Nights*) and the collection of poems, the *Ruba'iyat*, originated in Persia. Yet this heritage is often obscured to Westerners and even Arabs in the region.

Richard Nelson Frye, an American scholar of Iran, recognized this issue. He wrote, "Arabs no longer understand the role of Iran and the Persian language in the formation of Islamic culture. Perhaps they wish to forget the past, but in so doing they remove the bases of their own spiritual, moral and cultural being… without the heritage of the past and a healthy respect for it…there is little chance for stability and proper growth."

LESSON **1** REVIEW

Fact Follow-Up

1. How has Bedouin life changed?
2. How have the people of Saudi Arabia changed the physical environment of their arid homeland?
3. Who lives in the United Arab Emirates?
4. Describe the cultures of the Northern Tier.
5. Who were the Persians?

Talk About It

1. What does "We Turks resemble ourselves" mean?
2. What does Professor Frye mean when he says that "without the heritage of the past and a healthy respect for it…there is little chance for stability and proper growth"?

Chapter 14

LESSON **1** REVIEW

Fact Follow-Up Answers

1. Long ago, the Bedouin used to move with their herds of animals in search of grazing land and water. The government later encouraged nomads to settle in cities and towns.
2. Saudis have built cities in the desert, and they have drilled for oil. Oil production meant the construction of wells, pipelines, and storage tanks. Oil wealth has allowed the Saudis to change their land in many ways. They have drilled deeps wells to tap underground water and pipe it to remote locations. The Saudis have also built desalination plants to take the salt out of seawater. The freshwater produced by desalination can be used for irrigation and for drinking. More agriculture is now possible in the nation.
3. People from across Southwest and South Asia have settled in the United Arab Emirates. Non-citizens make up about 80 percent of its population.

4. Both Turkey and Iran are Muslim nations, though their people are not Arabs. Most Turks are Sunni Muslims; most Iranians are Shiites. Turkey has brought together peoples of many ethnic backgrounds.
5. Persians descended from Aryan tribes that migrated from Central Asia around 2000 B.C.

Talk About It Answers

1. Turkey is made up of many different peoples, many of whom reject ethnic or ancestral labels. "We Turks resemble ourselves" means that Turks want to be seen for the individuals that they are and not judged by predetermined ideas about who people might think they are.
2. Important points: Students should state their opinion and support it. Encourage students to discuss why a sense of history is important and what we can learn from it.

LESSON ② Islamic Societies and Cultures

Arabic is a musical language well suited to poetry. Long before Islam, Arabs valued poetry as the highest art form. Poets were honored everywhere.

Poems carried listeners away from the hardships of everyday life. In beautiful words and phrases, poets vividly described glorious battles and brave heroes. They entertained people with verses about romances or swift horses. Poems showed how Arabs prized such virtues as courage, honor, and hospitality.

Facing Change

Arab poets today are caught up in the struggles of the modern world. They face the same battle between "traditional" and "modern" that is occurring throughout the Islamic world. The Kuwaiti poet Sulaiman al-Fulayyih writes of that conflict:

*When will we strive, my friend, to be
Not as others imagine us
But as we wish ourselves to be?*

In Saudi Arabia, Kuwait, and other Gulf States, grandparents have seen their world change. They might tell their grandchildren how people used to earn their living as pearl divers. Today, artificially cultured pearls from Japan have replaced pearls found in the Persian Gulf. Motors now power fishing boats that once were driven by wind and sails.

Where donkeys and camels once carried loads on well-worn paths, pickup trucks and cars drive along paved roads. Houses have modern appliances, radios, satellite dishes, and imported goods. Children attend school. Most of their grandparents never had learned to read and write. In today's world, children need these educational tools.

Old traditions and new customs exist side by side. Families celebrate feast days, such as Eid al-Fitr, at the end of Ramadan. Village women and girls wear clothes they or their grandmothers have embroidered by hand. Sometimes, they buy ready-made clothes. Children sport T-shirts with Disney characters. Few believe that centuries of tradition are about to be swept away.

The Quran (above) inspires many poets in Southwest Asia. **What is a major subject of Southwestern Asian poets today?**

Society and Culture

KEY IDEAS

- Desert traditions such as hospitality and family honor are important in Saudi society.

- Islamization is the creation of governments based on conservative Muslim traditions.

KEY TERMS

patriarchal
Islamists
Islamization

Muslim women pray on the last day of Ramadan outside the Dome of the Rock mosque in Jerusalem. **What keeps such traditions alive?**

Discussion Questions

1 Why have Islamists been so successful in gaining support for their cause?

2 How would our lives be different if we had a religiously conservative government?

3 How does religion influence art?

4 What problems could result if you were a girl raised in the United States but then had to move to a country run by an Islamist regime?

Research Activity

Stories of Southwest Asian Culture

OBJECTIVES: 7.02, 12.01

The Day of Ahmed's Secret by Florence Parry Heide and Judith Heide Gilliland, illustrated by Ted Lewin, (Mulberry Books, 1995. ISBN 0688140238.) is a story of a young Egyptian boy going about his daily chores in noisy and bustling Cairo. The illustrations make this book an excellent tool for teaching about Arabic culture.

After reading the book out loud have the students draw a vertical line to separate a piece of paper. One side should be labeled "modern" and the other "ancient." Share the book again and have the students find examples of modern and ancient culture and conveniences. With two copies of the book (or more) the class could work in groups to see the different responses they had when they come back together. For example, on pages 2 and 3 ancient culture could include many of the men wearing fezzes and robes; the women's heads are covered; and Ahmed is riding through town on a cart pulled by a donkey. Students should describe how the market is a blend of traditional and modern influences.

Sami and the Time of Troubles, by the same authors (Clarion, 1992. ISBN 0395720850.), is about a ten-year-old boy who lives in Beirut, Lebanon. This book reinforces the reality of the conflicts in Southwest Asia. Prior to reading this book some background regarding the Lebanese-Israeli conflict would be helpful, or pictures showing

The Islamic Revival

Many people in the Middle East are disturbed by some effects of modernization. They blame poverty on unjust and corrupt governments and on Western values. They argue that foreign ideas have undermined Islamic traditions and values.

"Islam is the answer," some have decided. American newspapers often call these people "Islamic fundamentalists," but a more accurate term is *Islamists*. Islamists want *Islamization,* the creation of governments based on conservative Islamic traditions. They demand a strict moral code and religious observance. In city slums, Islamists provide social services, such as medical care. They have set up schools where children learn the Quran along with other subjects.

A key issue has been how women appear and behave in public. For several years some young women from wealthy Muslim families abandoned traditions governing their dress and behavior. Many stopped wearing a veil to cover their faces. Some wore Western hair styles and short skirts. Many attended universities in Europe or the United States. Muslim women joined hospital staffs as nurses and doctors. Female engineers worked alongside men. Islamists were outraged. Many wanted to limit women's role in public life. Others just wanted women and men to be more modest in public.

Some Islamic reformers have put together a strong political movement. It has won support in countries throughout the Islamic world. Yet Islamists have gained power only in one country, Iran.

In an effort to keep Islamists out of power, most Middle Eastern governments have adopted parts of the Islamists' program. Some have overturned laws that gave women certain rights. Many women have returned to wearing traditional dress, at least in public.

CONNECTIONS • GEOGRAPHY & THE ARTS •

Visions of Beauty

Early Muslims shunned drawing images of humans or animals because they believed it may lead to idolatry (worshipping of images or idols). Followers found a way to express their faith for Allah in other ways. Islamic artists demonstrated their visions of beauty in mosaic and cloth while obeying the rules of Islam.

Mosaic, bits of colored glass or tile, became a way to decorate the mosques. Complicated geometric forms, in brilliant colors and puzzlelike in design, made patterns symbolizing life and worship. The patterns symbolize the infinity of God with their seemingly never-ending repetition. Mosques, such as the Blue Mosque of Turkey, were places of reflection and silence, and the mosaic patterns added to the atmosphere of quiet.

Prayer rugs also reflect the art of Islam (right). The prayer rug has a solid arch-shaped block of color and represents the *mihrab*, or prayer niche that faces Mecca in a mosque wall. Prayer rugs are used only for prayer. Some have arrows woven into them pointing to Mecca.

Rug making is an art and industry in the region. Persian rugs woven by hand are prized around the world. Turks and others produce their own patterns and styles. Rugs may be made of silk, wool, or cotton, usually dyed bright colors. Years ago, weavers used natural dyes from berries, roots, bark, and minerals. Today, they use a variety of natural and synthetic dyes.

Lebanon before and after the conflict began.

Sitti's Secret by Naomi Shihab Nye, illustrated by Nancy Carpenter (Simon & Schuster, 1997. ISBN 0689817061.), is about a young girl in America who has a grandmother who lives in a Palestinian village on the West Bank. When Mona returns from visiting her grandmother, she writes a letter to the president of the United States regarding her concern about the situation in the Middle East. Students could write letters to the United Nations or world leaders expressing their concern for various conflicts occurring at that time. Addresses for embassies and other government offices can be found in an almanac.

Customs

Iranians celebrate New Year's Day late in March. Villages are decorated. Villagers buy candles, household goods, and gifts. Old pottery is broken. People eat special dishes off new plates. During the six-day holiday, dancers dressed in baggy red trousers perform to the rhythms of drums and tambourines.

Desert Traditions

Paradise is described in the Quran as a place constantly "watered by rivers. Its food is perpetual, endless, and its shade also." That view of heaven suggests the physical comforts that Arabs of an earlier age valued—water, food, and shade. Many traditions developed among Arabs that reflected their desert environment.

Hospitality

Today, as in the past, hospitality is offered both to friend and stranger. Desert Arabs freely share food and water with anyone who asks. After three days a stranger is expected to leave.

Special occasions still demand feasts or banquets. Guests are welcomed with great ceremony. Dishes are heaped with meat such as lamb or goat, rice, and probably dates. Plates and utensils are not used, unless perhaps for Western guests. Instead, diners help themselves. They use only the right hand; the left is considered unclean. Guests are offered the best morsels or tastiest portion of each dish.

A final course includes fruit and *halwah*, a sweet, flaky dessert made from crushed sesame seeds and honey. Strong black coffee or sweet tea ends the meal. Sometimes burning incense signals guests that it is time to leave.

Women prepare and serve all meals. They carry in platters of food to serve the male family members and guests. In rural areas they may sit separately from the men and eat the leftover food. Traditionally, most foods are cooked in a single pot to save scarce fuel.

Family

Loyalty to family and family honor are highly valued among Arabs. The family protects its members and accepts the responsibility of caring for old, sick, widowed, or jobless family members. In Saudi Arabia, the extended family might include three generations: parents, and sons along with their wives and children. Today, family patterns are changing, especially among city dwellers. Younger couples often set up their own households.

Arab families are *patriarchal*. The oldest male is the head of the household. He makes decisions but asks other family members for their views. Older women often have great influence.

Early on, children learn that family interests are more important than individual wishes. Even when they are older, they accept decisions made by their elders even if they disagree with them.

Family entertainment in Arab nations often includes large meals or banquets. Meals such as the one in this photo are rarely held outside of rural villages today. **Why is family so important in Arabic society?**

Society and Culture

279

Discussion Questions

1 How does the role of the Arab woman compare to the role of women in your household?

Caption Answer

Loyalty to family and family honor are highly valued among Arabs. The family protects its members and accepts the responsibility of caring for old, sick, widowed, or jobless family members.

Activity

Clothing and Culture

🏴 OBJECTIVES: 11.01, 12.02, 12.03

Discuss as a class the physical, political, traditional, and cultural aspects of clothing. What are the messages clothes may send to others? Have students look through news magazines, *National Geographic,* and social studies textbooks for pictures that represent these different aspects of clothing. Share the pictures with the class and speculate how or why that type of clothing may have achieved importance in its society.

Have students compare the clothing of the United States, Northern Africa, Sub-Saharan Africa, and Southwest Asia. What purposes do the types of clothing serve? How are they alike and different? Finally, discuss the role of clothing in our society. How do we identify people based upon clothing (uniforms/jobs, fashion/wealth, style/sophistication)? Is that a good thing? Should we as Americans judge people of other cultures based upon their clothing?

Teacher Notes

Women and Islam

Islam sees a woman, either single or married, as an individual in her own right, with the right to own and dispose of her property and earnings. A marriage dowry is given by the groom to the bride for her own personal use, and she keeps her own family name rather than taking her husband's.

Both men and women are expected to dress in a way that is modest and dignified; the traditions of female dress found in some of the Muslim countries are often the expression of local customs.

Review with students the photographs in our textbook and other resources of women in different Muslim nations, including the nations of Southwest Asia, South Asia, and Southeast Asia. Notice how the dress varies from region to region and nation to nation. The type of dress and degree of seclusion is dictated more by local custom and the national government's degree of Islamization than by the Quran itself.

Discussion Questions

1 Polygamy is practiced in Muslim countries. Arranged marriages are also common. What impact do you think these practices have on marriages?

2 How successful do you think the National Organization for Women (NOW) would be in Southwest Asia?

 Caption Answer

Local interpretations of Islamic law require traditional dress of women.

 Activity

Falafel

🔺 **OBJECTIVES:** 11.01

2 cups dried chickpeas
1 medium onion, quartered
¼ cup parsley
¾ teaspoon black pepper
2 teaspoons ground coriander
¼ cup water
1 teaspoon red hot pepper flakes
2–3 cloves garlic
⅛ head sweet red pepper
2 teaspoons cumin
4 teaspoons flour
2 teaspoons baking powder
2–3 slices stale bread
2 teaspoons salt
2 teaspoons oregano
1 teaspoon baking powder
½ cup water

Place in a large bowl, cover chickpeas-generously with water, and soak overnight. Drain. Add onion, garlic, bread, parsley, and red sweet pepper. Run through the fine blade of a meat grinder or process in food processor until mealy. Add spices, flour, baking powder, and water. Mix well.

In a small dish mix the remaining baking powder and water. Use it to moisten the palm of your hands and form balls of the chickpea mixture the size of walnuts, then flatten a bit. Deep-fry in oil at medium high heat until golden brown. Serve piping hot. Arrange in halved loaves of pita, topped with salad vegetables and Tahini sauce. Hot pepper may also be sprinkled on top.

Female chemical engineers in Kuwait wear contrasting styles of clothing. **Why are women of the Arabian Peninsula expected to wear traditional dress?**

woman's father or brother ensures those rights are protected in the marriage contract. Divorce is easier for men than for women, but Saudi Arabia has a low divorce rate.

Clothing

Desert Arabs developed clothes suited to the climate. Tight trousers and shirts are uncomfortable in a hot, dusty environment. Instead, men and women wear long loose robes that let the air circulate and protect them from the sun.

At first glance, we may think all Arab robes are alike, but styles vary in each country. In Saudi Arabia, men wear a long white or blue robe. They cover their heads with a red-and-white-checkered cloth held in place by a black or white cord. On cold nights, men wear a sleeveless coat made of camel hair or sheepskin.

Women's clothing also varies from country to country. In Saudi Arabia, women are expected to wear traditional clothing. A wealthy young woman, however, can find ways to avoid the requirement. A university student walking to class wears a long black wool cloak reaching to her ankles. Her head and face are covered. When she steps inside her classroom building, she slips out of these outer garments. Beneath the black cloak is a brightly colored, fashionable dress. In Egypt, women working outside their homes openly wear Western dress.

Arab society differs from Western cultures that promote the value of the individual.

In Saudi Arabia, social activities take place at home within the family. There are few public entertainments. Relatives visit one another at home. At home, women talk to their female friends and relatives in one room and men talk in another. Men and women do not mix in public.

Although the Quran allows men to have more than one wife, most Saudi men today have only one. Women have divorce rights and property rights. Usually, a

LESSON ② REVIEW

Fact Follow-Up

1. What are some contrasts between traditional and modern in both the Arabian Peninsula and Northern Tier?
2. What are some traditional dining and family customs in the Arabian Peninsula?
3. What Arab traditions reflect the desert environment?
4. Describe the life of women in traditional Arab society.

Talk About It

1. What do you think is the greatest strength of the extended family system in the Arabian Peninsula. Why?
2. Suppose a guest from Saudi Arabia were to visit in your home or school. What are the most important customs of our society that you would need to explain to your visitor? Why would the visitor need to know about these customs?

LESSON ② REVIEW

Fact Follow-Up Answers

1. Technology, transportation, and communications are modern, but family and social life are traditional. Turkey is the least traditional of the Northern Tier nations.
2. Arabs gather to eat around a large dish, sitting on the floor and helping themselves to food with the right hand. Women prepare and serve the meals but eat separately. Arab families are patriarchal. The oldest male is head of the household and is responsible for making decisions, but he asks other family members for their views.
3. The sharing of food and water and the wearing of loose clothing make sense in the desert.
4. Women do not mix with men in public. They eat and visit at home separately from the men. They are responsible for the cooking and serving of food, and often advise men in their family privately. Although divorce is easier for men, women do have property rights and divorce rights. Although the Quran allows men to have more than one wife, this practice is not widespread.

Jericho. Damascus. Baghdad. Tyre. These cities of the Fertile Crescent are rooted in ancient history. Today, factories and modern apartments nudge up against ancient city walls. If the stones could speak, they would tell much about the men, women, and children of other ages.

Because the Fertile Crescent was a crossroads of trade, its cities prospered. They were centers for the exchange of goods and ideas. Of the region's many cities, Jerusalem is perhaps the most famous. It is a holy city for Jews, Christians, and Muslims.

"Jerusalem the Golden"

Visitors to Jerusalem marvel at the glistening white stones that cover its buildings. At sunset, the stones glow like gold. "Jerusalem the Golden" is one of its nicknames.

A thousand years ago, a Muslim writer noted that "Jerusalem is a golden basin filled with scorpions." His words reflected a sad truth. Since ancient times,

many people have valued the city, but violence has haunted it.

Jerusalem, ancient capital of the Hebrews, has been conquered by many armies. Romans, Arabs, Christian Crusaders, and Ottomans all have ruled it. Today, Jerusalem sits at the center of a new conflict. Israelis call it their capital. Palestinian Arabs and others say that Israel has no right to make it their capital. So this holy city has yet to see a peaceful future.

KEY IDEAS

- Jerusalem is a sacred city for Jews, Christians, and Muslims.
- Israel is a Jewish state, but Arabs live there as well.

KEY TERMS

Sabbath
secular

Jerusalem is home to Jews, such as this boy, as well as Christians and Muslims. **Why has Jerusalem been the center of conflict?**

Society and Culture

281

Discussion Questions

1 How do you think the conflict over Jerusalem could be peacefully resolved?

Caption Answer

It is a holy site for three religions. Israel claims it as its capital, but Palestinian Arabs disagree.

Talk About It Answers

1. Important points: Remind students to select one strength and give reasons for their selection. Note: The support system the family provides is a great help to family members.
2. Important points: Remind students to select customs they think are most important and explain why visitors would need to know about them. Note: Girls and boys in school together, dress, music television, and other entertainment, ways of eating, position of women, attitudes toward the elderly.

Activity

Fishbowl

⬧ **OBJECTIVES:** 8.01, 12.01

On slips of paper, write the names of religious sites such as the Western Wall, Dome of the Rock, St. Mary Magdalen, and the religions and important people of the religions—Judaism, Christianity, Islam—Jesus, and Muhammad. Place the slips of paper in a bowl and after reading the eyewitness account, have individual students draw a slip of paper from the bowl and ask them to explain why that place, religion, or person, is important to Jerusalem.

Extension Novice ELL students should observe.

For a writing prompt, ask students to explain why Jerusalem is considered one of the world's holiest cities using information from the text as supporting details.

For additional information on Jerusalem, read *Jerusalem, Shining Still* by Karla Kuskin (HarperCollins Children's Books, 1987. ISBN 0060235489.).Large amounts of rainfall mean more vegetation.

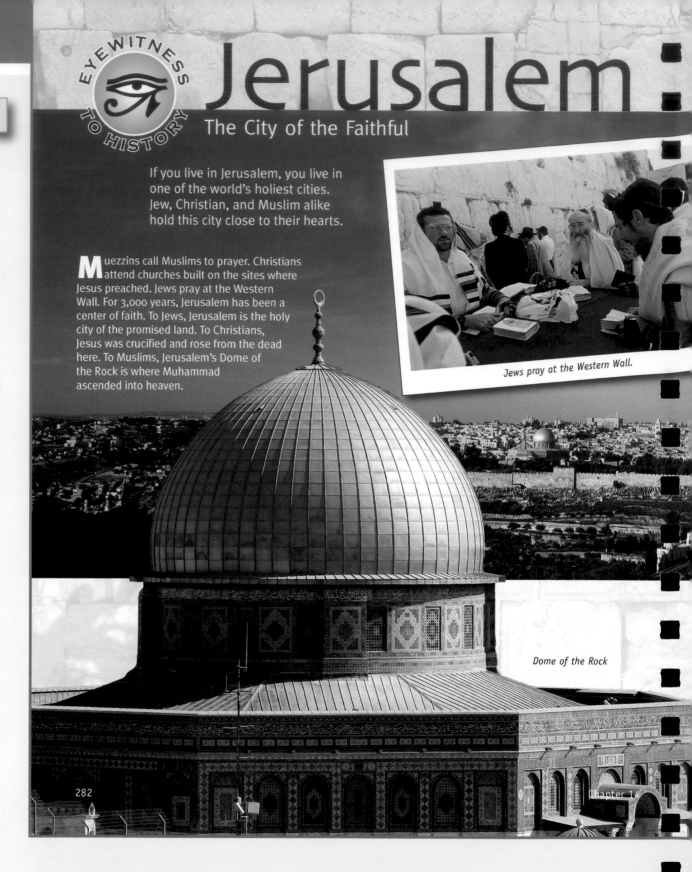

EYEWITNESS TO HISTORY

Jerusalem
The City of the Faithful

If you live in Jerusalem, you live in one of the world's holiest cities. Jew, Christian, and Muslim alike hold this city close to their hearts.

Muezzins call Muslims to prayer. Christians attend churches built on the sites where Jesus preached. Jews pray at the Western Wall. For 3,000 years, Jerusalem has been a center of faith. To Jews, Jerusalem is the holy city of the promised land. To Christians, Jesus was crucified and rose from the dead here. To Muslims, Jerusalem's Dome of the Rock is where Muhammad ascended into heaven.

Jews pray at the Western Wall.

Dome of the Rock

282

Chapter 14

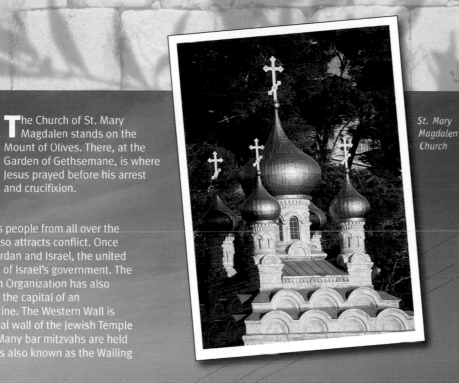

The Church of St. Mary Magdalen stands on the Mount of Olives. There, at the Garden of Gethsemane, is where Jesus prayed before his arrest and crucifixion.

St. Mary Magdalen Church

Jerusalem attracts people from all over the world. The city also attracts conflict. Once divided between Jordan and Israel, the united city is now the seat of Israel's government. The Palestine Liberation Organization has also declared Jerusalem the capital of an independent Palestine. The Western Wall is said to be an original wall of the Jewish Temple built by Solomon. Many bar mitzvahs are held at this wall, which is also known as the Wailing Wall.

Jerusalem is called al-Quds (the Holy) by Muslims who believe in the city's importance because of its role during the time of the Prophet Muhammad and the early prophets. The city is surrounded by walls (above) built by the Muslim ruler Suleiman the Great in the sixteenth century.

Women on their way to prayer at a mosque

 Eyewitness Activity

Jerusalem: The City of the Faithful

OBJECTIVES: 12.01

Give students a web graphic organizer to illustrate Jerusalem's importance to Islam, Christianity, and Judaism. An example of a web diagram is in the Teacher's Resource Guide.

National Geographic's video *Within These Walls* is an excellent source for showing students how important Jerusalem is to the three major monotheistic religions and would integrate well with this Eyewitness.

Extension Assign the video only for novice and intermediate ELL students unless the graphic organizer is completed together in class. Do not assign them further research.

Discussion Questions

1 Israel has a policy of allowing Jews from across the world to become Israeli citizens. What would be the advantages and disadvantages of this policy?

2 People emigrate to Israel for religious reasons. What are some reasons why people emigrate to the United States?

3 What are some of the differences that separate people of the Jewish faith?

4 Everyone in Israel must serve in the military, even women. Do you think women should be made to serve in the armed forces in the United States?

5 Do you think women serving in the armed forces would make it stronger?

6 Why would the United States give military aid to Israel?

7 How are Orthodox Jews and Islamists similar?

Caption Answer

Sephardic and Ashkenazi

Israel's People

Like its neighbors Jordan and Lebanon, Israel has limited fertile land and few minerals. Unlike its neighbors, it is a Jewish state. Most Israelis are Jewish immigrants from all over the world. Israel allows Jews from any land to settle there.

Israeli Culture

Several factors—such as the country of origin, length of time in Israel, and religious practices—influence Jewish lifestyles. In general, family life and religious celebrations play an important role in society. Popular recreational activities include camping, hiking, and going to the beach, as well as visiting sports facilities, libraries, and theaters.

Israeli Jews are diverse. Because they come from many lands, they speak many languages. Sephardic (seh·FAR·dic) Jews come from Arab and Mediterranean countries. They make up a large percentage of the population, but are also typically less educated and poorer than other Israelis.

Ashkenazi (ash·ken·AH·zee) Jews—of European origin—dominated Israel's early years and still fill top jobs. Differences between Ashkenazi and Sephardic Jews have sometimes led to conflict.

Israeli law guarantees religious freedom. Religious faith and practice differ widely among Israeli Jews. Orthodox Jews, about 15 percent of the population, follow strict religious law in all aspects of life. Yet many Israelis observe no religious practices. The majority of Jews lie somewhere in between, practicing their faith according to personal preferences and ethnic traditions.

Orthodox and non-Orthodox groups sometimes disagree over observance of the *Sabbath,* a holy day of rest, military service, and other aspects of daily life. Tensions between Orthodox and non-Orthodox groups are rising.

These people enjoy time at a park with the skyline of Tel Aviv, Israel, in the background. **What are the two main Jewish ethnic groups?**

Education The quality of Israel's educational system and its high literacy rate reflect the importance of education. Because Jewish immigrants from all over the world move to Israel, education helps unify the nation. Jewish children attend either state *secular* (nonreligious) or religious schools. Both types of schools teach Hebrew.

Some secondary schools specialize in technological, agricultural, military, or religious studies. There are also private schools sponsored by Orthodox groups and Christian denominations.

Arabs in Israel

Many Christian and Muslim Arabs also live in Israel, making up about 20 percent of the population. They have the same legal rights as Jewish citizens, although they may face other challenges. A large number of these Arabs have family roots that go back hundreds of years in the lands that eventually became Israel.

The founding of Israel as a Jewish state is sometimes at odds with the idea of Israel as a democracy with a large Arab minority. Because of this, Israel has sometimes been called an "ethnic democracy." Jews and Arabs in Israel lead largely separate lives.

Arabs in Israel are divided along religious lines although they share a common language and other cultural ties. Muslim Arabs, mostly Sunnis, live mainly in small towns and villages and follow many traditions of the Islamic world. Christian Arabs reside mostly in the cities.

Arab children attend separate schools emphasizing their history, religions, and culture. They learn Arabic and Hebrew.

Young people from the United States often go to Israel to live on a kibbutz. Like members of the kibbutz, these visitors feel that they are serving Israel. They are willing to work hard, share almost everything with others, and follow instructions from community leaders. If there were communities like this in the United States, would you join one? Why?

These young Israeli boys are Orthodox Jews. They attend a Jewish day school that teaches secular subjects and religion. **Why is education important in Israel?**

Discussion Questions

1 Imagine that someone from another country comes to visit you. What customs of our country would you need to explain to your visitor so they can fit in more easily?

Caption Answer

Jewish people from all over the world immigrate to Israel. Education helps to unite them.

Activity

Potato Latkes for Hanukkah Recipe

OBJECTIVES: 12.01

Latkes are a favorite treat served during Hanukkah, the Jewish Festival of Lights.

4 large peeled and grated potatoes
2 eggs
¼ cup flour
¼ teaspoon pepper
1 teaspoon salt
vegetable oil
¼ teaspoon baking powder

Mix grated potatoes and eggs in a large mixing bowl. Add flour, salt, pepper, and baking powder and mix well. Heat about ½-cup oil in skillet. Drop mixture by spoonfuls into hot oil, flattening with a spoon. Cook until browned, approximately three minutes on each side. Remove from skillet and drain on paper towels. This recipe makes about 24 small latkes. Serve with sour cream or apple sauce.

Extension For ELL students, model and provide additional explanations

---

LESSON **3** REVIEW

Fact Follow-Up

1. To what three faiths is Jerusalem the holy city?
2. To which ethnic group do Arab Jews belong?
3. Describe the diversity of Israelis.

Talk About It

1. Would you consider Arabs to be second-class citizens in Israel? Why or why not?
2. Why has Israel been both a center of religion and of conflict?

Society and Culture

285

LESSON **3** REVIEW

Fact Follow-Up Answers

1. Judaism, Christianity, and Islam all claim Jerusalem as a holy city.
2. Arab Jews belong to the Sephardic group.
3. Some Israelis are Orthodox Jews, and some observe no religious practices; most Israeli Jews lie somewhere in between. Because they come from many lands, Israeli Jews speak many languages from Europe, Africa, and Asia. Several factors, such as the country of origin, length of time in Israel, and religious practices influence Jewish lifestyles. Arabs and Jews lead largely separate lives.

Talk About It Answers

1. Important points: Students should take a position and support it. Arabs have some limitations in the "ethnic democracy." However, Arabs choose to stay in Israel rather than move to another nation.
2. Jerusalem was a center of religious ideas in ancient times, and today is regarded as a holy city by Islam, Judaism, and Christianity. Many nations and religions have sought to control it over the centuries.

Teaching This Skill Lesson

Materials Needed textbooks, paper, pencils

Classroom Organization whole class, individuals and small groups (if desired)

Beginning the Lesson ask: "How would you feel if I told you this was the most diverse class I'd ever taught?" Probe to make sure students have a working understanding of the concept of diversity.

Developing the Lesson Compare students' statements about diversity (above) to the notion of diversity in the Middle East. Have students skim Chapters 11, 12, and 13 for examples of diversity in the region. List examples on the chalkboard and lead students to group these examples into categories. Use a sketch of the chart in the skill lesson to demonstrate how students should begin to complete the chart. Have students complete the chart individually or by working in small groups.

Conclusion In a general class discussion, ask which example(s) of diversity offer the most potential for peace? for conflict? Which diversity is most recent, longest-lasting? Ask what examples of diversity should be managed to avoid future conflicts.

Extension Make a homework assignment: have students write letters to imaginary pen pals in a specific location in the Middle East suggesting ways conflicts might be managed.

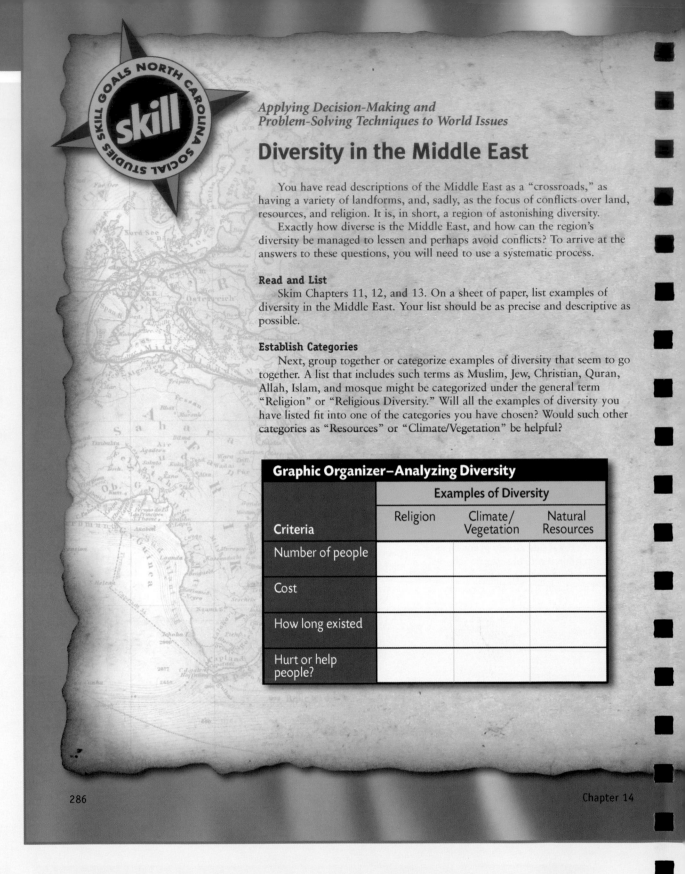

Applying Decision-Making and Problem-Solving Techniques to World Issues

Diversity in the Middle East

You have read descriptions of the Middle East as a "crossroads," as having a variety of landforms, and, sadly, as the focus of conflicts over land, resources, and religion. It is, in short, a region of astonishing diversity.

Exactly how diverse is the Middle East, and how can the region's diversity be managed to lessen and perhaps avoid conflicts? To arrive at the answers to these questions, you will need to use a systematic process.

Read and List

Skim Chapters 11, 12, and 13. On a sheet of paper, list examples of diversity in the Middle East. Your list should be as precise and descriptive as possible.

Establish Categories

Next, group together or categorize examples of diversity that seem to go together. A list that includes such terms as Muslim, Jew, Christian, Quran, Allah, Islam, and mosque might be categorized under the general term "Religion" or "Religious Diversity." Will all the examples of diversity you have listed fit into one of the categories you have chosen? Would such other categories as "Resources" or "Climate/Vegetation" be helpful?

Graphic Organizer–Analyzing Diversity			
	Examples of Diversity		
Criteria	Religion	Climate/ Vegetation	Natural Resources
Number of people			
Cost			
How long existed			
Hurt or help people?			

This traditional parade marks the end of the carnival period in Limassol, Cyprus.

Evaluate categories

Third, examine and then evaluate the categories you have established. Should some categories be changed? Then, evaluate the potential of each category for causing conflict by asking such questions as these:

1. How many people are involved?
2. How expensive would it be to deal with this situation?
3. How long has this situation existed?
4. Does this diversity help or hurt all people?

You might use pluses or minuses to evaluate the categories using these questions. Which examples of diversity in the region hold potential for peace? Which is most likely to cause conflict? Which diversity is recent or long-lasting?

Finally, examine your answers to each of these questions. Based upon this examination, what might be the role of government or other organizations in managing society? What type of diversity should be managed to avoid future conflicts?

 Skill Lesson Review

1. Which category affected the most people? the fewest people? *Important points: Possible answers might include religious diversity, ethnic diversity, political diversity. Students should share their categories with the class.*

2. Which of your categories of diversity do you believe have the most potential for conflict? the least? *Important points: Students should share their categories. Economic diversity, religious diversity, and diversity of resources are potential sources of conflict*

3. Which step of the process was easiest for you? most difficult for you? Why? *Answers will vary according to learning styles. Students should reflect on why a particular step was easy or difficult.*

4. Is this process a useful way of examining diversity? *Important points: Students should be encouraged to express their opinions. This process may move us toward ways diversity might lead to cooperation.*

5. What are some other areas to which this process can be applied? *Important points: Students should be encouraged to suggest other areas. Examples may include diversity inside the United States, even within a school or classroom.*

Talk About It

1. Important points: Students should choose either physical or cultural and support the choice with explanations. Note: At one time, physical characteristics were more important than they have become with the introduction of technology in the area.

2. Important point: Students should choose one reason and then support their choice. Note: A reaction against Westernization and European influences and a return to tradtional Muslim values are reasons for the revival.

3. Jerusalem has been a center of religious feeling for centuries. Many nations and religions have sought and still seek to control it.

4. Important points: Islamization continues to be strong, new leaders have taken steps to rebuild the economy, improve international relations, and allow their people new freedoms.

5. Important points: Students should choose one nation and explain the choice. Note: Turkey, Cyprus, Lebanon, or Israel are likely nations for students to choose.

Mastering Mapwork

1. San'a

2. Mecca is located to the south and slightly to the west of Medina in western Saudi Arabia. Neither is very far from the Red Sea.

3. Oman is located in the southeastern corner of the Arabian Peninsula. It is bordered on the north by the United Arab Emirates, on the northwest by Saudi Arabia, and on the west by Yemen. It is bordered on the east by the Gulf of Oman and on the south and southeast by the Arabian Sea.

4. The An Nafud Desert is located in extreme northwestern Saudi Arabia.

5. Muscat, Oman, lies just south of the Tropic of Cancer.

6. The United Arab Emirates are located in the southeastern portion of the Arabian Peninsula. They are bounded on the north by the Persian Gulf and on the south and west by Saudi Arabia.

7. Yemen has the most southerly location.

8. Turkey is the most northerly and most westerly.

9. The Caspian Sea forms a part of the northern border of Iran.

CHAPTER 14 REVIEW

Lessons Learned

LESSON 1
Many Different Cultures
Arab cultures have adapted to the desert environment. Saudi Arabia and the United Arab Emirates are both Arab nations with different societies. Turkey and Iran are non-Arab nations with their own identities. Persians are an ethnic group in Iran with a rich heritage.

LESSON 2
Islamic Societies and Cultures
Desert traditions of hospitality and entertainment within the home are strong on the Arabian Peninsula. Clothing, food, housing, and customs are dictated by the desert environment. Islamists have led an Islamic revival in the region. Islamists are conservative Muslims who want their nations to be governed by traditional Islamic principles.

LESSON 3
Israeli Society and Culture
Followers of Judaism, Christianity, and Islam think of Jerusalem as a sacred city. Although Israel is a Jewish nation, Arabs and Christians also live there. The Jews of Israel practice their faith in varying ways.

Talk About It

1. Which do you think is more important in explaining how people live in Saudi Arabia—the physical or cultural characteristics of place? Explain why.

2. What do you think is the most important reason for the Islamic revival? Why?

3. Why is Jerusalem both a holy city and a city of conflict?

4. In 20 years, how will life in Iran resemble life today? Give reasons for your answer.

5. In which nation of the region do you think women have the most freedom? Explain.

Mastering Mapwork

LOCATION
Use the map on page 271 to answer these questions:

1. What is the name of the city located nearest 15°N and 45°E?

2. What is the location of Mecca relative to the location of Medina?

3. Describe the relative location of Oman.

4. What is the relative location of the An Nafud Desert in Saudi Arabia?

5. What city is located nearest the Tropic of Cancer?

6. Describe the relative location of the Persian Gulf.

7. What country has the most southerly location on the Arabian Peninsula?

8. Which nation in the region is both most northerly and most westerly?

9. What body of water forms a part of the northern border of Iran?

Go to the Source

Following Recipes

It has been said that there are three major kinds of cuisines in the world: Turkish, Chinese, and French. This means that these cuisines have influenced the foods of other nations.

Dugun Corbasi, or Turkish Wedding Soup, is traditionally served at Turkish wedding celebrations. It features lamb, which is a cornerstone of Turkish cuisine. Read the recipe and answer the questions below.

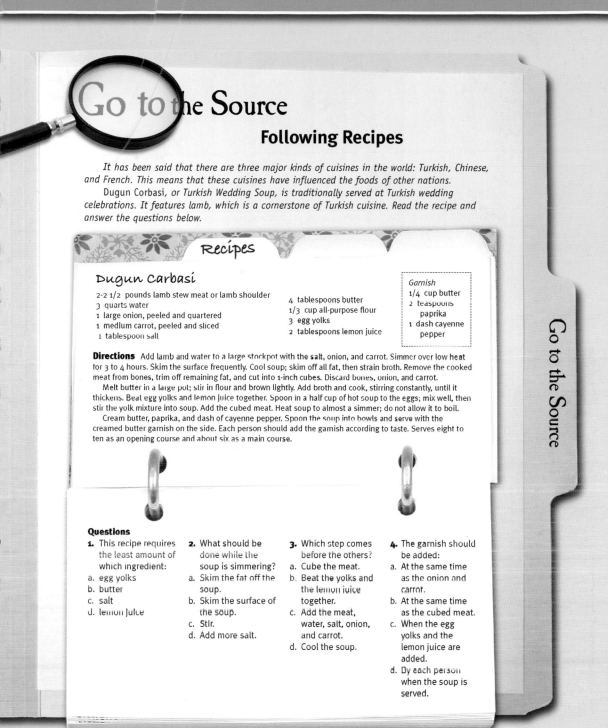

Recipes

Dugun Carbasi

2-2 1/2 pounds lamb stew meat or lamb shoulder
3 quarts water
1 large onion, peeled and quartered
1 medium carrot, peeled and sliced
1 tablespoon salt

4 tablespoons butter
1/3 cup all-purpose flour
3 egg yolks
2 tablespoons lemon juice

Garnish
1/4 cup butter
2 teaspoons paprika
1 dash cayenne pepper

Directions Add lamb and water to a large stockpot with the salt, onion, and carrot. Simmer over low heat for 3 to 4 hours. Skim the surface frequently. Cool soup; skim off all fat, then strain broth. Remove the cooked meat from bones, trim off remaining fat, and cut into 1-inch cubes. Discard bones, onion, and carrot.

Melt butter in a large pot; stir in flour and brown lightly. Add broth and cook, stirring constantly, until it thickens. Beat egg yolks and lemon juice together. Spoon in a half cup of hot soup to the eggs; mix well, then stir the yolk mixture into soup. Add the cubed meat. Heat soup to almost a simmer; do not allow it to boil.

Cream butter, paprika, and dash of cayenne pepper. Spoon the soup into bowls and serve with the creamed butter garnish on the side. Each person should add the garnish according to taste. Serves eight to ten as an opening course and about six as a main course.

Questions

1. This recipe requires the least amount of which ingredient:
a. egg yolks
b. butter
c. salt
d. lemon juice

2. What should be done while the soup is simmering?
a. Skim the fat off the soup.
b. Skim the surface of the soup.
c. Stir.
d. Add more salt.

3. Which step comes before the others?
a. Cube the meat.
b. Beat the yolks and the lemon juice together.
c. Add the meat, water, salt, onion, and carrot.
d. Cool the soup.

4. The garnish should be added:
a. At the same time as the onion and carrot.
b. At the same time as the cubed meat.
c. When the egg yolks and the lemon juice are added.
d. By each person when the soup is served.

Society and Culture

289

Go to the Source

OBJECTIVES: 12.02; Skills 1.01, 3.05

Turkey's cuisine has been influenced by Turkic, Arabic, Greek and Persian cuisines. In turn, Turkish cuisine also influenced these cuisines, other neighboring cuisines, and also west European cuisines. Each region of Turkey also has its own specialties.

Until recently, meat was rarely eaten except at wedding celebrations and special holidays. This was due to the fact that it was expensive and hard to come by. This Wedding Soup features lamb as its main ingredient.

ANSWERS

1. c
2. b
3. c
4. d

How to Use the Chapter Review

There are three sections in the Chapter Review: Talk About It, Mastering Mapwork, and Go to the Source. Use the Vocabulary Worksheets and the Chapter Review Worksheet in the Teacher's Resource Guide for additional reinforcement and preparation for the Chapter Assessments. The chapter and lesson reviews and the Chapter Review Worksheets are the basis of the assessment for each chapter.

Talk About It questions encourage students to speculate about the content of the chapter and are suitable for class or small-group discussion. They are not intended to be assigned for homework.

Mastering Mapwork has students apply one or more of the Five Themes of Geography to maps within the chapter.

Go to the Source activities allow students to analyze a primary source that relates to the content of the chapter. The questions and activities familiarize students with different types of primary sources and also build content-reading skills.